D1569574

HIGH-PERFORMANCE COMPUTING

WILEY SERIES ON PARALLEL AND DISTRIBUTED COMPUTING
Albert Y. Zomaya, Series Editor

Parallel and Distributed Simulation Systems / Richard Fujimoto

Surviving the Design of Microprocessor and Multimicroprocessor Systems: Lessons Learned / Veljko Milutinović

Mobile Processing in Distributed and Open Environments / Peter Sapaty

Introduction to Parallel Algorithms / C. Xavier and S. S. Iyengar

Solutions to Parallel and Distributed Computing Problems: Lessons from Biological Sciences / Albert Y. Zomaya, Fikret Ercal, and Stephan Olariu (*Editors*)

New Parallel Algorithms for Direct Solution of Linear Equations / C. Siva Ram Murthy, K. N. Balasubramanya Murthy, and Srinivas Aluru

Practical PRAM Programming / Joerg Keller, Christoph Kessler, and Jesper Larsson Traeff

Computational Collective Intelligence / Tadeusz M. Szuba

Parallel and Distributed Computing: A Survey of Models, Paradigms, and Approaches / Claudia Leopold

Fundamentals of Distributed Object Systems: A CORBA Perspective / Zahir Tari and Omran Bukhres

Pipelined Processor Farms: Structured Design for Embedded Parallel Systems / Martin Fleury and Andrew Downton

Handbook of Wireless Networks and Mobile Computing / Ivan Stojmenoviić (*Editor*)

Internet-Based Workflow Management: Toward a Semantic Web / Dan C. Marinescu

Parallel Computing on Heterogeneous Networks / Alexey L. Lastovetsky

Tools and Environments for Parallel and Distributed Computing / S. Hariri and M. Parashar (*Editors*)

Distributed Computing: Fundamentals, Simulations and Advanced Topics, Second Edition / Hagit Attiya and Jennifer Welch

High-Performance Computing: Paradigm and Infrastructure / Laurence T. Yang and Minyi Guo (*Editors*)

HIGH-PERFORMANCE COMPUTING
Paradigm and Infrastructure

Edited by

LAURENCE T. YANG
MINYI GUO

A JOHN WILEY & SONS, INC., PUBLICATION

Library of Congress Cataloging-in-Publication Data:

High performance computing : paradigm and infrastructure / [edited by] Laurence Tianruo Yang and
Minyi Guo.
    p. cm.
   Includes bibliographical references.
   ISBN-13 978-0-471-65471-1 (cloth : alk. paper)
   ISBN-10 0-471-65471-X (cloth : alk. paper)
   1. High performance computing. 2. Parallel processing (Electronic computers) 3. Electronic data
processing—Distributed processing. I. Yang, Laurence Tianruo. II. Guo, Minyi.
   QA76.88.H538 2005
   0004′.35—dc22
                     2004028291

Printed in the United States of America.

10 9 8 7 6 5 4 3 2 1

Contents

PART 4   Clusters and Grid Computing

PART 6   Wireless and Mobile Computing

PART 7   High Performance Applications

■■■ Preface

The field of high-performance computing has obtained prominence through advances in electronic and integrated technologies beginning in the 1940s. With hyperthreading in Intel processors, hypertransport links in next-generation AMD processors, multicore silicon in today's high-end microprocessors from IBM, and emerging cluster and grid computing, parallel (and distributed) computing have moved into the mainstream of computing. To fully exploit these advances, researchers and industrial professionals have started to design parallel or distributed software systems and algorithms to cope with large and complex scientific and engineering problems with very tight timing schedules.

This book reports the recent important advances in aspects of the paradigm and infrastructure of high-performance computing. It has 41 chapters contributed by prominent researchers around the world. We believe all of these chapters and topics will not only provide novel ideas, new results, work-in-progress, and state-of-the-art techniques in the area, but also stimulate the future research activities in the area of high-performance computing with applications.

This book is divided into seven parts: programming model, architectural and system support, scheduling and resource management, clusters and grid computing, peer-to-peer computing, wireless and mobile computing, and high-performance applications. For guidance to readers, we will outline the main contributions of each chapter so that they can better plan their perusal of the material. Extensive external citations can be found in the individual chapters. Supplemental material can be found on the following ftp site: ftp://ftp.wiley.com/public/sci_tech_mea/high-performance_computing.

PART I PROGRAMMING MODEL

It has been noted that the acceptance of parallel computing mainly depends on the quality of a high-level programming model, which should provide powerful abstractions in order to free the programmer from the burden of dealing with low-level issues. In the first chapter, Chan et al. describe a high-level, graph-oriented programming model called GOP and a programming environment called ClusterGOP, for building and developing message-passing parallel programs. In the second chapter, Chapman reviews the nature of HPC platforms and programming models that have been designed for use on them. She particularly considers OpenMP, the most recent high-level programming model that successfully uses compiler technology to support the complex task of parallel application development, and she discuss the challenges to its broader deployment in the HPC arena, as well as some possible strategies for overcoming them. In the third chapter, written by Gorlatch, the author describes the SAT (Stages and Transformations) approach to parallel programming, whose main objective is to systematize and simplify the programming process. In Chapter 4, Tikin surveys the state of the art in computation models and programming tools based on the bulk-synchronous parallel (BSP) model, which has now become one of the mainstream research areas in parallel computing, as well as a firm foundation for language and library design.

In Chapter 5, Morris et al. examine the use of two different parallel programming models in heterogeneous systems: MPI, a popular message passing system; and Cilk, an extension to C with dataflow semantics. They consider both the performance of the two systems for a set of simple benchmarks representative of real problems and the ease of programming these systems. The chapter by Gonzalez et al. describes two proposals for the OpenMP programming model arising from the detected lacks in two topics: nested parallelism and pipelined computations. It also presents a proposal introducing the precedence relations in the OpenMP programming model, which allows the programmers to specify explicit point-to-point thread synchronizations, being general enough to manage with any pipelined computation. The emergence of system-on-chip (SOC) design shows the growing popularity of the integration of multiple processors into one chip. In the chapter by Liu et al., the authors propose that a high-level abstraction of parallel programming like OpenMP is suitable for chip multiprocessors. They also present their solutions to extend OpenMP directives to tackle the heterogeneity problem. Several optimization techniques are proposed to utilize advanced architecture features of the target SOC, the Software Scalable System on Chip (3SoC).

PART 2 ARCHITECTURAL AND SYSTEM SUPPORT

The challenge in compiling programs for distributed memory systems is to determine data and computation decompositions so that load balance and low communication overhead can be achieved. In Chapter 8, Lee et al. describe their different compiler techniques for both regular and irregular programs. Hardware prefetching is an effective technique for hiding cache-miss latency and thus improving the overall performance. In Chapter 9, Zhang et al. propose a new prefetching scheme that improves performance without increasing memory traffic or requiring prefetch buffers. For concurrent I/O operations, atomicity defines the results in the overlapped file regions simultaneously read/written by multiple processes. In Chapter 10, Liao et al. investigate the problems arising from the implementation of MPI atomicity for concurrent overlapping write operations. To avoid serializing the I/O, they examine two alternatives: (1) graph-coloring and (2) process-rank ordering. Compared to file locking, these two approaches are scalable and each presents different degrees of I/O parallelism.

For SOR-like PDE solvers, loop tiling either helps little in improving data locality or hurts performance. Chapter 11 by Xue et al. presents a novel compiler technique called code tiling for generating fast tiled codes for these solvers on uniprocessors with a memory hierarchy. This "one-size-fits-all" scheme makes their approach attractive for designing fast SOR solvers without having to generate a multitude of versions specialized for different problem sizes. To enable the process/thread migration and checkpointing schemes to work in heterogeneous environments, Liu and Chaudhary (Chapter 12) have developed an application-level migration and checkpointing package, MigThread, to abstract computation states at the language level for portability. To save and restore such states across different platforms, their chapter proposes a novel "receiver makes right" (RMR) data conversion method called coarse-grain tagged RMR (CGT-RMR), for efficient data marshalling and unmarshalling. In Chapter 13, Baba et al. address comprehensive techniques in receiving message-prediction and its speculative execution in message passing parallel programs. As communication cost is one of the most crucial issues in parallel computation and it prevents highly parallel processing, the authors focus on reduction of idle time in reception processes in message passing systems. They propose prediction algorithms and evaluate them by using NAS Parallel Benchmarks. In the last chapter of this part, Morrison et al. discuss the experiences and lessons learned from applying reconfigurable computing (FPGAs) to high-performance computing. Some example applications are then outlined. Finally, some speculative thoughts on the future of FPGAs in high-performance computing are offered.

PART 3   SCHEDULING AND RESOURCE MANAGEMENT

In Chapter 15, Hong and Prasanna consider the resource allocation problem for computing a large set of equal-sized independent tasks on heterogeneous computing systems. This problem represents the computation paradigm for a wide range of applications such as SETI@home and Monte Carlo simulations. In the next chapter, Antonopoulos et al. first present experimental results that prove the severity of bus saturation effects for the performance of multiprogrammed workloads on SMPs. The performance penalty is often high enough to nullify the benefits of parallelism. Driven by this observation, they introduce two gang-like, kernel-level scheduling policies that target bus bandwidth as a primary shared-system resource. The new policies attained an average 26% performance improvement over the native Linux scheduler. The most common objective function of task scheduling problems is makespan. However, on a computational grid, the second optimal makespan may be much longer than the optimal makespan because the computing power of a grid varies over time. So, if the performance measure is makespan, there is no approximation algorithm in general for scheduling onto a grid. In Chapter 17, Fujimoto and

Hagihara propose a novel criterion of a schedule. The proposed criterion is called total processor cycle consumption, which is the total number of instructions the grid could compute until the completion time of the schedule. The proposed algorithm does not use any prediction information on the performance of underlying resources.

The genetic algorithm has emerged as a successful tool for optimization problems. Vidyarthi et al. (Chapter 18) propose a task allocation model to maximize the reliability of distributed computing systems (DCSs) using genetic algorithms. Their objective in the chapter is to use the same GA proposed in their earlier work to minimize the turnaround time of the task submitted to the DCS and to compare the resultant allocation with the allocation in which reliability is maximized. Heterogeneous computing systems have gained importance due to their ability to execute parallel program tasks. In many cases, heterogeneous computing systems have been able to produce high performance for lower cost than a single large machine in executing parallel program tasks. However, the performance of parallel program execution on such platforms is highly dependent on the scheduling of the parallel program tasks on to the platform machines. In Chapter 19, Hagas and Janecek present a task scheduling algorithm on a bounded number of machines with different capabilities. The algorithm handles heterogeneity of both machines and communication links. A new model for classifying and extracting the application behavior is presented by Senger et al. in Chapter 20. The extraction and classification of process behavior are conducted through the analysis of data that represent the resource occupation. These data are captured and presented on an artificial self-organizing neural network, which is responsible for extracting the process behavior patterns. This architecture allows the periodic and on-line updating of the resource occupation data, which adapts itself to classify new behaviors of the same process. The proposed model aims at providing process behavior information for the load balancing algorithms that use this information in their selection and transference policies.

PART 4   CLUSTERS AND GRID COMPUTING

Computational grids that couple geographically distributed resources are becoming the de-facto computing platform for solving large-scale problems in science, engineering, and commerce. Chapter 21 by Luther et al. introduces design requirements of enterprise grid systems and discusses various middleware technologies that meet them. It mainly presents a .NET-based grid framework called Alchemi, developed as part of the Gridbus project. In the next chapter, the grid middleware issue is discussed. Grid middleware provide users with seamless computing ability and uniform access to resources in the heterogeneous grid environment. Several software toolkits and systems have been developed, most of which are results of academic research projects all over the world. Asadzadeh et al. focus on four of these middleware technologies: UNICORE, Globus, Legion, and Gridbus. They also present their implementation of a resource broker for UNICORE, as this functionality was not supported in it. A comparison of these systems on the basis of the architecture, implementation model, and several other features is included. A Distributed Java

Virtual Machine (DJVM) is a clusterwide virtual machine that supports parallel execution of a multithreaded Java application on clusters. The DJVM hides the physical boundaries between the cluster nodes and allows executed Java threads in parallel to access all cluster resources through a unified interface. In Chapter 23, Zhu et al. address the realization of a distributed Java virtual machine, named JESSICA2, on clusters, and detail its performance analysis.

The goal of data grids is to provide a large virtual storage framework with unlimited power through collaboration among individuals, institutions, and resources. In Chapter 24, Qin and Jiang first review a number of data grid services such as metadata service, data access service, and performance measurement service. They then investigate various techniques for boosting the performance of data grids; these key techniques fall into three camps: data replication, scheduling, and data movement. Since security issues become immediately apparent and critical in grid computing, they also review two intriguing issues related to security in data grids. Finally and importantly, they have identified five interesting open issues, and pointed out some potential solutions to the open problems. In Chapter 25, Bhardwaj discusses how the effect of the "I/O bottleneck" can be mitigated with parallel I/O operations using ROMIO MPI-IO implementation over parallel virtual file systems (PVFSs) on Linux clusters. As an application example, a seismic imaging algorithm has been shown to perform better with Parallel I/O.

Indiana University's AVIDD (Analysis and Visualization of Instrument-Driven Data) facility is the only geographically distributed cluster on the Top 500 list. It ranked 50th by June of 2003, achieving over 1 TFlops of LINPACK performance. In Chapter 26 by Wang et al., AVIDD's hardware and software setup are introduced, and their experience of performance tuning and benchmarking under the guidance of the existing LINPACK performance model is reported. In the end, the advantages of the distributed cluster-building approach are discussed based on the performance measurements. In Chapter 27, the porting on a Globus equipped platform of a hierarchically distributed, shared-memory parallel version of an application for particle-in-cell (PIC) simulation of plasma turbulence is described by Briguglio et al., based on the hierarchical integration of MPI and Open MP, and originally developed for generic (nongrid) clusters of SMP nodes. The service-oriented architectures generally, and web services in particular, have become important research areas in distributed and grid computing. For well-known reasons, a significant number of users have started to realize the importance of "trust" management for supporting business and scientific interactions electronically in service-oriented architectures. The last chapter of this part, authored by Ali et al., investigates the role of "trust" and "reputation" in the context of service provision and use, and proposes an architecture for utilizing these concepts in scientific applications.

PART 5 PEER-TO-PEER COMPUTING

In Chapter 29, Hsiao and King present two types of peer-to-peer (P2P) resource-discovery systems, namely, unstructured and structured P2P systems. Specially, the authors discuss how to perform routing and joining operations in a structured P2P overlay. Additionally, they discuss how a structured P2P system can be enhanced to support searches by keyword, attribute-value pairs, and range. Blind flooding is a popular search mechanism used in current commercial P2P systems because of its simplicity. However, blind flooding among peers or superpeers causes large volumes of unnecessary traffic, although the response time is short. In some search mechanisms, not all peers may be reachable, creating the so-called partial coverage problem. Aiming at alleviating the partial coverage problem and reducing the unnecessary traffic, Liu et al. propose an efficient and adaptive search mechanism, Hybrid Periodical Flooding (HPF), in Chapter 30. HPF retains the advantages of statistics-based search mechanisms, alleviates the partial coverage problem, and provides the flexibility to adaptively adjust different parameters to meet different performance requirements. In order to improve the DHT-based P2P system routing performance, a routing algorithm called HIERAS, taking into account of the hierarchical structure, is proposed by Xu et al. in Chapter 31. In the last chapter of this part, Enokido and Takizawa discuss a group protocol that supports applications with group communication service when QoS supported by networks or required by applications is changed. An autonomic group protocol is realized by cooperation of multiple autonomous agents. Each agent autonomously takes a class of each protocol function. They make clear what combination of classes can be autonomously used by agents in a view. They also present how to autonomously change the manner of retransmission.

PART 6   WIRELESS AND MOBILE COMPUTING

Mobility management is important for both the 2G personal communications services (PCS) networks and the 3G cellular networks. The research presented by Patury et al. in Chapter 33 aims at implementing the gateway location register (GLR) concept in the 3G cellular networks by employing a caching location strategy at the location registers for certain classes of users meeting certain call and mobility criteria. Results obtained without any cache are compared with those from the three cases when a cache is applied only at the GLR, only at the visitor location register (VLR), and at both. Their study indicates when a cache is preferred in 3G cellular networks. Due to the limitation of available energy in the battery-driven devices in wireless ad hoc networks (WANETs), the longevity of the network is of prime concern. Chapter 34, written by Deng and Gupta, reviews the research on maximizing the lifetime of tree-based multicasting in WANETs. The problem can be divided into two categories. When a single tree is used throughout the multicast session, maximum multicast time can be found in polynomial time. In the other situation, where more than one multicast tree is used alternately, a quantized-time version of this problem has been proven to be NP-hard. In the next chapter, authored by Kim et al., first proposes two QoS-aware scatternet scheduling algorithms: a perfect algorithm for bipartite scatternets and a distributed local algorithm for general scatternets. Then, they analyze the QoS performance of the proposed algorithms and evaluate the quantitative performance by simulation. For the objective performance evaluation, they devise a random scheduling algorithm and compare the performance results of both algorithms.

PART 7   HIGH-PERFORMANCE APPLICATIONS

In the first high-performance applications chapter, Harvey et al. present MinEX, a novel latency-tolerant partitioner that dynamically balances processor workloads while minimizing data movement and runtime communication for applications that are executed in a parallel distributed-grid environment. The chapter also presents comparisons between the performance of MinEX and that of METIS, a popular multilevel family of partitioners. These comparisons were obtained using simulated heterogeneous grid configurations. A solver for the classical N-body problem is implemented to provide a framework for the comparisons. In Chapter 37, by Cirne et al., the authors discuss how to run bag-of-tasks applications (those parallel applications whose tasks are independent) on computational grids. Bag-of-tasks applications are both relevant and amenable for execution on grids. However, few users currently execute their bag-of-tasks applications on grids. They investigate the reason for this state of affairs and introduce MyGrid, a system designed to overcome the identified difficulties. MyGrid also provides a simple, complete, and secure way for a user to run bag-of-tasks applications on all resources she or he has access to. In the next chapter, Tabirca et al. present an efficient method to calculate in parallel the values of the Smarandache function. The computation has an important constraint, which is to have consecutive values computed by the same processor. This makes the dynamic scheduling methods inapplicable. The proposed solution in the chapter is based on a balanced workload block scheduling method. Experiments show that the method is efficient and generates a good load balance.

In Chapter 39, Orendt et al. present a case study on the design, implementation, and deployment of a low-cost cluster for periodic comparisons of gene sequences using the BLAST algorithms. This work demonstrates that it is possible to build a scalable system that can accommodate the high demands imposed by the need for continuous updating of the existing comparisons due to newly available genetic sequences. Branch & bound applications represent a typical example of irregularly structured problems whose parallelization using hierarchical computational architectures (e.g., clusters of SMPs) involves several issues. In Chapter 40, Aversa et al. show how the combined use of PVM and OpenMP libraries allow us to develop hybrid code in order to introduce an additional dynamic distribution among the shared memory nodes of the system. Both coarse-grain and fine-grain parallelization are based on the coordinator/workers paradigm. In the last of the whole book, Bonifacio and Spinillo describe an advanced telecommunication service, based on a convergent architecture between TDM networks and IP networks. The service makes use of advanced protocols and a layered architecture, for the fast delivery of new features and the best leaveraging of existing legacy solutions. The chapter gives a short overview of advanced elephony architectures and protocols, focusing then on describing the detailed implemented solutions.

ACKNOWLEDGMENTS

Of course, our division of this book into parts is arbitrary. The represented areas, as well, are not an exhaustive representation of the world of current high-performance computing. Nonetheless, they represent a rich and many-faceted body of knowledge that we have the pleasure of sharing with our readers. We would like to thank the authors for their excellent contributions and patience in assisting us. Last but not the least, we thank Professor Albert Y. Zomaya very much for helping and encouraging us to finish this work. All the great help and patience from Val Moliere and Emily Simmons of Wiley throughout this project are also very warmly acknowledged.

LAURENCE T. YANG
MINYI GUO

Antigonish, Nova Scotia, Canada
Fukushima, Japan
September 2005

Contributors

Rashid J. Al-Ali, School of Computer Science and Welsh eScience Centre, Cardiff University, Cardiff, United Kingdom

Ali Shaikh Ali, School of Computer Science and Welsh eScience Centre, Cardiff University, Cardiff, United Kingdom

Alejandro Sanchez Alvarado, Department of Neurobiology and Anatomy, University of Utah, Salt Lake City, Utah

Christos D. Antonopoulos, High Performance Information Systems Lab, Computer Engineering and Informatics Department, University of Patras, Patras, Greece

Anish Arora, Department of Computer and Information Science, The Ohio Statue University, Columbus, Ohio

Parvin Asadzadeh, Grid Computing and Distributed Systems Lab, Department of Computer Science and Software Engineering, University of Melbourne, Melbourne, Australia

R. Aversa, Department of Engineering Information, Second University of Naples, Aversa, Italy

E. Ayguade, Computer Architecture Department, Technical University of Catalonia, Barcelona, Spain

Takanobu Baba, Department of Information Science, Faculty of Engineering, Utsunomiya University, Utsunomiya, Tochigi, Japan

Carla Osthoff Barros, Department of Computer Systems, Federal University of Campina Grande, Campina Grande, Brazil

Dheeraj Bhardwaj, Department of Computer Science and Engineering, Indian Institute of Technology, Delhi, India

Laxmi Bhuyan, Department of Computer Science and Engineering, University of California, Riverside, California

Rupak Biswas, NAS Division, NASA Ames Research Center, Moffett Field, California

Anna Bonifacio, Covansys, Rome, Italy

Francisco Brasileiro, Department of Computer Systems, Federal University of Campina Grande, Campina Grande, Brazil

Sergio Briguglio, Association EURATOMENEA, Frascati, Rome, Italy

Rajkumar Buyya, Grid Computing and Distributed Systems Lab, Department of Computer Science and Software Engineering, University of Melbourne, Melbourne, Australia

Jiannong Cao, Department of Computing, Hong Kong Polytechnic University, Hung Hom, Kowloon, Hong Kong, China

Regina Helena Carlucci Santana, Department of Computer Science and Statistics, Mathematics and Computer Science Institute, University of Sao Paulo, Sao Carlos, Brazil

Fan Chan, Department of Computing, Hong Kong Polytechnic University, Hung Hom, Kowloon, Hong Kong, China

Barbara Chapman, Department of Computer Science, University of Houston, Houston, Texas

Vipin Chaudhary, Institute for Scientific Computing, Wayne State University, Detroit, Michigan

Alok Choudhary, Electrical and Computer Engineering Department, Northwestern University, Evanston, Illinois

Walfredo Cirne, Department of Computer Systems, Federal University of Campina Grande, Campina Grande, Brazil

Kenin Coloma, Electrical and Computer Engineering Department, Northwestern University, Evanston, Illinois

Lauro Costa, Department of Computer Systems, Federal University of Campina Grande, Campina Grande, Brazil

Sajal K. Das, Department of Computer Science, University of Texas at Arlington, Arlington, Texas

Guofeng Deng, Department of Computer Science and Engineering, Arizona State University, Tempe, Arizona

Beniamino Di Martino, Department of Engineering Information, Second University of Naples, Aversa, Italy

Tomoya Enokido, Department of Computers and Systems Engineering, Tokyo Denki University, Ishizaka, Hatoyama, Hiki, Saitama, Japan

Julio C. Facelli, Center for High Performance Computing, University of Utah, Salt Lake City, Utah

Weijian Fang, Department of Computer Science, University of Hong Kong, Pokfulam Road, Hong Kong, China

Rodrigo Fernandes de Mello, Department of Computer Science and Statistics, Mathematics and Computer Science Institute, University of Sao Paulo, Sao Carlos, Brazil

Giulana Fogaccia, Association EURATOMENEA, Frascati, Rome, Italy

Noriyuki Fujimoto, Graduate School of Information Science and Technology, Osaka University, Toyonaka, Osaka, Japan

Fumihito Furukawa, Venture Business Laboratory, Utsunomiya University, Tochigi, Japan

Marc Gonzalez, Computer Architecture Department, Technical University of Catalonia, Barcelona, Spain

Sergei Gorlatch, Institute for Information, University of Munster, Munster, Germany

Minyi Guo, Department of Computer Software, University of Aizu, Aizu-Waka-matsu-Shi, Japan

Rajiv Gupta, Department of Computer Science, University of Arizona, Tucson, Arizona

Sandeep K. S. Gupta, Department of Computer Science and Engineering, Arizona State University, Tempe, Arizona

Kenichi Hagihara, Graduate School of Information Science and Technology, Osaka University, Toyonaka, Osaka, Japan

Tarek Hagras, Department of Computer Science and Engineering, Czech Technical University, Praha, Czech Republic

Dave Hart, University Information Technology Services, Indiana University, Bloomington, Indiana

Daniel J. Harvey, Department of Computer Science, Southern Oregon University, Ashland, Oregon

Brian Haymore, Center for High Performance Computing, University of Utah, Salt Lake City, Utah

Philip D. Healy, Department of Computer Science, The Kane Building, The University of College Cork, Cork, Ireland

Bo Hong, Department of Electrical Engineering—Systems, University of California, Los Angeles, California

Hung-Chang Hsiao, Department of Computer Science, National Tsing Hua University, Hsinchu, Taiwan

Yiming Hu, Electrical and Computer Engineering, and Computer Science, University of Cincinnati, Cincinnati, Ohio

Qingguang Huang, School of Computer Science and Engineering, University of New South Wales, Sydney, Australia

Yohsiyuki Iwamoto, Nasu-Seiho High Schoo, Tochigi, Japan

Jan Janeček, Department of Computer Science and Engineering, Czech Technical University, Praha, Czech Republic

Hai Jiang, Institute for Scientific Computing, Wayne State University, Detroit, Michigan

Hong Jiang, Department of Computer Science and Engineering, University of Nebraska, Lincoln, Nebraska

Chun Ling Kei, Grid Computing and Distributed Systems Lab, Department of Computer Science and Software Engineering, University of Melbourne, Melbourne, Australia

JunSeong Kim, School of Electrical and Electronics Engineering, Chung-Ang University, Seoul, Korea

Young Man Kim, School of Computer Science, Kookmin University, Seoul, South Korea

Chung-Ta King, Department of Computer Science, National Tsing Hua University, Hsinchu, Taiwan

J. Labarta, Computer Architecture Department, Technical University of Catalonia, Barcelona, Spain

Ten H. Lai, Department of Computer and Information Science, The Ohio Statue University, Columbus, Ohio

Francis C. M. Lau, Department of Computer Science, University of Hong Kong, Pokfulam Road, Hong Kong, China

KyuHo Lee, School of Electrical and Electronics Engineering, Chung-Ang University, Seoul, Korea

PeiZong Lee, Institute of Information Science, Academia Sinica, Taipei, Taiwan

Jie Li, Department of Computer Science, Graduate School of Systems and Information Engineering, University of Tsukuba, Tsukuba Science City, Ibaraki, Japan

Wei-Keng Liao, Electrical and Computer Engineering Department, Northwestern University, Evanston, Illinois

Xiaola Lin, Department of Computer Science, City University of Hong Kong, Kowlon, Hong Kong, China

Feng Liu, Institute for Scientific Computing, Wayne State University, Detroit, Michigan

Yunhao Liu, Department of Computer Science and Engineering, Michigan State University, East Lansing, Michigan

Akshay Luther, Grid Computing and Distributed Systems Lab, Department of Computer Science and Software Engineering, University of Melbourne, Melbourne, Australia

X. Martorell, Computer Architecture Department, Technical University of Catalonia, Barcelona, Spain

N. Mazzocca, Department of Engineering Information, Second University of Naples, Aversa, Italy

John Morris, Department of Computer Science, The University of Auckland, Auckland, New Zealand

John P. Morrison, Department of Computer Science, The Kane Building, The University of College Cork, Cork, Ireland

Deepa Nayar, Grid Computing and Distributed Systems Lab, Department of Computer Science and Software Engineering, University of Melbourne, Melbourne, Australia

Lionel M. Ni, Department of Computer Science, Hong Kong University of Science and Technology, Hong Kong, China

Dimitrios S. Nikolopoulos, Department of Computer Science, The College of William and Mary, Williamsburg, Virginia

Padraig O'Dowd, Department of Computer Science, The Kane Building, The University of College Cork, Cork, Ireland

Kanemitsu Ootsu, Department of Information Science, Faculty of Engineering, Utsunomiya University, Utsunomiya, Tochigi, Japan

Anita M. Orendt, Center for High Performance Computing, University of Utah, Salt Lake City, Utah

Yi Pan, Department of Computer Science, Georgia State University, Atlanta, Georgia

Mary Papakhian, University Information Technology Services, Indiana University, Bloomington, Indiana

Theodore S. Papatheodorou, Department of Computer Science, The College of William and Mary, Williamsburg, Virginia

Daniel Paranhos, Department of Computer Systems, Federal University of Campina Grande, Campina Grande, Brazil

Krishna Priya Patury, Department of Computer Science, Georgia State University, Atlanta, Georgia

Viktor K. Prasanna, Department of Electrical Engineering—Systems, University of California, Los Angeles, California

Neil Pundit, Scalable Computing Systems Department, Sandia National Laboratories, Albuquerque, New Mexico

Xiao Quin, Department of Computer Science, New Mexico Institute of Mining and Technology, Socorro, New Mexico

Kirti Rani, Department of Computer Science, Rani Durgavati University, Jabalpur, India

Omer F. Rana, School of Computer Science, Cardiff University, Cardiff, United Kingdom

Rajiv Ranjan, Grid Computing and Distributed Systems Lab, Department of Computer Science and Software Engineering, University of Melbourne, Melbourne, Australia

Kieran Reynolds, Department of Computer Science, The Kane Building, The University of College Cork, Cork, Ireland

David Richardson, Center for High Performance Computing, University of Utah, Salt Lake City, Utah

Sofia Robb, Department of Neurobiology and Anatomy, University of Utah, Salt Lake City, Utah

Eric Russell, Scalable Computing Systems Department, Sandia National Laboratories, Albuquerque, New Mexico

Marcos José Santana, Department of Computer Science and Statistics, Mathematics and Computer Science Institute, University of Sao Paulo, Sao Carlos, Brazil

Elizeu Santos-Neto, Department of Computer Systems, Federal University of Campina Grande, Campina Grande, Brazil

Biplab Kume Sarker, Department of Computer and Engineering, Kobe University, Kobe, Japan

Luciano José Senger, Department of Informatics, State University of Ponta Grossa, Ponta Grossa, Brazil

Steven Simms, University Information Technology Services, Indiana University, Bloomington, Indiana

G. Spinillo, Covansys, Rome, Italy

Craig Stewart, University Information Technology Services, Indiana University, Bloomington, Indiana

Sabin Tabirca, Department of Computer Science, The Kane Building, The University of College Cork, Cork, Ireland

Tatiana Tabirca, Department of Computer Science, The Kane Building, The University of College Cork, Cork, Ireland

Makoto Takizawa, Department of Computers and Systems Engineering, Tokyo Denki University, Ishizaka, Hatoyama, Hiki, Saitama, Japan

Alexander Tiskin, Department of Computer Science, University of Warwick, Conventry, United Kingdom

Anil Kumar Tripathi, Department of Computer Science, Faculty of Science, Banaras Hindu University, Varanasi, India

George Turner, University Information Technology Services, Indiana University, Bloomington, Indiana

Salvatore Venticinque, Department of Engineering Information, Second University of Naples, Aversa, Italy

Srikumar Venugopal, Grid Computing and Distributed Systems Lab, Department of Computer Science and Software Engineering, University of Melbourne, Melbourne, Australia

Deo Prakash Vidyarhi, Department of Computer Science, Faculty of Science, Banaras Hindu University, Varanasi, India

Gregorio Vlad, Association EURATOMENEA, Frascati, Rome, Italy

John Paul Walters, Institute for Scientific Computing, Wayne State University, Detroit, Michigan

Chien-Min Wang, Institute of Information Science, Academia Sinica, Taipei, Taiwan

Cho-Li Wang, Department of Computer Science, University of Hong Kong, Pokfulam Road, Hong Kong, China

Peng Wang, University Information Technology Services, Indiana University, Bloomington, Indiana

Lee Ward, Scalable Computing Systems Department, Sandia National Laboratories, Albuquerque, New Mexico

Jan-Jan Wu, Institute of Information Science, Academia Sinica, Taipei, Taiwan

Li Xiao, Department of Computer Science and Engineering, Michigan State University, East Lansing, Michigan

Yang Xiao, Computer Science Division, The University of Memphis, Memphis, Tennessee

Zhiyong Xu, Department of Computer Science and Engineering, University of California, Riverside, California

Jingling Xue, School of Computer Science and Engineering, University of New South Wales, Sydney, Australia

Laurence T. Yang, Department of Computer Science, St. Francis Xavier University, Antigonish, Nova Scotia, Canada

Takashi Yokota, Department of Information Science, Faculty of Engineering, Utsunomiya University, Utsunomiya, Tochigi, Japan

Youtao Zhang, Department of Computer Science, University of Texas at Dallas, Richardson, Texas

Wenzhang Zhu, Department of Computer Science, University of Hong Kong, Pokfulam Road, Hong Kong, China

Zhenyun Zhuang, Department of Computer Science and Engineering, Michigan State University, East Lansing, Michigan

## CHAPTER 1

ClusterGOP: A High-Level Programming Environment for Clusters

FAN CHAN, JIANNONG CAO, and MINYI GUO

1.1 INTRODUCTION

Traditionally, parallel programs are designed using low-level message-passing libraries, such as PVM [18] or MPI [29]. Message-passing (MP) provides the two key aspects of parallel programming: (1) synchronization of processes and (2) read/write access for each processor to the memory of all other processors [23]. However, programmers still encountered difficulties when using MP facilities to develop parallel programs, especially for large-scale applications. First, MP facilities such as MPI and PVM provide low-level programming tools. Their interfaces are simple but force the programmer to deal with low-level details, and their functions are too complicated to use for a nonprofessional programmer. The low-level parallel primitives make the writing of real-world parallel applications tedious and error-prone. Second, often, the main implementation complexity arises from the process management of MP facilities. Applications require the programming of process management, which is not an easy task. Third, MPMD (multiple program multiple data) programming is difficult in many situations without good support. For example, MPI is mainly for SPMD (single program multiple data) programming. Even with some new and enhanced features in MPI-2 [20], the support is not sufficient for programmers to take advantage of the MPMD paradigm. Consequently, programming parallel applications requires special techniques and skills, which are different for each MP facility, and programmers have to rely on their experience, quite often in an ad-hoc way.

It has been agreed that the acceptance of parallel computing mainly depends on the quality of a high-level programming model, which should provide powerful abstractions in order to free the programmer from the burden of dealing with low-level issues [3]. Several high-level models have been developed for message-pass-

High-Performance Computing: Paradigm and Infrastructure. Edited by L. T. Yang and M. Guo
Copyright © 2006 John Wiley & Sons, Inc.

1

ing programming. Ensemble [12, 13, 14] supports the design and implementation of message-passing applications (running on MPI and PVM), particularly MPMD and those demanding irregular or partially regular process topologies. In Ensemble, the applications are built by composition of modular message-passing components. There are some other high-level languages (e.g., Mentat [19], C++ [9], and Fortran-M [16]), and runtime systems (e.g., Nexus [17]), which support combinations of dynamic task creation, load balancing, global name space, concurrency, and heterogeneity. Programming platforms based on an SPMD model (e.g., Split-C [15] and CRL [22]) usually have better performance than MPMD-based ones. MPRC [11, 10] is an MPMD system that uses RPC as the primary communication abstraction and can produce good results compared with the SPMD model. Some proramming tools integrate message passing with other parallel programming paradigms to enhance the programming support. The Nanothreads Programming Model (NPM) [21] is such a programming model; it integrates shared memory with MPI and offers the capability to combine their advantages. Another example is Global Arrays (GA) [26], which allows programmers to easily express data parallelism in a single, global address space. GA provides an efficient and portable shared-memory programming interface for parallel computers. The use of GA allows the programmer to program as if all the processors have access to the same data in shared memory.

Graphical programming environments have also been developed to ease parallel programming using visual and interactive approaches. CODE [2, 24] provides a visual programming environment with a graphical parallel programming language. The programmer can create a parallel program by drawing a dataflow graph that shows the communication structure of the program. HeNCE [1] is a graphical environment for creating and running parallel programs in graphs over a heterogeneous collection of computers. Differing from CODE, the graph in HeNCE shows the control flow of a program [28]. VPE [25] is a visual parallel programming environment. It provides a simple GUI for creating message-passing programs and supports automatic compilation, execution, and animation of the programs.

In this chapter, we describe a high-level, graph-oriented programming model called GOP and a programming environment called ClusterGOP for building and developing message-passing parallel programs. GOP [5, 4] supports high-level design and programming of parallel and distributed systems by providing built-in support for a language-level construct and various operations on a high-level abstraction called the *logical graph*. With GOP, the configuration of the interacting processes of a parallel/distributed program can be represented as a user-specified logical graph that is mapped onto the physical network topology. The programming of interprocess communication and synchronization between local processors is supported by built-in primitives for graph-based operations. ClusterGOP is a programming environment built on top of the GOP model, providing a high-level programming abstraction through the ClusterGOP library for building parallel applications in clusters, It contains tools for development of GOP-based parallel programs with intelligent, visual support and a run-time system for deployment, execution, and management of the programs. ClusterGOP supports both SPMD and MPMD parallel computing paradigms [7, 8]. Also, with ClusterGOP, developing large parallel programs can be simplified with the predefined graph types and scalability support. The ClusterGOP system is portable as its implementation is based almost exclusively on calls to MPI, a portable message-passing standard.

The rest of chapter is organized as follows. Section 1.2 presents an overview of the ClusterGOP framework, including the GOP model and the ClusterGOP architecture. Section 1.3 describes the main features of the VisualGOP tool for supporting visual program development, from program construction to process mapping and compilation. In Section 1.4, we describe the ClusterGOP library of programming primitives. Support for MPMD programming in ClusterGOP is discussed in Section 1.5. Section 1.6 illustrates how parallel program development is done in ClusterGOP by using an example. Finally Section 1.7 concludes the chapter with a discussion of our future work.

1.2   GOP MODEL AND ClusterGOP ARCHITECTURE

ClusterGOP is based on the GOP model. In developing GOP for parallel programming, it was our observation that many parallel programs can be modeled as a group of tasks performing local operations and coordinating with each other over a logical graph, which depicts the program configuration and intertask communication pattern of the application. Most of the graphs are regular ones such as tree and mesh. Using a message-passing library, such as PVM and MPI, the programmer needs to manually translate the design-level graph model into its implementation using low-level primitives. With the GOP model, such a graph metaphor is made explicit at the programming level by directly supporting the graph construct in constructing the program.

The key elements of GOP are a logical graph construct to be associated with the local programs (LPs) of a parallel program and their relationships, and a collection of functions defined in terms of the graph and invoked by messages traversing the graph. In GOP, a parallel program is defined as a collection of LPs that may execute on several processors [4, 5]. Parallelism is expressed through explicit creation of LPs and communication between LPs is solely via message passing. GOP allows programmers to configure the LPs into a logical graph, which can serve the purpose of naming, grouping, and configuring LPs. It can also be used as the underlying structure for implementing uniform message passing and LP coordination mechanisms. The code of the LPs can be implemented using a set of high-level operations defined over the graph. As shown in Figure 1.1, the GOP model consists of the following parts:

- A logical graph (directed or undirected) whose nodes are associated with LPs, and whose edges define the relationships between the LPs.
- An LPs-to-nodes mapping, which allows the programmer to bind LPs to specific nodes.

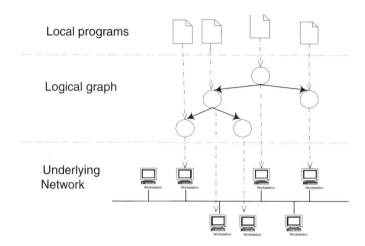

Local programs

Logical graph

Underlying
Network

Figure 1.1   The GOP conceptual model.

- An optional nodes-to-processors mapping, which allows the programmer to explicitly specify the mapping of the logical graph to the underlying network of processors. When the mapping specification is omitted, a default mapping will be performed.
- A library of language-level, graph-oriented programming primitives.

The GOP model provides high-level abstractions for programming parallel applications, easing the expression of parallelism, configuration, communication, and coordination by directly supporting logical graph operations (GOP primitives). GOP programs are conceptually sequential but augmented with primitives for binding LPs to nodes in a graph, with the implementation of graph-oriented, inter-node communications completely hidden from the programmer. The programmer first defines variables of the graph construct in a program and then creates an instance of the construct. Once the local context for the graph instance is set up, communication and coordination of LPs can be implemented by invoking operations defined on the specified graph. The sequential code of LPs can be written using any programming language such as C, C++, or Java.

1.2.1   The ClusterGOP Architecture

The framework of the ClusterGOP programming environment is illustrated in Figure 1.2. The top layer is VisualGOP, the visual programming tool [6]. The ClusterGOP Application Programming Interface (API) is provided for the programmer to build parallel applications based on the high-level GOP model. The ClusterGOP library provides a collection of routines implementing the ClusterGOP API, with a very simple functionality to minimize the package overhead [7].

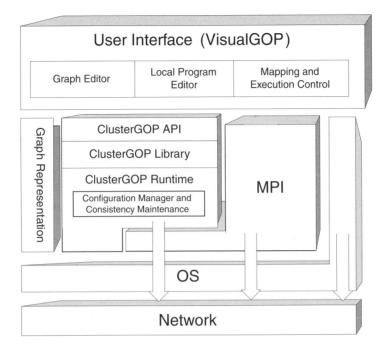

Figure 1.2   The ClusterGOP framework.

The ClusterGOP Runtime is responsible for compiling the application, maintaining the logical graph structure, and executing the application. On each machine, there exist two runtimes. The first one is the ClusterGOP runtime, a background process that provides graph deployment, update, querying, and synchronization. The second is the MPI runtime, which is used by ClusterGOP as the low-level parallel programming facility for the ClusterGOP implementation.

As shown in Figure 1.3, the architecture of ClusterGOP is divided into three layers: the programming layer, the compilation layer, and the execution layer. In the programming layer, the programmer develops a ClusterGOP program using GOP's high-level abstraction. ClusterGOP exports a set of APIs with supporting library routines that provides the implementation of the parallel applications with traditional programming languages, e.g., the C language.

In the compilation layer, LPs will be transformed into an executable program in the target's execution environment. The LPs are compiled with both the MPI and the ClusterGOP libraries.

The bottom execution layer is realized through the services of two important runtimes, the MPI runtime and the ClusterGOP runtime. The MPI runtime is used by ClusterGOP for implementing process communication through the network. The ClusterGOP runtime is developed as a daemon process on top of the operating system on each node. It helps the ClusterGOP processes to dynamically resolve the

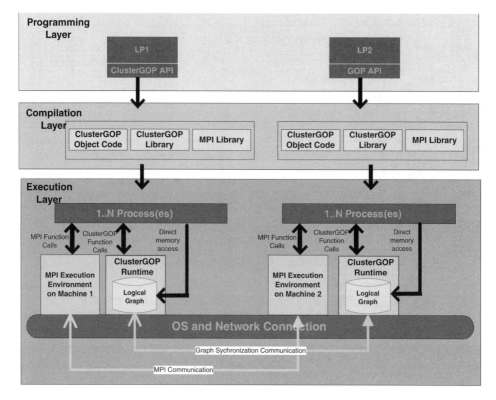

Figure 1.3   The ClusterGOP program communication implementation.

node names into process IDs and to prepare for MPI communication. A graph representation is used for the operations defined by ClusterGOP primitives. The ClusterGOP runtime provides the synchronization among all the nodes, so that each node can maintain the most updated logical graph for running ClusterGOP primitives. The ClusterGOP runtime system is implemented by the C language with socket communication and synchronization functions. Nodes in the same machine use the shared memory to access the graph. Nodes on different machines use a memory coherence protocol called the Sequential Consistency Model [27] to synchronize graph updating.

1.3   VISUALGOP

VisualGOP is a visual tool that supports the design, construction, and deployment of ClusterGOP programs. It helps the programmer further eliminate many coding details and simplify many of the program development tasks.

The organization of ClusterGOP components is shown in Figure 1.4. There are two levels: the visual level and the nonvisual level. Figure 1.5 shows a screen of

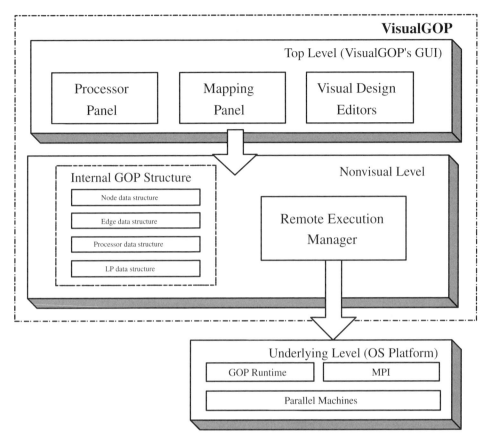

Figure 1.4   The VisualGOP architecture.

the main visual interface of VisualGOP. The components for visual program construction provide graphical aids (visual design editors) for constructing a ClusterGOP program. The graph editor is used to build the logical graph, representing the program structure from a visual perspective. The LP editor is used for editing the source code of LPs in a ClusterGOP program. The components for mapping and resource management provide the programmer the control over the mapping of LPs to graph nodes and the mapping of graph nodes to processors (through the mapping panel). They also allow the programmer to access the information about the status of the machine and network elements (through the processor panel).

The nonvisual level contains components responsible for maintaining a representation of GOP program design and deployment information. This representation is kept in memory when program design takes place, and is later stored in a file. Components in this level are also responsible for compilation and execution of the constructed programs. Compilation transforms the diagrammatic representations

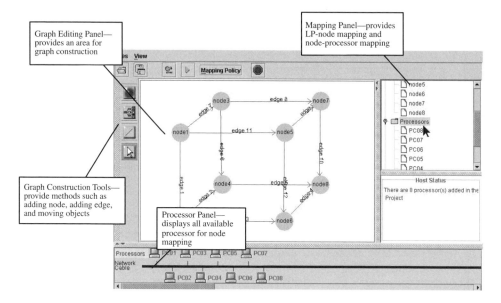

Figure 1.5   The main screen of VisualGOP.

and GOP primitives in the LPs into the target machines code. The remote execution manager makes use of the stored information to execute the constructed GOP program on a given platform.

With VisualGOP, the programmer starts program development by building a highly abstracted design and then transforms it successively into an increasingly more detailed solution. The facilities provided help the programmer to separate program design and configuration (i.e., the definition of the logical graph) from implementing the program components (i.e., the coding of the LPs). VisualGOP also supports the automation of generating a large portion of GOP code such as declaration and initialization of graph constructs and generation of message templates. The visual programming process under VisualGOP consists of the following iterative stages:

1. Visual programming. The programmer interacts with VisualGOP through a visual representation of the design of a parallel program. The design is presented as a logical graph that consists of a set of nodes representing LPs and a set of edges representing the interactions between the LPs in the program. The graph editor supports the creation and modification of a logical graph and the LP editor is used to visually manipulate the textual LP source code.

2. Binding of LPs to graph nodes. The programmer specifies the binding of LPs of a parallel program to the nodes of the logical graph. The programmer has two ways of doing this. The first way is to create the LPs and then bind them to the graph nodes. Another way is to combine the two steps into one: click

on a node of the graph to open the program editor by which the code of the LP mapped to the node can be entered.

3. Mapping of graph nodes to processors. The programmer specifies the mapping of the nodes in the graph to the processors in the underlying network. The mapping panel of VisualGOP displays the GOP program elements (nodes, processors, LPs) in a hierarchical tree structure. The programmer can use drag-and-drop to bind and unbind the LPs to graph nodes and the graph nodes to processors. Detailed binding information concerning a node can be viewed by selecting and clicking the node. The processor panel displays processors and their connections, and also provides the drag-and-drop function to bind and unbind graph nodes to one of the processors.

4. Compile the LPs. The programmer uses this function to distribute the source files to the specified processors for compilation.

5. Execute the program. The programmer uses this function to execute the constructed GOP program on the specified processors. Outputs will be displayed on the VisualGOP.

During the program design process, VisualGOP provides the user with automated, intelligent assistance. Facilities provided include the generation of ClusterGOP primitives in editing LP code, checking the consistency of LP code against the logical graph specified by the programmer, and support for scalability [6]. All of these are achieved through visual interactions with the tools in VisualGOP.

1.4   THE ClusterGOP LIBRARY

The ClusterGOP runtime has been implemented on top of MPI. Graph-oriented primitives for communications, synchronization, and configuration are perceived at the programming level and their implementation hides the programmer from the underlying programming activities associated with accessing services through MPI. The programmer can thus concentrate on the logical design of an application, ignoring unnecessary low-level details.

The implementation of ClusterGOP applications is accomplished through wrapping functions (ClusterGOP library) to native MPI software. In general, ClusterGOP API adheres closely to MPI standards. However, the ClusterGOP library simplifies the API by providing operations that automatically perform some MPI routines. It also allows the argument list to be simplified.

ClusterGOP provides a set of routines to enable graph-oriented point-to-point and collective communications (in both blocking and nonblocking modes). The API follows the MPI standard, but it is simpler and the implementation is specifically designed for the graph-oriented framework. For example, graph node ID is used instead of process ID to represent different processes, so the LP bound to a node can be replaced without affecting other LPs. ClusterGOP API also hides the complexity of low-level addressing and communication, as well as initializing processes from the programmer. Three types of communication and synchronization primitives are provided [7]:

1. *Point-to-point communication* consists of a process that sends a message and another process that receives the message—a send/receive pair. These two operations are very important as well as being the most frequently used operations. To implement optimal parallel applications, it is essential to have a model that accurately reflects the characteristics of these basic operations. ClusterGOP provides primitives for a process to send a message to and receive a message from a specific graph node, as well as primitives for sending messages to nodes with relationships defined in terms of the graph, such as parents, children, neighbors, and so on.

2. *Collective Communication* refers to message passing involving a group (collection) of processes. Sometimes, one wishes to gather data from one or more processes and share this data among all participating processes. At other times, one may wish to distribute data from one or more processes to a specific group of processes. In ClusterGOP API, another type of collection communication primitives using the parent and child relationships is provided. It is used for finding the parent or child nodes, and then broadcasts the data to all the corresponding nodes.

3. *Synchronization operations* are provided to support the synchronization of processes.

ClusterGOP also provides a set of operations to query the information about nodes and edges in the graph. The information can be generated during the running of the application. Programmers can use the query information in communication. For example, when programmers want to find the neighbor node connected to the current node, they can use an API function to retrieve the node name of a connected edge. Programming in this way helps programmers dynamically assign the node names in the communication procedures, without specifying static node names in the LP code. Therefore, it helps programmers design the LP structure freely, and produces a more readable code for software maintenance.

1.5 MPMD PROGRAMMING SUPPORT

MPMD is advantageous when the application becomes large and complex with heterogeneous computations requiring irregular or unknown communication patterns. MPMD separates the application into different loosely coupled functional modules with different program sources for concurrent tasks, thus promoting code reuse and the ability to compose programs.

With the MPMD programming model under ClusterGOP, each LP is associated with a separate source code. Data can be distributed and exchanged among the LPs. ClusterGOP also has a better node-group management than MPI so that the processes can form groups easily and efficiently. The main features in ClusterGOP to support high-level MPMD programming include forming process groups, data distribution among the processes, and deployment of processes for execution. With these features, programmers can program group communication by using Node-Group, manage distributed tasks and processors through visual interfaces, map resources to tasks, and compile and execute programs automatically. The underlying implementation using MPI is hidden from the programmer.

In ClusterGOP, we use a NodeGroup to represent a group of processes, providing the same functionality as the MPI communicator. NodeGroup helps the programmer to write code for group communications and is implemented using MPI's communicator. A NodeGroup consists of a set of member processes. Each process in the group can invoke group communication operations such as collective communications (gather, scatter, etc.). In the design phase, VisualGOP provides a visual way for representing the NodeGroup involved in a MPMD program. The programmer can highlight the NodeGroup in the logical graph to specify the nodes that belong to the NodeGroup. When the programmer wants to use the collective operations, VisualGOP provides the valid NodeGroup for programmer to select. It also hides the programming details that are used for constructing the NodeGroup in the MPMD programs so that the programmer can concentrate on programming the nodes' tasks. As a result, the program is easier to understand.

In the MPMD programming model, tasks have different programs to execute but usually need to exchange or share some data. MPI provides API functions for distributing data to different processes, but the programmer still has to write the code for the data distribution procedure. In ClusterGOP, tasks share data by keeping a portion of the global memory in each node that is involved in the communication. The node can update the memory without having to communicate with other nodes. Using VisualGOP, data distribution can be performed by the programmer through the visual interface. The global memory can be created by selecting an option in VisualGOP: vertical, horizontal, or square memory distribution. By default, the memory is distributed to the nodes in a balanced way such that each node will almost share the same amount of the distributed data object. VisualGOP also provides a visual interface to allow the programmer to manually specify the memory distribution on each node. ClusterGOP translates the data distribution specified by the programmer into MPI code.

In many exisiting systems, the distributed memory object is a built-in function and most of the objects are distributed in the whole environment. However, due to its complex design nature, overheads occur frequently that reduce its efficiency. ClusterGOP implements the DSM in a different way in that distributed objects are used only if programmer explicitly demands them. ClusterGOP implements the global memory functions by using the GA toolkit [26], which is based on MPI for communications. GA provides an efficient and portable shared-memory programming interface. In ClusterGOP, before compiling the application, all distributed objects are converted into Global Array (GA) codes.

In MPMD programming, managing the mapping of nodes (tasks) to processors can be a complicated task. VisualGOP provides the support for visually mapping LPs to nodes and nodes to processors, and for automatic compilation and execution of the applications. This facilitates the development process and simplifies the running of the large-scale MPMD application.

1.6 PROGRAMMING USING ClusterGOP

1.6.1 Support for Program Development

In VisualGOP, programmers are provided with a variety of abstractions that are useful in developing parallel programs. When designing a parallel program, the programmer starts by constructing a graph that shows the program structure. A graph is constructed in VisualGOP as a structure containing data types for describing a conceptual graph. The programmer can use the graph editing panel to draw the graph, which will be translated to the textual form. The graph editing panel displays the graphical construction view of VisualGOP, and this is where all of the editing of the program's logical graph structure takes place. Controls are provided for drawing the graph components within this panel. These controls include functions for adding nodes, subgraph nodes, and edges, as well as for moving nodes. Also, edges can be added between two nodes by joining the source and the destination nodes.

The programmer then can use the LP editor to define source code for LPs attached to the graph nodes (see Figure 1.6). The programmer can type in the code or

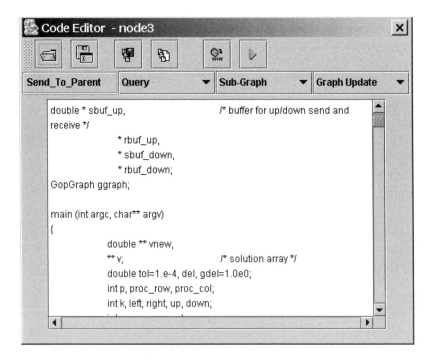

Figure 1.6 Editing the LP.

load the existing program source into the editor. After that, the new LP will be bound to the node automatically. ClusterGOP primitives can be automatically generated from visual icons. Also, the LP editor provides consistency checking to prevent the creation of graph semantic errors. For example, the programmer is not allowed to make incorrect connections, such as connecting a node to a nonexistent node. To assist the programmer with graph-oriented programming, the editor has features to ensure that newly created or modified node or edge names are correct within the logical graph structure.

The LPs of the parallel program need to be bound to the nodes of a logical graph for naming, configuration, and communication purposes. They also need to be distributed to processors in the underlying network for execution through the Cluster-GOP runtime system. Therefore, after the logical graph and LPs are created, the programmer needs to bind the LPs to the nodes, and to set up a processor list for binding the nodes to the processors. These are achieved by using VisualGOP's LP-to-node mapping and node-to-processor mapping functions. When the programmer selects the status of a specific node, an LP can be chosen from the node property's pull-down menu. After the selection, the LP is mapped to that node. When using the node-to-processor function, the programmer can explicitly specify the mapping by dragging and dropping the node into one of the processors in the processor panel, or let the GOP system automatically perform task allocation. Once mapped, the graph node has all this required information such as IP address/hostname, compiler path, and so on.

The mapping panel presents the graph component properties in a simple tree structure. The components are classified into one of three categories: node, processor, or local program. Each component shows its properties in the program, and the mapping relationship that it belongs to. It is updated automatically whenever the program structure is modified in the graph editing panel.

Let us look at an example (see Figure 1.7). We first define a mapping, M1, for a MPMD program, which defines the relationships between the graph nodes and the LPs for the program. In the map, there are several types of LPs: the distributor, which receives and distributes the data, and the calculator, which calculates and submits its own partial data to the distributor and receives data from the neighbor nodes and from the distributor. Our definition of M1 is (given in the C language, where LV-MAP is the corresponding map data type):

LV-MAP M1 =
{ {0, "distributor"}, {1, "calculatorA"}, {2, "calculatorA"}, {3, "calculatorB"},
{4, "calculatorA"}, {5, "calculatorA"}, {6, "calculatorB"}, {7, "calculatorC"},
{8, "calculatorC"}, {9, "calculatorD"} }

Then, we can specify a mapping, M2, of the graph nodes onto the processors. With the aid of the processor panel, the node is mapped onto the target processor. It is assumed that each node will be executed on a different processor. The processor panel displays information about processor availability. If it is currently assigned, the relevant node is indicated.

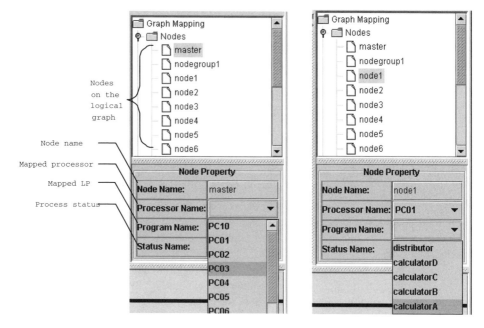

Figure 1.7   LP-to-node and node-to-processor mapping.

The final step in building an application is to compile and execute the LPs on the target processors. VisualGOP automatically generates the compiled machine code and starts the program execution remotely. It recognizes the LP's implementation language type and invokes the corresponding remote compilation and execution procedures. Remote ClusterGOP runtimes installed on the target machines are listening for incoming requests.

When the programmer selects the remote compilation option for a node, he/she can specify the processor to be used as the target for compiling the program source for execution. The machine's name is the same as that of the processor that the programmer specified in the graph panel. After a processor is selected, the program source is made ready for compilation. The programmer is only required to input the command argument that is used for compiling or executing the LP on the target machine. After that, the remote compilation and execution will be done automatically. The execution results can be viewed through VisualGOP.

1.6.2   Performance of ClusterGOP

Serveral example applications have been implemented on ClusterGOP, including the finite difference method, parallel matrix multiplication, and two-dimensional fast Fourier transform [8]. The performance of the applications are evaluated using MPI and ClusterGOP. We use Parallel Matrix Multiplication to show how ClusterGOP supports the construction and running of parallel programs on clusters.

In this example, we consider the problem of computing $C = A \times B$, where A, B, and C are dense matrices of size $N \times N$ (see Equation 1.1).

$$C_{ij} = \sum_{k=0}^{N-1} A_{ik} \times B_{kj} \qquad (1.1)$$

As shown in Figure 1.8, a 3×3 mesh is defined in this example. Besides $N \times N$ nodes in the mesh, there is an additional node, named "master," which is connected to all the nodes of the mesh. There are two types of programs in this example: "distributor" and "calculator." There is only one instance of "distributor," which is associated with the "master" node. Each mesh node is associated with an instance of "calculator." The "distributor" program first decomposes the matrices A and B into blocks, whose sizes are determined by the mesh's dimension. It then distributes the blocks to the nodes on the left-most column and the nodes on the bottom rows, respectively. Each "calculator" receives a block of matrix A and matrix B from its left edge and bottom edge, and also propagates the block along its right edge and top edge. After data distribution, each "calculator" calculates the partial product and sends it back to the "distributor." The "distributor" assembles all the partial products and displays the final result.

The experiments used a cluster of twenty-five Linux workstations; each workstation running on a Pentium-4 2GHz. The workstations are set up with MPICH 1.2 and all the testing programs are written in C. Execution times were measured in sec-

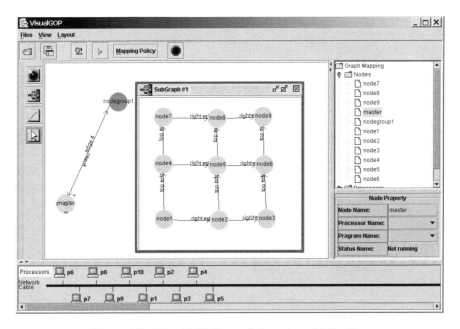

Figure 1.8   VisualGOP for parallel matrix multiplication.

onds using the function MPI Wtime(). Measurements were made by inserting instructions to start and stop the timers in the program code. The execution time of a parallel operation is the greatest amount of time required by all processes to complete the execution. We choose to use the minimum value from ten measurements.

Figure 1.9 shows the performance result in execution time. We can see that the MPI program runs slightly faster than the ClusterGOP program. This may be the result of conversion overheads (nodes to the rank ID) in the ClusterGOP library. However, there are no significant differences between MPI and ClusterGOP when the problem size and processor number are getting larger.

1.7   SUMMARY

In this chapter, we first described the GOP approach to providing high-level abstraction in message-passing parallel programming. The GOP model has the desirable features of expressiveness and simple semantics. It provides high-level abstractions for programming parallel programs, easing the expression of parallelism, configuration, communication, and coordination by directly supporting logical graph operations. Furthermore, sequential programming constructs blend smoothly and easily with parallel programming constructs in GOP. We then presented a programming environment called ClusterGOP that supports the GOP model. ClusterGOP supports both SPMD and MPMD programming models with various tools for the programmer to develop and deploy parallel applications. We showed the steps of programming parallel applications using ClusterGOP and reported the results of the evaluation on how ClusterGOP performs compared with the MPI. The results showed that ClusterGOP is as efficient as MPI in parallel programming.

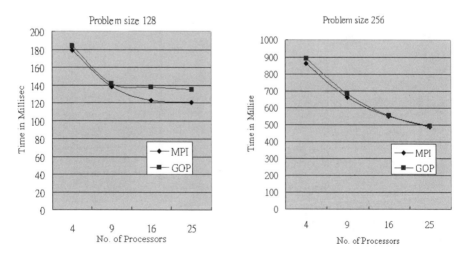

Figure 1.9   Execution time per input array for the parallel matrix multiplication application.

For our future work, we will enhance the current implementation with more programming primitives, such as update and subgraph generation. We will also define commonly used graph types as builtin patterns for popular programming schemes. Finally, we will develop real-world scientific and engineering computing applications using ClusterGOP.

ACKNOWLEDGMENTS

This work was partially supported by Hong Kong Polytechnic University under HK PolyU research grants G-H-ZJ80 and G-YY41.

REFERENCES

1. C. Anglano, R. Wolski, J. Schopf, and F. Berman. Developing heterogeneous applications using zoom and HeNCE. In *Proceedings of the 4th Heterogeneous Computing Workshop,* Santa Barbara, 1995.

2. D. Banerjee and J. C. Browne. Complete parallelization of computations: Integration of data partitioning and functional parallelism for dynamic data structures. In *Proceedings of 10th International Parallel Processing Symposium (IPPS '96),* pp. 354–360, Honolulu, Hawaii, 1996.

3. M. Besch, H. Bi, P. Enskonatus, G. Heber, and M.Wilhelmi. High-level data parallel programming in PROMOTER. In *Proceedings of 2nd International Workshop on High-level Parallel Programming Models and Supportive Environments,* pp. 47–54, Geneva, Switzerland, 1997.

4. J. Cao, L. Fernando, and K. Zhang. DIG: A graph-based construct for programming distributed systems. In *Proceedings of 2nd International Conference on High Performance Computing,* New Delhi, India, 1995.

5. J. Cao, L. Fernando, and K. Zhang. Programming distributed systems based on graphs. In M.A. Orgun and E.A. Ashcroft, (Eds.), *Intensional Programming I,* pp. 83–95. World Scientific, 1996.

6. F. Chan, J. Cao, A. T.S. Chan, and K. Zhang. Visual programming support for graph-oriented parallel/distributed processing. Accepted by *Software—Practice and Experiences, 2004,* 2002.

7. F. Chan, J. Cao, and Y. Sun. High-level abstractions for message-passing parallel programming. *Parallel Computing, 29*(11–12), 1589–1621, 2003.

8. F. Chan, A. T.S. Chan J. Cao, and M. Guo. Programming support forMPMDparallel computing in ClusterGOP. *IEICE Transactions on Information and Systems,* E87-D(7), 2004.

9. K. Chandy and C. Kesselman. Compositional C++: Compositional parallel programming. In *Proceedings of 6th International Workshop in Languages and Compilers for Parallel Computing,* pp. 124–144, 1993.

10. C. Chang, G. Czajkowski, and T. Von Eicken. MRPC: A high performance RPC system for MPMD parallel computing. *Software—Practice and Experiences, 29*(1), 43–66, 1999.

11. C. Chang, G. Czajkowski, T. Von Eicken, and C. Kesselman. Evaluating the performance limitations of MPMD communication. In *Proceedings of ACM/IEEE Supercomputing,* November 1997.

12. J. Y. Cotronis. Message-passing program development by ensemble. In *PVM/MPI 97,* pp. 242–249, 1997.

13. J. Y. Cotronis. Developing message-passing applications on MPICH under ensemble. In *PVM/MPI 98,* pp. 145–152, 1998.

14. J. Y. Cotronis. Modular MPI components and the composition of grid applications. In *Proceedings of the 10th Euromicro Workshop on Parallel, Distributed and Network-Based Processing 2002,* pp. 154–161, 2002.

15. D. Culler,A. Dusseau, S. Goldstein, A. Krishnamurthy, S. Lumeta, T.Von Eicken, and K. Yelick. Parallel programming in Split-C. In *Proceedings of ACM/IEEE Supercomputing,* pp. 262–273, 1993.

16. I. Foster and K. Chandy. FORTRAN M: A language for modular parallel programming. *Journal of Parallel and Distributed Computing, 26*(1), 24–35, 1995.

17. I. Foster, C. Kesselman, and S. Tuecke. The nexus approach for integrating multithreading and communication. *Journal of Parallel and Distributed Computing, 37*(1), 70–82, 1996.

18. A. Geist, A. Beguelin, J. Dongarra, W. Jiang, R. Manchek, and V.S. Sunderam. *PVM: Parallel Virtual Machine: A Users' Guide and Tutorial for Networked Parallel Computing.* MIT Press, Cambridge, MA, 1994.

19. A. Grimshaw. An introduction to parallel object-oriented programming with Mentat. Technical Report 91-07, University of Virginia, July 1991.

20. W. Gropp, S. Huss-Lederman, A. Lumsdaine, E. Lusk, B. Nitzberg, W. Saphir, and M. Snir. *MPI: The Complete Reference, volume 2, The MPI Extensions.* MIT Press, Cambridge, MA, 1998.

21. P.E. Hadjidoukas, E.D. Polychronopoulos, and T.S. Papatheodorou. Integrating MPI and nanothreads programming model. In *Proceedings of the 10th Euromicro Workshop on Parallel, Distributed and Network-Based Processing 2002,* pp. 309–316, 2002.

22. K. Johnson, M. Kaashoek, and D.Wallach. CRL: High-performance all-software distributed shared memory. In *Proceedings of the 15th ACM Symposium on Operating Systems Principles (SOSP),* pp. 213–226, 1995.

23. O. McBryan. An overview of message passing environments. *Parallel Computing, 20*(4), 417–447, 1994.

24. P. Newton. *A Graphical Retargetable Parallel Programming Environment and Its Efficient Implementation.* PhD thesis, University of Texas at Austin, Department of Computer Science, 1993.

25. P. Newton and J. Dongarra. Overview of VPE: A visual environment for messagepassing. In *Proceedings of the 4th Heterogeneous Computing Workshop,* 1995.

26. J. Nieplocha, R. J. Harrison, and R. J. Littlefield. Global arrays: A nonuniform memory access programming model for high-performance computers. *The Journal of Supercomputing, 10*(2), 197–220, 1996.

27. C. Scheurich and M. Dubois. Correct memory operation of cache-based multiprocessors. In *Proceedings of the 14th annual international symposium on Computer Architecture,* pp. 234–243. ACM Press, 1987.

28. V.Y. Shen, C. Richter, M.L. Graf, and J.A. Brumfield. VERDI: a visual environment for designing distributed systems. *Journal of Parallel and Distributed Computing,* 9(2), 128–137, 1990.

29. M. Snir, S. Otto, S. Huss-Lederman, D. Walker, and J. Dongarra. *MPI: The Complete Reference.* MIT Press, Cambridge, MA, USA, 1996.

## CHAPTER 2

The Challenge of Providing a High-Level Programming Model for High-Performance Computing

BARBARA CHAPMAN

2.1 INTRODUCTION

High-performance computing (HPC) is a critical technology that is deployed to design many engineering products, from packaging for electronics components to aeroplanes and their component parts. It is also needed in the design of computers themselves, and in safety testing of automobiles and reactors. It is used in modern drug development and in the creation of synthetic materials. It has helped us investigate global climate change and understand how to preserve rare books. In order to be able to solve these important problems with the required degree of accuracy, HPC codes must efficiently exploit powerful computing platforms. Since these are frequently the newest, and fastest, machines of the day, HPC application developers often become the pioneers who work with engineers and system software designers to identify and overcome a variety of bugs and instabilities. They learn how to write code for new kinds of architectures, and serve as the pilot users of new programming languages, libraries, compilers, and tools for application development and tuning. However, this reprogramming is labor-intensive and inefficient, and HPC applications experts are scarce. High-level programming standards are essential to reduce the human effort involved when applications target new platforms.

But providing a high-level standard for HPC application creation is a major challenge. At any given time, there are a variety of architectures for large-scale computing, with specific features that should be exploited to achieve suitable performance levels. HPC programmers are reluctant to sacrifice performance for ease of programming, and a successful standard must be capable of efficient implementation across these platforms. Moreover, there are additional constraints: sufficient understanding of the programming model is needed so that performance bugs can be identified and strategies for overcoming them designed. Applications must be able to scale, at least in the sense that performance is sustained when both problem and machine size are increased. Finally, HPC is a relatively small market and vendors cannot support a multiplicity of programming models that target it, so a standard must be usable for a large fraction of HPC codes.

In this chapter, we briefly discuss recent HPC hardware technology and then consider attempts to define programming standards for the creation of such applications. We first review the programming models MPI and HPF, and the lessons that were learned from these significant standardization efforts. We then consider more recent models, with a particular focus on OpenMP, and discuss its strong points and problems. We then speculate on what is needed to obtain a useful high-level programming model for HPC. The final part of this chapter discusses a strategy for implementing OpenMP on clusters, which we refer to as DMPs, and show that it has great potential, but that a compiler-oriented approach remains a challenge. There is a mismatch between the traditional behavior of HPC applications developers, who are accustomed to the hard work of low-level, machine-specific programming, and the declared goal of high-level approaches that attempt to provide a reduction in development effort. In the future, there may not be the luxury of a choice and it is important that this technology be further improved.

2.2 HPC ARCHITECTURES

2.2.1 Early Parallel Processing Platforms

The 1990s saw the emergence of the first parallel programming "standards" for HPC, and hardware that was deployed at the time dictated the nature of these activities. At the start of the decade, vector supercomputing systems such as those marketed by Cray Research, Fujitsu, and NEC, were widely used to run large-scale applications. Two to four vector processors were combined to form particularly powerful systems with a single shared memory that were efficiently exploited by major numerical computations in weather forecasting, fluid dynamics, and more. Bus-based shared-memory parallel systems (SMPs), consisting of small numbers of RISC CPUs that share memory, were also available, but their uptake faltered when it became clear that it would be hard to extend this technology to larger CPU counts. Transputers had given rise to simple, low-cost clusters that gave some early adopters their first taste of inexpensive parallel computing, and a number of HPC researchers had migrated to the new distributed-memory parallel platforms (DMPs), produced by companies such as Intel, Meiko, and nCUBE. SIMD (single instruction, multiple data) computers (e.g., from Thinking Machines and Maspar), which execute an instruction on all the elements of an array simultaneously, were in use, and there had been experiments with cache-coherent platforms, notably by Kendall Square Research.

Vector systems were expensive to purchase and operate. As a result, they were usually operated by centers that serviced the needs of a number of paying customers. DMPs could be built in many different sizes, from small to (in principle) arbitrarily large configurations, and so it was possible to build machines to suit the budgets of individual organizations. They appeared to be the most suitable basis for the massive parallelism envisioned by leaders of the day. As the technology stabilized, organizations increasingly procured their own DMP supercomputers. Thus, the use of distributed memory platforms, as well as the size of systems built, continued to grow steadily throughout the decade and their share of the HPC market rose accordingly [49]. However, vendor-supplied systems such as the Meiko CS2, Cray T3D and T3E, and IBM's SP architectures, were not the only DMPs in use throughout the 1990s. Such systems essentially consist of a number of individual computers, complete with CPU and memory, connected via a custom high-speed network and with system support to ensure that data is rapidly transported between the different memories. Similarly, workstations connected by a local-area network began to be used together to compute a single job, a trend that was greatly encouraged by the emergence of third-party software to simplify parallel job submission. They became known as clusters of workstations (COWs). Although the Ethernet networks used to build COWs were slow in comparison to the custom networks of true DMPs, they were much cheaper to build.

In the latter half of the 1990s, most U.S. hardware vendors began to produce SMPs. In contrast to those built in the late 1980s, these relatively inexpensive systems are intended for wide usage as desktop computers and powerful servers. With the tremendous increase in clock speed and size of memory and disk storage, some applications that formerly required HPC hardware could be executed on a single SMP. Perhaps more significantly, for the first time, parallel computers were accessible to a broad swathe of users.

2.2.2 Current HPC Systems

Today, vector supercomputers continue to provide highest levels of performance for certain applications, but remain expensive. SMPs are widely marketed, with CPU counts from two to over a hundred, as with the Sun Microsystems 6800 series. Most hardware vendors now combine DMP and SMP technologies to provide the cycles demanded by large-scale computations. As a result, they have two distinct levels of architectural parallelism.

COWs have become commonplace; clusters consisting of many thousands of processors are now deployed in laboratories as well as industry (e.g., for seismic processing). The cost of networking has decreased and its performance has increased rapidly, so that the performance penalty associated with early COWs is much reduced. Since COWs may be configured as clusters of SMPs, they no longer differ substantially from custom architectures in structure. The availability of low-cost COWs built on the open-source Linux operating system, commodity chips, and commodity networks is driving most hardware vendors to offer similar solutions, in addition to proprietary platforms. A recent survey of hardware vendors [17] showed that they expect the trend toward use of clustered SMPs for HPC to continue; systems of this kind already dominate the Top500 list.

However, there are interesting alternatives. Some HPC platforms enable code running on a CPU to directly access the entire system's memory, that is, to directly reference data stored on another SMP in the system. Some have global addressing schemes and others provide support for this in the network. The so-called ccNUMA (cache coherent nonuniform memory access) systems marketed by HP and SGI [46] transparently fetch data from remote memory when needed, storing it in the local cache and invalidating other copies of the same dataset as needed. They can be thought of as large virtual SMPs, although code will execute more slowly if it refers to data stored on another SMP (hence the nonuniform cost of access). The size of such machines has continued to grow as the technology matures, and they have become an important platform for HPC applications.

Current research and development in high-end architectures considers large-scale platforms with global memory and huge numbers of concurrently executing threads. Early platforms with these characteristics include IBM's BlueGene and the Cray Research Tera. In another recent development, hardware manufacturers are now producing chips that provide additional parallelism in the form of multiple cores and multiple simultaneously executing threads that share a single processor (e.g., Intel's hyperthreading). This introduces a different kind of shared-memory parallelism that will need to be exploited by HPC applications. No machine has thus far convincingly closed the "memory gap," despite the introduction of hierarchies of cache and mixtures of shared and private cache. The trend toward global memory and concurrently executing threads has intensified interest in shared- (global-) memory programming models.

The HPC market does not dominate the agenda of hardware vendors. Although it remains an important test bed for new technologies, its market share is declining. Further, even traditional HPC players have become price conscious, and many now exploit relatively inexpensive commodity technologies rather than custom HPC platforms. Thus, many CPUs configured in HPC systems today were designed for the mass market. The power of an HPC platform is derived solely from the exploitation of multiple CPUs. We now discuss the application programming interfaces (APIs) that have been created for this purpose and discuss their benefits and limitations.

2.3   HPC PROGRAMMING MODELS: THE FIRST GENERATION

Creating a parallel application that utilizes the resources of a parallel system well is a challenging task for the application developer, who must distribute the computation involved to a (possibly large) number of processors in such a way that each performs roughly the same amount of work. Moreover, the parallel program must be designed to ensure that data is available to a processor that requires it with as little delay as possible. This implies that the location of the data in the memory system must be carefully chosen and coordinated with the distribution of computation. Overheads for global operations, including start-up times, may be significant, especially on machines with many processors, and their impact must be minimized. The programming models presented here and in the next section all involve the user in the process of distributing work and data to the target machine, but differ in the nature of that involvement.

During the infancy of parallel computing, researchers proposed a variety of new languages for parallel programming, but few experienced any real use. The major hardware vendors created programming interfaces for their own products. Although a standards committee met, with the goal of defining a portable API for shared memory programming [52], no agreement emerged. The providers of DMPs developed library interfaces for their systems that enabled applications to exchange data between processors (e.g., Intel's NX library). It was common practice for programmers to rewrite HPC applications for each new architecture, a laborious procedure that often required not only prior study of the target machine but also the mastery of a new set of language or library features for its programming.

The 1990s saw the first de facto standardization of parallel programming APIs. Vendor extensions for vector and SIMD machines were fairly well understood and commonalities were identified among the different sets of features provided. Several of these were standardized in the array extensions that are part of Fortran 90. Broad community efforts produced HPF and MPI and a subsequent vendor consortium defined OpenMP for parallel application development. The APIs that we discuss below have not (with the exception of a few features of HPF) been adopted by the relevant ISO committees, and thus are standards only in the sense that they have been endorsed by a significant community of hardware and compiler vendors and their users.

2.3.1 The Message Passing Interface (MPI)

When a DMP is used to execute an application (we include COWs implicitly in this category from now on), data stored in memory associated with a processor must be transferred via the system's network to the memory associated with another processor whenever the code executing on the latter needs it. The most popular solution to programming such machines gives full control over this data transfer to the user. In an analogy to human interaction, it is referred to as message passing; a "message" containing the required data is sent from the code running on one processor to the remote code that requires it. MPI, or Message Passing Interface, was developed by a group of researchers and vendors to codify what was largely already established practice when their deliberations began in 1993 [32]. It consists of a set of library routines that are invoked from within a user code written in Fortran or C to transfer data between the processes involved in a computation. MPI was designed for DMPs at a time when the use of SMP, SIMD, and vector technology had begun to decline. It was soon available on all parallel platforms of interest, in both public domain and proprietary implementations.

MPI realizes a *local* model of parallel computing, as the user must write program code for each participating processor, inserting MPI routines to send or receive data as needed. Most MPI programs are created according to the so-called SPMD (single program, multiple data) model, where the same code runs on each processor, parameterized by the MPI-supplied process identification number. Although it is possible to write an MPI program using few library routines, the API provides rich functionality that enables optimization of many common kinds of communication. It provides for modularity in program design, particularly via the notion of groups of processes and subsequently introduced features for parallel I/O. It is applicable to both Fortran and C.

Considerable work is involved in creating an MPI code, and the cost of program maintenance is high. The programmer must set up buffers, move communications in order to minimize delays, modify code to minimize the amount of data communicated, and decide when it is advantageous to replicate computations to save communication. New kinds of errors, such as deadlock and livelock, must be avoided; debugging is nontrivial, especially for high CPU counts. Unless exceptional care is taken, the selected data distribution is hardwired into the program code, as it determines the placement and content of communications. The most appropriate MPI implementation of a program may differ between platforms; it is not uncommon to see multiple MPI versions of an application, each tuned for a target system of interest.

MPI functionality was already partially implemented on most platforms of the day at the time of its introduction. Open-source implementations rapidly became available. Application developers found that they could understand the model and its performance characteristics, and that it had the generality to describe the parallelism required to solve a great variety of problems. Thus, it is not ease of programming, but good performance, coupled with wide availability of the API, that led to its popularity. Programming models that assume a distributed memory can be very reasonably implemented on shared-memory platforms also, and thus it remained applicable to virtually all HPC architectures, even after the reintroduction of SMPs into the marketplace. MPI versions of a large number of important applications have been developed and are in broad use. It remains the most widely used API for parallel programming.

2.3.2 High-Performance Fortran (HPF)

On an architecture in which the memory is physically distributed, the time required to access nonlocal data may be significantly higher than the time taken to access locally stored data, and the management of data assumes great importance. This was the insight that resulted in the design of High Performance Fortran (HPF) [21], the first effort to provide a high-level programming model for parallel computing that received broad support.

Many researchers and vendor representatives took an active part in the definition of HPF, which appeared at approximately the same time as MPI. The HPF Forum began meeting regularly from early 1992 to design an implicit parallel programming model, that is, a model in which the user provides information to the compiler so that the latter can generate the explicitly parallel code. The forum kept to a tight schedule, producing its first language definition in just over a year. As the name implies, the features were designed for use with Fortran, and in particular with Fortran 90.

HPF realizes a *global* model of parallel computing: there is one program with a single thread of control that will be translated into multiple processes by the compiler. The core of HPF consists of a set of compiler directives with which the user may describe how a program's data is to be distributed among the CPUs of a machine. The API also provides two forms of *parallel loop,* as well as intrinsic functions and library routines that permit the user to query the system (e.g., to obtain information on the number of executing processors) and to perform certain arithmetical computations. It supports interoperability via a so-called extrinsic interface that enables HPF code to invoke procedures written under a different API. The central constructs of HPF offer a wide variety of options for mapping the program's data structures to the target platform. The platform may be represented by one or more user-declared logical *processor arrays,* which serve to give them a shape (and possibly size) and enable arrays to be distributed to them. Arrays in the program may be directly distributed to processors or they may be aligned with a *template* in order to ensure that they are mapped in a coordinated fashion. Templates are logical structures that are introduced for this purpose only; they may not appear in executable statements. The initial HPF definition provided for block and cyclic distributions that are applied to dimensions of an array or template. Any or all dimensions of an array may be left undistributed, in which case all elements of the corresponding dimensions are mapped to all processors. HPF defines a *block distribution* that maps a contiguous segment of an array dimension to each target processor; segments are the same size, with the possible exception of the last one. The *cyclic distribution* maps segments of a user-specified length in round-robin fashion to the target processors. It is relatively easy to compute the location of a given array element from its indices and the distribution's specification, particularly for block distributions. It is also a simple matter to compute the set of array elements that are local to a given process. These are often referred to as data *owned* by that process, and the basic strategy for compiling HPF code is to generate the code to be computed by each processor according to the *"owner computes"* rule. Thus, in HPF the user-specified data distribution determines the work distribution.

The task of the compiler is to generate the explicitly parallel processes, one of which will run on each participating processor. It must allocate storage for local data, based upon the user-inserted directives as well as for copies of nonlocal data needed by a process, and must assign computations to each processor. Storage for nonlocal data cannot be efficiently created without knowledge of its extent; thus, notation was introduced to permit specification of the *"shadow"* region of an array. The default strategy for distributing the work is then derived from the data distribution as indicated above. This requires a translation of global data references into local and nonlocal data references. The compiler must moreover insert the necessary communications to satisfy nonlocal references. If a computation includes indirect referencing, some of the corresponding analysis must be performed at run time. It is essential for performance that the communications be optimized to reduce their impact on performance, typically by aggregating them and starting them as early as possible to permit data transfer to be overlapped with computation. Separate compilation of procedures results in the need to specify mappings for formal procedure parameters and a costly reorganization of data is liable to be incurred whenever it does not verifiably match the distribution of the corresponding actual arguments.

The HPF translation process is complex and easily impaired if sufficient information is not available to do one of these tasks well. For instance, if it is not clear that a communication statement can be removed from an inner loop and combined with other data transfers, the resulting code may spend too much time transferring data. Run-time testing may alleviate some of the problems associated with lack of information, but in some cases, severe performance degradation may result from an inability to perform optimizations in the compiler.

HPF requires extensive program analysis and, in particular, accurate data dependence analysis to perform this translation. It also requires a full set of loop transformations to improve the translation process. For example, loop interchange might permit communications to be fused. If the data defined by two statements in a loop nest have different owners, then loop distribution might be able to split them into multiple loops, for which individual iterations can be assigned to processes without conditionals, otherwise, each of these statements would be conditionally executed in every iteration and the evaluation of the conditional would increase the overhead of the translation.

The HPF effort was preceded by a number of research projects that had the ambitious goal of enabling application developers to design programs for DMPs in much the same way as they were accustomed to on a sequential machine (e.g. [11]), and by several prototypes that demonstrated some of the compiler technology needed for their implementation (e.g. [15, 20]) . The standardization activity sparked off a good deal more research into a variety of compilation techniques that are needed to support any high-level parallel programming API. In addition to further work on loop transformations and their application, the benefits of interprocedural analysis for this and other complex translations became apparent. Fortran array reshaping and the passing of noncontiguous data, such as a strided array section, at procedure boundaries cause difficulties that have parallels in other contexts. Realignment and redistribution may occur implicitly at procedure boundaries, and a variety of efforts worked on the problem of optimizing the required all-to-all data exchange, which is particularly expensive when cyclic distributions are involved. Other activities aimed to reduce the implementation cost of reduction operations. Work to translate the HPF independent loop, the iterations of which are spread among the processes, required that the nonlocal data accesses be determined and the data fetched prior to the loop's execution. A strategy was developed to handle indirect array references, for which these datasets cannot be determined at compile time. Referred to as the *inspector–executor* strategy [24, 39], it essentially consists of a new "inspector" loop that partially executes the loop's code to determine the required data, then determines which elements are nonlocal and communicates with other processes to exchange information on the required elements, and, finally, exchanges the actual data. Only then is the original loop executed. This strategy is prohibitively expensive and is only appropriate if the constructed communication sets can be reused. The problem it attempts to solve is incurred in other high-level models, particularly when arrays are indirectly referenced.

The HPF Forum created a powerful and extensive programming API that was intended to be an easy means for creating parallel code. It led to much progress in compiler technology for DMPs and for parallel systems in general. Yet the introduction of data distributions into a sequential program is not sufficient to enable the compiler to achieve consistently efficient code. At the time HPF was introduced, the cost of exchanging data between processes on a DMP was extremely high and the penalty for a compiler's insertion of excessive communications was significant. Moreover, as a result of the complexity of the compilation process and the need to develop Fortran 90 compiler technology concurrently, HPF products were slow to emerge.

The task of modifying a program to perform well under HPF was poorly understood, and the apparent simplicity was deceptive. There were exceptional penalties for "getting it wrong." It required a great deal of insight into the HPF translation process and a commitment that few were willing to bring to a new and relatively untested technology. HPF compilers had different strengths and weaknesses. Performance results and experiences were inconclusive and sometimes contradictory. Moreover, the stringent time constraints adhered to by the HPF Forum did not permit HPF1.0 to adequately address the needs of unstructured computations; these were of great importance at the time in the HPC community. Although HPF2.0 introduced generalized block distribution and indirect array distributions, these came much later and the latter proved to be very hard to implement. Finally, HPF did not address the needs of the growing fraction of HPC codes that were written in C.

MPI implementations were available by the time HPF compilers emerged, and they applied a technology that was already successfully deployed in HPC. Thus, HPF did not enjoy the success achieved by MPI despite the conveniences it provided (cf. Figure 2.1). Nevertheless, work on this API led to an upsurge of research into a variety of compiler optimizations and provided compiler technology that is useful for the realization of other high-level parallel programming APIs.

```
!HPF$ DISTRIBUTE (*,BLOCK)::A,B
!HPF$ SHADOW(0,1:1):: A
!HPF$ INDEPENDENT
    do j = 2, SIZE-1
      do i = 2, SIZE-1
        a(i, j) = (b(i - 1, j) + b(i + 1, j) + b(i, j - 1) +
b(i, j + 1)) / 4
      enddo
    enddo
!HPF$ INDEPENDENT
    do j = 2, SIZE-1
      do i = 2, SIZE-1
        b(i, j) = a(i, j)
      enddo
    enddo
!HPF$ INDEPENDENT REDUCTION(sum)
    do j = 1,SIZE
      do i = 1,SIZE
        sum = sum + b(i,j)
      end do
    end do
```

(a)

```
Double precision a(0:SIZE,SIZE/nproc+1), b(0:SIZE,SIZE/nproc+1)
Call MPI_INIT()
Call MPI_Comm_size(MPI_COMM_WORLD, nproc, ierr)
Call MPI_Comm_rank(MPI_COMM_WORLD, myid, ierr)
do j = 2, SIZE/nproc-1
    do i = 2, SIZE-1
      a(i, j) = (b(i - 1, j) + b(i + 1, j) + b(i, j - 1) +b(i, j + 1)) / 4
    enddo
enddo
If (myid .lt. npes-1) Send my last column to my east neighbor myid+1,
If (myid .ne. 0)      Receive a column from my west neighbor myid-1
If (myid .ne. 0)      Sends my first column to west neighbor myid-1
If (myid .ne. npes-1) Receives data from my east neighbor myid+1
do j = 2, SIZE/nproc-1
    do i = 2, SIZE-1
      b(i, j) = a(i, j)
    enddo
enddo
do j = 1,SIZE/nproc
    do i = 1,SIZE
      sum = sum + b(i,j)
    end do
end do
Call MPI_Reduce(...)
Call MPI_FINALIZE(ierr)
```

(b)

Figure 2.1   (a) Jacobi HPF program and (b) Jacobi pseudo-MPI code.

2.4   THE SECOND GENERATION OF HPC PROGRAMMING MODELS

The next generation of programming models for HPC has focused on shared memory. On a shared memory platform, the main goal is to perform an even distribution of the work in a program to the executing processors. The relatively low penalty incurred when accessing nonlocal data on DSM systems has led to notable successes in the deployment of shared-memory APIs on these platforms too. A shared-memory programming style has also been realized on DMPs. The shared-memory model is generally considered to be more user-friendly than its distributed-memory counterparts.

2.4.1   OpenMP

Both HPF and MPI were introduced to support application development on DMPs. Yet shortly thereafter, SMPs were being sold in large quantities. OpenMP was introduced to fulfill the need for an API for this class of platforms [37]. First introduced with an interface for Fortran late 1997 by an influential group of computer vendors, it was extended by C and C++ versions just a year later. The OpenMP programming model is based upon earlier attempts to provide a standard API for shared-memory parallel programming and was thus already familiar to many in the HPC community; it primarily supports the parallelization of loops needed for many scientific and engineering computations. It is much easier to parallelize unstructured computations under OpenMP than under either of the above-mentioned APIs, since there is no need to partition unstructured data.

   Like HPF, OpenMP is an implicit parallel programming model, consisting of a set of compiler directives and several library routines, that realizes a global model of parallel computing. It is based upon the fork–join execution model, in which a single master thread begins execution and spawns a team of worker threads to perform computations in parallel regions. It is the task of the user to specify the parallel regions and to state how the work is to be shared among the team of threads that will execute them. The directives enable the declaration of such regions, the sharing of work among threads, and their synchronization. Loop iterations may be statically or dynamically distributed in blocks or in cyclic fashion, array computations distributed, and work divided into a set of parallel sections. Parallel regions may differ in the number of threads assigned to them at run time. The user is responsible for detecting and dealing with race conditions in the code, as well as for thread coordination. Critical regions and atomic updates may be defined; variable updates may be ordered, or a set of statements executed by the first thread to reach them only. The OpenMP library implements locks. An innovative feature of OpenMP is the inclusion of orphan directives, directives that are dynamically, rather than lexically, within the scope of a parallel region. They greatly simplify the code migration process, since there is no need to extract code from subprograms for worksharing, and they enable large parallel regions to be created. OpenMP permits private variables, with potentially different values on each thread, within parallel regions. Other data is shared. Fortran programs may have thread-private common blocks, and private variables may be SAVEd. Since OpenMP is a shared memory model, sequence and storage association is not affected by its directives. A conditional compilation feature facilitates the maintenance of a single source code for both sequential and parallel execution.

The basic compilation strategy for OpenMP is relatively simple, as the language expects the application developer to indicate which loops are parallel and, therefore, this analysis is not required. No communications need be inserted. The main focus is on the generation of thread-specific code to implement the parallel regions. Most often, parallel regions are converted to procedures that are then adapted via the insertion of calls to a thread library such as pThreads [33]. Since iterations are distributed, there is no need for compiler analysis to determine the locus of computation.

OpenMP can be used in several different ways. The straightforward approach does not require the user to analyze and possibly modify an entire application, as is the case with both HPF and MPI. Instead, each loop is parallelized in turn. Although this does require the user to deal with data dependencies in small regions of a program, it is generally considered appropriate for nonexpert application developers [5]. If the implicit barriers after many constructs are not eliminated where possible, they may degrade performance. Problems arise when data being updated is stored in more than one cache of an SMP and if attention is not paid to this, performance gains may be moderate only. Even nonexpert users may need to learn about cache. However, the requirements of HPC applications generally necessitate a different strategy for using OpenMP, which relies on the user to explicitly distribute work and data among the threads that will execute it. Thread-private data structures are created to hold local data and shared-data structures are only declared to hold data needed by more than one thread. Since OpenMP provides thread identification, work can be explicitly allocated to threads as desired. The strategy minimizes interactions between threads and can yield high performance and scalability [50]. Although fewer details need be specified than with MPI, this so-called SPMD-style OpenMP presupposes a more extensive program modification, but it is likely to be easier to maintain than a corresponding MPI code, since fewer lines are added.

The OpenMP developers did not present the specification until compilers were nearly ready, in an effort to avoid the frustrations caused by the slow arrival of HPF compilers. Tools quickly became available for OpenMP application development, debugging, and performance analysis (e.g. [26, 38]). This, its applicability to all major HPC programming languages, the relative ease of its use, its support for single-source as well as incremental-application development facilitated its rapid adoption as the de facto standard for shared memory parallel programming by the remaining hardware vendors and the community.

However, the current language was primarily designed to facilitate programming of modest-sized SMPs, and OpenMP parallel programs cannot be executed on DMPs. Many codes executed on large clusters of SMPs are programmed using a combination of MPI and OpenMP, such that MPI performs synchronization and data transfer takes place between the different SMPs, whereas OpenMP is used to program within each SMP. Where more than one kind of parallelism is naturally present in an application, this is a strategy that can work well. Unfortunately, the easiest way to develop such a program, particularly if development begins with an MPI code, is to create OpenMP parallel regions between MPI library calls. This is not an efficient way to use OpenMP, and performance results can be disappointing. Several hybrid strategies are discussed in [9, 25, 48].

2.4.1.1   OpenMP on DSM Platforms. OpenMP is also implementable on cc-NUMA systems. The threads that execute a parallel region may run on processors across multiple nodes (e.g. [28]) of the machine. When a loop is parallelized via a worksharing construct, for instance, loop iterations are executed on threads distributed across the system, and the program data may also be spread across the different node memories. It is likely that a thread will reference data stored in nonlocal memory. Unfortunately, large numbers of remote memory accesses can lead to significant network traffic and substantial delays.

In order to obtain high performance from ccNUMA systems [44], coordinated placement of data and computations over the memories is needed [7, 18, 43] to ensure that the data accessed by each thread is largely local to the processor on which that thread is currently executing. OpenMP does not provide any mechanisms for controlling the placement of data relative to computation, so vendors have supplied means by which this may be influenced. One of these is a default "first touch" strategy that allocates data in memory local to the first thread that accesses it; if the application developer carefully distributes the initial data references across threads, this simple mechanism may suffice. An alternative is to automatically migrate pages of data so that they are near to threads that reference them. This is appealing, as it is transparent to the user. However, pages of memory are fairly large, and without application insight it can be hard for the system to determine when it is appropriate to move data. Thus, more research into this area is needed [36]. Finally, both HP and SGI have provided custom extensions to OpenMP to permit the user to express the data locality requirements of an application (e.g. [6, 12, 13, 47]), although it is not easy to provide these features in an API that permits incremental program development. The basic approach embodied by HPFD has been used, but page-based data distributions have also been included. Despite considerable overlap of functionality, the syntax and a number of details differ substantially in these vendor-specific features. Partly as a result of this, they are not widely used; most application developers rely on "first touch" allocation and privatization of data, although the specification of thread affinity appears to be a useful concept. SPMD-style codes on DSM platforms have been shown to outperform MPI and to scale better, so that the difference increases with large CPU counts [50].

2.4.2   Other Shared-Memory APIs

Other APIs have been developed recently that are important to some sectors of the community. One of these is Global Arrays (GA), which applies a shared-memory programming model to DMPs, and another is Unified Parallel C (UPC), which focuses on providing support for DSM platforms. The latter in particular introduces several ideas that may influence future programming models for HPC.

2.4.2.1 *Global Arrays (GA)*. GA is a library [34] that was designed to simplify the programming methodology on DMPs by providing a shared-memory abstraction. It provides routines that enable the user to specify and manage access to shared data structures, called *global arrays,* in a FORTRAN, C, C++, or Python program. A GA program consists of a collection of independently executing processes, each of which is thus able to access data declared to be shared without interfering with other processes. Programmers can write their parallel program using this *local* model as if they have shared-memory access, specifying the layout of shared data at a higher level. GA permits the user to specify block-based data distributions corresponding to HPF BLOCK and GEN_BLOCK distributions, which map identical-length chunks and arbitrary-length chunks of data to processes, respectively. *Global arrays* are accordingly mapped to the processors executing the code. Each GA process is able to independently and asynchronously access these distributed data structures via *get* or *put* routines. GA combines features of both message-passing and shared-memory programming models, leading to both simple coding and efficient execution. The GA programming model forces the programmer to determine the needed locality for each phase of the computation. By tuning the algorithm to maximize locality, portable high performance is easily obtained. GA has been widely implemented and has been used to develop several HPC applications.

2.4.2.2 *Unified Parallel C (UPC)*. UPC [8, 14] is an extension of C that aims to support application development on DSMs or other systems by providing for a global address space and multithreaded programming. In contrast to OpenMP, it provides data mappings and expects the programmer to consider and express data locality explicitly. UPC code is *global,* and roughly equivalent to SPMD-style OpenMP code in that it typically combines some shared data with largely local computations. Arrays and pointers may be declared as shared and given an HPF-like data distribution; all other data objects are private. A parallel loop is defined, the iterations of which are assigned to threads by the compiler rather than via a user-specified loop schedule. An interesting feature of UPC is that it allows the user to specify whether strict or relaxed consistency is to be applied to memory references, whereby the former refers to sequential consistency and the latter requires a thread-local consistency only, so that computations may be reorganized so long as there are no dependencies within that thread (only) to prevent it. Threads execute asynchronously unless the user explicitly inserts a fence, barrier, or a split barrier that permits the execution of local code while waiting for other threads to reach the same point in their execution. UPC can be implemented on systems that provide support for asynchronous read and write operations, such that a processor is able to independently fetch nonlocal data. It is thus more easily implemented on DMPs than OpenMP is, but lacks the simpler development approach, including incremental development, and does not support single-source operation. Implementations of UPC exist on several platforms. *Co-Array Fortran* (CAF) is often considered to be the Fortran equivalent to UPC. This is not altogether true; CAF does not provide global data and provides a *local* model of computation.

2.4.3   Is A Standard High-Level API for HPC in Sight?

Although MPI is a de facto standard for DMPs, it is error-prone and, above all, time-consuming. The HPC community is small and its ability to sustain even a single specific high-level programming model has been questioned. But the importance of a parallel programming API for DMPs that facilitates programmer productivity is increasingly recognized. If such an API is to be broadly used in HPC, it must be expressive enough to allow application developers to specify the parallelism in their applications, it must be capable of efficient implementation on most HPC platforms, and it must enable users to achieve performance on these machines. OpenMP is designed for shared-memory systems and emphasizes usability, but does not provide similar levels of portability. However, it enjoys strong and ongoing vendor support and for this reason it is currently the best candidate for developing a truly portable high-level API. Moreover, it may also facilitate exploitation of chip multithreading and multicore systems. It potentially has a much larger market since it may satisfy the needs of a range of applications that do not necessarily belong to HPC but can exploit single SMPs.

But there are a number of challenges that must be met if OpenMP is to become a widely used API in the HPC community. Unlike MPI, which can be implemented on SMPs with reasonable efficiency, OpenMP is hard to realize efficiently on DMPs. The current approach is to implement OpenMP on top of software that provides virtual shared memory on a DMP, a so-called software-distributed shared-memory (DSM) system, such as Omni [40, 42] or TreadMarks [1, 22]. Although this technology does not yet provide the performance levels required for HPC applications, it is the subject of a good deal of ongoing work and a production version of TreadMarks is expected to appear soon. Other proposals have been made that extend OpenMP to DMPs [31].

OpenMP is not without other difficulties. One of these is the relative ease with which erroneous codes can be produced. It is up to the application developer to insert all necessary synchronization to coordinate the work of the independently executing threads. In particular, this requires the error-prone, manual recognition of data dependencies and the correct ordering of accesses. The power of OpenMP lies in the ease with which large parallel regions may be created and these may span many procedures, complicating this task. Although the solution may lie in tool support rather than language modification, it is an issue that requires attention.

OpenMP currently supports only the simplest expression of hierarchical parallelism [2]. There is no facility for the distributed execution of multiple levels of a loop nest in parallel within a single parallel region, let alone the ability to assign work to threads within the same SMP. Yet being able to exploit this hierarchy could be critical to achieving scalable performance. This might be realized by the provision of means to indicate how resources should be allocated to nested parallel regions, possibly with some architectural description. Other challenges include the need to provide additional features that support the creation of codes for very large platforms. Starting up threads across an entire machine, for example, can become very costly, as can the allocation of shared data and global operations such as reductions. There is currently no concept corresponding to the MPI process groups, and this is certainly needed. Unstructured computations will require more language and compiler support for efficient execution across large numbers of SMPs. Some applications require synchronization that is hard to express in the current OpenMP language [45]. On the other hand, a compiler could, in some circumstances, automatically determine which variables can be safely privatized in a parallel region to relieve the user of this task. A number of proposals exist for extending OpenMP in these and other ways (e.g. [3, 27, 29, 36]).

A slight relaxation of the semantics of OpenMP might also improve its performance for some applications. The current standard requires that the user state that there are no dependencies between a pair of consecutive parallel loops. Otherwise, the compiler will ensure that one loop has been completed in its entirety via an expensive barrier before the next loop can be computed. But, in reality, it is often possible do better than that and languages such as UPC provide finer grain synchronization. A more flexible OpenMP translation strategy [51] might determine the dependencies between the sets of loop iterations that will be executed by a single thread. At run time, an iteration set may then be executed as soon as those it depends on have completed. This replaces many of the barriers in an OpenMP code by synchronization between pairs of threads.

2.5 OPENMP FOR DMPS

We now turn to the most challenging of the problems facing OpenMP, that of extending it for execution on DMPs. The most straightforward approach to do so relies on the memory management capabilities of software DSMs to handle a code's shared data. Under this approach, an OpenMP program does not need to be modified for execution on a DMP; the software DSM is responsible for creating the illusion of shared memory by realizing a shared address space and managing the program data that has been declared to be shared. However, there are inherent problems with this translation. Foremost among these is the fact that the management of shared data is based upon pages, which incurs high overheads. Software DSMs perform expensive data transfers at explicit and implicit barriers of a program, and suffer from false sharing of data at page granularity. They typically impose constraints on the amount of shared memory that can be allocated. One effort [16] translates OpenMP to a hybrid MPI and software DSM in order to overcome some of the associated performance problems. This is a difficult task, and the software DSM could still be a performance bottleneck. Much better performance can be obtained if the user creates an SPMD-style OpenMP code prior to this parallelization, in order to minimize the shared data. Array padding may then help reduce some of the memory conflicts. Few, if any, language extensions are needed to apply this translation.

In the following, we describe an alternative approach to translating OpenMP to DMPs in order to provide some insight into this translation. Its strong point is that the compiler inserts explicit communications and is thus able to control the data that is transferred as well as the point of transfer. The weakness of the approach is that it is rather complex, introducing some of the difficulties that proved problematic for HPF, albeit with lower penalties. A major challenge is the need to determine a data distribution for shared data structures. It relies on a translation from OpenMP to Global Arrays, described above [23].

2.5.1   A Basic Translation to GA

It is largely straightforward to translate OpenMP programs into GA programs because both have the concept of shared data and the GA library features match most OpenMP constructs. However, before the translation occurs, it is highly beneficial to transform OpenMP code into the so-called SPMD style [30] in order to improve data locality. The translation strategy [23] follows OpenMP semantics. OpenMP threads correspond to GA processes and OpenMP shared data are translated to global arrays that are distributed among the GA processes; all variables in the GA code that are not global arrays are called private variables. OpenMP private variables will be translated to GA private variables as will some OpenMP shared data. OpenMP scalars and private variables are replicated to each GA process. Small or constant shared arrays in OpenMP will also be replicated; all other shared OpenMP arrays must be given a data distribution and they will be translated to global arrays.

Shared pointers in OpenMP must also be distributed. If a pointer points to a shared array, it must be determined whether the contents of the current pointer are within the local portion of the shared memory. Otherwise, *get* or *put* operations are required to fetch and store nonlocal data and the pointer will need to point to the local copy of the data. If a shared pointer is used directly, an array can be substituted for it and distributed according to the loop schedule because GA does not support the distribution of C pointers.

The basic translation strategy assigns loop iterations to each process according to OpenMP static loop schedules. For this, the iteration sets of the original OpenMP parallel loops must be calculated for each thread. Furthermore, the regions of shared arrays accessed by each OpenMP thread when performing its assigned iterations must be computed. After this analysis, we determine a block-based data distribution and insert the corresponding declarations of global arrays. The loop bounds of each parallel loop are modified so that each process will work on its local iterations. Elements of global arrays may only be accessed via *get* and *put* routines. Prior to computation, the required global array elements are gathered into local copies. If the local copies of global arrays are modified during the subsequent computation, they must be written back to their unique "global" location after the loop has completed. GA synchronization routines replace OpenMP synchronization to ensure that all computation as well as the communication to update global data have completed before work proceeds.

An example of an OpenMP program and its corresponding GA program is given in Figure 2.2. The resulting code computes iteration sets based on the process ID. Here, array *A* has been given a block distribution in the second dimension, so that each processor is assigned a contiguous set of columns. Nonlocal elements of global array *A* in Figure 2.2(b) are fetched using a *get* operation followed by synchronization. The loop bounds are replaced with local ones. Afterward, the nonlocal array elements of *A* are put back via a *put* operation with synchronization.

Unfortunately, the translation of synchronization constructs (CRITICAL, ATOMIC, and ORDERED) and sequential program sections (serial regions outside parallel regions, OpenMP SINGLE and MASTER) may become nontrivial. GA has several features for synchronization that permit their expression; however, the translated codes may not be efficient.

2.5.2 Implementing Sequential Regions

Several different strategies may be employed to translate the statements enclosed within a sequential region of OpenMP code, including I/O operations, control flow constructs (IF, GOTO, and DO loops), procedure calls, and assignment statements. A straightforward translation of sequential sections would be to use exclusive master process execution, which is suitable for some constructs including I/O operations. Although parallel I/O is permitted in GA, it is a challenge to transform OpenMP sequential I/O into GA parallel I/O. The control flow in a sequential region must be executed by all the processes if the control flow constructs enclose or are enclosed by any parallel regions. Similarly, all the processes must execute a procedure call if the procedure contains parallel regions, either directly or indirectly. The properties of the data involved are used to determine the different GA execution

```
1 !$OMP PARALLEL
SHARED(a)
2 do k = 1 , MAX
3 !$OMP DO
4  do j = 1 , SIZE_J ( j )
5    do i = 2 , SIZE-1
6      a(i,j)= a(i-1,j)+a(i+1,j)+ ...
7    enddo
8  enddo
9 !$OMP END DO
10 enddo
11 !$OMP END PARALLEL
```

```
1 OK=ga_create (MT_DBL, SIZE_X , SIZE_Y , 'A' ,
2             SIZE_X, SIZE_Y/ nproc , g_a )
3 do k = 1 , MAX
4 ! compute new lower bound and upper bound for each process
5 (new_low, new_upper) = ...
6 ! compute the remote array region read for each thread
7 (jlo, jhi)= ...
8 call  ga_get ( g_a, 1, SIZE , jlo , jhi , a, ld )
9 call ga_sync ( )
12 do j = new_low , new_upper
13   do i = 2 , SIZE-1
14     a (i, j) = a(i-1, j) +a(i+1,j)...
15   enddo
16 enddo
18 ! compute remote array region written
19 call ga_put ( g_a , 1 , SIZE , jlo , jhi , a , ld)
20 call ga_sync ( )
21 enddo
```

Figure 2.2   (a) An OpenMP program and (b) the corresponding GA program.

strategies chosen for an assignment statement in sequential parts of an OpenMP program:

1. If a statement writes to a variable that will be translated to a *GA private* variable, this statement is executed redundantly by each process in a GA program; each process may fetch the remote data that it will read before executing the statement. A redundant computation can remove the requirement of broadcasting results after updating a GA private variable.
2. If a statement writes to an element of an array that will be translated to a global array in GA (e.g., S[i]=. . .), this statement is executed by a single process. If possible, the process that owns the shared data performs the computation. The result needs to be put back into the "global" memory location.

Data dependences need to be maintained when a global array is read and written by different processes. To ensure this, synchronization may be inserted after each write operation to global arrays during the translation stage; at the code optimization stage, we may remove redundant *get* or *put* operations, and aggregate communications of neighboring data if possible.

2.5.3 Data and Work Distribution in GA

GA provides simple block-based data distributions only and supplies features to make them as efficient as possible. There are no means for explicit data redistribution. GA's asynchronous one-sided communication transfers the required array elements, rather than pages of data, and it is optimized to support the transfer of sets of contiguous or strided data, which are typical for HPC applications. These provide performance benefits over software DSMs. With block distributions, it is easy to determine the location of an arbitrary array element. However, since these distributions may not provide maximum data locality, they may increase the amount of data that needs to be gathered and scattered before and after execution of a code region, respectively. In practice, this tends to work well if there is sufficient computation in such code regions. GA only requires that the regions of global arrays that are read or written by a process be calculated to complete the communication; GA handles the other details. It is fast and easy for GA to compute the location of any global data element. We may optimize communication by minimizing the number of *get/put* operations and by merging small messages into larger ones.

It is the task of the user to specify the distribution of global data in a GA program; when converting OpenMP programs to the corresponding GA ones, the compiler must, therefore, choose the distribution. A suitable strategy for doing so may be based upon simple rules such as the following:

1. If most loop index variables in those loop levels immediately enclosed by PARALLEL DO directives sweep over the same dimension of a shared array in an OpenMP program, we perform a one-dimensional distribution for the corresponding array in this dimension.

2. If different dimensions of a shared array are swept over almost evenly by parallel loops, we may perform multidimensional distribution for this array.

3. If parallel loops always work on a subset of a shared array, we may distribute this shared array using a GEN_BLOCK distribution; otherwise, a BLOCK distribution may be deployed. In the former case, the working subset of the shared array is distributed evenly to each thread; the first and last threads will be assigned any remaining elements of arrays at the start and end, respectively.

This translation could be improved with an interactive tool that collaborates with the user. Another possible improvement would be to perform data distribution based on the most time-consuming parallel loops. Statically, we may estimate the importance of loops. However, user information or profile results, even if based on a partial execution, are likely to prove much more reliable. A strategy that automates the instrumentation and partial execution of a code with feedback directly to the compiler might eliminate the need for additional sources of information.

OpenMP static loop scheduling distributes iterations evenly. When the iterations of a parallel loop have different amounts of work to do, dynamic and guided loop scheduling can be deployed to balance the workload. It is possible to translate all forms of the OpenMP loop schedule. However, the GA code corresponding to dynamic and guided-loop scheduling may have unacceptable overheads, as it may contain many *get* and *put* operations transferring small amounts of data. Other work distribution strategies need to be explored that take data locality and load balancing into account.

For irregular applications, it may be necessary to gather information on the global array elements needed by a process; whenever indirect accesses are made to a global array, the elements required in order to perform its set of loop iterations cannot be computed. Rather, an inspector–executor strategy is needed to analyze the indirect references at run time and then fetch the data required. The resulting datasets need to be merged to minimize the number of required *get* operations. We enforce static scheduling and override the user-given scheduling for OpenMP parallel loops that include indirect accesses. The efficiency of the inspector–executor implementation is critical. In a GA program, each process can determine the location of data read/written independently and can fetch it asynchronously. This feature may substantially reduce the inspector overhead compared with HPF or any other paradigm that provides a broader set of data distributions. Here, each process independently executes an inspector loop to determine the global array elements (including local and remote data) needed for its iteration set and their locations. The asynchronous communication can be overlapped with local computations, if any.

2.5.4 Irregular Computation Example

FIRE™ is a fully interactive fluid-dynamics package for computing compressible and incompressible turbulent fluid. *gccg* is a parallelizable solver in the FIRE™

Benchmarks [4] that uses orthomin and diagonal scaling. It is used here to illustrate how to translate codes with irregular data accesses to GA.

Figure 2.3 displays the most time-consuming part of the *gccg* program. In the approach described above, we perform array region analysis to determine how to handle the shared arrays in OpenMP. Shared arrays *BP, BS, BW, BL, BN, BE, BH, DIREC2,* and *LCC* are privatized during the initial compiler optimization to improve locality of OpenMP codes, since each thread performs work only on an individual region of these shared arrays. In the subsequent translation, they will be replaced by GA private variables. In order to reduce the overhead of the conversion between global and local indices, global indices may be preserved for the list of arrays above when declaring them and we may allocate memory for array regions per process dynamically if the number of processes is not a constant. Shared array *DIREC1* is distributed via global arrays according to the work distribution in the two parallel do loops in Figure 2.3. A subset of array *DIREC1* is updated by all threads in the first parallel loop; the second parallel loop accesses *DIREC1* indirectly via *LCC*. We distribute *DIREC1* using a GEN_BLOCK distribution according to the static loop schedule in the first parallel loop in order to maximize data locality, as there is no optimal solution of data distribution for *DIREC1* in the second loop. The array region *DIREC1*[*NINTC1*:*NINTCF*] is mapped to each process evenly in order to balance the work. Since *DIREC1* is declared as [1:*N*], the array regions [1:*NINTC1*] and [*NINTCF*:*N*] must be distributed as well. We distribute these two regions to process 0 and the last process for contiguity, thus using a GEN_BLOCK distribution (as in HPF) as shown in Figure 2.4, assuming four processors are involved.

As before, work distribution is based on the OpenMP loop schedule. In the case in which all data accesses will be local (the first loop of Figure 2.3), loop iterations

```
!$OMP PARALLEL
      DO I = 1, iter
!$OMP DO
         DO 10 NC=NINTCI,NINTCF
            DIREC1(NC)=DIREC1(NC)+RESVEC(NC)*CGUP(NC)
      10 CONTINUE
!$OMP END DO
!$OMP DO
         DO 4 NC=NINTCI,NINTCF
            DIREC2(NC)=BP(NC)*DIREC1(NC)
      X        - BS(NC)  * DIREC1(LCC(1,NC))
      X        - BW(NC)  * DIREC1(LCC(4,NC))
      X        - BL(NC)  * DIREC1(LCC(5,NC))
      X        - BN(NC)  * DIREC1(LCC(3,NC))
      X        - BE(NC)  * DIREC1(LCC(2,NC))
      X        - BH(NC)  * DIREC1(LCC(6,NC))
       4 CONTINUE
!$OMP END DO
      END DO
!$OMP END PARALLEL
```

Figure 2.3 An OpenMP code segment in *gccg* with irregular data accesses.

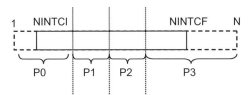

Figure 2.4   GEN_BLOCK distribution for array DIREC1.

are divided evenly among all the threads and data are referenced contiguously. If a thread reads or writes some nonlocal data in a parallel loop, array region analysis enables us to calculate the contiguous nonlocal data for regular accesses and we can fetch all the nonlocal data within one communication before these data are read or written. Fortunately, we do not need to communicate for the first loop in Figure 2.3 due to completely local accesses. But in the second loop of Figure 2.3, some data accesses are indirect and thus actual data references are unknown at compiling time. Therefore, we cannot generate efficient communications based upon static compiler analysis, and at least one communication per iteration has to be inserted. This would incur very high overheads. Hence, an inspector–executor strategy [24, 39] is employed to avoid them.

The inspector–executor approach is a simplification of the strategy developed within the HPF context, as it can be realized by a fully parallel loop, as shown in Figure 2.3. We detect the values for each indirection array in the allocated iterations of each GA process. One way to handle this is to let a hash table save the indices of nonlocal accesses and generate a list of communications for remote array regions. Each element in the hash table represents a region of a global array, which is the minimum unit of communication. Using a hash table can remove duplicated data communications that will otherwise arise if the indirect array accesses from different iterations refer to the same array element. We need to choose the optimal region size of a global array to be represented by a hash table element. This will depend on the size of the global array, data access patterns, and the number of processes, and needs to be further explored. The smaller the array regions, the more small communications are generated. But if we choose a larger array region, the generated communication may include more unnecessary nonlocal data. Another task of the inspector is to determine which iterations access only local data, so that we may overlap nonlocal data communication with local data computation.

A straightforward optimization of the inspector is to merge neighboring regions into one large region in order to reduce the number of communications. The inspector loop in Figure 2.5 only needs to be performed once during execution of the *gccg* program, since the indirection array remains unmodified throughout the program. Our inspector is lightweight because:

1. The location of global arrays is easy to compute in GA due to the simplicity of GA's data distributions.

```
DO iteration=local_low, local_high
    If (this iteration contains non-local data) then
        Store the indices of non-local array elements into a hash table
        Save current iteration number in a nonlocal list
    Else
        Save current iteration number in a local list
    Endif
Enddo
Merge contiguous communications given in the hash table
```

Figure 2.5   Pseudocode for an inspector.

2. The hash table approach enables us to identify and eliminate redundant communications.

3. All of the computations of the inspector are carried out independently by each process.

These factors imply that the overheads of this approach are much lower than is the case in other contexts and that it may be viable even when data access patterns change frequently, as in adaptive applications. For example, an inspector implemented using MPI is less efficient than our approach as each process has to generate communications for both sending and receiving, which rely on other processes' intervention.

The executor shown in Figure 2.6 performs the computation in a parallel loop following the iteration order generated by the inspector. It prefetches nonlocal data via nonblocking communication, here using the nonblocking *get* operation *ga_nbget*() in GA. Simultaneously, the iterations that do not need any nonlocal data are executed so that they are performed concurrently with the communication.

```
! non-local data gathering
Call ga_nbget(....)
DO iteration1=1, number_of_local_data
    Obtain the iteration number from the local list
    Perform the local computation
Enddo
! wait until the non-local data is gathered
Call ga_nbwait()
Do iteration2=1, number_of_nonlocal_data
    Obtain the iteration number from the non-local list
    Perform computation using non-local data
enddo
```

Figure 2.6   Pseudocode for an executor.

ga_nbwait(), which is used to ensure that the nonlocal data is available before we perform the corresponding computation.

An essential part of this strategy is the optimization of the resulting GA code. In particular, GA *get* and *put* operations created before and after each parallel construct may be redundant. If a previous *put* includes the data of a subsequent *get* operation, we may remove the *get* operation; if the data in a *put* operation contains the content of a following *put* operation, the latter may be eliminated. It is advantageous to move *get* and *put* operations to positions that are as early as possible in order to reduce delays incurred waiting for data. Extensive optimizations require accurate array region analysis and parallel control flow analysis [10] in order to obtain context-sensitive array region communication information.

2.6 EXPERIMENTS WITH OpenMP ON DMPS

Initial experiments that evaluated the translation of regular, small OpenMP codes to the corresponding GA ones achieved encouraging results on a cluster of Itanium2s and an IBM SP RS/6000 and were reported in [23]. The Itanium2 cluster at the University of Houston has twenty-four two-way SMP nodes and a single four-way SMP node; each of the 24 nodes has two 900 MHz CPUs and 4 GB memory. The Scali interconnect has a system bus bandwidth of 6.4 GB/s and a memory bandwidth of 12.8 GB/s. The NERSC IBM SP RS/6000 is composed of 380 nodes, each of which consists of 16 375 MHz POWER 3+ CPUs and 16 GB to 64 GB memory. These nodes are connected to an IBM "Colony" high-speed switch via two "GX Bus Colony" network adapters. OpenMP programs can be run on a maximum of four CPUs on the Itanium2 and on 16 processors of the IBM SP.

Figure 2.7 displays the performance of the well-known Jacobi kernel with a 1152 by 1152 matrix on these two DMPs. Both the OpenMP program and the corresponding GA code achieved linear speedup because of the data locality inherent in

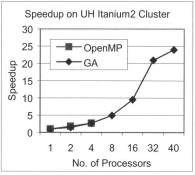 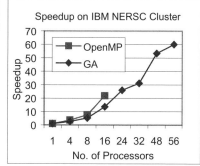

Figure 2.7   The performance of a Jacobi OpenMP program and its corresponding GA program.

the Jacobi solver. LBE [19] is a computational fluid dynamics code that solves the lattice Boltzmann equation. The numerical solver employed by this code uses a nine-point stencil. Unlike the Jacobi solver, the neighboring elements are updated at each iteration. Figure 2.8 displays the performance of an LBE program with a 1024 by 1024 matrix in OpenMP and its corresponding GA program, both on the IBM SP. The performance of LBE is lower than that of Jacobi as a result of updates to nonlocal global array elements. Note that optimization of the GA version of our LBE program removed a large amount of synchronization; otherwise, the performance does not scale.

The *gccg* benchmark previously introduced was used to explore the efficiency of our simple data distribution, work distribution, and inspector-executor strategies. Figure 2.9 depicts the performance of the OpenMP and corresponding GA programs for *gccg* on the IBM SP. The performance of the OpenMP version is slightly better than the corresponding GA program within an SMP node, but the corresponding GA program with a large input data set achieves a speedup of 26 with 64 processors in four nodes. The steady performance gain here can be attributed to the fact that the inspector is only calculated once and reused throughout the program, and the communication and computation are well overlapped.

2.7 CONCLUSIONS

OpenMP is actively maintained by the OpenMP ARB, a consortium including the major hardware vendors and independent compiler companies. It continues to improve this API, particularly in order to increase its range of applicability. Given the wide availability of compilers and tools for this model, it is the most suitable starting point for a high-level programming model for HPC. However, this would require that an implementation strategy be provided that permits OpenMP code to execute well on DMPs. Most existing efforts attempt to do so by exploiting software DSM to handle the shared data. In this chapter, we describe an alternative approach that relies on a compiler translation. Nevertheless, it has a number of features in

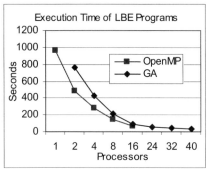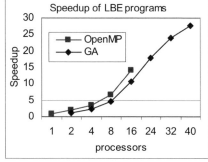

Figure 2.8 The performance of LBE program in OpenMP and corresponding GA form.

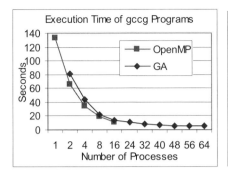 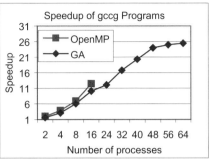

Figure 2.9   The performance of *gccg* in OpenMP and its corresponding GA version.

common with approaches that translate OpenMP to Software DSMs [22, 41] or Software DSM plus MPI [16] for DMP execution. All of these methods must adopt a strategy for distributing data across the system. Also, the work distribution has to be implemented for both parallel and sequential regions, and it is typically the latter that leads to problems. On the other hand, our translation to GA is distinct from other approaches in that it promises higher levels of efficiency, via the construction of precise communication sets, if done well. The difficulty of the translation itself lies somewhere between a translation to MPI and the translation to software DSMs. The shared memory abstraction is supported by GA and software DSMs, but is not present in MPI. Since only the local portion of the original data can be seen by each process in MPI, manipulating nonlocal variables in that model requires that the owner process and the local indices of arrays have to be calculated, introducing inefficiencies. The fast nonblocking and blocking one-sided communication mechanisms offered in GA allow for flexible and efficient programming. MPI will soon provide these features, but they are unlikely to be as efficient as their GA counterparts. With MPI-1, care must be taken with the ordering of communications to avoid deadlocks. Also, extra data transfers may occur with software DSMs due to the fact that data is moved at a page granularity [1]. GA is able to efficiently transfer sets of contiguous or strided data, which avoids the overheads of the transfers at the page granularity of software DSMs. Besides, for the latter, the different processes must synchronize when merging their modifications to the same page, even if those processes write to distinct locations of that page. In contrast, such synchronizations are not necessary in the GA translation scheme. Our GA approach relies on compiler analyses to obtain precise information on the array regions accessed; otherwise, synchronization must be inserted conservatively to protect the accesses to global arrays.

Although most work attempting to translate OpenMP for DMPs largely avoids the introduction of new language features, several may be beneficial. First, it may help if in this context program data is private by default. Help may also be needed to support the reuse of data access patterns generated in inspector loops. The Portland Group Inc. has proposed data distribution extensions for OpenMP, along with

ON HOME directives for DMPs [31]. INDIRECT directives were proposed in [27, 35] for irregular applications. The idea is to create inspectors to detect data dependencies at runtime and to generate executors to remove the unnecessary synchronization; the overhead of the inspector can be amortized if a SCHEDULE reuse directive is present.

Compiler technology has improved, in no small measure as a result of the HPF development effort, and the cost of accessing nonlocal data is reduced both as a result of improved networking and the provision of efficient single-sided communication. However, this approach requires extensive optimization and for this a good deal of program analysis is required. Some improvements call for parallel data flow analysis, a technique that is still in its infancy. Thus, even though the progress is encouraging, there is plenty of work to do before we can reliably provide the required levels of performance on many platforms. We believe that this work is essential if a high-level programming model is to be realized.

2.8 ACKNOWLEDGMENTS

My colleagues in the DOE Programming Models project, especially Ricky Kendall, helped me understand GA and discussed the translation from OpenMP to GA. Lei Huang performed the GA experiments and designed the basic translation described here, and Zhenying Liu considered several of the language implications.

REFERENCES

1. C. Amza, A. L. Cox, S. Dwarkadas, P. Keleher, H. Lu, R. Rajamony, W. Yu, and W. Zwaenepoel, TreadMarks: Shared Memory Computing on Networks of Workstations, *IEEE Computer, 29*(2), 18–28, 1996.

2. E. Ayguade, M. Gonzalez, J. Labarta, X. Martorell, N. Navarro, and J.Oliver, NanosCompiler. A Research Platform for OpenMP extensions, in *Proceedings of First European Workshop on OpenMP (EWOMP '99), Lund, Sweden, September 30–October 1, 1999.*

3. E. Ayguade, X. Martorell, J. Labarta, M. Gonzalez, and N. Navarro, Exploiting Multiple Levels of Parallelism in OpenMP: A Case Study, in *Proceedings of International Conference on Parallel Processing, Aizu, 1999.*

4. G. Bachler and R. Greimel, *Parallel CFD in the Industrial Environment,* Unicom Seminars, London, 1994.

5. R. Baxter, P. Graham and M. Bowers, Rapid Parallelisation of the Industrial Modelling Code PZFlex, in *Proceedings of European Workshop on OpenMP (EWOMP 2000), Edinburgh, UK, September 2000.*

6. J. Bircsak, P. Craig, R. Crowell, Z. Cvetanovic, J. Harris, C. A. Nelson and C. D. Offner, Extending OpenMP for NUMA machines, *Scientific Programming 8*(3), 2000.

7. R. Blikberg and T. Sorevik, Early Experiences with OpenMP on the Origin 2000, in *Proceedings of European Cray MPP meeting, Munich, September 1998.*

8. W. W. Carlson, J. M. Draper, D. E. Culler, E. B. K. Yelick, and K. Warren, Introduction to UPC and Language Specification, CCS-TR-99-157, IDA Center for Computing Sciences, Bowie, MD, May 1999.

9. F. Cappello and D. Etiemble, MPI versus MPI+OpenMP on IBM SP for the NAS Benchmarks, in *Proceedings of Supercomputing(SC2000), Dallas, TX, November 2000.*

10. S. Chakrabarti, M. Gupta, and J.-D. Choi, Global Communication Analysis and Optimization, in *SIGPLAN Conference on Programming Language Design and Implementation,* pp. 68–78, 1996.

11. B. Chapman, P. Mehrotra, and H. Zima, Programming in Vienna Fortran, *Scientific Programming 1*(1), 31–50 1992.

12. B. Chapman, P. Mehrotra, and H. Zima. Enhancing OpenMP with Features for Locality Control, in W. Zwieflhofer (Ed.), *Towards TeraComputing,* World Scientific Publishing Co. 1999, pp. 301–313.

13. B. Chapman, F. Bregier, A. Patil, and A. Prabhakar, Achieving High Performance under OpenMP on ccNUMA and Software Distributed Share Memory Systems, *Concurrency and Computation Practice and Experience 14,* 1–17, 2002.

14. W.-U. Chen, D. Bonachea, J. Duell, P. Husbands, C. Iancu, and K. Yelick, A Performance Analysis of the Berkeley UPC Compiler, in *Proceedings of 17th Annual ACM International Conference on Supercomputing, San Francisco, CA, June 23–26, 2003,* ACM Press, 2003.

15. R. Das, M. Uysal, J. Saltz, and Y.-S. Hwang, Communication Optimizations for Irregular Scientific Computations on Distributed Memory Architectures, *Journal of Parallel and Distributed Computing 22*(3), 462–479, 1994.

16. R. Eigenmann, J. Hoeflinger, R. H. Kuhn, D. Padua, A. Basumallik, S.-J. Min, and J. Zhu, Is OpenMP for Grids? in *Workshop on Next-Generation Systems, International Parallel and Distributed Processing Symposium (IPDPS'02), Fort Lauderdale, FL, April 15–19, 2002.*

17. J. Fagerström, Münger P. Faxen, A. Ynnerman, and J-C. Desplat, High Performance Computing Development for the Next Decade, and Its Implications for Molecular Modeling Applications. *Daily News and Information for the Global Grid Community, 1,* 20, October 28, 2002.

18. T. Faulkner, Performance Implications of Process and Memory Placement Using a Multi-Level Parallel Programming Model on the Cray Origin 2000, Available at http://www.nas.nasa.gov/~faulkner.

19. X. He and L.-S. Luo, Theory of the Lattice Boltzmann Method: From the Boltzmann Equation to the Lattice Boltzmann Equation. *Physical Review Letters E 6*(56), 6811, 1997.

20. S. Hiranandani, K. Kennedy, and C.-W. Tseng, Compiling Fortran D for MIMD Distributed-Memory Machines, *Communications of ACM 35*(8), 66–80, 1992.

21. HPF Forum, High Performance Fortran language specification, Version 2.0, Rice University, 1997.

22. Y.C. Hu, H. Lu, A. L. Cox, and W. Zwaenepoel, OpenMP for Networks of SMPs, *Journal of Parallel and Distributed Computing 60,* 1512–1530, 2000.

23. L. Huang, B. Chapman, and R. Kendall, OpenMP for Clusters, in *Proceedings of the Fifth European Workshop on OpenMP (EWOMP'03), Aachen, Germany September 22–26, 2003.*

24. Y.-S. Hwang, B. Moon, S. D. Sharma, R. Ponnusamy, R. Das, and J. H. Saltz, Run-time and Language Support for Compiling Adaptive Irregular Problems on Distributed Memory Machines, *Software Practice and Experience 25*(6), 597–621, 1995.

25. P. Kloos, F. Mathey, and P. Blaise, OpenMP and MPI Programming with a CG Algorithm, in *Proceedings of European Workshop on OpenMP (EWOMP 2000), Edinburgh, UK, September 2000.*

26. Kuck and Associates. KAP/Pro Toolset for OpenMP. See www.kai.com/kpts/.

27. J. Labarta, E. Ayguadé, J. Oliver, and D. Henty: New OpenMP Directives for Irregular Data Access Loops, in *Proceedings of 2nd European Workshop on OpenMP (EWOMP'00), Edinburgh, UK, September 2000.*

28. J. Laudon and D. Lenoski, The SGI Origin ccNUMA Highly Scalable Server, SGI Published White Paper, March 1997.

29. M. Leair, J. Merlin, S. Nakamoto, V. Schuster, and M. Wolfe, Distributed OMP—A Programming Model for SMP Clusters, in *Proceedings of Compilers for Parallel Computers (CPC2000), Aussois, France, January 2000.*

30. Z. Liu, B. Chapman, T.-H. Weng, and O. Hernandez, Improving the Performance of OpenMP by Array Privatization, in *Proceedings of Workshop on OpenMP Applications and Tools (WOMPAT 2002), Fairbanks, AK, 2002,* pp. 244–259.

31. J. Merlin (The Portland Group, Inc.), Distributed OpenMP: Extensions to OpenMP for SMP Clusters, in *Proceeding of 2nd European Workshop on OpenMP (EWOMP'00), Edinburgh, UK, September 2000.*

32. Message Passing Interface Forum, MPI: A Message-Passing Interface Standard. Version 1.1, June 1995.

33. B. Nichols, D. Buttlar, and J. Proulx Farrell, *Pthreads Programming,* O'Reilly Publishers, 1996.

34. J. Nieplocha, R. J. Harrison, and R. J. Littlefield, Global Arrays: A Non-uniform Memory Access Programming Model for High-Performance Computers, *The Journal of Supercomputing 10,* 197–220, 1996.

35. D. S. Nikolopoulos, C. D. Polychronopoulos, and E. Ayguadé, Scaling Irregular Parallel Codes with Minimal Programming Effort, in *Proceedings of the ACM/IEEE SC 2001 Conference (SC'01), Denver, CO, November 10–16, 2001.*

36. D. S. Nikolopoulos, T.S. Papatheodorou, C.D. Polychronopoulos, J. Labarta, and E. Ayguade, Is Data Distribution Necessary in OpenMP? in *Proceedings of Supercomputing (SC2000), Dallas, TX, November 2000.*

37. OpenMP Architecture Review Board, OpenMP Fortran Application Program Interface. Version 2.0, http://www.openmp.org, 2000.

38. P. Petersen and S. Shah, OpenMP Support in the Intel® Thread Checker, in *Proceedings of International Workshop on OpenMP Applications and Tools (WOMPAT 2003), Toronto, Canada, June 2003,* pp. 1–12.

39. J. Saltz, H. Berryman, and J. Wu, Multiprocessors and Run-Time Compilation, *Concurrency: Practice and Experience 3*(6), 573–592, 1991.

40. M. Sato, H. Harada, and Y. Ishikawa, OpenMP Compiler for a Software Distributed Shared Memory System SCASH, in *Proceedings of Workshop on OpenMP Applications and Tools (WOMPAT 2000), San Diego, July 2000.*

41. M. Sato, H. Harada, A. Hasegawa, and Y. Ishikawa, Cluster-Enabled OpenMP: An

OpenMP Compiler for SCASH Software Distributed Shared Memory System, *Scientific Programming, Special Issue: OpenMP, 9*(2-3), 123–130, 2001.

42. M. Sato, S. Satoh, K. Kusano, and Y. Tanaka, Design of OpenMP Compiler for an SMP Cluster, in *Proceedings of First European Workshop on OpenMP (EWOMP '99), Lund, Sweden, September 30–October 1, 1999,* pp. 32–39.

43. A. Sawdey, SC-MICOM, Software and documentation available from ftp://ftp-mount.ee.umn.edu/pub/ocean/.

44. S. Seidel, Access Delays Related to the Main Memory Hierarchy on the SGI Origin2000, in *Proceedings of Third European CRAY-SGI Workshop, Paris, France, September 1997.*

45. S. Shah, G. Haab, P. Petersen, and J. Throop, Flexible Control Structures for Parallelism in OpenMP, in *Proceedings of First European Workshop on OpenMP (EWOMP '99), Lund, Sweden, September 30–October 1, 1999.*

46. H. Shan and J. Singh, A Comparison of MPI, SHMEM and Cache-Coherent Shared Address Space Programming Models on the SGI Origin 2000, in *Proceedings of International Conference on Supercomputing, Rhodes, Greece, June 20–25,1999,* ACM, 1999 .

47. Silicon Graphics Inc. *MIPSpro 7 FORTRAN 90 Commands and Directives Reference Manual,* Chapter 5: Parallel Processing on Origin Series Systems, *Documentation number 007-3696-003.* http://techpubs.sgi.com.

48. L. A. Smith and J. M. Bull, Development of Mixed Mode MPI/OpenMP Applications, in *Proceedings of Workshop on OpenMP Applications and Tools (WOMPAT 2000), San Diego, July 2000.*

49. Top500 Organization, The Top500 Supercomputers and historical lists Top 500 Supercomputer Sites, http://www.top500.org/.

50. A. J. Wallcraft, SPMD OpenMP vs MPI for Ocean Models, in *Proceedings of First European Workshop on OpenMP (EWOMP '99), Lund, Sweden, September 30–October 1, 1999.*

51. T.-H. Weng and B. Chapman, Implementing OpenMP Using Dataflow Execution Model for Data Locality and Efficient Parallel Execution, in *Proceedings of 7th International Workshop on High-Level Parallel Programming Models and Supportive Environments (HIPS '02), Ft. Lauderdale, FL, April 15, 2002.*

52. X3H5 Committee, Parallel Extensions for Fortran, TR X3H5/93-SD1 Revision M, ANSI Accredited Standards Committee X3, April 1994.

## CHAPTER 3

SAT: Toward Structured Parallelism Using Skeletons

SERGEI GORLATCH

3.1 INTRODUCTION

Parallel and distributed systems have been a continuously growing class of computing facilities for decades. On the one hand, the demand for such systems has been strong and is steadily increasing. In addition to traditional time- and data-intensive applications, the recent growth of the Internet has given rise to geographically distributed high-performance systems (*grids*) and to new classes of commercial applications with parallelism on both the server and client sides. On the other hand, bigger and more powerful systems are being built that offer several levels of parallelism to the user: multithreading within a processor, multiprocessing in an SMP or a cluster, as well as distributed parallelism among remote machines cooperating via the Internet.

In spite of such a favorable combination of conditions—strong demand and good hardware availability—program development for parallel systems remains a difficult and challenging task. Today's programmers rely mostly on the programming culture of the 1980s and 1990s, the Message Passing Interface (MPI) still being the instrument of choice for demanding applications. However, its unstructured programming model based on explicit, individual communications between processors is notoriously complicated and error-prone.

This chapter explores an alternative model of parallel programming that avoids individual communications. Our approach, called *SAT (stages and transformations)*, is based on *skeletons*—high-level parallel constructs. Skeletons are typical patterns of parallelism, abstracted and offered to the application programmer as reusable program components. These components are provided with prepackaged implementations for main classes of parallel machines. To develop a specific application, the programmer chooses one or several suitable skeletons, customizes them for the application and, finally, composes customized components together to obtain the executable target program.

High-Performance Computing: Paradigm and Infrastructure. Edited by L. T. Yang and M. Guo **51**
Copyright © 2006 John Wiley & Sons, Inc.

The chapter is organized as follows. Section 3.2 outlines the SAT methodology by introducing basic skeletons as abstract constructs and collective operations as concrete programming means. In Section 3.3, we introduce a more complex skeleton called homomorphism, and present semantics-preserving transformations for skeletons and collective operations. Section 3.4 describes our case study, the maximum segment sum problem, in which we demonstrate how this problem is specified using skeletons and its solution developed by transformation toward an imperative program. Section 3.5 discusses both absolute performance of the programs developed in SAT and their performance predictability. We conclude in Section 3.6 by summarizing the main features and contributions of the SAT methodology and discussing future work.

3.2   SAT: A METHODOLOGY OUTLINE

Parallelism has traditionally had a rather contradictory standing in computer programming research. On the one hand, parallel activity both within and between computational entities is a phenomenon reflecting the natural world; furthermore, it is often desirable as a means to achieve higher performance. On the other hand, humans usually perceive the specification, control, and analysis of parallel activity as inherently hard. Many attempts have been undertaken to hide parallelism behind some kind of abstraction.

3.2.1   Motivation and Methodology

The main idea of the approach described in this chapter is simple: we recognize that parallelism in practice follows a number of recurring patterns of computation and interaction, such as pipelines, processor farms, and so on. The term skeleton originates from this observation: a skeleton abstracts a common pattern of parallelism and offers it to the application programmer as a programming construct. The study of skeletons (as opposed to specific applications) has an advantage of offering higher-level programming interfaces, opportunities for formal analysis and transformation, and the potential for "generic" machine implementations that are both portable and efficient.

Arguably, the main advantage of using skeletons is the availability of a formal framework for reasoning about programs. Skeletons can be modeled as higher-order functions and thus possess a rich set of semantics-preserving transformations, for example, for transforming one program into an equivalent but more efficient one. In addition, cost measures can be associated with skeletons and their compositions, thus enabling performance considerations.

The SAT approach stands for "stages and transformations." It addresses two contradictory requirements in parallel programming: whereas abstraction from low-level details simplifies the programming process, these details must be taken into account to achieve high performance. We, therefore, distinguish between the *abstraction view* and the *performance view* of a program.

3.2.2 Abstraction View: Basic Skeletons and Compositions

For the purpose of abstraction, SAT makes use of higher-order functions (function-als) on lists. These functionals capture general idioms of parallel programming that are independent of the parallel architecture and use elementary operators and functions as (customizing) parameters. A functional expression usually represents a class of programs that can be reasoned about, either taking into account particular properties of the customizing functions or not. This style of programming is called generic [14] or skeleton-based [1, 6].

Let us introduce the notation used in this chapter, restricting ourselves for simplicity to nonempty lists as our data structure, with concatenation denoted by #. A function application is denoted by juxtaposition. It binds most tightly and associates to the left. For the sake of simplicity, we define the skeletons informally and illustrate them with examples.

Map. Probably the simplest—and at the same time the "most parallel"—skeleton is *map,* which applies a unary function f to each element of a list, producing a list of the same size:

$$map\, f[x_1, x_2, \ldots, x_n] = [fx_1, fx_2, \ldots, fx_n] \tag{3.1}$$

In the following example, the doubling function is applied to each element of a list, yielding a result list of the same length, which is expressed using the *map* skeleton as follows:

$$map\ (*2)\ [0, 1, 2] = [0, 2, 4]$$

The independence of the individual function applications enables the following natural data-parallel interpretation of *map*: each processor of a parallel machine computes function f on the piece of data residing in that processor, in parallel with the computations performed in all other processors.

Reduction. The function *reduction* (*red*) takes a binary, associative operation $\oplus$ as parameter to reduce a list of values to a single value:

$$red(\oplus)\ [x_1, x_2, \ldots, x_n] = x_1 \oplus x_2 \oplus \ldots \oplus x_n \tag{3.2}$$

Two examples of particular instances of the reduction skeleton are as follows:

$$sum = red(+)\ \text{sum of list elements}$$

$$concat = red(\#)\ \text{flattening a list of lists}$$

Reduction can be computed in parallel in a tree-like manner with logarithmic time complexity, owing to the associativity of the base operation. Each processor applies function $\oplus$ to the element it owns and the element it receives from another processor.

Scan. In many practical applications, all intermediate results of a reduction are required, for example, in a carry–lookahead computation. Skeleton *scan* serves this purpose. It is specified by applying *red* to all prefixes of the input list:

$$scan(\oplus)\,[x_1, x_2, \ldots, x_n] = [x_1, x_1 \oplus x_2, \ldots, x_1 \oplus \ldots \oplus x_n] \qquad (3.3)$$

Despite an apparently sequential data dependence between the components of the result list, there are parallel algorithms for computing the scan functional with logarithmic time complexity [12, 8].

Composition. Individual skeletons, represented formally as higher-order functions, are composed in SAT by means of backward functional composition ∘, such that $(f \circ g)x = f(gx)$, which represents the sequential execution order on (parallel) stages.

3.2.3   Performance View: Collective Operations

To ensure competitive target performance, the design process should result in a program that can be implemented directly and efficiently on a wide variety of parallel machines. We call such a representation of the parallel target program the *performance view*.

Following the current practice of parallel programming, the SAT methodology adopts a performance view based on the SPMD (single program, multiple data) model and the MPI standard. To free the performance view from unimportant details, we represent it in simplified, MPI-like pseudocode. This code comes in two types of statements: *Computations* are represented as sequential function calls, for example, Call f(a), which implement the map functional of the abstraction view. *Communications* are restricted to collective operations.

Figure 3.1 shows the main collective operations of MPI for a group of four processes, P0 to P3. The top two rows of Figure 3.1 contain collective operations that specify pure communication (e.g., Broadcast, Gather). The operations at the bottom of the figure, Reduce and Scan, perform both communication and computation, and implement the reduction and scan skeleton of the abstraction view, respectively. The binary operator specifying computations (+ in Figure 3.1) is a parameter of the collective operation; it may be either predefined, like addition, or user defined. If this operator is associative, as required by MPI, then the corresponding collective operation can be efficiently implemented in parallel.

Note that the performance view of the SAT methodology is based exclusively on collective operations, that is, we avoid the send–recv commands. This "send–recv considered harmful" attitude was discussed by me in detail elsewhere [10].

3.2.4   SAT: Combining Abstraction with Performance

The ultimate goal of the SAT methodology is to mediate between the functional abstraction view and the imperative performance view in the program design process.

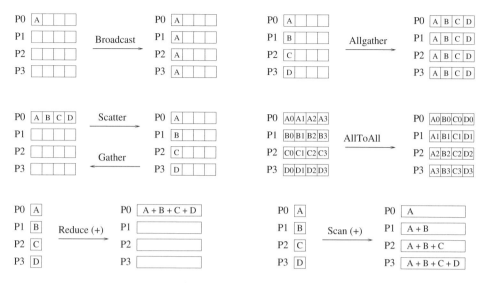

Figure 3.1   Collective operations on four processes. A box row shows data in one process.

To do so, the SAT methodology is based on two eponymous concepts, stages and transformations:

Stages are building blocks of both the abstraction view and the performance view: a program is always a sequence of stages. Each stage encapsulates parallelism of a possibly different kind.

Transformations support program design and optimization. They are correctness-preserving transitions, either between different abstraction views or from an abstraction view to a performance view.

An important goal of the SAT design process is to shield the user from the underlying transformational formalism; the transformations are proved "behind the scenes" and are made freely available to the user. If a high-quality parallel implementation is offered for each skeleton, the only remaining task for the user is to express the particular problem using available skeletons. The user need not be aware of which particular steps were taken to obtain their efficient implementation.

Structured, compositional programming works best if there is a supply of schemata which cover all needs of the application programmer. Our concept of a computational schema is the skeleton, and the programming paradigm in which we realize it is functional programming. One aspect in which functional programming surpasses many other programming paradigms is its powerful type system. To exploit this strength, a skeleton must be a function with a fully specified, executable body, and the only way of customizing a schema is via the actual parameters of a function call. This supplies both the implementation and runtime system with added power for optimization.

In the SAT approach, we distinguish two communities of programmers:

1. Application programmers are experts in their application domain and can express their computational solutions using skeletons.
2. System programmers (skeleton implementers) are experts in program compilation and optimization and in issues of computer architecture, like memory management, parallelism, and communication.

Application programmers work at the abstract level of skeletons rather than at the machine level. Their responsibility in program optimization is in the choice and customization of skeletons. System programmers are responsible for making a skeleton implementation perform well on a given machine.

3.3 SKELETONS AND COLLECTIVE OPERATIONS

The second-order functions introduced in the previous section are basic skeletons: each of them describes a class of functions, obtainable by substituting application-specific operators for parameters $\oplus$ and f. The need to manage important classes of applications leads to the introduction of more complex skeletons, for example, different variants of divide and conquer.

In this section, we take the generalization step from particular functions on lists with data-parallel semantics, like *map* and *red*, to a class of functions called *homomorphisms* that possess the common property of being well parallelized in a data-parallel manner. Introduced by Bird [4] in the constructive theory of lists, they have been studied extensively [13, 15, 8]. Our particular interest in homomorphisms is due to their direct correspondence to the divide-and-conquer paradigm that is used in the development of both sequential and parallel algorithms.

The primary motivation for defining a (new) skeleton is to identify a new or a more general, useful pattern of parallelism, to create an efficient parallel implementation for it, and to thereby obtain efficient implementations for its various instantiations. We show a twofold connection between skeletons and collective operations. On the one hand, some collective operations are instances of particular skeletons and thus enjoy their implementation properties. On the other hand, some collective operations are used as building blocks for implementing skeletons.

3.3.1 The H Skeleton and Its Standard Implementation

Let us introduce the H (homomorphism) skeleton. Definition 1, illustrated by the figure to the right of it, describes a class of functions with the parameter operation $\circledast$. Both *map* and *red* can obviously be obtained by an appropriate instantiation of the H skeleton; therefore, they are called H instances.

Definition 1 (Homomorphism)
A function h on lists is called a homomorphism with combine operation $⊛$, iff for arbitrary lists x, y:

$$h(x \# y) = (hx) ⊛ (hy)$$

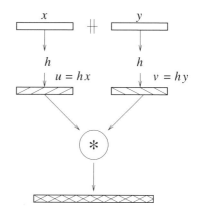

The key property of homomorphisms is given by the following theorem.

Theorem 1 (Factorization [4])   A function h on lists is a homomorphism with combine operation $⊛$, iff it can be factorized as follows:

$$h = red(⊛) \circ map\ \phi \qquad (3.4)$$

where $\phi a = h[a]$.

The practical importance of the theorem lies in the fact that the right-hand side of the Equation (3.4) is a good candidate for parallel implementation. This term has a typical SAT structure consisting of two stages. In the first stage, function ϕ is applied in parallel on each processor (*map* functional). The second stage constructs the end result from the partial results in the processors by applying the *red* functional. Therefore, if we can express a given problem as an H instance, this problem can be solved in a standard manner as two consecutive parallel stages—*map* and *red*.

The standard implementation [Equation (3.4)] of the H skeleton is time-optimal, but only under the assumption that makes it impractical: the required number of processors must grow linearly with the size of the data. A more practical approach is to consider a bounded number p of processors, with a data block assigned to each of them. We introduce the type $[\alpha]_p$ of lists of length p, and affix functions defined on such lists with the subscript p, for example, map_p. The partitioning of an arbitrary list into p sublists, called *blocks,* is done by the *distribution function, dist(p)* : $[\alpha] \rightarrow [[\alpha]]_p$. In practice, one tries to obtain blocks of approximately the same size.

Theorem 2 (Promotion [4])   If h is a homomorphism w.r.t. $⊛$, then

$$h \circ red(\#) = red(⊛) \circ map\ h \qquad (3.5)$$

This general result about homomorphisms is useful for parallelization via data partitioning. From Equation (3.5), we obtain:

$$h = red(⊛) \circ map_p\ h \circ dist(p) \qquad (3.6)$$

which is the standard implementation of a homomorphism on a fixed number p of processors.

3.3.2 Transformations for Performance View

According to the SAT design methodology, programs with collective operations are sequential compositions of stages. We shall outline some semantics-preserving transformations for specific compositions of collective operations; for more details, see [9].

Our first rule states that if binary operators $\otimes$ and $\oplus$ are associative and $\otimes$ distributes over $\oplus$, then the following transformation of a composition of scan and reduction is applicable:

$$
\begin{bmatrix} \texttt{MPI\_Scan}\,(\otimes); \\ \texttt{MPI\_Reduce} \end{bmatrix} \Rightarrow \begin{bmatrix} \texttt{Make\_pair:} \\ \texttt{MPI\_Reduce}\,(f(\otimes, \oplus)); \\ \texttt{if my\_pid==ROOT then} \end{bmatrix} \tag{3.7}
$$

Here, the functions `Make_pair` and `Take_first` implement simple data arrangements that are executed locally in the processes, that is, without interprocess communication. The binary operator $f(\otimes, \oplus)$ on the right-hand side is built using the operators from the left-hand side of the transformation. The definition of f, as well as other similar transformations can be found in [9].

The effect of such transformations on an MPI program is that two subsequent collective operations are fused into one, with simple local computations beforehand and afterward. This is illustrated in Figure 3.2 for a program with p processes, where each process either follows its own control flow, depicted by a down arrow, or participates in a collective operation, depicted by a shaded area. Since collective operations involve communication and sometimes synchronization as well, fusing two collective operations into one may save execution time; more details on that are given in Section 3.5.1.

Rule (3.7) and other similar transformations have the following advantages:

1. They are formulated and proved formally as mathematical theorems.
2. They are parameterized by the occurring operators $\oplus$ and $\otimes$, and are therefore usable for a wide variety of applications.

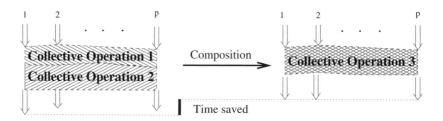

Figure 3.2 Fusing two collective operations by a transformation like Equation (3.7).

3. They are valid for all possible implementations of the collective operations involved.
4. They can be applied independently of the parallel target architecture.

3.4   CASE STUDY: MAXIMUM SEGMENT SUM (MSS)

In this section, we demonstrate how transformations are used in the design process toward predictable, better performance.

We consider the famous *maximum segment sum* (MSS) problem—a *programming pearl* [2], studied by many authors [4, 5, 15, 16, 17]. Given a list of numbers, function *mss* finds a contiguous list segment, whose members have the largest sum among all such segments, and returns this sum. For example:

$$mss[2, -4, 2, -1, 6, -3] = 7$$

where the result is contributed by the segment $[2, -1, 6]$.

Specification. We start with an intuitive, obviously correct specification:

$$mss = red(\uparrow) \circ map(red(+)) \circ segs \qquad (3.8)$$

which consists of three stages, from right to left:

segs yields the list of all segments of the original list.
map $(red(+))$ for each segment computes the sum of its elements by the reduction with the usual addition, +; the list of segment sums is thus obtained.
red($\uparrow$) the maximum segment sum, is computed by the reduction with operator $\uparrow$ that computes the maximum of its two arguments.

We introduce functions yielding all initial and all closing segments of a list:

$$inits[x_1, x_2, \ldots, x_n] = [[x_1], [x_1, x_2], \ldots, [x_1, x_2, \ldots, x_n]]$$
$$tails[x_1, x_2, \ldots, x_n] = [[x_1, x_2, \ldots, x_n], \ldots, [x_{n-1}, x_n], [x_n]]$$

Now, function *segs* can be specified formally using these functions:

$$segs = red(\#) \circ map\ tails \circ inits$$

Substituting this into Equation (3.8), we obtain our first algorithm for computing *mss*:

$$mss = red(\uparrow) \circ map(red(+)) \circ red(\#)\ map\ tails \circ inits \qquad (3.9)$$

Algorithm (3.9) is correct, but it has a poor time complexity—$O(n^3)$ for an input list of length n—due to the communication costs of stage $red(\#)$ [15].

Optimizing Abstraction View. To design a better algorithm, we start from Equation (3.9) and make use of the rules provided by Rule 3.7 and also of some standard equalities on higher-order functions from [15]. We omit some intermediate steps of the transformation process (see [9] for details):

$$mss = red(\uparrow) \circ map(red(+)) \circ red(\#) \circ map\ tails \circ inits$$

$$= red(\uparrow) \circ map(red(\uparrow)) \circ map(map(red(+))) \circ map\ tails \circ inits$$

$$= \ldots$$

$$= red(\uparrow) \circ map\ \pi_1 \circ (<\uparrow, +>) \circ map\ pair$$

$$= \pi_1 \circ red(\Uparrow) \circ scan(<\uparrow, +>) \circ map\ pair$$

$$= \pi_1 \circ \pi_1 \circ red((\Uparrow, <\uparrow, +>)) \circ map(pair \circ pair)$$

The derivation first arrives at the underlined expression for mss; its time complexity is $O(n)$ sequentially and $O(\log n)$ in parallel, which is a substantial improvement compared with the cubic complexity of the algorithm (3.9).

The corresponding performance view (MPI program) reads as follows:

```
Program MSS-1(my_pid,...);
Make_pair;
MPI_Scan (<↑, +>);                    (3.10)
Take_first;
MPI_Reduce (↑);
```

This program still has two collective communications, and that suggests as the next design step to try and merge those communications together. The derivation continues from the underlined expression. Denoting $\pi_1^2 \overset{\text{def}}{=} \pi_1 \circ \pi_1$ and $pair^2 \overset{\text{def}}{=} pair \circ pair$, we obtain the following target program:

$$mss = \pi_1^2 \circ red((\Uparrow, <\uparrow, +>)) \circ map(pair^2) \qquad (3.11)$$

The semantics of operator $(\Uparrow, <\uparrow, +>)$, which works on pairs of pairs (quadruples), can be expressed in terms of $\uparrow$ and $+$:

$$((r_1, s_1), (t_1, u_1)) (\Uparrow, <\uparrow, +>) ((r_2, s_2), (t_2, u_2)) \overset{\text{def}}{=}$$

$$((r_1 \uparrow r_2 \uparrow (t_1 + s_2), s_1 \uparrow (u_1 + s_2)), (t_2 \uparrow (t_1 + u_2), u_1 + u_2))$$

The elements of a quadruple in the above definition, that is r, s, t, u, all have an intuitive meaning related to the MSS problem: mss itself, maximum sum of an initial segment, and so on. However, unlike other derivations for *mss* [5], our approach proceeds without using this problem-specific knowledge.

The MPI representation of target program (1.11) is as follows:

$$
\begin{aligned}
&\texttt{Program MSS-2 (my-pid,...);} \\
&\texttt{Make\_quadruple;} \\
&\texttt{MPI\_Reduce ((}⇑\texttt{, <}↑\texttt{, +>));} \\
&\texttt{if my\_pid==ROOT then Take\_first;\~}
\end{aligned}
\tag{3.12}
$$

with the creation and projection functions for quadruples.

MSS as Homomorphism. Another possibility for the MSS problem is to use the standard H implementation [Equation (3.6)]. Since the quadruple (*mss*, *mis*, *mcs*, *ts*) is shown in [5] to be a homomorphism, that is, an H instance in our terminology, we can apply equality (3.6), which leads to the following expression for the *mss* function:

$$
mss = \pi_1 \circ red(\circledast) \circ map_p \,(mss,\, mis,\, mcs,\, ts) \circ dist(p)
\tag{3.13}
$$

Let us transform Equation (3.13) into a performance view for the case in which the input list is distributed evenly among the processors. In the performance view below, program `MSS-Dist`, the partitioned input is expressed by an HPF-like [7] annotation, `Block`, which means that array `list` is distributed blockwise, `list-block` being the block stored locally in a processor:

```
Program MSS-Dist (mypid);
/+ Input: list (Block) */
  Call quadruple (list-block);
  MPI_Reduce (⊛, root);
  if mypid == root then Output (mss);
```

The three stages of the SPMD program `MSS-Dist` are obtained directly from the stages of the abstraction view (3.13), offering a good chance that the generation of the performance view can be mechanized:

map_p (*mss*, *mis*, *mcs*, *ts*) is implemented by calling the program `quadruple` in each of the *p* processors on the processor's block of the input list.

red(⊛) is implemented by the collective operation `MPI_Reduce` with the user-defined operation ⊛, which, in this case, is the combine operation of the homomorphism. The resulting quadruple is stored in processor `root`.

Projection, π_1, is performed by processor `root`, which picks the first component of the quadruple, thus yielding the result of the program.

The asymptotic time complexity of program `MSS-Dist` can be predicted by estimating the complexity of each of its three stages:

1. The sequential program `quadruple` has linear complexity and works on a block of size n/p, which takes time $O(n/p)$.

2. Reduction over p processors, with a constant-time basic operation ⊛, takes time $O(\log p)$.

3. The last stage, projection, is obviously constant-time. Therefore, the time complexity of our target program, `MSS-Dist`, is $O(n/p + \log p)$—the best that can be expected in practice—with the constants depending on the concrete parallel machine.

3.5 PERFORMANCE ASPECTS IN SAT

High performance is the first and foremost reason for using parallel machines. However, the performance of parallel programs is known to be an inexhaustible source of contradictory discussions that show how difficult it is to discuss performance matters in the parallel setting.

3.5.1 Performance Predictability

Performance predictability for parallel programs is often viewed as even more difficult to achieve than the absolute performance itself. The main advantage of collective operations is that we can design programs by using the transformations presented in the previous section, and also estimate the impact of every single transformation on the program's performance.

In Table 3.1, obtained using the approach of [11], we summarize the results on the performance impact of particular transformation rules for collective operations. In the composition `Scan; Reduce`, both collective operations use the same base operator, whereas in `Scan_1; Reduce_2` the operators are different. Operation `Comcast` is defined in [11].

The parameters in the table are as follows: m is the block size in a processor, and t_s is the start-up time of communication, and t_w is the per-word transfer time. The estimates were validated in experiments on different parallel machines.

Table 3.1 Impact of transformations on performance

Composition rule	Improvement if
`Scan_1; Reduce_2` → `Reduce`	always
`Scan; Reduce` → `Reduce`	$t_s > m$
`Scan_1; Scan_2` → `Scan`	$t_s > 2m$
`Scan; Scan` → `Scan`	$t_s > m(t_w + 4)$
`Bcast; Scan` → `Comcast`	always
`Bcast; Scan; Reduce` → `Local`	$t_w + \frac{1}{m} \cdot t_s \geq \frac{1}{3}$

Summarizing, if we detect a composition of scan and reduction in the abstraction view of an algorithm, or the following term in a performance view:

$$\texttt{MPI\_Scan}(\otimes); \texttt{MPI\_Allred}(\oplus);$$

we can either leave it unchanged or transform it using the rules presented in the table in one of the following three ways (for details see [9]):

1. Applying the composition rule results in time complexity:

$$\log p \cdot (t_s + m \cdot (2 \cdot t_w + 3))$$

2. Applying the combined rule yields time:

$$2 \cdot t_s \cdot \log p + 3 \cdot m \cdot (t_w + 1) \cdot (p - 1)/p$$

   which is better than the first solution if $t_s < 2 \cdot m \cdot t_w \cdot (\log p - 1)/\log p$, for a sufficiently big p.
3. One other possibility is to decompose the reduction stage. This design decision provides a slower solution than the first two. However, it does not impose an additional restriction of distributivity on the involved operators and can thus be applied in a broader context. The decomposition rule improves performance if

$$t_s < m \cdot (t_w + 1 - (2 \cdot t_w + 1)/\log p)$$

Since the performance impact of a particular transformation depends on the parameters of both the application and the machine, there are several alternatives to choose from in a particular design. Usually, the design process can be captured as a tree, one example of which is shown in Figure 3.3.

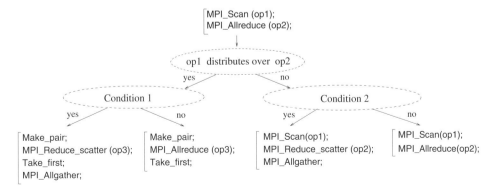

Figure 3.3   The tree of design alternatives.

The conditions in the figure read as follows (see [9] for details):

$$\text{Condition } 1 = t_s < 2 \cdot m \cdot t_w \cdot (\log p - 1)/\log p$$
$$\text{Condition } 2 = t_s < m \cdot (t_w + 1 - (2 \cdot t_w + 1)/\log p)$$

The best design decision is obtained by checking the design conditions. For example, if the distributivity condition holds, it takes us from the root into the left subtree in Figure 3.3. If the block size in an application is small, `Condition 1` yields "no," and we thus end up with the second (from left to right) design alternative, where `op3 = f(op1,op2)` according to rule (3.7). Note that the conditions in the tree may change for a different implementation of the involved collective operations on the same parallel machine.

3.5.2   Absolute Performance

Let us discuss whether our restriction of the imperative view to exclusively collective operations might lead to a lower absolute performance than when using traditional, low-level individual communication described by send–receive:

1. The implementations of collective operations in terms of *send–recv* are written by the implementers who are much more familiar with the parallel machine and its network than application programmers. Recently, hybrid algorithms have been proposed, (*library MagPIe*), which switch from one implementation of a collective operation to another, depending on the message size, number of processors involved, and so on. Such optimizations are practically impossible at the user level in programs using *send–recv*. Some implementations of collectives exploit machine-specific communication commands that are usually inaccessible to an application programmer.

2. Very often, collective operations are implemented not via *send–recv*, but rather directly in hardware, which is simply impossible at the user level. This allows all machine resources to be fully exploited and sometimes leads to rather unexpected results; for example, a simple bidirectional exchange of data between two processors using *send–recv* on a Cray T3E takes twice as long as a version with two broadcasts [3]. The explanation for this phenomenon is that the broadcast is implemented directly on top of the shared-memory support of the Cray T3E.

3.6   CONCLUSIONS AND RELATED WORK

The diversity of parallel computers and the complexity of their software call for portable, tractable, and efficiently implementable parallel-programming models and languages. The SAT methodology is an attempt to propagate the use of higher-order programming constructs as program building blocks in such models. The SAT methodology focuses on two orthogonal aspects of parallel programming: abstraction and performance. They are reconciled within a programming model that recasts a traditional parallel composition of sequential processes into a sequential composition of parallel stages, expressed using higher-order skeletons.

There are similarities between design patterns used in the object-oriented programming and skeletons in SAT. For example, the published Pipes-and-Filters and the Master–Slave patterns correspond to the pipeline and farm skeletons. However, although skeletons tend to be described in a formal way, patterns are usually loosely described in English and/or a combination of UML diagrams. Another difference is that a skeleton's "raison d'être" is in the design of high-performance systems, whereas design patterns tend to tackle other aspects such as fault tolerance, timeliness, and quality of service.

Application programmers benefit from abstraction in SAT, which hides much of the complexity of managing massive parallelism. They are provided with a set of abstract skeletons whose parallel implementations have a well-understood behavior and predictable efficiency. Expressing an application in terms of skeletons is usually significantly simpler than developing a low-level parallel program for it.

The SAT approach changes the program design process in several ways. First, it liberates the user from the practically unmanageable task of making the right design decisions based on numerous, low-level details of a particular application and a particular machine. Second, by providing standard implementations, it increases confidence in the correctness of the target programs, for which traditional debugging is hard on massively parallel machines. Third, it offers predictability instead of an a posteriori approach to performance evaluation. Fourth, it provides semantically sound methods for program composition and refinement, which open up new perspectives in software engineering. And last but not least, abstraction, that is, going from the specific to the general, gives new insights into the basic principles of parallel programming.

An important feature of the SAT methodology is that the underlying formal framework remains largely invisible to application programmers. The programmers are given a set of methods for instantiating, composing, implementing, and transforming diverse skeletons, but the development of these methods is delegated to the community of system programmers.

The task of a system programmer in SAT can be formulated more precisely, and alternative solutions can be compared more systematically than in the case of an unrestricted variety of parallel architectures, programming styles, and implementation tricks. This paves the way for a gradual transition from largely ad hoc implementation efforts to an integrated compiler technology for parallel machines.

Future work should concentrate on the adaptation of concepts across disciplines and the integration of these concepts within all phases of a well-defined development cycle. Considering adaptation, new theories and models must be developed to express requirements such as quality of service, dynamic change management, and dependability. Although middleware platforms have proved useful for applications with loosely coupled tasks and low communication requirements, their appropriateness for highly coordinated tasks that make large demands on communication and synchronization still requires investigation. The case for integration should give a greater role to such tools that use formal notation, provide a rich set of design abstractions, allow model checking, and offer automatic code generation. Integration of existing or new techniques should be achieved through formally defined, generic, reusable entities. Some of these entities have already been described in this chapter as skeletons. Also, standards like CORBA and MPI contain "patterns" that support location transparency and decouple processes from the underlying communication mechanism. It is expected that similar approaches will be adopted at a much higher level in the development cycle.

REFERENCES

1. B. Bacci, S. Gorlatch, C. Lengatter, and S. Pelagatti, Skeletons and transformations in an integrated parallel programming environment, in *Parallel Computing Technologies (PaCT-99)*, LNCS 1662, pp. 13–27. Springer-Verlag, 1999.

2. J. Bentley, Programming pearls, *Communications of ACM, 27,* 865–871, 1984.

3. M. Bernashi, G. Iannello, and M. Lauria, Experimental results about MPI collective communication operations. In *High-Performance Computing and Networking,* LNCS 1593, pp. 775–783, 1999.

4. R. Bird, Lectures on constructive functional programming. In M. Broy (Ed.), *Constructive Methods in Computing Science,* NATO ASI Series F: Vol. 55, pp. 151–216, Springer-Verlag, 1988.

5. M. Cole, Parallel programming with list homomorphisms, *Parallel Processing Letters, 5*(2), 191–204, 1994.

6. M. I. Cole, *Algorithmic Skeletons: A Structured Approach to the Management of Parallel Computation,* Pitman, 1989.

7. I. Foster, *Designing and Building Parallel Programs,* Addison-Wesley, 1995.

8. S. Gorlach, Extracting and implementing list homomorphisms in parallel program development, *Science of Computer Programming, 33*(1), 1–27, 1998.

9. S. Gorlach, Towards formally-based design of message passing programs, *IEEE Transactions on Software Engineering, 26*(3), 276–288, March 2000.

10. S. Gorlatch, Send-receive considered harmful: Myths and realities of message passing, *ACM TOPLAS, 26*(1), 47–56, 2004.

11. S. Gorlatch, C. Wedler, and C. Lenganer, Optimization rules for programming with collective operations, In M. Atallah (Ed.), *Proceedings of IPPS/SPDP'99,* pp. 492–499, IEEE Computer Society Press, 1999.

12. R. Ladner and M. Fischer, Parallel prefix computation, *Journal of ACM, 27,* 831–838, 1980.

13. E. Meijer, M. Fokkinga, and R. Paterson, Functional programming with bananas, lenses, envelopes and barbed wire, In J. Hughes (Ed.), *Proceedings of 5th ACM Conference on Functional Programming and Computer Architecture (PPCA'91),* pp. 124–144, Springer-Verlag, 1991.

14. D. Musser and A. Stepanov, Algorithm-oriented generic libraries, *Software—Practice and Experience, 24*(7), 623–642, 1994.

15. D. Skillicorn, *Foundations of Parallel Programming,* Cambridge University Press, 1994.

16. D. Smith, Applications of a strategy for designing divide-and-conquer algorithms, *Science of Computer Programming, 8*(3), 213–229, 1987.

17. D. Swierstra and O. de Moor, Virtual data structures, In B. Möller, H. Partsch, and S. Schuman (Eds.), *Formal Program Development,* LNCS 755, pp. 355–371, Springer-Verlag, 1993.

## CHAPTER 4

Bulk-Synchronous Parallelism: An Emerging Paradigm of High-Performance Computing

ALEXANDER TISKIN

4.1 THE BSP MODEL

A computation model is an abstract computing device used to reason about computation. An algorithm in a specific model processes an input into an output in a finite number of steps. Algorithm complexity depends on the computational model in which the algorithm is defined. Some models are designed with code performance prediction accuracy as the primary concern (so-called performance models, see e.g. [7]). Such models are necessarily elaborate and include a large number of parameters. Our approach is complementary, emphasizing model and algorithm simplicity, relative (but not necessarily absolute) accuracy, and the model's ability to guide algorithm design.

4.1.1 General-Purpose Parallelism

The model of bulk-synchronous parallel (BSP) computation [71, 53] provides a simple and practical framework for general-purpose parallel computing. Its main goal is to support the creation of architecture-independent and scalable parallel software. Key features of BSP are its treatment of the communication medium as an abstract, fully connected network, and strict separation of all interaction between processors into point-to-point asynchronous data communication and barrier synchronization. This separation allows an explicit and independent cost analysis of local computation, communication, and synchronization.

A BSP computer (see Figure 4.1) contains

- *p processors;* each processor has a local memory and is capable of performing an elementary operation or a local memory access in every time unit.

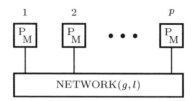

Figure 4.1 The BSP computer.

- A communication network, capable of accepting a word of data from every processor, and delivering a word of data to every processor, every g time units.
- A barrier synchronization mechanism, capable of synchronizing all processors every l time units.

The processors may follow different threads of computation, and have no means of synchronizing with one another between the global barriers.

A BSP computation is a sequence of supersteps (see Figure 4.2). The processors are synchronized between supersteps; the computation within a superstep is completely asynchronous. Consider a superstep in which every processor performs up to w local operations, sends up to h_{out} words of data, and receives up to h_{in} words of data. We call w the local computation cost, and $h = h_{out} + h_{in}$ the communication cost of the superstep. The total superstep cost is defined as $w + h \cdot g + l$, where the communication gap g and the latency l are parameters of the network defined above. For a computation comprising S supersteps with local computation costs w_s and communication costs h_s, $1 \leq s \leq S$, the total cost is $W + H \cdot g + S \cdot l$, where

- $W = \sum_{s=1}^{S} w_s$ is the total local computation cost.
- $H = \sum_{s=1}^{S} h_s$ is the total communication cost.
- S is the synchronization cost.

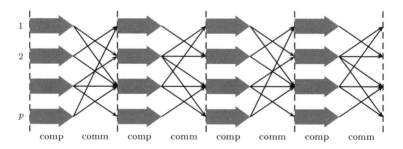

Figure 4.2 BSP computation.

The values of W, H, and S typically depend on the number of processors p and on the problem size.

In order to utilize the computer resources efficiently, a typical BSP program regards the values p, g, and l as configuration parameters. Algorithm design should aim to minimize local computation, communication, and synchronization costs for any realistic values of these parameters. The main BSP design principles are

- Load balancing, which helps to minimize both the local computation cost W and the communication cost H.
- Data locality,[1] which helps to minimize the communication cost H.
- Coarse granularity, which helps to minimize (or sometimes to trade off) the communication cost H and the synchronization cost S.

The values of network parameters g and l for a specific parallel computer can be obtained by benchmarking. The benchmarking process is described in [6]; the resulting lists of machine parameters can be found in [60, 6]

4.1.2 BSP Versus Traditional Parallelism

Traditionally, much of theoretical research in parallel algorithms has been done using the Parallel Random Access Machine (PRAM) [24]. The model contains

- A number of processors, each capable of performing an elementary operation in every time unit
- Global shared memory, providing uniform access for every processor to any location in one time unit

A PRAM computation proceeds in a sequence of synchronous parallel steps, each taking one time unit. Concurrent reading or writing of a memory location by several processors within the same step may be allowed or disallowed. The number of processors is potentially unbounded, and is often considered to be a function of the problem size. If the number of processors p is fixed, the PRAM model can be viewed as a special case of the BSP model, with $g = l = 1$ and communication realized by reading from/writing to the shared memory.

Since the number of processors in a PRAM can be unbounded, a common approach to PRAM algorithm design is to associate a different processor with every data item. Often, the processing of every item is identical; in this special case, the computation is called data-parallel. Programming models and languages designed for data-parallel computation can benefit significantly from the BSP approach to cost analysis; see [37] for a more detailed discussion.

---

[1]The term "data locality" refers here to placing a piece of data in the local memory of a processor that "needs it most." It has nothing to do with the locality of a processor in a specific network topology, which is actively discouraged from use in the BSP model. To distinguish these concepts, some authors use the terms "strict locality" [36] or "colocality" [65].

It has long been recognized that in order to be practical, a model has to impose a certain structure on the communication and/or synchronization patterns of a parallel computation. Such a structure can be provided by defining a restricted set of collective communication primitives, called skeletons, each with an associated cost model (see, e.g. [13]). In this context, a BSP superstep can be viewed as a simple generalized skeleton (see also [37]). However, current skeleton proposals concentrate on more specialized, and somewhat more arbitrary, skeleton sets (see, e.g. [14]).

The CTA/Phase Abstractions model [2], which underlies the ZPL language, is close in spirit to skeletons. A CTA computation consists of a sequence of phases, each with a simple and well-structured communication pattern. Again, the BSP model takes this approach to the extreme, where a superstep can be viewed as a phase allowing a single generic asynchronous communication pattern, with the associated cost model.

4.1.3 Memory Efficiency

The original definition of BSP does not account for memory as a limited resource. However, the model can be easily extended by an extra parameter m, representing the maximum capacity of each processor's local memory. Note that this approach also limits the amount of communication allowed within a superstep: $h \leq m$. One of the early examples of memory-sensitive BSP algorithm design is given in [55].

An alternative approach to reflecting memory cost is given by the model CGM, proposed in [20]. A CGM is essentially a memory-restricted BSP computer in which memory capacity and maximum superstep communication are determined by the size of the input/output N: $h \leq m = O(N/p)$. A large number of algorithms have been developed for the CGM; see, for example, [68].

4.1.4 Memory Management

The BSP model does not directly support shared memory, which is often desirable for algorithmic and programming reasons. Furthermore, the BSP model does not properly address the issue of input/output, which can also be viewed as accessing an external shared memory. Virtual shared memory can be obtained by PRAM simulation, a technique described in [71]. An efficient simulation on a p-processor BSP computer is possible if the simulated virtual PRAM has at least $p \log p$ processors, a requirement know as slackness. Memory access in the randomized simulation is made uniform by address hashing, which ensures a nearly random and independent distribution of virtual shared memory cells.

In the automatic mode of BSP programming proposed in [71] (see also [22]), shared memory simulation completely hides the network and processors' local memories. The algorithm designer and the programmer can enjoy the benefits of virtual shared memory; however, data locality is destroyed, and, as a result, performance may suffer. A useful compromise is achieved by the BSPRAM model [69]. This model can be seen as a hybrid of BSP and PRAM, where each processor keeps its local memory, but, in addition, there is a uniformly accessible shared (possibly external) memory. Automatic memory management can still be achieved by the address hashing technique of [71]; additionally, paper [69] identifies large classes of algorithms for which simpler, slackness-free solutions are possible.

In contrast to the standard BSP model, the BSPRAM is meaningful even with a single processor ($p = 1$). In this case, it models a sequential computation that has access both to main and external memory (or the cache and the main memory). Further connections between parallel and external-memory computations are explored in [63].

Paper [19] introduces a more elaborate model EM-BSP, in which each processor, in addition to its local memory, can have access to several external disks, which may be private or shared. Paper [72] proposes a restriction of BSPRAM, called BSPGRID, in which only the external memory can be used for persistent data storage between supersteps, a requirement reflecting some current trends in processor architecture. Paper [61] proposes a shared-memory model QSM in which normal processors have communication gap g, and each shared memory cell is essentially a "miniprocessor" with communication gap d. Naturally, in a superstep every such "miniprocessor" can "send" or "receive" at most p words (one for each normal processor), hence the model is similar to BSPRAM with communication gap g and latency $dp + l$.

Virtual shared memory is implemented in several existing or proposed programming environments offering BSP-like functionality (see, e.g. [49, 46]).

4.1.5 Heterogeneity

In the standard BSP model, all processors are assumed to be identical. In particular, all have the same computing speed (which is an implicit parameter of the model), and the same communication gap g. In practice, many parallel architectures are heterogeneous, that is, they include processors with different speed and communication performance. This fact has prompted heterogeneous extensions of the BSP model, such as HBSP [73] and HCGM [57]. Both make the processor speed an explicit parameter. Each processor has its own speed and communication gap; these two parameters can be independent or linked (e.g., proportional). The barrier structure of computation is kept in both models.

4.1.6 Subset Synchronization

Barrier synchronization is perceived by many to be too restrictive. Valiant's seminal paper [71] mentions briefly the possibility of synchronizing a subset, rather than the complete set of processors, but this possibility is not explored any further. Subset synchronization is a feature of various other parallel computation models, either independent of BSP (e.g., LogP [16], LPRAM [1], Y-PRAM [17], Asynchronous PRAM [26], H-PRAM [36], WPRAM [58], CLUMPS [10]), or designed as extensions of BSP (e.g., D-BSP and Y-BSP [18], WFBP [47], dBSP [5], BSPWB [62], CCM [28], H-BSP [11], OBSP [29]). Programming primitives for synchronizing processor subsets are defined in the MPI standard [67] and implemented in several existing or proposed programming environments offering BSP-like functionality (see, e.g. [64, 46, 8]).

Subset synchronization is usually justified by the following concerns:

- Adapting the algorithm to network topology
- Accommodating load imbalance and reducing processors' idle time, especially in irregular applications
- Overlapping computation and communication
- Recursively decomposing the computation into independent subproblems, a technique commonly known as divide and conquer.

The first two concerns are analyzed in detail in [66, 33, 51]. It is shown that for typical applications, exploiting network topology (as opposed to data locality) has little or no effect on program efficiency, while making programming and debugging much more difficult.[2] The question of reducing processors' idle time is in fact independent from the synchronization mechanism, both barrier and subset-synchronizing approaches require careful load balancing. The third concern is addressed in [66]. It is argued that the loss of efficiency due to the lack of computation–communication overlap is more than outweighed by the advantages of bulk data transfer. Furthermore, for sufficiently large problems it is possible to achieve computation–communication overlap and bulk data transfer simultaneously by controlling the size of communication buffers (see [8]). Papers [70, 50] propose a mechanism for bulk-synchronous divide and conquer, answering the final concern from the list above.

4.1.7 Other Variants of BSP

The BSP* model [4] is a refinement of BSP with an alternative cost formula for small h-relations. Recognizing the fact that communication of even a small amount of data incurs a constant-sized overhead, the model introduces a parameter b, defined as the minimum communication cost of any, even zero-sized, h-relation. Since the overhead reflected by the parameter b can also be counted as part of superstep latency, the BSP* computer with communication gap g and latency l is asymptotically equivalent to a standard BSP computer with gap g and latency $l + b$.

The E-BSP model [43] is another refinement of BSP in which the cost of a superstep is parametrized separately by the maximum amount of data sent, the maximum amount of data received, the total volume of communicated data, and the network-specific maximum distance of data travel. The OBSP* model [7] is an elaborate extension of BSP that accounts for varying computation costs of individual instructions, and allows the processors to run asynchronously while maintaining "logical supersteps." Although E-BSP and OBSP* may be more accurate on some

---

[2]An opposing argument is made in [44], which gives some examples of efficiency loss due to global synchronization. However, each of these examples is either highly machine dependent or has a relatively small input size.

architectures (paper [43] considers a linear array and a 2D mesh), they lack the generality and simplicity of pure BSP. A simplified version of E-BSP, asymptotically equivalent to pure BSP, is defined in [44].

The PRO approach [25] is introduced as another parallel computation model, but can perhaps be better understood as an alternative BSP algorithm design philosophy. It requires that algorithms be work optimal, disregards point-to-point communication efficiency by setting $g = 1$, and instead puts emphasis on synchronization efficiency and memory optimality.

4.2 BSP PROGRAMMING

4.2.1 The BSPlib Standard

Based on the experience of early BSP programming tools [56, 31, 54], the BSP programming community agreed on a common library standard BSPlib [40]. The aim of BSPlib is to provide a set of BSP programming primitives, striking a reasonable balance between simplicity and efficiency. BSPlib is based on the single program/multiple data (SPMD) programming model, and contains communication primitives for direct remote memory access (DRMA) and bulk-synchronous message passing (BSMP). Experience shows that DRMA, due to its simplicity and deadlock-free semantics, is the method of choice for all but the most irregular applications. Routine use of DRMA is made possible by the barrier synchronization structure of BSP computation.

The two currently existing major implementations of BSPlib are the Oxford BSP toolset [60] and the PUB library [8]. Both provide a robust environment for the development of BSPlib applications, including mechanisms for optimizing communication [41, 21, 21], load balancing and fault tolerance [38]. The PUB library also provides a few additional primitives (oblivious synchronization, processor subsets, multithreading). Both the Oxford BSP toolset and the PUB library include tools for performance analysis and prediction. Recently, new approaches have been developed to BSPlib implementation [59, 48, 45] and performance analysis [39, 74].

4.2.2 Beyond BSPlib

The Message Passing Interface (MPI) is currently the most widely accepted standard of distributed-memory parallel programming. In contrast to BSPlib, which is based on a single programming paradigm, MPI provides a diverse set of parallel programming patterns, allowing the programmer to pick and choose a paradigm most suitable for the application. Consequently, the number of primitives in MPI is an order of magnitude larger than in BSPlib, and the responsibility to choose the correct subset of primitives and to structure the code rests with the programmer. It is not surprising that a carefully chosen subset of MPI can be used to program in the BSP style; an example of such an approach is given by [6].

The ZPL language [12], already mentioned in Subsection 4.1.2, is a global-view array language based on a BSP-like computation structure. As such, it can be considered to be one of the earliest high-level BSP programming tools. Another growing trend is the integration of the BSP model with modern programming environments. A successful example of integrating BSP with Python is given by the package Scientific Python [42], which provides high-level facilities for writing BSP code, and performs communication by calls to either BSPlib or MPI. Tools for BSP programming in Java have been developed by projects NestStep [46] and JBSP [32]; a Java-like multithreaded BSP programming model is proposed in [70]. A functional programming model for BSP is given by the BSMLlib library [34]; a constraint programming approach is introduced in [3]. Projects InteGrade [27] and GridNestStep [52] are aiming to implement the BSP model using grid technology.

4.3 CONCLUSIONS

Parallel computers are a powerful tool of modern science and engineering. A parallel computer may have tens, hundreds or thousands of processors, making the computation inherently more complex than single-processor computation. Much effort has been spent trying to tackle this complexity, both in theory and in practice. One of the most important recent advances is the model of bulk-synchronous parallel (BSP) computation, proposed in 1990 by L. Valiant. Due to its elegance and simplicity, the BSP model has now become one of the mainstream research areas in parallel computing, as well as a firm foundation for language and library design.

In this chapter, we have surveyed the state of the art in two particular areas of BSP research: computation models and programming tools. Much work has also been done in BSP algorithms and applications. For an account of recent progress in these areas, we refer the reader to [23, 68, 6, 9].

The field of BSP computing is developing rapidly, pursuing the goals of efficient parallel algorithms, general-purpose parallel programming and, ultimately, scalable parallel applications. Based on a few simple underlying principles, through the advances in BSP architecture, BSP programming and BSP algorithms, we are seeing the emergence of the BSP computing discipline.

REFERENCES

1. A. Aggarwal, A. K. Chandra, and M. Snir, Communication complexity of PRAMs, *Theoretical Computer Science, 71*(1), 3–28, March 1990.
2. G. A. Alverson, W. G. Griswold, C. Lin, D. Notkin, and L. Snyder, Abstractions for portable, scalable parallel programming, *IEEE Transactions on Parallel and Distributed Systems, 9*(1), 71–86, January 1998.
3. O. Ballereau, G. Hams, and A. Lallouet, BSP constraint programming, S. Gorlatch and C. Lengauer (Eds.), *Constructive Methods for Parallel Programming, volume 10 of Advances in Computation: Theory and Practice,* Nova Science Publishers, 2002.
4. A. Bäumker, W. Dittrich, and F. Meyer auf der Heide, Truly efficient parallel algorithms: 1-optimal multisearch for an extension of the BSP model, *Theoretical Computer Science, 203*(2), 175–203, 1998.

5. M. Beran, Decomposable bulk synchronous parallel computers, in *Proceedings of SOFSEM,* volume 1725 of *Lecture Notes in Computer Science,* pp. 349–359, Springer-Verlag, 1999.

6. R. H. Bisseling, *Parallel Scientific Computation: A structured approach using BSP and MPI,* Oxford University Press, 2004.

7. V. Blanco, J. A. González, C. León, C. Rodríguez, G. Rodríguez, and M. Printista, Predicting the performance of parallel programs, *Parallel Computing, 30,* 337–356, 2004.

8. O. Bonorden, B. Juurlink, I. von Otte, and I. Rieping, The Paderborn University BSP (PUB) library, *Parallel Computing, 29,* 187–207, 2003.

9. BSP Worldwide, http://www.bsp-worldwide.org.

10. D. K. G. Campbell, On the CLUMPS model of parallel computation, *Information Processing Letters, 66,* 231–236, 1998.

11. H. Cha and D. Lee, H-BSP: A hierarchical BSP computation model, *The Journal of Supercomputing, 18,* 179–200, 2001.

12. B. L. Chamberlain, S.-E. Choi, E. C. Lewis, C. Lin, L. Snyder, and W. D. Weathersby, ZPL: A machine independent programming language for parallel computers, *IEEE Transactions on Software Engineering, 26*(3), 197–211, 2000.

13. M. Cole, Algorithmic skeletons, in K. Hammond and G. Michaelson (Eds.), *Research Directions in Parallel Functional Programming,* Springer-Verlag, pp. 289–303.

14. M. Cole, Bringing skeletons out of the closet: A pragmatic manifesto for skeletal parallel programming, *Parallel Computing, 30,* 389–406, 2004.

15. R. Corrêa et al. (Eds.), *Models for Parallel and Distributed Computation: Theory, Algorithmic Techniques and Applications,* volume 67 of *Applied Optimization,* Kluwer Academic Publishers, 2002.

16. D. E. Culler, R. M. Karp, D. Patterson, A. Sahay, B. B. Santos, K. E. Schauser, R. Subramonian, and T. von Eicken. LogP: A practical model of parallel computation, *Communications of ACM, 39*(11), 78–85, November 1996.

17. P. de la Torre and C. P. Kruskal, Towards a single model of efficient computation in real parallel machines, *Future Generation Computer Systems, 8,* 395–408, 1992.

18. P. de la Torre and C. P. Kruskal, Submachine locality in the bulk synchronous setting, in L. Bougé et al. (Eds.), *Proceedings of Euro-Par (Part II),* volume 1124 of *Lecture Notes in Computer Science,* pp. 352–358, Springer-Verlag, 1996.

19. F. Dehne, W. Dittrich, and D. Hutchinson, Efficient external memory algorithms by simulating coarse-grained parallel algorithms, *Algorithmica, 36,* 97–122, 2003.

20. F. Dehne, A. Fabri, and A. Rau-Chaplin, Scalable parallel computational geometry for coarse grained multicomputers, *International Journal on Computational Geometry, 6,* 379–400, 1996.

21. S. R. Donaldson, J. M. D. Hill, and D. Skillicorn, Predictable communication on unpredictable networks: implementing BSP over TCP/IP and UDP/IP, *Concurrency: Practice and Experience, 11*(11), 687–700, 1999.

22. C. Fantozzi, A. Pietracaprina, and G. Pucci, A general PRAM simulation scheme for clustered machines, *International Journal of Foundations of Computer Science, 14*(6), 1147–1164, 2003.

23. A. Ferreira and I. Guérin-Lassous, Discrete computing with coarse grained parallel systems: An algorithmic approach, in R. Corrêa et al. (Eds.), *Models for Parallel and Dis-*

tributed Computation: Theory, Algorithmic Techniques and Applications, volume 67 of Applied Optimization, Kluwer Academic Publishers, pp. 117–143.

24. S. Fortune and J. Wyllie, Parallelism in random access machines, in *Proceedings of ACM STOC,* pp. 114–118, 1978.

25. A. H. Gebremedhin, I. Guérin Lassous, J. Gustedt, and J. A. Telle. PRO: A model for parallel resource-optimal computation, in *Proceedings of IEEE HPCS,* pp. 106–113, 2002.

26. P. B. Gibbons, Asynchronous PRAM algorithms, in J. H. Reif (Ed.), *Synthesis of Parallel Algorithms,* pp. 957–997, Morgan Kaufmann, 1993.

27. A. Goldchleger, F. Kon, A. Goldman, M. Finger, and C. C. Bezerra, InteGrade: Object-oriented Grid middleware leveraging idle computing power of desktop machines, *Concurrency and Computation: Practice and Experience, 16,* 449–454, 2004.

28. J. A. González, C. Leon, F. Piccoli, M. Printista, J. L. Roda, C. Rodríguez, and F. Sande, The Collective Computing Model, *Journal of Computer Science and Technology, 3,* October 2000.

29. J. A. González, C. Leon, F. Piccoli, M. Printista, J. L. Roda, C. Rodríguez, and F. Sande, Performance prediction of oblivious BSP programs, in R. Sakellariou et al. (Eds.), *Proceedings of Euro-Par,* volume 2150 of *Lecture Notes in Computer Science,* pp. 96–105, Springer-Verlag, 2001.

30. S. Gorlatch and C. Lengauer (Eds.), *Constructive Methods for Parallel Programming, volume 10 of Advances in Computation: Theory and Practice,* Nova Science Publishers, 2002.

31. M. W. Goudreau, K. Lang, S. B. Rao, T. Suel, and T. Tsantilas, Portable and efficient parallel computing using the BSP model, *IEEE Transactions on Computers, 48*(7), 670–689, 1999.

32. Y. Gu, B.-S. Lee, and W. Cai. JBSP: A BSP programming library in Java, *Journal of Parallel and Distributed Computing, 61,* 1126–1142, 2001.

33. G. Hains. Subset synchronization in BSP computing, in H. R. Arabnia (Ed.), *Proceedings of PDPTA,* volume 1, pp. 242–246. CSREA Press, 1998.

34. G. Hains and F. Loulergue, Functional bulk synchronous parallel programming using the BSMLlib library, in S. Gorlatch and G. Lengauer (Eds.), *Constructive Methods for Parallel Programming, volume 10 of Advances in Computation: Theory and Practice,* Nova Science Publishers, 2002.

35. K. Hammond and G. Michaelson (Eds.), *Research Directions in Parallel Functional Programming,* Springer-Verlag, 1999.

36. T. Heywood and S. Ranka, A practical hierarchical model of parallel computation I: The model, *Journal of Parallel and Distributed Computing, 16*(3), 212–232, November 1992.

37. J. Hill, Portability of performance in the BSP model, in K. Hammond and G. Michaelson, *Research Directions in Parallel Functional Programming,* Springer-Verlag, pp. 267–287.

38. J. M. D. Hill, S. R. Donaldson, and T. Lanfear, Process migration and fault tolerance of BSPlib programs running on a network of workstations, in D. Pritchard and J. Reeve (Eds.), *Proceedings of Euro-Par,* volume 1470 of *Lecture Notes in Computer Science,* pp. 80–91, Springer-Verlag, 1998.

39. J. M. D. Hill, S. A. Jarvis, C. Siniolakis, and V. P. Vasilev, Analysing an SQL application with a BSPlib call-graph profiling tool, in D. Pritchard and J. Reeve (Eds.), *Proceed-*

ings of Euro-Par, volume 1470 of *Lecture Notes in Computer Science,* pp. 157–165, Springer-Verlag, 1998.

40. J. M. D. Hill, W. F. McColl, D. C. Stefanescu, M. W. Goudreau, K. Lang, S. B. Rao, T. Suel, T. Tsantilas, and R. H. Bisseling, BSPlib: The BSP programming library, *Parallel Computing, 24,* 1947–1980, 1998.

41. J. M. D. Hill and D. B. Skillicorn, Lessons learned from implementing BSP, *Future Generation Computer Systems, 13,* 327–335, 1997/98.

42. K. Hinsen, High-level parallel software development with Python and BSP, *Parallel Processing Letters, 13*(3), 473–484, 2003.

43. B. H. H. Juurlink and H. A. G. Wijshoff, The E-BSP model: Incorporating general locality and unbalanced communication into the BSP model, in L. Bougé et al. (Eds.), *Proceedings of Euro-Par (Part II),* volume 1124 of *Lecture Notes in Computer Science,* pp. 339–347, Springer-Verlag, 1996.

44. B. H. H. Juurlink and H. A. G. Wijshoff, A quantitative comparison of parallel computation models, *ACM Transactions on Computer Systems, 16*(3), 271–318, August 1998.

45. Y. Kee and S. Ha, An efficient implementation of the BSP programming library for VIA, *Parallel Processing Letters, 12*(1), 65–77, 2002.

46. C. W. Keßler, NestStep: Nested parallelism and virtual shared memory for the BSP model, *The Journal of Supercomputing, 17,* 245–262, 2000.

47. J.-S. Kim, S. Ha, and C. S. Jhon, Relaxed barrier synchronization for the BSP model of computation on message-passing architectures, *Information Processing Letters, 66,* 247–253, 1998.

48. S.-R. Kim and K. Park, Fully-scalable fault-tolerant simulations for BSP and CGM, *Journal of Parallel and Distributed Computing, 60,* 1531–1560, 2000.

49. D. S. Lecomber, C. J. Siniolakis, and K. R. Sujithan, PRAM programming: in theory and in practice, *Concurrency: Practice and Experience, 12,* 211–226, 2000.

50. F. Loulergue, Parallel superposition for bulk synchronous parallel ML, in P. M. A. Sloot et al. (Eds.), *Proceedings of ICCS (Part III),* volume 2659 of *Lecture Notes in Computer Science,* pp. 223–232, Springer-Verlag, 2003.

51. J. M. R. Martin and A. V. Tiskin, BSP modelling of two-tiered parallel architectures, in B. M. Cook (Ed.), *Proceedings of WoTUG, volume 57 of Concurrent Systems Engineering Series,* pp. 47–55, 1999.

52. H. Mattsson and C. W. Kessler, Towards a virtual shared memory programming environment for grids, in *Proceedings of PARA, Lecture Notes in Computer Science,* Springer-Verlag, 2004.

53. W. F. McColl, Scalable computing, in J. van Leeuwen, (Ed.), *Computer Science Today: Recent Trends and Developments,*volume 1000 of *Lecture Notes in Computer Science,* pp. 46–61, Springer-Verlag, 1995.

54. W. F. McColl and Q. Miller, Development of the GPL language. Technical report (ESPRIT GEPPCOM project), Oxford University Computing Laboratory, 1995.

55. W. F. McColl and A. Tiskin, Memory-efficient matrix multiplication in the BSP model, *Algorithmica, 24*(3/4), 287–297, 1999.

56. R. Miller, A library for bulk-synchronous parallel programming, in *Proceedings of General Purpose Parallel Computing,* pp. 100–108, British Computer Society, 1993.

57. P. Morin, Coarse grained parallel computing on heterogeneous systems, in *Proceedings of ACM SAC,* pp. 628–634, 2000.

58. J. M. Nash, P. M. Dew, M. E. Dyer, and J. R. Davy, Parallel algorithm design on the WPRAM model, in *Abstract Machine Models for Highly Parallel Computers,* pp. 83–102, Oxford University Press, 1996.

59. M. V. Nibhanupudi and B. K. Szymanski, Adaptive bulk-synchronous parallelism on a network of non-dedicated workstations, in *High Performance Computing Systems and Applications,* pp. 439–452, Kluwer Academic Publishers, 1998.

60. The Oxford BSP Toolset, http://www.bsp-worldwide.org/implmnts/oxtool, 1998.

61. V. Ramachandran, A general purpose shared-memory model for parallel computation, in M. T. Heath, A. Ranade, and R. S. Schreiber (Eds.), *Algorithms for Parallel Processing,* volume 105 of *IMA Volumes in Mathematics and Applications,* 1999.

62. C. Rodriguez, J. L. Roda, F. Sande, D. G. Morales, and F. Almeida, A new parallel model for the analysis of asynchronous algorithms, *Parallel Computing, 26,* 753–767, 2000.

63. J. Sibeyn and M. Kaufmann, BSP-like external-memory computation, in G. C. Bongiovanni, D. P. Bovet, and G. Di Battista (Eds.), *Proceedings of CIAC,* volume 1203 of *Lecture Notes in Computer Science,* pp. 229–240, Springer-Verlag, 1997.

64. D. B. Skillicorn, miniBSP: A BSP language and transformation system manuscript, 1996.

65. D. B. Skillicorn, Predictable parallel performance: The BSP model, in R. Corrêa et al. *Models for Parallel and Distributed Computation: Theory, Algorithmic Techniques and Applications,* volume 67 of *Applied Optimization,* Kluwer Academic Publishers, pp. 85–115.

66. D. B. Skillicorn, J. M. D. Hill, and W. F. McColl, Questions and answers about BSP, *Scientific Programming, 6*(3), 249–274, 1997.

67. M. Snir and W. Gropp, *MPI: The Complete Reference,* 2nd ed., MIT Press, 1998.

68. S. W. Song, Parallel graph algorithms for coarse-grained multicomputers, in R. Corrêa et al. *Models for Parallel and Distributed Computation: Theory, Algorithmic Techniques and Applications,* volume 67 of *Applied Optimization,* Kluwer Academic Publishers, pp. 147–178.

69. A. Tiskin, The bulk-synchronous parallel random access machine, *Theoretical Computer Science, 196*(1–2), 109–130, April 1998.

70. A. Tiskin, A new way to divide and conquer, *Parallel Processing Letters, 11*(4), 409–422, 2001.

71. L. G. Valiant, A bridging model for parallel computation, *Communications of the ACM, 33*(8), 103–111, August 1990.

72. V. Vasilev, BSPGRID: Variable resources parallel computation and multi-programmed parallelism, *Parallel Processing Letters, 13*(3), 329–340, 2003.

73. T. L. Williams and R. J. Parsons, The heterogeneous bulk synchronous parallel model, in J. Rolim et al. (Eds.), *Proceedings of IPDPS Workshops,* volume 1800 of *Lecture Notes in Computer Science,* pp. 102–108, Springer-Verlag, 2000.

74. W. Zheng, S. Khan, and H. Xie, BSP performance analysis and prediction: Tools and applications, in V. Malyshkin, (Ed.), *Proceedings of PaCT,* volume 1662 of *Lecture Notes in Computer Science,* pp. 313–319, Springer-Verlag, 1999.

## CHAPTER 5

Cilk Versus MPI: Comparing Two Parallel Programming Styles on Heterogeneous Systems

JOHN MORRIS, KYUHO LEE, and JUNSEONG KIM

5.1 INTRODUCTION

The most cost-effective raw processing power is now found in commodity personal computers as a consequence of high production volumes and competition among manufacturers. Since personal computers are usually connected to networks of some type, economic networking hardware (interfaces, routers, switches, etc.) is also readily available. Thus powerful inexpensive parallel processors or networks of workstations (NoWs) can be built from commodity PCs.

Continual technological improvements also mean that more powerful processors rapidly become available as manufacturers release new, faster processor chips. Market pressures ensure that these chips soon appear in systems. Thus, unless a system has been built over a very short period of time, it will inevitably be a heterogeneous one. As processors (PEs) are added or replaced, processors that are more cost-effective than those used initially will be available [Kwok, 2003].[1]

If the parallel processing run-time system (which could be a message passing one such as MPI [Snir, 1996], one which creates an illusion of shared memory [Amza et al., 1996], or the RTS supporting Cilk's dataflow mode of operation [Blumofe et al., 1995]) naively distributes equal amounts of work to each PE in a heterogeneous NoW, then the presence of a final barrier at which results are gathered to generate the ultimate result leads to an n-PE system equivalent, at best, to n of the slowest PEs. Parallel overheads will often considerably reduce the NoW system's power. This clearly represents a waste of resources in a system where individual PE powers may vary by large factors. Thus, the ability to effectively ex-

---

[1]In this work, we only consider commodity components that contain very small numbers (say 1–2) processors on each system bus so that there is no shared memory. The programs that we used here will, of course, run easily on small clusters sharing a common memory, but they do not systematically exploit the shared memory to increase performance.

High-Performance Computing: Paradigm and Infrastructure. Edited by L. T. Yang and M. Guo **81**

ploit the more powerful PEs in a heterogeneous system allows efficient systems to be built, maintained, and augmented. Heterogeneity may come from sources other than raw CPU clock speed. Cache sizes and speeds, the mix of processing units in a superscalar, bus speeds, peripheral interface efficiency (particularly network cards), and memory speed and capacity may all change the relative power of a PE. Relative powers are also problem dependent, so that simple load balancing schemes that rely on knowledge of relative powers are unlikely to be effective over a wide range of problems, as well as requiring significant setup or calibration effort.

5.1.1 Message-Passing Run-Time Systems

A message-passing run-time system provides one basic capability: the ability to transmit a message from one PE to another, that is, `send` and `receive` primitives. Generally, these provide synchronization also: a process blocks, a `receive` until the sending process has executed the `send`. Providing very low level semantic support, message-passing systems require more programmer effort to manage data, threads of computation, and synchronization. This is usually reflected in higher program complexity, confirmed by our measurements in Section 1.3.6.

5.1.2 Cilk's Dataflow Model

Although Cilk is based on a weakly typed programming language, it has a strong semantic model. Threads are "fired" (become ready for execution) when all their data is available. Thus, Cilk programs are data driven as far as the main computational units—the threads—are concerned and control driven within each thread. A quite small extension to C, Cilk is easy to learn but its safety (based on the strict dataflow model) is compromised by the ability to use C pointers (particularly global ones). On the other hand, it is able to leverage extensive experience in optimizing C compilers. A safer version of Cilk—Dataflow Java—has been implemented and has been demonstrated to run in fully heterogeneous environments consisting of processors running different operating systems [Lee and Morris, 1998], but its performance could not match that of C-based Cilk.

5.1.3 Terminology

Cilk operates by spawning threads that may be stolen for execution on some other PE. Our MPI programs ran as a single program (i.e., single thread of execution) on individual PEs. We built a small support library for MPI that placed work descriptors in a queue and distributed those descriptors to individual PEs in messages. In the general description of the benchmark problems, we use the term subtask to describe either a Cilk thread or a work descriptor generated for MPI. We also use the term spawning level to describe—for problems with recursive solutions—the level in the tree of subtasks to which subtasks that could be distributed to other PEs were generated. Below this level, "core" sequential code routines were invoked for execution on the local processor. *sp_level* = 0 generates no subtasks for execution on other PEs and corresponds to sequential execution on a single processor.

5.2 EXPERIMENTS

We selected several simple problems with varying computation and communication requirements and wrote programs in both C using an MPI library [Gropp et al., 1996] and Cilk. We selected a problem size so that the slowest PE took ~ 60 seconds to solve the problem. This ensured that, even when speedups close to the expected maximum (~ 25, see Table 5.1) were observed, minor perturbations—for example, those introduced by occasionally probing CPUs—had negligible effect on the overall results. Any effect of random asynchronous eventswas further minimized by running each experiment five times and reporting means.

5.2.1 Programs

To ensure accurate comparison, the same "core" code for each problem (compiled with the same compiler optimizations) was used in both Cilk and MPI programs. These core routines were invoked by individual tasks on each PE when no further distributable tasks were to be generated. In several problems, the number of subtasks generated can be relatively easily changed; this affects both load-balancing and communication:computation ratios, so we measured the effects of increasing the number of subtasks. The degree of subtask creation is characterized by the spawning level, defined in Section 5.1.3.

We also assessed program complexities by counting lines of code (separated into core algorithm code and support code, that is, code to manage work queues) and variables. We discuss the effort needed to change a basic problem solution to use the heterogeneous environment and report gains resulting from these changes.

MPI lends itself to simple work distribution schemes in which blocks of computation are sent to individual PEs. Aversa and coworkers used their Ps simulator to predict optimal PE loads [Aversa et al., 2003], but simulation, especially of multiple PE systems, is slow. The real system used here enabled us to obtain better insights into performance through the ability to rapidly explore wide parameter spaces. Our experiments with various spawning levels produced some unexpected results and new guidelines for efficient PE use. Simulation is also more difficult to

Table 5.1 Characteristics of our NoW testbed

Name	Clock (MHz)	Memory (Mbytes)	Relative power	Linux version
ant1-6	400(P-II)	128	1.00	v7.3
ant7-8	450(P-III)	128	1.07–1.13	v7.3
ant9-10	800(P-III)	128	1.93–2.47	v9.0
ant11-16	800(P-III)	128	1.93–2.20	v7.3

use in situations in which PE "powers" are dynamic, for example, when some PEs are being used in random, unpredictable fashions for other work. This happens when a NoW is operating in an idle-cycle-stealing mode; this is discussed further in Section 5.4.

We measured the relative performance of the PEs in our test bed when solving the test problems and observed a range of relative "powers" (see Table 5.1). Thus any assumption of fixed powers is treacherous. We partly overcame this problem by probing: each PE was asked to solve the problem individually and the performance factors were used to determine load balancing factors. Using these factors produced, as expected, much better speedups. Without them (that is, with equal work loads) the system was essentially constrained to be *n* copies of the slowest processor. However, conflicts for the communications network, queuing of large packets, and so on, mean that simple predetermined loading factors are not ideal; better results can be obtained with dynamic load-balancing schemes. The Cilk RTS's "work-stealing" mode of operation is well suited to this and can lead to near-optimum use of the system (cf. Figure 5.1 and Figure 5.5). Its ability to create work on slave processors further helps load balancing. To achieve a similar effect with MPI, we built a small work packet management suite of routines, which were sufficiently generic that they could be used with many problems. They provided a simple queue to which work descriptors could be added by the work generator (usually the master PE) and extracted for dispatch to slaves as needed.

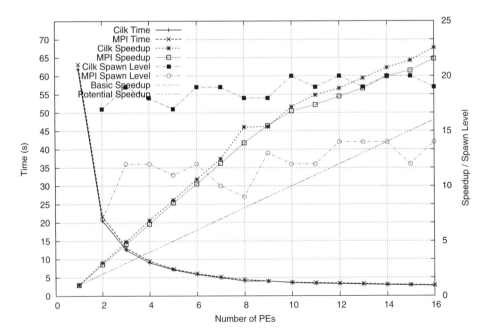

Figure 5.1   Fibonacci. Times and speedups for best spawning level. Spawning levels are also shown.

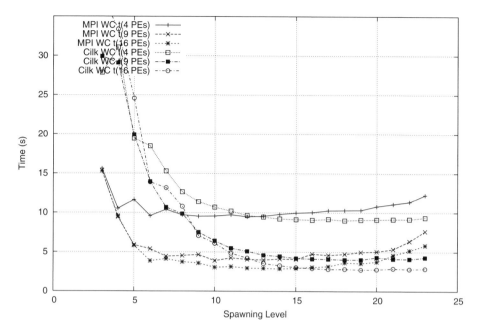

Figure 5.2 Fibonacci. Effect of varying the spawning level.

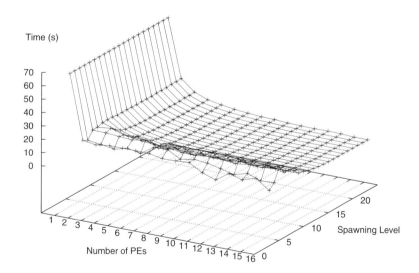

Figure 5.3 Fibonacci. Varying spawning level for Cilk (wall clock times).

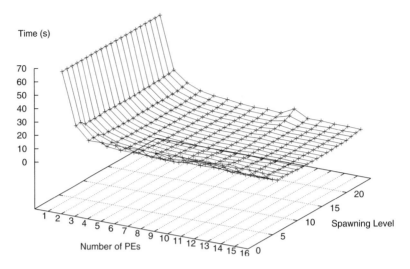

Figure 5.4 Fibonacci. Varying spawning level for MPI (wall clock times).

Because this suite could have been transferred to a library and used without further alteration for many problems, its code was tallied separately in the code volume comparisons (see Table 5.2).

5.2.2 Test Bed

Following usual practice, we collected PCs of varying ages and capabilities. Components were replaced as necessary to build working systems, not to produce a homogeneous system. The memory of each system was increased to at least 128 Mbytes. Again, no attempt was made to ensure equality or fairness, except with respect to the minimum amount of memory. None of the programs had working sets large enough to cause significant amounts of paging. None of the benchmark programs used the disc system for anything except initial program loading (which was not included in the timed results) and trivial amounts of result logging. Thus, the performance (or lack of it) of individual discs did not affect the results. Each PE was connected to a Nortel BayStack 70-24T Ethernet switch operating at 100 Mbps. Note that the Cilk program distribution system adds PEs to the system in the order in which they responded to the initial broadcast. No attempt was made to control this order as it mimics a real heterogeneous system in which PEs are upgraded as old components are replaced. This causes the varying slope of the "potential" speedup line in the following figures. One of the slower processors was always used as the master and speedups were always referred to it. This arrangement is the optimal one for MPI in which the simplest programming solution often uses a master PE for synchronization and data distribution but not for any significant amounts of computation.

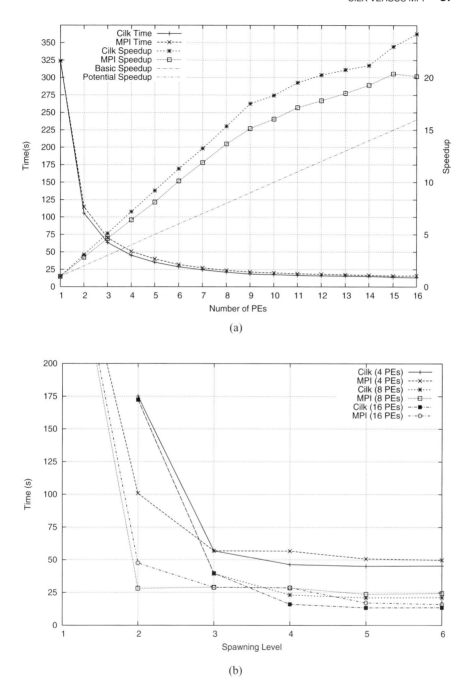

Figure 5.5   Traveling salesman problem. (a) Times and speedups, $n = 13$. (b) Times versus spawning level.

5.3 RESULTS

With a heterogeneous NoW, there are two possible bases for a speedup metric:

1. Counting each PE as a unit so that a 16-PE system's "ideal" speedup is 16
2. Weighting PEs by their powers (see Table 5.1)

Two target speedup lines have been placed on speedup graphs—"basic speedup" assumes that all PEs are equal and "potential speedup" considers individual PE powers. In our 16-PE testbed, the potential speedup relative to the slowest PE was ~ 25; it varies slightly from problem to problem due mainly to differing cache utilization.

5.3.1 Fibonacci

Despite its known poor performance, the recursive algorithm was used because the core code is trivial and thus provides a good comparison of the relative overheads of Cilk and MPI programs. Furthermore, by introducing an additional parameter—the spawning level—we generated a wide range of computation:communication ratios in each problem.

In previous work, MPI showed a slight performance edge [Baek et al., 2004]. However, those experiments used a low spawning level. Here, we fully investigated the effect of spawning larger numbers of threads by increasing the spawning level; see Figure 5.3 and 5.4, which plot time versus number of PEs *and* spawning level. In Fibonacci, increasing the spawning level by one doubles the number of subtasks (Cilk threads or MPI work descriptors) generated. Figure 5.3 shows that, for Cilk, run times continue to decrease as the spawning level increases up to 23 (although at this level, improvements are hard to measure—they are buried in experimental noise). However, with MPI, best results were achieved with significantly lower spawning levels (see Figure 5.1 and Figure 5.2). Larger systems require higher spawning levels to achieve best results.

When sufficiently large spawning levels were used, Cilk shows a slight performance edge over MPI. A simple model based on task granularity suggests that to get within 10% of the best obtainable result, each "PE equivalent" should receive on the order of 10 subtasks, yielding a total of ~ 250 tasks for our test bed with a total power equivalent to ~ 25 times the slowest PE. With Cilk in particular, the number of threads that are spawned to achieve the best results far exceeds this prediction. Changing $sp\_level = 11$ to $sp\_level = 13$ (or 2048 to 8192 tasks) decreases the time by ~ 20% for 16 Pes (see Figure 5.2). In Cilk, these additional threads do not necessarily migrate to another PE, but wait to be either executed locally or stolen by an idle PE. A large pool of fine-grain threads ensures that any idle PE is able to obtain work quickly by randomly targetting another PE, ensuring that PEs do not stay idle for long, leading to close to ideal speedups (see Figure 5.1).

With Cilk, adding the code for switching to the "core" (fast) function involved four additional lines of code, so that implementing a large spawning depth is simply a matter of choosing a (suitably large!) value. In the MPI version, generated sub-tasks were placed in a queue using library code—used in other programs, so that there was no additional effort for the queue management code—but the distribution code was more complex than the Cilk version (see Table 5.2).

5.3.2 Traveling Salesman Problem

The traveling salesman problem (TSP) is a typical NP-complete problem, requiring a search of $n!$ permutations of a list. It is solved with a simple recursive program. Good speedups are trivially obtained with little communication overhead by dispatching subtours to be evaluated to individual PEs. The cost matrix is moderately large [$\mathcal{O}(n^2)$], but it only needs to be distributed to each PE once. Subtour descriptors are short integer lists requiring short messages. Optimizations dramatically affect the efficiency of TSP programs; many have been discovered, starting with the work of Dantzig and coworkers [Dantzig et al., 1954]. However, since our aim was not to solve very large TSP problems but rather to compare Cilk and MPI and their effectiveness on heterogeneous systems, we used a simple unoptimized program.

The Cilk TSP programs deviate slightly from a pure dataflow model in the initialization phase, which distributes the cost matrix to a global location on each PE. Thus, this setup phase was handled almost identically in both Cilk and MPI programs. Even though it is very small for the TSP, the time to distribute the cost matrix was included in measured times in both cases.

TSP shows excellent speedups because each subtask at the top level represents a large amount of work for a small communication effort. The results are shown in Figure 5.5(a). For Cilk, speedups approached the potential speedup. Note again the importance of creating sufficient threads. As Figure 5.5(b) shows, significant improvement is obtained by increasing the spawning level from 2 to 3, which increases the number of threads generated from 132 to 1320. Again, MPI programs exhibited their best performance with fewer subtasks, but Cilk programs performed even better when sufficient threads were spawned.

The MPI version did not distribute the generated subcomputations in as efficient a way as the Cilk program and its speedup suffered. To complete any subtour computation, Cilk threads deposit data in any order (i.e., as other PEs complete) into the closure for the thread, which proceeds to choose the minimum. In contrast, MPI reads results from other PEs in order. At best, this requires additional I/O buffer space to manage completions that occur in an order other than the programmed one and, at worst, PEs may be blocked while waiting for the receiver to execute a read.

The Cilk program is particularly simple: it has only two parallel statements, one to spawn the initial thread and the other to spawn threads to work on subtours. Two sync statements are also needed.[2]

---

[2]The Cilk compiler could infer the need for these from a simple dataflow analysis of the code (detecting definition–use pairs), but its authors presumably considered that a programmer could do a better job of deciding the optimum placement of the minimum number of sync's.

5.3.3 *N*-Queens Problem

Another "hard" problem, *N*-Queens, requires an exhaustive search to find all the possible placements of nonthreatening queens on an $N \times N$ chess-board. It has no setup costs (e.g., distribution of a cost matrix for TSP) and spawns $O(N)$ threads recursively at every stage; thus, it has a "pure" recursive code solution.

With this problem, both systems performed similarly, with the Cilk system exhibiting a slight edge, but differences were generally similar to run-to-run variations and thus not very significant (Figure 5.6). The fan-out for *N*-Queens is irregular, with varying numbers of subtasks being generated at each level. There is also the small amount of computation needed to decide whether a path is safe so far (and, therefore, should by evaluated further by a subtask), which slows down the generation of subtasks. This irregular fan-out benefited MPI, which achieved better speedups than observed for the more regular TSP problem, albeit by a small margin (21.2 versus 20.2). Again, best speedups were observed with large numbers of generated subtasks, with MPI reaching its best performance at lower spawning levels. This is a repeat of the pattern already observed for Fibonacci and the TSP.

5.3.4 Matrix Multiplication

A simple but important problem, matrix multiplication is trivially parallelized: to compute the matrix product, *AB*, first the *B* matrix is sent to all PEs, then bands of

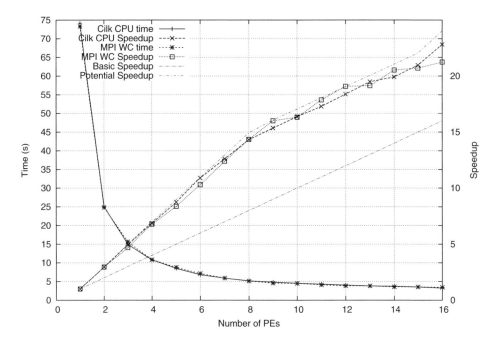

Figure 5.6 Times and speedup for *N*-Queens, $N = 14$. Varying sequential depth.

rows of the A matrix are sent to PEs, which compute a submatrix of the product and transmit it back to the host. It has $\mathcal{O}(n^2)$ communication cost and $\mathcal{O}(n^3)$ computation cost. With modern fast CPUs and relatively slow networks, this implies that speedup will only be observed with matrices large enough to overcome fixed overheads. Large blocks of data are also transmitted: in our test problem, which multiplies two 1100×1100 matrices of floats, a 4.8 Mbyte block of data (the B matrix) is transferred to each PE at startup. The Cilk program used the ability to specify which PE should run a thread to distribute bands to specific PEs. Two variants were compared: one in which equal sized bands were distributed to each PE (i.e., the system was assumed to be homogeneous), and the other in which relative PE power factors were determined for this problem (see Table 5.1) and the band "widths" were weighted by these factors. In both cases, the measured times include the time needed to distibute the B matrix and the time to reassemble the product on the original PE.

Since matrix multiplication is very regular, with simple, predictable load patterns, it might be expected that MPI's direct message passing would have lower overheads and produce better results. However, in a previous study [Tham, 2003], Cilk performed better. This was attributed to Cilk's synchronize-in-any-order dataflow model resulting in cheaper synchronization for the final result. We repeated these experiments for the current heterogeneous system with different approach-

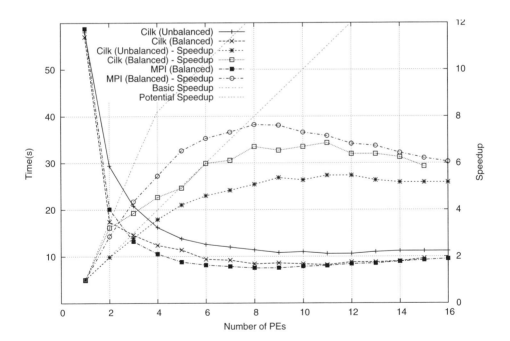

Figure 5.7 Times and speedup for matrix multiplication (1100×1100), Cilk (wall clock times).

es to load balancing: equal loads and balanced (or power-weighted) loads (with no work stealing).

As expected, a simple balancing algorithm that divided the A matrix into bands of width proportional to PE powers provided a significant benefit with higher maximum speedup with fewer PEs. Cilk programs exhibited very high initial speedups, achieving near ideal speedup with two PEs despite the large sequential communication overhead. This is due to cache effects—a system of n PEs has $\sim n$ times as much cache. Thus, splitting a large matrix multiplication into smaller bands allows larger fractions of the critical matrix (the one accessed by columns, B in our experiments) to remain within data caches.

Speedups reached peaks at 8 PEs (balanced) and 10 PEs (even distribution), reflecting the increased competition for the common network in the initialization and completion stages of the algorithm. However, in the heterogeneous system, MPI exhibited significantly larger maximum speedup. This was attributed to better I/O handling by the underlying MPI routines, as most of the work is done in the same core routine in both cases. Cilk's I/O system uses two threads to manage communications: this provides significant benefits when large numbers of small messages are involved. However, in this problem, computation is blocked while the large initial and final messages are transmitted, so that MPI's direct handling of data transmission has no deleterious effect. Cilk's ability to handle messages in any order in the RTS no longer provides the benefit reported previously [Tham, 2003]; our CPUs are faster, but the network speed remains the same.

5.3.5   Finite Differencing

This problem solves several physical systems. One example is that of heat flow through a conducting plate. Laplace's equation is solved in a discrete form by dividing the region of interest into a rectangular array of cells and iteratively updating the value of each cell (representing temperature in the heat flow example) with the average of the four nearest-neighbor cells. Each PE is assigned a band of cells (a set of rows of the array) to solve. A solution is reached when the system converges to a stable set of values, that is, when the cell values change by less than some error criterion in each iteration. Rows of boundary cells are shared between pairs of PEs; in each iteration, each PE only needs to update its two neighbors with new cell values. Several synchronization schemes are possible:

- "Master" synchronization. A master PE communicates with the others and decides when all PEs have converged. If any of the bands is yet to converge, the master signals each PE to calculate one more iteration.
- "Distributed" synchronization. When a PE has reached convergence, it passes a token to its neighbor, which passes it on if it has also converged. As soon as a token returns "home," that is, to its originating PE, then the whole computation has converged and all PEs are notified. This allows a degree of asynchronous processing—PEs may overlap computation and boundary value communication more efficiently.

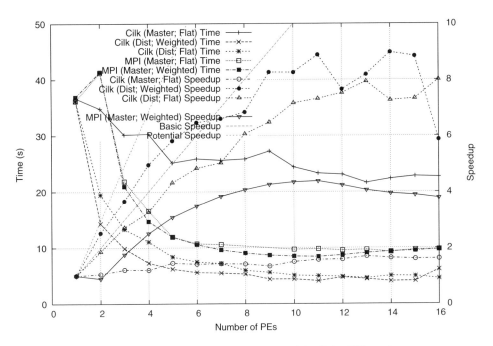

Figure 5.8 Time and speedup for several variants of the finite differencing program.

- Fully asynchronous. Each PE commences a new iteration whether or not boundary updates have arrived from neighbors. Boundary updates are dispatched to neighbors when they are available.

The simple, regular communication patterns required for synchronous versions of this problem match MPI's capabilities well and this problem is easily coded using MPI. The Cilk version departs from a strict dataflow model[3] and was relatively harder to code. The master synchronization MPI code only transmitted the convergence signals to the master; boundaries were transmitted directly to neighbours. Coding the transmission of the boundaries through the master would have required additional effort *and* slowed the program down. This was the easiest way to code the Cilk version, though. As a consequence, MPI was superior in both coding effort and performance for a master synchronized system. A Cilk program that used fully distributed synchronization was written, and debugged with considerable effort because the current Cilk RTS requires all spawned threads to be fired and does not provide any mechanism for killing them directly![4] However, this version performed better than its simpler MPI counterpart. In addition to direct communication of the boundaries, it allows a degree of asynchronous computation—a PE can receive the

---

[3]A pure dataflow solution is possible, but it involves excessive copying of data in a parallel environment and was not considered.
[4]Cilk does not keep direct references to spawned threads, only to empty data slots within them.

next boundary from a neighbour while it is completing the current iteration, a significant benefit in a heterogeneous environment. Comparing the Cilk results for the two synchronization styles is a textbook example of the cost of synchronization in parallel systems. We did not implement the fully distributed synchronization scheme in MPI because Cilk's capability to send Active Messages [von Eicken et al., 1992] makes the detection of convergence easy and efficient. Computation continues while the convergence tokens are being passed from PE to PE. An MPI system would need to use "out-of-band" communication to permit the simple, random interleaving of boundary updates and convergence tokens that Cilk allows. (Our programming time was consumed by the need to ensure that any spawned Cilk thread was eventually fired. The convergence code was simple!)

5.3.6   Program Complexity

Although they are far from perfect metrics, we used counts of lines of code (LOC) and variables to provide some estimate of relative programming difficulty. The counts in Table 5.2 are for the "core" code that solves the problem. Code that generated the test dataset and code used for instrumentation (timing or measuring other aspects of performance, e.g., counting Laplace iterations) was not included. The tallies were divided into two groups: basic code needed to solve the problem (code that would be present in a sequential version of the same problem) and parallel overhead (code to initialize and configure the system, create threads, transmit data, synchronize, etc.). *Disclaimer: software metrics is not an exact science!*[5] The figures provided here are very basic and simply provide an indication of programming effort. A small amount of "noise" in the form of individual programming style was also added by the several authors of the programs used. However, the lower parallel programming overhead of Cilk is clear: by providing a simple semantic model, it provides considerably more support for a programmer than MPI. It is also notable that some of the optimizations are trivially added to Cilk programs.

With MPI, in order to obtain good speedups, we built queues of "work packets" that were distributed to each PE. The queue management code was counted in the column marked "Library" in Table 5.2 because generic code was placed in a library so that each program only saw `create`, `add`, and `get` methods; these methods could become part of the MPI library.

5.4   CONCLUSION

With the exception of the finite differencing program, Cilk versions of the programs were considerably easier to write. Implicit synchronization using a dataflow model means that fewer statements directing parallel execution are needed. Most Cilk pro-

[5]Our counts were generated by hand: we considered that the additional effort required to remove instrumentation and diagnostic code in order to use a tool to obtain more sophisticated counts was unwarranted.

Table 5.2 Code complexities

| Problem | Cilk | | | | MPI | | | | |
| | Algorithm | | Overhead | | Algorithm | | Overhead | | Lib |
	LOC	var	LOC	var	LOC	var	LOC	var	LOC
Fibonacci	6	2	1	0	[a]				
+sp level	10	2	3	1	7	3	12	5	52
TSP	20	13	9	0	[a]				
+sp level	23	13	9	1	18	10	14	6	59
MM	9	6	27	21	9	6	11	6	51
N-Queens	19	13	2	1	[a]				
+sp level	26	12	2	2	19	10	11	4	55
Laplace									
master synch	17	10	42	44	15	6	18	2	
dist synch	30	5	20	10	[b]				

[a]Spawning level is fundamental to MPI version.
[b]Not implemented.

grams (Fibonacci, TSP, and N-Queens in the set used here) will run on any number of processors (including a single PE) without any explicit consideration of the current size of the NoW system. The program that we used for distributing Cilk programs to individual PEs simply counts the number of PEs responding to a broadcast request and the RTS uses this number when making work-stealing requests. Thus, Cilk programs work well in "flexible" environments where the number of PEs may change from day to day.

Our results clearly show that measurable additional performance can be obtained by spawning more threads or creating more work packets than simple load balancing calculations would require. With Cilk programs, the improvement is gradual and continues until thousands of threads that could be shifted from PE to PE have been generated. With MPI programs, the improvement is rapid and best results were achieved with smaller values of the spawning level (i.e., smaller numbers of work packets), but these best results were also achieved with larger numbers of work packets than a simple work-balancing model suggests. Thus, performance depends critically on creating large numbers of fine-grain computations, even when these computations are explicitly distributed to individual PEs as they were with our MPI programs. With Cilk, even though large numbers of threads are created, not many of them actually migrate (they are executed locally unless an idle PE steals them). However, there is always a pool of threads available to an idle PE. The current Cilk RTS makes an idle PE choose another PE randomly to steal work. The large pool of available threads ensures that the first steal request is satisfied, ensuring that PEs waste little time idling, producing good work-balancing and allowing Cilk programs to obtain an edge over MPI ones. This edge is likely to be more pronounced in truly dynamic systems, where competing work loads effectively change the power (or cycles available to any one program) continually. Cilk programs that have spawned large pools of fine-grained threads should tolerate this situation considerably better than MPI programs.

In cases where explicit distribution of work to PEs is appropriate because obvious simple distribution policies are readily coded (MM, Laplace), both Cilk and MPI require similar numbers of statements, that is, MPI has no significant advantage when it might be expected to have one.

When a strict dataflow model requires excessive data copying (Laplace), MPI both allows simpler implementations and provides better performance. We note that both systems are C-based, so that hybrid programs that, for example, used Cilk's dataflow model when it was effective and MPI's "direct" transfer of data from source to destination when it provided better performance, could readily be put together.

One of the major lessons learned from this study came from the availability of the two very different computation models. Since it was trivial to change the spawning level in Cilk programs, we were led to study its effect on performance carefully. When we discovered that more threads than originally expected were needed to achieve best performance, we were motivated to check whether MPI programs exhibit the same phenomenon in this environment and found that although the effect is less marked, it can be used to extract significant additional performance fromMPI programs. The lessons learned from the distributed Laplacian synchronization in Cilk should also translate to MPI systems. We are currently evaluating techniques such as multithreading to implement these ideas.

ACKNOWLEDGMENTS

John Morris was supported by the Foreign Professors Invitation Program of the Institute of Information Technology Assessment (IITA) at Chung-Ang University, Seoul, Korea. SunHo Baek set up the system on which these experiments were run.

REFERENCES

Amza, C., Cox, A. L., Dwarkadas, S., Keleher, P., Lu, H., Rajamony, R., Yu, W., and Zwaenepoel, W. (1996), TreadMarks: Shared Memory Computing on Networks of Workstations, *IEEE Computer, 29*(2), 18–28.

Aversa, R., Mazzocca, N., and Villano, U. (2003), A case study of application analytical modeling in heterogeneous computing environments: Cholesky factorization in a NOW, *The Journal of Supercomputing, 24*(1), 5–24.

Baek, S., Lee, K., Kim, J., and Morris, J. (2004), Heterogeneous networks of workstations. Technical report, School of Electrical and Electronics Engineering, ChungAng University, Seoul, Korea.

Blumofe, R. D., Joerg, C. F., Kuszmaul, B. C., Leiserson, C. E., Randall, K. H., and Zhou, Y. (1995), Cilk: An efficient multithreaded runtime system, in *PPoPP'95,* Santa Barbara, CA.

Dantzig, G. B., Fulkerson, R., and Johnson, S. M. (1954), Solution of a large-scale travelling salesman problem, *Operations Research, 2,* 393–410.

Gropp,W., Lusk, E., Doss, N., and Skjellum, A. (1996), A highperformance, portable implementation of the MPI message passing interface standard, *Parallel Computing, 22*(6), 789–828.

Kwok, Y.-K. (2003), On exploiting heterogeneity for cluster based parallel multithreading using task duplication, *Journal of Supercomputing, 25,* 63–72.

Lee, G. and Morris, J. (1998), Dataflow Java: Implicitly parallel Java, in *Proceedings of the Australasian Computer Systems Architecture Conference,* pp. 151–158.

Snir, M. (1996), *MPI: The Complete Reference,* MIT Press, Cambridge, MA.

Tham, C. K. (2003), *Achilles: A High Bandwidth, Low Latency, Low Overhead Network Interconnect for High Performance Parallel Processing Using a Network of Workstations.* PhD thesis, The University of Western Australia.

von Eicken, T., Culler, D. E., Goldstein, S. C., and Schauser, K. E. (1992), Active Messages: a Mechanism for Integrated Communication and Computation, in *Proceedings of the 19th Annual International Symposium on Computer Architecture, Gold Coast, Australia,* pp. 256–266.

## CHAPTER 6

Nested Parallelism and Pipelining in OpenMP

M. GONZÁLEZ, E. AYGUADE, X. MARTORELL, and J. LABARTA

This chapter describes two topics missing from the current OpenMP programming model: nested parallelism and pipelined computations. The contributions in this chapter point out the situations in which nested parallelism appears as the way for increasing performance and the heuristics for an efficient parallel execution under a multilevel strategy. Some applications, although containing some amount of parallelism, cannot be expressed through OpenMP directives due to data dependences. Usually, the available parallelism is organized in the form of a pipeline, requiring complex thread synchronizations not available in the current OpenMP definition. The chapter presents a proposal for introducing precedence relations in the OpenMP programming model. The proposal allows programmers to specify explicit point-to-point thread synchronizations, being general enough to manage with any pipelined computation.

6.1 INTRODUCTION

OpenMP [7] has emerged as the standard programming model for shared-memory parallel programming. The OpenMP organization has joined the main parallel vendors in an effort to standardize parallel directives. The resulting definition for the OpenMP programming model contains the main features included in the parallel environments of each main vendor. It follows an SPMD programming model, in which parallel tasks are specified by work-sharing constructs that define the work distribution among the available threads. The current OpenMP definition offers support for loop and sections parallelism, plus some thread synchronization schemes, like barrier synchronizations, mutual exclusions, or atomic operations. Its simplicity and portability across a range of parallel platforms are achieved without sacrificing performance.

The task of parallelizing a sequential code it is not easy to do. Programmers have to make significant efforts in the detection of the available parallelism. Much hard-

High-Performance Computing: Paradigm and Infrastructure. Edited by L. T. Yang and M. Guo **99**

er is the work dedicated to the tuning of the application. In many cases, programmers see how the available parallelism is restricted because the parallel environment does not offer enough support for its efficient exploitation, or even for its exploitation itself. Since the birth of OpenMP, there have been several research works on the most common topics in any parallel programming model. A lot of previous ideas in the literature on HPF and MPI have now been developed for OpenMP. Typically, OpenMP research works present the evaluation of the current programming model through the parallelization of several real applications that point out the benefits and deficiencies of the model. The evaluation of the model is done by measuring the impact of several factors like data placement, work distribution, thread synchronization, and the overheads of the parallel runtime system. All of these measurements are always matched to the available functionalities in the model that allow the programmers to tune their applications to get the best performance. In that context, most of the OpenMP research works end up with the definition of new constructs in the language to cover the detected deficiencies.

One of the most significant OpenMP functionalities is the possibility of expressing multiple levels of parallelism [2, 4, 6, 8, 9, 17]. This is achieved by nesting parallel constructs, including parallel loops and sections. The possibility of nesting parallel constructs is the natural way to express, using a single programming paradigm, the integration of task and data parallelism or even the exploitation of multiple levels of data parallelism. Exploiting just a single level of parallelism may incur low performance returns when the number of processors to run the application is increased [2]. The solution to that is the exploitation of the multilevel parallelism in the application. Typically, scientific applications contain multilevel parallelism. This parallelism is organized in several computations operating over independent data structures, where the work to be done can be performed in parallel too (task and data parallelism). In some situations, the computations present some dependences that restrict the available parallelism, but not to the point of eliminating the possibility of having a multilevel strategy.

It has only been very recently that OpenMP commercial systems (compiler and runtime) have supported the nested parallelism exploitation [13, 14]. Because of this, one can find several research works that combine two programming models in order to achieve a multilevel execution. Typically, MPI is used in the outermost level, and then OpenMP is used in the innermost level. Examples of this kind of work are found in [15, 16]. From our point of view, this work just demonstrates the usefulness of nested parallelism. We are going to show that there is no need to mix two programming models; OpenMP is enough, but with several modifications.

This chapter summarizes our research activity in the nested parallelism exploitation and thread synchronization. We have carried out several experiments that have helped us to point out other issues related to nested parallelism exploitation [2]. Work allocation appears to be an important issue in achieving performance. Current work allocation schemes in OpenMP seem to be incapable of efficiently exploiting the parallelism in the innermost level. The deficiencies of the model lead to a loss of performance due to several factors. Applications might suffer from a poor locality exploitation caused by a wrong work placement. Applications might not be suitable for the grain size obtained in a multilevel parallel strategy. The resulting grain size might be too small to make worthwhile the parallelism exploitation with large numbers of threads. Our experience has shown that it is necessary to include in the model new mechanisms to avoid the default work allocation. The programmer has to be able to define the appropriate work distribution schemes that fit well in the application.

We have detected that when looking for nested parallelism, data dependencies might appear through the different levels of parallelism. Although the data dependencies provide some parallelism, this cannot be specified through the existing directives in the programming model. Typically, this situations appear in codes containing irregular access patterns or an available parallelism in the form of a pipeline [3, 5, 10, 12]. The parallel computations are characterized by a data-dependent flow of computation that implies serialization. In this direction, the specification of generic task graphs as well as complex pipelined structures is not an easy task in the framework of OpenMP. In order to exploit the available parallelism, the programmer has to define complex synchronization data structures and use synchronization primitives along the program, sacrificing readability and maintainability.

6.2 OpenMP EXTENSIONS FOR NESTED PARALLELISM

OpenMP extends the Fortran sequential programming model with single-program multiple data (SPMD) constructs, work-sharing constructs, and synchronization constructs, and provides support for the sharing and privatization of data. The parallelism is specified through the definition of a parallel region. A parallel region is a portion of code that is going to be executed by several threads. The code in the parallel region is somehow replicated and executed by the threads, but several mechanisms allow different work distribution schemes. The OpenMP execution model follows the fork/join model. A program written with OpenMP begins executing as a single process, which is called the master thread. The program executes sequentially until a parallel region is encountered. The master thread creates a team of threads and becomes the master of the team. The statements in the parallel region are executed in parallel by all threads. Upon completion of the parallel region, the threads in the team synchronize and only the master thread continues execution. Any number of parallel constructs can be specified in a single program. As a result, a program may fork and join many times during execution.

6.2.1 Parallelism Definition

OpenMP provides two directives for the definition of the parallelism: PARALLEL and END PARALLEL. The programmer defines the parallel region by enclosing the parallel code between these two directives. The syntax of the construct is

```
!$OMP PARALLEL [ clauses ]
c Parallel code
!$OMP END PARALLEL
```

When a thread encounters a parallel region, it creates a team of threads and becomes the master of the team. The master thread belongs to the team. The number of threads in the team is controlled by environment variables, the NUM THREADS clause, and/or library calls. Only the use of the NUM THREADS clause is going to be described. Following the current OpenMP definition, the behavior of the program is implementation dependent when more threads are requested than can be successfully created. We will see in Section 6.2.2 that our proposal supports this situation and does not introduce any restriction on the number of threads to be used in a parallel region. Once created, the number of threads in the team remains constant for the duration of that parallel region. It can be changed either explicitly by the user or automatically by the runtime system from one parallel region to another.

Within the dynamic extent of a parallel region, threads are numbered consecutively ranging from zero (for the master thread) up to one less than the number of threads within the team. The intrinsic `omp_get_num_threads` returns the number of executing threads in the team. It is possible to obtain the value of a thread identifier by invoking the library routine `omp_get_thread_num`. Between two consecutive parallel regions, the thread numbers for the two regions are consistent. This means that a thread identified with a given thread number in the first parallel region will be identified with the same thread number in the second region. This allows the programmer to maintain data locality for the two parallel regions. The PARALLEL construct accepts several clauses. The most common are PRIVATE, FIRSTPRIVATE, and REDUCTION.

Work-sharing constructs (DO, SECTIONS, and SINGLE) are provided to divide the execution of the enclosed code region among the members of a team. All threads are independent and may synchronize at the end of each work-sharing construct or at specific points (specified by the BARRIER directive). Exclusive execution mode is also possible through the definition of CRITICAL regions. The SECTIONS directive is a noniterative work-sharing construct that specifies the enclosed sections of code (each one delimited by a SECTION directive) divided among threads in the team. Each section becomes a task that is executed once by a thread in the team. The DO work-sharing construct is used to divide the iterations of a loop into a set of independent tasks, each one executing a chunk of consecutive iterations. Finally, the SINGLE work-sharing construct informs that only one thread in the team is going to execute the work.

The END PARALLEL directive denotes the end of the parallel region. There is an implied barrier at this point, so that only when all threads in the team have reached the END PARALLEL directive does the master thread continue the execution past the end of the parallel region.

6.2.1.1 *Nested Parallelism* OpenMP considers nested parallelism by allowing the programmer to nest PARALLEL constructs. The nested parallelism appears because a thread already executing inside an outer parallel region might encounter a PARALLEL construct, defining an inner parallel region. If a thread in a team executing a parallel region encounters another parallel region, it creates a new team, and it becomes the master of that new team. The thread name space is defined in the

same manner independently of the level at which a parallel region is spawned; threads get numbered from zero to the number of available threads minus one. The work allocation schemes associated with the work-sharing constructs are equally defined, whether or not they appear in a nested parallel construct.

6.2.2 Thread Groups

In the fork/join execution model defined by OpenMP, a program begins execution as a single process or thread. This thread executes sequentially until a PARALLEL construct is found. At this time, the thread creates a team of threads and it becomes its master thread. All threads execute the statements enclosed lexically within the parallel constructs. Work-sharing constructs (DO, SECTIONS, and SINGLE) are provided to divide the execution of the enclosed code region among the members of a team. All threads are independent and may synchronize at the end of each work-sharing construct or at specific points (specified by the BARRIER directive).

In this study, a group of threads is composed of a subset of the total number of threads available in the team to run a parallel construct. In a parallel construct, the programmer may define the number of groups and the composition of each group. When a thread in the current team encounters a parallel construct defining groups, the thread creates a new team and it becomes its master thread. The new team is composed of as many threads as there are groups defined; the rest of the threads are reserved to support the execution of nested parallel constructs. In other words, the groups' definition establishes the threads that are involved in the execution of the parallel construct and the allocation strategy or scenario for the inner levels of parallelism that might be spawned. When a member of this new team encounters another parallel construct (nested in the one that caused the group definition), it creates a new team and deploys its parallelism to the threads that compose its group. The GROUPS clause allows the user to specify thread groups. It can only appear in a PARALLEL construct or combined PARALLEL DO and PARALLEL SECTIONS constructs:

```
C$OMP PARALLEL [DO|SECTIONS] [GROUPS(gspec)]
```

Different formats for the groups specifier `gspec` are allowed. In this chapter, we only comment on the two more relevant. For additional details concerning alternative formats as well as implementation issues, please refer to [2].

6.2.2.1 Weighted Group Definition In this case, the user specifies the number of groups (`ngroups`) and an integer vector (`weight`) indicating the relative amount of computation that each group has to perform. The syntax is

```
GROUPS(ngroups,weight)
```

Vector `weight` is allocated by the user in the application address space and it has to be computed from information available within the application itself (for instance, iteration space, computational complexity, or even information collected at runtime). The runtime library determines, from this information, the composition of the groups. The algorithm assigns all the available threads to the groups and ensures that each group at least receives one thread. The main body of the algorithm is shown in Figure 6.1 (using Fortran90 syntax). The library generates two internal vectors (`masters` and `howmany`). In this algorithm, `nthreads` is the number of threads that are available to spawn the parallelism in the parallel construct containing the group definition.

6.2.2.2 *Most General Group Definition*   This syntax corresponds to the most general format for the groups definition. Its syntax is

```
GROUPS(ngroups, masters, howmany)
```

The first argument (`ngroups`) specifies the number of groups to be defined and consequently the number of threads in the team that is going to execute the parallel construct. The second argument (`masters`) is an integer vector with the identifiers (using the active numeration in the current team) of the threads that will compose the new team. Finally, the third argument (`howmany`) is an integer vector whose elements indicate the number of threads that will compose each group. The vectors have to be allocated in the memory space of the application, and their content and correctness have to be guaranteed by the programmer. Notice that this format must be used when the default mapping described before does not provide the expected performance.

6.2.3 Evaluation of the Proposal

In this section, we present some evaluation of the proposal for the thread groups. We want to show that exploiting nested parallelism is worthy but has to be done through certain scheduling decisions, achieved by the thread grouping. The presented results also show that there is no need for mixing OpenMP programming with any other programming paradigm. By including the new constructs in the OpenMP language, it is possible to avoid hybrid models for the nested parallelism exploitation. We think this is quite important, compared to the results that have appeared in recent research works around OpenMP nested parallelism.

```
howmany(1:ngroups) = 1
do while (sum(howmany(1:ngroups)) .lt. nthreads)
  pos = maxloc(weight(1:ngroups)/howmany(1:ngroups))
  howmany(pos(1)) = howmany(pos(1)) + 1
end do
masters(1) = 0
do i = 1, ngroups-1
  masters(i+1) = masters(i) + howmany(i)
end do
```

Figure 6.1   Skeleton of the algorithm used to compute the composition of groups.

6.2.3.1 MGPOM Application MGPOM is a standard Fortran77 multiblock grid code. A parallel version of MGPOM uses MPI asynchronous sends and receives to exchange data between adjacent blocks at the interfaces. OpenMP has been used as a second level of parallelization within each MPI process to improve the load balance in the simulation of the Arabian Gulf. This area extends from 48 East to 58 East in longitude and from 23.5 North to 30.5 North in latitude. The computation is defined over a grid structure formed by 20 blocks, covering the Gulf area. OpenMP with NanosCompiler [1] extensions is used to parallelize the serial version of the MGPOM code at the outer levels (block to block) as well as at the inner levels (within each block). The number of threads used to exploit the inner level of parallelism depends on the size of each grid block. Figure 6.2 shows the use of the OpenMP directives and GROUPS construct implemented into the main program and a subroutine of the serialMGPOMcode version. This figure shows a version in which the runtime library, using the default algorithm described in Section 6.2.2, determines the composition of the groups. The GROUPS clause has as input arguments the number of blocks (`maxb`) and a vector with the number of grid points in each block (`work`). Notice that the GROUPS clause is the only nonstandard use of OpenMP. The exploitation of multiple levels of parallelism is achieved through the nesting of PARALLEL DO constructs. Table 6.1 shows the number of grid points in each block for the 20-block grid. This is the composition of the work vector. The runtime library supporting the code generated by the NanosCompiler

```
          SUBROUTINE baropg(drhox,drhoy,drx2d,dry2d,nb)
          . . .
C$OMP PARALLEL DO PRIVATE (i,j,k)
          DO 200 j = 1, jm
          DO 200 k = 1 kb
          DO 200 I = 1, im
          rho(i,j,k,nb)=rho(i,j,k,nb)-rmean(i,j,k,nb)
          200 CONTINUE
          . . .
          RETURN
          END
          . . .

          PROGRAM main
          . . .
C$OMP PARALLEL DO PRIVATE(n) GROUPS(maxb, work)
          DO 414 n = 1, maxb
          . . .
          IF (mode .ne. 2) THEN
          CALL baropg (drhox, drhoy, drx2d, dry2d, n)
          . . .
          ENDIF
          414 CONTINUE
          . . .
          END
```

Figure 6.2 Excerpt of the OpenMP implementation.

Table 6.1 Number of grid points in each block of the 20-block case

Block	1	2	3	4	5	6	7	8	9	10
Size	1443	1710	1677	2150	700	989	2597	2862	2142	1836

Block	11	12	13	14	15	16	17	18	19	20
Size	1428	1881	1862	2058	1470	1280	1848	2318	999	2623

would generate the allocation of threads to groups shown in Tables 6.2 and 6.3 assuming 20 and 30 processors, respectively. Who and Howmany are the two internal vectors generated by the library with the master of each group (who) and the number of threads to be used in each group (howmany). With 20 processors, the critical path is determined by the largest block (i.e., block number 8) yields a theoretical speedup of 12.5. With 30 processors, the critical path is determined by the block with the largest ratio size/howmany (i.e., block number 17), with a theoretical speedup of 19.4. According to the allocation of threads to groups shown in Table 6.3, the average work per thread has a large variance (from 1848 in block 17 to 700 in block 5). This variance results in a noticeable load imbalance. To reduce this load imbalance, several blocks could be gathered into a cluster such that the work distribution is equally divided among groups. To achieve this, the users can define their own composition of groups, as shown in Figure 6.3. User function compute groups decides how many OpenMP threads are devoted to the execution of each block and which OpenMP thread is going to be the master in the exploitation of the inner level of parallelism inside each block. This function has as input arguments the number of blocks (maxb) and a vector with the number of grid points in the block (work). It returns two vectors with the master of each group (who) and the number of threads to be used in each group (howmany). This is the information that is later used in the GROUPS clause. Table 6.4 shows the allocation of the threads to groups as well as the identities of blocks in a cluster. A cluster of two

Table 6.2 Default allocation of threads to groups with 20 threads

Block	1	2	3	4	5	6	7	8	9	10	11	12	13	14	15	16	17	18	19	20
Howmany	1	1	1	1	1	1	1	1	1	1	1	1	1	1	1	1	1	1	1	1
Who	0	1	2	3	4	5	6	7	8	9	10	11	12	13	14	15	16	17	18	19

Table 6.3 Default allocation of threads to groups with 30 threads

Block	1	2	3	4	5	6	7	8	9	10	11	12	13	14	15	16	17	18	19	20
Howmany	1	1	1	2	1	1	2	2	2	2	1	2	2	2	1	1	1	2	1	2
Who	0	1	2	3	5	6	7	9	11	13	15	16	18	20	22	23	24	25	27	28

```
          PROGRAM main
          ...
          CALL compute_groups(work, maxb, who, howmany)
          ...
   C$OMP PARALLEL DO PRIVATE(n) GROUPS(maxb, who, howmany)
          DO 414 n = 1, maxb
             ...
             IF (mode .ne. 2) THEN
                 CALL baropg (drhox, drhoy, drx2d, dry2d, n)
                 ...
             ENDIF
      414 CONTINUE
          ...
          END
```

Figure 6.3 Excerpt of the OpenMP implementation with user-defined groups.

blocks with 20 processors is shown in this case. In this case, the work imbalance is noticeably reduced.

6.2.3.2 *Performance*   In this section, we evaluate the behavior of two parallel versions of MGPOM. The MPI-OpenMP version exploits two levels of parallelism by combining the two programming paradigms: MPI to exploit the interblock parallelism and OpenMP to exploit the intrablock parallelism. The OpenMP-Only version exploits the two levels of parallelism using OpenMP and the extensions offered by the NanosCompiler and supporting OpenMP runtime system. For the compilation of the multilevel OpenMP version, we use the NanosCompiler to translate from extended OpenMP Fortran77 to plain Fortran77, with calls to the supporting runtime library NthLib. We use the native f77 compiler to generate code for an SGI Origin2000 system [11]. The flags are set to -mips4 -64 -O2. The experiments have been performed on system with 64 R10k processors,running at 250MHzwith 4Mb of secondary cache each. Table 6.5 shows the speed-up achieved by the two versions of the program. Notice that the performance of the nested OpenMP version is equivalent to the original mixed MPI-OpenMP. In order to conclude this section, Table 6.6 shows the relative performance (w.r.t the execution with 20 processors of the OpenMP-only version) for three OpenMP versions of the application: no groups exploits two levels of parallelism but does not define groups (similar to using the NUM_THREADS clause), groups performs a homogeneous distribution of the available threads among the groups, and weighted performs a weight-

Table 6.4 Allocation of threads to groups with 20 threads after clustering

Cluster	1	2	3	4	5	6	7	8	9	10
Blocks	1,9	2,13	3,12	4,11	5,8	6,20	7,19	10,17	14,15	16,18
Howmany	2	2	2	2	2	2	2	2	2	2
Who	0	2	4	6	8	10	12	14	16	18

Table 6.5 Speedup with respect to the sequential execution for the multilevel OpenMP and the mixed MPI-OpenMP versions

Number of threads	OpenMP-Only	MPI-OpenMP
20	15.3	14.7
40	23.9	22.2
60	27.8	23.0

Table 6.6 Speedup (relative to the execution with 20 threads for OpenMP-Only) for three different OpenMP versions

Number of threads	No groups	Groups	Weighted
20	0.44	1	1
40	0.33	1.5	1.7
60	0.26	1.51	1.9

ed distribution of the available threads among the groups. Notice that the performance of both groups and weighted versions is greater than no groups. Also, the weighted performs better due to load unbalance that exists among blocks. In summary, additional information is needed in the NUM THREADS clause to boost the performance of applications with multiple levels of parallelism.

6.3 OPENMP EXTENSIONS FOR THREAD SYNCHRONIZATIONS

In this section, we describe the OpenMP extensions proposed to support the specification of explicit point-to-point thread synchronizations. Although the proposal is general enough to cover any kind of synchronization scheme, the extensions are in the framework of nested parallelism and target the definition pipelined executions. The proposal is based on the introduction of the precedence relations in the OpenMP programming model. An initial definition of the extensions to specify precedences was described in [3].

6.3.1 Precedence Relations

The proposal is divided into two parts. The first one consists of the definition of a name space for the tasks generated by the OpenMP work-sharing constructs. The second one consists of the definition of precedence relations among those named tasks.

6.3.1.1 The NAME Clause
The NAME clause is used to provide a name to a task that comes out of a work-sharing construct. Its syntax of use for the OpenMP work-sharing constructs is

```
C$OMP SECTIONS                          C$OMP SINGLE NAME(name_ident)
C$OMP SECTION NAME(name_ident)          ...
...                                     C$OMP END SINGLE
C$OMP END SECTIONS
C$OMP DO NAME(name_ident)
...
C$OMP END DO
```

The name ident identifier is supplied by the programmer and follows the same rules that are used to define variable and constant identifiers. In a SECTIONS construct, the NAME clause is used to identify each SECTION. In a SINGLE construct the NAME clause is used in the same manner. In a DO work-sharing construct, the NAME clause only provides a name to the whole loop. We propose to define each iteration of the loop as a parallel task. This means that the name space for a parallel loop has to be large enough to identify each loop iteration. This is done by identifying each iteration of the parallelized loop with the identifier supplied in the NAME clause plus the value of the loop-induction variable for that iteration. Notice that the number of tasks associated to a DO work-sharing construct is not determined until the associated do statement is going to be executed. This is because the number of loop iterations is not known until the loop is executed. Depending on the loop scheduling, the parallel tasks (iterations) are mapped to the threads. The programmer simply defines the precedences at the iteration level. These precedences are translated at runtime to task precedences that will cause the appropriate thread synchronizations, depending on the SCHEDULE strategy specified to distribute iterations.

6.3.1.2 The PRED and SUCC Clauses and Directives

Once a name space has been created, the programmer is able to specify a precedence relation between two tasks using their names:

```
[C$OMP] PRED(task_id[,task_id]*) [IF(exp)]
[C$OMP] SUCC(task_id[,task_id]*) [IF(exp)]
```

PRED is used to list all the task names that must release a precedence to allow the thread encountering the PRED directive to continue its execution. The SUCC directive is used to define all those tasks that, at this point, may continue their execution. The IF clause is used to guard the execution of the synchronization action. Expression exp is evaluated at runtime to determine if the associated PRED or SUCC directive applies.

As clauses, PRED and SUCC apply at the beginning and end of a task (because they appear as part of the definition of the work-sharing itself), respectively. The same keywords can also be used as directives, in which case they specify the point in the source program where the precedence relationship has to be fulfilled. Code before a PRED directive can be executed without waiting for the predecessor tasks. Code after a SUCC directive can be executed in parallel with the successor tasks.

The PRED and SUCC constructs always apply inside the enclosing work-sharing construct where they appear. Any work-sharing construct affected by a precedence clause or directive has to be named with a NAME clause.

The `task id` is used to identify the parallel task affected by a precedence definition or release. Depending on the work-sharing construct where the parallel task was coming from, the `task_id` presents two different formats:

```
task_id = name_ident | name_ident,expr
```

When the `task id` is only composed of a `name ident` identifier, the parallel task corresponds to a task coming from a SECTIONS or SINGLE work-sharing construct. In this case, the `name ident` corresponds to an identifier supplied in a NAME clause that annotates a SECTION/SINGLE construct. When the `name_ident` is followed by one expression, the parallel task corresponds to an iteration coming from a parallelized loop. The expression evaluation must result in an integer value identifying a specific iteration of the loop. The precedence relation is defined between the task being executed and the parallel task (iteration) coming from the parallelized loop with the name supplied in the precedence directive. Notice that once the precedence has been defined, the synchronization that is going to ensure it will take place between the threads executing the two parallel tasks involved in the precedence relation. Therefore, implicit in the precedence definition, there is a translation of task identifiers to the threads executing the tasks, depending on the scheduling that maps tasks to threads.

In order to handle nested parallelism, we extend the previous proposal. When the definition of precedence appears in the dynamic extend of a nested parallel region caused by an outer PARALLEL directives, multiple instances of the same name definition (given by a NAME clause/directive) exist. In order to differentiate them, the `name ident` needs to be extended with as many `task_ids` as outer levels of parallelism:

```
name_ident[:task_id]+
```

Therefore, the `task_id` construct might take the following syntax:

```
task_id = name_ident | name_ident,expr | [(task_id):]*task_id
```

Figure 6.4 shows a multilevel example. Two nested loops have been parallelized, although they are not completely parallel. Some parallelism might be exploited according to the data dependences caused by the use of `A(k-1,j-1)` in iteration `(k,j)`. Both parallel loops have been named and the appropriate precedences have been defined to ensure that data dependents are not violated. Notice that the task name space in the innermost loop (`innerloop`) is replicated for each iteration of the outermost loop (`outerloop`). To distinguish between different instances of the same name space, a task identifier is extended with the list of all task identifiers in the immediate upper levels of parallelism.

```
C$OMP PARALLEL DO NAME (outerloop)
   do k = 1, N
C$OMP PARALLEL DO NAME (innerloop)
      do j = 1, N
C$OMP PRED((outerloop,k-1):(inner_loop, j-1))
      ...
         A(k,j)=A(k-1,j-1)*A(k,j)
      ...
C$OMP SUCC((outerloop,k+1):(inner_loop, j+1))
      enddo
   enddo
```

Figure 6.4   Example of multilevel code with precedences.

6.3.2   Evaluation of the Proposal

This section shows two parallelization strategies for one of the NAS benchmarks that make use of the proposed precedence directives. The objective is to point out the simplicity of the directives compared to the transformations that programmers usually do to adapt their codes to OpenMP programming style. As before, the evaluation has been done on a SGI Origin2000 with 64 R10000 processors (250 MHz) and Irix 6.5. The parallel code is automatically generated using the NanosCompiler [1] to transform the source code annotated with the new precedence directives to run on NthLib [18, 17].

6.3.2.1   NAS LU   LU is a simulated CFD application that comes with the NAS benchmarks [19]. It uses a symmetric successive overrelaxation (SSOR) method to solve a diagonal system resulting from a finite-difference discretization of the Navier–Stokes equations. Two parallel regions are defined for the solver computation. Both have the same structure in terms of data dependences, so only one will be described. The computation is performed over a three-dimensional matrix by a nest of three do loops, one per dimension. The matrix size is $31 \times 31 \times 31$ elements. The computation defines that there is a dependence from the element (k, j, i) to elements $(k + 1, j, i)$, $(k, j + 1, i)$, and $(k, j, i + 1)$. We have evaluated three different versions of the LU benchmark for class W: two versions using a single-level parallel strategy, and a third version exploiting two levels of parallelism.

Single-Level omp   This version corresponds to the one distributed in the NAS benchmarks. It exploits loop-level parallelism in the outermost dimension (k). As this loop is not completely parallel, the benchmark contains the necessary thread synchronizations to preserve the dependences in the k dimension. These synchronizations are coded by the programmer in the source code using vectors allocated in the application address space. Once a thread working on a k iteration has performed some iterations on the j loop, it signals the thread working on the $k + 1$ iteration for the same set of j iterations and allows its execution. Thus, a pipeline is created.

Figure 6.5 shows the structure of the source code for this version. Notice that the programmer has to introduce the FLUSH construct to ensure memory consistency

```
!$OMP PARALLEL DEFAULT(SHARED) PRIVATE(k,iam)          subroutine blts(...)
!$OMP MASTER                                             ...
      mthreadnum=omp_get_num_threads()-1                iam = omp_get_thread_num()
      if (mthreadnum .gt. (jend-jst)) then              if (iam.gt.0 .and. iam.le.mthreadnum)
        mthreadnum=jend-jst                                 neigh=iam-1
      endif                                                 do while (isync(neigh).eq.0)
!$OMP END MASTER                                      !$OMP FLUSH(isync)
                                                        end do
      iam = omp_get_thread_num()                        isync(neigh)=0
      isync(iam) = 0                                  !$OMP FLUSH(isync)
                                                        endif
!$OMP BARRIER
      do k = 2, nz -1                                 !$OMP DO
        call jacld(k)                                     do j=jst,jend
        call blts( isiz1, isiz2,                          ...
     1             isiz3,                                 enddo
     2             nx, ny, nz, k,                     !$OMP END DO NOWAIT
     3             omega,
     4             rsd, tv,                                if (iam .lt. mthreadnum) then
     5             a, b, c, d,                                 do while (isync(iam) .eq. 1)
     6             ist, iend, jst,                     !$OMP FLUSH(isync)
     7             jend,nx0, ny0)                          end do
      end do                                              isync(iam) = 1
!$OMP END PARALLEL                                    !$OMP FLUSH(isync)
                                                        endif
                                                        ...
                                                        end
```

Figure 6.5   Source code for NAS LU application.

for the integer vector `isync` used for synchronization. The vector is not padded, so false sharing problems may appear in the synchronization execution, degrading performance. The leftmost column in Table 6.7 shows the performance numbers for this version in terms of speedup. Notice that for this version only up to 31 processors might be used, as the k loop only contains 31 iterations.

Single Level with Precedences   This version follows a similar parallel strategy as the `Single level omp` version. To design this version, the extensions described in Section 6.3 have been introduced in the source code replacing the original synchronization code. False sharing problems disappear and the programmer does not have to be concerned with memory consistency issues as both things are handled by the runtime system. A blocking scheduling to the k, j, i do loops has been done and only the blocked k loop has been parallelized. The blocking allows the programmer to control the amount of work performed between two thread synchronizations. Figure 6.6 shows the new source code with precedence directives. The middle column in Table 6.7 shows the performance numbers for this version. Notice that it behaves very similar to the `Single level omp` version, so no performance is lost due to possible runtime overheads. Both versions, `Single level omp` and `Single level nth`, are not exploiting all the available parallelism in the computation. After computing an element (k, j, i), the computation can continue on elements $(k + 1, j, i)$, $(k, j, + 1, i)$, and

Table 6.7   Performance for LU NAS application

Number of threads	Single-level pure omp	Single-level precedences	Two levels precedences
4	3.86	4.25	3.83
9	7.02	6.95	7.15
16	11.14	10.52	11.17
25	10.77	10.43	12.78
36	12.29	13.28	15.07
49	12.29	13.28	17.43
64	12.29	13.28	11.53

$(k, j, i + 1)$ in parallel. Those versions only exploit the parallelism between the $(k + 1, k, i)$ and $(k, j, + 1, i)$ elements.

Two Levels with Precedences   This version exploits nearly all the parallelism present in the computation. Figure 6.6 shows the new source code with precedence directives. In this version, once a thread ends its computation on a block (bk, bj, bi) composed by a set of k, j, and i iterations, it signals two threads: the ones that are going to work on the blocks $(bk + 1, bj, bi)$ and $(bk, bj + 1, bi)$. Notice that this version, as it is exploiting more parallelism, is able to take advantage of more than 31 processors and, even more than that, it is able to fill the pipeline faster than the `Single level omp` and `Single level precedences` versions. The performance numbers in the rightmost column in Table 6.7 show that the `Two levels precedences` reaches the maximum speed-up with 49 threads, 20% more than the best performance in the `Single level precedences` versions.

6.4   SUMMARY

In this chapter we present two proposals for extending the OpenMP programming model. The first one is oriented toward one of the most studied OpenMP topics: nested parallelism exploitation. Recent OpenMP research works showed that some OpenMP applications cannot be speeded up while the number of available threads increases. This behavior has been seen when more than 32 threads are available and the parallel strategy is based on the exploitation of a single level of parallelism. In this situation, multilevel strategies appear as a good solution for increasing performance. It has been also shown that with the current OpenMP support, those applications cannot benefit from nested parallelism. The reason for this is that OpenMP does not provide the appropriate mechanisms to control the thread distribution among the different levels of parallelism. Other recent works tried to solve the problem by mixing two programming paradigms: MPI for the outermost level and OpenMP in the inner levels. Those works showed the usefulness of nested parallelism, but their solution requires the mixing of two programming models very dif-

```
!$OMP PARALLEL DEFAULT(SHARED)
!$OMP& PRIVATE(a,b,c,d,bk,bj,bi)
!$OMP DO NAME (l_bk)
      do bk = 1, nblocksk


      do bj=1,nblocksj
!$OMP PRED (l_bk, bk-1)
      do bi=1,nblocksi
        call jacld(bk,bj,bi,a,b,c,d)
        call blts( isiz1, isiz2, isiz3,
   1          nx, ny, nz, bk,bj,bi,
   2          omega,rsd, tv,
   3          a, b, c, d,
   4          ist, iend, jst, jend,
   5          nx0, ny0)
      enddo !bi
!$OMP SUCC (l_bk, bk+1)
      enddo !bj
      end do !bk
!$OMP END DO NOWAIT
!$OMP END PARALLEL



a) Single level version
```

```
!$OMP PARALLEL DEFAULT(SHARED)
!$OMP& PRIVATE(tv,a,b,c,d,bk,bj)
!$OMP DO NAME (l_bk)
      do bk = 1, nblocksk
!$OMP PARALLEL
!$OMP DO NAME (l_bj) PRIVATE(bi)
      do bj=1,nblocksj
        do bi=1,nblocksi
!$OMP PRED ( (l_bk,bk-1):(l_bj,bj) )
!$OMP PRED ( (l_bk,bk):(l_bj,bj-1) )
          call jacld(bk,bj,bi,a,b,c,d)
          call blts(isiz1, isiz2, isiz3,
   1          nx, ny, nz, bk,bj,bi,
   2          omega,
   3          rsd, tv,
   4          a, b, c, d,
   5          ist, iend, jst, jend,
   6          nx0, ny0)
!$OMP SUCC ( (l_bk,bk+1):(l_bj,bj) )
!$OMP SUCC ( (l_bk,bk):(l_bj,bj+1) )
          enddo !bi
        enddo !bj
!$OMP END DO NOWAIT
!$OMP END PARALLEL
        enddo !bk
!$OMP END DO NOWAIT
!$OMP END PARALLEL

b) Two levels version
```

Figure 6.6 NAS LU application with precedences.

ferent in their bases: MPI targets distributed memory architectures, while OpenMP was initially defined for shared-memory architectures. The proposal in this chapter solves the OpenMP deficiencies in a purely OpenMP manner. The proposal introduces thread grouping inside the OpenMP programming model. New constructs are defined that allow programmers to explicitly set the number of threads to be used in each parallel level and a thread distribution for the execution of the nested parallel levels.

The second proposal in the chapter focuses on OpenMP support for thread synchronizations. The current OpenMP definition covers simple synchronization schemes like the barrier synchronization, mutual exclusion execution, and ordered execution. It is quite common that the applications contain some amount of parallelism but not in the form that the OpenMP directives allow one to specify. In such situations, it is necessary to code explicit thread synchronizations that usually define a computational wavefront in the form of a pipeline. Current synchronization constructs seem inadequate to deal with these situations, thus the proposal in the chapter tries to cover the OpenMP deficiencies. The proposal is based on the introduction of the precedence relations between the parallel tasks arising from the worksharing constructs. Programmers are allowed to define explicit point-to-point thread synchronizations, general enough to organize the computations under a pipelined structure.

ACKNOWLEDGMENTS

This research has been supported by the Ministry of Science and Technology of Spain and the European Union (FEDER funds) under contract: TIC2001-0995-C02-01, TIN 2004-07739-C02-01, and by the ESPRIT POP project under contract IST-2001-33071.

REFERENCES

1. M. González, E. Ayguadé, J. Labarta, X. Martorell, N. Navarro, and J. Oliver, NanosCompiler: A Research Platform for OpenMP Extensions," in *First European Workshop on OpenMP,* Lund (Sweden), October 1999.

2. M. González, J. Oliver, X. Martorell, E. Ayguade, J. Labarta, and N. Navarro, OpenMP Extensions for Thread Groups and Their Runtime Support, in *Workshop on Languages and Compilers for Parallel Computing,* August 2000.

3. M. González, E. Ayguadé, X. Martorell, and J. Labarta, Defining and Supporting Pipelined Executions in OpenMP, in *Workshop on OpenMP Applications and Tools (WOMPAT'01),* August 2001.

4. M. González, E. Ayguadé, X. Martorell, J. Labarta, and P-V. Luong, Dual-Level Parallelism Exploitation with OpenMP in Coastal Ocean Circulation Modeling, in *Second Workshop on OpenMP: Experiences and Implementations (WOMPEI'02,* part of ISHPC-02), Kyoto (Japan), May 2002.

5. M. González, E. Ayguadé, X. Martorell, and J. Labarta, Exploiting Pipelined Executions in OpenMP, in *Proceedings of the International Conference of Parallel Processing (ICPP03),* Kaohsiuug (Taiwan), 6–9 October 2003.

6. T. Gross, D. O'Halloran, and J. Subhlok, Task Parallelism in a High Performance Fortran Framework, *IEEE Parallel and Distributed Technology, 2,* 3, 1994.

7. OpenMP Organization, OpenMP Fortran Application Interface, v. 2.0, www.openmp.org, June 2000.

8. A. Radulescu, C. Nicolescu, A. J. C. van Gemund, and P. P Jonker, CPR: Mixed Task and Data Parallel Scheduling for Distributed Systems, in *15th International Parallel and Distributed Processing Symposium (IPDPS'2001),* April 2001.

9. S. Ramaswamy, *Simultaneous Exploitation of Task and Data Parallelism in Regular Scientific Computations,* Ph.D. Thesis, University of Illinois at Urbana-Champaign, 1996.

10. T. Rauber and G. Runge, Compiler Support for Task Scheduling in Hierarchical Execution Models, *Journal of Systems Architecture, 45,* 483–503, 1998.

11. Silicon Graphics Computer Systems SGI, Origin 200 and Origin 2000, Technical Report, 1996.

12. J. Subhlok, J. M. Stichnoth, D. R O'Hallaron, and T. Gross, Optimal Use of Mixed Task and Data Parallelism for Pipelined Computations, *Journal of Parallel and Distributed Computing, 60,* 297–319, 2000.

13. XL Fortran for AIX, Language Reference, version 8.11, IBM, 2nd ed., June 2003.

14. *Intel Technology Journal Hyper on Threading Technology, 6,* February 14, 2002.

15. T. Boku, S. Yoshikawa, M. Sato, C. G. Hoover, and W. G. Hoover, Implementation and Performance Evaluation of SPAM Particle Code with OpenMP-MPI Hybrid Programming, in *Proceedings of the 3rd EuropeanWorkshop on OpenMP (EWOMP2001),* Barcelona, Sept. 2001.

16. P. Kloos, F. Mathey, and P. Blaise, OpenMP and MPI Programming with a CG Algorithm, in *Proceedings of the 3rd EuropeanWorkshop on OpenMP (EWOMP2001),* Barcelona, Sept. 2001.

17. X. Martorell, E. Ayguadé, N. Navarro, and J. Labarta, A Library Implementation of the Nano-Threads Programming Model, in *Proceedings of the 2nd Europar* Conference 1996.

18. X. Martorell, E. Ayguadé, J. I. Navarro, J. Corbalán, M. González, and J. Labarta, Thread Fork/join Techniques for Multi-level Parallelism Exploitation in NUMA Multiprocessors, in *13th International Conference on Supercomputing ICS'99,* Rhodes (Greece), June 1999.

19. A. Waheed and J. Yan, Parallelization of NAS Benchmarks for Shared Memory Multiprocessors, Technical Report, NAS-98-010, March 1998, http://www.nas.nasa.gov/Research/Reports/Techreports/1998/nas-98-010-abstract.html.

## CHAPTER 7

OpenMP for Chip Multiprocessors

FENG LIU and VIPIN CHAUDHARY

7.1 INTRODUCTION

Modern system-on-chip (SOC) design shows a clear trend toward integration of multiple processor cores, and the SOC System Section of the "International Technology Roadmap for Semiconductors" (http://public.itrs.net/) predicts that the number of processor cores will increase dramatically to match the processing demands of future applications. Providers like Intel, IBM, TI, Motorola, and Cradle have their own approaches for their high volume markets. Prior chip-level SOCs have been proposed using multiple copies of the same core (i.e., homogeneous), but core diversity offers better performance and greater ability to adapt to the demands of applications.

Developing a standard programming paradigm for parallel machines has been a major objective in parallel software research. Such standardization would not only facilitate the portability of parallel programs, but reduce the burden of parallel programming as well. Two major models for parallel machines are clusters or distributed memory machines and symmetric multiprocessor (SMP) machines. Several parallel programming standards have been developed for individual architecture, such as the Message-Passing Interface (MPI) for distributed-memory machines, and OpenMP or thread libraries (i.e., Pthread) for shared-memory machines.

Chip multiprocessors has become an emerging parallel machine architecture. Currently, there are no programming standards for SOCs or heterogeneous chip multiprocessors. Developers are required to write complex assembly language and/or C programs for SOCs. It is beneficial to incorporate high-level standardization like OpenMP to improve program effectiveness. OpenMP is an industrial standard for shared-memory parallel programming agreed on by a consortium of software and hardware vendors [1, 2]. It consists of a collection of compiler directives, library routines, and environment variables that can be easily inserted into a sequential program to create a portable program that will run in parallel on shared-memory architectures.

In this chapter, we propose extensions to OpenMP to deal with the heterogeneity of chip multiprocessors. The heterogeneity is an important feature for most chip

High-Performance Computing: Paradigm and Infrastructure. Edited by L. T. Yang and M. Guo **117**

multiprocessors in the embedded space. Typical SOCs incorporate different types of processors into one die (RISC or DSP-like processors). For parallel chips like the Software Scalable System on Chip (3SoC) from Cradle, the parallelism is divided among processors; each processor may have a different instruction set. By extending OpenMP, we can deploy different types of processors for parallel programming. We also focus on extending OpenMP for optimization. Our implementation of the OpenMP compiler shows that OpenMP extensions can be used for optimization of parallel programs on chip multiprocessor architecture. The current version of our compiler accepts standard OpenMP programs and our extensions to OpenMP. Our performance evaluation shows scalable speedup using different types of processors and performance improvement through individual optimization extension on 3SoC.

The rest of this chapter is organized into eight sections. Section 7.2 introduces the 3SoC architecture. In Section 7.3, we discuss our compiler/translator for chip multiprocessors. Section 7.4 describes our extensions to OpenMP to deal with the heterogeneity. Optimization techniques to improve OpenMP performance on CMP are discussed in Section 7.5. Section 7.6 discusses the general implementation of this compiler. Performance evaluation and results are showed in Section 7.7. Finally, we summarize our conclusions in Section 7.8.

7.2   3SoC ARCHITECTURE OVERVIEW

Cradle's Software Scalable System on Chip (3SoC) architecture consists of dozens of high-performance RISC-like and digital signal processors on a single chip with fully software-programmable and dedicated input–output processors. The processors are organized into small groups, with eight digital signal processors and four RISC-like processors each sharing a block of local data and control memory; all groups have access to global information via a unique on-chip bus—the global bus. Data, signal, and I/O processors are all available on a single chip, and that the chip is thereby capable of implementing entire systems [3]. The block diagram is shown as Fig. 7.1.

The 3SoC is a shared-memory MIMD (multiple instruction/multiple data) computer that uses a single 32-bit address space for all register and memory elements. Each register and memory element in the 3SoC has a unique address and is uniquely addressable.

7.2.1   Quads

The quad is the primary unit of replication for 3SoC. A 3SoC chip has one or more quads, with each quad consisting of four processing elements (PEs), eight digital signal engines (DSEs), and one memory transfer engine (MTE) with four memory transfer controllers (MTCs). In addition, PEs share 32 KB of instruction cache and Quads share 64 KB of data memory, 32 KB of which can be optionally configured as cache. Thirty-two semaphore registers within each quad provide the synchronization mechanism between processors. Figure 7.2 shows a quad block diagram.

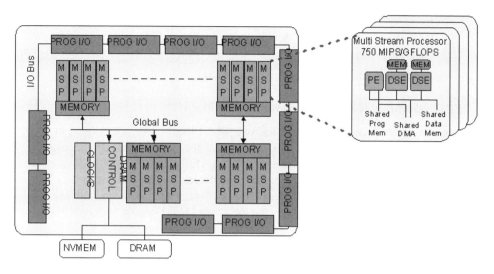

Figure 7.1   3SoC block diagram.

Note that the media stream processor (MSP) is a logical unit consisting of one PE and two DSEs:

- **Processing Element.** The PE is a 32-bit processor with 16-bit instructions and 32 32-bit registers. The PE has a RISC-like instruction set consisting of both integer and IEEE 754 floating-point instructions. The instructions have a variety of addressing modes for efficient use of memory. The PE is rated at approximately 90 MIPS.
- **Digital Signal Engine.** The DSE is a 32-bit processor with 128 registers and local program memory of 512 20-bit instructions optimized for high-speed-

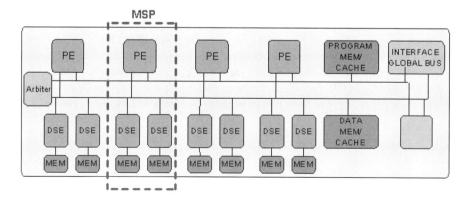

Figure 7.2   Quad block diagram.

fixed and floating-point processing. It uses MTCs in the background to transfer data between the DRAM and the local memory. The DSE is the primary computing engine and is rated at approximately 350 MIPS for integer or floating-point performance.

7.2.2   Communication and Synchronization

- **Communication.** Each quad has two 64-bit local buses: an instruction bus and a data bus. The instruction bus connects the PEs and MTE to the instruction cache. The data bus connects the PEs, DSEs, and MTE to the local data memory. Both buses consist of a 32-bit address bus, a 64-bit write-data bus, and a 64-bit read-data bus. This corresponds to a sustained bandwidth of 2.8 Gbytes/s per bus. The MTE is a multithreaded DMA engine with four MTCs. An MTC moves a block of data from a source address to a destination address. The MTE is a modified version of the DSE with four program counters (instead of one) as well as 128 registers and 2 KB of instruction memory. MTCs also have special functional units for BitBLT, Reed Solomon, and CRC operations.
- **Synchronization.** Each Quad has 32 globally accessible semaphore registers that are allocated either statically or dynamically. The semaphore registers associated with a PE, when set, can also generate interrupts to the PE.

7.2.3   Software Architecture and Tools

The 3SoC chip can be programmed using standard ANSI C or a C-like assembly language ("CLASM") or a combination thereof. The chip is supplied with GNU-based optimizing C compilers, assemblers, linkers, debuggers, a functional and performance-accurate simulator, and advanced code profilers and performance analysis tools. Please refer to the 3SoC programmer's guide [4].

7.3   THE OpenMP COMPILER/TRANSLATOR

There are a number of OpenMP implementations for C and FORTRAN on SMP machines today. One of the approaches is to translate a C program with OpenMP directives to a C program with Pthreads [5]. Design of portable OpenMP compilers and translations of OpenMP directives have been studied [7, 8, 9, 10]. Our OpenMP prototype compiler consists of three phases as described in the following subsections.

7.3.1   Data Distribution

In OpenMP, there are several clauses to define data privatization. Two major groups of variables exist: shared and private data. Private data consists of variables that are accessible by a single thread or processor that doesn't need communication, such as variables defined in "PRIVATE" and "THREADPRIVATE" clauses. Some private data needs initialization or combination before or after parallel constructs, like "FIRSTPRIVATE" and "REDUCTION." Access to these data should be synchronized among different processors.

7.3.2 Computation Division

The computation needs to be split among different processors. The only way to represent parallelism in OpenMP is by means of a PARALLEL directive, as shown below:

```
#pragma omp parallel
{
    /* code to be executed in parallel */
}
```

In the 3SoC architecture, a number of processors can be viewed as a number of "threads" compared to normal shared-memory architectures. Each processor or "thread" has its own private memory stack. At the same time, each processor is accessing the same blocks of shared local memory within the quad or SDRAM outside the quad. In a typical 3SoC program, PE0 will initiate and start several other processors like PEs or DSEs, so that PE0 acts as the "master" thread and all other processors act as "child" threads. Then PE0 will transfer parameters and allocate data among different processors. It will also load the MTE firmware and enable all MTCs. Through data allocation PE0 tells each processor to execute specific regions in parallel. PE0 will also execute the region itself as the master thread of the team. At the end of a parallel region, PE0 will wait for all other processors to finish and collect required data from each processor, similar to a "master" thread.

The common translation method for parallel regions uses a microtasking scheme. Execution of the program starts with the master thread, which during initialization creates a number of spinner threads that sleep until they are needed. The actual task is defined in other threads that are waiting to be called by the spinner. When a parallel construct is encountered, the master thread wakes up the spinner and informs it of the parallel code section to be executed and the environment to be set up for this execution. The spinner then calls the task thread to switch to a specific code section and execute.

For a chip multiprocessor environment, each "thread" unit is one processor. The number of "threads" is the actual processor number instead of a team of virtual threads, which can be created at the discretion of the user in a normal shared-memory model. It is not practical to create two threads—one for spinning and another for actual execution. Moreover, each processor has its own processing power and doesn't wait for resources from other processors. In our approach, we simply assign each parallel region in the program with a unique identifying function. The code inside the parallel region is moved from its original place and replaced by a function statement, by which its associated region calls this function and processors with correct IDs to execute selected statements in parallel (See Figure 7.3).

7.3.3 Communication Generation

In OpenMP specifications, several communications and synchronizations need to be guaranteed and inserted into the parallel regions at certain points. For example, only one processor is allowed access to the global "REDUCTION" variable at the end of the parallel construct at a time before an implicit barrier. Hardware synchronization features like semaphores in 3SoC are the most important features that distinguish normal multiprocessor chips from "parallel" chips. On 3SoC platforms, the semaphore library (Semlib) has procedures for allocating global semaphores and quad semaphores and for locking and unlocking. Reading a semaphore register, which also sets the register, is an atomic operation that cannot be interrupted. Sample barrier code is shown below:

```
semaphore_lock(Sem1.p);
    done_pe++;                    //global shared variable
semaphore_unlock(Sem1.p);
while(done_pe<(PES)); //PES is total
number of PEs
    _pe_delay(1);
```

7.4 EXTENSIONS TO OpenMP FOR DSES

Programming for PEs is similar to conventional parallel programming. The programs start with one PE (PE0) that is responsible for the environment setup and initialization of all other PEs. Afterward, PEs are involved in execution of selected statements within each parallel region by its associated processor ID. PEs are the primary processing units. Our implementation of OpenMP compiler could accept standard C programs with OpenMP directives and successfully convert them to parallel programs for PEs. The heterogeneity is based on DSE processors.

7.4.1 Controlling the DSEs

The controlling PE for a given DSE has to load the DSE code into the DSE instruction memory. Thereafter, the PE initializes the DSE DPDMs with the desired variables and starts the DSE. The PE then either waits for the DSE to finish, by polling, or can continue its work and get interrupted when the DSE finishes its task. Several DSE library calls are invoked. Sample code is shown in Figure 7.4.

First, the PE initializes the DSE library calls via dse_lib_init(&LocalState). Then the PE does a quad I/O check and data allocation such as assigning an initial value for the matrix. In the next for-loop, the PE allocates a number of DSEs and loads the DSE code into the DSE instruction memory by dse_instruction_load(). This is done by allocating within one quad first, dse_id[i]= dse_alloc(0); if failed, it will

```
int main() {
  //..
  #pragma omp parallel
  {
    #pragma omp single
    {
      printf("hello world!\n");
    }
    //only one thread execute this
  }
  //..
}
```

```
void function1() {
  {
    my_quadid=_QUAD_INDEX;
    my_peid=(my_quadid*4)+_PE_INDEX;
    //identify each processor ID

    ..
    if(my_peid==3)
    {
      printf("hello world!\n");
    }
    //only one processor execute this, not necessary master
processor
    <communication and synchronization for this parallel
region>
  }
}

int main() {
  {
  if(my_peid==0)
  {
    <allocate and initialize number of processors>
    <start all other processors>
  }
  // PE0 initialize and start all other processors

  function1();
  // each processor will run parallel region,
  // PE0 will also execute this function

  <end all processors>
  }
}
```

Figure 7.3   Translation of an OpenMP program (left) to a 3SoC parallel region (right).

load from other quads. Afterward, the PE loads the DPDMs onto the allocated DSEs with dse_loadregisters(dse_id). After all initializations are done, the PE starts all DSEs and tells DSEs to execute from the zeroth instruction, via the function call dse_start(dse_id[i], 0). The PE then waits for the DSEs to finish and automatically releases all DSEs by dse_wait(dse_id[i]). When all tasks finish, the DSE terminate library call dse_lib_terminate() is invoked.

7.4.2   Extensions for DSEs

The main parallel region is defined as #pragma omp parallel USING_DSE(parameters). When the OpenMP compiler encounters this parallel region, it will switch to the corresponding DSE portion. The four parameters declared here are: number of DSEs, number of registers, starting DPDM number, and data register array, such as (8, 6, 0, dse mem). For OpenMP compiler, the code generation is guided by the parameters defined in parallel USING_DSE construct. The compiler will

```
void main() {
        ..
        int dse_id[NUM_DSE];

        dse_lib_init(&LocalState); //DSE library initialization

        pe_in_io_quad_check();

        <Data allocation>

        _MTE_load_default_mte_code(0x3E); // load the MTE firmware

        for(i = 0; i < NUM_DSE; i++) {

                dse_id[i] = dse_alloc(0);  // allocate a dse in this quad

                if(dse_id[i] < 0) {
                        // no dse free in our quad, allocate from any quad
                        dse_id[i] = dse_alloc_any_quad(0);
                        if(dse_id[i] < 0) {
                                printf("Dse could not be allocated !");
                        }
                }

                // load the instructions on the allocated DSEs
                dse_instruction_load(dse_id[i], (char *)&dse_function, (char
*)&dse_function_complete, 0);
        }

        DSE_loadregisters(dse_id); // Load the Dpdm's on the allocated DSEs

        for(i = 0; i < NUM_DSE; i++) {
                // Start the DSEs from the 0th instruction
                dse_start(dse_id[i], 0);
        }

        for(i = 0; i < NUM_DSE; i++) {
                // Wait for the Dse's to complete, frees the DES
                dse_wait(dse_id[i]);
        }
        ..
        dse_lib_terminate();      // DSE library call to terminate
        ..
}
```

Figure 7.4   Sample code for controlling DSEs.

generate environment setups like dse_lib_init, dse_ alloc(0), DSE startup, and wait call dse_start(), dse_wait(), and termination library call dse_lib_terminate(). So users are not required to do any explicit DSE controls like startup DSE dse_start() (Figure 7.5).

The benefit of using extensions is that it helps to abstract highlevel parallel programs, and allows the compiler to insert initialization code and data environment

```
int main() {
        //other OpenMP parallel region
        #pragma omp parallel
        {
        }
        ...
        //OpenMP parallel region for number of DSEs, with parameters
        #pragma omp parallel USING_DSE(8,6,0,dse_mem)
           {
                       #pragma omp DSE_DATA_ALLOC
                       {
                  <initialization functions>
                       }

                       #pragma omp DSE_LOADCOMREG
                       {
                  <define data registers to be transferred to DSE>
                       }

                       #pragma omp DSE_LOADDIFFREG(i)
                       {
                  <define DSE data registers with different value>
                       }

                       #pragma omp DSE_OTHER_FUNC
                       {
                  <other user defined functions>
                       }

              //main program loaded and started by PE0
                       #pragma omp DSE_MAIN
                       {
                  <order of executing user defined functions or other code>
                       }
           }
        ...
}
```

Figure 7.5   Extensions to OpenMP for DSEs.

setup, if required. This hides DSE implementation details from the programmer and greatly improves the code efficiency for parallel applications.

7.5 OPTIMIZATION FOR OpenMP

In a chip multiprocessor environment, several unique hardware features are specially designed to streamline the data transfer, memory allocations, and so on. Such features are important for improving the performance for parallel programming on CMP. Some optimizations use a thread library for OpenMP that provides runtime optimization of parallel regions [11]. In this section, we present some optimization techniques that can be deployed to fully utilize advanced features of 3SoC, thus improving the performance of OpenMP.

7.5.1 Using the MTE Transfer Engine

Memory allocation is critical to the performance of parallel programs on SOCs. Given the availability of local memory, programs will achieve better performance in local memory than in SDRAM. On-chip memory is of limited size for SOCs or other equivalent DSP processors. Data locality is not guaranteed. One approach is to allocate data in DRAM first, then move data from DRAM to local memory at run time. Thus, all the computation is done in on-chip memory instead of in the slow SDRAM. In 3SoC, a developer can invoke one PE to move data between the local memory and DRAM at run time.

3SoC also provides a better solution for data transfer using the MTE transfer engine (detailed in Section 7.2.2). Note that the MTE processor runs in parallel with all other processors. It transfers data between local data memory and SDRAM in the background. We use extensions to OpenMP to incorporate the MTE transfer engine. The OpenMP directives are:

```
#pragma omp MTE_INIT(buffer size, data structure, data slice)
#pragma omp MTE_MOVE(count, direction)
```

MTE_INIT initializes a local buffer for data structure with specified buffer size. MTE_MOVE will perform actual data movement with the MTE engine. Data size equaling count*slice will be moved with respect to the direction (from local $\rightarrow$ DRAM or DRAM $\rightarrow$ local). Within a parallel region, a developer can control data movement between local memory and SDRAM before or after the computation. The MTE firmware needs to be loaded and initiated by PE0 at the beginning of the program. A number of MTE library calls will be generated and inserted by the compiler automatically. The results show significant performance speedup using the MTE to do data transfer, especially when the size of target data structure is large. Performance evaluation of using the MTE versus using the PE to do data transfer is given in Section 7.7.

7.5.2 Double Buffer and Data Prefetching

Data prefetching is a popular technique to improve the memory access latencies. Besides using the MTE to do data transfer in 3SoC, we can also apply a data prefetching approach through double buffering.

For nondouble buffering, as discussed in Section 7.5.1, we assume data is allocated in SDRAM first. Before the PE starts to perform computations, it invokes the MTE engine to populate or move the data from DRAM to local memory. When the MTE is done, it will interrupt the PE, informing it that data is ready and computation can be started. The interrupts used are semaphore interrupts. The PE locks a semaphore before calling on the MTE to move data. Once the MTE is done, it unlocks the semaphore, thus causing an interrupt. To reduce the memory access latencies, double buffering is used to improve the performance. Instead of using one buffer as in the previous example, it uses two local buffers that work in round-robin manner; each time one buffer is being computed, data in another buffer is being transferred, and vice versa.

Figure 7.6 shows how to perform matrix multiplication using double buffering. We are multiplying matrices A and B, and the result is kept in matrix C. Matrix B is in the local memory, whereas matrices A and C are both in DRAM. However, instead of one local buffer per matrix, we allocate two buffers in the local memory for both matrices A and C. The PE calls the MTE to populate the first local buffer of matrix A. The PE then calls the MTE to populate the second local buffer of matrix A. While the MTE is moving data, the PE starts to perform computations, storing the result in the first local buffer of matrix C. Sometime during the computations, the PE will be interrupted by the MTE. When the PE finishes the first round of computation, it can start on the second local buffer of matrix A, and store the result in the second local buffer of matrix C. As a result, at any given time, while the PE is performing computations, the MTE will be moving data from the DRAM into a local buffer of matrix A and also will be moving the completed results from a local buffer of matrix C into the DRAM.

To implement double buffering to improve the performance of OpenMP, we provide extensions to OpenMP. Users are required to perform explicit control of data movement between local memory and SDRAM. The directives are:

```
#pragma omp DB_INIT(buffer1 size, buffer2 size, data structure1,
data structure2, data slice1, data slice2)
#pragma omp
DB_MOVE(buffer ID1, direction1, buffer ID2, direction2)
```

DB INIT initializes two buffers for each data structure with specified size, totalling four buffers. DB_MOVE at a certain point controls the actual data movement between SDRAM and local memory. Each time, DB_MOVE will move one slice for both data structure 1 and structure 2, with specified direction (from local $\rightarrow$ DRAM or DRAM $\rightarrow$ local) and buffer ID (1 or 2) for each data structure. Concurrently, PE will do computation against another buffer of each structure. The OpenMP compiler automatically sets up the environment, initializes the MTE, allocates necessary buffers, and inserts the required library calls. With the help of these extensions, users can write OpenMP parallel programs that control data movement dynamically at run time.

7.5.3   Data Privatization and Other Functions

OpenMP provides few features for managing data locality. The method provided for enforcing locality in OpenMP is to use the PRIVATE or THREADPRIVATE clauses. However, systematically applied privatization requires good programming practices. Some researchers have proposed several approaches to provide optimiza-

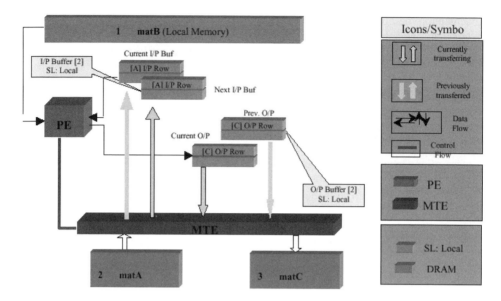

Figure 7.6   Extensions to OpenMP for DSEs.

tion with modest programming effort, including the removal of barriers that separate two consecutive parallel loops [12], improving cache reuse by means of privatization, and other improvements [13, 14].

In order to improve the performance of OpenMP on 3SoC, we apply these optimization techniques. For the time being, not all techniques discussed here are available in our first-version compiler.

For barrier elimination, it may be possible to remove the barrier separating two consecutive loops within a parallel region. Barriers require a lot of communication and synchronization so that this optimization can greatly improve the performance. For data privatization, shared data with read-only accesses in certain program sections can be made "PRIVATE" and treated as "FIRSTPRIVATE," which has a copy-in value at the beginning of parallel regions. For the 3SoC architecture, all synchronization is carried out by means of hardware semaphores. It is helpful to combine these semaphores together when encountered with a consecutive barrier and critical section, thus reducing the overall synchronization. For example, at the end of the parallel region, the "REDUCTION" variable needs to be synchronized and modified by each thread to reflect the changes, which can be combined with an implicit barrier at the end of parallel region, as illustrated in Figure 7.7.

7.6   IMPLEMENTATION

In this section, we discuss our implementation of the OpenMP compiler/translator for 3SoC. However, this chapter is not focused on implementation details. To implement an OpenMP compiler for 3SOC, there are four major steps [6].

```
{
  #pragma omp parallel for reduction(+:sum)
    for (i=0; i < n; i++)
      sum = sum + (a[i] * b[i]);
}
```

OpenMP code

```
{
  for(..) {
  }
  //critical session
  semaphore_lock(Sem1.p);
    sum=sum+sum_pri;
  semaphore_unlock(Sem1.p);

  //barrier
  semaphore_lock(Sem2.p);
    sum=sum+sum_pri;
    done_pe1++;
  semaphore_unlock(Sem2.p);
  while(done_pe2<(PES));
    _pe_delay(1);
}
```

Before Optimization

```
{
  for(..) {
  }
  //combine barrier semaphore and
  //critical session semaphore together
    semaphore_lock(Sem1.p);
      sum=sum+sum_pri;
      done_pe1++;
    semaphore_unlock(Sem1.p);
    while(done_pe1<(PES));
      _pe_delay(1);
}
```

After Optimization

Figure 7.7   Optimization (semaphore elimination).

1. **Parallel regions.** Each parallel region in the OpenMP program will be assigned a unique identifying function number. The code inside the parallel region is moved from its original place into a new function context. The parallel construct code will be replaced by code of PE0s allocating multiple PEs or DSEs, setting up the environment, starting all processors, assigning workload to each processor, and waiting for all other processors to finish.

2. **Data range.** Through analysis of all the data attributes in the OpenMP data environment clause—"SHARED," "PRIVATE," "FIRSTPRIVATE," "THREADPRIVATE," and "REDUCTION"—the compiler determines the data range for separate functions and assigns memory allocation like "_SL" or "_SD" in 3SOC. Related global variable replication such as "REDUCTION" is also declared and implemented.

3. **Work-sharing constructs.** These are the most important constructs for OpenMP, referred to as for-loop directive, sections directive, and single directive. Based on the number of processors declared at the beginning of the 3SOC program, each processor will be assigned its portion of work distinguished by processor ID. During run time, each processor will execute its own slice of work within designated functions. For example, for the "sections" construct, each subsection defined in #pragma omp section will be assigned a distinct processor ID, and run in parallel by different processors.

4. **Synchronization.** There are a number of explicit or implicit synchronization points for OpenMP constructs—critical or parallel construct. Correspondingly, these constructs are treated by allocating a number of hardware semaphores in 3SOC. Allocation is achieved statically or dynamically.

Our current version of the OpenMP compiler can take standard OpenMP programs. Provided with extensions to OpenMP, users can also write OpenMP code to utilize advanced chip multiprocessor features, like different processors, MTE, or double buffering on 3SoC.

7.7 PERFORMANCE EVALUATION

Our performance evaluation is based on 3SoC architecture; the execution environment is the 3SoC cycle accurate simulator, Inspector (version 3.2.042), and the 3SoC processor. Although we have verified the programs on the real hardware, we present results on the simulator as it provides detailed profiling information.

To evaluate our OpenMP compiler for 3SoC, we take parallel applications written in OpenMP and compare the performance on multiple processors under different optimization techniques. The first parallel application is matrix multiplication. By applying different optimizations at compilation, we compare the performance of parallel application among:

No data locality (matrices in SDRAM)

No optimization, with data locality (matrices in local memory)

Using the MTE for data transfer

Using the PE for data transfer and double buffering separately

The second application is LU decomposition that follows the same approach. We also show the compiler overhead by comparing the result with hand-written code in 3SoC.

Figure 7.8 shows the results of matrix multiplication using multiple PEs. The speedup is against sequential code running on a single processor (one PE). Figure

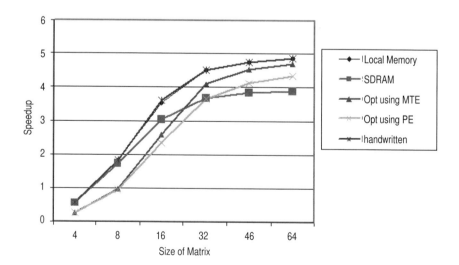

Figure 7.8   Matrix multiplication using four PEs.

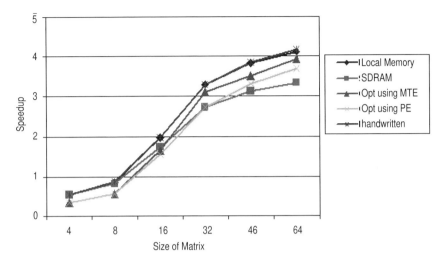

Figure 7.9   LU decomposition using four PEs.

7.9 shows the result for LU decomposition using multiple PEs against one PE. We use four PEs within one quad for both figures. By analysis of both charts, we conclude the following:

- **Local memory versus SDRAM.** As expected, memory access latencies affect the performance significantly. When the size of the data structure (matrix size) increases, speedup by allocation of data in local memory is obvious. For 64×64 matrix LU decomposition, the speedup is 4.12 times in local memory versus 3.33 times in SDRAM.

- **Using the MTE versus SDRAM.** As discussed in Section 7.5, we can deploy the MTE data transfer engine to move data from SDRAM to local memory at run time, or we can leave the data in SDRAM only and never transfer it to local during execution. Due to the limited size of the local memory, it is not practical to put all data within the local memory. For small-size matrices below 32×32, the MTE transfer has no benefit; in fact, it downgrades the performance in both examples. The reason is that the MTE environment setup and library calls need extra cycles. For larger-size matrices, it shows speedup compared to data in SDRAM only. For 64×64 matrix multiplication, the speedup is 4.7 versus 3.9. Actually, 64×64 using MTE engine is only a 3.2% degradation compared to storing data entirely in the local memory. Therefore, moving data using the MTE will greatly improve performance for large amounts of data.

- **Using the MTE versus using the PE.** We observed scalable speedup by using the MTE over the PE to move data. The extra cycles used in MTE movement do not grow much as the matrix size increases. For large dataset movements, the MTE will achieve greater performance over the PE.

- **Using compiler-generated versus handwritten code.** The overhead of using the OpenMP compiler is addressed here. Since the compiler uses a fixed allocation to distribute computation, combined with extra code added to the program, it is not as good as manual parallel programming. In addition, some algorithms in parallel programming cannot be represented in OpenMP. The overhead for the OpenMP compiler is application dependent. Here, we only compare the overhead of the same algorithm deployed by both the OpenMP compiler and handwritten code. It shows that overhead is within 5% for both examples.

Figure 7.10 shows the result of matrix multiplication using multiple DSEs. Double buffering techniques are used here. The matrix size is 128 × 128.

- **Scalable speedup by using a number of DSEs.** Four DSEs achieve a 3.9 times speedup over one DSE for the same program without double buffering, and 32 DSEs obtain a 24.5 times speedup over one DSE. This shows that 3SoC architecture is suitable for large intensive computation on multiple processors within one chip and that performance is scalable.

- **Double buffering.** Double buffering shows great performance improvement, especially for smaller numbers of DSEs. For one DSE, the speedup is 1.8 times by using double buffering over one DSE without double buffering, almost equivalent to using two DSEs. We expect the speedups with larger numbers of DSEs to be in the same range with larger matrices.

In Figure 7.11, we implemented parallelized FFT using multiple DSEs. For most applications, computation time plays an important role in the use of the FFT algorithm. The computation time can be reduced using parallelism in FFT, in 3SoC employing multiple DSEs. Figure 7.11 shows the scalable scheme of FFT using different numbers of DSEs. From the computation cycles taken, the time for computation

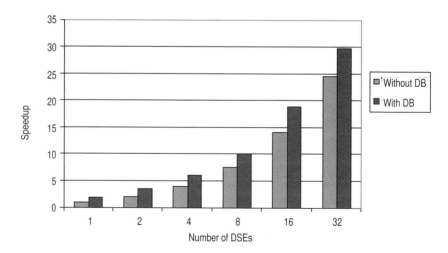

Figure 7.10 Matrix multiplication using DSEs.

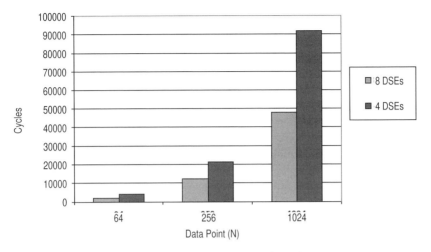

Figure 7.11   Parallelized FFT using DSEs.

of 1024 complex points using eight DSEs is approximately 240 microseconds (with the current 3SoC clock speed of 200 MHz), which is comparable to other DSP processors. For 64 fixed-size data points, using 8 DSEs achieves a 1.95 times speedup over four DSEs. It is clear from Figure 7.11 that FFT implementation in OpenMP is scalable.

7.8   CONCLUSIONS

In this chapter, we propose an OpenMP compiler for chip multiprocessors (3SoC as an example), especially targeted at extending OpenMP directives to cope with the heterogeneity of CMPs. In view of this emerging parallel architecture, advanced architecture features are important. By extending OpenMP for CMPs, we provide several optimization techniques. The OpenMP compiler hides the implementation details from the programmer, thus improving the overall code efficiency and ease of parallel programming on CMPs.

ACKNOWLEDGMENT

This research was supported in part by the Institute for Manufacturing Research and the Institute for Scientific Computing, Wayne State University.

REFERENCES

1. OpenMP Architecture Review Board, OpenMP C and C++ Application Program Interface, Version 2.0, http://www.openmp.org, March 2002.

2. R. Chandra, L. Dagum, D. Kohr, D. Maydan, J. McDonald, and R. Menon, *Parallel Programming in OpenMP,* Morgan Kaufmann Publishers, 2001.

3. 3SoC Documentation–3SoC 2003 Hardware Architecture, Cradle Technologies, Inc. March 2003.

4. *3SoC Programmer's Guide,* Cradle Technologies, Inc., http://www.cradle.com, March 2002.

5. C. Brunschen and M. Brorsson, OdinMP/CCp—A Portable Implementation of OpenMP for C, in *European Workshop on OpenMP,* Sepetember 1999.

6. F. Liu and V. Chaudhary, A practical OpenMP Compiler for System on Chips, in *Workshop on OpenMP Applications and Tools,* pp. 54–68, June 2003.

7. D. Quinlan, M. Schordan, Q. Yi, and B. R. De. AC++ Infrastructure for Automatic Introduction and Translation of OpenMP Directives, in *Workshop on OpenMP Applications and Tools,* June 2003.

8. M. Sato, S. Satoh, K. Kusano, and Y. Tanaka. Design of OpenMP Compiler for an SMP Cluster, in *European Workshop on OpenMP,* September 1999.

9. S. J. Min, S. W. Kim, M. Voss, S. I. Lee, and R. Eighmann, Portable Compilers for OpenMP. In *Workshop on OpenMP Applications and Tools,* 2001.

10. X. Tian, A. Bik, M. Girkar, P. Grey, H. Saito, and E. Su, Intel OpenMP C++/Fortran Compiler for Hyper-Threading Technology: Implementation and Performance, *Intel Technology Journal,* 6(1), 36–46, 2002.

11. M. Burcea and M. J. Voss, A Runtime Optimization System for OpenMP, in *Workshop on OpenMP Applications and Tools,* June 2003.

12. C. Tseng, Compiler Optimization for Eliminating Barrier Synchronization, in *Proceedings of the 5th ACM Symposium on Principles and Practice of Parallel Programming,* July 1995.

13. S. Satoh, K. Kusano, and M. Sato, Compiler Optimization Techniques for OpenMP Programs, in *2nd European Workshop on OpenMP,* pp. 14–15, 2000.

14. A. Krishnamurthy and K. A. Yelick, Optimizing Parallel Programs with Explicit Synchronization, in *SIGPLAN Conference on Programming Language Design and Implementation,* pp. 196–204, 1995.

## CHAPTER 8

Compiler and Run-Time Parallelization Techniques for Scientific Computations on Distributed-Memory Parallel Computers

PEIZONG LEE, CHIEN-MIN WANG, and JAN-JAN WU

The challenge in compiling programs for distributed-memory systems is to determine data and computation decompositions so that load balance and low communication overhead can be achieved. For regular programs, when all necessary information is known at compiling time, we present compiler techniques to generate data and computation decompositions without using any programming language directives. Communication codes can then be generated based on data distribution. For irregular programs, when data reference patterns are unknown at compiling time, programming language directives are helpful for assigning data and/or computation decompositions. In addition, inspector and executor preprocessing is a useful run-time support technique to minimize the communication overhead. For irregular programs when data reference patterns have some rules, such as unstructured mesh applications in which only geometrically neighboring data are accessed, programming language interfaces to support special-purpose data partitioning libraries are needed to help programmers improve the efficiency and shorten the development life cycle of parallel programs.

8.1 INTRODUCTION

Workstation clusters and personal computer clusters are becoming the main tools for running scientific computations in research laboratories as they are relatively easy to scale. Also, given the large number of processing elements (PEs), they are well suited for effectively solving large problems such as grand challenge problems [51]. However, program development for these types of distributed memory parallel computers (DMPCs) is time-consuming and error-prone, as the programmer is forced to manage both parallelism and communication [14, 94, 118]. There is an urgent need, therefore, to develop compiler and run-time parallelization techniques to transform a sequential program (code) with some compiler directives into an effective parallel code for DMPCs.

A sequential program written by imperative programming languages, such as FORTRAN or C, defines the iteration space for executing the target computation in sequence, as well as the communication patterns among the data. As computation arrangement and data allocation among PEs influence load balance and communication overhead, computation decomposition and data distribution should be considered simultaneously in order to maximize load balance and minimize communication overhead.

In this chapter, we present compiler techniques for computation decomposition and data distribution based on the gap of communication penalties, which includes the communication overhead of data alignment among different data arrays and data access due to the spatial data localities of each data array. If the compiler can find all data dependence relations, it can determine an optimal partial-order execution sequence that satisfies those relations and minimizes the execution time on shared-memory computers [24, 107]. If the compiler can further optimize data alignment among data arrays, it can distribute the arrays and computations among PEs on DMPCs, such that both load balance is achieved and communication overhead is minimized [74].

However, in many application programs, indirect array references are frequently used to access irregular or dynamic data structures. For example, in unstructured mesh applications, an array subscript may involve references to other array elements. Since the values of the array elements are not known at compiling time, it is impossible for a compiler to decide on an effective alignment for data arrays that are accessed through indirect references. A naive data-distribution strategy may incur high communication overhead. A program is called "irregular" if its data reference patterns depend on run-time computed values, or change during program execution; otherwise, it is called "regular."

We discuss run-time support techniques to reduce the communication overhead of irregular programs. Inspector/executor preprocessing is a commonly used run-time support technique for irregular computation on distributed-memory architectures. The PARTI library was the first library to support inspector/executor preprocessing [13], and the ARF compiler [113] was the first compiler to support irregularly distributed arrays. The ARF compiler relies on the PARTI library to implement nonuniform data mapping and coordinate interprocessor data movement. It transforms a program annotated with parallel loops and data distribution directives by embedding calls in the PARTI primitives in the original program. A Do-loop with irregular array references is transformed into a pair comprised of inspector and executor. In this chapter, we use the ARF/PARTI compilation system to demonstrate inspector/executor type preprocessing on a computational fluid dynamics simulation code.

The ARF/PARTI system implements a general-purpose compilation technique. It was designed to handle parallel loops with irregular array references. However, in many applications, such as unstructured mesh computations, data access has a spatial locality with respect to their coordinates. Therefore, data distributions should be amenable to a geometrically spatial locality. A naive ordering of data elements and a naive "block," "cyclic," or "block–cyclic" data distribution may incur substantial communication overhead. In these cases, programmers may not have the ability to develop a special-purpose data partitioner (software tool) for data distribution. Library supports are therefore necessary for programmers to use existing well-known software tools for partitioning data and solving sparse linear systems. We have found that compiler directives are crucial for helping compilers decide on suitable data alignments and data distributions. We have also found that special-purpose libraries, such as data partitioning tools and sparse linear solvers, are very useful for improving the efficiency and shortening the development life cycle of parallel programs.

The rest of this chapter is organized as follows. Section 8.2 provides some definitions and the background of this research. Section 8.3 presents our method for compiling a regular program on DMPCs. Section 8.4 presents compiler and runtime support techniques for irregular computation. Section 8.5 presents library support for irregular computation. Section 8.6 surveys related works. Finally, some concluding remarks are given in Section 8.7.

8.2 BACKGROUND MATERIAL

The abstract target machine we adopt is a q-D grid of $N_1 \times N_2 \times \cdots \times N_q$ PEs, where D stands for dimensional. A PE on the q-D grid is represented by the tuple $(p_1, p_2, \ldots, p_q)$, where $0 \leq p_i \leq N_i - 1$ for $1 \leq i \leq q$. The parallel program generated from a sequential program for a grid corresponds to the SPMD (single program, multiple data) model, in which large data arrays are partitioned and distributed among PEs, and in which each PE executes the same program, but operates on distinct data items [36, 46, 79].

8.2.1 Data Distribution and Data Alignment

On DMPCs, data are distributed among PEs and related data are aligned together.

8.2.1.1 Cyclic(b), Block, and Cyclic Data Distributions
In order to support data-parallel programming, the current HPF (High Performance Fortran) standard only allows data arrays in each dimension to be distributed in block, cyclic, block-cyclic, replicated, fixed, or not-distributed fashions [61]. Block-cyclic data distribution, or `cyclic`(b) distribution, is the most general regular distribution in which blocks of size b of a 1-D data array are distributed among a 1-D processor array of N PEs in a round-robin fashion.

For example, let array $x(l : u)$ be indexed from l to u, where x is a 1-D array, or, in general, some specific dimension of a high-dimensional array. Then, under `cyclic`(b) distribution, the set of elements $x(l + pb : l + pb + b - 1)$, $x(l + (p + N)b : l + (p + N)b + b - 1)$, etc. is stored in pth PE, denoted by PE_p. Thus, the ith entry of

x is stored in PE$_p$, where $p = \lfloor (i - l)/b \rfloor \bmod N$. We say that array x is distributed in a *cyclic* fashion if $b = 1$; in a *block* fashion if $b = \lceil (u - l + 1)/N \rceil$; and in a *block-cyclic* fashion if $1 < b < \lceil (u - l + 1)/N \rceil$.

8.2.1.2 Communication Overhead Due to Accessing Different Data Arrays

If two data (variables) of different data arrays appear in a statement, which is not in a cycle of Do-across dependence within a Do-loop, then we can use a collective communication to fetch data. If, however, the statement is in a cycle of Do-across dependence within a Do-loop, iterations in the Do-loop will be executed conservatively in a sequential manner. In this case, the communication overhead can be analyzed in a similar manner to the "dependence" cases in Table 8.2.

Suppose that two dimensions, each from a different data array, are distributed along the same dimension of the target q-D grid. From the relationship between left-hand-side (LHS) and right-hand-side (RHS) array subscript reference patterns in the original sequential program, we can specify the communication primitives used in the SPMD program when RHS data are sent to the owner of the LHS data, based on the pattern-matching techniques in Table 8.1. These communication primitives have also been adopted by [36, 67, 68, 79, 114]. We use "message no.(message length)" to represent each penalty based on two two-dimensional data arrays accessed with each other in a depth-two nested Do-loop. We assume that both dimensions of these two data arrays have the same problem size m and that the mentioned two dimensions are distributed among N PEs in the same block fashion.

In Table 8.1, the communication primitive *transfer* specifies that a message be sent from one PE to the other PE. *Shift* means a circular shift of data among neigh-

Table 8.1 Communication primitives used in the SPMD program when LHS and RHS array subscripts of two dimensions, each from a different data array, have certain specific patterns, where these two data array dimensions are distributed along the same grid dimension in a block fashion and the communication cost is represented by "message no.(message length)"

Case	LHS	RHS	Communication primitive	Cost on network
1	$f(i)$	$f(i)$	no	no
2	c_1	c_2	transfer	$1(m)$
3	i	$i \pm c$	shift	$1(\min\{c, m/N\}m)$
4	$f_1(i)$	$f_2(i)$	affine-transform	exist algorithms*
5	i	c	broadcast	$\log N(m)$
6	c	i	reduction	$\log N(m)$
7	i or $f_3(i)$	j or $f_4(j)$	many-to-many-multicast	$N(m^2/N)$
8	i	unknown	gather	$N(m^2/N)$
9	unknown	i	scatter	$N(m^2/N)$

*[39, 60, 71] have presented fast algorithms for generating communication sets.

Notes: i and j are loop control index variables; c, c_1, and c_2 are constants at compiling time; "unknown" means that the value is unknown at compiling time; $f_1(i)$ and $f_2(i)$ are two affine functions of the form $s_1 \times i + c_1$ and $s_2 \times i + c_2$, respectively; $f(i)$, $f_3(i)$, and $f_4(j)$ are three functions of i and j, respectively.

boring PEs along the specified grid dimension. *Affine-transform* indicates sending data from each PE on the specified grid dimension(s) to a distinct PE according to an affine transform. *Broadcast* represents sending a message to all PEs on the specified dimension(s) of the processor grid. *Reduction* stands for reducing data using a simple associative and commutative operator over all the PEs lying on the specified grid dimension(s). *Many-to-many-multicast* represents replication of data from all PEs on the specified grid dimension(s) to themselves. *Gather* means to receive a message from each PE lying on the specified grid dimension(s). Finally, *scatter* means sending a different message to each PE lying on the specified grid dimension(s).

Case 3 is a special instance of Case 4. There exist algorithms for generating communication sets for Case 4 [39, 60, 71]. Therefore, in the following, we say that two dimensions, each from a different array, have an affinity relation if the two subscripts of these two dimensions are affine functions of the same (single) loop-control index variable of a Do-loop. As to the costs of Case 7 through Case 9, they are considerably higher than those of Case 1 through Case 6.

As Case 7 can be identified at compiling time, it should avoid distributing dimensions of different data arrays that do not have an affinity relation to the same grid dimension. If Case 7 only appears in some parts of the program, performing data redistribution is another choice [68]. In Case 8 and Case 9, subscripts are unknown at compiling time; for example, subscripts are array elements. In these cases, as compilers cannot determine data alignment, they can only assign a naive data distribution for each data array and conservatively replicate data among all PEs. The codes' communication penalties are therefore high. Even so, the penalties of Cases 8 and 9 may be reduced using run-time support techniques, such as inspector–executor techniques [113], which are explained in Section 8.4.

8.2.1.3 *Data Alignment and Axis Alignment*

We say that $x(i)$ is aligned with $y(i + c)$ for a constant integer c, which means that $x(1)$ is aligned with $y(1 + c)$, $x(2)$ is aligned with $y(2 + c)$, and so on, for all $x(i)$ and $y(i + c)$ defined in the data domain. In addition, $x(i)$ and $y(i + c)$ are stored in the same PE.

The axis alignment technique was introduced in [80], and further developed in, for example, [36, 68, 74]. It emphasizes that related data arrays should be aligned together and data distributions of these related arrays should be based on the alignment relations among components of arrays. More specifically, if two dimensions, each from a different array, have an affinity relation, then it is advantageous for them to be aligned with each other in order to avoid communication.

A component affinity graph is used to represent affinity relations among dimensions of data arrays, where each node represents one dimension of a data array and each edge represents an affinity relation between two dimensions of two different arrays. The weight of an edge is an estimate of the communication that is required if dimensions of two arrays are distributed along different dimensions of the target grid. The component-alignment problem is defined as an optimal partitioning of the node set of the component affinity graph into k disjointed subsets, where k is the dimension of the highest dimensional data array. The objective is to minimize the total weight of the edges across nodes in different subsets, under the constraint that no two nodes corresponding to the same array are in the same subset. Array dimensions within each of the above-mentioned k disjointed subsets are then aligned together. Data distributions of these array dimensions will share the same pattern. To avoid excessive details, we do not discuss weights here; for this, see [36, 37, 38, 68, 78, 79, 80].

Example 1
Consider the program in Figure 8.1(a). The first dimension of y is aligned with the second dimension of x because subscripts of these two dimensions are affine functions (j and $j - 1$) of the same (single) innermost loop-control index variable j. Meanwhile, the second dimension of y is aligned with the first dimension of x because subscripts of these two dimensions are affine functions (i and $i - 1$) of the same outermost loop-control index variable i. Figure 8.1(b) shows the component affinity graph of the program, where x1 and y1 represent the first dimension of arrays x and y, respectively; and x2 and y2 represent the second dimension of arrays x and y, respectively. Suppose that the target machine is a linear processor array of $N = 3$ PEs and the problem size is $m = 6$. Figure 8.1(c) shows the data layouts of arrays x and y under a well-aligned data distribution scheme: $x(\text{block}, \times)$ and $y(\times, \text{block})$, where the symbol "$\times$" means that the specified array dimension is not distributed. Clearly, during computation, communication is only required to access read-only boundary data from neighboring PEs. Figure 8.1(d) shows the data layouts of arrays x and y under a nonaligned data distribution scheme: $x(\text{block}, \times)$ and $y(\text{block}, \times)$. It is also clear that, during computation, data reorganization access among PEs is needed to perform a transpose operation.

8.2.2 Data Temporal Dependency and Spatial Locality

We now discuss the dependence relations between the iteration space and the data space.

8.2.2.1 Temporal Dependence Vectors and Temporal use Vectors
In the iteration space of a nested Do-loop, each array variable may appear once, twice, or more times, resulting in its traces within the iteration space. If an array variable is first generated in some iteration α and then used in another iteration β, it induces one temporal dependence vector $d = \beta - \alpha$. In addition, if an array variable is used in different iterations α and β, it also induces one temporal use vector $d = \beta - \alpha$. We use d_x to represent a temporal dependence vector and d_x^r to represent a temporal use vector, both for array x. (Superscript "r" stands for "read-only".)

Example 1 (continued)
In Figure 8.1(a), the pair $\langle x(i, j), x(i, j - 1)\rangle$ induces one temporal dependence vector $d_x = (0, 1)$, whereas the pair $\langle y(j, i), y(j, i - 1)\rangle$ induces one temporal use vector $d_y^r = (1, 0)$, both in the iteration space $\mathcal{L}^{(2)} = \{(i, j), \mid 1 \leq i, j \leq m\}$.
    We say that a vector is regular if it is a constant vector, and irregular if it cannot be represented by a constant number of regular vectors. Note that a temporal depen-

(a) {* x(i, 0) and y(j, 0) are zero's. *}
  do i = 1, m
    do j = 1, m
      x(i, j) = x(i, j1) + y(j, i) + y(j, i1)
  enddo enddo

$d_x = (0, 1)$ $d_y^r = (1, 0)$ $s_x = (0, c3)$ $s_y^r = (0, c1)$

(b)

$x1$ $y1$

$x2$ $y2$

(c)

	x11 x12 x13 x14 x15 x16 x21 x22 x23 x24 x25 x26	PE0	y11 y21 y31 y41 y51 y61 y12 y22 y32 y42 y52 y62
	x31 x32 x33 x34 x35 x36 x41 x42 x43 x44 x45 x46	PE1	y13 y23 y33 y43 y53 y63 y14 y24 y34 y44 y54 y64
	x51 x52 x53 x54 x55 x56 x61 x62 x63 x64 x65 x66	PE2	y15 y25 y35 y45 y55 y65 y16 y26 y36 y46 y56 y66

(d)

	x11 x12 x13 x14 x15 x16 x21 x22 x23 x24 x25 x26	PE0	y11 y12 y13 y14 y15 y16 y21 y22 y23 y24 y25 y26
	x31 x32 x33 x34 x35 x36 x41 x42 x43 x44 x45 x46	PE1	y31 y32 y33 y34 y35 y36 y41 y42 y43 y44 y45 y46
	x51 x52 x53 x54 x55 x56 x61 x62 x63 x64 x65 x66	PE2	y51 y52 y53 y54 y55 y56 y61 y62 y63 y64 y65 y66

(e)

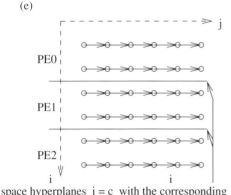

space hyperplanes i = c with the corresponding
iteration space mapping vector iv = (1, 0)

(f)

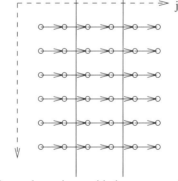

space hyperplanes j = c with the corresponding
iteration space mapping vector iv = (0, 1)

Figure 8.1 (a) A depth-two nested Do-loop and its temporal vectors and spatial vectors. (b) A component affinity graph representing alignment relations among dimensions of arrays x and y. When the problem size m = 6 and the number of PEs $N = 3$, data layouts of arrays x and y under data distribution schema are (c) x(block, ×) and y(×, block), and (d) x(block, ×) and y(block, ×). Cases of iteration space mapping vectors are (e) **iv** = (1, 0), and (f) **iv** = (0, 1).

dence vector is the same as a data dependence vector, and a temporal use vector is the same as an input dependence vector [72, 73, 112, 117]. We use the phrases "temporal vectors" and "spatial vectors," which we introduce next, as we feel they match the intuition guiding our approach.

8.2.2.2 Spatial Dependence Vectors and Spatial Use Vectors

Focusing on data arrays, we are interested in whether different variables in the same dimension are accessed simultaneously in the same iteration. For example, if $y(j, i)$ and $y(j, i-4)$ both appear in the loop body of an iteration, we associate with y a spatial vector $(0, c)$, where c is a penalty defined in Table 8.2. We say that all pairs $y(j, i)$ and $y(j, i-4)$ are located at a constant distance $(0, 4)$ for all indices i and j defined in the iteration space, because the difference in the first dimension is $j - j = 0$ and the difference in the second dimension is $i - (i-4) = 4$. This indicates that for the same value (j) of the first dimension, several elements located at a constant distance with different subscripts in the second dimension will be accessed while performing an iteration.

Spatial vectors allow us to decide which dimension of an array should be fixed in PEs so that communication is not incurred. It is especially convenient to use spatial vectors when there is no nontrivial temporal vector or when temporal vectors are irregular. For example, the pair $\langle x(i, k), x(k, k) \rangle$ for $i > k$, arising from Gaussian elimination with partial pivot, incurs a broadcast operation that cannot be represented by

Table 8.2 Seven different penalties $(0, c_1, c_2, c_3, c_4, c_5, c_6)$ for different ranks of communication overhead based on two subscripts of the same data array dimension of a pair of occurrences of that data array if the mentioned (data array) dimension is distributed in a block fashion.

Subscripts		Communication	Penalty Dependence	Use
$f(i)$	$f(i)$	no	0	0
$f(i)$	$f(i) - c$	shift	c_3	c_1
$f(i)$	c	broadcast	c_5	c_2
c	$f(i)$	reduction	c_5	c_2
$f_1(i)$	$f_2(j)$	many-to-many-multicast	c_6	c_4
$f(i)$	unknown	gather	c_6	c_4
unknown	$f(i)$	scatter	c_6	c_4

Notes: $c_1 = 1(\min\{c, m/N\}m)$; $c_2 = \log N(m)$; $c_3 = N\lceil c/N \rceil (\min\{c, m/N\}m)$; $c_4 = N(m^2/N)$; $c_5 = m \log N(1)$; and $c_6 = mN(m/N)$. i and j are loop control index variables; $f(i)$ is an affine function of the form $a \times i + b$; $f_1(i)$ and $f_2(j)$ are functions of i and j, respectively; c is a constant at compiling time; and "unknown" means that the value is unknown at compiling time. We use "message no.(message length)" to represent each penalty based on a two-dimensional data array generated or used in a depth-two nested Do-loop. Then, $0 < c_1 < c_2 < c_3 < c_4 < c_5 < c_6$, where m is the size in each data array dimension and N is the number of PEs.

a constant number of temporal vectors. But it is easy to use one spatial use vector $(c_2, 0)$, where c_2 is a penalty defined in Table 8.2, to indicate that it is better not to distribute array x along the first dimension in order to avoid communication overhead due to irregular data access. Note that a symbolic array variable, which appears in the program, is called an array occurrence. For example, $x(i, k)$ and $x(k, k)$ are two occurrences of array x.

Formally, we say that a pair of data array occurrences induces a spatial dependence vector if one occurrence is on the LHS and the other is on the RHS and they induce one temporal dependence vector. It induces a spatial use vector if both occurrences are on the RHS or if one occurrence is on the LHS and the other occurrence is on the RHS, but they do not induce any temporal dependence vector.

For a spatial vector, we use seven penalties $(0, c_1, c_2, c_3, c_4, c_5, c_6)$ to represent seven different ranks (gaps) of communication overhead incurred along a data dimension, if that data dimension is distributed. The penalties depend on whether access patterns are "regular" or "irregular" and on "dependence" or "use" characteristics, as shown in Table 8.2, where $0 < c_1 < c_2 < c_3 < c_4 < c_5 < c_6$. Also, c_1 through c_6 are different ranks of communication overhead due to a two-dimensional data array, which is generated or used in a depth-two nested Do-loop. We assume that m is the problem size for the data array, N is the number of PEs, and the data array is distributed among PEs in a block fashion.

We use s_x to represent a spatial dependence vector and s_x^{r} to represent a spatial use vector, both for array x.

Example 1 (continued)
In Figure 8.1(a), the pair $\langle x(i, j), x(i, j - 1) \rangle$ induces one spatial dependence vector $s_x = (0, c_3)$ for array x and the pair $\langle y(j, i), y(j, i - 1) \rangle$ induces one spatial use vector $s_y^{\mathrm{r}} = (0, c_1)$ for array y.

8.2.3   Computation Decomposition and Scheduling

On DMPCs, the data distributions of all data arrays have to be determined for the entire computation before the execution starts. The same holds for the computation distributions of all the iterations in the nested Do-loops. Computation decomposition in each nested Do-loop is based on the data distribution of the dominant data array in that Do-loop. After partitioning the iterations among PEs according to the owner computes rule or owner stores rule with respect to the dominant data array, the iterations in each individual PE are scheduled for satisfying dependence constraints.

8.2.3.1   *The Dominant Data Array in a Nested Do-loop*   If an iteration is assigned to a PE, the data for that iteration must be in the PE during the execution of the iteration. Ideally, the distributions are such that the computational load is balanced and there is no redistribution (migration) of data during computation. As this is not generally possible, we try to minimize the migration of data by finding those data arrays that are accessed the most often (later referred to as "dominant") and try

not to change their assignment for as large fragments of computation as possible, while following either the owner computes rule or the owner stores rule, so that when they are accessed during the fragments, they, and other "related" arrays are in the PEs that need to access them.

A program may include generated-and-used arrays, which induce temporal dependence relations, write-only arrays, read-only arrays, and privatization arrays, which only occur within a Do-loop. In each Do-Loop, we rank data arrays in descending order, according to the following characteristics: generated-and-used > write-only > read-only > privatization; data arrays of equal status are ranked by decreasing dimensionality; and data arrays of equal characteristics and dimensionality are ranked by decreasing frequency of being generated and/or used in Do-loops.

We nominate one of the highest ranked arrays as the *dominant* array in the Do-loop. Its distribution is decided first because it influences the decomposition of the computation (partitioning of the iteration space). Other data arrays are then distributed, based on their alignment with the dominant array, which has the largest volume of accessed data. It is better not to migrate the dominant array in order to avoid excessive data communication.

8.2.3.2 *Owner Computes Rule and Owner Stores Rule*   If an iteration is to be executed in a PE based on the data distribution of the LHS array, the iteration scheduling is based on the owner computes rule. If an iteration is assigned to be executed in a PE based on the data distribution of a RHS array, the iteration scheduling is based on the owner stores rule. If the LHS and the RHS arrays are aligned well, then both under the owner computes rule and the owner stores rule, the communication overhead incurred is not significant. However, if the LHS array and some RHS arrays are not aligned well, significant communication overhead cannot be avoided, no matter which rule is applied. In order to minimize communication, we use the owner computes rule or the owner stores rule, depending on whether we prefer not to move data elements of the dominant data array which possibly is the LHS array or a specific RHS array.

8.2.3.3 *Iteration-Space Mapping Vectors*   An affine function $s \times i + c$ of a single-loop control index variable i increases monotonously with respect to i when $s > 0$ and decreases monotonously with respect to i when $s < 0$, where s and c are constant integers. If the subscript of a distributed dimension of the dominant array in a Do-loop is an affine function of a single-loop control index variable, the iteration space of the Do-loop will be partitioned (based on either the owner computes rule or the owner stores rule with respect to the dominant array) by a set of parallel hyperplanes. This can be represented by an elementary vector, known as an iteration space mapping vector.

In a Do-loop, q dimensions of the dominant array are distributed. Therefore, we define q iteration space mapping vectors, which are q elementary vectors, for the target q-D grid. That is, for each distributed dimension of the dominant array, we define an iteration-space-mapping vector that corresponds to a distributed dimension of the iteration space of that Do-loop. The dimensionality of an iteration-space-mapping vector is equal to the dimensionality of the Do-loop. The value of the entry (of the iteration space mapping vector) corresponding to the loop control index variable appearing in a distributed dimension of the dominant array is 1; the value of all other entries is zero.

Example 1 (continued)

Figure 8.1(e) shows the temporal dependence relations in the iteration space, which is partitioned by the iteration-space-mapping hyperplanes $i = c$, whose normal vector (the iteration-space-mapping vector) is $\mathbf{iv} = e_1 = (1, 0)$. Figure 8.1(f) shows that the iteration space is partitioned by the iteration-space-mapping hyperplanes $j = c$, whose normal vector is $\mathbf{iv} = e_2 = (0, 1)$.

8.3 COMPILING REGULAR PROGRAMS ON DMPCS

Table 8.1 (in Section 8.2.1) shows that if the subscripts of two dimensions, each from a different data array, are not affine functions of the same (single) loop-control index variable, these two dimensions are not suitable for axis alignment. In addition, if the subscript of a distributed dimension of a data array is neither a constant nor an affine function of a single-loop-control index variable, we can only assign a naive data distribution for this data array and rely on run-time support techniques (which will be presented in Section 8.4) to reduce communication overhead.

However, if the subscript of each dimension of a data array is an affine function of a single-loop-control index variable, we can use axis alignment techniques to align dimensions among different data arrays. In addition, each iteration-space-mapping vector corresponds to a dimension of data array that is distributed. Therefore, the problem of determining data distributions for all data arrays is reduced to the problem of finding a set of iteration-space-mapping vectors. These are based on either the owner computes rule or the owner stores rule, following the data distribution of the dominant data array in each Do-loop.

The complete procedure for determining data and computation decompositions and performing computation consists of four steps, of which, the second step is an alignment phase, the third step is a distribution phase, and the fourth step is an optimization phase for a coarse-grain pipeline:

Step 1. According to the data-dependence graph, we apply loop-fission techniques among statements [6], to make the original program more amenable to parallel execution.

Step 2. We construct a component affinity graph for each Do-loop, and apply the dynamic programming algorithm for axis alignments to decide whether data realignment between adjacent program fragments is needed [68]. All Do-loops in a program fragment will then share a static data-distribution scheme.

Step 3. We find a data-distribution scheme for each program fragment. In each fragment, we first determine a static data-distribution scheme for some of the dominant generated-and-used data arrays, based on finding iteration-space-mapping vectors from some of the most computationally intensive nested Do-loops, in which these data arrays are generated or used. Based on the alignment relations, a static data-distribution scheme is then determined for all data arrays throughout all Do-loops in each program fragment.

Step 4. For the computation in each Do-loop, based on the owner computes rule or the owner stores rule, we find the corresponding iteration-space-mapping vectors (which represent distributed dimensions of the iteration space) from the data distribution of a target (the dominant) data array. If communication cannot be avoided due to regular temporal dependences, we find tiling vectors and determine tile sizes so that iterations can be executed in a coarse-grain pipeline fashion. If, however, the computation only induces temporal use vectors, then there can be a communication-free computation decomposition, provided that we can replicate the required remote read-only data.

8.3.1 The Algorithm to Perform Step 1

In the following, we briefly describe the algorithm for performing loop fission. The structure of Do-loops in a general program can be treated as a tree or a forest, in which assignment statements are leaves and Do statements are internal nodes. We assume that statements within each Do-loop have been topologically sorted according to dependence precedences among statements in a preprocessing step. Loop fission, which is based on the dependence level of a Do-loop to detect whether each level-j Do-loop is parallel or not, has been proposed for vectorization [6]. But even in the case when some level-j Do-loops are sequential, if temporal dependence vectors are regular, we can exploit parallelism using tiling techniques. In addition, loop fission can separate unrelated dependences in a Do-loop and thus potentially investigate more parallelism. Furthermore, after loop fission, we can easily generate aggregate message-passing communication primitives before the outermost loop, which does not induce dependence relations for read-only data. In this chapter, we apply loop fission to identify the execution order of nested Do-loops in sequence.

If a Do-loop contains assignment statements and other Do-loops, we apply loop fission techniques top-down as follows. Suppose that dependence relations among all k children of a parent induce k' strongly connected components. If $k' > 1$, we apply loop fission for the parent Do-loop so that the grandparent loses one child but gains k' children. After that, we recursively deal with each of the k' children. If $k' = 1$, we do not apply loop fission for the parent Do-loop, but recursively deal with each of the k children.

8.3.2 The Algorithm to Perform Step 2

Using the tree-structure of Do-loops obtained in Step 1, we apply a dynamic programming algorithm bottom-up to decide whether consecutive Do-loops can share the same data-distribution scheme. Based on axis alignments, we construct a component affinity graph for each Do-loop and various component affinity graphs for consecutive Do-loops. It can then be heuristically determined whether data redistribution is needed between adjacent program fragments. If it is better for child Do-loops to use different data distribution schemes, we do not proceed to the parent Do-loop; but if it is better for them to share a static data distribution scheme, the parent Do-loop will adopt this static scheme. We repeatedly check whether the parents' and their siblings' Do-loops can share a static distribution scheme, proceeding up to the root if possible [68].

8.3.3   The Algorithm to Perform Step 3

For each program fragment, we want to find the data distribution for the dominant array (which is one of the highest-dimensional generated and used arrays). That is, in the most computationally intensive nested Do-loop, which dominates the total execution time, where the target data array variables are generated or used, we want to find q iteration-space-mapping vectors. These correspond to q dimensions of the target data array, such that all the iterations can be mapped into the q-D grid with the execution requiring as little communication as possible.

First, we analyze the spatial dependence/use vectors of the dominant array. A dimension of the dominant array is distributed if its communication penalty (shown in Table 8.2 for spatial vectors) is lower than those of other dimensions that are not distributed.

Second, if there are two or more dimensions whose penalties are the same, we analyze their corresponding iteration-space-mapping vectors. We find the temporal dependence vectors for all data arrays appearing in this Do-loop and study the inner products between these space-mapping vectors and all temporal dependence vectors. The dimension, whose corresponding space-mapping vector causes more inner products to be zero, will be distributed in order to reduce dependence communication during execution.

Third, if there are still two or more dimensions whose conditions are the same, we find temporal use vectors for all data arrays appearing in this Do-loop, and study the inner products between their corresponding space-mapping-vectors and all temporal use vectors. The dimension, whose corresponding space-mapping vector causes more inner products to be zero, will be distributed in order to reduce prefetching communication during execution.

Fourth, if there are still two or more dimensions whose conditions are the same, we analyze the spatial vectors of the dominant array for other Do-loops. We then choose the dimension whose communication penalty (shown in Table 8.2 for spatial vectors) is the lowest in order to reduce communication during the execution of other Do-loops.

Fifth, if there are still two or more dimensions whose conditions are the same, we choose the dimension based on a data-storage method to enhance cache performance. For instance, as Fortran adopts the column-major data-storage method, we will distribute the "column" dimension if possible; and as C adopts the row-major data-storage method, we will distribute the "row" dimension if possible.

According to the alignment relations, data distributions for other aligned data arrays can then be determined. If there are still some data arrays whose data distributions are not yet determined, we determine the data distribution for one of the high-est-dimensional generated and used data arrays from the remaining data arrays until data distributions for all data arrays are determined [74].

8.3.4   The Algorithm to Perform Step 4

The parallel hyperplanes corresponding to the iteration space mapping vectors par-tition the iteration space into N partitions, where N is the number of PEs. When communication is needed due to regular dependences, each partition can be further divided into tiles. The tiles have to satisfy the atomic computation constraint, so that the dependence relations among tiles do not induce a cycle [53]. A small tile corresponds to a fine-grain solution, incurring a large number of small communica-tion messages among PEs, whereas a large tile corresponds to a coarse-grain solu-tion, incurring a long delay time among PEs due to dependent data.

The execution time can be formulated as a function of tile sizes, the size of itera-tion space, CPU speed, and communication speed. Optimal tile sizes may be found when the execution time is minimized [74, 115]. After tiling, each PE sequentially executes all the iterations in a tile, and then sends/receives boundary data to/from neighboring PEs. The next tile can then be executed by the PE using a coarse-grain pipeline, which overlaps computation time and communication time.

Loop fission and data redistribution are necessary for dealing with large applica-tions with long program codes. In this chapter, we use short program codes as ex-amples. Therefore, loop fission and data redistribution are not discussed further. In-terested readers, however, can find these topics elsewhere [68, 74].

Example 1 (continued)
Consider again the program in Figure 8.1(a). There are two two-dimensional arrays x and y; x is a generated-and-used array and y is a read-only array. Therefore, x is the dominant array in this program. It has a spatial dependence vector $s_x = (0, c_3)$, which indicates that if x is distributed along the first dimension, it will not incur communication overhead for x. If, however, x is distributed along the second di-mension, it will incur communication overhead c_3, due to certain regular depen-dence. Consequently, x is distributed along the first dimension.

Since the iteration space is rectangular, block distribution is used. Therefore, x is distributed under data-distribution schema $x(\texttt{block}, \times)$. Since y is aligned with x as shown in Figure 8.1(b), y is distributed under data-distribution schema $y(\times, \texttt{block})$ as shown in Figure 8.1(c). The subscripts appearing in the first dimension of x are the same affine function of the loop-control index variable i. Therefore, the corre-sponding iteration-space-mapping vector is $\mathbf{iv} = (1, 0)$ and the iteration space is par-titioned along its first dimension of Do-i loop, based on the owner computes rule of x, as shown in Figure 8.1(e).

On the other hand, suppose that y is the dominant array (as y may be used more frequently in other places). y has a spatial use vector $s_y^r = (0, c_1)$, which indicates that if it is distributed along the first dimension, it will not incur communication overhead for y. If, however, y is distributed along the second dimension, it will incur communication overhead c_1, due to prefetch read-only data. Therefore, y is distributed along the first dimension.

Again, since the iteration space is rectangular, block distribution is used. Therefore, y is distributed under data-distribution schema $y(\texttt{block}, \times)$. Since x is aligned with y, as shown in Figure 8.1(b), x is distributed under data-distribution schema $x(\times, \texttt{block})$, as shown in Figure 8.2(a). The subscripts appearing in the first dimension of y are the same affine function of the loop-control index variable j. Therefore, the corresponding iteration-space-mapping vector is $\mathbf{iv} = (0, 1)$ and the iteration space is partitioned along its second dimension of Do-j loop, based on the owner stores rule of y, as shown in Figure 8.1(f).

Since x has a temporal dependence vector $d_x = (0, 1)$, $\mathbf{iv} \cdot d_x = (0, 1) \cdot (0, 1) = 1$, the temporal dependences of x will induce communication between neighboring PEs. To avoid sending many small messages between neighboring PEs, we tile the iteration space. The tiles have to satisfy the atomic computation constraint, so that the dependence relations among tiles do not induce a cycle. Here, we tile the iteration space using two sets of tiling hyperplanes. The first is the set of iteration-space-mapping hyperplanes represented by $j = c$, which corresponds to iteration-space-mapping vector $\mathbf{iv} = (0, 1)$. The second is represented by $i = c$, which corresponds to the vector $(1, 0)$. A coarse-grain pipeline is scheduled as shown in Figure 8.2(b).

Example 2

Figure 8.3(a) shows the Dgefa program in Linpack for computing Gaussian elimination with partial pivoting. Because there are true backward dependences from line 28 to lines 6, 8, 17, 18, 22, and 24, the outermost Do-k loop has to be executed sequen-

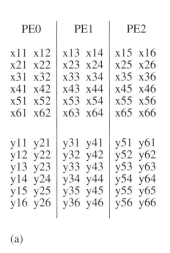

(a)

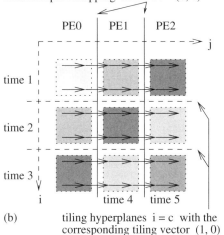

(b)

space hyperplanes $j = c$ with the corresponding iteration space mapping vector $\mathbf{iv} = (0, 1)$

tiling hyperplanes $i = c$ with the corresponding tiling vector $(1, 0)$

Figure 8.2 (a) Data layout based on the schema: $x(\times, \texttt{block})$ and $y(\texttt{block}, \times)$, (b) tiling the iteration space.

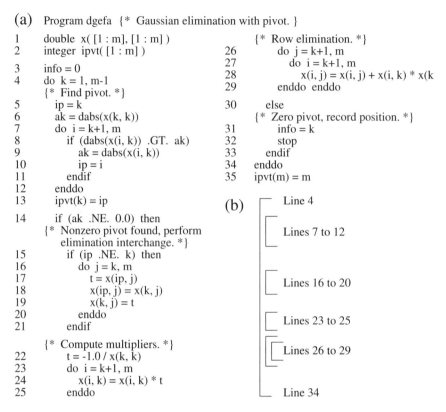

Figure 8.3   (a) A program computes Gaussian elimination with partial pivoting. (b) Structure of Do-loops including statements from lines 4 to 34.

tially, as shown in Figure 8.3(b). Within each outermost iteration, there is no temporal dependence relation for array x, but there are several spatial use vectors. The pair $\langle x(i, k), x(k, k)\rangle$ for $i > k$, due to lines 6, 8, and 9, induces one spatial use vector, $s_x^r(1) = (c_2, 0)$; the pair $\langle x(\text{ip}, j), x(k, j)\rangle$ for $\text{ip} > k$, due to lines 17, 18, and 19, induces the same spatial use vectors; the pair $\langle x(i, k), x(k, k)\rangle$ for $i > k$, due to lines 22 and 24, induces another same spatial use vector; and two pairs $\langle x(i, j), x(k, j)\rangle$ for $i > k$ and $\langle x(i, j), x(i, k)\rangle$ for $j > k$, due to line 28, induce two spatial use vectors $s_x^r(1) = (c_2, 0)$ and $s_x^r(2) = (0, c_2)$, respectively. Because the most computationally intensive Do-loop includes lines from 26 to 29, both dimensions have the same communication penalty c_2.

If the target machine is a two-dimensional grid so that $q = 2$, then both dimensions are distributed. Because the iteration space is a pyramid, in order to satisfy a load balance constraint, both dimensions are distributed as a cyclic(b) distribution as $x(\text{cyclic}(b), \text{cyclic}(b))$, where b is a small positive integer.

On the other hand, if the target machine is a one-dimensional linear processor array so that $q = 1$, we have to give up one degree of parallelism. However, computation decomposition cannot be determined on the basis of a nonexistent temporal dependence relation. Nor can it be determined on the basis of two spatial use vectors induced from the most computationally intensive Do-loop of lines 26 through 29, as these two spatial vectors have the same weight. However, based on the spatial use vector, $s_x^r(1) = (c_2, 0)$, induced from three other less computationally intensive Do-loops, we can decide to distribute array $x(i, j)$ along its second dimension among PEs as $x(\times, \texttt{cyclic}(b))$. Then, based on the owner computes rule, the iteration space for the most computationally intensive Do-loop of lines 26 through 29 is decomposed along its first dimension of Do-j loop, as subscripts appearing in the second dimension of x only involve loop-control index variable j.

8.4   COMPILER AND RUN-TIME SUPPORT FOR IRREGULAR PROGRAMS

If a compiler can gather enough information through analysis of the source code, it can generate highly efficient codes for data and computation decompositions automatically, as presented in Section 8.3. However, when crucial information is not available until a program executes, compile-time analysis fails. There are a variety of applications in which array subscript functions are not known at compiling time, for example, the subscripts shown in Cases 8 and 9 in Table 8.1 in Section 8.2.1. In these cases, compilers do not have information about how to align data arrays with one another effectively. A compiler, therefore, can only assign a naive data distribution for each data array, or rely on programmers using programming language directives, to specify a user-defined data distribution. In many applications, some subscript functions are given by integer arrays. Consider the occurrence $y(\texttt{idx}(i))$ in the High Performance Fortran (HPF) code segment below.

```
real x(1000), y(1000)
integer idx(1000)
TEMPLATE blocks(1000)
ALIGN x, y, idx WITH blocks
DISTRIBUTE blocks(BLOCK)
 ... idx gets assigned values at run-time ...
do i = 1, 500
   x(i) = y(idx(i))
enddo
```

The model of data mapping in HPF is a two-level mapping of array elements to logical processors. The user can ALIGN array elements to a TEMPLATE, which is then partitioned and distributed (DISTRIBUTE) onto an array of logical processors. In the example above, although the arrays are distributed into regular blocks, the indirect array references given by $y(\texttt{idx}(i))$ make it impossible for a compiler to predict what data could be communicated at compiling time.

Compile-time analysis is also difficult when there are irregular array distributions or irregular partitions of loop iterations. In the example illustrated in Figure

8.4, template reg is partitioned into equal-sized blocks, with one block assigned to each PE. Array map is aligned with template reg and used to specify how distribution irreg is partitioned among PEs. An irregular distribution is specified using an integer array, whereby map(i) is set equal to p, and element i of the distribution irreg is assigned to PE p. Array x and array y are distributed irregularly as given by map. Obviously, it is impossible to predict at compiling time the data that need to be communicated, even though the subscript expression is a simple linear function, because the distribution of x and y are not known until run time.

The ARF/PARTI run-time compilation system [113], which consists of two layers, was one of the first efforts to support the efficient execution of irregular computations. The bottom layer is the library of PARTI run-time procedures that are designed to: (1) support a shared name space, (2) provide the infrastructure needed to implement nonuniform data mapping efficiently, (3) coordinate interprocessor data movement, and (4) manage the storage of, and access to, copies of off-processor data. The top layer is a compiler that carries out program transformations by embedding calls in the PARTI primitives in the original program. A Do-loop with irregular array references is transformed into a pair made up of inspector and executor [97].

8.4.1 The Inspectors and Executors

Inspectors and executors perform optimizations to reduce communication costs for nonlocal access arising from irregular array references. Each PE precomputes which data have to be sent or received. Communication volume can be reduced by prefetching a single copy of each off-processor datum, even if it is referenced several times. The number of messages can be reduced by prefetching large quantities of off-processor data in a single message.

8.4.1.1 Inspector   The inspector loop carries out the preprocessing needed to reduce the volume of communication and the number of messages transmitted. Figure 8.8 in Section 8.4.2 shows how the inspector is generated by the ARF compiler

```
real x(1000), y(1000)
integer map(1000)
TEMPLATE reg(1000), irreg(1000)
ALIGN map WITH reg
DISTRIBUTE reg(BLOCK)
   ... set values of map array using a mapping method ...
ALIGN x, y WITH irreg
DISTRIBUTE irreg(map)
do i = 1, 500
   x(i) = y(i+2)
enddo
```

Figure 8.4   An example code for irregular data distribution.

for a parallel loop. The main data structures are hash tables, called hashed-caches [45], which are used for temporary storage. Run-time primitives initialize the hashed caches, store and retrieve data from them and flush the hashed caches when appropriate. During program execution, a hash table records off-processor fetches and stores them so as to enable every PE to recognize when more than one reference is being made to the same off-processor distributed-array element. Using this method, only one copy of that element needs to be fetched or stored.

During the inspector phase, the inspector loop performs a set of interprocessor communications that allows it to anticipate exactly which "send" and "receive" communication calls each PE must execute before and after executing the loop. To carry out the inspector loop, we must be able to find the owner of each distributed-array element. Regular data distributions comprise those that require simple functions to compute the PE and local index of a particular array element. On the other hand, irregular data distributions are those in which the ARF/PARTI system attempts to partition in a way that balances the following two objectives:

1. To have each PE perform approximately the same amount of work
2. To minimize communication overhead

Typically, it is impossible to express the resulting array partitions in a simple way. By allowing an arbitrary assignment of distributed-array elements to PEs, ARF/PARTI takes on the additional burden of maintaining a data structure that describes the partitioning. The size of this data structure must be the same as the size of the irregularly distributed array. This data structure is called a distributed translation table. Distributed translation tables are partitioned among PEs in equal-sized blocks, that is, the first m/N elements are on the first PE, the second m/N elements are on the second PE, and so on, where m is the number of data elements and N is the number of PEs. When an element A(i) of the distributed array A is accessed, the home processor and local index are found in the portion of the distributed translation table stored in PE $\lfloor (i-1)/(m/N) \rfloor$, where the array index starts from 1 in Fortran. Each lookup in a translation table, which aims to discover the home processor and the local index associated with a global distributed array index, is referred to as a dereference request. Translation tables are accessed during the inspector phase to determine where each data element resides. Once preprocessing is completed, every PE knows exactly which nonlocal data elements it needs should be sent to and received from the other PEs. After that, the necessary communication and computation can be carried out.

8.4.1.2 Executor   The original Do-loop is transformed into an executor loop. The initial data-exchange phase follows the plan established by the inspector. When a PE obtains copies of nonlocal distributed array elements, the copies are written into the PE's hashed cache. Once the communication phase is over, each PE carries out its computation using locally stored portions of distributed arrays, along with nonlocal distributed array elements stored in the hashed cache. When the computation phase is finished, distributed array elements to be stored off-processor are obtained from the hashed cache and sent to the appropriate off-processor locations.

8.4.1.3 PARTI Primitives   The PARTI run-time primitives [13] can be divided into three categories: primitives that may be invoked during the inspector phase, the executor phase, or both the inspector and executor phases. The scheduler primitive, invoked during the inspector phase, determines the "send" and "receive" calls that are needed during the executor phase. These calls may be used to scatter data, gather data, or perform reduction operations during the executor phase. The distributed translation table mentioned earlier is used during the inspector phase. The hashed cache primitives are used during both the inspector and the executor phases.

8.4.2   The ARF Compiler

The ARF compiler transforms the source program into an SPMD form. Data distribution specifications given by programmers are used to partition the program and generate appropriate communication. The compiler incorporates the PARTI primitives to carry out the computations on each PE efficiently.

We use an unstructured mesh application for computing a Euler flow solver to illustrate how the ARF compiler generates the corresponding inspector and executor. A practical two-dimensional unstructured mesh normally includes from 10,000 to 200,000 triangular elements, depending on resolution [69, 70, 76]. In this chapter, we use a simple blunt body as our example to illustrate data structures, data distributions, and the arising irregular computations.

Figure 8.5 shows the data structures and numbering of data elements for the unstructured mesh of a blunt-body example used in the Euler solver. It includes 30 nodes, 66 edges, and 36 triangular cells (elements). The nodes, edges, and cells are ordered in a way that forms wavefronts, that is, according to their coordinates. For two coordinates (i_1, j_1) and (i_2, j_2), (i_1, j_1) is ahead of (i_2, j_2) if $i_1 < i_2$, or $i_1 = i_2$ but $j_1 < j_2$. Each node keeps track of the cells that joint at this node (by array `CellNearNode`); each edge has the information of its two vertices (by array `NodeOfEdge`) and two adjacent cells (by array `CellNearEdge`); and each cell keeps information about its three vertices (by array `NodeOfCell`), its three edges (by array `EdgeOfCell`), and its three adjacent cells (by array `CellNearCell`). Each edge has an orientation (direction); for each cell, three nodes, three edges, and three adjacent cells are stored counterclockwise. In Figure 8.5(d), negative integers in `EdgeOfCell` represent edges with opposite directions. For example, if the edge 9 (node1, node2) is represented by "9," then the edge "-9" (node2, node1) is in the opposite direction to edge 9.

Figure 8.6 shows the HPF-like program that executes a Euler flow solver based on Frink's scheme. This kernel is from an iterative solver produced for a program designed to calculate fluid flow for geometries defined by an unstructured mesh using a finite-volume method [69, 70]. For the finite-volume method, state variables are defined at nodes, edges, and cells. State variables of nodes are updated based on the state variables of their surrounding cells, which can be implemented by a Do-all loop without loop-carry dependences. State variables of edges will be updated based on the state variables of their adjacent cells, which can also be implemented

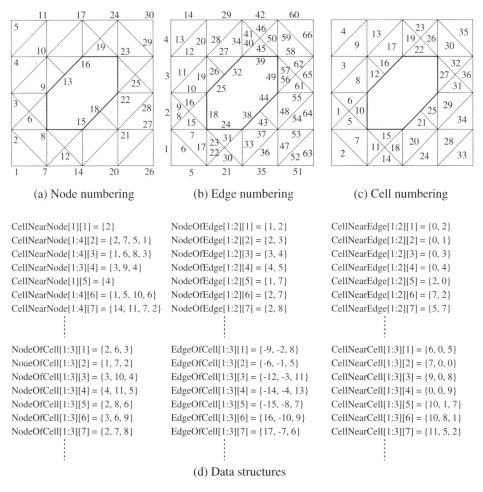

(a) Node numbering   (b) Edge numbering   (c) Cell numbering

CellNearNode[1][1] = {2}   NodeOfEdge[1:2][1] = {1, 2}   CellNearEdge[1:2][1] = {0, 2}
CellNearNode[1:4][2] = {2, 7, 5, 1}   NodeOfEdge[1:2][2] = {2, 3}   CellNearEdge[1:2][2] = {0, 1}
CellNearNode[1:4][3] = {1, 6, 8, 3}   NodeOfEdge[1:2][3] = {3, 4}   CellNearEdge[1:2][3] = {0, 3}
CellNearNode[1:3][4] = {3, 9, 4}   NodeOfEdge[1:2][4] = {4, 5}   CellNearEdge[1:2][4] = {0, 4}
CellNearNode[1][5] = {4}   NodeOfEdge[1:2][5] = {1, 7}   CellNearEdge[1:2][5] = {2, 0}
CellNearNode[1:4][6] = {1, 5, 10, 6} NodeOfEdge[1:2][6] = {2, 7}   CellNearEdge[1:2][6] = {7, 2}
CellNearNode[1:4][7] = {14, 11, 7, 2} NodeOfEdge[1:2][7] = {2, 8}   CellNearEdge[1:2][7] = {5, 7}

⋮   ⋮   ⋮

NodeOfCell[1:3][1] = {2, 6, 3}   EdgeOfCell[1:3][1] = {-9, -2, 8}   CellNearCell[1:3][1] = {6, 0, 5}
NodeOfCell[1:3][2] = {1, 7, 2}   EdgeOfCell[1:3][2] = {-6, -1, 5}   CellNearCell[1:3][2] = {7, 0, 0}
NodeOfCell[1:3][3] = {3, 10, 4}   EdgeOfCell[1:3][3] = {-12, -3, 11} CellNearCell[1:3][3] = {9, 0, 8}
NodeOfCell[1:3][4] = {4, 11, 5}   EdgeOfCell[1:3][4] = {-14, -4, 13} CellNearCell[1:3][4] = {0, 0, 9}
NodeOfCell[1:3][5] = {2, 8, 6}   EdgeOfCell[1:3][5] = {-15, -8, 7} CellNearCell[1:3][5] = {10, 1, 7}
NodeOfCell[1:3][6] = {3, 6, 9}   EdgeOfCell[1:3][6] = {16, -10, 9} CellNearCell[1:3][6] = {10, 8, 1}
NodeOfCell[1:3][7] = {2, 7, 8}   EdgeOfCell[1:3][7] = {17, -7, 6}   CellNearCell[1:3][7] = {11, 5, 2}

⋮   ⋮   ⋮

(d) Data structures

Figure 8.5 Data structures and numbering of data elements for the unstructured mesh of a blunt-body example used in the Euler solver.

by a Do-all loop. State variables of cells will be updated based on the state variables of their nodes, edges, and adjacent cells. The updates based on the nodes and edges can be implemented by two Do-all loops. The updates based on adjacent cells need to solve a sparse linear system.

In the program, line 1 defines state variables on nodes, edges, and cells; lines 2 through 4 define data structures of the unstructured mesh and mapping arrays of irregular data distributions for nodes, edges, and cells; lines 5 through 13 define data alignment and data distribution using programming language directives. Lines 14 through 57 form the main iterative loop, wherein lines 15 through 20 form a Do-loop that updates nodeQg, the node state variables, based on the values of the surrounding cells' states. The partitioning of computational work is specified in lines

```
       {* A Euler flow solver based on Frink's scheme.    nodeQg(), edgeFlx(), and
          cellQs() are state variables representing density, velocity, and energy. *}
 1     real*8 nodeQg(MaxNode), edgeFlx(MaxEdge), cellQs(MaxCell)
 2     integer nodemap(MaxNode), CellNearNode(9, MaxNode), NodeOfCell(3, MaxCell)
 3     integer edgemap(MaxEdge), NodeOfEdge(2, MaxEdge), CellNearEdge(2, MaxEdge)
 4     integer cellmap(MaxCell), EdgeOfCell(3, MaxEdge), CellNearCell(3, MaxCell)
 5     TEMPLATE nodereg(MaxNode), edgereg(MaxEdge), cellreg(MaxCell)
 6     TEMPLATE nodeirreg(MaxNode), edgeirreg(MaxEdge), cellirreg(MaxCell)
 7     ALIGN nodemap WITH nodereg, edgemap WITH edgereg, cellmap WITH cellreg
 8     ALIGN nodeQg WITH nodemap, edgeFlx WITH edgemap, cellQs WITH cellmap
 9     ALIGN CellNearNode(j, i) WITH nodemap(i)
10     ALIGN NodeOfEdge(j, i), CellNearEdge(j, i) WITH edgemap(i)
11     ALIGN NodeOfCell(j, i), EdgeOfCell(j, i), CellNearCell(j, i) WITH cellmap(i)
12     DISTRIBUTE nodereg(BLOCK), edgereg(BLOCK), cellreg(BLOCK)
13     DISTRIBUTE nodeirreg(nodemap), edgeirreg(edgemap), cellirreg(cellmap)
       {* Preprocessing step: set initial values. *}
       ......................
14     do iter = 1, iterations
       {* Step 1: update node state variables based on surrounding cells' state values. *}
15       do iNode = 1, nNode on nodeirreg
16         nodeQg(iNode) = 0.0
17         do i = 1, nCellNearNode(iNode)
18           iCell = CellNearNode(i, iNode)
19           nodeQg(iNode) = nodeQg(iNode) + cellQs(iCell)
             ......................
20       enddo  enddo
       {* Step 2: update edge state variables based on adjacent cells' state values. *}
21       do iEdge = 1, nEdge on edgeirreg
22         iCell = CellNearEdge(1, iEdge)
23         if (iCell .NE. OUTSIDE_DOMAIN) then
24           QL = cellQs(iCell)
25         else QL = boundary_function(iEdge)
26         endif
27         iCell = CellNearEdge(2, iEdge)
28         if (iCell .NE. OUTSIDE_DOMAIN) then
29           QR = cellQs(iCell)
30         else QR = boundary_function(iEdge)
31         endif
32         edgeFlx(iEdge) = function1(QL, QR)
33       enddo


       {* Step 3: update cell state variables based on nodes', edges' and cells' state values. *}
34       do iCell = 1, nCell on cellirreg
35         Qx = 0.0
36         do i = 1, 3
37           iNode = NodeOfCell(i, iCell)
38           Qx = Qx + nodeQg(iNode)
39         enddo
40         Qj = a * cellQs(iCell)
41         do i = 1, 3
42           jCell = CellNearCell(i, iCell)
43           if (jCell .NE. OUTSIDE_DOMAIN) then              (continued)
```

Figure 8.6   Euler flow solver based on Frink's scheme.

```
44                    Qj = Qj + b * cellQs(jCell)
45                endif
46              enddo
47              cellQs(iCell) = function2(Qx, Qj)
48          enddo
49          do iCell = 1, nCell on cellirreg
50              RHS(iCell) = 0.0
51              do i = 1, 3
52                  iEdge = abs(EdgeOfCell(i, iCell))
53                  dtemp = (double)sign(EdgeOfCell(i, iCell))
54                  RHS(iCell) = RHS(iCell) - dtemp * edgeFlx(iEdge)
55              enddo  enddo
              ..................
56          solve a sparse linear system with respect to adjacent cells' state variables
57      enddo
```

Figure 8.6   *continued.*

15, 21, 34, and 49 using an *on* clause, where in each Do-loop a distributed array is used to specify the loop iterations to be carried out on each PE. The on clause "on nodeirreg" in line 15 specifies that the loop iterations are distributed in the same way as nodeQg (because nodeQg is aligned with nodemap in line 8 and nodeirreg is distributed according to nodemap in line 13). Therefore, each reference to nodeQg(iNode) within the Do-loop from lines 15 through 20 is local. The computation decomposition of this Do-loop can be treated based on the owner computes rule with respect to nodeQg. The reference to cellQs(iCell) in line 19 may require off-processor data access.

Lines 21 through 33 form a Do-loop which updates edgeFlx, the edge state variables, based on the values of adjacent cells' states. Similarly, the loop iterations are distributed in the same way as edgeFlx, that is, the computation decomposition of this Do-loop can be treated based on the owner computes rule with respect to edgeFlx. The reference to cellQs(iCell) may require off-processor data access. Lines 34 through 48 and 49 through 55 form two Do-loops that sweep over the cells in the unstructured mesh and update the physical states of the cells, based on the values on their nodes, edges, and adjacent cells. The on clause "on cellirreg" specifies that the distribution of the loop iterations are identical to that of cellQs, that is, the computation decomposition of these two Do-loop can be treated based on the owner computes rule with respect to cellQs. The references to node-Qg(iNode), edgeFlx(iEdge), and cellQs(jCell) may require off-processor data access. Line 56 calls up a library routine to solve a sparse linear system based on the state variables of cells and their adjacent cells.

The physical states of the nodes, edges and cells are stored in data arrays node-Qg, edgeFlx and cellQs, respectively. The arrays nodemap, edgemap, and cellmap specify the mapping of these data arrays. It is assumed that the arrays nodeirreg, edgeirreg, and cellirreg are passed to the Euler solver kernel after being generated by a data partitioner in a preprocessing step (which is not presented in Figure 8.6) between lines 13 and 14. In this presentation, the mesh is partitioned using a recursive coordinate bisection (RCB) method. Figures 8.7(a) and (b) show the mesh partitioned into two partitions and four partitions, respectively.

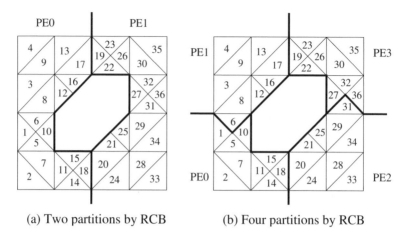

(a) Two partitions by RCB   (b) Four partitions by RCB

Figure 8.7 Data partitioning for the blunt-body example based on the recursive coordinate bisection method.

Each partition is assigned to a PE, where the nodes and the edges at the partitioning boundary are assigned to the PE (partition) with a smaller PE (partition) id.

The compiler uses the information in `nodeirreg`, `edgeirreg`, and `cellirreg` to generate code to set up the distributed translation tables. These distributed translation tables are used to describe the mapping of the data distributions of `nodeQg`, `edgeFlx`, `cellQs`, `CellNearNode`, `NodeOfEdge`, `CellNearEdge`, `NodeOfCell`, `EdgeOfCell`, and `CellNearCell`. For each (global) index, both the PE and the local index are stored explicitly in the distributed translation table as `global(PA, LA)`. Table 8.3 shows the three distributed translation tables for the blunt-body example on four PEs. For example, cellmap(27) is distributed to (and thus stored in) PE_3 which records that cell 27 is stored at the local cell 5 in PE_4, represented by 27(4, 5).

We now describe the inspector and the executor for the Euler solver. For simplicity of presentation, we focus on the Step-3 loops from lines 34 through 55 that update the states of the cells. The references `nodeQg(iNode)` in line 38, `cellQs(jCell)` in line 44, and `edgeFlx(iEdge)` in line 54 may require off-processor references. The compiler generates an inspector to produce a schedule and a hash table to handle access to the distributed arrays `nodeQg`, `cellQs` and `edgeFlx`. The compiler generates an inspector and an executor to run on each PE. The code executed on each PE to generate the inspector is shown in Figure 8.8.

Statements S1, S2, and S3 show the generation of the translation tables using `nodeirreg`, `edgeirreg`, and `cellirreg` arrays. Translation tables for the blunt-body example can be seen in Table 8.3. Statements S4, S5, and S6 show the dereference calls that compute the addresses of various data elements. Statements S7 through S12 in the inspector code generate the hash tables and data communication schedules. Array pairs (NPA and NLA, EPA and ELA, and CPA and CLA) store

Table 8.3   Distributed translation tables for the blunt-body example on four PEs

map	PE$_1$ global (PA, LA)	PE$_2$ global (PA, LA)	PE$_3$ global (PA, LA)	PE$_4$ global (PA, LA)
cellmap	1 (1,1)	10 (1,5)	19 (4,1)	28 (3,5)
	2 (1,2)	11 (1,6)	20 (3,1)	29 (3,6)
	3 (2,1)	12 (2,6)	21 (3,2)	30 (4,6)
	4 (2,2)	13 (2,7)	22 (4,2)	31 (3,7)
	5 (1,3)	14 (1,7)	23 (4,3)	32 (4,7)
	6 (2,3)	15 (1,8)	24 (3,3)	33 (3,8)
	7 (1,4)	16 (2,8)	25 (3,4)	34 (3,9)
	8 (2,4)	17 (2,9)	26 (4,4)	35 (4,8)
	9 (2,5)	18 (1,9)	27 (4,5)	36 (4,9)
nodemap	1 (1,1)	9 (1,7)	17 (2,7)	24 (4,3)
	2 (1,2)	10 (2,3)	18 (3,1)	25 (3,5)
	3 (1,3)	11 (2,4)	19 (4,1)	26 (3,6)
	4 (2,1)	12 (1,8)	20 (3,2)	27 (3,7)
	5 (2,2)	13 (2,5)	21 (3,3)	28 (3,8)
	6 (1,4)	14 (1,9)	22 (3,4)	29 (4,4)
	7 (1,5)	15 (1,10)	23 (4,2)	30 (4,5)
	8 (1,6)	16 (2,6)		
edgemap	1 (1,1)	18 (1,11)	35 (3,1)	51 (3,9)
	2 (1,2)	19 (2,8)	36 (3,2)	52 (3,10)
	3 (2,1)	20 (2,9)	37 (3,3)	53 (3,11)
	4 (2,2)	21 (1,12)	38 (3,4)	54 (3,12)
	5 (1,3)	22 (1,13)	39 (4,1)	55 (3,13)
	6 (1,4)	23 (1,14)	40 (4,2)	56 (3,14)
	7 (1,5)	24 (1,15)	41 (4,3)	57 (4,9)
	8 (1,6)	25 (2,10)	42 (4,4)	58 (4,10)
	9 (1,7)	25 (2,11)	43 (3,5)	59 (4,11)
	10 (2,3)	27 (2,12)	44 (3,6)	60 (4,12)
	11 (2,4)	28 (2,13)	45 (4,5)	61 (3,15)
	12 (2,5)	29 (2,14)	46 (4,6)	62 (4,13)
	13 (2,6)	30 (1,16)	47 (3,7)	63 (3,16)
	14 (2,7)	31 (1,17)	48 (3,8)	64 (3,17)
	15 (1,8)	32 (2,15)	49 (4,7)	65 (4,14)
	16 (1,9)	33 (1,18)	50 (4,8)	66 (4,15)
	17 (1,10)	34 (2,16)		

the PEs and local indices of off-processor array access to `nodeQg`, `edgeFlx`, and `cellQs`, respectively.

The executor generated by the compiler is depicted in Figure 8.9. Off-processor elements of `nodeQg`, `edgeFlx`, and `cellQs` are gathered and stored in hash tables HN, NE, and HC, respectively. Values for `nodeQg`, `edgeFlx`, and `cellQs` are obtained either from hash tables HN, HE, and HC, respectively, or from local memory. The global index "jCell" in line 19 has to be computed for testing and to

```
S1   TN = build_translation_table(nodeirreg)
S2   TE = build_translation_table(edgeirreg)
S3   TC = build_translation_table(cellirreg)
S4   call dereference(NPA,NLA, TN, NodeOfCell)
S5   call dereference(EPA,ELA, TE, EdgeOfCell)
S6   call dereference(CPA,CLA, TC, CellNearCell)

S7   HN = setup_hashed_cache(NPA,NLA)
S8   HE = setup_hashed_cache(EPA,ELA)
S9   HC = setup_hashed_cache(CPA,CLA)
S10  SN = scheduler(HN,NPA,NLA)
S11  SE = scheduler(HE,EPA,ELA)
S12  SC = scheduler(HC,CPA,CLA)
```

Figure 8.8   Inspector for the Step-3 loops in the Euler flow solver.

determine whether it is in the computing domain in line 20. The global indices "iNode" in line 9 and "iEdge" in line 34 are not generated if they are not used in the program.

Since the development of ARF, a significant amount of work has been done in standardizing extensions to the Fortran language. The High Performance Fortran Forum (HPFF), a joint effort between the academic community and industry, has agreed on a set of language extensions called HPF [5]. It has been heavily influenced by experimental languages such as Fortran D [31, 102], Vienna Fortran [17], Crystal [77], Kali [63], and DINO [95]. The HPFF decided to defer consideration of language extensions targeting irregular problems.

8.4.3   Language Interfaces for Data Partitioners

The difficulty with the data distribution specification depicted in Figure 8.4 is that the map array that gives the distribution pattern of irreg has to be generated separately by running a partitioner. Although there is a wealth of partitioning methods available, coding such methods from scratch can represent a significant effort. A better solution is to provide suitable language interfaces for the user to couple existing data partitioners (for generating the map array) to the compiler. The Fortran-90D/Chaos compilation system [90] was one of the first methods to provide such language interfaces.

Fortran 90D links partitioners to programs by using a data structure that stores information on which data partitioning is to be based. Data partitioners can make use of different kinds of program information. Graph-based partitioners operate on data structures that represent undirected graphs. In spatial-location-based partitioners, each graph vertex is assigned a set of coordinates that describe its spatial location. Vertices may also be assigned weights to represent estimated computational costs. In some cases, vertex weights can be used as the sole partitioning criterion in problems in which computational costs dominate. A partitioner can make use of a combination of connectivity, geometrical, and weight information. A data structure,

```
1    call gather_exchange(SN, HN, nodeQg)
2    call gather_exchange(SE, HE, edgeFlx)
3    call gather_exchange(SC, HC, cellQs)

4    do iter = 1, iterations
5        ncount = 1, ecount = 1, ccount = 1
     {* Step 1 and Step 2 are not presented here, only Step 3 is presented here. *}

     {* For all cells assigned to processor p. *}
6        do iCell = 1, nCell(p)
7            Qx = 0.0
8            do i = 1, 3
9    {*         iNode = NodeOfCell(i, iCell)  *}
10               if (NPA(ncount) .EQ. p) then
11                   vx = nodeQg(NLA(ncount))
12               else  use NPA(ncount), NLA(ncount) to get vx from the hash table HN
13               endif
14               Qx = Qx + vx
15               ncount = ncount + 1
16           enddo

17           Qj = a * cellQs(iCell)
18           do i = 1, 3
19               jCell = CellNearCell(i, iCell)
20               if (jCell .NE. OUTSIDE_DOMAIN) then
21                   if (CPA(ccount) .EQ. p) then
22                       vx = cellQs(CLA(ccount))
23                   else  use CPA(ccount), CLA(ccount) to get vx from the hash table HC
24                   endif
25                   Qj = Qj + b * vx
26               endif
27               ccount = ccount + 1
28           enddo
29           cellQs(iCell) = function2(Qx, Qj)
30       enddo

31       do iCell = 1, nCell(i)
32           RHS(iCell) = 0.0
33           do i = 1, 3
34   {*          iEdge = abs(EdgeOfCell(i, iCell)  *}
35               dtemp = (double)sign(EdgeOfCell(i, iCell))
36               if (EPA(ecount) .EQ. p) then
37                   vx = edgeFlx(ELA(ecount))
38               else  use EPA(ecount), ELA(ecount) to get vx from the hash table HE
39               endif
40               RHS(iCell) = RHS(iCell) - dtemp * vx
41               ecount = ecount + 1
42       enddo  enddo
         .....................
43       solve a sparse linear system with respect to adjacent cells' state variables
44   enddo
```

Figure 8.9   Executor for the Do-loops of Step 3 in the Euler flow solver.

called `GeoCol`, is used to record this information. It consists of a set of vertices, a set of undirected edges, a set of vertex weights, edge weights, and a set of coordinates information for each vertex. The user can use: (a) the directive CONSTRUCT to direct the compiler to generate a GeoCol data structure; (b) the keyword GEOM-ETRY to specify spatial information; (c) the keyword LOAD to specify vertex weights; and (d) the keyword LINK to specify the edges associated with the Geo-Col graph. We extend the `GeoCol` concept by adding a keyword CELL to specify the cells formed by the vertices in the GeoCol graph. The concept of cells is important for unstructured mesh computations with finite-volume methods.

The following code segment calls up a data partitioner and generates data distribution:

```
S1 DISTRIBUTE reg(block)
S2 CONSTRUCT G(GEOMETRY(nNodes,xcord,ycord),
              CELL(nCells,cnode1,cnode2,cnode3))
S3 SET dist BY PARTITIONING G USING RCB
S4 REDISTRIBUTE reg(dist)
```

In statement S1, template `reg` is originally partitioned into blocks. Statement S2 defines a GeoCol data structure called G having nNodes vertices with coordinates specified by two arrays xcord and ycord, and nCells cells specified by three arrays cnode1, cnode2, and cnode3 for the three boundary vertices for all cells. Each pair of vertices also forms the boundary edges of the cells. Statement S3 chooses the recursive coordinate bisection (RCB) method for partitioning. At compiling time, the compiler generates calls to the run-time support that, when the program executes, generates the GeoCol data structure and passes it to the RCB partitioner. The partitioner partitions the GeoCol graph into N subgraphs, where N is the number of PEs, and passes the new distribution information to a run-time procedure to redistribute data.

8.5 LIBRARY SUPPORT FOR IRREGULAR APPLICATIONS

The use of library routines can improve the efficiency and shorten the development life cycle of parallel programs. In this section, we present three library routines used in our sample unstructured mesh application for computing a Euler flow solver. They perform data partitioning, data reordering, and sparse linear system solving.

8.5.1 Data Partitioning and Reordering

In Figure 8.7 in Section 8.4.2, we adopt a RCB method for data partitioning. It works as follows. In the first step, 36 cells are decomposed into two parts based on the x-coordinates of their gravity centers (x_i, y_i), so that each part has 18 cells, as shown in Figure 8.7(a). In the second step, each part is decomposed into two partitions based on the y-coordinates of their gravity centers, so that each partition finally has 9 cells, as shown in Figure 8.7(b). We then apply a "bucket sort" to reorder the cells in each partition, as shown in Figure 8.10(c). Similarly, nodes and edges are reordered by bucket sorts, as shown in Figures 8.10(a) and (b).

The purpose of using the RCB method and the bucket sort is to give a simple presentation of data partitioning and data reordering. In effect, when a minimum number of cut edges between adjacent partitions is required, partitioning unstructured meshes can be treated as a graph-based partitioning problem, which has been shown to be NP-complete [32]. Hence, optimal solutions are computationally intractable for large problems. However, several heuristic methods have been proposed, such as recursive coordinate bisection [30, 41], geometric bisection [84], recursive spectral bisection [91], multilevel recursive spectral bisection [11], recursive Kernighan-Lin min-cut bipartitioning [29, 106], multilevel k-way partitioning [56, 57], multilevel quadtree-based partitioning [75], and other techniques

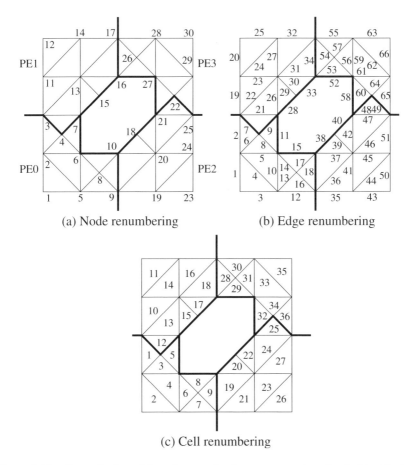

(a) Node renumbering   (b) Edge renumbering

(c) Cell renumbering

Figure 8.10.   Renumbering of data elements for the unstructured mesh of a blunt-body example used in the Euler solver.

[85, 99]. In addition, load balancing and repartitioning of adaptive meshes have been studied [25, 27, 86, 86, 98, 101], and quality measurements for graph partitioning have been reported [87]. Complete surveys of partitioning irregular graphs can be found in [43, 55].

Data-reordering methods have different considerations. The wavefront method (mentioned in Section 8.4.2) can improve convergence of the target partial differential equation solver. This is probably because elements (nodes, edges, or cells) in the mesh are iterated along a particular direction, for example, from west to east or from south to north, according to the elements' coordinates.

Cuthill and McKee suggested another renumbering method based on a breadth-first search on a graph [26]. Starting from a vertex of minimal degree, they applied a breadth-first search level by level, where vertices with a small degree (of adjacent edges) within each level were numbered first, followed by vertices with a large degree (of adjacent edges). Cuthill and McKee's sequence is well known for reducing the bandwidth of a sparse matrix. Liu and Sherman further pointed out that the reverse Cuthill–McKee sequence, in which level construction was restarted from a vertex of minimal degree in the final level, was always at least as good as its corresponding Cuthill–McKee sequence in terms of minimizing the bandwidth of a sparse matrix [81].

Heber, Biswas, and Gao introduced self-avoiding walks (SAWs) for renumbering unstructured meshes and improving data locality for accessing neighboring data [42]. As two consecutive triangles in a SAW sequence shared an edge or a vertex, SAWs were also used to partition data for sparse matrix applications over unstructured meshes on parallel computers. The effectiveness of any ordering is dependent upon its applications [76].

8.5.2   Solving Sparse Linear Systems

A system of linear equations can be modeled in matrix form as $Ax = b$, where A is an $m \times m$ matrix and x and b are both vectors of length m. Given the coefficient matrix A and the scalar vector b, the problem is to find values for the vector x such that the given system of linear equations can be satisfied. A matrix is sparse if there are relatively few nonzero elements in the matrix, and a linear system is called sparse if the original coefficient matrix is sparse. Two approaches are used to solve linear systems. The direct methods compute $x = A^{-1}b$, where A is nonsingular by directly using methods such as LU factorization, Gaussian elimination with partial pivoting, and Cholesky factorization [12, 28, 88]. However, there are several disadvantages of using direct methods to solve large-size sparse linear systems. The time complexity of computing the inverse of the coefficient matrix A can be upwards of $O(m^3)$; the nonzero fill-in caused by the factorization may break the sparsity of the original coefficient matrix, which will result in the need for more memory than can be afforded.

The iterative methods that use successive approximations to obtain more accurate solutions at each step are quite attractive, especially in saving memory space [12, 44, 96]. In many situations when the coefficient matrix satisfies positive definite or diagonal dominant conditions, the solution converges very quickly. A matrix A is called positive definite if it satisfies $x^\mathsf{T}Ax > 0$ for all vectors x, where x^T is the transposition of x. A matrix A is called diagonal dominant if it satisfies both $\mathrm{abs}(A_{ii}) > \Sigma_{j\neq i}\,\mathrm{abs}(A_{ij})$ and $\mathrm{abs}(A_{ii}) > \Sigma_{j\neq i}\,\mathrm{abs}(A_{ji})$ for $1 \leq i, j \leq m$, where m is the problem size. Unfortunately, no single iterative method is robust enough to solve all sparse linear systems accurately and efficiently. Generally, an iterative method is suitable only for a specific class of problem, since the rate of convergence depends heavily on special properties of the matrix.

Solving sparse linear systems plays an important role in scientific and engineering computation. For example, in the Euler program in Figure 8.6 in Section 8.4.2, line 56 calls up a library routine to solve a sparse linear system. However, because "compressed" data structures are used to store sparse matrices, compilers cannot determine effective data alignment among data arrays. In this section, we describe how to use compiler techniques to design efficient parallel implementations for sparse linear systems, and take the Jacobi iterative method as our example [33].

The Jacobi method is the simplest stationary iterative method, which performs, in each iteration, the same operations on the current iteration vectors. It is derived from examining each of the equations in the linear system in isolation. If we solve the ith equation, while assuming other entries of x remain unchanged, this suggests an iterative method defined by

$$x_i^{(k)} = \left(b_i - \sum_{j\neq i} A_{ij}\, x_j^{(k-1)} \right) \Big/ A_{ii}, \qquad \text{for } 1 \leq i, j \leq m$$

where $x_i^{(k)}$ will become $x_i^{(k'-1)}$ in the $(k' = k + 1)$-th iteration.

Figure 8.11 shows the component affinity graph of the Jacobi iterative method, where A1 and A2 represent the first and the second dimensions of the matrix A, respectively. Applying the component alignment algorithm mentioned in Section 8.2.1, $x^{(k)}$, A1, and b are aligned together; and $x^{(k-1)}$ and A2 are aligned together. Suppose that the target machine is a linear processor array. If matrix A is distributed along its first dimension among PEs, $x_i^{(k)}$ can be computed independently after we prefetch off-processor $x_j^{(k-1)}$. If matrix A is distributed along its second dimension among PEs, $x_i^{(k)}$ cannot be computed independently, as it has to perform a (relatively expensive) reduction operation among PEs. Therefore, matrix A is determined to

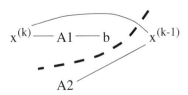

Figure 8.11   Component affinity graph representing alignment relations among dimensions of arrays $x^{(k)}$, $x^{(k-1)}$, and b, and dimensions of the matrix A.

be distributed along its first dimension among PEs in order to reduce communication overhead. We adopt a compressed row storage (CRS) format to store the sparse matrix A. (If matrix A is distributed along its second dimension among PEs, we will adopt a compressed column storage format to store the sparse matrix A.)

Figure 8.12 shows the CRS representation for a blunt-body example shown in Figure 8.10(c). Let w be the number of non-zero elements in the $m \times m$ coefficient

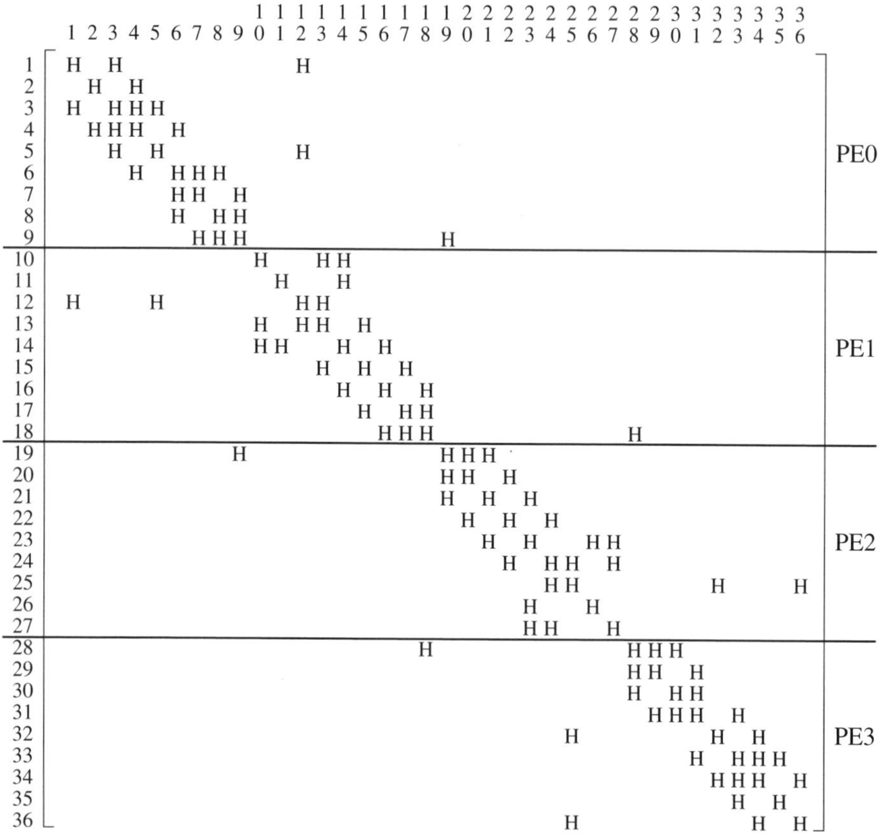

(a) The coefficient matrix

```
array
index 1  2  3   4  5  6  7  8  9  10  11 12 13 14 15 16  17 18 19 20 21 22 23 24 25 26 27 28 29 30

RO    1  4  6   10 14 17 21 24 27 31

CO    1  3  12  2  4  1  3  4  5  2   3  4  6  3  5  12  4  6  7  8  6  7  9  6  8  9  7  8  9  19

DA    H H H  H  H  H  H  H  H  H  H   H H H H H H  H H H H H H H H H H H H H H
```

(b) The CRS representation in PE0

Figure 8.12   The sparse matrix of a blunt-body example shown in Figure 8.10(c) and its CRS representation in PE_0. A nonzero element is represented by an "H."

matrix A. The CRS format is composed of the following three arrays: DA($1:w$), CO($1:w$), and RO($1:m+1$). The data array DA stores the nonzero values of the coefficient matrix A in a row-wise fashion. The column array CO stores the column indices of the corresponding nonzero elements in the sparse matrix. Finally, the row array RO stores the indices for the data arrays DA and CO that correspond to the first nonzero element of each row if such an element exits. Precisely, the jth nonzero element in the ith row of the matrix, located at the CO(RO(i) + j – 1)-th column of the matrix, is stored in DA(RO(i) + j – 1). The storage savings achieved by this approach are usually significant. Instead of requiring $m \times m$ storage locations, we only need $2w + m + 1$ storage locations.

Figure 8.13 shows a sequential version program for the Jacobi iterative method, whereas Figure 8.14 shows an SPMD version program for comparison. In the sequential version program, array y represents $x^{(k)}$, and array x represents $x^{(k-1)}$. In line 13, compilers cannot determine how to align array y with arrays x, DA, and CO. This points out that using current compiler techniques is not sufficient to decompose compressed data structures automatically. However, programmers can use compiler techniques to help them analyze data alignment and data distribution from a "dense" version program. In the SPMD version program, some global data gx(CO(j)) required in the computation phase are not in the local memory. Therefore, we have to prefetch these off-processor data before the computation phase. After that, the computation phase can be performed independently for each Do-i loop.

For a "dense" version program, it is appropriate to use a many-to-many-multicast communication primitive to replicate local array "y" to every other PE so as to get the global array "gx." However, for a "sparse" version program, we only

```
1     real*8  x(m), y(m), b(m), DA(MaxNonzero)
2     integer RO(m+1), CO(MaxNonzero)
3     {*  Fill initial values of y(1 : m) . *}
4     do  k = 1, iterations
5         do  i = 1, m  {* Copy phase. *}
6             x(i) = y(i)
7         enddo

8         do  i = 1, m  {* Computation phase. *}
9             y(i) = 0.0
10            do  j = RO(i), RO(i+1) - 1
11                if  (CO(j) .EQ. i) then
12                    aii = DA(j)
13                else  y(i) = y(i) + DA(j) * x(CO(j))
14                endif
15            enddo
16            y(i) = (b(i) - y(i)) / aii
17        enddo

18        if  (convergence criteria fulfilled) then
19            stop
20        endif
21    enddo
```

Figure 8.13   A sequential version Jacobi iterative method for sparse linear systems.

```
1     real*8  y(PE_MaxRow), b(PE_MaxRow)
2     real*8  gx(m), DA(PE_MaxNonzero)
3     integer RO(PE_MaxRow+1), CO(PE_MaxNonzero)
4     {*  The inspector loop. *}
5     count = 1
6     do  i = 1, MyRowNum
7        do  j = RO(i), RO(i+1) - 1
8           use a local table which records the number of
            rows assigned to each PE to decide the
            processor-local index pair for index CO(j)

9              count = count + 1
10    enddo  enddo
11    HV = setup_hashed_cache(PA, LA)
12    SV = scheduler(HV, PA, LA)

13    RowOffset = the number of rows in preceding PEs
14    {*  Fill initial values of y(1 : MyRowNum) . *}
15    do  k = 1, iterations

16       call gather_exchange(HV, SV, y)
17       extract data from HV and store them into array 'gx'

18       do  i = 1, MyRowNum  {* Computation phase. *}
19          y(i) = 0.0
20          do  j = RO(i), RO(i+1) - 1
21             if  (CO(j) .EQ.  i + RowOffset) then
22                aii = DA(j)
23             else  y(i) = y(i) + DA(j) * gx(CO(j))
24             endif
25          enddo
26          y(i) = (b(i) - y(i)) / aii
27       enddo

28       if  (convergence criteria fulfilled) then
29          stop
30       endif
31    enddo
```

Figure 8.14   An SPMD version Jacobi iterative method for sparse linear systems.

need those necessary elements, instead of the whole array. For example, in Figure 8.12(a), PE_0 only needs to fetch one off-processor datum from PE_1 and this datum will be stored in gx(12); PE_0 only needs to send two data, $y(1)$ and $y(5)$, to PE_1. Therefore, many-to-many-multicast communication overworks, which results in copying unnecessary data, wasting I/O bandwidth, and lengthening execution time.

In our implementation, before the main iterative loop, in lines 4 through 12, we adopt PARTI routines to implement an inspector loop. According to a local table that records the number of rows assigned to each PE, we can find the processor-local index pair for the index CO(j). Meanwhile, within the main iterative loop but before the computation phase, in lines 16 and 17, we use PARTI routines to fetch off-processor data and store them into a global array "gx."

To implement an efficient parallel algorithm for the solution of sparse linear systems from scratch is usually difficult work. Fortunately, with the aid of compiler techniques, it is much easier now, as demonstrated above. In addition, there are many numerical and communication libraries that can help programmers implement an efficient parallel version of numerical algorithms. For example, the BLAS (Basic Linear Algebra Subprograms) [2] library provides high-quality "building block" routines for performing basic vector and matrix operations, such as inner product and matrix–vector product. On top of BLAS, a parallel version of BLAS called PBLAS [3] is developed to perform basic vector and matrix operations on parallel machines. There is another project called BLACS (Basic Linear Algebra Communication Subprograms) [1], whose purpose is to create a linear-algebra-oriented message-passing interface that may be implemented efficiently and uniformly across a wide range of distributed-memory platforms. With PBLAS and BLACS as building blocks, a collaborative project called ScaLAPACK contains routines for solving systems of linear equations, least-squares problems, and eigenvalue problems on distributed-memory message-passing MIMD computers and networks of workstations. The reader is referred to [4] for more details.

8.6 RELATED WORKS

The challenge in compiling programs for DMPCs is to determine data and computation decompositions so that load balance and low communication overhead can be achieved. In effect, communication overhead is dependent on data distribution. However, there is a cyclical dependence while formulating cost models for data distribution and communication. A data-distribution scheme must be given before analyzing communication cost, but the determination of whether a data-distribution scheme is good or not really depends on which communication primitives are involved. Li and Chen proved that the problem of determining an optimal static alignment between the dimensions of distinct arrays is NP-complete [80]. Mace showed that a class of dynamic-data layout problems for interleaved memory machines are NP-complete [82]. Anderson and Lam presented another formulation of the dynamic-data layout problem that is NP-hard [7]. Kremer also identified that the problem of dynamic data remapping (the interphase data-layout problem) is NP-complete [64]. Therefore, early parallelizing compiler research emphasized allowing programmers to specify the data distribution using language extensions, such that compilers could then generate all the communication instructions according to these language extensions [14, 83, 119]. Callahan and Kennedy showed that message-passing programs on distributed-memory systems could be derived from sequential shared-memory programs, along with directions on how elements of shared arrays were distributed to processors [14]. Hiranandani, Kennedy, and Tseng developed an enhanced version of Fortran called Fortran D, which allowed programmers to specify data decomposition [46]. Balasundaram, Fox, Kennedy, and Kremer designed an interactive environment for guiding data partition and distribution, and for estimating performance [9, 10].

Koelbel and Mehrotra proposed the global name space, in which the compiler permitted programmers to express their algorithms using the global name space and specify them at a high level [62]. In High Performance Fortran (HPF), programmers had the obligation to provide *TEMPLATE, ALIGN,* and *DISTRIBUTE* directives to specify data distribution [61]. Other similar works, which allowed programmers to explicitly specify the data decomposition by using language extensions and could generate all the communication instructions by compilers, included ASPAR [52], ParaScope [59], AL [103], SUPERB [119], and others.

For regular problems (in which data access and data dependencies can be determined at compiling time), there has been research on the use of compiler techniques to automatically determine sequential programs' data distribution on distributed-memory systems. Chen, Choo, and Li studied compiling a functional programming language—Crystal—on various distributed-memory systems, such as the iPSC, the nCUBE, and the Connection Machine [22]. They showed that it is possible to use compiler techniques to automatically transform shared-memory programs to message-passing programs on distributed-memory systems. Furthermore, they invented a component-alignment algorithm for data distribution [80], and derived an algorithm for matching syntactic reference patterns with appropriate aggregate communication primitives [79]. Gupta and Banerjee, on the other hand, have generalized the above compiler techniques for dealing with Fortran. They especially discussed the contiguous or cyclic data-partitioning method and emphasized finding optimal communication costs at compiling time [35, 36]. Su, Palermo, and Banerjee, in addition, developed a compiler, PARADIGM, for automating parallelization of regular computations on distributed-memory computers [100].

Chapman, Fahringer, Mehrotra, Moritsch, and Zima adopted Li and Chen's component alignment algorithm [80] for handling distributed data in Vienna Fortran [15]. In addition, they used language extension for handling dynamic data distribution [16]. Kennedy, Kremer, Meller-Crummey, and Carle proposed an automatic data-layout strategy that is implemented in their D programming tools. In their strategy, they first explored several possible data layouts for each program phase, and then defined the communication cost between candidate data layouts of adjacent phases. The problem of finding dynamic data layouts for the entire program is thus reduced to a single-source, shortest-paths problem [58, 66]. Very soon after that, using path-finding techniques to determine whether data redistributions were necessary or not became a trend [19, 20, 21, 40, 68, 89]. Among them, methods by Chatterjee et al., Gupta and Krishnamurthy, and Palermo adopted a top-down approach, while Lee adopted a bottom-up approach.

There are other works related to the compilation of programs for distributed-memory computers. Kremer developed techniques for using 0-1 integer programming for automatic data layout in the interphase data layout problem [65]. Kalns, Xu, and Ni suggested a cost model for determining a small set of appropriate data distribution patterns among many possible choices [54]. Hovland and Ni determined data distribution using augmented data-access descriptors [48]. Chen and Sheu [23], Huang and Sadayappan [49], Ramanujam and Sadayappan [92, 93], and Wolf and Lam [110, 111] determined computation decomposition and/or degree of parallelism based on the hyperplane method. Furthermore, Gong, Gupta, and Melhem [34], Hudak and Abraham [50], and Hou, Wang, Ku, and Hsu [47] developed compile-time techniques for optimizing communication overhead. Other papers, which addressed the problem of determining initial data distributions and/or distributions for temporaries, include [18, 21, 108].

In summary, there are two major methods for compiling regular problems. The first focuses on determining the computation decomposition for each Do-loop independently, using the hyperplane method and tiling techniques, and thus implicitly determines a corresponding data decomposition. This approach can utilize the most parallelism for each Do-loop. However, this may cause data arrays to be stored among PEs in a skewed manner, which violates data-layout standards in HPF, or different Do-loops to have different data distributions, which may incur a heavy data-redistribution cost.

The second method focuses on determining data distributions among PEs first, so that computation decompositions can be implemented based on the owner computes rule. For this class of methods, component alignment approaches are very promising for DMPCs, because dimensions on each data array can be distributed independently of each other, following the HPF standard.

There is a need to combine the above two methods. Our approach provides a framework for doing this. It includes an alignment phase and a distribution phase. The alignment phase identifies data realignment between program fragments and determines axis alignments for a program fragment, with consecutive Do-loops within the fragment sharing the same data-distribution scheme. Meanwhile the distribution phase determines data distributions for data spaces and computation decompositions for iteration spaces.

We use both temporal and spatial dependence vectors to determine which dimensions of a data array should be distributed. Temporal vectors come from data dependence/use relations in the iteration space of a single nested Do-loop. Therefore, they are useful for determining computation decomposition for that Do-loop. Spatial vectors come from data dependence/use relations in the data space of data arrays within a program fragment, which may include several nested Do-loops, so they are useful for determining data distribution for the whole program fragment.

In our method, we focus on determining data and computation decompositions simultaneously by identifying the correspondence between the distributed dimensions of a dominant data array and the distributed dimensions of the iteration space of a Do-loop. The latter can be represented by iteration-space-mapping vectors. The core idea is to analyze the communication overhead for each dimension of the dominant data array, if that dimension is distributed. We start by determining the axis alignments for a program fragment, with consecutive Do-loops within the fragment sharing the same data-distribution scheme. To decide on data decomposition, we rank the "importance" of all data arrays, and refer to some as dominant. Dominant arrays are those that we do not want to migrate during computation. We establish correspondence between the distributed dimensions of the dominant data array and the iteration-space-mapping vectors (which correspond to the distributed dimensions of the iteration space) in each nested Do-loop. A dimension of a dominant data array is distributed if the communication penalties of that dimension in the spatial vectors of the dominant data array are low, or if the corresponding space-mapping vector can cause more inner products to be zero with all temporal vectors in the most computationally intensive Do-loop.

The data distributions of other data arrays are determined based on the alignment relations with the dominant data array. Once data distributions are determined, based on either the owner computes rule or the owner stores rule with respect to the dominant data array, computation decomposition for each nested Do-loop is determined. If all temporal dependence relations across iteration partitions are regular, we can find tiling vectors and tile sizes, so that tiles satisfy the atomic computation constraint [74]. Hence, iterations can be executed with a coarse-grain pipeline, overlapping the computation and communication time.

For irregular or adaptive problems, several researchers have also developed programming environments. Williams and Glowinski [109] describe a programming environment (DIME) for calculations with unstructured triangular meshes. Baden [8] has developed a programming environment targeting particle computations. These programming environments, however, are highly customized for use in specific application areas.

The PARTI library [13] was the first general-purpose run-time support for irregular computation on distributed-memory architectures. It was designed for use by compilers to handle parallel loops with irregular array references, and can also be used by programmers in a wide range of applications. The PARTI run-time support provides primitives that support the inspector- and executor-type execution. The scheduler primitive, invoked during the inspector phase, determines the "send" and "receive" calls that are needed during the executor phase. The data-exchange primitives, invoked during the executor phase, are used to scatter data, gather data, or perform reduction operations over the distributed data. The CHAOS library [90] is an extended version of the PARTI library, enhanced with a new set of storage management functions.

Since the development of the PARTI run-time support, there have been a lot of research efforts in developing compilation techniques for computation with irregular data references. The Kali compiler [63] was the first compiler to incorporate PARTI-type run-time preprocessing, but it only allows uniformly distributed arrays. A Do-loop with irregular array references is transformed into a pair of inspector and executor [97].

The ARF/PARTI compilation system [113], which consists of two layers, was the first compiler to support irregularly distributed arrays. The bottom layer is the library of PARTI run-time procedures that are designed to provide the infrastructure needed to implement nonuniform data mapping efficiently and to coordinate interprocessor data movement. The top layer is a compiler that carries out program transformations by embedding calls in the PARTI primitives in the original program. A Do-loop with irregular array references is transformed into an inspector and executor pair.

Although the ARF compiler supports computation with irregularly distributed arrays, it does not support on-line partitioning of data arrays. The map array that gives the distribution results of the data arrays has to be generated separately by running a partitioner. It is desirable for a compiler to provide suitable language interfaces for the user to couple existing data partitioners to the compiler and allow the generated code to perform data partitioning at run time.

In this line of works, von Hanxleden [105] developed compiler-linked partitioners that decompose arrays based on distributed-array element values. These partitioners are called value-based decompositions. One example is decomposing based on the geometry values of the mesh nodes, that is, the coordinates of the vertices.

Fortran 90D [90] links partitioners to programs by using a data structure that stores information on which data partitioning is based. As data partitioners can make use of different kinds of program information, a data structure called GeoCol is used to record this information. The directive CONSTRUCT directs the compiler to generate a GeoCol data structure. At compiling time, the compiler generates calls to the run-time support that, when the program executes, generates the GeoCol data structure and passes it to the specified partitioner. The partitioner then partitions the GeoCol graph in N subgraphs, where N is the number of PEs, and passes the new distribution information to a run-time procedure to redistribute the data.

Vienna Fortran [116] also provides language constructs for the user to specify a customized data-distribution function. The Vienna Fortran compiler adopts the Fortran-90D/CHAOS compilation techniques to implement user-defined distribution. Vienna Fortran also proposes new language features that permit the user to characterize a matrix as "sparse" and specify the associated representation [104]. Together with data distribution of the matrix, this feature enables the compiler and run-time system to transform sequential sparse codes into parallel message-passing codes.

8.7 CONCLUDING REMARKS

In this chapter, we have presented compiler and run-time parallelization techniques for scientific computations on DMPCs. We studied three categories of programs that depend on information obtained at compiling time. First, when a program is regular and all necessary information is known at compiling time, we identify the correspondence between distributed dimensions of a data array and distributed dimensions of the iteration space of a Do-loop. In addition, we analyze the communication overhead of data alignments among different data arrays and data access due to the spatial data localities of each data array. These allow us to provide automatic compilation techniques to generate load-balanced data and computation decompositions, without using any programming language directives. Communication code can then be generated based on data distribution.

Second, for irregular programs in which data-reference patterns depend on run-time computed values or change during program execution, compile-time analysis for data alignments fails. When data-reference patterns are random (and thus do not follow any rule), no compiler can deliver load-balanced data and computation decompositions. In this case, programming-language directives are helpful for assigning data and/or computation decomposition. In addition, inspector and executor preprocessing is a useful run-time support technique to minimize the communication overhead.

Finally, for some irregular programs, such as unstructured mesh applications, data-reference patterns have geometrically spatial locality. When data-reference patterns have some rules, special-purpose data-partitioners can be used to achieve load-balanced data and computation decompositions, thereby minimizing communication overhead. In this case, a programming-language interface to support libraries is needed to help programmers improve the efficiency and shorten the development life cycle of parallel programs. We use a blunt-body example for the Euler flow solver to illustrate libraries for data partitioning, data reordering, and a sparse linear-system solver. We found that because "compressed" data structures are used to store sparse matrices, compilers cannot determine effective data alignment among data arrays. However, it is possible to use compiler techniques to design efficient parallel implementations for sparse linear systems.

It is instructive to compare computation decompositions and communication sets for these three categories. For the first and third categories, computation decomposition depends heavily on data distribution. For example, computation decomposition is based on the owner computes rule or the owner stores rule of some data array. Computation decomposition is load balanced, as compilers or data partitioners can generate load-balanced data distribution. However, for the second category, both data-distribution and data-access patterns may be unknown at compiling time, as shown in Figure 8.4. In this case, two methods can be used. First, we still adopt the owner computes rule or owner stores rule for assigning computations; for example, we use "on clause" directives, as shown in Figure 8.6. Although this may reduce a certain amount of communication overhead, the computation loads are not guaranteed to be balanced. In the second method, computations can be decomposed evenly among PEs. For example, the first iteration block is assigned to the first PE, the second iteration block is assigned to the second PE, and so on. Therefore, computation decomposition is load balanced. However, we may have to both fetch off-processor data using "gather" communication primitives and store off-processor data using "scatter" communication primitives. As shown in Tables 8.1 and 8.2, the overhead of these communication primitives is high.

The communication set for the first category can be represented by the union of closed forms [71], and an array can be used to store off-processor data. The communication set for the second category has a random pattern, so we can use a hash table to store off-processor data. Finally, in the third category, the communication set lies in the boundary between adjacent partitions, so we can use an overlap region to store off-processor data.

ACKNOWLEDGMENTS

This work was partially supported by the NSC under Grants NSC 92-2213-E-001-012 (Jan-Jan Wu), NSC 92-2213-E-001-013 (PeiZong Lee and Chien-Min Wang), and NSC 93-2213-E-001-007 (PeiZong Lee and Chien-Min Wang).

REFERENCES

1. Basic linear algebra communication subprograms, http://www.netlib.org/blacs/index. html.

2. Basic linear algebra subprograms, http://www.netlib.org/blas/faq.html.

3. Parallel basic linear algebra subprograms, http://www.netlib.org/scalapack/pblas_qref. html.

4. The scalapack project, http://www.netlib.org/scalapack/.

5. High performance Fortran language specification, *Scientific Programming, 2,* 1–170, 1993.

6. J. R. Allen and K. Kennedy, Automatic translation of Fortran programs to vector form, *ACM Transactions on Programming Languages and Systems, 9*(4), 491–542, Oct. 1987.

7. J. M. Anderson and M. S. Lam, Global optimizations for parallelism and locality on scalable parallel machines, in *Proceedings of ACM-SIGPLAN PLDI,* pp. 112–125, Albuquerque, N.M., June 1993.

8. S. Baden, Programming abstractions for dynamically partitioning and coordinating localized scientific calculations running on multiprocessors, *SIAM Journal of Scientific and Statistical Computation, 12,* 145–157, Jan. 1991.

9. V. Balasundaram, G. Fox, K. Kennedy, and U. Kremer, An interactive environment for data partition and distribution, in *Proceedings of Fifth Distributed Memory Comput. Conference,* pp. 1160–1170, Charleston, SC, Apr. 1990.

10. V. Balasundaram, G. Fox, K. Kennedy, and U. Kremer, A static performance estimator to guide data partitioning decisions, in *Proceedings ACM SIGPLAN Symposium on Principles and Practices of Parallel Programming,* pp. 213–223, Williamsburg, VA, Apr. 1991.

11. S. T. Barnard and H. D. Simon, Fast multilevel implementation of recursive spectral bisection for partitioning unstructured problems, *Concurrency and Computation: Practice and Experience, 6*(2), 101–117, Apr. 1994.

12. R. Barrett, M. Berry, T. Chan, J. Demmel, J. Donato, J. Dongarra, V. Eijkhout, V. Pozo, C. Romime, and H. van der Vorst, *Templates for the Solution of Linear Systems: Building Blocks for Iterative Methods*, SIAM Press, Philadelphia, PA, 1994.

13. H. Berryman, J. Saltz, and J. Scroggs, Execution time support for adaptive scientific algorithms on distributed memory architectures, *Concurrency and Computation: Practice and Experience, 3,* 159–178, 1991.

14. D. Callahan and K. Kennedy, Compiling programs for distributed-memory multiprocessors, *The Journal of Supercomputing, 2,* 151–169, 1988.

15. B. Chapman, T. Fahringer, and H. Zima, Automatic support for data distribution on distributed memory multiprocessor systems, in *Lecture Notes in Computer Science 768, Sixth International Workshop on Languages and Compilers for Parallel Computing,* pp. 184–199, Portland, Oregon, Aug. 1993.

16. B. Chapman, P. Mehrotra, H. Moritsch, and H. Zima, Dynamic data distributions in Vienna Fortran, in *Proceedings of Supercomputing '93,* pp. 284–293, Portland, Oregon, Nov. 1993.

17. B. Chapman, P. Mehrotra, and H. Zima, Programming in Vienna Fortran, *Scientific Programming, 1*(1), 31–50, 1992.

18. S. Chatterjee, J. R. Gilbert, and R. Schreiber, Mobile and replicated alignment of arrays in data-parallel programs, in *Proceedings of Supercomputing '93,* Nov. 1993.

19. S. Chatterjee, J. R. Gilbert, R. Schreiber, and T. J. Sheffler, Array distribution in data-parallel programs, in *Lecture Notes in Computer Science 892, Seventh International Workshop on Languages and Compilers for Parallel Computing,* pp. 76–91, 1994.

20. S. Chatterjee, J. R. Gilbert, R. Schreiber, and T. J. Sheffler, Modelling data-parallel programs with the alignment-distribution graph, *Journal of Programming Language, 2,* 227–258, 1994.

21. S. Chatterjee, J. R. Gilbert, R. Schreiber, and S. H. Teng, Automatic array alignment in data-parallel programs, in *Proceedings of ACM SIGACT/SIGPLAN Symposium on Principles of Programming Languages,* Charleston, SC, Jan. 1993.

22. M. Chen, Y. I. Choo, and J. Li, Compiling parallel programs by optimizing performance, *The Journal of Supercomputing, 2,* 171–207, 1988.

23. T. Chen and J. Sheu, Communication-free data allocation techniques for parallelizing compilers on multicomputers, *IEEE Transactions Parallel Distributed Systems, 5*(9), 924–938, Sept. 1994.

24. Y. S. Chen, S. D. Wang, and C. M. Wang, Tiling nested loops into maximal rectangluar blocks, *Journal of Parallel and Distributed Computing, 35*(2), 123–132, June 1996.

25. Y.-C. Chung, C.-J. Liao, and D.-L. Yang, A prefix code matching parallel load-balancing method for solution-adaptive unstructured finite element graphs on distributed memory multicomputers, *The Journal of Supercomputing, 15,* 25–49, 2000.

26. E. Cuthill and J. McKee, Reducing the bandwidth of sparse symmetric matrices, in *Proceedings 24th Nat. Conference of the ACM,* pp. 157–172, 1969.

27. R. Diekmann, R. Preis, F. Schlimbach, and C. Walshaw, Shape-optimized mesh partitioning and load balancing for parallel adaptive FEM, *Parallel Computing, 26*(12), 1555–1581, Dec. 2000.

28. J. Dongarra, I. S. Duff, D. C. Sorensen, and H. A. van der Vorst, *Solving Linear System on Vector and Shared Memory Computers,* SIAM Press, Philadelphia, PA, 1991.

29. F. Ercal, J. Ramanujan, and P. Sadayappan, Task allocation onto a hypercube by recursive mincut bipartitioning, *Journal of Parallel and Distributed Computing, 10*(1), 35–44, 1990.

30. C. Farhat and M. Lesoinne, Automatic partitioning of unstructured meshes for the parallel solution of problems in computational mechanics, *International Journal for Numerical Methods in Engineering, 36,* 745–764, 1993.

31. G. Fox, S. Hiranandani, K. Kennedy, C. Koelbel, U. Kremer, C. Tseng, and M. Wu, Fortran D language specification, Technical Report TR90-141, Dept. Computer Science, Rice University, Dec. 1990.

32. M. R. Garey and D. S. Johnson, *Computers and Intractability,* W. H. Freeman, San Francisco, 1979.

33. G. H. Golub and C. F. van Loan, *Matrix Computations,* The John Hopkins Press, Baltimore, MD, 2nd ed., 1989.

34. C. Gong, R. Gupta, and R. Melhem, Compilation techniques for optimizing communication on distributed-memory systems, in *Proceedings International Conference on Parallel Processing,* pp. II, 39–46, St. Charles, IL, Aug. 1993.

35. M. Gupta and P. Banerjee, Compile-time estimation of communication costs on multi-computers, in *Proceedings International Parallel Processing Symposium,* pp. 470–475, Beverly Hills, CA, Mar. 1992.

36. M. Gupta and P. Banerjee, Demonstration of automatic data partitioning techniques for parallelizing compilers on multicomputers, *IEEE Transactions Parallel Distributed Systems, 3*(2), 179–193, Mar. 1992.

37. M. Gupta and P. Banerjee, A methodology for high-level synthesis of communication on multicomputers, in *Proceedings of ACM International Conference on Supercomputing,* Washington DC, July 1992.

38. M. Gupta and P. Banerjee, Compile-time estimation of communication costs of programs, *Journal of Programming Language, 2,* 191–225, 1994.

39. S. K. S. Gupta, S. D. Kaushik, C. H. Huang, and P. Sadayappan, Compiling array expressions for efficient execution on distributed-memory machines, *Journal of Parallel and Distributed Computing, 32,* 155–172, 1996.

40. S. K. S. Gupta and S. Krishnamurthy, An interprocedural framework for determining efficient array data redistributions, *Journal of Information Science and Engineering, 14*(1), 27–51, Mar. 1998.

41. M. T. Heath and P. Raghavan, A Cartesian parallel nested dissection algorithm, *SIAM Journal of Matrix Analysis Applications, 16,* 235–253, 1995.

42. G. Heber, R. Biswas, and G. R. Gao, Self-avoiding walks over adaptive unstructured grids, *Concurrency and Computation: Practice and Experience, 12,* 85–109, 2000.

43. B. Hendrickson and T. G. Kolda, Graph partitioning models for parallel computing, *Parallel Computing, 26*(12), 1519–1534, Dec. 2000.

44. M. R. Hestenes and E. Stiefel, Methods of conjugate gradients for solving linear systems, *Journal of Research of National Bureau of Standards, 49,* 409–436, 1954.

45. S. Hiranandani, K. Kennedy, and C.-W. Tseng, Compiler optimizations for Fortran D on MIMD distributed-memory machines, in *Proceedings Supercomputing,* pp. 86–100, Nov 1991.

46. S. Hiranandani, K. Kennedy, and C-W. Tseng, Compiling Fortran D for MIMD distributed-memory machines, *Communications of the ACM, 35*(8), 66–80, Aug. 1992.

47. Y. Hou, C.-M. Wang, C.-Y. Ku, and L.-H. Hsu, Optimal processor mapping for linear-complement communication on hypercubes, *IEEE Transactions Parallel Distributed Systems, 12*(5), 514–527, May 2001.

48. P. D. Hovland and L. M. Ni, A model for automatic data partitioning, in *Proceedings International Conference on Parallel Processing,* pp. II, 251–259, St. Charles, IL, Aug. 1993.

49. C. H. Huang and P. Sadayappan, Communication-free hyperplane partitioning of nested loops, *Journal of Parallel and Distributed Computing, 19,* 90–102, 1993.

50. D. E. Hudak and S. G. Abraham, *Compiling Parallel Loops for High Performance Computers,* Kluwer Academic Publishers, Norwell, Massachusetts, 1993.

51. K. Hwang, *Advanced Computer Architecture: Parallelism, Scalability, Programmability,* McGraw-Hill, New York, 1993.

52. K. Ikudome, G. C. Fox, A. Kolawa, and J. W. Flower, An automatic and symbolic parallelization system for distributed memory parallel computers, in *Proceedings of Fifth Distributed Memory Computing Conference,* pp. 1105–1114, Charleston, SC, Apr. 1990.

53. F. Irigoin and R. Triolet, Supernode partitioning, in *Proceedings ACM SIGACT-SIG-PLAN Symposium on Principles of Programming Languages,* pp. 319–329, San Diego, CA, January 1988.

54. E. T. Kalns, H. Xu, and L. M. Ni, Evaluation of data distribution patterns in distributed-memory machines, in *Proceedings International Conference on Parallel Processing,* pp. II, 175–183, St. Charles, IL, Aug. 1993.

55. G. Karypis and V. Kumar, A fast and high quality multilevel scheme for partitioning irregular graph, *SIAM Journal of Scientific Computing, 20*(1), 359–392, 1998.

56. G. Karypis and V. Kumar, Multilevel *k*-way partitioning scheme for irregular graphs, *Journal of Parallel and Distributed Computing, 48,* 96–129, 1998.

57. G. Karypis and V. Kumar, Parallel multilevel *k*-way partitioning scheme for irregular graphs, *SIAM Review, 41*(2), 278–300, 1999.

58. K. Kennedy and U. Kremer, Initial framework for automatic data layout in Fortran D: A short update on a case study, Technical Report CRPC-TR93324-S, Center for Research on Parallel Computation, Rice University, July 1993.

59. K. Kennedy, K. S. Mckinley, and C. W. Tseng, Interactive parallel programming using the ParaScope editor, *IEEE Transactions Parallel Distributed Systems, 2*(3), 329–341, July 1991.

60. K. Kennedy, N. Nedeljković, and A. Sethi, Communication generation for cyclic(*k*) distributions, in *Proceedings Third Workshop on Languages, Compilers, and Runtime Systems for Scalable Computers,* pp. 185–197, Troy, New York, May 1995.

61. C. Koelbel, D. Loveman, R. Schreiber, G. Steele, Jr., and M. Zosel, *The High Performance Fortran Handbook,* MIT Press, Cambridge, MA, 1994.

62. C. Koelbel and P. Mehrotra, Compiling global name-space parallel loops for distributed execution, *IEEE Transactions Parallel Distributed Systems, 2*(4), 440–451, Oct. 1991.

63. C. Koelbel, P. Mehrotra, and J. V. Rosendale, Supporting shared data structures on distributed memory architectures, in *Proceedings ACM SIGPLAN Symposium on Principles and Practices of Parallel Programming,* pp. 177–186, March 1990.

64. U. Kremer, NP-completeness of dynamic remapping, in *Proceedings of the Fourth Workshop on Compilers for Parallel Computers,* Delft, The Netherlands, Dec. 1993.

65. U. Kremer, Automatic data layout using 0–1 integer programming, in *Proceedings of International Conference on Parallel Architectures and Compilation Techniques,* Montréal, Canada, Aug. 1994.

66. U. Kremer, J. Mellor-Crummey, K. Kennedy, and A. Carle, Automatic data layout for distributed-memory machines in the D programming environment, in *Automatic Parallelization—New Approaches to Code Generation, Data Distribution, and Performance Prediction,* pp. 136–152, Vieweg Advanced Studies in Computer Science, Verlag Vieweg, Wiesbaden, Germany, 1993.

67. P.-Z. Lee, Techniques for compiling programs on distributed memory multicomputers, *Parallel Computing, 21*(12), 1895–1923, 1995.

68. P.-Z. Lee. Efficient algorithms for data distribution on distributed memory parallel computers. *IEEE Transactions Parallel Distributed Systems, 8*(8), 825–839, Aug. 1997.

69. P.-Z. Lee, C.-H. Chang, and M.-J. Chao, A parallel Euler solver on unstructured meshes, in *Proceedings ISCA 13th International Conference on Parallel and Distributed Computing Systems,* pp. 171–177, Las Vegas, NV, Aug. 2000.

70. P.-Z. Lee, C.-H. Chang, and J.-J. Wu, Parallel implicit Euler solver on homogeneous and heterogeneous computing environments, AIAA paper 2001–2588, American Institute of Aeronautics and Astronautics, June 2001. Presented at the 15th AIAA Computational Fluid Dynamics Conference, Anaheim, CA, June 11–14, 2001.

71. P.-Z. Lee and W.-Y. Chen, Generating communication sets of array assignment statements for block-cyclic distribution on distributed memory machines, *Parallel Computing, 28*(9), 1329–1368, Sept. 2002.

72. P.-Z. Lee and Z. M. Kedem, Synthesizing linear-array algorithms from nested For loop algorithms, *IEEE Transactions Comput., C-37,* 1578–1598, December 1988.

73. P.-Z. Lee and Z. M. Kedem, Mapping nested loop algorithms into multi-dimensional systolic arrays, *IEEE Transactions Parallel Distributed Systems, 1,* 64–76, Jan. 1990.

74. P.-Z. Lee and Z. M. Kedem, Automatic data and computation decomposition on distributed memory parallel computers, *ACM Transactions on Programming Languages and Systems, 24*(1), 1–50, Jan. 2002.

75. P.-Z. Lee, J.-J. Wu, and C.-H. Chang, Partitioning unstructured meshes for homogeneous and heterogeneous parallel computing environments, in *Proceedings International Conference on Parallel Processing,* pp. 315–322, Vancouver, Canada, Aug. 2002.

76. P.-Z. Lee, C.-H. Yang, and J.-R. Yang, Fast algorithms for computing self-avoiding walks and mesh intersections over unstructured meshes, AIAA paper 2003-4125, American Institute of Aeronautics and Astronautics, June 2003. This was been presented at *the 16th AIAA Computational Fluid Dynamics Conference,* Orlando, FL, June 23-26, 2003.

77. J. Li, *Compiling Crystal for Distributed Memory Machines,* PhD thesis, Dept. of Computer Science, Yale University, 1991.

78. J. Li and M. Chen, Generating explicit communication from shared-memory program references, in *Proceedings of Supercomputing '90,* pp. 865–876, 1990.

79. J. Li and M. Chen, Compiling communication-efficient problems for massively parallel machines, *IEEE Transactions Parallel Distributed Systems, 2*(3), 361–376, July 1991.

80. J. Li and M. Chen, The data alignment phase in compiling programs for distributed-memory machines, *Journal of Parallel and Distributed Computing, 13,* 213–221, 1991.

81. W.-H. Liu and A. H. Sherman, Comparative analysis of the Cuthill-McKee and the reverse Cuthill-McKee ordering algorithms for sparse matrices, *SIAM Journal on Numerical Analysis, 13*(2), 198–213, Apr. 1976.

82. M. Mace, *Memory Storage Patterns in Parallel Processing,* Kluwer Academic Publishers, Boston, MA, 1987.

83. P. Mehrotra and J. Van Rosendale, Programming distributed memory architectures using Kali, in A. Nicolau, D. Gelernter, T. Gross, and D. Padua (Eds.), *Advances in Languages and Compilers for Parallel Computing,* pp. 364–384. Pitman/MIT-Press, 1991.

84. G. L. Miller, S.-H. Teng, W. Thurston, and S. A. Vavasis, Automatic mesh partitioning, in *Graph Theory and Sparse Matrix Computation,* volume 56 of *The IMA Volumes in Mathematics and Its Applications,* pp. 57–84. Springer-Verlag, 1993.

85. B. Monien, R. Preis, and R. Diekmann, Quality matching and local improvement for multilevel graph-partitioning, *Parallel Computing, 26*(12), 1609–1634, Dec. 2000.

86. L. Oliker and R. Biswas, PLUM: Parallel load balancing for adaptive unstructured meshes, *Journal of Parallel and Distributed Computing, 52,* 150–177, 1998.

87. L. Oliker, R. Biswas, and H. N. Gabow, Parallel tetrahedral mesh adaptation with dynamic load balancing, *Parallel Computing, 26*(12), 1583–1608, Dec. 2000.

88. J. Ortega and C. Romine, The *ijk* forms of factorization ii, *Parallel Computing, 7*(2), 149–162, 1988.

89. D. J. Palermo, *Compiler Techniques for Optimizing Communication and Data Distribution for Distributed-Memory Multicomputers,* PhD thesis, University of Illinois at Urbana-Champaign, Urbana, IL, 1996.

90. R. Ponnusamy, J. Saltz, A. Choudhary, Y.-S. Hwang, and G. Fox, Runtime support and compilation methods for user-specified irregular data distributions, *IEEE Transactions Parallel Distributed Systems, 6*(8), 815–831, 1995.

91. A. Pothen, H. D. Simon, and K. P. Liou, Partitioning sparse matrices with eigenvectors of graphs, *SIAM Journal of Matrix Anaylsis Applications, 11,* 430–452, 1990.

92. J. Ramanujam and P. Sadayappan, Compile-time techniques for data distribution in distributed memory machines, *IEEE Transactions Parallel Distributed Systems, 2*(4), 472–482, Oct. 1991.

93. J. Ramanujam and P. Sadayappan, Tiling multidimensional iteration spaces for multicomputers, *Journal of Parallel and Distributed Computing, 16,* 108–120, 1992.

94. A. Rogers and K. Pingali, Compiling for distributed memory architectures, *IEEE Transactions Parallel Distributed Systems, 5*(3), 281–298, Mar. 1994.

95. M. Rosing, R. B. Schnabel, and R. P. Weaver, The DINO parallel programming language, *Journal of Parallel and Distributed Computing, 13,* 30–42, 1991.

96. Y. Saad, *Iterative Methods for Sparse Linear Systems,* PWS Publishing Company, Boston, MA, 1996.

97. J. Saltz, K. Crowley, R. Mirchandaney, and H. Berryman, Run-time scheduling and execution of loops on message passing machines, *Journal of Parallel and Distributed Computing, 8,* 303–312, 1990.

98. K. Schloegel, G. Karypis, and V. Kumar, Wavefront diffusion and LMSR: Algorithms for dynamic repartitioning of adaptive meshes, *IEEE Transactions Parallel Distributed Systems, 12*(5), 451–466, May 2001.

99. K. Schloegel, G. Karypis, and V. Kumar, Parallel static and dynamic multi-constraint graph partitioning, *Concurrency and Computation: Practice and Experience, 14,* 219–240, 2002.

100. E. Su, D. J. Palermo, and P. Banerjee, Automating parallelization of regular computations for distributed-memory multicomputers in the paradigm compiler, in *Proceedings International Conference on Parallel Processing,* pp. II, 30–38, St. Charles, IL, Aug. 1993.

101. N. Touheed, P. Selwood, P. K. Jimack, and M. Berzins, A comparison of some dynamic load-balancing algorithms for a parallel adaptive flow solver, *Parallel Computing, 26*(12), 1535–1554, Dec. 2000.

102. C.-W. Tseng, *An Optimizing Fortran D Compiler for MIMD Distributed-Memory Machines,* PhD thesis, Dept. of Computer Science, Rice University, 1993.

103. P. S. Tseng, *A Systolic Array Parallelizing Compiler,* Kluwer Academic Publishers, Boston, MA, 1990.

104. M. Ujaldon, E. L. Zapata, B. M. Chapman, and H. Zima, Vienna Fortran/HPF exten-

sions for sparse and irregular problems and their compilation, *IEEE Transactions Parallel Distributed Systems, 8*(10), 1068–1083, Oct. 1997.

105. R. von Hanxleden, Compiler support for machine independent parallelization of irregular problems, Technical Report CRPC-TR92301-S, Center for Research on Parallel Computation, Rice University, Nov. 1992.

106. C. Walshaw and M. Cross, Parallel optimisation algorithms for multilevel mesh partitioning, *Parallel Computing, 26*(12), 1635–1660, Dec. 2000.

107. C. M. Wang and S. D. Wang, Efficient processor assignment algorithms and loop transformations for executing nested parallel loops on multiprocessors, *IEEE Transactions Parallel Distributed Systems, 3*(1), 71–82, January 1992.

108. S. Wholey, Automatic data mapping for distributed-memory parallel computers, in *Proceedings of ACM International Conference on Supercomputing,* pp. 25–34, July 1992.

109. R. D. Williams and R. Glowinski, Distributed irregular finite elements, Technical Report C3P 715, Caltech Concurrent Computation Program, Feb. 1989.

110. M. E. Wolf and M. S. Lam, A data locality optimizing algorithm, in *Proceedings of ACM SIGPLAN '91 Conference on Programming Language Design and Implementation,* pp. 30–44, Toronto, Ontario, Canada, June 1991.

111. M. E. Wolf and M. S. Lam, A loop transformation theory and an algorithm to maximize parallelism, *IEEE Transactions Parallel Distributed Systems, 2*(4), 452–471, Oct. 1991.

112. M. Wolfe, *High Performance Compilers for Parallel Computing,* Addison-Wesley, Redwood City, CA, 1996.

113. J. Wu, R. Das, J. Saltz, H. Berryman, and S. Hirandan, Distributed memory compiler design for sparse problems, *IEEE Transactions Comput., 44*(6), 737–753, June 1995.

114. J.-J. Wu, *Optimization and Transformation Techniques for High Performance Fortran,* PhD thesis, Yale University, 1995.

115. J. Xue, Communication-minimal tiling of uniform dependence loops, *Journal of Parallel and Distributed Computing, 42,* 42–59, 1997.

116. E. L. Zapata, O. Plata, R. Asenjo, and G. P. Trabado, Data-parallel support for numerical irregular problems, *Parallel Computing, 25*(13–14), 1971–1994, Dec. 1999.

117. H. Zima and B. Chapman, *Supercompilers for Parallel and Vector Computers,* Addison-Wesley, Redwood City, CA, 1990.

118. H. Zima and B. Chapman, Compiling for distributed-memory systems, *Proceedings of the IEEE, 81*(2), 264–287, Feb. 1993.

119. H. P. Zima, H-J. Bast, and M. Gerndt, SUPERB: A tool for semi-automatic MIMD/SIMD parallelization, *Parallel Computing, 6,* 1–18, 1988.

## CHAPTER 9

Enabling Partial-Cache Line Prefetching through Data Compression

YOUTAO ZHANG and RAJIV GUPTA

9.1 INTRODUCTION

Due to the increasing CPU and memory performance gap, off-chip memory accesses have become increasingly expensive and can take hundreds of cycles to finish.
Since load instructions usually reside on the critical path, a single load miss could
block all of its dependent instructions and stall the pipeline. To improve memory performance, hardware prefetching [3, 2, 7, 1] has been proposed for use in high-performance computer systems. Prefetching overlaps long memory access latency with pri-
or computations such that at the time the data is referenced, it is present in the cache.

Different prefetching approaches vary in *where* they hold the prefetched data,
what data they prefetch, and *when* they prefetch the data. A prefetch scheme can
simply prefetch the next cache line or, with additional hardware support, prefetch
cache lines with a dynamically decided stride. Since hardware speculatively
prefetches data items, these data items may and may not be used by later accesses.
In order to avoid the pollution of the data cache, prefetched data is usually kept in a
separate prefetch buffer. A cache line is moved from the prefetch buffer to the data
cache if a memory access references data in the cache line. Since the prefetch buffer
is of limited size, new prefetched cache lines have to kick out old ones in the buffer
if the buffer is full. If a cache line is prefetched too early, it might be replaced by the
time it is referenced. On the other hand, if a cache line is prefetched too late, we are
unable to fully hide the cache miss latency. If a prefetched cache line is never
moved from the prefetch buffer to the data cache, the memory bandwidth used in
bringing it into the prefetch buffer is wasted. Although prefetching is a simple and
effective technique, it results in increased memory traffic and thus requires greater
memory bandwidth.

In this chapter, we propose a prefetching technique that does not increase memory traffic or memory bandwidth requirements. By transferring values in compressed

High-Performance Computing: Paradigm and Infrastructure. Edited by L. T. Yang and M. Guo **183**
Copyright © 2006 John Wiley & Sons, Inc.

form, memory bandwidth is freed and, whenever possible, this extra bandwidth is used to prefetch other compressed values. In addition, the scheme we propose does not require introduction of extra prefetch buffers.

The compression scheme is designed based upon characteristics of dynamically encountered values that were observed in our studies [8, 9, 6]. In particular, dynamic values can be categorized as small values and big values. Positive small values share the prefix of all zeros and negative small values share the prefix of all ones. Als, pointer addresses that account for a significant percentage of big values share the same prefix if they are in the same memory chunk of certain size. Using small amount of space to remember these prefixes, we can store the values in compressed form and easily reconstruct the original values when they are referenced.

The prefetching scheme works as follows. With each line in memory, another line that acts as the prefetch candidate is associated. When a cache line is fetched, we examine the compressibility of values in the cache line and the associated prefetch candidate line. If the ith word of the line and the ith word from its prefetched candidate line are both compressible, the two words are compressed and transferred, using up bandwidth of one word. This is done for each pair of corresponding words in the two lines. This approach clearly does not increase the memory bandwidth requirements. However, in general, it results in prefetching of a partial cache line. By studying a spectrum of programs from different benchmark suites, we found that the compressible words are frequent and prefetching a partial cache line helps to improve the performance. In addition, we derived a parameter to characterize the importance of different cache misses. We found that a cache miss from a compressible word normally blocks more instructions than that from an uncompressible word. Thus, prefetching of compressible words shortens the critical path length and improves the processor throughput.

The rest of this chapter is organized as follows. We motivate our design by a small example in Section 9.2. Cache details and access sequences are discussed in Section 9.3. Implementation and experimental results are presented in Section 9.4. Related work is reviewed in Section 9.5. Finally, Section 9.6 summarizes our conclusions.

9.2 MOTIVATION FOR PARTIAL-CACHE LINE PREFETCHING

We first discuss the representation of compressed values used by in our hardware design and then illustrate how the cache performance is improved by enabling prefetching of partial caches lines.

9.2.1 Dynamic Value Representation

Although a single machine word of 32 bits can represent 2^{32} distinct values, these values are not used with equal frequency by programs. Memory addresses, or pointer values, account for a significant percentage of dynamically used values. Recent studies showed that dynamically allocated heap objects are often small [11] and, by applying different compiler optimization techniques [10, 11], these objects can be grouped together to enhance spatial locality. As a result, most of these pointer values point to reasonably sized memory regions and, therefore, they share a common prefix. For nonaddress values, studies show that many of them are small values, either positive or negative, and close to the value zero [9]. The higher-order bits of small positive values are all zeros, whereas the higher-order bits of small negative values are all ones.

Given the above characteristics of values, it is clear that they can be stored in compressed formats in caches and reconstructed into their uncompressed forms when referenced by the processor. Figure 9.1(a) shows the case when the prefix of a pointer value can be discarded. If an address pointer stored in memory and the memory address at which the address pointer is stored share a prefix, then the prefix need not be stored in memory. When a shortened pointer is accessed from memory, by concatenating it with the prefix of the address from which the pointer is read, the complete address pointer can be constructed. For example, in Figure 9.1(a), when we access pointer Q using pointer P, we could use the prefix of pointer P to reconstruct the value of Q. Figure 9.1(b) shows the case in which the prefix of a small value can be discarded if these bits are simply sign extensions. We save only the sign bit and could extend this bit to all higher-order bits when reconstructing the value.

According the above observations, compression is achieved by eliminating higher-order bits of the values. The next question we must answer is, how many of the higher-order bits should be eliminated to achieve compression? On one hand, the elimination of a greater number of higher-order bits reduces the space required to store a compressible value. On the other hand, requiring a longer prefix reduces the total number of values that are classified as compressible. Through a study of a spectrum of programs, we found that compressing a 32 bit value down to 16 bits strikes a good balance between the two competing effects described above [16]. We use the 16th bit to indicate whether the lower-order 15 bits represent a small value or a memory address. The remaining 15 bits represent the lower order bits of the ac-

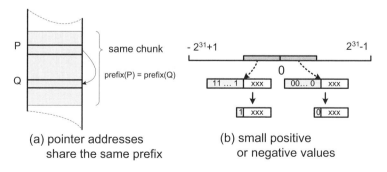

Figure 9.1   Representing a 32-bit value using fewer than 32 bits.

tual value. Thus, pointers within a 32 K memory chunk and small values within the range [−16384, 16383] are compressible.

Figure 9.2 shows in more detail the value representation we use. A value could be stored in either compressed or uncompressed form, and if it is stored in compressed form, it could be a compressed pointer or a compressed small value. Thus, two flags are used for handling compressed values. Flag "VC" indicates whether the stored value is in compressed form. When it is set, which represents a compressed value, the second "VT" flag is used to indicate if the original value is a small value or pointer address. The "VT" flag is stored as part of the compressed value in the cache, whereas the "VC" flag is stored separately from the value.

Although the above compression scheme is very simple, it is very effective in practice. We studied the compression opportunities for a spectrum of programs chosen from the Olden, SPEC95Int, and SPEC2000Int benchmark suites. The results are summarized in Figure 9.3. We examined all accessed values as a result of word-level memory accesses and categorized the values as compressible and uncompressible according to our scheme. If the higher-order 18 bits are all 0s or 1s, we consider it to be a compressible small value. If a value and its address share the same 17-bit prefix, we consider it to be a compressible address pointer. Otherwise, the value is categorized as a noncompressible value. From the figure, we can see that, on average, 59% of dynamic accessed values are compressible under the definition of this compression scheme.

9.2.2 Partial Cache Line Prefetching

Consider the commonly used prefetch on miss policy. If a referenced cache line l is not in the cache, the cache line l is loaded into the data cache and cache line $l + 1$ is brought into the prefetch buffer. Thus, the demand on the memory bandwidth is increased. On the other hand, by exploiting the dynamic-value representation redundancy, we can perform hardware prefetching that exploits the memory bandwidth saved through data compression. Our method stores values in the cache in compressed form, and in the space freed up by compressing values to 16 bits, additional compressible values are prefetched and stored. If a word in fetched line l at some

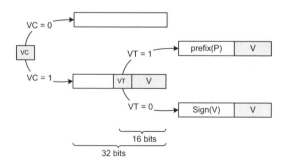

Figure 9.2 Representing compressed values.

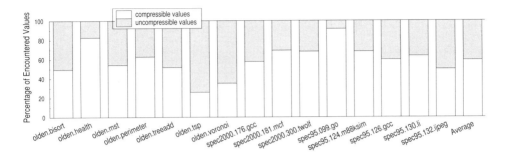

Figure 9.3 Values encountered by CPU-generated memory accesses.

offset is compressible, and so is the word at the same offset in the prefetched line l + 1, then the two words are compressed and held in the data cache at that offset. On the other hand, if the word at a given offset in line l or line l + 1 is not compressible, then only the word from from line l is held in the cache. Thus, when all words in line l are fetched into the cache, some of the words in line l + 1 are also prefetched into the cache.

Let us consider the example shown in Figure 9.4 where, for illustration purposes, it is assumed three out of four words are compressible in each cache line. The space made available by compression in each cache line is not enough to hold another cache line. Therefore, we choose to prefetch only part of another line. If the compressible words from another cache line with corresponding offsets are prefetched, then three additional compressible words can be stored, which covers seven out of eight words from two cache lines.

The example in Figure 9.5 illustrates how compression enabled prefetching can improve performance. Figure 9.5(b) shows a code fragment that traverses a link list whose node structure is shown in Figure 9.5(a). The memory allocator would align the address allocation and each node takes one cache line (we assume 16 bytes per line cache). There are four fields, of which two are pointer addresses, one is a type

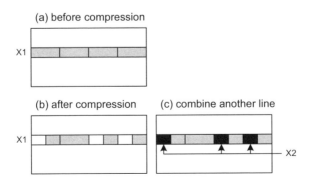

Figure 9.4 Holding compressed data in the cache.

```
struct node {
        int type;
        int info;
        struct node *prev;
        struct node *next;
};
```

(a) node declaration

```
        ...
(1)     while ( p ) {
(2)         if (p→type == T)
(3)             sum += p→info;
(4)         p = p→next;
        }
        ...
```

(b) sample code

Figure 9.5   Dynamic data structure declaration.

field, and the other one contains a large value. Except for this large information value field, the other three fields are identified as highly compressible. The sample
code shown in Figure 9.5(b) calculates the sum of the information field for all nodes
of type T. Without cache line compression, each node takes one cache line. To traverse the list, the next field is followed to access a new node.

A typical access sequence for this piece of code would generate a new cache
miss at statement (2) for every iteration of the loop [see Figure 9.6(a)]. All accesses
to other fields in the same node fall into the same cache line and thus are all cache
hits. However, if all compressible fields are compressed, a cache line would be able
to hold one complete node and three fields from another node. Now an access sequence will have cache hits at statements (2) and (4), plus a possible cache miss at
statement (3), as shown in Figure 9.6(b). Partial cache line prefetching can improve
performance in two ways. First, if the node is not of the type T, we do not need to
access the large information field. This saves one cache miss. Second, even in the
case in which we do need to access the information field, the cache miss happens at
statement (3). Although the new and old schemes generate the same number of
cache misses, the miss at statement (3) is less important. The critical program execution path is "(1)(2)(4)" and (3) is not on this path. Thus, a miss at (3) will have
less impact on the overall performance.

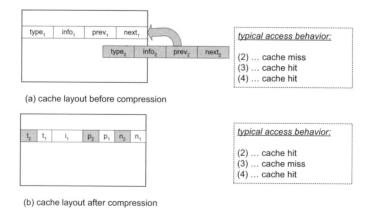

(a) cache layout before compression

(b) cache layout after compression

Figure 9.6   Cache layout before and after compression.

9.3   CACHE DESIGN DETAILS

In this section, we will first discuss the design of our compression-based data cache. Next we will present the fast compression and decompression logic. Handling of data accesses to our new cache design will also be discussed.

9.3.1   Cache Organization

In this section, we consider a two-level cache hierarchy shown in Figure 9.7. Both L1 and L2 caches are on-chip. Moreover partial cache line prefetching is implemented for both caches. At the interface between the CPU and L1, cache compression and decompression are performed so that the CPU always sees values in uncompressed form while the cache stores the values in compressed form. Similarly the off-chip memory holds values in uncompressed form, but before these values are transferred on-chip, they are compressed. A value is considered to be compressible if it satisfies either of the following two conditions:

1. If the 18 higher-order bits are all ones or all zeros, the 17 higher-order bits are discarded.
2. If the 17 higher-order bits are the same as those of the value's address, the 17 higher-order bits are discarded.

Compressible words are stored in the cache in their compressed forms. Potentially, one physical cache block could hold content from two lines, identified here as the primary cache line and the affiliated line. The primary cache line is defined as the line mapped to the physical cache line/set by a normal cache of the same size

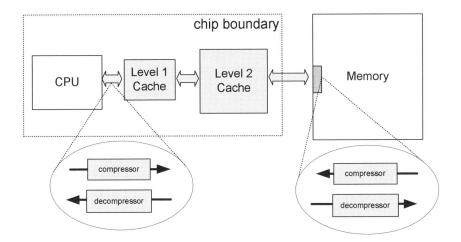

Figure 9.7   Two-level compression cache design.

and associativity. Its affiliated cache line is the unique line that is calculated through a single operation as shown below:

$$<Tag_{affiliated}, Set_{affiliated}> = <Tag_{primary}, Set_{primary}> \oplus mask$$

where *mask* is a predefined value. The mask is chosen to be 0x1 which means the primary and affiliated cache lines are consecutive lines of data. Thus, this choice of the mask value corresponds to the next-line prefetch policy. Accordingly, given a cache line, there are two possible places it can reside in the cache, referred to as the primary location and the affiliated location. The cache access and replacement policy ensure that at most one copy of a cache line is kept in the cache at any time.

In comparison to a traditional cache design, the major difference is at the interface between L1 and L2 cache. In a standard two-level cache hierarchy, the requests from the upper-level cache are line based. For example, if there is a miss at the first-level cache, a request for the whole line is issued to the second-level cache. In the compression cache design, the requested line might appear as an affiliated line in the second-level cache and thus only be partially present in the L2 cache. To maximize the benefits from partially prefetched cache line, we do not always get a complete line from L2 cache as long as the requested data item can be found. So the compression cache design keeps the requests to the second-level cache as word based and a cache hit at the second-level cache returns a partial cache line. The returned line might be placed as a primary line or an affiliated line. In either case, flags are needed to indicate whether a word is available in the cache line or not. A flag PA (primary availability) for the primary cache line is associated with one bit for each word and another flag AA (affiliated availability) for the affiliated cache line is provided. As discussed, a value compressibility flag (VC) is used to identify if a value is compressible or not. For the values stored in the primary line, a one-bit VC flag is associated for each word. On the other hand, if a value can appear in the affiliated line, it must be compressible and thus no extra flag is needed for these values. The design details of the first-level compression cache are shown in Figure 9.8.

When compared to other prefetching schemes, partial cache line prefetching adds 3 bits for every machine word, about a 10% cache size increase; however, it completely removes the prefetch buffer. Thus, the hardware costs introduced from the extra flags are not high. In the next section, we will compare our scheme to hardware prefetching with prefetch buffer.

9.3.2 Dynamic Value Conversion

Since a value held by a memory location can dynamically change from an uncompressible one to a compressible and vice versa, it is important to support fast compression and decompression, especially between the CPU and L1 cache. Dynamic values are compressed before writing to L1 cache and decompressed before sending back to the CPU. In Figure 9.9, we present the hardware implementation of the compressor and decompressor. To compress a value, three possible cases are

Address:

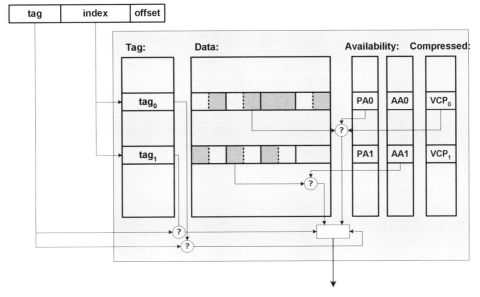

Figure 9.8   Compression cache.

checked in parallel: (i) the higher-order 17 bits of value and address are the same, (ii) the higher-order 18 bits are all ones, and (iii) the higher-order 18 bits are all zeros. Each of the checks can be performed using $\log(18)$ = five levels of two input gates. In addition, extra delay is introduced in form of three levels of gates to distinguish these cases. The total delay is eight gate delays. Since compression is associated with write instructions, the data is usually ready before the pipeline reaches the write back stage. As a result, compression delay can be hidden before writing back to the cache.

It is more critical to quickly decompress a value that is associated with a read instruction. As shown in Figure 9.9(b), we need at least two levels of gates to decompress the higher-order 17 bits. Each gate is enabled by a flag input. The delay associated with decompression can be hidden. Typically, the delay associated with the reading of the data array is smaller than the delay associated with tag matching. Therefore, after data has been read, some time is available to carry out the decompression while the tag matching is still in progress. This approach for hiding decompression delay is essentially similar to the approach used in [15] to hide the delay associated with the decoding of read values.

9.3.3   Cache Operation

Next, we discuss further details of how the cache operates. First, we describe the interactions at interface points (CPU/L1, L1/L2, and L2/Memory) and next we dis-

(a) Compress a value

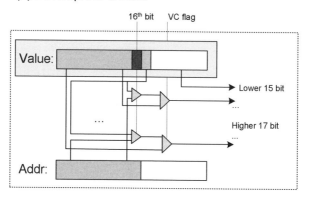

(b) Decompress a value

Figure 9.9 Value compression and decompression.

cuss how the situation in which a value stored in a location changes from being compressible to uncompressible is handled.

9.3.3.1 CPU–L1 Interface When a read request is sent from the CPU, both the primary cache line and its affiliated line are accessed simultaneously. The set index of the primary cache line is flipped to find its affiliated line. If found in the primary cache line, we return the data item in the same cycle, and if it is found in the affiliated line, the data item is returned in the next cycle (with one extra cycle latency). A compressed word is decompressed and sent back to the CPU. In the case of writing a value to the cache, a write hit in the affiliated cache line will bring the line to its primary place.

9.3.3.2 L1–L2 Interface For cache accesses from L1 cache to L2 cache, if the accessed word is available in L2, it is a cache hit and only the available words in the cache line are returned. Since the block size of L2 cache is two times that of L1 cache, the primary and affiliated cache lines in L1 cache reside in the same cache line block in L2 cache. Since they are already organized in their compressed format, words from the affiliated line are returned only when they and their corresponding words in primary line are compressible.

When a new cache line arrives to the L1 from L2 cache, the prefetched affiliated line is discarded if it is already in the cache (it must be in its primary place in this situation). On the other hand, before discarding a replaced cache line, we check to see if it is possible to put the line into its affiliated place. If the dirty bit is set, we still write back its contents and only keep a clean partial copy in its affiliated place.

9.3.3.3 L2–Memory Interface   For accesses from L2 cache to memory, both the primary and the affiliated lines are fetched. However, before returning the data, the cache lines are compressed and only available places from the primary line are used to store the compressible items from the affiliated line. The memory bandwidth is still the same as before. The arrival of the new line to L2 cache is handled in a manner similar to the arrival of a new cache line to L1 cache.

9.3.3.4 Changes in Values from Compressible to Uncompressible
When a word in a primary cache line changes from compressible word to uncompressible word, and the corresponding word in the affiliated cache line already resides in the word, we have a choice between keeping either the primary line or the affiliated line in the cache line. Our scheme gives priority to the words from the primary line. The words from the affiliated line are evicted. The affiliated line must be written back if the dirty bit is set.

When a word in an affiliated cache line changes from compressible to uncompressible, we move the line to its primary place and update its corresponding word. The effect is the same as that of bringing a prefetched cache line into the cache from the prefetch buffer in a traditional cache.

9.4   EXPERIMENTAL RESULTS

In this section, we first briefly describe our experimental setup and then present the results of our experimental evaluation. To evaluate the effectiveness of our cache design, we compare its performance with a variety of other cache implementations.

9.4.1   Experimental Setup

We implemented a compression-enabled partial cache line prefetching scheme using Simplescalar 3.0 [4]. The baseline processor is a four-issue superscalar with two levels of on-chip cache (Figure 9.10). Except the basic cache configuration, we used the same parameters for implementations of all different cache designs.

We chose a spectrum of programs from the Olden [13], SPEC2000, and SPEC95 [14] benchmark suites. Olden contains pointer-intensive programs that allocate and operate on dynamically allocated data structures. The results were collected with

Parameter	Value
Issue width	4 isssue, out of order
Instruction fetch queue	16 intructions
Branch predictor	Bimod
LD/ST queue	8 entry
Function units	4 ALUs, 1 Mult/Div, 2 Mem ports
	4 FALU, 1 Fmult/Fdiv
I-cache hit latency	1 cycle
I-cache miss latency	10 cycles
L1 D-cache hit latency	1 cycle
L1 D-cache miss latency	10 cycles
Memory access latency	100 cycles (L2 cache miss latency)

Figure 9.10 Baseline experimental setup.

representative input sets provided with the benchmark. SPEC programs were run with the reference input set.

We compared the performances of cache configurations described below. The comparisons were made in terms of overall execution time, memory traffic, and miss rates.

- **Baseline cache (BC).** L1 cache is 8 K direct mapped and 64 bytes/line. L2 cache is 64 K two-way associative and 128 bytes/line.
- **Baseline cache with compression (BCC).** L1 and L2 caches are the same as baseline the configuration. We add compressors and decompressors at the interfaces of CPU and L1 cache, L2, cache and memory. This does not affect the cache performance but it does reduce the memory traffic.
- **Higher associative cache (HAC).** L1 cache is 8 K two-way associative and 64 bytes/line. L2 cache is 64 K four-way associative and 128 bytes/line. Since two cache lines may be accessed if the required word is in the affiliated cache, we model a cache with double the associativity at both cache levels for comparison.
- **Baseline cache with prefetching (BCP).** L1 and L2 caches are the same as the baseline configuration; however, we invest the hardware cost of our scheme to cache prefetch buffers. A eight-entry prefetch buffer is used to help L1 cache and a 32-entry prefetch buffer is used to help L2 cache. Both are designed to be fully associative with LRU replacement policy.
- **Compression-enabled partial line prefetching (CPP).** L1 cache is 8 K direct mapped, 64 bytes per cache line. L2 cache is 64 K two-way associative, 128 bytes per cache line. Partial cache lines are prefetched, as we discussed.

9.4.2 Memory Traffic

The memory traffic comparison of different cache configurations is shown in Figure 1.11; memory traffics for all cache configurations are normalized with respect

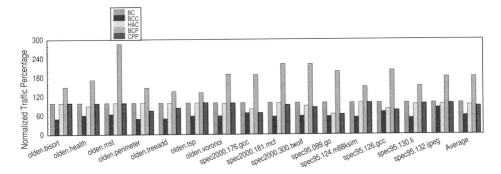

Figure 9.11   Comparison of memory traffic.

to the memory traffic of baseline cache, which appears as 100% in the graph. It is clear from the graph that the simple data-compression technique, as discussed in this chapter, greatly reduces the memory traffic; the reduction as shown by BCC is on average 60% of BC configuration. On the other hand, the hardware prefetching technique increases memory traffic significantly, with an average increase of about 80%. The new CPP design makes use of the saved memory bandwidth from data compression to carry out prefetching. It generates, on average, 90% of the traffic of the BC configuration. Thus, while traditional prefetching increases memory traffic, our CPP design reduces traffic even though it carries out prefetching.

The CPP design is not a simple combination design of prefetching and data compression at the memory bus interface. It stores the prefetch data inside the cache, which effectively provides a larger prefetch buffer than the scheme that puts all hardware overhead into supporting a prefetch buffer (BCP).As a result, the memory traffic for CPP is lower than the average of BCC and BCP's traffic [(60% + 180%)/2 = 120%].

As discussed earlier, the only access sequence in BCP that could increase memory traffic happens if a store instruction writes to the primary place or the affiliated place and changes a compressible value to an uncompressible one. Either this action will generate a cache miss (if the value is written to the affiliated place) or it will cause the eviction of a dirty affiliated line (if the value is written to the primary place). However, this situation does not occur often enough in practice. As a result, our CPP design results in an overall reduction in memory traffic in comparison to the baseline cache.

9.4.3   Execution Time

The overall execution time comparisons of different cache configurations, normalized with respect to the baseline configuration (BC), are shown in Figure 9.12. The difference between the BC bar and other bars gives the percentage speedup.

First, we observe that data compression itself affects neither the memory access sequence nor the availability of cache lines in the data cache. As a result, it has the

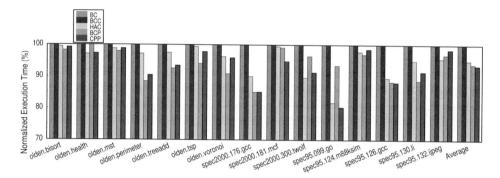

Figure 9.12 Performance comparison.

same performance results as baseline. It is also clear HAC consistently does better than BC, which is to be expected. Hardware prefetching is very effective and gives better performance than HAC for 11 out of 14 programs.

The proposed CPP design does consistently better than the baseline cache. This is expected since CPP never kicks out a cache line in order to accommodate a prefetched line and, thus, prefetching in CPP can never cause cache pollution. On average, programs run 7% faster on the CPP configuration when compared to the baseline configuration. While HAC has a better replacement policy, CPP can hold more words in the cache. For example, although a two-way associative cache can hold two cache lines in a set, CPP can hold the content from four lines in these two physical lines. Thus, CPP reduces the capacity misses in comparison to HAC and improves the performance. From the figure, we can also see that CPP does better than BCP for five out 14 programs. Generally, CPP does slightly worse than BCP since CPP only prefetches partial cache lines and thus is less aggressive in its prefetching policy in comparison to BCP. However, if conflict misses are dominant, that is, a higher associative cache has better performance than BCP (e.g., olden.health and spec2000.300.twolf), CPP performs better than BCP. CPP reduces the conflict misses and thus improves the effectiveness of prefetching.

9.4.4 Cache Miss Comparison

The comparison of L1 and L2 cache misses for different configurations are shown in Figure 9.13 and Figure 9.14, respectively. As we can see, prefetching techniques (BCP and CPP) greatly reduce cache misses in comparison to the baseline configuration. In comparison to HAC, prefetching techniques generally have comparable or more L1 cache misses, but in many cases fewer L2 cache misses. HAC greatly reduces the conflict misses. For BCP, since the prefetch buffer of L1 cache is small, new prefetched items sometimes replace old ones before they are used. For CPP, a new fetched cache line kicks out a primary line and its associated prefetched line. Thus, conflict misses are not effectively removed. For L2 cache, BCP sometimes

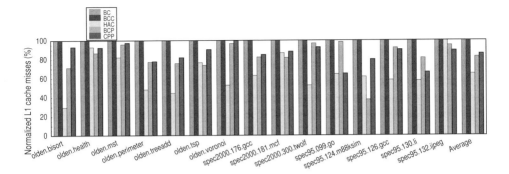

Figure 9.13   Comparison of L1 cache misses.

performs better than CPP since it has a larger prefetch buffer and can hide the miss penalty more effectively.

An interesting phenomenon is that although CPP sometimes has more L1 or L2 cache misses than HAC, it still achieves better overall performance (e.g., for 130.li from SPECint95, although CPP has more L1 and L2 cache misses than HAC, the overall performance using CPP is 6% better than HAC). As was mentioned in the previous sections, this suggests that different cache misses have different performance impacts, that is, some cache misses hurt the performance more than other cache misses.

Additional experiments were designed to further analyze this phenomenon. We first derive a new parameter for this purpose. Given a set of memory access instructions m, the importance of this set of memory references is defined as the percentage of total executed instructions that directly depend on m. In case that m is the set of cache miss instructions from a program execution, its importance parameter indicates how many directly dependent instructions are blocked by the cache misses. A higher number means that the cache misses block more instructions and thus can

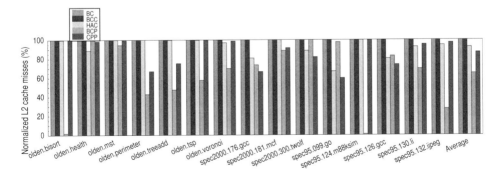

Figure 9.14   Comparison of L2 cache misses.

hurt the performance more. The method to approximately compute this percentage is as follows. According to Amdahl's law, we have

$$Speedup_{overall} = \frac{Execution_{old}}{Execution_{new}} = \frac{1}{(1 - Fraction_{enhanced}) + \dfrac{Fraction_{enhanced}}{Speedup_{enhanced}}}$$

$$\therefore Fraction_{enhanced} = \frac{Speedup_{enhanced}\left(1 - \dfrac{1}{Speedup_{overall}}\right)}{Speedup_{enhanced} - 1}$$

In the Simplescalar simulator, without speculative execution, the memory address generated and their accesses are affected by the following factors: the executable program, the input, the seed for the random generator. If all these factors are fixed, two runs with different cache configurations will generate exactly the same instruction execution sequence as well as the memory address access sequence. Thus, by varying only the cache miss penalty and running the program twice, we would observe that the same number of cache misses happen at the same instructions. Moreover, given this fixed set of instructions that have cache misses, their directly dependent instructions are also fixed. As we know, by shortening the miss penalty, the main change to the execution is the reduced dependence length from a cache miss instruction to its directly dependent instructions, the enhanced fraction could thus be considered as the percentage of the instruction that are directly depending on these cache misses.

Now, for different cache configurations, this fraction is computed as follows. First, the cache miss latency is reduced in half, which means $Speedup_{enhanced} = 2$. Second, the overall performance speedup is measured, which is $Speedup_{overall}$. It is computed from the total number of cycles before and after changing the miss penalty. Now, the value of $Fraction_{enhanced}$ can be obtained. The results for different configurations are plotted in Figure 9.15.

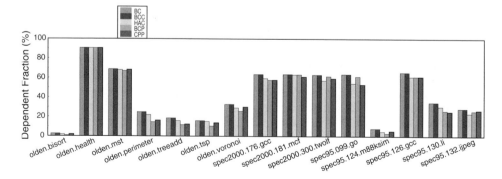

Figure 9.15   The estimation of cache miss importance.

From the comparison results, for different benchmark programs shown in Figure 9.15, it can be seen that CPP reduces the importance of the cache misses for most benchmarks. For the benchmarks that are slower than HAC, it is seen that they have larger importance parameters. This estimation is consistent with the result shown in Figure 9.12.

For the benchmarks with significant importance reduction, further study of the average ready queue length in the processor, when there is at least one outstanding cache miss, was carried out. The queue length increase of CPP over the HAC was studied. The results are shown in Figure 9.16. The results indicate that the average queue length is improved by up to 78% for these benchmarks. This parameter tells us when there is a cache miss in the new cache design, the pipeline still has a lot of work to do.

To summarize, we conclude that CPP design reduces the importance of caches misses when compared to BC and HAC configurations. That is the reason why CPP sometimes has higher cache misses but still gives better overall performance.

9.5   RELATED WORK

Different prefetching techniques have been proposed to hide cache miss penalty and improve the cache performance. Hardware prefetching [2, 7, 1] does not require compiler support as well as the modification of existing executable code. Simple schemes [3] prefetch the data of next cache line while more sophisticated schemes use dynamic information to find data items with fixed stride [2] or arbitrary distance [1]. However, prefetching techniques significantly increase the memory traffic and memory bandwidth requirements. Our new proposed scheme, on the other hand, employs data compression and effectively transmits more words with the same memory bandwidth. It does not explicitly increase the memory traffic or improve the overall performance.

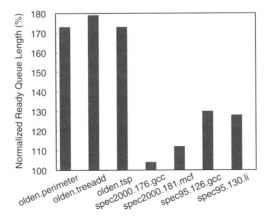

Figure 9.16   Average ready queue length in miss cycles.

Currently, data compression has been adapted into cache design mainly for the purpose of reducing power consumption. Existing designs [5, 6] improve the data density inside the cache with compression schemes of different dynamic cost and performance gain. In [5] a relatively complex compression algorithm is implemented in hardware to compress two consecutive lines. As a complicated compression scheme, it is employed at level 2 cache and data items are decompressed to level 1 cache before its access. In [6], data could be compressed at both levels by exploiting frequent values found from programs. If two conflicting cache lines can be compressed, both are stored within the cache; otherwise, only one of them is stored. Both of the above schemes operate at the cache line level and do not distinguish the importance of different words within a cache line. As a result, they cannot exploit the saved memory bandwidth for partial cache line prefetching.

The pseudoassociative cache [12] also has primary and a secondary cache lines. Our new design has similar access sequence. However, the cache line is updated very differently. For pseudoassociative cache, if a cache line enters its secondary place, it has to kick out the original line. Thus, it introduces the danger of degrading the cache performance by converting a fast hit to a slow hit or even a cache miss. On the contrary, the new cache design only stores a cache line to its secondary place if there are free spots. Also, it will not pollute the cache line or degrade the original cache performance.

9.6 CONCLUSION

A novel cache design was discussed in this chapter that removes the memory traffic obstacle of hardware prefetching. It partially prefetches compressible words from the next cache line from the lower level memory hierarchy. By exploiting the memory bandwidth saved by data compression, this scheme does not explicitly increase memory traffic. It removes the prefetch buffer by storing the prefetched data within the cache, which could effectively store more content with the same size of data cache. On an average, the new cache improves the overall performance by 7% over the baseline cache and by 2% over the higher associativity cache configuration.

ACKNOWLEGMENTS

This work was supported by DARPA award no. F29601-00-1-0183 and National Science Foundation grants CCR-0220262, CCR-0208756, CCR-0105535, and EIA-0080123 to the University of Arizona.

REFERENCES

1. A. Roth, A. Moshovos, and G. S. Sohi, Dependence Based Prefetching for Linked Data Structures, in *ACM Proceedings of the Eighth International Conference on Architectural*

Support for Programming Languages and Operating Systems, pp. 116–126, San Jose, CA, 1998.

2. J. L. Baer and T. Chen, An Effective On-Chip Preloading Scheme to Reduce Data Access Penalty, in *Proceedings of Supercomputing '91,* pp. 178–186, Nov. 1991.

3. N. P. Jouppi, Improving Direct-mapped Cache Performance by the Addition of Small Fully Associative Cache and Prefetch Buffers, in *Proceeding of 17th Annual International Symposium on Computer Architecture,* pp. 364–373, Seattle, WA, May 1990.

4. D. Burger and T. Austin, The SimpleScalar Tool Set, Version 2.0, *Technical Report CS-TR-97-1342,* University of Wisconsin-Madison, June 1997.

5. J-S. Lee, W-K. Hong, and S-D. Kim, Design and Evaluation of a Selective Compressed Memory System, in *IEEE International Conference on Computer Design,* Austin, TX, pp. 184–191, Oct. 1999.

6. J. Yang, Y. Zhang and R. Gupta, "Frequent Value Compression in Data Caches," *IEEE/ACM International Symposium on Microarchitecture,* Monterey, CA, pp. 258–265, Dec 2000.

7. A. Smith, Cache memories, *ACM Computing Survey, 14,* 473–530, Sept. 1982.

8. Y. Zhang and R. Gupta, Data Compression Transformations for Dynamically Allocated Data Structures, in *International Conferenceon Compiler Construction,* pp. 14–28, Grenoble, France, Apr. 2002.

9. Y. Zhang, J. Yang, and R. Gupta, Frequent Value Locality and Value-Centric Data Cache Design, in *ACM 9th International Conference on Architectural Support for Programming Languages and Operating Systems,* pp. 150–159, Cambridge, MA, Nov. 2000.

10. T. M. Chilimbi, M. D. Hill, and J. R. Larus, Cache-Conscious Structure Layout, in *ACM SIGPLAN Conference on Programming Language Design and Implementation* (PLDI), pp. 1–12, Atlanta, GA, May 1999.

11. T. M. Chilimbi, M. D. Hill, and J. R. Larus, Cache-Conscious Structure Definition, in *ACM SIGPLAN Conference on Programming Language Design and Implementation* (PLDI), pp. 13–24, Atlanta, GA, May 1999.

12. D. Patterson and J. Hennessy, *Computer Architecture: A Quantitative Approach,* 2nd ed., Morgan Kaufmann Publishers, San Francisco, CA, 1995.

13. M. Carlisle, *Olden: Parallelizing Progrms with Dynamic Data Structures on Distributed-Memory Machines,* PhD Thesis, Princeton Univ., Dept. of Computer Science, June 1996.

14. http://www.spec.org/.

15. J. Yang and R. Gupta, Energy Efficient Frequent Value Data Cache Design, in *IEEE/ACM International Symposium on Microarchitecture,* Istanbul, Turkey, pp. 197–207, Nov. 2002.

16. Y. Zhang, *The Design and Implementation of Compression Techniques for Profile Guided Compilation,* PhD Thesis, University of Arizona, Dept. of Computer Science, Tucson, AZ, August 2002.

## CHAPTER 10

MPI Atomicity and Concurrent Overlapping I/O

WEI-KENG LIAO, ALOK CHOUDHARY, KENIN COLOMA,
LEE WARD, ERIC RUSSELL, and NEIL PUNDIT

10.1 INTRODUCTION

Parallel file access has been an active research topic for many years. Efforts were made in both software development and hardware design to improve the I/O bandwidth between computational units and storage systems. Although most of these works only consider exclusive file access among the concurrent I/O requests, more scientific applications nowadays require data partitioning with overlap among the requesting processes [1, 6, 9, 10]. A typical example of concurrent overlapping access uses ghost cells in a multidimensional array partitioning in which the subarray partitioned in one process overlaps with its neighbors near the boundary and the file read–write requests for the subarrays are simultaneously issued from more than one process. The ghosting technique is commonly used in large-scale simulations, such as earth climate, N-body astrophysics, and hydrodynamics, in which a strong spatial domain partitioning relationship is present. Figure 10.1 illustrates an example of a two-dimensional array in a block–block partitioning pattern in which a ghost cell represents data "owned" by more than one process. A typical run of this large-scale type of application can take from days to months and data is usually output periodically for the purposes of check pointing as well as progressive visualization. During check pointing, the output of ghost cells creates overlapping I/O from all processes concurrently. The outcome of the overlapped file regions from a concurrent I/O is commonly referred as atomicity.

The focus of this chapter is to examine the implementation issues for concurrent overlapping I/O operations that abide by the atomicity semantics of the Message Passing Interface (MPI) standard. At first, the differentiation of the MPI atomicity semantics from the definition in the Portable Operating System Interface (POSIX) standard is illustrated. The POSIX definition only considers atomicity at the granularity of read()/write() calls in which only a contiguous file space can be specified in a single I/O request. In MPI, a process can define a noncontiguous file view

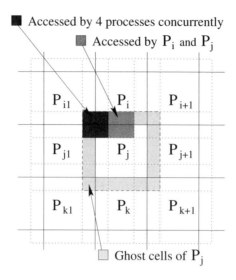

Figure 10.1   A two-dimensional array partitioned with overlaps. The ghost cell of P_j overlaps with its eight neighbors, resulting in some areas accessed by more than one process.

using MPI-derived data types and subsequent I/O calls can then implicitly access noncontiguous file regions. Since the POSIX definition is not aware of noncontiguous I/O access, it alone cannot guarantee atomic access in MPI, and additional efforts are needed above the file system to ensure the correct implementation of atomic MPI access. Two potential approaches for atomicity implementation will be studied: using byte-range file locking and a process handshaking strategy. Using a byte-range file-locking mechanism is a straightforward method to ensure atomicity. In many situations, however, file locking can serialize what were intended to be concurrent I/O calls and, therefore, it is necessary to explore alternative approaches. Process handshaking uses interprocess communication to determine the access sequence or agreement on the overlaps. Two methods are studied: graph coloring and process-rank ordering methods. These two methods order the concurrent I/O requests in a sequence such that no two overlapping requests can perform at any instance. Experimental performance results are provided for running a test code using a column-wise partitioning pattern on three machine platforms: a Linux cluster running an extended NFS file system, an SGI Origin2000 running XFS, and an IBM SP running GPFS. The results show that, in general, using file locking generates the worst performance and process-rank ordering performs the best on all three machines.

10.2   CONCURRENT OVERLAPPING I/O

The concurrent overlapping I/O referred to in this chapter occurs when I/O requests from multiple processes are issued simultaneously to the file system and overlaps exist among the file regions accessed by these requests. If all the requests are read requests, the file system can use the disk cache to duplicate the overlapped data for the requesting processes and no conflict will exist when obtaining file data among the processes. However, when one or more I/O requests are write requests, the outcome of the overlapped regions, either in file or in process's memory, can vary depending on the implementation of the file system. This problem is commonly referred as I/O atomicity.

10.2.1   POSIX Atomicity Semantics

The Portable Operating System Interface (POSIX) standard defines atomicity such that all the bytes from a single file I/O request that start out together end up together, without interleaving from other I/O requests [3, 4]. The I/O operations confined by this definition include the system calls that operate on regular files. In this chapter, the focus is on the effect of the read and write calls on atomicity.

The POSIX definition can be simply interpreted as that either all or none of the data written by a process is visible to other processes. The none case can occur when the write data is cached in a system buffer and has not been flushed to the disk or the data is flushed but overwritten by other processes. Hence, when POSIX semantics are applied to the concurrent overlapping I/O operations, the resulting data in the overlapped regions in the disk shall consist of data from only one of the write requests. In other words, no mixed data from two or more requests shall appear in the overlapped regions. Otherwise, in the nonatomic mode, the result of the overlapped region is undefined, that is, it may comprise mixed data from multiple requests. Many existing file systems support the POSIX atomicity semantics, such as NFS, UFS, IBM PIOFS, GPFS, Intel PFS, and SGI XFS.

The POSIX read and write calls share a common characteristic: one I/O request can only access a contiguous file region specified by a file pointer and the amount of data starting from the pointer. Therefore, the overlapped data written by two or more POSIX I/O calls can only be a contiguous region in the file. Many POSIX file systems implement the atomic I/O by serializing the process of the requests such that the overlapped regions can only be accessed by one process at any moment. By considering only the contiguous file access, the POSIX definition is suitable for file systems that mainly handle nonparallel I/O requests. For I/O requests from parallel applications that frequently issue noncontiguous file access requests from multiple processes, POSIX atomicity may improperly describe such parallel access patterns and impose limitation for the I/O parallelism.

10.2.2   MPI Atomicity Semantics

The Message Passing Interface (MPI) standard 2.0 [5] extends the atomicity semantics by taking into consideration the parallel I/O operations. The MPI atomic mode is defined as: In concurrent overlapping MPI I/O operations, the results of the overlapped regions shall contain data from only one of the MPI processes that participates in the I/O operations. Otherwise, in the MPI nonatomic mode, the result of the overlapped regions is undefined. The difference of the MPI atomicity from the POSIX definition lies in the use of MPI file view, a new file concept introduced in MPI 2.0. A process's file view is created by calling up `MPI_File_set_view()` through an MPI-derived data type that specifies the visible file range to the process. When used in message passing, the MPI-derived data type is a powerful mechanism for describing the memory layout of a message buffer. This convenient tool is extended in MPI 2.0 for describing the file layout for the process's file view. Since a derived data type can specify a list of noncontiguous file segments, the visible data to a process can also be noncontiguous. In an MPI I/O operation, all visible segments to a requesting process are logically considered as a continuous data stream from/to the file system. In addition, each process can independently define its own file view independently from others in a collective MPI I/O operation.

In the MPI atomicity semantics, a call to `MPI_File_read_xxx()` or `MPI_File_writ_xxx()` is regarded as a single I/O operation. A single collective MPI I/O operation can contain requests from multiple processes. Since each process can define its own file view with a list of noncontiguous file segments, the overlapped file regions between two processes can also be noncontiguous in the file. If the underlying MPI I/O implementation considers the access to each file segment as a single `read()/write()` call, then there will be multiple calls issued simultaneously from a process to the file system. Although the atomicity of accessing to a contiguous overlapped region is guaranteed in the POSIX-compliant file systems, the MPI atomicity that demands atomicity across one or more regions of overlap cannot simply rely on the POSIX I/O calls. Additional effort is required to implement a correct MPI atomicity semantics. The fact that MPI-derived data types provide more programming flexibility when specifying noncontiguous file layouts increases the complexity of enforcing atomicity in MPI.

Figure 10.2 shows an example of a concurrent write from two processes in MPI atomic and nonatomic modes. The file views of both processes consist of six noncontiguous file segments, assuming that the two-dimensional array is stored in row-major. If writing each of the file segment uses a single call to `write()`, then there will be 12 write calls issued in total. Since the processing order of these 12 calls in the file system can be arbitrary, the result in the overlapped columns can contain interleaved data, as illustrated in the MPI nonatomic mode. The same outcome will occur in a POSIX file system since POSIX atomicity only considers the `read()/write()` calls individually. Therefore, the MPI implementation cannot simply rely on the file system to provide the correct file atomicity.

10.3 IMPLEMENTATION STRATEGIES

In many distributed-memory parallel computing systems in use today, dedicated compute nodes are often used as file servers to process the file requests from the application nodes. The designs of such file systems seldom consider concurrent overlapping I/O requests and many optimization strategies can actually hinder the parallelism of overlapping I/O. For example, the read-ahead and write-behind strategies

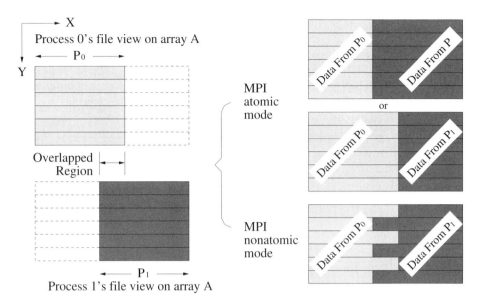

Figure 10.2 A two-dimensional column-wise partitioning with overlaps on two processes. In MPI atomic mode, overlapped data can only come from either P_0 or P_1. Otherwise, the result is undefined; for example, interleaved.

are adopted, in which read-ahead prefetches several file blocks following the data actual requested to the client's system cache in anticipation of the program's sequential reading pattern, and write-behind accumulates several requests in order to better utilize the available I/O bandwidth. The read-ahead and write-behind policies often work against the goals of any file system relying on random-access operations that are used commonly in parallel I/O operations. Under these two policies, two overlapping processes in a concurrent I/O operation can physically cache more overlapping data than logically overlaps in their file views. It is also possible that the overlapping data of two processes is cached by a third process because of the read-ahead.

The cache coherence problem has been studied extensively in many client–server-based file systems. The most commonly implemented caching scheme is to consult the server's modification time for the data cached on the clients before issuing the I/O requests. Obviously, communication overhead between server and clients for cache validation and refreshing can become significant for a concurrent overlapping I/O request due to the unnecessary data transfers. Although this problem can be alleviated by disabling the use of read-ahead/write-behind, the performance gain from the reduced overhead may not offset the performance loss due to disabling caching. In this chapter, our discussion is not limited to specific file systems and we assume the general I/O requests can start at arbitrary file spaces. We now examine two potential implementation strategies for MPI atomicity and analyze their performance complexity:

1. **Using byte-range file locking.** This approach uses the standard Unix byte-range file locking mechanism to wrap the read/write call in each process such that the exclusive access permission of the overlapped region can be granted to the requesting process. While a file region is locked, all read/write requests to it will directly go to the file server. Therefore, the written data of a process is visible to other processes after leaving the locking mode and the subsequent read requests will always obtain fresh data from the servers because of the use of the read locks.

2. **Using process handshaking.** This approach uses MPI communication to perform interprocess negotiation for writing to the overlapped file regions. The idea is a preferable alternative to using file locking. However, for file systems that perform read-ahead and write-behind, a file synchronization call immediately following every write call may be required to flush out all information associated with the writes in progress. Cache invalidation may also be needed before reading from the overlapped regions to ensure that there is fresh data coming from the servers. Under this strategy category, we further discuss two negotiation methods: graph coloring and process-rank ordering.

In order to help describe the above three approaches in terms of data amount and file layouts, two concurrent overlapping I/O cases are used as examples. These two cases employ access patterns commonly seen in many scientific applications: row-wise and column-wise partitioning on a two-dimensional array.

10.3.1 Row- and Column-Wise Two-Dimensional Array Partitioning

Given P processes participating a concurrent I/O operation, the row-wise partitioning pattern divides a two-dimensional array along its most significant axis, whereas the column-wise divides it along the least significant axis. To simplify the discussion, we assume all I/O requests are write requests and the following assumptions are also made:

- All P processes concurrently write their subarrays to a single shared file.
- The layouts of the two-dimensional array in both memory and disk storage are in row-major order, where axis Y is the most significant axis and X is the least.
- The subarrays partitioned in every two consecutive processes overlap with each other for a few rows or columns on the boundary along the partitioning axis.
- The global array is of size $M \times N$ and the number of overlapped rows or columns is R, where $R < M/P$ and $R < N/P$.

Figure 10.3 illustrates the two partitioning patterns on $P = 4$ processes. In the row-wise case, the file view of process P_i is a subarray of size $M' \times N$, where $M' = (M/P) + R$, if $0 < i < P - 1$. In the column-wise case, the file view of P_j is of size M

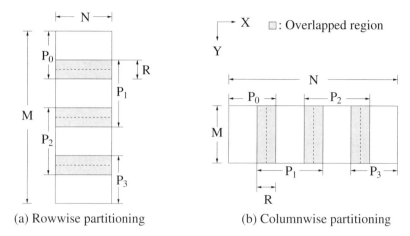

(a) Rowwise partitioning   (b) Columnwise partitioning

Figure 10.3 Row-wise and column-wise partitioning on a two-dimensional array. The file views of every two consecutive processes overlap with each other in R rows or columns along the Y/X axis.

$\times N'$, where $N' = (N/P) + R$ for $0 < j < P - 1$. Both P_0 and P_{P-1} contain $R/2$ rows or columns less in row and column-wise cases, respectively.

10.3.2 Byte-Range File Locking

Byte-range file locking is a mechanism provided by a file system within its locking protocol. This mechanism can be used to ensure the exclusive access to a locked file region. If a set of concurrent I/O calls contains only read requests, the locking protocol is usually implemented to allow a shared read lock so that more than one process can read the locked data simultaneously. If at least one of the I/O requests is a write request, the write lock is often granted exclusively to the requesting processes. Most of the existing locking protocols are centrally managed and their scalability is, hence, limited. A distributed locking protocol used in the IBM GPFS file system relieves the bottleneck by having a process manage its granted locked file region for the further requests from other processes [8]. When it comes to the overlapping requests, however, concurrent writes to the overlapped data must be still sequential.

10.3.2.1 *Row-wise Partitioning* We now use the row-wise partitioning example shown in Figure 10.3(a) to describe the atomicity implementation using file locking. In this example, the file view of a process overlaps R rows with its previous and successive processes. Since the file storage layout is assumed to be in a row-major order, that is, each row of size N is stored consecutively to its previous and successive row, every process' file view actually covers a single contiguous file space. Therefore, the concurrent overlapping I/O can be implemented using a single `write()` call in each process. On the file system that supports only the atomic

mode, atomic file results are automatically guaranteed for the row-wise partitioning case. On file systems that do no support the atomic mode, wrapping the I/O call in each process with byte-range locking of the file region will also generate atomic results. ROMIO, an MPIIO implementation developed at Argonne National Laboratory, relies on the use of byte-range file locking to implement the correct MPI atomicity in which processes must obtain an exclusive write lock to the overlapped file regions before they perform the write [12, 11].

10.3.2.2 Column-Wise Partitioning

In the column-wise partitioning case shown in Figure 10.3(b), the file view of each process is a subarray of size $M \times N'$ overlapping R columns with its left and right processes. Note that each of the M rows of size N' in the file view is not contiguous with its previous or successive row in the file-storage layout. The distance between the first elements of two consecutive rows in each process's file view is N. Therefore, the overlapped file regions of two consecutive processes consist of M noncontiguous rows of size R each. Figure 10.4 shows an MPI code fragment that creates the file view for each process using a derived data type to specify the column-wise partitioning pattern and a collective MPIIO call to perform the concurrent write.

An intuitive implementation for the column-wise case is to regard each contiguous I/O request as a single `read()`/`write()` call. This approach results in M write calls fromeach process and PM calls in total. On a POSIX file system, if all PM requests are processed concurrently without any specific order, interleaved results may occur in the overlapped regions. Since the processing order of these write requests can be arbitrary, the same scenario can also occur on other file systems even if file locking wraps around each I/O call. Enforcing the atomicity of individual `read()`/`write()` calls is not sufficient to enforce MPI atomicity. One solu-

```
1.   MPI_File_open(comm, filename, io_mode, info, &fh);
2.   MPI_File_set_atomicity(fh, 1);
3.   sizes[0] = M;          sizes[1] = N;
4.   sub_sizes[0] = M;    sub_sizes[1] = N / P;
5.   if (rank == 0 || rank == P-1)  sub_sizes[1] -= R/2;
6.   starts[0] = 0;          starts[1] = (rank == 0) ? 0 : rank * (N/P - R/2);
7.   MPI_Type_create_subarray(2, sizes, sub_sizes, starts, MPI_ORDER_C,
8.                         MPI_CHAR, &filetype);
9.   MPI_Type_commit(&filetype);
10.  MPI_File_set_view(fh, disp, MPI_CHAR, filetype, "native", info);
11.  MPI_File_write_all(fh, buf, buffer_size, etype, &status);
12.  MPI File close(&fh);
```

Figure 10.4   An MPI code fragment that performs the column-wise access. The shaded area illustrates the construction of the derived data type, to define process's file view.

tion is for each process to obtain all M locks before performing any write calls. However, this approach can easily cause deadlock when waiting for the requesting locks to be granted. An alternative is to have the file lock start at the process's first file offset and end at the very last file offset the process will write, virtually the entire file. In this way, all M rows of the overlapped region will be accessed atomically.

Though the POSIX standard defines a function, lio listio(), to initiate a list of noncontiguous file accesses in a single call, it does not explicitly indicate if its atomicity semantics are applicable. If POSIX atomicity is extended to `lio_listio()`, the MPI atomicity can be guaranteed by implementing the noncontiguous access on top of `lio-listio()`. Otherwise, additional effort such as file locking is necessary to ensure the MPI atomicity.

10.3.3   Processor Handshaking

An alternative approach to avoid using file locking is through process handshaking, in which the overlapping processes negotiate with each other to obtain the desirable access sequence to the overlapped regions. In this section, we discuss two possible implementations of process handshaking: graph coloring and process-rank ordering methods.

10.3.3.1   Graph-Coloring Approach   Given an undirected graph $G = (V, E)$ in which V represents a set of vertices and E represents a set of edges that connect the vertices, a k-coloring is a function $C : V \rightarrow \{1, 2, \ldots, k\}$ such that for all $u, v \in V$, if $C(u) = C(v)$, then $(u, v) \notin E$; that is, no adjacent vertices have the same color. The graph-coloring problem is to find the minimum number of colors, k, to color a given graph. Solving the MPI atomicity problem can be viewed as a graph-coloring problem if the I/O requesting processes are regarded as the vertices and the overlapping between two processes represents the edge. When applying graph-coloring to the MPI atomicity implementation, the I/O processes are first divided into k groups (colors) in which no two processes in a group overlap their file views. Then, the concurrent I/O is carried out in k steps. Note that process synchronization between any two steps is necessary to ensure that no process in one group can proceed with its I/O before the previous group's I/O completes. The graph-coloring approach fulfills the requirement of MPI atomicity while maintaining at least a degree of I/O parallelism.

The graph-coloring methodology is a heuristic that has been studied for a long time and has proved to be NP-hard for general graphs [2]. Because the overlapping I/O patterns present in most science applications are hardly arbitrary, a greedy solution may suffice. Figure 10.5 gives a simple, greedy graph-coloring algorithm that first uses a $P \times P$ overlapping matrix, W, to indicate if there is an overlap between two processes, and starts coloring the processes by looking for the lowest-ranked processes whose file views do not overlap with any process in that color. Let us now consider the column-wise partitioning example. Figure 10.6 shows the overlapping matrix using this greedy algorithm. It is obvious that two colors are enough

Given an overlapping P x P matrix, W, where

$$W[i][j] = \begin{cases} 1 & \text{if process i overlaps j and } i \neq j \\ 0 & \text{otherwise} \end{cases}$$

R_i : the ith row of W $R_i[j]$: the jth element of R

R' : an array of size P   C : an array of size P, initial all -1

```
1.    maxColor ← 0
2.    for  each row i = 0 . . . P-1
3.        for  j = 0 . . . P-1
4.            if  W[i][j] = 0  and  C[i] < 0  then
5.                C[j] ← maxColor
6.                break
7.        R' ← R_j
8.        for  k = j+1 . . . P-1
9.            if  R'[k] = 0  and  C[k] < 0  then
10.               C[k] ← maxColor
11.               R' ← R' ∨ R_k
12.       maxColor ← maxColor + 1
13.   myColor ← C[self]
```

Figure 10.5   A greedy graph-coloring algorithm that finds the color id for each I/O process in variable myColor.

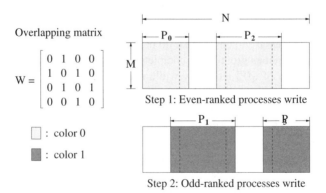

Figure 10.6   For the two-dimensional column-wise access, the graph-coloring algorithm divides the I/O requests into two steps: even-ranked processes write first, followed by the odd-ranked ones.

to maintain MPI atomicity; the even-ranked processes perform their I/O requests prior to the odd-ranked processes.

10.3.3.2   *Process-Rank Ordering*   Another process handshaking approach is to have all processes agree on a certain access priority to the overlapped file regions. An example is to use a policy in which the higher-ranked process wins the right to access the overlapped regions while others surrender their writes. A couple of immediate advantages of this approach are the elimination of overlapping access, so that all I/O requests can proceed concurrently, and the reduction of the overall I/O amount. The overhead of this method is the recalculation of each process's file view by marking down the overlapped regions with all higher-rank processes's file views. Considering the column-wise partitioning example, Figure 10.7 illustrates the new processes's file views generated from the process-rank ordering approach. The new file view for process P_i, $0 < i < P-1$, is a $M \times N/P$ subarray, whereas the file views for P_0 and P_{P-1} are $M \times [(N/P) - (R/2)]$ and $M \times [(N/P) + (R/2)]$, respectively. Compared to Figure 10.6, each process surrenders its write for the rightmost R columns.

10.3.4   Scalability Analysis

In the column-wise partition case, the file locking approach results in $MN - (N - N')$ bytes, nearly the entire file, being locked while each process is writing. In fact, once a process is granted its write locking request, no other processes can access to the file. As a result, using byte-range file locking serializes the I/O and dramatically degrades the performance. The purpose of proposing the two process-handshaking approaches is to try to maintain the I/O scalability without the use of file locking. The overhead of the graph-coloring approach is the construction of the overlapping matrix using all processes's file views. In the column-wise partitioning case, the graph-coloring approach maintains half of the I/O parallelism. In the process-rank ordering approach, the exact overlapped byte ranges must be known in order to generate the new local file view. Once the new file views are obtained, I/O requests can proceed with full parallelism. The overhead of both approaches is expected to be negligible when compared to the performance improvement resulting from the removal of all overlapping requests. Additionally, the overall I/O amount on the file system is reduced since the lower-rank processes surrender their accesses to the overlapped regions.

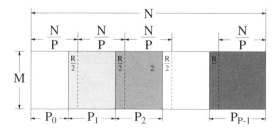

Figure 10.7   The new process-file views for the column-wise overlapping I/O resulting from the process-rank ordering approach.

10.4 EXPERIMENTAL RESULTS

We now examine the performance of the approaches discussed previously. The implementation of the column-wise partitioning example used standard Unix I/O calls and experimental results were obtained from three parallel machines: ASCI Cplant™, an Alpha Linux cluster at Sandia National Laboratory; the SGI Origin 2000 at the National Center for Supercomputing Applications (NCSA); and Blue Horizon, the IBM SP at San Diego Supercomputing Center (SDSC). The machine configurations are briefly described in Table 10.1. Cplant is a Linux cluster running the Extended Network File System (ENFS), in which each compute node is mapped to one of the I/O servers in a round-robin selection scheme at boot time [7]. Basically, ENFS is an NFS file system with a few changes. The most notable is the absence of file locking on Cplant. Accordingly, our performance results on Cplant do not include the experiments that use file locking. ENFS also performs the optimization that NFS usually does, including read-ahead and write-behind.

The experiments were obtained by running three array sizes: $4096 \times 8192(32$ MB), $4096 \times 32{,}768$ (128 MB), and $4096 \times 262{,}144$ (1 GB). On all three machines, we used 4, 8, and 16 processors, and the results are shown in Figure 10.8. Note that the performance of file locking is the worst of the implementations of MPI atomicity. The poor results are also expected, as discussed in Section 10.3.2, because file locking hinders the I/O concurrency. In most of the cases, the process-rank ordering strategy outperformed graph coloring. The overheads of calculating the overlapping matrix for both the graph-coloring and process-rank ordering approaches are less than 1% of the execution time in all the experiments.

10.5 SUMMARY

In this chapter, we examined the atomicity semantics for both the POSIX and MPI specifications. The difference between them is the number of noncontiguous regions in each I/O request. Although the POSIX considers only one contiguous file space I/O, a single MPI I/O request can access noncontiguous file space using MPI's file view facility. We compared a few implementation strategies for en-

Table 10.1 System configurations for the three parallel machines on which the experimental results were obtained

	Cplant	Origin 2000	IBM SP
File system	ENFS	XFS	GPFS
CPU type	Alpha	R10000	Power3
CPU speed	500 MHz	195 MHz	375 MHz
Network	Myrinet	Gigabit Ethernet	Colony switch
I/O servers	12	—	12
Peak I/O bandwidth	50 MB/s	4 GB/s	1.5 GB/s

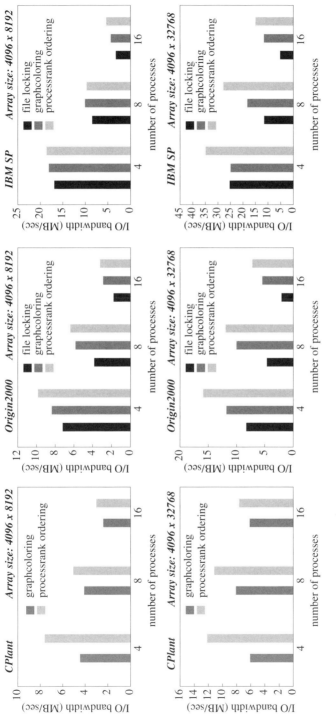

Figure 10.8 Performance results of running the column-wise partitioning experiments on a Linux Cluster, an IBM SP, and an SGI Origin200. Three file sizes were used: 32 MB, 128 MB, and 1GB. (*Continued on next page.*)

215

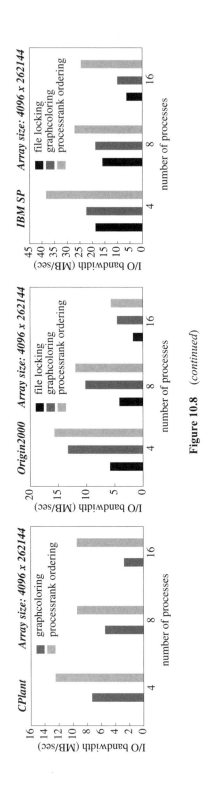

Figure 10.8 (*continued*)

forcing atomic writes in MPI, including file locking, graph coloring, and process-rank ordering. The experimental results showed that using file locking performed the worst when running a two-dimensional, column-wise partitioning case. Since file locking is basically a centrally managed mechanism, the parallelism of concurrent I/O requests, especially for overlapping I/O, can be significantly degraded by using it. The two alternatives proposed in this chapter negotiate process's I/O requests in order of access priority through process handshaking. Without using a centralized locking mechanism, these two approaches greatly improve the I/O performance.

The strategies of graph coloring and process-rank ordering require that every process be aware of all the processes participating in a concurrent I/O operation. In the scope of MPI, only collective calls have this property. Note that MPI collective I/O is different from the concurrent I/O, in which a concurrent I/O is for the more general I/O case. An MPI noncollective I/O operation can also be concurrent. File locking seems to be the only way to ensure atomic results in noncollective I/O calls in MPI, since the concurrent processes are unknown. Otherwise, given the participating processes, I/O optimizations such as the process handshaking approach proposed in this chapter can be applied to improve performance.

ACKNOWLEDGMENTS

This work was supported in part by DOE laboratories, SNL, LANL, and LLNL under subcontract No. PO28264, and in part by NSF EIA0103023. It was also supported in part by NSF cooperative agreement ACI9619020 through computing resources provided by the National Partnership for Advanced Computational Infrastructure at the San Diego Supercomputer Center. We also acknowledge the use of the SGI Origin2000 at NCSA.

REFERENCES

1. P. Crandall, R. Aydt, A. Chien, and D. Reed, Input-Output Characteristics of Scalable Parallel Applications, in *Supercomputing '95,* Dec. 1995.

2. M. Garey and D. Johnson, *Computers and Intractability: A Guide to the Theory of NP-Completeness,* W.H. Freeman, New York, 1979.

3. IEEE Std. 1003.12001, *System Interfaces,* 2001.

4. IEEE/ANSI Std. 1003.1, *Portable Operating System Interface (POSIX)-Part 1: System Application Program Interface (API) [C Language],* 1996.

5. Message Passing Interface Forum, *MPI2: Extensions to the Message Passing Interface,* http://www.mpiforum.org/docs/docs.html, July 1997.

6. N. Nieuwejaar, D. Kotz, A. Purakayastha, C. Ellis, and M. Best. File-Access Characteristics of Parallel Scientific Workloads, *IEEE Transactions on Parallel and Distributed Systems,* 7(10), 1075–1089, Oct. 1996.

7. Sandia National Laboratories, *Computational Plant,* http://www.cs.sandia.gov/Cplant.

8. F. Schmuck and R. Haskin, GPFS: A Shared-Disk File System for Large Computing Clusters, in *The Conference on File and Storage Technologies (FAST'02)*, pp. 231–244, Jan. 2002.

9. E. Smirni, R. Aydt, A. Chien, and D. Reed, I/O Requirements of Scientific Applications: An Evolutionary View, in *The Fifth IEEE International Symposium on High Performance Distributed Computing*, pp. 49–59, 1996.

10. E. Smirni and D. Reed, Lessons from Characterizing the Input/Output Behavior of Parallel Scientific Applications, *Performance Evaluation: An International Journal, 33*(1), 27–44, June 1998.

11. R. Thakur, W. Gropp, and E. Lusk, On Implementing MPIIO Portably and with High Performance, in *The Sixth Workshop on I/O in Parallel and Distributed Systems*, pp. 23–32, May 1999.

12. Rajeev Thakur, William Gropp, and Ewing Lusk, *Users Guide for ROMIO: A High-Performance, Portable MPI-IO Implementation*, Mathematics and Computer Science Division, Argonne National Laboratory, October 1997, Technical Report ANL/MCSTM234.

## CHAPTER 11

Code Tiling: One Size Fits All

JINGLING XUE and QINGGUANG HUANG

11.1 INTRODUCTION

As the disparity between processor and memory speeds continues to increase, the importance of effectively utilizing caches is becoming widely recognized. Loop tiling (or blocking) is probably the most well-known loop transformation for improving data locality. This transformation divides the iteration space of a loop nest into uniform tiles (or blocks) and schedules the tiles for execution. Under an appropriate choice of tile sizes, loop tiling often improves the execution times of array-dominated loop nests, sometimes significantly.

However, loop tiling is not known to be very useful (or even not considered to be needed [15]) for two-dimensional PDE (partial differential equation) solvers. In addition, tile-size-selection algorithms [5, 6, 12, 14, 18] target only the two-dimensional arrays accessed in tiled codes. To address these limitations, Song and Li [16] propose a new tiling technique for handling two-dimensional Jacobi solvers. However, their technique is not applicable to SOR (successive overrelaxation) PDE solvers. Rivera and Tseng [15] combine loop tiling and padding to tile three-dimensional PDE codes, but they do not exploit a large amount of the temporal reuse carried by the outermost time loop. In this chapter, we present a new technique for improving the cache performance of a class of loop nests, which includes multidimensional SOR PDE solvers as a special case.

Our compiler technique, called *code tiling,* emphasizes the joint restructuring of the control flow of a loop nest through loop tiling and of the data it uses through a new array-layout transformation called *data tiling*. Although loop tiling is effective in reducing capacity misses, data tiling reorganizes the data in memory by taking into account both the cache parameters and the data-access patterns in tiled code. By taking control of the mapping of data to memory, we can reduce the number of capacity and conflict misses (which are referred to collectively as *replacement misses*) methodically. In the case of SOR-like PDE solvers assuming a direct-mapped cache, our approach guarantees the absence of replacement misses in two consecutively executed tiles in the sense that no memory line will be evicted from the cache as long as it will still be accessed later in the two tiles (see Theorems 4

High-Performance Computing: Paradigm and Infrastructure. Edited by L. T. Yang and M. Guo   **219**

and 6). Furthermore, this property carries over to the tiled code we generate for two-dimensional SOR during the computation of all the tiles in a single execution of the innermost tile loop (see Theorem 5). Existing tile-size-selection algorithms [5, 6, 12, 14, 18] cannot guarantee this property.

The synergy of loop tiling and data tiling allows us to find a problem-size-independent tile size that minimizes a cache-miss objective function independently of the problem-size parameters. This "one-size-fits-all" scheme makes our approach attractive for designing fast SOR solvers for a given cache configuration without having to generate a multitude of versions specialized for different problem sizes.

We have evaluated code tiling for a two-dimensional SOR solver on four representative architectures. In comparison with nine published loop-tiling algorithms, our tiled codes have low cache misses, high performance benefits, and smooth performance curves across a range of problem sizes. In fact, code tiling has succeeded in eliminating a significant amount of cache misses that would otherwise be present in tiled codes.

The rest of this chapter is organized as follows. Section 11.2 defines our cache model. Section 11.3 introduces our program model and gives a high-level view of our code-tiling strategy. Section 11.4 describes how to construct a data-tiling transformation automatically. Section 11.5 focuses on finding optimal problem-size-independent tile sizes. Section 11.6 discusses performance results. Section 11.7 reviews related work. Section 11.8 concludes and discusses some future work.

11.2 CACHE MODEL

In this chapter, a data cache is modeled by three parameters: C denotes its size, L its line size, and $\mathcal{K}$ its associativity. C and L are in array elements unless otherwise specified. Sometimes, a cache configuration is specified as a triple $(C, L, \mathcal{K})$. In addition, we assume a fetch-on-write policy so that reads and writes are not distinguished.

A *memory line* refers to a cache-line-sized block in the memory, whereas a *cache line* refers to the actual block in which a memory line is mapped.

From an architectural standpoint, cache misses fall into one of three categories: *cold, capacity,* and *conflict.* In this chapter, cold misses are used as before but capacity and conflict misses are combined and called *replacement misses.*

11.3 CODE TILING

We consider the following program model:

$$\text{for } I_1 = p_1, q_1$$

$$\cdots \tag{11.1}$$

$$\text{for } I_m = p_m, q_m$$
$$A(I) = f(A(MI + c_1), \ldots, A(MI + c_\eta))$$

where $I = (I_1, \ldots, I_m)$ is known as the *iteration vector; M* is an $n \times m$ integer matrix; the loop bounds p_k and q_k are affine expressions of the outer loop variables I_1, $\ldots$, I_{k-1}; the vectors $c_1, \ldots, c_\eta$ are *offset* integer vectors of length n; and f symbolizes some arbitrary computation on the η array references. Thus, A is an n-dimensional array accessed in the loop nest. In this chapter, all arrays are assumed to be in row major. As is customary, the set of all iterations executed in the loop nest is known as the *iteration space* of the loop nest:

$$S = \{I = (I_1, \ldots, I_m) : p_k \leq I_k \leq q_k, k = 1, \ldots, m\} \qquad (11.2)$$

This program model is sufficiently general to include multidimensional SOR solvers. Figure 11.1 depicts a two-dimensional version, where the t loop is called the *time loop*, whose loop variable does not appear in the subscript expressions of the references in the loop body. In addition, the linear parts M of all subscript expressions are the identity matrix, and the offset vectors $c_1, \ldots, c_\eta$ contain the entries drawn from $\{-1, 0, 1\}$. These solvers are known as *stencil* codes because they compute values using neighboring array elements in a fixed stencil pattern. The stencil pattern of data accesses is repeated for each element of the array.

Without loss of generality, we assume that the program given in Equation (11.1) can be tiled legally by rectangular tiles [19]. For the two-dimensional SOR code, tiling the inner two loops is not beneficial since a large amount of temporal reuse carried by the time loop is not exploited. Due to the existence of the dependence vectors $(1, -1, 0)$ and $(1, 0, -1)$, tiling all three loops by rectangles would be illegal [19]. Instead, we skew the iteration space by using the linear transformation $\begin{bmatrix} 1 & 0 & 0 \\ 1 & 1 & 0 \\ 1 & 0 & 1 \end{bmatrix}$ and then permute the time step into the innermost position. This gives rise to the program in Figure 11.2. We choose to move the time step inside because a large amount of temporal reuse in the time step can be exploited for large values of P.

Loop tiling can be modeled as a mapping from the iteration space S to $\mathbb{Z}^{2m}$ such that each iteration $(I_1, \ldots, I_m) \in S$ is mapped to a new point in $\mathbb{Z}^{2m}$ [7, 19]:

$$(I_1, \ldots, I_m) \rightarrow \left(\left\lfloor \frac{I_1}{T_1} \right\rfloor, \ldots, \left\lfloor \frac{I_m}{T_m} \right\rfloor, I_1, \ldots, I_m \right) \qquad (11.3)$$

```
double A(0 : N + 1, 0 : N + 1)
for t = 0, P − 1
for i = 1, N
for j = 1, N
    A(i, j) = 0.2 × [A(i, j) + A(i − 1, j) + A(i, j − 1)
              + A(i + 1, j) + A(i, j + 1)]
```

Figure 11.1 Two-dimensional SOR code.

```
double A(0 : N + 1, 0 : N + 1)
for i = 0, P + N − 2
for j = 0, P + N − 2
for t = max(0, i − N + 1, j − N + 1), min(P − 1, i, j)
    A(i − t, j − t) = 0.2 × [A(i − t + 1, j − t) + A(i − t, j − t + 1)
                            + A(i − t, j − t) + A(i − t, j − t − 1) + A(i − t − 1, j − t)]
```

Figure 11.2   Skewed two-dimensional SOR code.

where $(T_1, \ldots, T_m)$ is called the *tile size* and $(\lfloor I_1/T_1 \rfloor, \ldots, \lfloor I_m/T_m \rfloor)$ identifies the tile that the iteration $(I_1, \ldots, I_m)$ belongs to. Viewed as a loop transformation, loop tiling decomposes an m-dimensional loop into a $2m$-dimensional loop nest, where the outer m loops are the *tile loops* controlling the execution of tiles and the inner m loops are the *element loops* controlling the execution of the iterations in a tile.

Definition 1 (Adjacent Tiles)   Two tiles identified by $(u_1, \ldots, u_m)$ and $(u_1', \ldots, u_m')$ are said to be *adjacent* if $u_1 = u_1', \ldots, u_{m-1} = u_{m-1}'$ and $u_m = u_m' - 1$.

Definition 2 (Intra-, Inter$_1$- and Inter$_2$-Tile (Replacement) Misses and Cold Misses)   Let u be a given tile and u' be its adjacent tile previously executed. Let there be k accesses, $a_1, \ldots, a_k$, to a memory line ℓ in the tile u. Any of the last $k - 1$ such accesses, a_i, where $i > 1$, is a replacement miss if ℓ is found not to be in the cache when a_i is executed. Such a replacement miss is called an *intratile (replacement) miss*. If the access a_1 is a miss, there are three cases. (a) If ℓ was also previously accessed in u', then the miss is called an *inter$_1$-tile (replacement) miss*. (b) If ℓ was previously accessed but not in u', then the miss is called an *inter$_2$-tile (replacement) miss*. (c) Otherwise, the miss is known as a cold miss in the standard manner.

By this definition, a miss is either a cold, intra-tile, inter$_1$-tile or inter$_2$-tile miss. Let u and u' be two adjacent tiles. If a tiled loop nest is free of intra- and inter$_1$-tile misses in both tiles, then no memory line will be evicted from the cache during their execution if it will still need to be accessed in u and u', and conversely.

Figure 11.3 gives a high-level view of code tiling for direct-mapped caches. In Step 1, the tiled code is generated with all the tile size parameters to be determined. In Step 2, we construct a data tiling g to map the n-dimensional array A to the one-dimensional array B such that the tiled code operating on B is free of intra- and inter$_1$-tile misses (see Definition 3). There can be many choices for such tile sizes. In Step 3 of Figure 11.3, we choose one such that the number of inter$_2$-tile misses is minimized. The optimal tile size found is independent of the problem size because our cost function is (Section 11.5). Our construction of g ensures that the number of cold misses in the tiled code increases only moderately (due to data remapping) with respect to that in the original program. Finally, in Steps 4 and 5, the final tiled code is generated.

Algorithm: CodeTiling
INPUT: • A program that conforms to the model (11.1)
  • Cache parameters $(C, L, 1)$ (in array elements)
OUTPUT: Tiled code for the given program

1. Generate the initial tiled code using loop tiling [19].

> The $2m$ loops go here // omitted
> $A(I) = f[A(MI + c_1), \ldots, A(MI + c_\eta)]$

2. Construct a data tiling transformation $g : \mathbb{Z}^n \to \mathbb{Z}$, to eliminate both intra- and inter_1-tile misses (Section 11.4).

3. Find the problem-size-independent tile size to miminize the inter_2-tile misses as described in Section 11.5.

4. Modify the tiled code obtained in (a) to get:

> The code to copy A to a new 1D array named B
> The same loop nest as in Step 1 goes here // omitted
> $B[g(I)] = f\{B[g(MI + c_1)], \ldots, B[g(MI + c_\eta)]\}$
> The code to copy the results in B to A

5. Compute g incrementally using additions/subtractions and apply loop distribution, if necessary, to avoid max and min.

Figure 11.3   Code tiling for a direct-mapped cache.

Definition 3 (Data Tiling)   Let a direct-mapped cache $(C, L, 1)$ be given. A mapping $g : \mathbb{Z}^n \to \mathbb{Z}$ (constructed in Step 2 of Figure 11.3) is called a *data tiling* if the tiled code given is free of intra- and inter_1-tile misses.

For a $\mathcal{K}$-way set-associative cache $(C, L, \mathcal{K})$, where $\mathcal{K} > 1$, we treat the cache as if it were the direct-mapped cache $[(\mathcal{K} - 1/\mathcal{K}) C, L, 1]$. As far as this hypothetical cache is concerned, g used in the tiled code is a data-tiling transformation. By using the effective cache size $(\mathcal{K} - 1/\mathcal{K})C$ to model the impact of associativity on cache misses, we are still able to eliminate all intratile misses for the physical cache (see Theorem 3). In the special case when $\mathcal{K} = 2$, the cache may be underutilized since the effective cache size is only $C/2$. Instead, we will treat the cache as if it were $(C, L, 1)$. The effectiveness of our approach has been validated by experiments.

11.4   DATA TILING

We describe an algorithm for constructing data-tiling transformations automatically. Throughout this section, we assume a direct-mapped cache, denoted by $(C, L, 1)$, where the cache size C and the line size L are both in array elements.

We will focus on a loop nest that conforms to the program model defined in Equation (11.1) with the iteration space S given in Equation (11.2). We denote by $offset(A)$ the set of the offset vectors of all η array references to A, that is, $offset(A) = \{c_1, \ldots, c_\eta\}$. The notation e_i denotes the i-th elementary vector whose i-th component is 1 and all the rest are 0.

Recall that a loop tiling is a mapping as defined in Equation (11.3) and that $T = (T_1, \cdots, T_m)$ denotes the tile size used. Let S_T be the set of all the tiles obtained for the program:

$$S_T = \left\{ u = (u_1, \ldots, u_m) : u = \left(\left\lfloor \frac{I_1}{T_1} \right\rfloor, \ldots, \left\lfloor \frac{I_m}{T_m} \right\rfloor \right), I \in S \right\} \qquad (11.4)$$

Let $T(u)$ be the set of all iterations contained in the tile u:

$$T(u) = \{v = (v_1, \ldots, v_m) : u_k T_k \le v_k \le (u_k + 1)T_k - 1, k = 1, \ldots, m\} \qquad (11.5)$$

where constraint $I \in S$ from Equation (11.4) is omitted. Thus, the effect of the iteration space boundaries on $T(u)$ is ignored. As a result, $|T(u)|$ is invariant with respect to u.

For notational convenience, the operator mod is used as both an infix and a prefix operator. We do not distinguish whether a vector is a row or column vector and assume that this is deducible from the context.

Let $addr$ be a memory address. In a direct-mapped cache $(C, \mathcal{L}, 1)$, the address resides in the memory line $\lfloor addr/\mathcal{L} \rfloor$ and is mapped to the cache line $\text{mod}(\lfloor addr/\mathcal{L} \rfloor, C/\mathcal{L})$.

In Section 11.4.1, we give a sufficient condition for a mapping to be a data tiling transformation. In Section 11.4.2, we motivate our approach by constructing a data-tiling transformation for the two-dimensional SOR program. In Section 11.4.3, we construct data-tiling transformations for the programs defined in Equation (11.1).

11.4.1 A Sufficient Condition

For a tile $u \in S_T$, its *working set,* denoted $D[T(u)]$, is given by:

$$D[T(u)] = \{MI + c : I \in T(u), c \in offset(A)\} \qquad (11.6)$$

It is easy to show that $D[T(u)]$ is a translation of $D[T(u')]$ for $u, u' \in S_T$. This property plays an important role in our development, which leads directly to Theorem 1.

Theorem 1 Let $u, u' \in S_T$ be two adjacent tiles, where $u' = u + e_m$. Then $|D[T(u)]\backslash D[T(u')]| = |D[T(u')]\backslash D[T(u)]|$ and $|D[T(u')]\backslash D[T(u)]|$ is independent of u (i.e., invariant with respect to u).

Figure 11.4 illustrates Theorem 1 using the example given in Figure 11.2. This theorem implies that the number of elements that are accessed in u but not in u', that is, $|D[T(u)]\backslash D[T(u')]|$, is exactly the same as the number of elements that are ac-

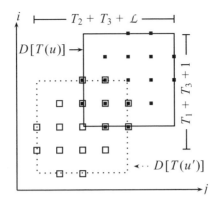

Figure 11.4   An illustration of Theorem 1 using the SOR in Figure 11.2. It is assumed $T_1 = T_2 = T_3 = L = 2$ and u and u' are two arbitrary adjacent tiles executed in that order. Thus, $|T(u)| = |T(u')| = 2 \times 2 \times 2 = 8$. The working sets $D[T(u)]$ and $D[T(u')]$ are depicted by the solid and dotted (larger) boxes, respectively. Thus, each (small) solid or plain box at (i, j) depicts an array element $A(i, j)$, identified by its array indices (i, j). The two "distance numbers" $T_1 + T_3 + 1$ and $T_2 + T_3 + L$ will be defined in Section 11.4.2.

cessed in u' but not in u, that is, $|D[T(u')]\backslash D[T(u)]|$. If we can find a one-to-one mapping $\psi : D(S) \to \mathbb{Z}$, such that $\psi : D[T(u')]\backslash D[T(u)] \to \psi[D(T(u)]\backslash D[T(u')]$ mod C and use it to map the element $A(MI + c)$ to $B[\psi(MI + c)]$, where $c \in \textit{offset}(A)$, then the two corresponding elements in the two sets will be mapped to the same cache line. By convention, $D(S)$ is the union of $D[T(u)]$ for all $u \in S_T$. As a result, the newly accessed data in $D[T(u')]\backslash D[T(u)]$ when u' is executed will evict from the cache exactly those data in $D[T(u)]\backslash D[T(u')]$ previously accessed in u.

However, this does not guarantee that all intra- and inter$_1$-tile misses are eliminated. Below we give a condition for data tiling to guarantee these two properties.

For a one-to-one mapping $g : \mathbb{Z}^n \to \mathbb{Z}$ and a subset $W \subset \mathbb{Z}^n$, $g : W \to g(W)$ is said to be a (C, L)-one-to-one mapping on W if whenever the following condition

$$\text{mod}\left(\left\lfloor \frac{g(w_1)}{L} \right\rfloor, C/L\right) = \text{mod}\left(\left\lfloor \frac{g(w_2)}{L} \right\rfloor, C/L\right) \tag{11.7}$$

holds, where $w_1, w_2 \in W$, then the following condition must hold:

$$\left\lfloor \frac{g(w_1)}{L} \right\rfloor = \left\lfloor \frac{g(w_2)}{L} \right\rfloor \tag{11.8}$$

A mapping $g : D(S) \to \mathbb{Z}$ is said to be (C, L)-one-to-one on S_T if g is (C, L)-one-to-one on $D[T(u)]$ for all $u \in S_T$.

Theorem 2   Let a direct-mapped cache $(C, L, 1)$ be given. A mapping $g : D(S) \to \mathbb{Z}$ is a data tiling if g is (C, L)-one-to-one on S_T.

Proof   Follows from Definition 3 and the definition of g.   □

Theorem 3   Consider a $\mathcal{K}$-way set-associative cache $(C, L, \mathcal{K})$ with an LRU replacement policy, where $\mathcal{K} > 1$. If a mapping $g : D(S) \rightarrow \mathbb{Z}$ is $[(\mathcal{K}_{-1}/\mathcal{K}) \, C, L]$-1-to-1 on S_T, then there are no intratile misses in the tiled code from Figure 11.3.

Proof   For the g given, there are at most $\mathcal{K} - 1$ distinct memory lines accessed during the execution of a single tile. By Definition 3, there are no intratile misses.   □

11.4.2 Constructing a Data Tiling for Two-Dimensional SOR

In this section, we construct a data-tiling transformation to eliminate all intra- and inter_1-tilemisses for two-dimensional SOR. We will continue to use the example given in Figure 11.4. Since the array A is stored in row major, the elements depicted in the same row are stored consecutively in memory. In Step 2 of Figure 11.3, we will construct a data tiling g to map A to B such that the elements of B will reside in the memory and cache lines as illustrated in Figure 11.5.

The basic idea is to divide the set of all elements of A into equivalence classes such that $A(i, j)$ and $A(i', j')$ are in the same class if $i = i' \bmod (T_1 + T_3 + 1)$ and $j = j' \bmod (T_2 + T_3 + L)$. For all array elements of A in the same equivalence class, we will construct g such that their corresponding elements in the one-dimensional array B have the same memory address (modulo C). In other words, $A(i, j)$ and $A(i', j')$ are

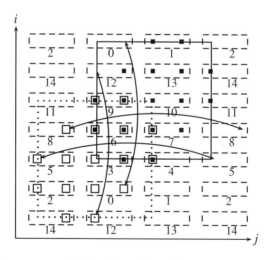

Figure 11.5   Memory reorganization effected by a data tiling g when $C = 30$ and $L = 2$. Continuing from Figure 11.4, g ensures that the elements of A are mapped to B so that all elements in B are aligned at the memory-line boundaries as shown. Each dashed box indicates that the two elements inside are in the same memory line; the number below indicates the cache line to which the memory line is mapped. The two elements connected by an arc are mapped to the same cache line (i.e., in the same equivalence class).

in the same class iff $g(i, j) = g(i', j')$ mod C. In Figure 11.5, the two elements of A connected by an arc are mapped to the same cache line. This ensures essentially that the unused elements that are accessed in a tile will be replaced in the cache by the newly accessed elements in its adjacent tile to be executed next. As mentioned earlier, this does not guarantee the absence of intra- and inter$_1$-tile misses. To eliminate them, we must impose some restrictions on (T_1, T_2, T_3). For example, a tile size that is larger than the cache size will usually induce intratile misses.

In the SOR program given in Figure 11.2, the linear part of an array reference is:

$$M = \begin{pmatrix} 1 & 0 & -1 \\ 0 & 1 & -1 \end{pmatrix}$$

and $offset(A) = \{c = (c_1, c_2) : |c_1| + |c_2| \leq 1\}$. Let $u = (ii, jj, tt)$, $u' = (ii, jj, tt + 1) \in S_T$ be two adjacent tiles, and $T(u)$ and $T(u')$ defined by Equation (11.5).

By Definition 3, it suffices to find a (C, L)-1-to-1 mapping on S_T. We introduce a two-parallelotope that contains $D[T(u)]$, which can be obtained by our algorithms, FindFacets and FindQ given in Figures 1.6 and 1.7, respectively. We denote this parallelotope by $[G, F(u), K]$. For the example shown in Figure 11.4, $\{G, F[(0, 0, 1)], K\}$ is defined by $\{I \in \mathbb{Z}^2 : -T_3 \leq G_1 I \leq T_1 + T_3, -T_3 \leq G_2 I \leq T_2 + T_3\}$, where $G_1 = (0, 1)$ and $G_2 = (1, 0)$, where $F[(0, 0, 1)] = (-T_3, -T_3)$, $K = (T_1 + T_3, T_2 + T_3)$ and the first and second rows of G are G_1 and G_2, respectively. According to $[G, F(u), K]$, we classify the points in the data space $[0, N + 1] \times [0, N + 1]$ (i.e., the set of array indices of A) such that the points in the same class are mapped into the same cache line. We say that two points (i, j) and (i', j') are *equivalent* if $G_1(i - i', j - j') = s(T_1 + T_3 + 1)$ and $G_2(i - i', j - j') = t(T_2 + T_3 + L)$, that is, if $i = i' + s(T_1 + T_3 + 1)$ and $j = j' + t(T_2 + T_3 + L)$, for some integers s and t. Two points are in the same class iff they are equivalent. For example, the two points connected by an arc in Figure 11.5 are in the same equivalence class.

Let $T_{13} = T_1 + T_3 + 1$ and $T_{23} = \lceil (T_2 + T_3 + 1)/L \rceil L$. We define:

$$g(i, j) = (\lfloor i/T_{13} \rfloor \lceil (N - 1)/T_{23} \rceil + \lfloor j/T_{23} \rfloor)C + \text{mod } (i, T_{13})T_{23} + \text{mod}(j, T_{23}) \quad (11.9)$$

Theorem 4 Let a direct-mapped cache $(C, L, 1)$ be given. Then g defined in (11.9) is a data tiling transformation for the two-dimensional SOR if the following two conditions hold:

1. L divides both T_2 and T_3
2. $(T_1 + T_3 + 1)\lceil (T_2 + T_3 + 1)/L \rceil L \leq C$

Proof By Theorem 2, we only need to prove that g is (C, L)-one-to-one on S_T. Let $u = (ii, jj, tt)$ and $T(u) = \{(i, j, t) : iiT_1 \leq i < (ii + 1)T_1, jjT_2 \leq j < (j + 1)T_2, ttT_3 < t < (tt + 1)T_3\}$. Thus, $D[T(u)] = \{(i - t, j - t) + c : (i, j, t) \in T(u), c \in offset(A)\}$. Let $(G, F(u), K)$ be the two-parallelotope containing $D[T(u)]$. Then $F(u) = (iiT_1 - ttT_3, jjT_2 - ttT_3)$. Suppose that $\text{mod}(\lfloor g(i, j)/L \rfloor, C/L) = \text{mod}(\lfloor g(i', j')/L \rfloor, C/L)$, where (i, j), $(i', j') \in D[T(u)]$. By the second hypothesis, $\lfloor \text{mod}(j, T_{23})/L \rfloor$, $\lfloor \text{mod}(j', T_{23})/L \rfloor < C$

holds. Thus, $\mathrm{mod}(i, T_{13})(T_{23}/L) + \lfloor \mathrm{mod}(j, T_{23})/L \rfloor = \mathrm{mod}(i', T_{13})(T_{23}/L) + \lfloor \mathrm{mod}(j', T_{23})/L \rfloor$. Since $\lfloor \mathrm{mod}(j, T_{23})/L \rfloor < T_{23}/L$ and $\lfloor \mathrm{mod}(j', T_{23})/L \rfloor < T_{23}/L$, we have that $i = i'$, and hence, that $\lfloor \mathrm{mod}(j, T_{23})/L \rfloor = \lfloor \mathrm{mod}(j', T_{23})/L \rfloor$. By the first hypothesis that L divides both T_2 and T_3, L must divide $g[F(u)]$ for all $u \in S_T$. Clearly, L divides $g[F(u) + (0, T_{23})]$ since L divides T_{23}. Since $g[F(u)] \le g(i, j)$, $g(i, j') < g[F(u) + (0, T_{23})]$ and $g[F(u) + (0, T_{23})] - g[F(u)] < C$, we have $\lfloor g(i, j)/L \rfloor = \lfloor g(i', j')/L \rfloor$. Hence, we have proved that g is (C, L)-one-to-one on S_T. $\square$

Therefore, g in Equation (11.9) for SOR guarantees the absence of intra- and inter$_1$-tile misses in the tiled code provided the two conditions in Theorem 4 are satisfied.

In the example illustrated in Figures 11.4 and 11.5, we have $T_1 = T_2 = T_3 = L = 2$ and $C = 30$. It can be verified that the two conditions in Theorem 4 are true. The resulting data tiling can be obtained by substituting these values into Equation (11.9).

In fact, our g has eliminated all inter$_2$-tile misses among the tiles in a single execution of the innermost tile loop.

Theorem 5   Under the same assumptions of Theorem 4, g defined in Equation (11.9) ensures that during any single execution of the innermost tile loop, every memory line, once evicted from the cache, will not be accessed during the rest of the execution.

Proof   Let $u = (ii, jj, tt)$ be an arbitrary tile and $D[T(u)]$ be defined as in the proof of Theorem 4. Let $\tilde{D}[T(u)]$ be the set of memory lines ℓ such that $\ell \in \tilde{D}[T(u)]$ iff there is $(i, j) \in D[T(u)]$ such that $B[g(i, j)]$ resides in ℓ. Let $u' = (ii, jj, tt + 1)$ and $u'' = (ii, jj, tt + m)$, where $m \ge 1$, and $\tilde{D}[T(u')]$ and $\tilde{D}[T(u'')]$ be similarly defined. From the proof of Theorem 4, we see that g is (C, L)-one-to-one. Thus, any memory line that is accessed in a tile cannot be evicted from the cache in that tile. If a memory line $\ell \in \tilde{D}[T(u)]$ is evicted from the cache when the tiles u and u' are executed, we prove next that ℓ must be contained in $\tilde{D}[T(u)] \backslash \tilde{D}[T(u')]$. In fact, if $\ell \notin \tilde{D}[T(u)] \backslash \tilde{D}[T(u')]$, then $\ell \in \tilde{D}[T(u')]$. Suppose that $\ell \in \tilde{D}[T(u')]$, then $\ell \in \tilde{D}[T(u)] \cap \tilde{D}[T(u')]$, and, hence, ℓ cannot be evicted from the cache in either u or u'. This contradicts the assumption on ℓ. Since $T_3 = L$, L divides both T_2 and T_{23}, and, by noting Equation (11.9), we have $(\tilde{D}[T(u)] \backslash \tilde{D}[T(u')]) \cap \tilde{D}[T(u'')] = \emptyset$. By noting that $\ell \in \tilde{D}[T(u)] \backslash \tilde{D}[T(u')]$, we conclude that ℓ cannot be accessed in u''. $\square$

11.4.3   Constructing a Data Tiling for Equation (11.1)

We give a data tiling, denoted g, for a program of the form of Equation (11.1). This time we need an r-parallelotope [17] that contains $D[T(u)]$, where r is the dimension of the affine hull of $D[T(u)]$. This parallelotope, denoted $P[T(u)]$, is found by FindFacets, given in Figure 11.6. We can see that $P[T(u)]$ is the smallest r-parallelotope containing $D[T(u)]$ if the components of the offset vectors in *offset*(A) are all from $\{-1, 0, 1\}$. Therefore, it is only necessary to map the ele-

Algorithm FindFacets
INPUT: M and $\mathit{offset}(A)$ in (11.1), T and $T(u)$
OUTPUT: The facets $[G, F(u), K]$ of $P[T(u)]$

For a subset σ of $[1, m]$ and $x = (x_1, \ldots, x_m)$, we write $x_\sigma = \Sigma_{i\in\sigma}x_ie_i$ and $x^\sigma = \Sigma_{i\in[1, m]\backslash\sigma}x_ie_i$.

1. Calculate the rank of M. Let $r = \mathrm{rank}(M)$. Let $M = [M_1, \ldots, M_m]$, where M_i is the i-th column of M.

2. $\tilde{K} = \{\{k_1, \ldots, k_s\} : 1 \le k_1 < \cdots < k_s \le m, \mathrm{rank}([M_{k_1}, \ldots, M_{k_s}]) = r - 1\}$.

3. $\max \tilde{K} = \{\sigma \in \tilde{K} : \nexists\, \sigma' \in \tilde{K}$ such that $\sigma \subset \sigma', \sigma \ne \sigma'\}$.

4. For $\sigma = \{\sigma_{i_1}, \ldots, \sigma_{i_s}\} \in \max \tilde{K}$, find a $G_\sigma \in \mathrm{IR}^m$ such that $G_\sigma M_{\sigma i} = 0$, $i = 1, \ldots, s$, $G_\sigma \ne 0$ and G_σ is a linear combination of $M_1, \ldots, M_m$.

5. Let $t_i = u_iT_i$ and $t'_i = (u_i + 1)T_i - 1$. Let $node[T(u)] = \{x = (x_1, \ldots, x_m) : x_i \in \{t_i, t'_i\}\}$. For $\sigma \in \max \tilde{K}$, find $x, z \in node[T(u)]$ such that $G_\sigma Mx^\sigma \le G_\sigma My^\sigma \le G_\sigma Mz^\sigma$ for all $y \in node[T(u)]$. Put $\sigma_- = x^\sigma$ and $\sigma_+ = z^\sigma$. Then $MT(u)^\pm_\sigma$ is a facet of $MT(u)$, where $T(u)^\pm_\sigma = \{y_\sigma + \sigma_\pm : y \in T(u)\}$.

6. Let $\max \tilde{K} = \{\sigma^1, \ldots, \sigma^p\}$, $G_i = G_{\sigma i}$ and $T^\pm_i = T(u)^\pm_{\sigma i}$. Let $\Gamma(M) = \{_\mathrm{r} = (\gamma_1, \ldots, \gamma_r) : 1 \le \gamma_1 < \cdots < \gamma_r \le p\}$. For $\gamma_r \in \Gamma(M)$, we have an r-parallelotope $(G^\gamma, F^\gamma, K^\gamma)$ containing $MT(u)$, where $(G^\gamma, F^\gamma, K^\gamma) = \{y \in H : F^\gamma_i \le G_{\gamma i}y \le F^\gamma_i + K^\gamma_i\}$, $F^\gamma_i = G_{\gamma i}MT^-_{\gamma i}$ and $K^\gamma_i = G_{\gamma i}MT^+_{\gamma i} - G_{\gamma i}MT^-_{\gamma i}$. Find a γ such that the volume of $(G^\gamma, F^\gamma, K^\gamma)$ is not smaller than the volume of $(G^{\gamma'}, F^{\gamma'}, \mathcal{K}^{\gamma'})$ for all $\gamma' \in \Gamma(M)$.

7. Let $(G^\gamma, F^\gamma, K^\gamma)$ be found in Step 6. Find $c^i_-, c^i_+ \in \mathit{offset}(A)$ such that $G^\gamma_i c^i_- \le G^\gamma_i c \le G^\gamma_i c^i_+$ for all $c \in \mathit{offset}(A)$.

8. An r-parallelotope $(G, F(u), K)$ that contains $\cup_{c\in\mathit{offset}(A)}(MT(u) + c)$ is found, where $G = G^\gamma$, $F(u) = (F_1, \ldots, F_r)$, $\mathcal{K} = (K_1, \ldots, K_r)$ and $F_i = F^\gamma_i + G^\gamma_i c^i_-$, $K_i = K^\gamma_i + G^\gamma_i c^i_+ - G^\gamma_i c^i_-$.

Figure 11.6   An algorithm for finding the facets of a parallelepiped.

ments of A that are accessed in the loop next to B. Hence, g is a mapping from $\mathbb{Z}^r$ to $\mathbb{Z}$, where $r \le n$.

Let $\phi(T)$ and $\psi(T)$ be the number of elements contained in $D[T(u)]$ and $P[T(u)]$, respectively. We assume that a tile fits into the cache, that is, $\psi(T) \le C$. Let $P[T(u)] = (G, F(u), \mathcal{K})$ be found by FindFacets and Q by FindQ given in Figure 11.7. Without loss of generality, we assume that $0 \in D(S)$ and $G\tilde{Q}S = \{v = (v_1, \ldots, v_r) : v_i = \lfloor G_i I/Q_i \rfloor, I \in S, i = 1, \ldots, r\}$, where $\tilde{Q} = \mathrm{diag}(\tilde{Q}_1, \ldots, \tilde{Q}_r)$, $\tilde{Q}_1 = Q_1, \ldots, \tilde{Q}_{r-1} = Q_{r-1}$ and $\tilde{Q}_r = \lceil (Q_r/\mathcal{L}) \rceil \mathcal{L}$. We call $G\tilde{Q}S$ the *data tile space*. For the SOR example, we have $r = 2$, $Q = \mathrm{diag}(T_1 + T_3 + 1, T_2 + T_3 + 1)$ and $\tilde{Q} = \mathrm{diag}(T_1 + T_3 + 1, \lceil (T_2 + T_3 + 1)/\mathcal{L} \rceil \mathcal{L})$. Assume that LB_i and UB_i are the smallest and largest of the i-th components of all the points in $G\tilde{Q}S$, respectively. For $I \in D(S)$, let $y(I) = [y_1(I), \ldots, y_r(I)] = \lfloor Q^{-1}GI \rfloor$ and $z(I) = [z_1(I), \ldots, z_r(I)] = GI - \tilde{Q}y(I)$.

Algorithm FindQ
INPUT: M and *offset*(A) in (11.1), $T(u)$ and $[G, F(u), K]$ of $P[T(u)]$
OUTPUT: Q

1. Put $G_i = G_{\sigma^{\gamma i}}$, where $\sigma^{\gamma i}$ is defined Step 6 of FindFacets. Let $1 \leq m_0 \leq m$ and $1 \leq r_0 \leq r$ such that $G_i M_{m_0} \neq 0, i = 1, \ldots, r_0, G_i M_{m_0} = 0, i = r_0 + 1, \ldots, r$ and $G_i M_s = 0, i = 1, \ldots, r, s = m_0 + 1, \ldots, m$. Let $\{G_i M y^{\sigma^{\gamma i}} + G_i c : y \in T(u), c \in offset(A)\} = \{h_1^i, \ldots, h_q^i\}$, where $h_1^i < \cdots < h_q^i$.

2. Let $\Delta = t'_{m_0} - t_{m_0} + 1$. If $G_i M_{m_0} > 0$, then take the smallest h_j^i such that $h_j^i + \Delta G_i M_{m_0} > h_q^i$ and define $Q_i = h_j^i + \Delta G_i M_{m_0} - h_1^i$. Otherwise, take the largest h_j^i such that $h_j^i + \Delta G_i M_{m_0} < h_1^i$ and define $Q_i = h_q^i - (h_j^i + \Delta G_i M_{m_0})$.

Figure 11.7   An algorithm for finding Q as required in Section 11.4.3.

Let $v = (v_1, \ldots, v_r)$ and

$$\text{rowLayout}(v_1, \ldots, v_r) = \sum_{j=1}^{r-1} \text{mod}\,(G_j v, \tilde{Q}_j) \prod_{k=j+1}^{r} (K_k + 1) + \text{mod}\,(G_r v, \tilde{Q}_r) \quad (11.10)$$

Let

$$g(v_1, \ldots, v_r) = \text{rowLayout}[z_1(v), \ldots, z_r(v)] + c\sum_{j=1}^{r} y_j(v) \prod_{k=j+1}^{r} (\text{UB}_k - \text{LB}_k) \quad (11.11)$$

where $\prod_{k=r+1}^{r}(\text{UB}_k - \text{LB}_k) = 0$.

Theorem 6   Let a direct-mapped cache $(C, L, 1)$ be given. Then g defined in Equation (11.11) is a data tiling transformation for Equation (11.1) if the following two conditions hold:

1. L divides $F_r(u)$ for all $u \in S_T$
2. $(\prod_{k=1}^{r-1} Q_k) \lceil Q_r \backslash L \rceil L \leq C$

Proof   Under the given two conditions, g is (C, L)-one-on-one on S_T. By Theorem 2, g is a data tiling as desired.   □

11.5   FINDING OPTIMAL TILE SIZES

Let a loop nest of the form of Equation (11.1) be given, where A is the array accessed in the nest. Let this loop nest be tiled by the tile size $T = (T_1, \ldots, T_m)$. Let $\tilde{T} = (T_1, \ldots, T_{m-1}, 2T_m)$. Using the notation introduced in Section 11.4.3, $\phi(T)$ represents the number of distinct array elements accessed in a tile and $\phi(\tilde{T})$ the number of distinct array elements accessed in two adjacent tiles. Thus, $\phi(\tilde{T}) - \phi(T)$ represents the number of new array elements accessed when we move from one tile to its adjacent tile to be executed next.

Our cost function is given as follows:

$$f(T) = \frac{T_1 \times \cdots \times T_m}{\phi(\tilde{T}) - \phi(T)} \tag{11.12}$$

For each tile size that induces no intra- and inter$_1$-tile misses, the number of cache misses (consisting of cold and inter$_2$-tile misses) in the tiled code is dominated by $|S_T|/f(T)$. Hence, the optimal tile size is a maximal point of f such that the conditions in Theorem 6 (or those in Theorem 4 for two-dimensional SOR) are satisfied. Of all tile sizes without intra- and inter$_1$-tile misses, we take the one such that the number of inter$_2$-tile misses is minimized. Hence, the total number of cache misses is minimized.

The set of all tile sizes is $\{(T_1, \ldots, T_m) : 1 \leqslant T_1, \ldots, T_m \leqslant C\}$. The optimal one can be found efficiently by an exhaustive search with a worst-time complexity being $O(C^m)$, where C is the cache size in array elements (rather than bytes). Essentially, we simply go through all tile sizes that satisfy the conditions mentioned above and pick the one that is a maximal point of f.

Next we provide a characterization of cache misses for a program p of the form of Equation (11.1) when $L = 1$; it can be generalized to the case when $L > 1$. Let $OMN(T)$ be the smallest among the cache miss numbers of all tiled codes for p obtained using the traditional loop tiling under a fixed T but all possible array layouts of A. Let $DTMN(T)$ be the cache miss number of the tiled code for p we generate when the layout of A is defined by a data-tiling transformation.

Theorem 7   Let a direct-mapped cache $(C, 1, 1)$ be given. Assume that $a_1 > 0, \ldots, a_m > 0$ are constants and the iteration space of Equation (11.1) is $[0, Na_1 - 1] \times \cdots \times [0, Na_m - 1]$. Let T and T' be two tile sizes. If $P[T(u)] = D[T(u)]$, then

$$OMN(T') - DTMN(T) \geq \prod_{s=1}^{m}(Na_s + 1)\left(\frac{\prod_{s=1}^{m}[1 - 2/(Na_s + 1)]}{f(T')} - \frac{1}{f(T)} - \frac{1}{Na_m + 1} \right)$$

Proof   When $L = 1$, we have the two inequalities:

$$OMN(T') \geq \prod_{s=1}^{m}\lfloor Na_sT'_s \rfloor[\phi(\tilde{T}) - \phi(T)]$$

$$= \prod_{s=1}^{m}\lfloor Na_sT'_s \rfloor \prod_{s=1}^{n} T'_s/f(T')$$

$$\geq \prod_{s=1}^{m}(Na_s - 1)/f(T')$$

$$DTMN(T) \leq \prod_{s=1}^{m-1}(Na_s + 1) + \prod_{s=1}^{m}(Na_s+1)/f(T)$$

which together imply the inequality in the theorem. $\square$

This theorem implies that when N is large and if we choose T such that $f(T) > f(T')$, then the number of cache misses in our tiled code is smaller than that obtained by loop tiling, regardless what array layout is used for the array A.

11.6   EXPERIMENTAL RESULTS

We evaluate code tiling using the two-dimensional SOR solver and compare its effectiveness with nine loop-tiling algorithms on the four platforms described in Table 11.1. In all our experiments, the two-dimensional SOR is tiled only for the first-level data cache in each platform.

All "algorithms" considered are referred to by the following names: `seq` denotes the sequential program, `cot` denotes code tiling, `lrw` is from [18], `tss` from [5], `ess` from [6], `euc` from [14], `pdat` from [12], and `pxyz` is the padded version of `xyz` with pads of 0–8 elements (the same upper bound used as in [14]).

Our tiled code is generated according to Figure 11.3. The program after its Step 1 is given in Figure 11.8. The data tiling g required in Step 2 is constructed according to Equation (11.9). The problem-size-independent tile sizes on the four platforms are found in Step 3 according to Section 11.5 and listed in Table 11.2. Note that in all platforms the optimal $T_3 = L$ holds. The final tiled code obtained in Step 4 is optimized as described in Step 5. Note that T_3 does not appear in the tiled code given in Figure 11.8 since the two corresponding loops are combined by loop coalescing.

All programs are in ANSI C, compiled and executed on the four platforms as described in Table 11.1. The last two platforms are SGI Origin 2000 and Compaq ES40 with multiple processors, but only one processor was used in our experiments. All our experiments were conducted when we were the only user on these systems.

The SOR kernel has two problem-size parameters P and N. In all our experiments except the one discussed in Figure 11.13, we fix $P = 500$ and choose N from 400 to 1200 at multiples of 57.

Table 11.1   Machine configurations

CPU	Pentium III	Pentium 4	MIPS R10K	Alpha 21264
Clock rate	933 MHz	1.8 GHz	250 MHz	500 MHz
L1 D-cache	16 kB/32 B/4	8 kB/64 B/4	32 kB/32 B/2	64 kB/64 B/2
L1 Replacement policy	LRU	LRU	LRU	FIFO
L2 D-cache	256 kB/32 B/8	512 kB/64 B/8	4 MB/128 B/2	4 MB/64 B/4
RAM	256 MB	512 MB	6 GB	6 GB
cc Version	gcc 3.2.1	gcc 3.2.1	MIPSpro 7.30	DEC C 5.6-075
cc Switches	-O2	-O2	-O2	-O2
OS	Debian Linux 3.0	Debian Linux 3.0	IRIX64 6.5	OSF1 4.0

for $ii = 0, (P + N - 2)/T_1$
for $jj = 0, (P + N - 2)/T_2$
for $t = \max(0, iiT_1 - N + 1, j \times T_2 - N + 1), \min(P - 1, (ii + 1) \times T_1 - 1, (jj + 1) \times T_2 - 1)$
for $i = \max(ii \times T_1, t), \min[(ii + 1) \times T_1, t + N] - 1$
for $j = \max(j \times T_2, t), \min[(j + 1) \times T_2, t + N] - 1$
$\quad A(i - t, j - t) = 0.2 \times [A(i - t + 1, j - t) + A(i - t, j - t + 1) + A(i - t, j - t)$
$\quad\quad\quad + A(i - t, j - t - 1) + A(i - t - 1, j - t)]$

Figure 11.8   Tiled two-dimensional SOR code.

Figure 11.9 shows the performance results on Pentium III. Figure 11.9(a) plots the individual execution times, showing that all tiled codes run faster than the sequential program except for ess at the larger problem sizes. But our tiled codes perform the best at all problem sizes (represented by the curve at the bottom). Figure 11.9(b) highlights the overall speedups of all tiled codes over the sequential program. This implies that code tiling is faster by factors of 1.98–2.62 than the other algorithms.

Figure 11.10 shows the results on Pentium 4. This time, however, loop tiling is not useful, as shown in Figure 11.10(a). Figure 11.10(b) indicates that neither of the existing algorithms yields a positive performance gain but code tiling attains a speedup of 1.56. Thus, code tiling is faster than these algorithms by factors of 1.56–1.59.

Figure 11.11 shows the results on R10K. Loop tiling helps little, but code tiling achieves a speedup of 2.01, which is in sharp contrast to the negligible positive speedups from the other tiling algorithms. Overall, code tiling is faster by factors of 1.92–1.95 over the other algorithms.

Figure 11.12 shows the results on Alpha 21264. Similar trends as in Pentium 4 can be observed. Code tiling is faster than the other algorithms by factors of 1.55–1.60.

Some other properties of code tiling are:

Copy Cost. All execution times include the copy overheads. In the tiled code for two-dimensional SOR, the copy cost contributes only $O(1/P)$ to the overall time complexity, where P is the number of time steps. We measured the copy

Table 11.2   Problem-size-independent tile sizes

Platform	(T_1, T_2, T_3)
Pentium III	(33, 32, 4)
Pentium 4	(15, 16, 8)
R10K	(50, 60, 4)
Alpha 21264	(76, 80, 8)

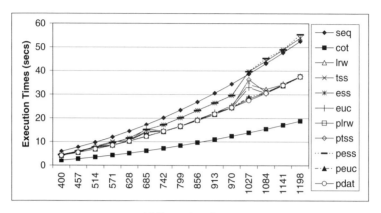

(a) Execution times

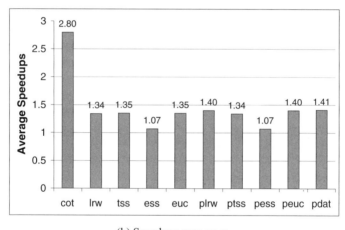

(b) Speedups over `seq`

Figure 11.9   Performance on Pentium III.

cost to be 0.8%–1.2% on Pentium III, 0.1–1.5% on Pentium 4, 0.1 – 1.0% on R10K and 0.1–1.3% on Alpha 21264 of the total execution time.

Address Calculation Cost. The data-tiling functions used involve integer division and remainder operations and are thus expensive. They are efficiently computed by using incremental additions/subtractions and distributing loop nests to avoid excessive max/min operations.

High and Smooth Performance Curves. Figures 11.9(a)–11.12(a) show clearly that code tiling produces high, smooth performance curves across a range of problem sizes on four platforms. To see the stability advantage further, Figure 11.13 plots the time differences Time(N) – Time(N – 3) between two adjacent problem sizes N and N – 3 at multiples of 3.

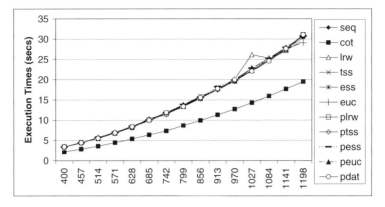

(a) Execution times

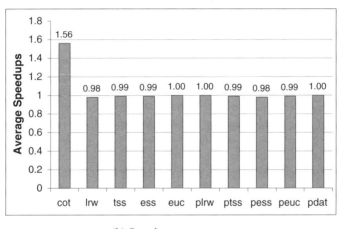

(b) Speedups over `seq`

Figure 11.10   Performance on Pentium 4.

Space Requirement. The size of the one-dimensional array B introduced in in Figure 11.3 is given by $g(N, N)$ in Equation (11.9). For the two-dimensional SOR, we find that $g(N, N) \leq N^2 + N\,C + C$, where C is the cache size in terms of array elements rather than bytes. For the problem sizes used in our experiments, $g(N, N)$ ranges from $1.03N^2$ to $1.16N^2$ on Pentium III. Note that the multiplier is only 1.33 when $N = 100$. When N is even smaller, tiling is usually not needed. The tiling technique for the Jacobi solvers [16] employs array duplication to remove anti and output dependencies, so their constant multiplier is 1.

Cache Misses. To support our claim that code tiling has eliminated a large amount of cache misses present in the tiled codes generated by loop tiling, we

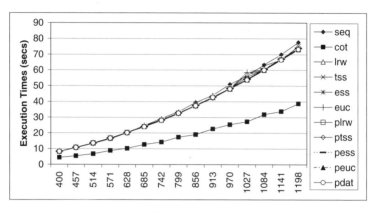

(a) Execution times

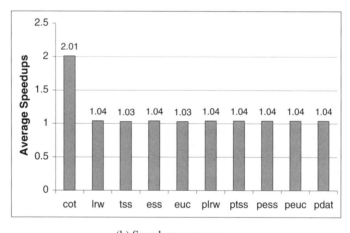

(b) Speedups over seq

Figure 11.11   Performance on R10K.

evaluated cache performance for all codes involved in our experiments using PCL [13]. Figure 11.14 plots the real L1 data cache misses for all methods on Pentium III. In comparison with Figure 11.9(a), the significant performance gains correlate well with the significant cache miss reductions at most problem sizes. Note that lrw has comparable or even smaller cache miss numbers at some problem sizes. This is because in our tiled codes, some temporaries are required to enable incremental computation of the data tiling function (see Step 4 in Figure 11.3) and they are not all kept in registers due to a small number of registers available on the x86 architecture. Despite of this problem, cot outperforms lrw at all problem sizes. This can be attributed to several reasons, such as the impact of TLB and L2 misses on the performance of the tiled code.

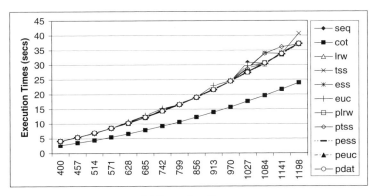

(a) Execution times

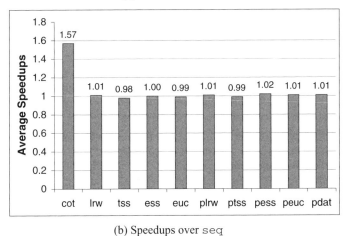

(b) Speedups over seq

Figure 11.12   Performance on Alpha 21264.

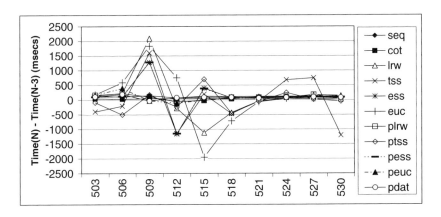

Figure 11.13   Performance stability on Pentium III ($P = 500$).

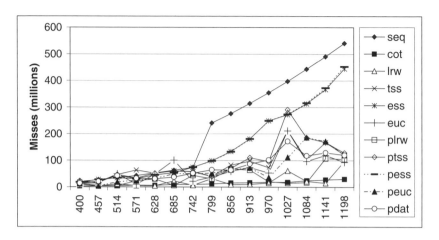

Figure 11.14   L1 data cache misses on Pentium III.

11.7   RELATED WORK

To the best of our knowledge, we are not aware of any previous work on applying a *global* data reorganization strategy to minimize the cache misses in tiled codes. Some earlier attempts on partitioning the cache and mapping arrays into distinct cache partitions can be found in [2, 10]. Manjikian and Abdelrahman [10] allocate arrays to equal-sized regions. Chang et al. [2] allow varying-sized regions but assume all arrays to be one-dimensional. These techniques cannot handle the two-dimensional SOR solvers since these kernels each use one single array—there is nothing to partition.

Compiler researchers have applied loop tiling to enhance data locality. Several tile-size-selection algorithms [5, 6, 12, 14, 18] find tile sizes to reduce the cache misses in tiled codes. Since these algorithms rely on the default linear layouts of the arrays, padding has been incorporated by many algorithms to help loop tiling stabilize its effectiveness [12, 14].

Although it promises performance gains in many programs, loop tiling is not very useful for two-dimensional PDE solvers and may even worsen their performance, as shown by our experiments. In recognizing this limitation, Song and Li [16] present a tiling technique for handling two-dimensional Jacobi solvers. This paper contributes a new technique for improving the performance of multidimensional SOR solvers. Rivera and Tseng [15] extend their previous work [14] to three-dimensional solvers but they do not exploit a large amount of temporal reuse carried at the time step as we do here.

Kodukula et al. [9] propose a data shackling technique to tile imperfect loop nests, but this technique itself does not tell which tile size to use. Like loop tiling, data shackling is a loop transformation. As such, it does not modify the actual layouts of the arrays used in tiled codes.

Chatterjee et al. [3] consider nonlinear array layouts and achieve impressive performance speedups in some benchmarks when they are combined with loop tiling. However, their technique is orthogonal to loop tiling; they rely on a tile-size-selection algorithm to find appropriate tile sizes. In addition, they choose nonlinear layouts for all the arrays without making any attempt at partitioning and reorganizing them in memory. In other words, they do not directly aim at reducing the cache misses in tiled codes. This may partially explain why they obtain increased cache misses in some benchmarks (due to conflict misses between tiles).

The importance of combining data transformations with loop transformations was recognized earlier [4]. Subsequently, several researchers [8, 11] permitted the coexistence of different array layouts (row major, column major, diagonal, or others) in a kernel- or program-wise fashion and obtain moderate performance gains for benchmark programs.

The PhiPAC project [1] uses an exhaustive search to produce highly tuned tiled codes for specific level-3 BLAS kernels, which are specialized not only for a given cache configuration but also a given problem size. Our code-tiling methodology generates automatically a single "optimised" version for an SOR PDE solver for all problem sizes.

11.8 CONCLUSION

We have presented a new compiler technique for improving the performance of a class of programs that includes multidimensional SOR PDE solvers as a special case. Code tiling combines loop tiling with data tiling in order to reduce cache misses in a predictable and methodical manner. We have evaluated its effectiveness using the classic two-dimensional SOR solver—for which loop tiling is ineffective—on four representative architectures. Our experimental results show that code tiling has eliminated a significant amount of cache misses that would otherwise be present in tiled codes. This translates to impressive performance speedups over nine loop-tiling algorithms for a range of problem sizes.

We believe that code tiling can be generalized to other programs, at least to dense matrix codes for which loop tiling is an appropriate means of control-flow restructuring for data locality. This will have the potential to eliminate a significant amount of conflict misses still present in tiled codes.

Acknowledgment. This work is supported by an ARC Grant DP0452623.

REFERENCES

1. J. Bilmes, K. Asanovic, C.-W. Chin, and J. Demmel, Optimizing matrix multiply using PHiPAC: A portable, high-performance, ANSI C coding methodology, in *International Conference on Supercomputing,* pp. 340–347, 1997.

2. C.-Y. Chang, J.-P. Sheu, and H.-C. Chen, Reducing cache conflicts by multi-level cache

partitioning and array elements mapping, in *7th International Conference on Parallel and Distributed Systems (ICPADS'00),* Iwate, Japan, 2000.

3. S. Chatterjee, V. V. Jain, A. R. Lebeck, S. Mundhra, and M. Thottethodi. Nonlinear array layout for hierarchical memory systems, in *ACM International Conference on Supercomputing (ICS'99),* pp. 444–453, Rhodes, Greece, June 1999.

4. M. Cierniak and W. Li, Unifying data and control transformations for distributed shared memory machines, in *ACM SIGPLAN'95 Conference on Programming Language Design and implementation,* California, 1995.

5. S. Coleman and K. S. McKinley, Tile size selection using cache organization and data layout, in *ACM SIGPLAN'95 Conference on Programming Language Design and Implementation (PLDI'95),* pp. 279–290, June 1995.

6. K. Esseghir, Improving data locality for caches, M.S. thesis, Rice University, Dept. of Computer Science, 1993.

7. F. Irigoin and R. Triolet, Supernode partitioning, in *15th Annual ACM Symposium on Principles of Programming Languages,* pp. 319–329, San Diego, California., Jan. 1988.

8. M. Kandemir and J. Ramanujam, A layout-concious iteration space transformation technique, *IEEE Transactions on Computers, 50*(12), 1321–1335, Dec. 2001.

9. I. Kodukula, N. Ahmed, and K. Pingali, Data-centric multi-level blocking, in *ACM SIGPLAN '97 Conference on Programming Language Design,* pp. 346–357, 1996.

10. N. Manjikian and T. Abdelrahman, Array data layout for the reduction of cache conflicts, in *8th International Conference on Parallel and Distributed Computing Systems,* 1995.

11. M. F. P. O'Boyle and P. M. W. Knijnenburg, Integrating loop and data transformations for global optimisation, in *International Conference on Parallel Architectures and Compilation Techniques (PACT'98),* 1998.

12. P. R. Panda, H. Nakamura, N. D. Dutt, and A. Nicolau, Augmenting loop tiling with data alignment for improved cache performance, *IEEE Transactions on Computers, 48*(2), 142–149, 1999.

13. PCL, The Performance Counter Library V2.2, 2003, http://www.fz-juelich.de/zam/PCL.

14. G. Rivera and C.-W. Tseng, A comparison of compiler tiling algorithms, in *8th International Conference on Compiler Construction (CC'99),* Amsterdam, The Netherlands, 1999.

15. G. Rivera and C.-W. Tseng, Tiling optimizations for 3D scientific computations, in *Supercomputing '00,* 2000.

16. Y. Song and Z. Li, New tiling techniques to improve cache temporal locality, in *ACM SIGPLAN'99 Conference on Programming Language Design and Implementation (PLDI'99),* pp. 215–228, May 1999.

17. R. Webster, *Convexity.* Oxford University Press, 1994.

18. M. E. Wolf and M. S. Lam, A data locality optimizing algorithm, in *ACM SIGPLAN'91 Conference on Programming Language Design and Implementation,* June 1991.

19. J. Xue, On tiling as a loop transformation, *Parallel Processing Letters, 7*(4), 409–424, 1997.

## CHAPTER 12

Data Conversion for Heterogeneous Migration/Checkpointing

HAI JIANG, VIPIN CHAUDHARY, and JOHN PAUL WALTERS

12.1 INTRODUCTION

Migration concerns saving the current computation state, transferring it to remote machines, and resuming execution at the statement following the migration point. Checkpointing concerns saving the computation state to file systems and resuming execution by restoring the computation state from saved files. Although the state-transfer medium differs, migration and checkpointing share the same strategy in state handling. To improve application performance and system resource utilization, they support load balancing, load sharing, data-locality optimization, and fault tolerance.

The major obstacle preventing migration/checkpointing from achieving wide-spread use is the complexity of adding transparent migration and checkpointing to systems originally designed to run as stand-alones [1]. Heterogeneity further complicates this situation. But migration and checkpointing are indispensable to the Grid [2] and other loosely coupled heterogeneous environments. Thus, effective solutions are needed.

To hide the different levels of heterogeneity, we have developed an application-level process/thread migration and checkpointing package called MigThread, which abstracts the computation state up to the language level [3, 4]. For applications written in the C language, states are constructed in the user space instead of being extracted from the original kernels or libraries for better portability across different platforms. A preprocessor transforms source code at compile time, whereas a run-time support module dynamically collects the state for migration and checkpointing.

The computation state is represented in terms of data. To support heterogeneity, MigThread is equipped with a novel "plug-and-play"-style data conversion scheme called coarse-grain tagged "receiver makes right" (CGT-RMR). It is an asymmetric data conversion method for performing data conversion only on the receiver side. Since common data representation standards are separate from user applications, programmers have to analyze data types, flatten down aggregate data types (such as structures), and encode/decode scalar types explicitly in programs. With help from

High-Performance Computing: Paradigm and Infrastructure. Edited by L. T. Yang and M. Guo **241**
Copyright © 2006 John Wiley & Sons, Inc.

MigThread's type system, CGT-RMR can detect data types, generate application-level tags for each data type, and ease the burden of data conversion work previously left to the programmer. Aggregate-type data are handled as a whole instead of being flattened down recursively in programs. Therefore, compared to common standards, CGT-RMR is more convenient in handling large data chunks. Inmigration and checkpointing, computation states spread out in terms of memory blocks, and CGT-RMR outperforms normal standards by a large margin. Also, no large routine groups or tables are constructed as in common RMR [8].

Architecture tags are generated on the fly so that new computer platforms can be adopted automatically. CGT-RMR takes an aggressive data-conversion approach between incompatible platforms. The low-level data-conversion failure events can be conveyed to the upper-level MigThread scheduling module to ensure the correctness of real-time migration and checkpointing. Empowered with CGT-RMR, MigThread can handle migration and checkpointing across heterogeneous platforms.

The remainder of this chapter is organized into seven sections. Section 12.2 provides an overview of migration and checkpointing. Section 12.3 discusses data conversion issues and some existing schemes. In Section 12.4, we provide the detail of designing and implementing CGT-RMR in MigThread. Section 12.5 presents some microbenchmarks and experimental results from real benchmark programs. In Section 12.6, we discuss related work. Section 12.7 discusses our conclusions and future work.

12.2 MIGRATION AND CHECKPOINTING

Migration and checkpointing concern constructing, transferring, and retrieving computation states. Despite the complexity of adding transparent support, migration and checkpointing continue to attract attention due to the potential for computation mobility.

12.2.1 MigThread

MigThread is an application-level, multigrained migration and checkpointing package [3] that supports both coarse-grained processes and fine-grained threads. MigThread consists of two parts: a preprocessor and a run-time support module.

The preprocessor is designed to transform a user's source code into a format from which the run-time support module can construct the computation state efficiently. It effectively improves the transparency in application-level schemes. The run-time support module constructs, transfers, and restores computation states dynamically [4].

Originally, the state data consists of the process-data segment, stack, heap, and register contents. In MigThread, the computation state is moved out from its original location (libraries or kernels) and is abstracted up to the language level. Therefore, the physical state is transformed into a logical form to achieve platform independence. All related information with regard to stack variables, function parameters, program counters, and dynamically allocated memory regions is collected into predefined data structures [3].

Figures 12.1 and 12.2 illustrate a simple example for such a process, with all functions and global variables transformed accordingly. A simple function **foo()** is defined with four local variables as in Figure 12.1. MigThread's preprocessor transforms the function and generates a corresponding **MTh_foo()** shown in Figure 12.2. All nonpointer variables are collected in a structure MThV, whereas pointers are moved to another structure, MThP. Within MThV, field MThV.MThP is the only pointer, pointing to the second structure, MThP, which may or may not exist. Field MThV.stepno is a logical construction of the program counter to indicate the program progress and where to restart. In process/thread stacks, each function's activation frame contains MThV and MThP to record the current function's computation status. The overall stack status can be obtained by collecting all of these MThV and MThP data structures spread in activation frames.

Since address spaces could be different on source and destination machines, values of pointers referencing stacks or heaps might become invalid after migration. It is the preprocessor's responsibility to identify and mark pointers at the language level so that they can easily be traced and updated later. MigThread also supports user-level memory management for heaps. Eventually, all state-related contents, including stacks and heaps, are moved out to the user space and handled by MigThread directly.

12.2.2 Migration and Checkpointing Safety

Migration and checkpointing safety concerns ensuring the correctness of resumed computation [4, 5]. In other words, computation states should be constructed precisely, and restored correctly on similar or different machines. The major identified unsafe factors come from unsafe systems (such as the one in C) and third-party libraries [4]. But for heterogeneous schemes, if data formats on different machines are incompatible, migration and resuming execution from checkpoint files might lead to errors, so it is important that upper-level migration/checkpointing schemes be aware of the situation in lower-level data conversion routines.

```
foo()
{
    int      a;
    double   b;
    int     *c;
    double **d;

            .
            .
            .
}
```

Figure 12.1 The original function.

```
          MTh_foo()
          {
            struct MThV_t {
                void    *MThP;
                int      stepno;

                int       a;
                double    b;
            } MThV;

            struct MThP_t {
                int       *c;
                double    **d;
            } MThP;

            MThV.MThP = (void *)&MThP;
                .
                .
                .

          }
```

Figure 12.2   The transformed function.

MigThread supports aggressive data conversion and aborts state restoration only when "precision loss" events occur. Thus, the third unsafe factor for heterogeneous schemes, incompatible data conversion, can be identified and handled properly.

12.3   DATA CONVERSION

Computation states can be transformed into pure data. If different platforms use different data formats and computation states constructed on one platform need to be interpreted by another, the data-conversion process becomes unavoidable.

12.3.1   Data-Conversion Issues

In heterogeneous environments, common data-conversion issues are identified as follows:

- **Byte Ordering**—Either big endian or little endian.
- **Character Sets**—Either ASCII or EBCDIC representation.
- **Floating-Point Standards**—IEEE 754, IEEE 854, CRAY, DEC, or IBM standard.
- **Data Alignment and Padding**—Data is naturally aligned when the starting address is on a "natural boundary." This means that the starting memory address is a multiple of the data's size. Structure alignment can result in unused

space, called padding. Padding between members of a structure is called *internal padding*. Padding between the last member and the end of the space occupied by the structure is called *tail padding*. Although a natural boundary can be the default setting for alignment, data alignment is actually determined by processors, operating systems, and compilers. To avoid such indeterministic alignment and padding, many standards flatten native aggregate data types and rerepresent them in their own default formats.

- **Loss of Precision**—When high-precision data are converted to their low-precision counterparts, loss of precision may occur.

12.3.2 Data-Conversion Schemes

Data representations can be either tagged or untagged. A tag is any additional information associated with data that helps a decoder unmarshal the data.

The canonical intermediate form is one of the major data-conversion strategies that provides an external representation for each data type. Many standards adopt this approach, such as XDR (External Data Representation) [6] from Sun Microsystems, ISO ASN.1 (Abstract Syntax Notation One) [7], CCSDS SFDU (Standard Formatted Data Units), ANDF (Architecture Neutral Data Format), IBM APPC GDS (General Data Stream), ISO RDA (Remote Data Access), and others [8]. Such common data formats are recognized and accepted by all different platforms to achieve data sharing. Even if both the sender and receiver are on the same machine, they still need to perform this symmetric conversion on both ends. XDR adopts the untagged data-representation approach. Data types have to be determined by application protocols and associated with a pair of encoding/decoding routines.

Zhou and Geist [8] took another approach, called "receiver makes it right" (RMR), which performs data conversion only on the receiver side. If there are n machines, each of a different type, the number of conversion routine groups will be $(n^2 - n)/2$. In theory, the RMR scheme will lead to bloated code as n increases. Another disadvantage is that RMR is not available for newly invented platforms.

12.4 COARSE-GRAIN TAGGED RMR IN MigThread

The proposed data conversion scheme is an RMR variant that only performs the conversion once. This tagged version can tackle data alignment, convert data structures as a whole, and eventually generate a lighter workload compared to existing standards.

An architecture tag is inserted at the beginning. Since the byte ordering within the network is big-endian, simply comparing data representation on the platform against its format in networks can detect the endianness of the platform. Currently, MigThread only accepts ASCII character sets and is not applicable on some IBM mainframes. Also, IEEE 754 is the adopted floating-point standard because of its dominance in the market, and MigThread can be extended to other floating-point formats.

12.4.1   Tagging and Padding Detection

For data-conversion schemes, the tagged approaches associate each data item with its type attribute so that receivers can decode each item precisely, thus, fewer conversion routines are required. But tags create an extra workload and slow down the whole process. However, untagged approaches maintain large sets of conversion routines and encoding/decoding orders have to be handled explicitly by the programmer. Performance improvement comes from the extra coding burden.

In existing data-format standards, both tagged and untagged approaches handle basic (scalar) data on a one-by-one basis. Aggregate data needs to be flattened down to a set of scalar types for data conversion. The main reason is to avoid the padding issue in aggregate types. Since the padding pattern is a consequence of the processor, operating system, and compiler, the padding situation only becomes deterministic at run time. It is impossible to determine a padding pattern in programs and impractical for programmers to convey padding information from programs to conversion routines at run time. This is because programs can only communicate with conversion routines in one direction and programming models have to be simple. Most existing standards choose to avoid padding issues by only handling scalar types directly.

MigThread is a combination of compile-time and run-time supports. Its programmers do not need to worry about data formats. The preprocessor parses the source code, sets up data-type systems, and transforms source code to communicate with the run-time support module through inserted primitives. With the data-type system, the preprocessor can analyze data types, flatten down aggregate data types recursively, detect padding patterns, and define tags as in Figure 12.3. But the actual tag contents can be set only at run time and they may not be the same on different

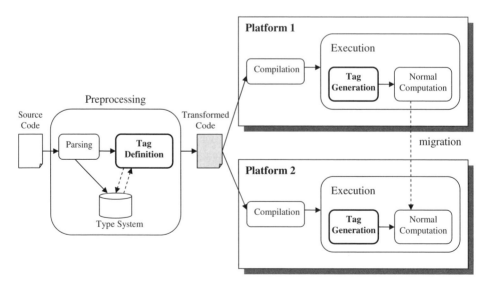

Figure 12.3   Tag definition and generation in MigThread.

platforms. Since all of the tedious tag definition work has been performed by the preprocessor, the programming style becomes extremely simple. Also, with the global control, low-level issues such as the data-conversion status can be conveyed to upper-level scheduling modules. Therefore, easy coding style and performance gains come from the preprocessor.

In MigThread, tags are used to describe data types and their padding situations so that data-conversion routines can handle aggregate data types as well as common scalar data types. As we discussed in Section 12.2, global variables and local function variables in MigThread are collected into their corresponding structure-type variables MThV and MThP, which are registered as the basic units. Tags are defined and generated for these structures as well as dynamically allocated memory blocks in the heap.

For the simple example in Section 12.2 (Figures 12.1 and 12.2), tag definitions of MThV_heter and MThP heter for MThV and MThP are shown in Figure 12.4. It is still too early to determine the content of the tags within programs. The preprocessor defines rules to calculate structure members' sizes and variant padding patterns, and inserts **sprintf()** to glue partial results together. The actual tag generation has to take place at run-time when the **sprintf()** statement is executed. On a Linux machine, the simple example's tags can be two character strings as shown in Figure 12.5.

A tag is a sequence of (m, n) tuples, and can be expressed in one of the following cases (where m and n are positive numbers):

- (m, n)—scalar types. The item "m" is simply the size of the data type. The "n" indicates the number of such scalar types.
- $[(m', n') \ldots (m'', n''), n]$—aggregate types. The "$m$" in the tuple (m, n) can be substituted with another tag (or tuple sequence) repeatedly. Thus, a tag can be expanded recursively for those enclosed aggregate data type fields until all fields are converted to scalar types. The second item "n" still indicates the number of the top-level aggregate data types.
- $(m, -n)$—pointers. The "m" is the size of pointer type on the current platform. The "$-$" sign indicates the pointer type, and the "n" still means the number of pointers.
- $(m, 0)$—padding slots. The "m" specifies the number of bytes this padding slot can occupy. The $(0, 0)$ is a common case and indicates no padding.

In programs, only one statement is issued for each data type, whether it is a scalar or aggregate type. The flattening procedure is accomplished by MigThread's preprocessor during tag definition instead of the encoding/decoding process at run time. Hence, programmers are freed from this responsibility.

12.4.2 Data Restoration

Each function contains one or two structures and corresponding tags, depending on whether MThP exists. In MigThread, all memory segments for these structures are

```
MTh_foo()
{
    struct MThV_t {
        void    *MThP;
        int     stepno;

        int     a;
        double  b;
    } MThV;

    struct MThP_t {
        int     *c;
        double  **d;
    } MThP;

    char MThV_heter[60];
    char MThP_heter[41];

    int MTh_so2 = sizeof(double);
    int MTh_so1 = sizeof(int);
    int MTh_so4 = sizeof(struct MThP_t);
    int MTh_so3 = sizeof(struct MThV_t);
    int MTh_so0 = sizeof(void *);

    MThV.MThP = (void *)&MThP;

    sprintf(MThV_heter,
"(%d,-1)(%d,0)(%d,1)(%d,0)(%d,1)(%d,0)(%d,1)(%d,0)", MTh_so0,
(long)&MThV.stepno-(long)&MThV.MThP-MTh_so0, MTh_so1,
(long)&MThV.a-(long)&MThV.stepno-MTh_so1, MTh_so1,(long)&MThV.b-
(long)&MThV.a- MTh_so1, MTh_so2,(long)&MThV+MTh_so3-(long)&MThV.b-
MTh_so2);

    sprintf(MThP_heter, "(%d,-1)(%d,0)(%d,-1)(%d,0)",
MTh_so0,(long)&MThP.d-(long)&MThP.c-MTh_so0,
MTh_so0,(long)&MThP+MTh_so4-(long)&MThP.d-MTh_so0);
                        .
                        .
                        .

}
```

Figure 12.4   Tag definition at compile time.

```
char MThV_heter[60]="(4,-1)(0,0)(4,1)(0,0)(4,1)(0,0)(8,0)(0,0)";
char MThP_heter[41]="(4-1)(0,0)(4,-1)(0,0)";
```

Figure 12.5   Tag calculation at run time.

represented in a "tag-block" format. The process/thread stack becomes a sequence of MThV, MThP, and their tags. Memory blocks in heaps are also associated with such tags to express the actual layout in memory space. Therefore, the computation state physically consists of a group of memory segments associated with their own tags in a "tag–segment" pair format. To support heterogeneity, MigThread executes data-conversion routines against these coarse-grained memory segments instead of the individual data object. Performance gains are guaranteed.

The receivers or reading processes of checkpointing files need to convert the computation state, that is, data, as required. Since activation frames in stacks are re-run and heaps are recreated, a new set of segments in "tag–block" format is available on the new platform. MigThread first compares architecture tags by strcmp(). If they are identical and blocks have the same sizes, this means the platform remains unchanged and the old segment contents are simply copied over by memcpy() to the new architectures. This enables prompt processing between homogeneous platforms whereas symmetric conversion approaches still suffer data-conversion overhead on both ends.

If platforms have been changed, conversion routines are applied on all memory segments. For each segment, a "walk-through" process is performed against its corresponding old segment from the previous platform, as shown in Figure 12.6. In these segments, according to their tags, memory blocks are seen to consist of scalar-type data and padding slots alternatively. The high-level conversion unit is data slots rather than bytes in order to achieve portability. The "walkthrough" process contains two index pointers pointing to a pair of matching scalar data slots in both blocks. The contents of the old data slots are converted and copied to the new data slots if byte ordering changes, and the index pointers are moved down to the next slots. In the meantime, padding slots are skipped over, although most of them are defined as (0, 0) to indicate that they do not physically exist. In MigThread, data items are expressed in a "scalar-type data–padding slots" pattern to support heterogeneity.

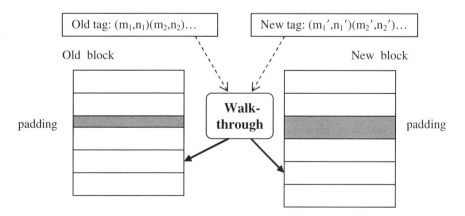

Figure 12.7 Walk-through "tag–block" format segments.

12.4.3   Data Resizing

Between incompatible platforms, if data items are converted from higher-precision formats to lower-precision formats, precision loss may occur. Stopping conversion is one option. Normally, higher-precision-format data are longer such that the high-end portion cannot be stored in lower-precision formats. But if the high-end portions contain all zero content for unsigned data, it is safe to throw them away since data values still remain unchanged, as shown in Figure 12.7. MigThread takes this aggressive strategy and intends to convert data until precision loss occurs. This is also a migration and checkpointing safety issue because continuous restoration might lead to incorrect results.

In MigThread, aggressive data conversion enables more programs to perform migration and checkpointing without aborting them too conservatively. Detecting incompatible data formats and conveying this low-level information up to the scheduling module can help abort data restoration promptly.

12.4.4   Address Resizing

Pointers are in fact memory addresses in C. Since they may become invalid after migration and checkpointing, pointer updating is required. MigThread chooses to record the physical memory addresses into the computation state instead of transforming them into logical representation formats. Base addresses of all data structures in stack frames and memory blocks in heaps are also transferred over so that old pointers can be identified by comparing their values against those base addresses.

Initially, pointers are also converted as any other regular type data. But if the data-flow direction is from high-precision formats to low-precision formats, unsafe precision loss may take place. Since pointers are actually addresses, their high-end portions are usually nonzero. Thus, the previous data-resizing technique is not applicable in this case. Before stack unfolding and heap recreation are complete, pointer updating might fail due to insufficient information. To prevent this, MigThread uses a "put-aside" strategy to save those old pointers somewhere else without immediately changing their lengths, as shown in Figure 12.8. Pointer updating starts after all memory segments in the stacks and heaps have been reestablished. The "walkthrough" module is called up again to search for pointers in stack frames

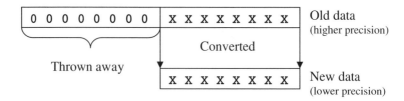

Figure 12.7   Safe precision-loss case for unsigned data.

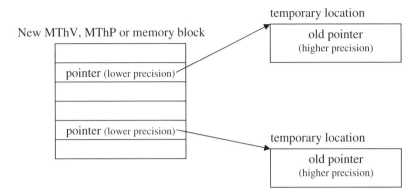

Figure 12.8   Address resizing of higher-precision pointers.

and heaps. If pointers have been put aside as in Figure 12.8, the values of the old pointers are fetched from the extra memory spaces and converted into valid pointer values for current data slots. The temporary spaces for higher-precision pointers will be released thereafter.

Each old pointer needs to compare against the old MThV and MThP of the current frame. The time complexity is $O(N_{ptr})$, where N_{ptr} is the pointer number. If failed, it becomes necessary to search through the old memory blocks in the heap, which are maintained on a red–black tree on the new platforms. The complexity will be $O(N_{ptr} \times \log N_{mem})$, where N_{mem} is the number of memory blocks in the heap. Only if they fail again do they need to go through stacks that are organized in a linkedlist fashion. The overhead is $O(N_{ptr} \times N_{frm})$, where N_{frm} is the number of activation frames. Therefore, the worst case will be $O[N_{ptr} \times (\log N_{mem} + N_{frm})]$.

12.4.5 Plug-and-Play

We declare CGT-RMR as a "plug-and-play"-style scheme even though it does not maintain tables or routine groups for all possible platforms. Since almost all forthcoming platforms are following the IEEE floating-point standard, no special requirement is imposed for porting code to a new platform. However, adopting old architectures such as IBM mainframe, CRAY, and DEC requires some special conversion routines for floating-point numbers.

12.5 MICROBENCHMARKS AND EXPERIMENTS

One of our experimental platforms is a SUN Enterprise E3500 with 330 Mhz Ultra-Sparc processors and 1 Gbyte of RAM, running Solaris 5.7. The other platform is a PC with a 550 Mhz Intel Pentium III processor and 128 Mbytes of RAM, running

Linux. The CGT-RMR scheme is applied for data conversion in migration and checkpointing between these two different machines.

PVM (Parallel Virtual Machine) uses the XDR standard for heterogeneous computing. Thus, some process migration schemes, such as SNOW [12], apply XDR indirectly by calling PVM primitives. Even the original RMR implementation was based on XDR's untagged strategy [8]. Since most existing systems adopt XDR or similar data conversion strategies [11, 5, 12], we compare our CGT-RMR with the XDR implementation in PVM to predict the performance of MigThread and other similar systems.

The costs of converting scalar data types are shown in Figure 12.9. Data are encoded on one platform and decoded on another platform. For scalar types, such as char, short, int, long and double, the PVM's XDR implementation (PVM-XDR) is slower than CGT-RMR, which is even faster in homogeneous environments since no conversion actually occurs. Also XDR forces the programmer to encode and decode data even on the same platforms. Figure 12.9 indicates that CGT-RMR can handle basic data units more efficiently than PVM-XDR.

To test the scalability, we apply the two schemes on integer and structure arrays. Figure 12.10 shows an integer array's behavior. In homogeneous environments (both encoding and decoding operations performed on either the Solaris or Linux machine), CGT-RMR demonstrates virtually no cost and excellent scalability. In heterogeneous environments, i.e., encoding data on Solaris or Linux and decoding

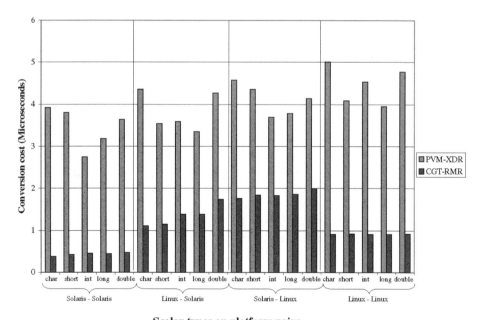

Scalar types on platform pairs

Figure 12.9 Conversion costs for scalar types.

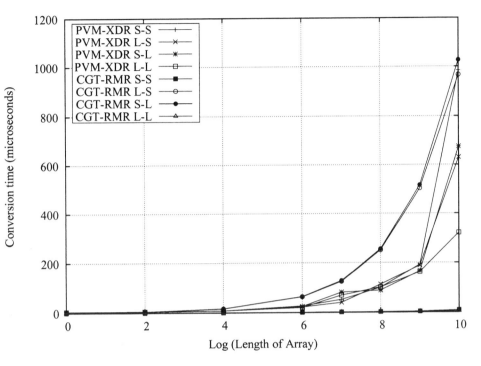

Figure 12.10   Conversion costs of integer arrays.

data on the other machine, CGT-RMR incurs a little more overhead, shown by the top two curves. The four curves in the middle are from PVM-XDR which does not vary much by different platform combinations, nor can it take advantage of homogeneous environments. This indicates that PVM-XDR has a little better scalability on scalar-type arrays in heterogeneous environments.

The conversion overheads of structure arrays are simulated in Figure 12.12. Figure 12.11 lists the sample structure array, which contains five common scalar-type fields with different data-alignment requirements. Again, in a homogeneous envi-

```
struct {
      char      a;
      short     b;
      int       c;
      long      d;
      double    e;
} s[n];
```

Figure 12.11   The structure array.

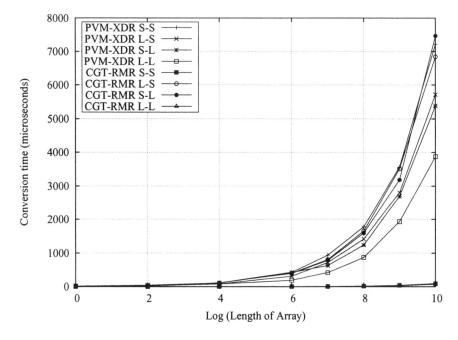

Figure 12.12   Conversion costs of structure arrays.

ronment, CGT-RMR causes virtually no overhead. In heterogeneous cases, the top two curves start merging with the four PVM-XDR curves. Because of the padding issue in structures, programmers have to encode/decode each field explicitly, which diminishes XDR's advantage in scalar arrays and incurs tremendous programming complexity. In the simple case shown in Figure 12.11, assuming that n is the number of scalar types, there will be 10n encoding and decoding statements hand-coded by programmers. In CGT-RMR, only one primitive is required on each side, and the preprocessor can handle all other tag generation details automatically. Therefore, CGT-RMR eases the coding complexity dramatically in complex cases such as migration and checkpointing schemes in which large computation states are common.

To evaluate the CGT-RMR strategy in real applications, we apply it on FFT, continuous and noncontinuous versions of LU from the SPLASH2 suite [15], and matrix multiplication applications. In order to compare CGT-RMR's data-conversion cost with that of XDR or other similar schemes in other migration and checkpointing systems [5, 11, 12], we extract pure data variables in stacks so that stack and heap management, pointer updating, and other issues will not affect our comparison. For each application, we create a corresponding skeleton program to simulate its stack variable situation. Figure 12.13 illustrates the real coding complexity of skeleton programs in terms of numbers of packing/unpacking instructions required in the program. The XDR and other similar data standards require programmers to add such instruction manually at each adaptation point, which is impractical for complex applications. On the other hand, CGT-RMR needs only one

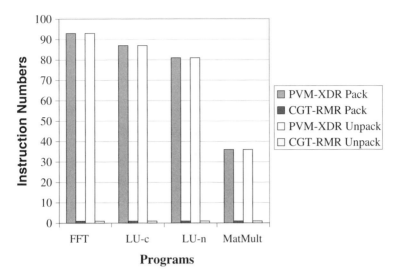

Figure 12.13   Instructions required for packing/unpacking in skeleton programs.

primitive and the preprocessor handles the remaining details automatically to improve the transparency drawback in the application-level migration and checkpointing schemes.

Figures 12.14 and 12.15 show the tag-generation and comparison costs for the stack variables in the skeleton programs. The processor of our Solaris machine is slower and causes longer tag-generation times, which is unavoidable in any case. In a homogeneous environment, tag-comparison time is negligible. However, even in

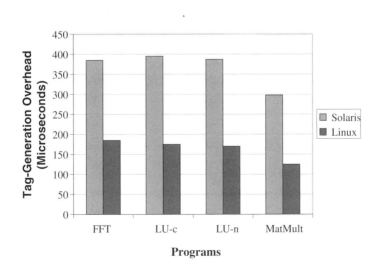

Figure 12.14   Tag-generation overhead in CGT-RMR.

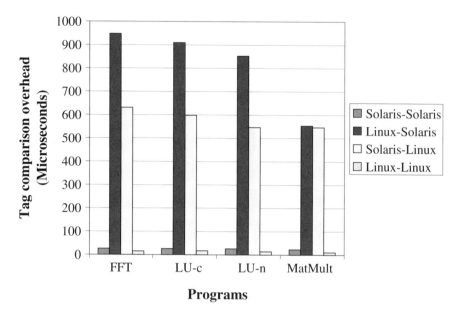

Figure 12.15   Tag comparison overhead in CGT-RMR. A tag generated on the first platform is compared with a tag on the second platform.

heterogeneous environments, both tag costs are much smaller in comparison with the application execution time.

The overall data-conversion costs of our skeleton programs are shown in Figure 12.16. Again, in homogeneous environments, CGT-RMR causes minimal overhead and outperforms PVM-XDR by a large margin. In heterogeneous environments, the two methods' overheads are close. In most cases, CGT-RMR is better or only causes minimal extra overheads. Only in the matrix multiplication program, XDR shows its advantage in scalar arrays since many "double"-type arrays exist. Fortunately, this is an implementation issue rather than a design defect. Our next release will resolve this issue. Still, the overall advanced performance of CGT-RMR is obvious.

The skeleton programs only provide a chance to compare stack variables since different migration and checkpoint schemes utilize various strategies on heaps and pointers. After the comparison against pure data, we analyze how CGT-RMR can affect the behavior of real applications. In our selected applications, we predefine the adaptation points for migration or checkpointing. The detailed overheads are listed in Table 12.1. With certain input sizes, applications are paused on one platform to construct computation states whose sizes can vary from 78 K to 2 M bytes in these sample programs. The computation states are then transferred to another platform for migration, or saved into file systems and read out by another process on another platform for checkpointing.

CGT-RMR plays a role in data conversion in stacks, data conversion in heaps, and pointer updating in both areas. In FFT and LUn, large numbers of memory

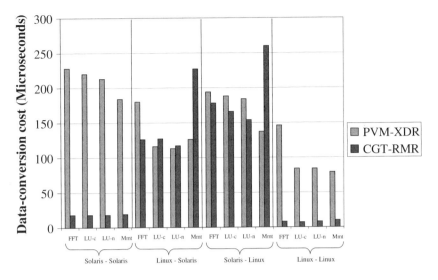

Programs on platform pairs

Figure 12.16 Data-conversion costs in abstract programs. Packing data on the first plat-form and unpacking them on the second platform.

Table 12.1 Migration and checkpointing overheads in real applications (microseconds)

Program (Act.)	OS Pair	State Size (B)	Save Files	Read Files	Send Socket	Convert Stack	Convert Heap	Update Pointers
FFT	Solaris-Solaris	78,016	96,760	24,412	26,622	598	1,033	364
(2,215)	Linux-Solaris	78,024	48,260	24,492	29,047	1,581	57,218	459
1,024	Solaris-Linux	78,016	96,760	13,026	16,948	923	28,938	443
	Linux-Linux	78,024	48,260	13,063	17,527	387	700	399
LUc	Solaris-Solaris	2,113,139	2,507,354	4,954,588	4,939,845	589	27,534	5,670,612
(2,868,309)	Linux-Solaris	2,113,170	1,345,015	4,954,421	5,230,449	1,492	3,158,140	6,039,699
512x512	Solaris-Linux	2,113,139	2,507,354	7,011,277	7,045,671	863	2,247,536	8,619,415
	Linux-Linux	2,113,170	1,345,015	7,058,531	7,131,833	385	19,158	8,103,707
LUn	Solaris-Solaris	135,284	165,840	51,729	53,212	528	2,359	306
(8,867)	Linux-Solaris	135,313	85,053	51,501	62,003	1,376	103,735	322
128x128	Solaris-Linux	135,284	165,840	40,264	44,901	837	52,505	359
	Linux-Linux	135,313	85,053	40,108	56,695	357	1,489	377
MatMult	Solaris-Solaris	397,259	501,073	166,539	164,324	136	2,561	484,149
(6)	Linux-Solaris	397,283	252,926	120,229	220,627	385	306,324	639,281
128x128	Solaris-Linux	397,259	501,073	166,101	129,457	862	604,161	482,380
	Linux-Linux	397,283	252,926	120,671	130,107	100	3,462	640,072

blocks are dynamically allocated in heaps. In homogeneous environments, stacks and heaps are recreated without data conversion, but in heterogeneous environments, converting data in large heaps dominates the CPU time. On the other hand, LUc and MatMult are deployed as pointer-intensive applications. When computation states are restored, pointer updating is an unavoidable task. In homogeneous environments with no data-conversion issues, the CPU simply devotes itself to pointer updating. Even in heterogeneous cases, pointer updating is still a major issue, although their large heaps also incur noticeable overheads. The time spent on stacks is negligible. It is clear that overhead distribution is similar for both homogeneous and heterogeneous environments in XDR or similar standards. CGT-RMR runs much faster in homogeneous environments and is similar in performance to XDR in heterogeneous environments.

From the microbenchmarks, we can see that CGT-RMR takes less time to convert scalar-type data and provides distinct advantages in programming complexity. XDR only shows limited advances in scalar array processing with tremendous coding effort from programmers. The experiments on real applications detail the overhead distribution and indicate that CGT-RMR helps provide a practical migration and checkpointing solution with minimal user involvement and satisfactory performance.

12.6   RELATED WORK

There have been a number of notable attempts at designing process migration and checkpointing schemes, however, few implementations have been reported in literature with regard to the fine-grain thread migration and checkpointing. An extension of the V migration mechanism is proposed in [9]. It requires both compiler and kernel support for migration. Data has to be stored at the same address in all migrated versions of the process to avoid pointer updating and variant padding patterns in aggregate types. Obviously, this constraint is inefficient or even impossible to meet across different platforms.

Another approach is proposed by Theimer and Hayes in [10]. Their idea was to construct an intermediate source-code representation of a running process at the migration point, migrate the new source code, and recompile it on the destination platform. An extra compilation might incur more delays. Poor efficiency and portability are the drawbacks.

The Tui system [5] is an application-level process-migration package that utilizes compiler support and a debugger interface to examine and restore process states. It applies an intermediate data format to achieve portability across various platforms. Just as in XDR, even if migration occurs on the same platform, data conversion routines are still performed twice.

Process Introspection (PI) [11] uses program annotation techniques as in MigThread. PI is a general approach for checkpointing and applies the "receiver makes right" (RMR) strategy. Data types are maintained in tables and conversion routines are deployed for all supported platforms. Aggregate data types are still flattened down to scalar types (e.g., int, char, long, etc.) to avoid dealing with data alignment and padding. MigThread does this automatically.

SNOW [12] is another heterogeneous process-migration system that tries to migrate live data instead of the stack and heap data. SNOW adopts XDR to encode and decode data, whereas XDR is slower than the RMR used in PI [8]. PVM installation is a requirement.

Virtual machines are the intuitive solution to provide abstract platforms in heterogeneous environments. Some mobile-agent systems such as the Java-based IBM Aglet [13] use such an approach to migrate computation. However, it suffers from slow execution due to interpretation overheads.

12.7 CONCLUSIONS AND FUTURE WORK

We have discussed a data-conversion strategy in MigThread, a process/thread migration and checkpointing scheme working across different platforms. Contrary to the fine-grain approaches adopted in many research projects, the proposed coarse-grain tagged "receiver makes right" scheme (CGT-RMR) enables MigThread to not flatten down aggregate types into scalar (primitive) data types within data-conversion routines. In fact, type flattening takes place in the tag-definition process that is conducted by MigThread's preprocessor. The contents of tags are determined at run time to eliminate possible alignment-affecting factors from CPUs, operating systems, and compilers. Since tags help resolve data alignment and padding, CGT-RMR provides significant coding convenience to programmers and contributes a feasible data-conversion solution in heterogeneous migration and checkpointing.

Another reason that CGT-RMR achieves performance gains is that it performs data conversion only on one side instead of both sides as in XDR. CGT-RMR exhibits tremendous efficiency in homogeneous environments and performance similar to XDR in heterogeneous environments. Since no tables or special data-conversion routines are required, CGT-RMR can be applied on new computer platforms directly. This "plug-and-play" design opens the door to future computer vendors.

CGT-RMR intends to convert data even between incompatible format platforms. This aggressive scheme stops conversion only when loss of precision actually occurs. Since MigThread provides support seamlessly at both compile and run time, such low-level conversion-error information can be conveyed to the upper-level scheduling module to abort the entire migration and checkpointing process. In address-space-decreasing cases, resized pointers can also be updated precisely.

We are currently building a new data conversion API so that programmers can use CGT-RMR directly rather than through MigThread. To accomplish a universal data-conversion scheme, CGT-RMR requires MigThread's preprocessor as its back end because the preprocessor's data type system is still indispensable. Working as a stand-alone standard such as XDR, CGT-RMR will benefit other migration and checkpointing schemes, and any application running in heterogeneous environments.

ACKNOWLEDGMENTS

This research was supported in part by NSF IGERT grant 9987598, NSF MRI grant 9977815, and NSF ITR grant 0081696.

REFERENCES

1. D. Milojicic, F. Douglis, Y. Paindaveine, R. Wheeler and S. Zhou, "Process Migration Survey," *ACM Computing Surveys, 32*(8), 241–299 (2000).

2. I. Foster, C. Kesselman, J. Nick, and S. Tuecke, "Grid Services for Distributed System Integration," *Computer, 35*(6), 37–46 (2002).

3. H. Jiang and V. Chaudhary, "Compile/Run-time Support for Thread Migration," in *Proceedings of 16th International Parallel and Distributed Processing Symposium,* pp. 58–66 (2002).

4. H. Jiang and V. Chaudhary, "On Improving Thread Migration: Safety and Performance," in *Proceedings of the International Conference on High Performance Computing,* pp. 474–484 (2002).

5. P. Smith and N. Hutchinson, "Heterogeneous Process Migration: the TUI System," Technical Report 96-04, University of British Columbia (1996).

6. R. Srinivasan, "XDR: External Data Representation Standard," RFC 1832, http://www.faqs.org/rfcs/rfc1832.html (1995).

7. C. Meryers and G. Chastek, "The use of ASN.1 and XDR for Data Representation in Real-Time Distributed Systems," Technical Report CMU/SEI-93-TR-10, Carnegie-Mellon University (1993).

8. H. Zhou and A. Geist, "'Receiver Makes Right' Data Conversion in PVM," in *Proceedings of the 14th International Conference on Computers and Communications,* pp. 458–464 (1995).

9. C. Shub, "Native Code Process-Originated Migration in a Heterogeneous Environment," in *Proceedings of the Computer Science Conference,* pp. 266–270 (1990).

10. M. Theimer and B. Hayes, "Heterogeneous Process Migration by Recompilation," in *Proceedings of the 11th International Conference on Distributed Computing Systems,* pp. 18–25 (1991).

11. A. Ferrari, S. Chapin, and A. Grimshaw, "Process Introspection: A Checkpoint Mechanism for High Performance Heterogeneous Distributed Systems," Technical Report CS-96-15, University of Virginia, Department of Computer Science (1996).

12. K. Chanchio and X. Sun, "Data Collection and Restoration for Heterogeneous Process Migration," *Software—Practice and Experience, 32*(9), pp. 845–871 (2002).

13. D. Lange and M. Oshima, *Programming Mobile Agents in Java with the Java Aglet API,* Addison-Wesley Longman: New York, 1998.

14. "PVM: Parallel Virtual Machine," http://www.csm.ornl.gov/pvm/pvm_home.html.

15. S.Woo, M. Ohara, E. Torrie, J. Singh, and A. Gupta, "The SPLASH-2 Programs: Characterization and Methodological Considerations," in *Proceedings of the 22nd Annual International Symposium on Computer Architecture* (1995).

CHAPTER 13

Receiving-Message Prediction and Its Speculative Execution

TAKANOBU BABA, TAKASHI YOKOTA, KANEMITSU OOTSU,
FUMIHITO FURUKAWA, and YOSHIYUKI IWAMOTO

13.1 BACKGROUND

Recently, prediction and speculative computation have attracted our attention, and there are many studies concerning this topic. In the field of computer architecture, for example, there have been many studies: branch prediction [1], memory-access prediction [2], and data-value prediction [3]. The hit ratio of current branch predictors is reaching nearly 100%. This saves the overhead caused by mispenalties, and contributes to the performance improvement.

Prediction and speculative computation techniques have also been applied to many other fields to enhance their performance [5]. These trends can be viewed as a kind of profile-based, dynamic optimization. It utilizes the past execution profile to predict the future as accurately as possible at run time, and speculatively executes the predicted events to tolerate the latencies of time-consuming operations.

Our basic motivation in this study is to explore the possibility of message prediction and its speculative execution [6, 7, 8, 9]. If the message to be received next can be predicted appropriately, the receiver can start its reception process before receiving the real message. This speculative execution utilizes an idle message-waiting time and, thus, enhances the performance. If the prediction was not correct, we need to flush the results of speculative computation and restart the reception process.

The success of this approach depends on the hit ratio of receiving-message prediction and the amount of idle time periods to be utilized for the speculative computation. In order to clarify these, we analyzed the message-passing patterns and idle-time lengths using NAS Parallel Benchmarks [11]. Figures 13.1, 13.2 and 13.3 illustrate typical message-passing characteristics in the benchmark. We found that there is regularity of message passings [12] and message sizes, and there are a lot of idle time periods before receiving messages. This work made us confident of possibility of using message prediction and its speculative computation during the idle time periods.

High-Performance Computing: Paradigm and Infrastructure. Edited by L. T. Yang and M. Guo **261**
Copyright © 2006 John Wiley & Sons, Inc.

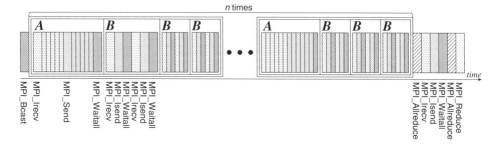

Figure 13.1   Sequence of MPI functions in the SP program.

As the reduction of internode communication overhead is crucial for parallel and distributed computation, this speculative computation will contribute to the improvement of the performance of parallel and distributed programs' execution.

We implemented our message-prediction method in the MPI libraries [9]. The MPI libraries are widely used, and there are many parallel programs that use them. Thus, if we can implement the method inside the libraries, the method can be applied to those programs without modifying them.

The rest of this chapter is organized as follows. Section 13.2 proposes the receiving-message-prediction method. The static and dynamic efforts for improving the success ratio of the prediction are described as well. Section 13.3 describes the implementation of the method in the MPI. The platform machines include a workstation (WS) cluster and the Sun Enterprise 3500 (E3500). Section 13.4 summarizes the experimental results, such as prediction ratios, success ratios, and speed-up ratios. Section 13.5 finalizes the chapter.

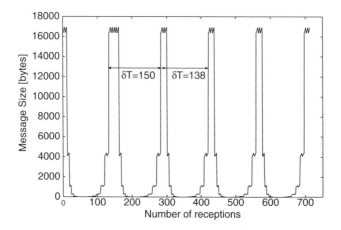

Figure 13.2   Sequence of message sizes in the MG program.

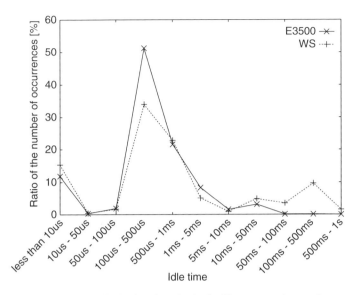

Figure 13.3   Distribution of idle-time lengths in the IS program. (us = microseconds, ms = milliseconds.)

13.2   RECEIVING-MESSAGE PREDICTION METHOD

Our basic idea is to utilize the idle state effectively by predicting the message to be received next using communication logs of the past messages. Figure 13.4 compares the normal execution process and the speculative execution process we have proposed. In speculative execution, the node in an idle state speculatively executes the message-receiving process and a part of the user program. When the message arrives, the header part is checked to see whether the prediction succeeds.

13.2.1   Prediction Method

This subsection describes the items to be predicted and the prediction algorithms. In order to avoid user-program modification, we implemented the method inside communication libraries. The speculative execution will not affect the user interface, that is, the specification of a message-passing library.

13.2.1.1   Message Items   Generally, the message consists of the header and the body. The message header contains information such as message size, sender ID, and selector ID. From these items, we selected the following items for the prediction:

1. Message size
2. Message type

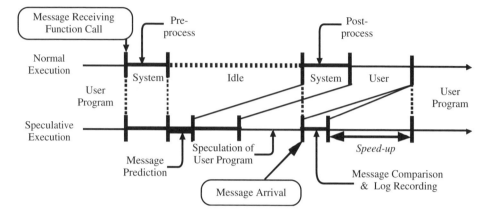

Figure 13.4   Flow of a receiving-message-prediction method.

3. Sender node number (sender node ID)
4. Function name
5. Method (selector ID)
6. Task ID

Predicting item (1) allows us to allocate a memory area for the message and to calculate the size of the message parameters (i.e., message size minus header size). If the predicted size is larger than the actual size, it is unnecessary to reallocate a memory area even though the prediction misses.

Predicting items (2) and (3) allow us to specify a node number to return a value. Predicting items (4), (5), and (6) allow us to allocate a memory area for temporary variables to start the method execution. In this study, we predict a whole message as one item in order to avoid overheads caused by the management of the message logs.

In the MPI library, some items such as source-node rank or message size (len) are described in a user program. In the prediction process, these items are preset into the predicted message.

Similar options exist when the node processor compares the arrived message with a predicted message. That is, it may compare the messages as one item, or compare the messages item by item. By the same reasoning as the unit of prediction, we compare the messages as one item.

13.2.1.2 Prediction Algorithms

In order to predict the items, we considered the following seven prediction algorithms [4].

Prev.: Use of the previous message
Max.: Maximum value of the past messages
Ave.: Average numeric value of the past messages

Mode: Frequency of the past messages

Markov: Use of the Markov chain

Log: Use of the execution log information

Linear: Use of the stride series

Among these seven algorithms, we selected two algorithms, *Prev.* and *Markov*. *Prev.* assumes that the next message is the same as the previous message. In this method, we have only to keep the previous message. We assumed that *Markov* would have the best success ratio compared with the other algorithms as it fully utilizes past history. However, it requires $O(m^{n+1})$ memory area (m represents the number of kinds within each item, and n represents the number of the previous messages to be referenced for the prediction). Further, it takes time to search the recorded logs. Thus, n will usually be 2 or 3.

The reasons why we selected *Prev.* and *Markov* are (i) they are expected to be the most comprehensive algorithms as described above, and (ii) they represent two extreme cases, namely, *Prev.* is easiest to implement as it just requires the previous message, and *Markov* is the most complex to implement as it requires us to keep and search the past sequence of message receptions.

13.2.2 Flow of the Prediction Process

In the normal execution process, the message-receiving process stops its execution to wait for message arrival. When a message arrives, a processor executes the postprocess for the arrived message and complete the reception process. We will explain the flow of the prediction process for *Prev.* and *Markov*.

Figure 13.5 shows the flow of the prediction process and postexecution process using the *Prev.* algorithm. If the message has already arrived, a processor records the message for the next prediction and executes the postprocess for the message. If the message has not arrived yet, the processor uses the recorded message as the next message (i.e., predicted message). Based on this predicted message, the processor executes the postprocess and waits for a message. After the message arrives, a processor compares the received message with predicted one. If the prediction succeeds, the processor completes the receiving process. Otherwise, the processor records the received message and reexecutes the postprocess with the received message.

Figure 13.6 shows a flow of the prediction process using the *Markov* algorithm. The differences from *Prev.* are the recording and prediction processes. In the recording process, the processor modifies the Markov table using the received message. In the prediction process, the processor refers to the Markov table.

13.2.3 Static Algorithm Selection by Profiling

An appropriate prediction algorithm may change, depending on a given parallel program. Profiling is a promising solution to find the algorithm by preexecuting a part of the program and recording the whole receiving message. We perform the

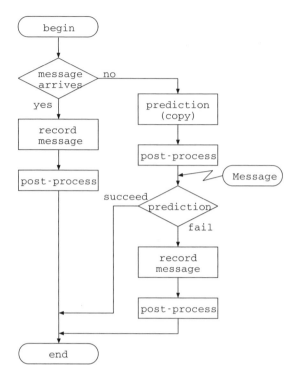

Figure 13.5   Flow of the prediction process (*Prev.*).

profiling as follows. At compile time, the preprocessor searches the MPI functions for message receiving. Then, the preprocessor inserts the profiling function [e.g., print_profile()] after the MPI function calls of the source program. After this process, the source program is preexecuted. In the profiling function, the processor executes the following processes:

1. Predicts a message based on all algorithms using the recorded messages
2. Compares the predicted message and received message
3. Counts the number of the successes and failures
4. Records the received message for the next prediction
5. Modifies the Markov table

When this preexecution finishes, the preprocessor checks the number of the successes, and decides on an algorithm that has the highest success ratio.

13.2.4   Dynamic Algorithm Switching

Profiling is not enough when a parallel program changes its behavior dynamically. The behavior may change, depending on the part of the program and on input data

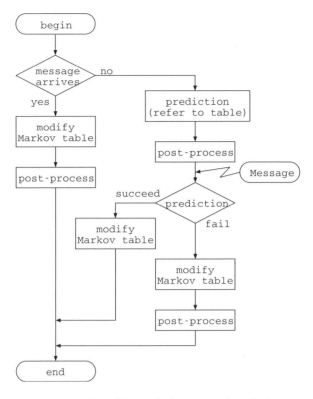

Figure 13.6   Flow of the prediction process (*Markov*).

to the program. In order to follow the change, the prediction algorithm should be changed dynamically.

Further, we should take care of cases in which the length of the idle time changes. If there is little idle time, the prediction itself should be stopped.

Figure 13.7 shows the flow of the dynamic switching process. There are two major differences from the usual prediction flows of Figures 13.5 and 13.6. First, we count the cases where there is no idle time, as the next message has arrived before the end of the current message's processing. When the counter, named *na* in the figure, reaches N, the node gives up the prediction. This allows us to avoid the overhead of the message recording.

Second, if the prediction fails M times, the processor switches the prediction algorithm to another algorithm. In this study, we start from the *Prev.* algorithm because it is simple and the overhead is lowest.

13.3   IMPLEMENTATION OF THE METHODS IN THE MPI LIBRARIES

The receiving-message-prediction method can be implemented on any parallel computer system, because the method is independent of the hardware and software

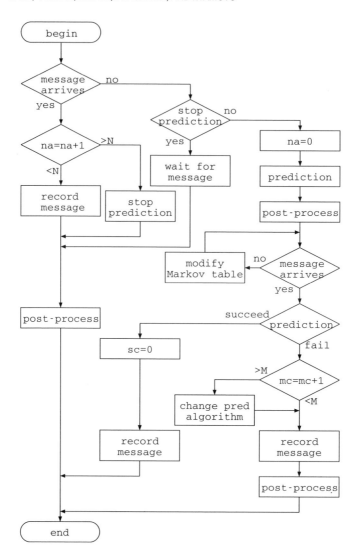

Figure 13.7   Flow of the dynamic switching process.

systems. In our research, we have implemented the method on various platforms, such as a workstation (WS) cluster, the Sun Enterprise 3500 (E3500), the NEC Cenju-3, the Fujitsu AP1000, and the A-NET multicomputer [13]. In order to show how to implement our method on general computer systems, this section describes the implementation of the MPI libraries on the WS cluster and the E3500.

We implemented our method by extending MPICH version 1.1.2. We added the function of the method to an MPI_Recv(), a frequently used function for receiving messages. In the MPICH, the MPI_Recv() is implemented as a basic communication function. It is called up by other MPI functions, such as MPI_Bcast(),

`MPI_Allreduce()`, `MPI_Alltoall()`, and `MPI_Wait()`, when these functions receive messages. Thus, all of these functions benefit from the receiving-message-prediction mechanism. In particular, when the reduction operations execute with the `MPI_Allreduce()` and `MPI_Alltoall()`, the communication routes are fixed statically. This is favorable for predicting the sender node IDs.

As discussed in Section 13.2, we execute only receiving processes speculatively. The node processor predicts only the message header, and executes the system process (postprocess) for the incoming message speculatively. If the message doesn't arrive after completing the prediction and the speculative execution, the processor sleeps until the message arrives. This strategy not only makes the implementation quite simple, but also requires no rollback of the user process.

The postprocess executes the following operations:

1. Convert the byte order
2. Identify the message type (control/ordinary message)
3. Search the queue of required messages, and dequeue from the queue
4. Identify the message size (short, long, vlong)
5. Copy the messages from the system reception buffer to user memory area
6. Set a receiving status (received size, sender node ID, error, etc.)

Operation (5) should be executed again after the message arrives, as this operation requires the message body.

13.4 EXPERIMENTAL RESULTS

13.4.1 Evaluation Environments

Before starting to discuss the practical effectiveness of receiving-message prediction, we first clarify our evaluation environments.

Two parallel processing platforms are used: a symmetric multiprocessor and a heterogeneous workstation cluster. The former is Sun Enterprise 3500 (E3500), in which eight UltraSPARC-II processors are connected via a 2.6 GB/s Gigaplane bus. The latter is a cluster of Sun workstations connected by 100Base-T Ethernet via a switching hub. The configuration of each environment is summarized in Table 13.1.

Table 13.1 Evaluation platforms

	CPU	Memory
E3500	UltraSPARC-II (400 MHz) × 8	3 GB
Workstation cluster (WS)	UltraSPARC-II (300 MHz) × 2	1 GB
	UltraSPARC (200 MHz) × 2	832 MB
	UltraSPARC-IIi (200 MHz)	128 MB
	UltraSPARC (167 MHz)	128 MB

The receiving-message-prediction method is implemented in the MPI libraries on the two platforms. The modified libraries predict message headers and no user process is speculatively executed. Execution time is measured from the beginning of the first node to the completion of whole nodes. Idle time is measured in the synchronous read function `MPI_Recv()`. Five applications from NAS Parallel Benchmarks are used: IS, SP, CG, EP, and MG.

13.4.2 Basic Characteristics of the Receiving-Message-Prediction Method

13.4.2.1 Actual Time Scale First, we measured the actual time scale in the receiving-message-prediction method. As shown in Figure 13.4, lengths of prediction and postprocess time are important for the method.

Prediction times are constant for each of prediction method, *Prev.* and *Markov*. It requires 6.1 μs for *Prev.* and 193 μs for *Markov*. The *Markov* method is expected to be high potential but, on the other hand, it requires large computation for prediction. This means the method may consume the potential gain of receiving-message prediction. The simpleness of the *Prev.* method shortens the prediction time.

Postprocess time varies due to the message granularity of each program, as shown in Table 13.2. Some programs (CG and EP) use small messages, thus, their postprocess time is short.

13.4.2.2 Basic Behavior Table 13.3 shows the prediction characteristics of each evaluation condition. We use a combination of platforms and prediction methods, for example, E3500 (*Prev.*). The second column of the table is the number of receptions through the program. "Pred." columns show the prediction ratios, that is, the percentage of predicted `MPI_Reads`. "Succ." columns illustrate the success ratios in the predicted receptions.

As described in Section 1.2, message prediction is performed only if the incoming message has not arrived at the beginning of the reception process. Thus the "Pred." columns indicate idle time lengths in the reception process of benchmark programs.

The CG and SP programs have very short (or no) idle time in the reception process and, thus, result in very low prediction ratios. In the CG row of Table 13.3, for example, 0.004% of prediction out of 23,618 receptions means that prediction is performed as little as only one time.

The EP program has a high prediction ratio and good success ratio for *Prev.* The program includes four reduction functions, which raises the prediction and success ratios.

Table 13.2 Postprocess time

	IS	SP	CG	EP	MG
Postprocess time (μs)	60,141	26,856	26	26	951

Table 13.3   Prediction characteristics

		E3500 (*Prev.*)		WS (*Prev.*)		WS (*Markov*)		WS (Chg.)	
Program	Number of Receptions	Pred. %	Succ. %	Pred. %	Succ. %	Pred. %	Succ. %	Pred. %	Succ. %
IS	2,322	4.46	1.46	3.55	1.38	3.87	6.64	3.79	6.18
SP	38,623	0.08	8.00	0.05	6.67	0.04	0.00	0.02	7.41
CG	23,618	0.004	25.00	0.008	0.00	0.004	0.00	0.00	0.00
EP	115	40.37	10.33	30.13	8.51	28.95	1.33	27.21	9.30
MG	35,108	3.48	1.43	3.19	2.34	2.49	2.19	0.22	7.14

The resulting speedup (or slowdown) comes actually from the idle time lengths. Figure 13.8 shows the speed-up ratio. About 5% of the acceleration of CG in E3500 (*Prev.*) means that a few successful predictions raise the performance, whereas the WS platform suffers from the high overhead of the prediction method.

Another example is the IS program. The prediction and success ratios of E3500 (*Prev.*) are similar to those of WS (*Prev.*). However, the idle time length of E3500 is very short and prediction overhead cancels the possible performance gain.

High prediction and success ratios are not necessarily reflected in the performance gain. The EP program is a typical example. The prediction and success ratios are high due to four series of reduction functions, as described above. However, the performance gain is not so large, as the functions are executed at the far end of the program.

13.4.2.3 *Idle-Time Reduction*

We can easily guess that idle time in a message-receiving process should be reduced if the receiving-message-prediction method is to use idle time efficiently. Figure 13.9 shows the numbers of occurrences of idle-time lengths. In this figure, receptions without any idle time are omitted. "No prediction" shows the original MPI library, and "w/prediction" shows the E3500 (*Prev.*) case. For example, there were 63 occurrences of "5–10ms" idle-time periods for "no prediction." After applying the receiving-message-prediction

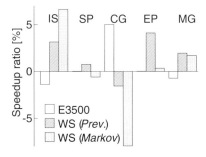

Fig. 13.8   Speedup ratio of benchmark programs.

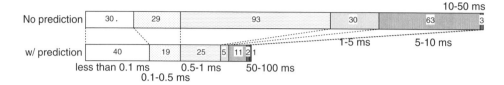

Fig. 13.9   Reduction of idle time.

method, this number is reduced to 11. The figure reveals considerable reduction of the idle time, which is due to the receiving-message-prediction process.

13.4.2.4   *Effects of Problem Size*   The postprocess time length depends on the message size, as shown in Table 13.2. This means that larger problems, whose message granularity is large, require longer postprocess times. This should result in more effective execution by receiving-message prediction. Figure 13.10 shows the speedup ratios of each program for class S and W problems. (Class S is smaller than W.) In all cases, speedup ratios are improved in class W.

13.4.3   Effects of Profiling

Table 13.4 shows examples of profiling results. Programs are executed on the E3500 platform with dataset class A and four nodes are used. We find that in the IS program, the tenth message is received at elapsed time 189.68 seconds and at that time 32.61% of predictions are successful with *Prev.* and 33.26 % with *Markov.*

From this table, we can easily find which prediction method is better for each benchmark program; the IS matches *Markov* and the SP and BT prefer *Prev.*, but the MG refuses both *Prev.* and *Markov*, since both success ratios are zero.

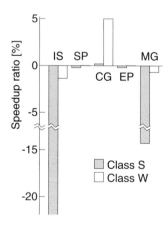

Fig. 13.10   Effects of problem size.

Table 13.4 Profiling results

Program	Received Counts	Elapsed Time, Seconds	Success Ratio *Prev.* %	*Markov* %
IS	4th	3.24	0.02	0.02
	5th	8.27	0.03	0.03
	6th	8.57	30.62	32.34
	10th	189.68	32.61	33.26
SP	100th	28.07	0.78	0.05
	200th	57.12	0.78	0.05
	300th	70.84	0.78	0.05
	400th	76.26	0.78	0.05
MG	100th	51.02	0.00	0.00
	200th	105.23	0.00	0.00
BT	100th	53.65	2.58	2.36
	200th	103.23	2.53	2.12
	300th	156.69	2.48	2.16

13.4.4 Dynamic Algorithm Changing

The WS (Chg.) column in Table 13.3 indicates characteristics of the dynamic algorithm changing method. Its performance graph is shown in Figure 13.11. In both of the table and graph, *Prev.* and *Markov* values are illustrated for comparison purposes. Figure 13.12 shows the timing flow of each of eight processors executing the IS program. The figure shows that *Chg.* performs proper selection of algorithms and thus allows us to obtain near-optimal performance benefit.

13.5 CONCLUDING REMARKS

This chapter describes the method for receiving-message prediction and its speculative execution. The method has been implemented with the MPI library, running on

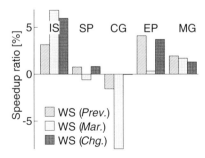

Fig. 13.11 Speedup ratios of dynamic algorithm switching.

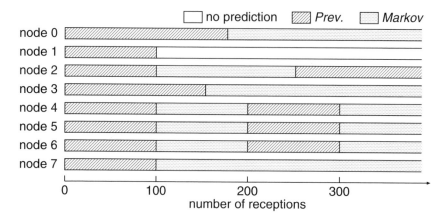

Fig. 13.12   Timing flow of dynamic algorithm switching.

two quite different platforms, that is, the WS cluster and the E3500 symmetric multiprocessor. The results of the performance evaluation can be summarized as follows:

- Our method is independent of any platforms. As this method can be implemented by modifying only the software inside message-passing libraries, it neither requires a change of hardware nor a change in the application software.

- The experimental results demonstrate that our method achieves up to a 6.8% speedup of applications described in the MPI library.

- The method utilizes the nodes effectively. This is evidenced by the decrease of the number of the idle-time occurrences and the lengths of the idle times after applying our method.

- The use of profiling, both for static algorithm selection and for dynamic switching, proves to increase the success ratio of predictions and decrease the overhead caused by mispredictions.

These results indicate not only the effectiveness of our method but also the applicability to various parallel and distributed platforms. Areas of future investigation include the application of various prediction methods we did not use, more aggressive prediction of a message body and its speculative execution, and the introduction of a new hardware mechanism that allows the receiving-message-prediction process to run in parallel with the other processes.

REFERENCES

1. S. McFarling, "Combining Branch Predictors," WRL Technical Note TN-36, Digital Western Research Laboratory, June 1993.

2. S. P. VanderWiel and D. J. Lijia, "Data Prefetch Mechanisms," *ACM Computing Surveys, 32,* 2, 174–199, June 2000.

3. K. Wang and M. Franklin, "Highly Accurate Data Value Prediction Using Hybrid Predictors," in *30th International Symposium on Microarchitecture,* pp. 281–290, Dec. 1997.

4. Y. Iwamoto, K. Suga, K. Ootsu, T. Yokota, and T. Baba, "Receiving Message Prediction Method," *Parallel Computing, 29,* 11–12, 1509–1538, Nov.–Dec. 2003.

5. T. Sasaki, T. Takayama, T. Hironaka, and S. Fujino, "Database Processing with Speculative Execution Reduction of Response Time in Multitransactions Environments," *Information Processing Society of Japan (IPSJ) SIG Notes, 97,* ARC–125, 127–132, 1997.

6. Y. Iwamoto, A. Sawada, D. Abe, Y. Sawada, K. Ootsu, T. Yoshinaga, and T. Baba, "Methodologies for High Performance Message Passing: Implementation and Evaluation," *Journal of Information Processing Society of Japan (IPSJ), 39,* 6, 1663–1671, 1998.

7. Y. Iwamoto, R. Adachi, K. Ootsu, T. Yoshinaga, and T. Baba, "High Speed Receiving Process of MPI by Receiving Message Prediction," *Journal of Information Processing Society of Japan (IPSJ), 42,* 4, 812–820, 2001.

8. Y. Iwamoto, K. Ootsu, T. Yoshinaga, and T. Baba, "Message Prediction and Speculative Execution of the Reception Process," in *Proceedings of the Eleventh IASTED International Conference on Parallel and Distributed Computing and Systems (PDCS'99),* pp. 329–334, 1999.

9. Y. Iwamoto, K. Ootsu, T. Yoshinaga, and T. Baba, "Prediction Methodologies for Receiving Message Prediction," *Journal of Information Processing Society of Japan, 41,* 9, 2582–2591, 2000.

10. Y. Iwamoto, K. Suga, K. Ootsu, and T. Baba, "Receiving Process of MPI by Receiving Message Prediction," in *Proceedings of the IASTED International Conference on Parallel and Distributed Computing and Systems (PDCS 2001),* pp. 486–490, 2001.

11. Available from: http://www.nas.nasa.gov/NAS/NPB.

12. J. Kim and D. J. Lilja, "Characterization of Communication Patterns in Message Passing Parallel Scientific Application Program," in *CANPC'98,* pp. 202–216, 1998.

13. T. Yoshinaga, A. Sawada, M. Hirota, D. Abe, Y. Iwamoto, and T. Baba, "System Performance Evaluation for the A-NET Multicomputer," *Transactions of the Institute of Electronics, Information and Communication Engineers, J81-D-I,* 4, pp. 368–376, 1998.

## CHAPTER 14

An Investigation of the Applicability of Distributed FPGAs to High-Performance Computing

JOHN P. MORRISON, PADRAIG O'DOWD, and PHILIP D. HEALY

14.1 INTRODUCTION

FPGAs (field-programmable gate arrays) are silicon chips that can be continuously reprogrammed with application-specific logic configurations. This interesting property gives them many advantages over ASICs (application-specific integrated circuits), which contain fixed hardware configurations and cannot be altered to implement different algorithms or updated if a bug is found. The first simple FPGAs were manufactured in 1986 and since then they have increased considerably in logic density and clock speed (however, FPGA clock speeds are not increasing at the same rate as microprocessor clock speeds; see below). As FPGA logic density and clock speeds increased, the field of reconfigurable computing, that is, using the reprogrammable aspect of FPGAs to implement different algorithms directly in hardware, grew in popularity.

In order to avoid confusion, it is instructive to clearly distinguish between the similar but distinct fields of reconfigurable computing in embedded computing and reconfigurable computing in high-performance computing. FPGAs have found widespread adoption in the Embedded Computing field as devices for prototyping ASIC designs, creating a steadily growing, multibillion-dollar industry. Despite the much greater complexity of FPGAs in comparison with ASICs, the economies of scale achieved during their production has led to them becoming a viable alternative to ASICs in many situations. With the release of the new Spartan 3 FPGA [1] it is expected that FPGAs will push even further into high-volume applications, offering a low-cost alternative to ASICs. FPGAs have also eroded the embedded-microprocessor market, as they can offer the advantage of reprogrammability but at increased execution speed. Indeed, FPGAs can be seen as blurring the distinction between hardware and software by merging the functionality of ASICs and microprocessors while maintaining the advantages of both. FPGAs containing embedded microprocessors, such as the Virtex II Pro [2], have become available, allowing applications to be created that are partitioned between hardware and software on the same logic device. Since embedded microprocessors and FPGAs operate at similar clock speeds (currently around 400 MHz), significant application speedups are easily attainable through the use of reconfigurable computing in embedded computing devices.

The goal of reconfigurable computing in high-performance computing is to decrease application execution time by utilizing FPGAs as coprocessors in desktop computers. There is a marked difference, however, between the clock speeds of desktop microprocessors and FPGAs. Relatively few applications can provide enough parallelism for the FPGA to exploit in order to close this performance gap. Despite this, applications do exist that can benefit greatly from FPGA implementation. This chapter discusses the experiences and lessons learned from trying to apply reconfigurable computing techniques to high-performance computing. The work-execution times of several applications on FPGAs (placed on PCI boards) and general-purpose desktop machines were compared (high-performance workstations or SMP machines were not considered). Comparisons of various cost factors are considered when comparing FPGAs to microprocessors, including speedups, ease of programming, and financial cost.

Unfortunately, the field of reconfigurable computing lacks clear benchmarks for comparing FPGAs to microprocessors. Such comparisons should include complete descriptions of the FPGA and microprocessor. For example, it is not useful to state that an FPGA can offer a five-fold decrease in application execution time over a microprocessor without specifying the relative clock speeds of the devices used. The development board on which the FPGA is placed is also of great importance. Since FPGAs can access several memory banks in parallel, the type and number of banks present on the board can have a significant effect on application performance. Also, the number of FPGAs placed on the board can obviously make a big difference. Boards with multiple FPGAs allows fine-grain parallelism between the FPGAs and, hence, may execute an algorithm much faster then a single FPGA alone.

The remainder of this chapter is organized as follows. High-performance computing with cluster computing is discussed in Section 14.2. In Section 14.3, the history of reconfigurable computing with FPGAs is discussed, including the different types of architectures used in reconfigurable systems. The Distributed Reconfigurable Metacomputer (DRMC) project is discussed in Section 14.4, the goal of which is to apply distributed FPGA acceleration to high-performance computing applications. Also discussed are the type of FPGAs used and the tools used to program them. Sections 14.5 and 14.6 present applications that were implemented on DRMC/FPGAs. The first shows how an application benefited from implementation on DRMC/FPGAs, and the second illustrates that not all applications benefited from implementation on DRMC/FPGAs with respect to application speedup, financial cost, and ease of programming. Section 14.7 presents conclusions of the DRMC project and speculates on the future of FPGAs in high-performance computing.

14.2 HIGH-PERFORMANCE COMPUTING WITH CLUSTER COMPUTING

A cluster can be defined as "a collection of computers that are connected over a local network and appear as a single computer system." Cluster computing has the goal of gathering many computers together to work as one high-performance computer.

Interest in cluster computing has grown rapidly in recent years, due the availability of powerful desktop machines and high-speed networks as off-the-self cheap commodity components. Clusters now provide a cheap alternative to supercomputers and offer comparable performance speeds on a broad range of high-performance computing applications. Today, free software can be downloaded from the Internet to allow groups of networked desktop machines to be easily combined into Beowulf-type PC clusters [3]. For some, cluster computing is now seen as the future of high-performance computing [4].

Traditional high-performance computing applications are diverse and are found in the scientific, engineering, and financial domains. To compete in these areas, much research has been done in the area of cluster design. The goal of the DRMC project was to take the idea of cluster computing (with desktop machines) one step further by adding reconfigurable computing hardware to form a reconfigurable cluster using only off-the-self components. A reconfigurable cluster (see Figure 14.1) retains all the advantages of a traditional cluster, but also allows algorithms to

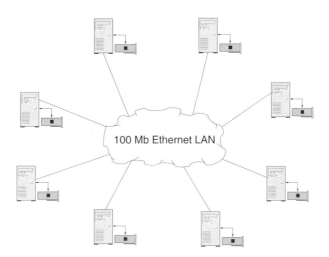

Figure 14.1 Cluster containing reconfigurable computing boards.

be implemented directly in hardware (on FPGAs), with the aim of improving application execution speeds.

14.3 RECONFIGURABLE COMPUTING WITH FPGAs

As of August 2003, state-of-the art FPGAs like the Xilinx Virtex II [5] had clock speeds of 400 MHz and up to 10 million gates. As FPGA capabilities increased and numerous early reconfigurable computing research projects reported that FPGAs could provide enormous performance gains, research activities in the area surged [6, 7]. Even after years of research, reconfigurable computing remains in the research domain, with very few examples of commercial use (one notable exception being that detailed in [8]). The main market for FPGAs is still ASIC prototyping and low-cost ASIC replacement.

Many different approaches to exploiting reconfigurable computing exist. Some of the most common are:

1. Adding a reconfigurable logic unit [9] as a functional unit to a microprocessor (similar to an ALU). The microprocessor still executes algorithms in the traditional von Neumann style, but parts of some algorithms can be implemented in hardware and executed using the reconfigurable logic unit. This requires building a new microprocessor from scratch and so is an expensive option.

2. Developing custom machines with specialized motherboards containing some number of FPGAs [8]. Algorithms are mapped onto the different FPGAs for execution. This approach is very different to the traditional von Neumann style. This type of reconfigurable architecture is suited to fine-grain parallelism between the FPGAs.

3. Adding reconfigurable computing boards to general desktop machines using the PCI bus. This is the approach taken by the DRMC project [10, 11]. Drivers running on the host processors allow the FPGAs to be configured with chosen algorithms and data can be transferred to and from the reconfigurable computing boards over the machines' PCI buses. Other projects such as that detailed in [12] use the more unusual approach of mixing the algorithm's logic with the networking logic in order to try to speed up execution even further. This requires a specialized reconfigurable computing board connected directly to the network.

An extensive list of reconfigurable computing projects and their target application areas can be found in [13–15]. The experiences described in this chapter are based on the DRMC approach, although, undoubtedly, particular approaches are more suitable to implementing some applications than others. It may, therefore, be claimed that specialized architectures result in the optimum implementation for certain problems (e.g., architectures that allow fine-grain parallelism between several

FPGAs). In the DRMC project, no specialist tuning was attempted, so applications that are not suited to DRMC may execute better on other reconfigurable architectures.

Reconfigurable computing boards such as the RC1000 contain one or more FPGAs; a number of external memory banks and PMC connectors are also usually present to allow other hardware to be connected to the board, if desired.

A significant factor mitigating against the increased adoption of reconfigurable hardware is the fact that FPGA clock speeds are increasing at a far lower rate than microprocessor clock speeds. In 1991, top-of-the-range microprocessors ran at 33 MHz, but FPGAs (Xilinx XC3090) could run as fast as reported in [17]. In June 2001, top-of-the-range microprocessors ran at 1.7 GHz, but FPGAs could only reach speeds of 200 MHz. In August 2003, top-of-the-range microprocessors ran at 3.08 GHz, but FPGAs (Xilinx Virtex II Pro [2]) could only reach maximum speeds of 400 MHz.

Figure 14.2 shows these comparisons and illustrates the different rates at which the clock speeds of both FPGAs and microprocessors are increasing. If this trend continues into the future, FPGAs will have a very hard time competing with microprocessors in the general-purpose high-performance computing arena. If FPGAs are to outperform microprocessors, they need applications that can offer tremendous amounts of parallelism. This challenge is compounded by the place and route tools currently available. These determine if a design can fit on an FPGA and at what clock speed the design can run. Very often, designs end up with very poor clock

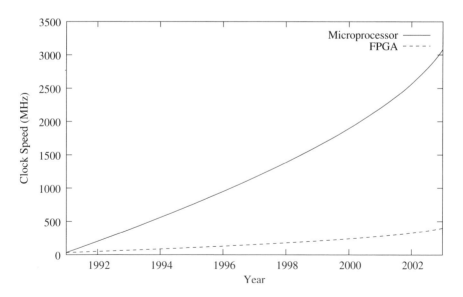

Figure 14.2 Graph comparing the rates at which FPGA and microprocessor clock speeds are increasing.

speeds, since it is virtually impossible to realize the maximum clock speed of an FPGA. Trying to increase the clock speeds of designs beyond what the place and route tools initially report can become a very laborious process, requiring significant knowledge of the underlying hardware by the designer. As a result, the speed at which the clock runs on an FPGA is often far slower than the theoretical maximum.

Notwithstanding the limitations outlined above, those applications that do exhibit the requisite level of parallelism will continue to see significant performance increases in the future. Figure 14.3 compares the rate at which FPGA and microprocessor densities have been increasing in recent years. If FPGA densities continue to increase at such a dramatic rate, those applications already suited to acceleration using FPGAs will see greater and greater speedups using reconfigurable computing techniques as time goes on. However, due to the limitations imposed by the relatively low clock speeds of FPGAs, there are many classes of application that are unlikely to benefit from FPGA implementation in the foreseeable future.

14.4 DRMC: A DISTRIBUTED RECONFIGURABLE METACOMPUTER

The Distributed Reconfigurable Metacomputer (DRMC) project [10, 11] provides an environment in which computations can be constructed in a high-level manner and executed on clusters containing reconfigurable hardware. DRMC is unique in

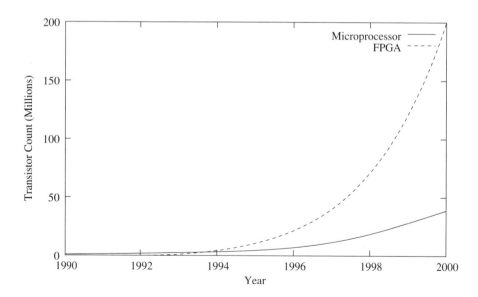

Figure 14.3   Graph comparing the rates at which the transistor count of FPGAs and the Intel Pentium family of microprocessors increased through the 1990s.

that applications are executed on clusters using the CONDENSED GRAPHS model of computing [18]. The DRMC system is comprised of several components: a meta-computing platform containing a condensed graphs engine capable of executing applications expressed as graphs, a condensed graphs compiler, a control program for initiating and monitoring computations, and a set of libraries containing components that simplify application development.

14.4.1 Application Development

A DRMC application consists of a set of graph definitions (expressed as XML, in a scheme similar to the one outlined in [19]) and a set of executable instructions. Instructions are implemented either in C or as FPGA configurations. Executable instructions are represented by object code (contained in .o files) or FPGA configurations (contained in .bit files).

The condensed graphs compiler compiles the set of definition graphs and links them with the set of executable instructions to produce a shared object (.so) file ready for dynamic linking and execution by the metacomputer. Any FPGA configurations required by the computation are loaded separately by the metacomputer as needed. Currently, application components are created manually, although tools to automate this process are under development.

14.4.2 Metacomputer Overview

The metacomputer is a peer-to-peer UNIX application composed of a daemon and, when an application is being executed, a multithreaded computation process. The daemon is lightweight and runs on each cluster node, listening for incoming messages. At an appropriate signal from the control program, the daemon spawns a computation process. The computation process essentially consists of a number of threads that exchange instructions and results (see Figure 14.4). At its core is

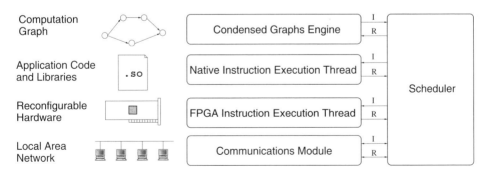

Figure 14.4 An overview of the various components comprising a DRMC computation process, along with the resources managed by each. Arrows indicate the flow of instructions (I) and results (R).

the scheduler, responsible for routing instructions and results between the various modules.

Instructions may arrive either from the condensed graphs engine or from the communications module. The scheduler sends native and condensed graph instructions to the native instruction execution thread. Likewise, FPGA instructions are sent to the FPGA instruction execution thread. Some instructions may have implementations in both software and hardware, in which case the scheduler is free to decide which thread is most appropriate. Instructions accumulate in the scheduler while awaiting execution. The scheduler will delegate instructions to other cluster nodes if this is deemed to be more expedient than waiting for an execution thread to become available.

Results arrive from the execution threads or, in the case of instructions executed remotely, the communications module. Results for instructions that initiated on the local machine are sent to the condensed graphs engine, progressing the computation. Results for instructions that originate remotely are sent to the appropriate machines.

14.4.3 Hardware Setup

The current metacomputer utilizes a standard Beowulf-type cluster [3], consisting of eight nodes, each a commodity desktop machine running the Redhat Linux operating system. The nodes were connected by a 100 Mb Ethernet switch.

A single Celoxica RC1000 reconfigurable computing board [20] was fitted to each cluster node (see Figure 14.5). These boards are PCI-based and incorporate a single Xilinx Virtex XCV2000E FPGA [21] as well as four banks (each 2 MBs in size) of on-board memory. The four memory banks can be accessed in parallel by the FPGA. This model of FPGA contains over 2.5 million gates and has a maximum clock rate of 100 MHz.

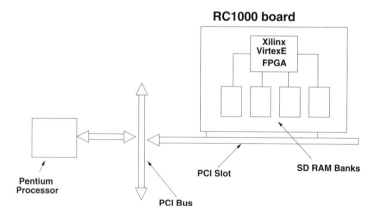

Figure 14.5 Celoxica's RC1000 board.

14.4.4 Operation

The execution of an application is initiated by sending the appropriate command from the control program to an arbitrary node in the cluster. This initiator node then spawns a computation process and broadcasts a message instructing the other cluster nodes to do likewise, specifying a shared directory containing the application code. Once the shared object containing the application code is loaded, a special registration function is called that informs the computation process of the instructions available and the libraries that the application depends on. The initiator node's computation process then commences execution of the application's top-level graph, which is equivalent to a C main function.

As instructions become available for execution, they form a queue that is managed by the scheduler. Some instructions are executed locally by sending them to the computation process's native-instruction-execution thread or FPGA instruction-execution-thread. If these local resources are busy, some instructions will be sent for execution to other cluster nodes. Instructions corresponding to condensed graphs may also be delegated to other cluster nodes, allowing parallelism to be exposed on remote machines.

Each cluster node regularly advertises its load to the others, allowing the schedulers to favor lightly loaded nodes when delegating instructions. If all the nodes are heavily loaded with long instruction queues, the computation is throttled, that is, no more new instructions are generated until the backlog has eased.

The control program (CP) monitors the execution of a computation, providing the user with real-time information on the state of each machine. The CP is also responsible for the display of log messages as well as user interaction with executing applications. In the event that a computation process exits prematurely (e.g., as the result of a badly written instruction causing a segmentation fault), the DRMC daemon executing on the affected node sends an appropriate error message to the CP before broadcasting a message to halt the computation.

14.4.5 Programming the RC1000 Board

The RC1000 boards were programmed using the Handel-C [22] language from Celoxica. Handel-C is a derivative of ANSI C specifically designed for translation to hardware. The language contains a number of extensions required for hardware development, including variable data widths and constructs for specifying parallelism and communications at the hardware level. Though Handel-C was chosen, other languages such as hardware description languages (HDLs) like Verilog [23] and VHDL [24] could have been used, but these languages are extremely low level and are very time-consuming to use compared to programming in C. Handel-C has the advantage of allowing software engineers with very little hardware knowledge to program FPGAs quickly.

Once an algorithm has been implemented in Handel-C, tested by the simulator in the Handel-C IDE [25], and found to be correct, it is compiled into EDIF [26] format. This EDIF design file is then passed to the Xilinx place and route tools [27] which produces a `.bit` (bitstream) file, which is used directly to configure the FPGA. Analysis with place and route tools reveals the longest paths in the resulting hardware design and, thus, the maximum clock speed at which a design can be run (sometimes the clock speed specified in the Handel-C code can not be met). If the clock rate was not set in the Handel-C code, the Handel-C compiler sets it to 20 MHz by default. Through a process of iterative refinement, various optimizations can be performed until an acceptable level of speed/efficiency is reached. This means that each time the clock speed is not met, the Handel-C code is modified and recompiled and the resultant EDIF design is again passed through the place and route tools. Place and route can be a long and cumbersome processes. When designs take up large amounts of the resources on the FPGA or/and have high clock speeds set, place and route can become a very long task. The example application in the next section took up large amounts of the logic of the FPGA, and it took well over a day to go through the process of going from the Handel-C code to a .bit file (on a 1.8 GHz Pentium 4 machine with 1 GB of RAM). Therefore, the iterative refinement to get the desired clock rate for large designs can be a slow process. As a result, the process of application development on an FPGA is considerably more difficult than on a microprocessor.

14.5   ALGORITHMS SUITED TO IMPLEMENTATION ON FPGAs/DRMC

An algorithm suited to implementation on DRMC/FPGAs is now presented. The chosen algorithm is a cryptographic key-crack application (of RC5), and is a good example of an embarrassingly parallel computation [28], that is, it can be divided into completely independent parallel tasks that require no intercommunication. The RC5 key-crack application running on DRMC is discussed in detail in [10]. The rest of this section presents a brief summary of that work.

RC5 is a simple and fast symmetric block cipher first published in 1994 [29]. The algorithm requires only three operations (addition, XOR, and rotation), allowing for easy implementation in hardware and software. Data-dependent rotations are used to make differential and linear cryptanalysis difficult, and, hence, provides cryptographic strength. The algorithm takes three parameters: the word size (w) in bits, the number of rounds (r), and the number of bytes (b) in the secret key. A particular (parameterized) RC5 algorithm is denoted RC5-w/r/b, with RC5-32/12/16 being the most common. As 64 bit chip architectures become the norm, it is likely that 64 bit word sizes will increase in popularity. In that case, it is suggested that the number of rounds be increased to 16. Variable length keys are accommodated by expanding the secret key to fill an expanded key table of $2(r + 1)$ words.

RC5 is extremely resistant to linear cryptanalysis, and is widely accepted as being secure (notwithstanding certain pathological examples that could yield to differential cryptanalysis and timing attacks) [30]. A brute-force attack (which this work focuses on) works by testing all possible keys in turn against an encrypted piece of known plain text. This type of attack is feasible when key lengths are small and have been successfully mounted on a number of occasions using networks of work-stations and distributed computing projects. For longer key lengths (128 bits or greater), the brute-force approach is totally inadequate, requiring millions of years to yield the key. Despite this, brute-force RC5 key cracking is a good choice of application in order to compare the possible speedup an FPGA can give with a traditional microprocessor implementation.

The RC5 application was implemented as a graph definition file, and a single `checkKeys` function implemented both as a native and an FPGA instruction, yielding a hardware and a software implementation. Other instructions required by the application were invoked directly from the DRMC libraries. The graph definition file was created using an XML editor. The computation graph is quite simple—it divides the key space into partitions (each containing 3 billion keys) that are then passed to instances of the `checkKeys` instruction. This instruction is responsible for encrypting the known plain text with all the keys in the supplied key-space partition, and comparing the encrypted plain text with the known cipher text. If a match is found, the key is returned.

The software and hardware implementations of `checkKeys` are based on the RC5 implementation contained in RFC 2040 [31]. To create the native implementation, this code was augmented with an extra function interfacing with DRMC to perform text conversions. The compiled object code and the graph definition file were passed to the condensed graphs compiler to create a shared object capable of being executed by the metacomputer.

The hardware implementation of `checkKeys` was created with Handel-C. The process of converting an ANSI C program to efficient Handel-C is relatively straightforward in comparison to traditional hardware design languages such as Verilog and VHDL. When the design was finished, it ran at 41 MHz and consisted of three identical pipelines operating in parallel, each consisting of eight stages. The longest stage took 72 clock cycles to execute, so the speed of the FPGA design is calculated as follows:

$$41 \text{ MHz}/72 \times 3 = 1.708333 \text{ million keys per second}$$

Figure 14.6 below shows the results of the execution speed of the FPGA (at 41 MHz) compared to a Pentium II 350 MHz and a Pentium IV 2.4 GHz.

As can be seen from Figure 14.6, the FPGA provided more than a ten-fold increase in speed over the Pentium IV and a 42-fold increase over the Pentium II. Newer FPGAs (such as the Virtex II) would offer even further speedups over the Virtex E FPGA used in this work, as the algorithm could not alone benefit from increased clock speeds but also from higher logic densities as well. Not even a (top-of-the-range) 3 GHz microprocessor could compete with an FPGA on this application.

A cluster containing eight Pentium II processors and eight RC1000 boards provides enough computing power to search the entire key space of a 40 bit RC5 key in less than 22 hours. That is over 350 times faster than if the eight Pentiums alone were used. This shows that FPGAs can offer significant speedups over traditional

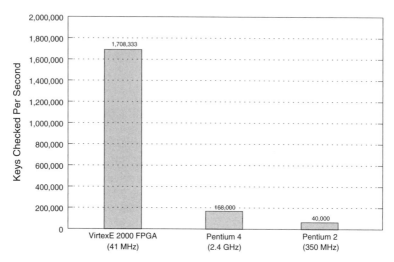

Figure 14.6 Comparison of the speed differences between microprocessors and FPGAs for searching RC5 key spaces.

microprocessors on this type of algorithm—highly parallel, easy to pipeline, little updating of a memory store (few memory accesses), and operations that a microprocessor does slowly.

Real-world applications that are similar to the RC5 key-crack application (and could benefit from implementation on DRMC/FPGAs) include encryption, compression, and image processing.

It must be noted that when creating the Handel-C design for the RC5 application, significant time was spent pipelining the design and that pipelining severely affected the readability of the Handel-C source code. As a result, unlike C code for a microprocessor, updating Handel-C code that has be extensively pipelined is a difficult process. Also, compiling the Handel-C code to a `.bit` file took a long time—over a day on a 1.8 GHz machine with 1 GB of RAM.

14.6 ALGORITHMS NOT SUITED TO IMPLEMENTATION ON FPGAs/DRMC

Some algorithms that were found not to be suited to implementation on DRMC's FPGA architecture are now presented. These include iterative matrix solvers [32, 33], Jacobi iteration, and Gauss–Seidel iteration. These applications differ from the RC5 example described above in that they require many memory accesses.

Iterative matrix solvers are used to solve systems of simultaneous linear equations, which are used extensively in scientific and engineering applications. The following presents a quick overview of the Jacobi and Gauss–Seidel algorithms; for a detailed discussion refer to [32] and [33]. The Jacobi iteration continuously applies the same iteration on a matrix until it converges. In each new iteration, the value of each entry in the matrix is calculated based on the values of its four neighbors in the previous iteration. As all the values calculated in iteration k depend on the values in the iteration $k - 1$, each entry in the matrix could be processed in parallel. Therefore, the Jacobi algorithm is highly parallel. The Gauss–Seidel iteration is similar to the Jacobi iteration, except it uses data as soon as it becomes available. When calculating the values for each entry of the matrix on iteration k, the new values of any neighbor that has already been calculated in the iteration k are used instead.

As these iterative matrix solvers involve floating-point math, the floating-point library [34] from Celoxica was used. The first problem encountered was that when these algorithms were implemented using the floating-point library, the place and route tools reported that the maximum clock rate could only be set as high as 20 MHz, even though the maximum clock speed of the FPGA used is 100 MHz. Although it is unrealistic to expect to get a design running this fast, 20 MHz was rather a poor result.

The following three algorithms were implemented on the RC1000 boards and their execution times were recorded:

1. **Gauss–Seidel Iteration.** One large matrix was placed into the four memory banks of the RC1000 board. The banks are not accessed in parallel due to the nature of the Gauss–Seidel algorithm. The algorithm reads enough data to compute the value of four entries in the matrix at a time and writes the results back into memory. Pipelining and parallelism were used as much as possible.

2. **Jacobi Iteration.** The Jacobi algorithm requires twice as much memory as the Gauss–Seidel algorithm so the matrix has to fit into just two memory banks. Due to the parallel nature of the Jacobi algorithm, the matrix is partitioned in two to allow the FPGA to operate on two memory banks in parallel. For each iteration, the algorithm computes the values of the matrices for the next iteration and writes them to the two empty banks. When the iteration is complete, the values on the boundaries of the two matrices are exchanged. On the next iteration, the data is read from the memory banks that were written to in the previous iteration and written to the banks that were read from in the previous iteration.

3. **Gauss–Seidel/Jacobi Hybrid.** This algorithm is based on the combination of the Gauss–Seidel algorithm and the Jacobi algorithm and is discussed in [32] (page 142). The matrix is broken into four; each submatrix is placed in one of the memory banks on the RC1000 board. In each iteration, the FPGA performs a Gauss–Seidel iteration on each of the memory banks in parallel. At the end of iteration, values on the boundaries of the matrices are exchanged (Jacobi iteration). This hybrid algorithm does not require many more iterations then the Gauss–Seidel algorithm to converge; in [32], it is stated that with a 128×128 matrix decomposed into eight submatrices, there is only a 5% increase in the number of iterations compared to performing the Gauss–Seidel algorithm on the entire 128×128 matrix.

Figure 14.7 shows and compares the execution times of these three algorithms to the Gauss–Seidel algorithm running on a 1.8 GHz microprocessor. Each algorithm was run on a 500 × 500 matrix for 1000 iterations. These measurements record the execution time of the algorithms on the FPGA. The time spent partitioning the matrix and transferring data over the PCI bus to the RC1000 board was not considered.

Reflecting on the poor execution times of the FPGA, its easy to see that even if the RC1000 board were to run at its maximum speed of 100 MHz (which would never be possible), it would not compete with the 1.8 GHz machine. Even though the FPGA can access the four memory banks in one clock cycle, for every clock cycle of the FPGA, the microprocessor can access its main memory 11 times. In addition, reconfigurable computing boards are considerably more expensive than general-purpose desktop machines. Any speedup that might be gained from reconfigurable computing must always be offset by the relative cost of the hardware. In this case, the FPGA implementation took longer and was more difficult to program than the microprocessor and could not compete with the microprocessor for speed—a poor result overall.

Even though these iterative matrix solver algorithms are very simple, many other algorithms exhibit the same characteristics, that is, they require many memory accesses. If an algorithm exhibits a lot of parallelism and if the data needed for this parallelism is all stored in the same memory bank, the FPGA can only access this data sequentially and slowly due to its relatively slow clock speed.

Although many general-purpose algorithms are similar to those discussed in this section, far fewer exhibit the characteristics of the RC5 algorithm discussed in the previous section. Except for a few specialized applications, when all factors are considered—cost, speedup, and ease of programming—it is hard to imagine how, with current technology, FPGAs (based on the model of PCI-based reconfigurable computing boards) can be considered a cost-effective general-purpose computing platform compared to top-of-the range desktop machines.

Ignoring the fact that several standard desktop machines could be purchased for the same price as one RC1000 board, combining multiple RC1000 boards to compete with one microprocessor is not efficient either, since the RC1000 board is con-

1000 iterations on a 500 × 500 Matrix	Execution time in seconds
Gauss–Seidel on 1.8 GHz Pentium 4 with 1 GB of 233 MHz RAM	11
Gauss–Seidel on a RC1000 board running at 20 MHz	134
Jacobi on a RC1000 board running at 20 MHz	56
Gauss–Seidel/Jacobi hybrid algorithm on a RC1000 board running at 20 MHz	43 (for 1050 iterations, 45)

Figure 14.7   Comparison of the execution speed of FPGAs and microprocessors while executing iterative matrix solvers.

nected to the PCI bus of the machine and fine-grain parallelism between boards is very inefficient. The reconfigurable architecture of DRMC is best suited to coarse-grain parallelism between the reconfigurable computing boards, in which the FPGAs execute algorithms at least as fast (but preferably faster) than the microprocessors of desktop machines. It is worth noting that other reconfigurable computing architectures would be a lot more suited to fine-grain parallelism between FPGAs and, thus, more suited to the iterative matrix solver algorithms mentioned above. For example, consider the development of custom machines with a specialized motherboard containing a very large number of FPGAs. This architecture allows for fine-grain parallelism between the FPGAs. Smaller (and cheaper) FPGAs could be used in these machines to reduce cost. This type of machine would be complicated to program and, despite its high cost, would potentially outperform any standard desktop machine while executing algorithms like the iterative matrix solvers. It is not being suggested that this type of machine would provide an efficient general computing platform since many sequential algorithms could not take advantage of the multiple FPGAs. However, for stand-alone applications that expose much parallelism, such an architecture would provide a high-performance alternative.

14.7 SUMMARY

In this chapter, experiences and lessons learned from trying to apply reconfigurable computing (FPGAs) to high-performance computing were discussed. This work compared execution speeds of FPGAs to general desktop machines (high-performance workstations or SMP machines were not considered). Top-of-the-range desktop machines currently run at over 3 GHz, so the gap in clock speeds between these and FPGAs is significant. It was found that an application would have to exhibit significant parallelism for the FPGA (on a PCI board) to outperform a modern microprocessor. The clock speed of microprocessors is increasing at a far greater rate then FPGA clock speeds and, as a result, big differences in clock speed between the FPGAs and microprocessors can diminish much of the FPGAs' advantages. This problem is not an issue in embedded computing, as embedded microprocessors run at a similar clock rate to FPGAs.

Speeding up some of the applications discussed in this paper might be possible using some advanced features like multiple clock domains on the FPGA, creating caches on the FPGA (to try to reduce memory access to external RAM banks), and programming with hardware description languages. These require specialized skills on the part of the programmer. To be widely accepted, FPGAs need to be as easy to program as microprocessors. Also, other reconfigurable architectures that allow fine-grain parallelism between multiple FPGAs would provide a better execution environment for certain algorithms.

FPGAs and their development boards are far more expensive than general desktop machines. Thus, when comparing reconfigurable computing boards to general desktop machines, the reconfigurable computing board would need to achieve a significant speedup to justify its cost. So, not only is fine-grain parallelism between reconfigurable computing boards inefficient because of communication over the PCI bus, but several desktop machines could be purchased for the price of one reconfigurable computing board.

There are many publications claiming significant speedups using FPGAs compared to microprocessor systems [13–15]. These claims need to be viewed in the correct context to ascertain absolute advantages. One thing is clear: proper benchmarks are needed when comparing the speed of FPGAs to microprocessors in order to paint a more accurate picture of their advantages and limitations.

In [16], it is stated that "a good speedup candidate for FPGA implementation is complex; it requires operations the microprocessor does slowly, and it has few memory accesses." Relatively few applications in high-performance computing meet these requirements. With current technology, when all factors are considered (execution speed, ease of programming, and financial cost), the idea of using distributed FPGAs (PCI-based reconfigurable computing boards) in cluster computing as a general-purpose computing platform faces many obstacles. Before FPGAs become a viable general-purpose alternative to microprocessors in high-performance computing, there needs to be a reduction in their cost, better programming tools have to be developed, and the clock speeds of FPGAs need to move closer to the clock speeds of microprocessors. The odds of these happening in the near future are small.

There are, however, many applications that are amenable to acceleration using FPGAs. These include cryptography, compression, searching, pattern matching, and image processing. As FPGA densities continue to increase at an impressive rate (much faster than microprocessor densities), the speedups attainable for these applications using reconfigurable computing will continue to increase dramatically. To sum up, although reconfigurable computing in high-performance computing will offer better and better speedups over time to those applications to which it is already suited, it is unlikely to break into new application domains due to the reasons outlined above.

ACKNOWLEDGMENTS

The support of IRCSET (through the Embark Initiative) and Enterprise Ireland (through grant no. IF/2001/318) is gratefully acknowledged.

REFERENCES

1. Xilinx, Inc., *Spartan-3 1.2V FPGA Family: Complete Data Sheet,* 2003.

2. Xilinx, Inc., *Virtex-II Pro™Platform FPGAs: Complete Data Sheet,* 2003.

3. T. Sterling, D. Savarese, D. J. Becker, J. E. Dorband, U.A. Ranawake, and C. V. Packer, BEOWULF: A parallel workstation for scientific computation, in *Proceedings of the 24th International Conference on Parallel Processing,* pp. I:11–14, Oconomowoc, WI, 1995.

4. http://www.clustercomputing.org.

5. Xilinx, Inc., *Virtex™-II Platform FPGAs: Complete Data Sheet,* 2003.

6. R. Hartenstein, A decade of reconfigurable computing: A visionary retrospective, in *Proceedings of the Conference on Design, Automation and Test in Europe,* Munich, Germany, 2001.

7. B. Radunovic, An overview of advances in reconfigurable computing systems, in *Proceedings of the 32nd Annual Hawaii International Conference on System Sciences, HIC-SS-32,* Hawaii, 1999.

8. http://www.starbridgesystems.com.

9. S. Hauck, T. W. Fry, M. M. Hosler, and J. P. Kao, The Chimaera reconfigurable functional unit, in Kenneth L. Pocek and Jeffery Arnold (Eds.), *Proceedings of the IEEE Symposium on FPGAs for Custom Computing Machines,* pp. 87–96, IEEE Computer Society Press, 1997.

10. J. P. Morrison, P. J. O'Dowd, and P. D. Healy, Searching RC5 keyspaces with distributed reconfigurable hardware, in *Proceedings of the 2003 International Conference on Engineering of Reconfigurable Systems and Algorithms,* pp. 269–272, Las Vegas, 2003.

11. J. P. Morrison, P. D. Healy and P. J. O'Dowd, DRMC: A distributed reconfigurable meta-computer, in *International Symposium on Parallel and Distributed Computing IS-PDC 2003,* Slovenia, 2003.

12. K. Underwood, R. R. Sass, and W. B. Ligon, Acceleration of a 2d-fft on an adaptable computing cluster, citeseer.nj.nec.com/536950.html.

13. http://www.io.com/ guccione/HW list.html.

14. http://www.eg3.com/WebID/soc/confproc/blank/univ/a-z.htm.

15. http://www.site.uottawa.ca/ rabielmo/personal/rc.html.

16. P. Kung, *Obtaining Performance and Programmability Using Reconfigurable Hardware for Media Processing,* PhD thesis, Technische Universiteit Eindhoven, 2002.

17. P. Bertin, D. Roncin, and J. Vuillemin, Programmable active memories: A performance assessment, Digital Paris Research Laboratory, 1993.

18. J. P. Morrison, *Condensed Graphs: Unifying Availability-Driven, Coercion-Driven and Control-Driven Computing,* PhD thesis, Technische Universiteit Eindhoven, 1996.

19. J. P. Morrison and P. D. Healy, Implementing the WebCom 2 distributed computing platform with XML, in *Proceedings of the International Symposium on Parallel and Distributed Computing,* pp. 171–179, Iasi, Romania, July 2002.

20. Celoxica Ltd., *RC1000 Hardware Reference Manual,* 2001.

21. Xilinx, Inc., *Virtex™-E 1.8V Field Programmable Gate Arrays Production Product Specification,* July 2002.

22. Celoxica Ltd., *Handel-C Language Reference Manual Version 3.1,* 2002.

23. P. R. Moorby and D. E. Thomas, *The Verilog Hardware Description Language,* Kluwer Academic Publishers, 1998.

24. P. J. Ashenden, *The Designer's Guide to VHDL, 2nd ed.,* Morgan Kaufmann, May 2001.

25. Celoxica Ltd., *DK Design Suite Datasheet,* 2001.

26. Electronic Industries Assn., *EDIF Electronic Design Interchange Format, Version 200,* June, 1989.

27. Xilinx, Inc., *Development System Reference Guide—ISE 4,* 2001.

28. G. V.Wilson, *Practical Parallel Programming (Scientific and Engineering Computation),* The MIT Press, 1996.

29. R. L. Rivest, The RC5 encryption algorithm, in William Stallings (Ed.), *Practical Cryptography for Data Internetworks,* IEEE Computer Society Press, 1996.

30. B. Kaliski and Y. Yin, On the security of the RC5 encryption algorithm, *CryptoBytes, 1*(2), 13–14, 1995.

31. R. Baldwin and R. Rivest, RFC 2040: The RC5, RC5-CBC, RC5-CBC-pad, and RC5-CTS algorithms, October 1996, ftp://ftp.internic.net/rfc/rfc2040.txt.

32. J. Zhu, *Solving Partial Differential Equations on Parallel Computers—An Introduction,* World Scientific Publishing, 1994.

33. G. H. Golub and C. F. Van Loan, *Matrix Computations, 2nd ed.,* The John Hopkins University Press, 1989.

34. Celoxica Ltd., *Handel-C Floating-Point Library Manual, Version 1.1,* 2002.

## CHAPTER 15

Bandwidth-Aware Resource Allocation for Heterogeneous Computing Systems to Maximize Throughput

BO HONG and VIKTOR K. PRASANNA

In this chapter, we consider the resource allocation problem for computing a large set of equal-sized independent tasks on heterogeneous computing systems. This problem represents the computation paradigm for a wide range of applications such as SETI@home and Monte Carlo simulations. We consider a general problem in which the interconnection between the nodes is modeled using a graph. Initially, the source data for all the tasks resides on the root node; other nodes in the system receive tasks from the root and/or some of their neighbors, compute some of these tasks, and push some tasks to some selected neighbors. We maximize the throughput of the system by using a linear programming formulation. This linear programming formulation is further transformed to an extended network flow representation, which can be solved efficiently using maximum-flow/minimum-cut algorithms. This leads to a simple protocol for the problem. The effectiveness of the proposed resource allocation approach is verified through simulations.

15.1 INTRODUCTION

We consider the problem of computing a large set of equal-sized independent tasks on a heterogeneous computing system. This problem represents the computation paradigm for a variety of research activities. Internet-based distributed computing projects are among the most well-known examples of this computation paradigm. Examples of such research projects include SETI@home [11], Folding@home [12], and data encryption/decryption [6]. This computation paradigm can also be applied to other more tightly coupled computations such as Monte Carlo simulations.

The system consists of a collection of heterogeneous compute resources, connected via heterogeneous network links. The network topology can be arbitrary and we model the system as an undirected graph, where each node in the graph represents a compute resource and each edge in the graph represents a network link. A

High-Performance Computing: Paradigm and Infrastructure. Edited by L. T. Yang and M. Guo

compute node needs to receive the source data for a task before executing the task. We assume that the source data for all the tasks initially reside on a single node in the system, which we call the root node. A compute node in the system can communicate with not only the root node (if such a network link exists), but also its neighbors. Every compute node thus needs to determine (1) where to get the tasks from and how many there are, (2) how many tasks to compute locally, and (3) where to transfer the rest of the tasks that it has received. We denote such a computation scheme as a graph-structured computation paradigm.

The proposed problem reduces to the scheduling of a set of independent tasks on heterogeneous computing systems. Many research efforts attempt to minimize the overall execution time (makespan) of all the tasks. This makespan minimization problem, in its general form, has been shown to be NP-complete [10]. We consider a related optimization objective: maximization of the system throughput. Maximization of the system throughput is not equivalent to the minimization of the makespan, since the system may not operate at full speed during the start-up and trailing time, during which some compute resources are waiting for initial task assignment or there are just not enough tasks to feed the compute resources. However, if the number of tasks is large, then the start-up and trailing time becomes negligible when compared with the overall computing time of all tasks. For applications that have a huge number of tasks such as SETI@home, system throughput, naturally, becomes the major concern. A restricted version of the throughput maximization problem has been studied in [2], where the compute nodes are considered to be connected via a tree topology.

In order to maximize the system throughput, we propose two approaches. We show that unlike the surprisingly difficult makespan minimization problem, the throughput maximization problem can be solved very efficiently. Our first approach reduces the throughput maximization problem to a linear programming problem. We then propose to model the computation as a special type of data flow. This leads to our extended network flow (ENF) representation for the throughput maximization problem. Based on our ENF representation, we find that the system throughput can be transformed to the network flow in a corresponding graph. Thus, the throughput maximization problem can be solved by using maximum flow/minimum cut algorithms.

Simulations are conducted to validate the motivation for utilizing graph-structured systems and verify the effectiveness the network-flow-representation-based resource allocation approach. Based on our solution for the throughput maximization problem, we develop a simple protocol to coordinate the compute nodes in the system. Simulations show that this protocol increases the system throughput by up to 41% when compared with a greedy protocol in which resources are allocated in a first-come, first-served fashion.

The rest of this chapter is organized as follows. Section 15.2 briefly reviews some related work. Section 15.3 describes our system model and formally states the optimization problem. In Section 15.4, we discuss our resource allocation approaches that maximize the system throughput. Experimental results are shown in Section 15.5. Concluding remarks are made in Section 15.6.

15.2 RELATED WORK

Task scheduling for heterogeneous computing systems has received a lot of attention recently. Unlike the research proposed in this chapter, many research efforts choose makespan as the optimization objective. Because the makespan minimization problem is known to be NP-complete [10], designing heuristics and evaluating their performance become the key issues. For example, static scheduling heuristics for a set of independent tasks are studied in [3], whereas the related dynamic scheduling problem has been studied in [14]. Other research efforts consider tasks with interdependencies. For example, a heuristic-based approach is studied in [20] to schedule multicomponent applications in heterogeneous wide-area networks. In [4], a software-in-the-loop approach is proposed to design and implement task scheduling algorithms for heterogeneous systems. In [16], an augmentation to Java is proposed to develop divide-and-conquer applications in distributed environments, and several scheduling heuristics are experimentally studied. Compared with these studies, the proposed method focuses on the maximization of system throughput. We show that unlike the surprisingly difficult makespan minimization problem, there exist efficient algorithms to maximize the system throughput.

There are some works that consider the system throughput. The Condor project [18] develops a software infrastructure so that heterogeneous resources with distributed ownerships can be utilized to provide large amounts of processing capacity over long periods of time. The master–slave paradigm is widely used in the Condor systems and has been exploited by various research efforts [8, 17] to maximize the throughput. In [2], a bandwidth-centric approach was proposed to maximize throughput for the multilevel master–slave computation paradigm in which the systems are considered to be connected via tree topologies. The problem of extracting a best spanning tree with optimal throughput out of a general graph-structured system was studied in [1]. Our study is also related to the divisible-load-scheduling problem, where the load can be partitioned into tasks with arbitrary sizes. The divisible load scheduling problem has been studied in [19] for systems with bus and tree network topologies. Compared with these efforts, the proposed work studies a more general problem that allows an arbitrary network topology. Not only does this graph-structured computation paradigm represent a wider range of real systems, it is also expected to result in a better utilization of the network resources since tasks can be transferred among the computing resources (see Section 15.5 for the comparison of graph-structured systems and tree-structured systems). The development of a distributed and adaptive task allocation algorithm for graph-structured computation has been addressed by another paper [9] that we published recently.

15.3 SYSTEM MODEL AND PROBLEM STATEMENT

The system is represented by a graph $G(V, E)$ Each node $V_i \in V$ in the graph represents a compute resource. The weight of V_i is denoted by w_i. w_i represents the processing power of node V_i, that is, V_i can perform one unit of computation in $1/w_i$ time. Each edge $E_{ij} \in E$ in the graph represents a network link. The weight of E_{ij} is denoted by l_{ij}. l_{ij} represents the communication bandwidth of link E_{ij}, that is, link E_{ij} can transfer one unit of data from V_i to V_j in $1/l_{ij}$ time. Links are bidirectional, so G is undirected and $E_{ij} = E_{ji}$. In the rest of the chapter, "edge" and "link" are interchangeably used. We use A_i to denote the adjacent nodes of V_i in G, that is, $A_i = \{V_j | \exists E_{ij} \in E\}$. This graph model is denoted as our base model.

We assume that the computation and communication can be overlapped on the compute nodes, the compute nodes can send and receive data concurrently, and the compute node can communicate with multiple neighbor nodes concurrently. These assumptions need to be further refined to model realistic computing and communication resources. Suppose a compute node connects to five other nodes, each through a 100 Mb/s link. It would be unrealistic to assume that this node can send or receive data at 500 Mb/s. A more reasonable scenario is that this node can communicate with only one of its neighbors at 100 Mb/s, or to all five neighbors concurrently, but at 20 Mb/s each. Therefore, for each compute node V_i, we introduce another two parameters: c_i^{in} and c_i^{out}. These two parameters indicate the capability of V_i's network interface to receive and send data: within one unit of time, at most $c_i^{in}(c_i^{out})$ units of data can flow into (out of) V_i.

Without loss of generality, we assume that each task has one unit of source data and requires one unit of computation. So a task is that transferred over a network link means one unit of data is transferred. A task that is computed by a compute node means that one unit of computation is performed. The tasks are independent of each other and do not share the source data. A compute node can compute a task only after receiving the source data of the task. Initially, node V_0 holds the source data for all the tasks. V_0 is called the root node. For each node V_i in the system, it receives tasks from a subset of its neighbors (V_0 could be the neighbor of some nodes), computes a subset of the tasks it received, and (possibly) sends the remaining tasks to another subset of its neighbors.

The throughput of the system is defined as the number of tasks processed by the system in one unit of time under steady-state conditions. We are now interested in the following problem: given a time interval T, what is the maximum number of tasks that can be processed by the system G? Let $f(V_i, V_j)$ denote the number of tasks transferred from V_i to V_j during this time interval. Note that $f(V_i, V_j)$ is directional, although the corresponding link E_{ij} is not. To simplify our discussion, if the actual data transfer is from V_i to V_j, we define $f(V_j, V_i) = -f(V_i, V_j)$. We have the following constraints:

1. $|f(V_i, V_j)/l_{ij}| \leq T$ for $\forall E_{ij} \in E$. This is because E_{ij} can transfer at most l_{ij} unit of data in one unit of time.

2. $\sum_{V_k \in A_i} [f(V_k, V_i)] \geq 0$ for $\forall V_i \in V - \{V_0\}$. This condition says that no intermediate node can generate tasks.

3. $\sum_{V_k \in A_i \& f(V_i, V_k) > 0} [f(V_i, V_k)] \leq T \times c_i^{out}$ for $\forall V_i \in V$. This means that V_i cannot send data at a rate higher than what is allowed by its network interface.

4. $\Sigma_{V_k \in A_i \& f(V_k, V_i) > 0}[f(V_k, V_i)] \leq T \times c_i^{in}$ for $\forall V_i \in V - \{V_0\}$. This means that V_i cannot receive data at a rate higher than what is allowed by its network interface.

5. $\Sigma_{V_k \in A_i}[f(V_k, V_i)/w_i] \leq T$ for $\forall V_i \in V - \{V_0\}$. We can see that $\Sigma_{V_k \in A_i}[f(V_k, V_i)]$ is the total number of tasks that V_i has kept locally (tasks received minus tasks sent out). This condition says that no intermediate node should keep more tasks than it can compute.

The total number of tasks computed by the system is $T \times w_0 + \Sigma_{V_i \in V - \{V_0\}}[\Sigma_{V_k \in A_i} f(V_k, V_i)]$ Since we are interested in the throughput of the system, we can normalize the time interval T to 1 and obtain the formal problem statement as follows.

Base Problem. Given an undirected graph $G(V, E)$, where node V_i has weight w_i and associated parameters c_i^{in} and c_i^{out}, and edge E_{ij} has weight l_{ij}, $w_i > 0$. $c_i^{in} > 0$. $c_i^{out} > 0$. $l_{ij} > 0$ if $E_{ij} \in E$ and $l_{ij} = 0$ otherwise. Find a real-valued function $f: V \times V \to R$ that satisfies:

1. $f(V_j, V_i) = -f(V_i, V_j)$ for $\forall\ V_i, V_j \in V$
2. $f(V_i, V_j) = \leq l_{ij}$ for $\forall\ V_i, V_j \in V$
3. $\Sigma_{V_k \in V} f(V_k, V_i) \geq 0$ for $\forall\ V_i \in V - \{V_0\}$
4. $\Sigma_{V_k \in V \& f(V_i, V_k) > 0} f(V_i, V_k) \leq c_i^{out}$ for $\forall\ V_i \in V$
5. $\Sigma_{V_k \in V \& f(V_k, V_i) > 0} f(V_k, V_i) \geq c_i^{in}$ for $\forall\ V_i \in V - \{V_0\}$
6. $\Sigma_{V_k \in V} f(V_k, V_i) \geq w_i$ for $\forall\ V_i \in V - \{V_0\}$

and maximizes

$$\mathcal{W} = w_0 + \sum_{V_i \in V - \{V_0\}} \left(\sum_{V_k \in V} f(V_k, V_i) \right) \tag{15.1}$$

Note that if edge E_{ij} does not exist, then $l_{ij} = 0$; thus conditions 1 and 2 imply that $f(V_i, V_j) = f(V_j, V_i) = 0$ if there is no edge between V_i and V_j.

If an instance of the Base Problem has G as the input graph and V_0 as the root node, we denote it as Base Problem (G, V_0).

This base problem is difficult to solve because of the constraints enforced by c_i^{in} and c_i^{out}. In the next section, we will derive two equivalent formulations for the base problem. The first formulation reduces the base problem to a linear programing problem. The second formulation reduces it to a network flow problem.

15.4 RESOURCE ALLOCATION TO MAXIMIZE SYSTEM THROUGHPUT

Let us first observe an important property of the base problem. Equation 1.1 shows that w_0 is just an additive constant to the system throughput; hence, we can ignore w_0 and maximize $\Sigma_{V_i \in V - \{V_0\}}[\Sigma_{V_k \in V} f(V_k, V_i)]$. We show that the system throughput is maximized only when V_0 "pumps out" tasks at the highest rate possible. Formally, we have the following proposition.

Proposition 15.4.1. Suppose $f: V \times V \to R$ is a feasible solution to the Base Problem, then

$$\sum_{V_i \in V - \{V_0\}} \left[\sum_{V_k \in V} f(V_k, V_i) \right] = \sum_{V_k \in V} f(V_0, V_k)$$

Proof

$\sum_{V_i \in V - \{V_0\}} [\sum_{V_k \in V} f(V_k, V_i)]$
$= \sum_{V_i \in V} \sum_{V_k \in V} f(V_k, V_i) - \sum_{V_i = V_0} \sum_{V_k \in V} f(V_k, V_i)$
$= 0 - [-\sum_{V_k \in V} f(V_0, V_k)]$
$= \sum_{V_k \in V} f(V_0, V_k)$ □

15.4.1   A Linear Programing Formulation

We first transform the base model to include the constraints enforced by c_i^{in} and c_i^{out}. We name the transformed model the intermediate representation as it will be further transformed in Section 15.4.2. The transformation is performed using the following procedure.

Procedure 1

1. Replace each node V_i in the base model by three nodes V_i^o, V_i', and V_i''. The weights of the three new nodes are w_i, 0, and 0, respectively. For the three new nodes, add a directed edge of weight c_i^{in} from V_i' to V_i^o, and another directed edge of weight c_i^{out} from V_i^o to V_i''. V_0^o is the root node in the intermediate representation.

2. Replace each edge E_{ij} in the base model by two directed edges E_{ij}' and E_{ji}', where E_{ij}' is from V_i'' to V_j' and E_{ji}' is from V_j'' to V_i'. Both E_{ij}' and E_{ji}' have weight l_{ij}.

Figure 15.1 illustrates an example for the base model and the corresponding intermediate representation. Each dotted large circle in Figure 15.1(b) contains three nodes, which are mapped from a single node in Figure 15.1(a). To simplify the notation, we omit the superscript "o" for nodes V_i^o in Figure 15.1(b). In Figures 15.1(a) and 15.1(b), the weight of the nodes are marked in the parenthesis after the node name. The edge names in Figure 15.1(b) are omitted; only the edge weights are marked in the parentheses.

Using the intermediate representation, we can reduce the Base Problem to a linear programing problem as follows.

Problem 1. Given a directed graph $G(V, E)$, where node V_i has weight $w_i > 0$ and edge E_{ij} has weight $l_{ij} > 0$, $l_{ij} = 0$ if $E_{ij} \notin E$. Find a real-valued function $f: V \times V \to R$ that satisfies:

1. $f(V_i, V_j) \leq l_{ij}$ for $\forall \ V_i, V_j \in V$
2. $f(V_j, V_i) = -f(V_i, V_j)$ for $\forall \ V_i, V_j \in V$
3. $0 \leq \Sigma_{V_k \in V} f(V_k, V_i) \leq w_i$ for $\forall \ V_i \in V - \{V_0\}$

and maximizes

$$W = w_0 + \sum_{V_k \in V} f(V_0, V_k) \tag{15.2}$$

The constraints c_i^{in} and c_i^{out} that were associated with compute nodes in the Base Problem have become the weights of the corresponding edges in Problem 1. To simplify the notation in Problem 1, we use l_{ij} uniformly to represent the weight of the edges, although some of edges may have weights c_i^{in} and c_i^{out}. We use V_i uniformly to denote the nodes in Problem 1, although they are named V_i^o, V_i', or V_i'' in Procedure 1. If an instance of Problem 1 has G as the input graph and V_0 as the root node, we denote it as Problem 1 (G, V_0).

The following proposition shows that the Base Problem and Problem 1 are equivalent. We use $W_B'(G, V_0)$ to represent the maximum throughput for Base Problem (G, V_0). We use $W_1(G, V_0)$ to represent the maximum throughput for Problem 1 (G, V_0).

Proposition 15.4.2. Suppose Base Problem (G, V_0) is converted to Problem 1 (G', V_0^o) using Procedure 1, then

$$W_B'(G, V_0) = W_1(G', V_0^o)$$

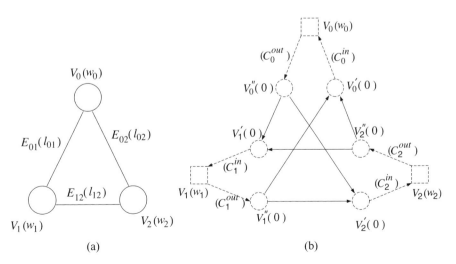

Figure 15.1 The base model and its intermediate representation. (a) The base model of a sample system. (b) The corresponding intermediate representation.

Proof. We use the notation used in Procedure 1 to denote the nodes/edges in G and their corresponding nodes/edges in G'.

Suppose $f \colon V \times V \to R$ is a feasible solution for Base Problem (G, V_0). We map it to a feasible solution $f' \colon V' \times V' \to R$ for Problem 1 (G', V_0^o) as follows:

1. if $f(V_i, V_j) \geq 0$, then set
$$f'(V_i'', V_j') = f(V_i, V_j), f'(V_j'', V_i') = 0,$$
$$f'(V_j', V_i'') = -f(V_i, V_j), f'(V_i', V_j'') = 0$$

2. $f'(V_i', V_i^o) = \Sigma_{V_k' \in V'} f'(V_k'', V_i'),$
$$f'(V_i^o, V_i') = -f'(V_i', V_i^o)$$

3. $f'(V_i^o, V_i'') = -\Sigma_{V_k' \in V'} f'(V_k', V_i''),$
$$f'(V_i'', V_i^o) = -f'(V_i^o, V_i'')$$

It is easy to verify that such an f' is a feasible solution for Problem 1 (G', V_0^o) and that f' leads to the same throughput as f.

Suppose $f' \colon V' \times V' \to R$ is a feasible solution for Problem 1 (G', V_0^o). We map it to a feasible solution $f \colon V \times V \to R$ for Base Problem (G, V_0) using the following equation:

$$f(V_i, V_j) = f'(V_i'', V_j') + f'(V_i', V_j'')$$

It is also easy to verify that such an f is a feasible solution for Base Problem (G, V_0) and that it has the same throughput as f'. $\qquad\square$

Problem 1 is a linear programming problem. Algorithms such as the simplex algorithm can be used to solve this problem. In the next section, we show that this problem can be further reduced to a network flow problem, which can be solved using efficient algorithms.

15.4.2 An Extended Network Flow Representation

From Proposition 15.4.1, we notice that the system throughput is the sum of V_0's compute power and the rate with which tasks flow out of V_0 After the data (tasks) flows out of V_0, it will be transferred in the system and finally be consumed (computed) by some nodes. If we model these data consumptions as a special type of data flow to a hypothetical node, then the throughput of the system is solely defined by the rate with which data flows out of V_0. This leads to our extended network flow (ENF) representation for the system throughput problem.

The following procedure transforms the intermediate representation to the ENF representation.

Procedure 2

1. For each node V_i in the intermediate representation, create a corresponding node V_i' in the ENF representation. Set the weight of V_i' as 0.

2. For each edge E_{ij} in the intermediate representation that goes from V_i to V_j, create an edge E'_{ij} in the ENF representation that goes from V'_i to V'_j. Set the weight of E'_{ij} as that of E_{ij}.
3. Add a node S to the ENF representation. S has weight 0.
4. For each node V'_i in the ENF representation, if the weight of V_i (V'_i's corresponding node in the intermediate representation) is greater than 0, add an edge E'_{iS} that goes from V'_i to S. Set the weight of E'_{iS} as w_i, the weight of node V_i in the intermediate representation.

We call the hypothetical node S the sink node of the ENF representation.

Figure 15.2 shows an example of the ENF representation obtained by applying Procedure 2 to the intermediate representation in Figure 15.1(b). To simplify the notation, we use the same node names as in the intermediate representation except node S, which is the newly added sink node. The weight of the nodes are marked in the parentheses after the node names. The edge names are omitted; only the edge weights are marked in the parentheses.

Based on our ENF representation, we have the following maximum flow problem.

Problem 2: Given a directed graph $G(V, E)$, where edge E_{ij} has weight $l_{ij} > 0$, $l_{ij} = 0$ if $E_{ij} \notin E$, a root node V_0, and a sink node s. Find a real-valued function $f : V \times V \to R$ that satisfies

1. $f(V_i, V_j) \leq l_{ij}$ for $\forall\ V_i, V_j \in V$
2. $f(V_j, V_i) = -f(V_i, V_j)$ for $\forall\ V_i, V_j \in V$
3. $\Sigma_{V_j \in V} f(V_i, V_j) = 0$ for $\forall\ V_i \in V - \{V_0, S\}$

and maximizes

$$\mathcal{W} = \sum_{V_i \in V} f(V_0, V_i) \tag{15.3}$$

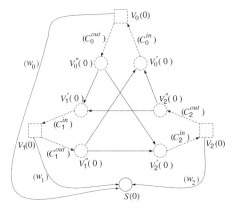

Figure 15.2   The ENF representation of the example system in Figure 15.1.

If an instance of Problem 2 has G as the input graph, V_0 as the root node, and S as the sink node, we denote it as Problem 2 (G, V_0, S).

The following proposition shows that Problem 1 can be reduced to Problem 2. We use $W_E(G, V_0, S)$ to represent the maximum flow for Problem 2 (G, V_0, S).

Proposition 15.4.3. Given Problem 1 (G, V_0), suppose it is converted to Problem 2 (G', V_0', S) using Procedure 2, then

$$W_1(G, V_0) = W_E(G', V_0', S)$$

To prove Proposition 15.4.3, we need to set up a mapping between the feasible solutions of Problem 1 and Problem 2 and show that corresponding solutions have the same throughput. The proof of Proposition 15.4.3 is similar to that for Proposition 15.4.2 and is hence omitted here.

Problem 2 is the well-studied network flow problem. There are several algorithms [5] to solve this problem [e.g., the Edmonds–Karp algorithm of $O(|V| \cdot |E|^2)$ complexity, the preflow-push algorithm of $O(|V|^2 \cdot |E|)$ complexity, and the lift-to-front algorithm of $O(|V|^3)$ complexity]. Similar to the mapping discussed in the proof of Proposition 15.4.2, we can define a mapping from the solution of Problem 2 to an optimal resource allocation for the Base Problem. This optimal resource allocation contains the following information: which compute nodes and which network links to use; in one unit of time, how many tasks to transfer on the network links; and how many tasks to compute at each node. Because our ENF-representation-based approach has taken into account the constraints on both the computation and the communication capabilities of the resources, it not only reflects the computing capability of the compute nodes, but is also bandwidth-aware.

Because we have normalized the time interval to 1 in our problem statement, the optimal resource allocation determined by our ENF-representation-based approach can assign a noninteger number of tasks to a compute node or transfer a noninteger number of tasks over a network link. However, as long as the w_i's and the l_{ij}'s are rational numbers, the optimal objective function f in Problem 2 determined by the maximum-flow/minimum-flow algorithms is rationally valued. Hence, the optimal objective function for the Base Problem is also rationally valued. Given these rational numbers, we can scale the time interval and find an implementation of the optimal resource allocation in which the number of tasks computed by the nodes and the number of tasks transferred over the links are all integers.

15.5 EXPERIMENTAL RESULTS

The first set of simulations compare the graph-structured computation and the well-known master–slave computation. In master–slave computations, all the compute nodes receive tasks only from the root node, ignoring the network links that may exist among the compute nodes.

For a fair comparison, we consider the scenario in which every compute node in the system has a network connection to the root node. The system is first created with a star topology in which each compute node has a single link connecting to the root node. Then, communication links are randomly added into the system with the requirement that any two nodes are connected by only one link. l_{ij}, c_{in}, and c_{out} are uniformly distributed between 0 and 1. w_i is uniformly distributed between 0 and w_{max}. Note that $1/w_{max}$ represents the average computation/communication ratio of a task. $w_{max} \geq 1$ represents a trivial scenario because the direct neighbors of the root node can consume, statistically, all the tasks flowing out of the root node. There is no need for other nodes to join the computation. The actual value of w_{max} depends on the application. For example, in SETI@home, it takes about 5 minutes to receive a task through a modem and about 10 hours to compute a task on a current-model home computer [11]. For this set of simulations, we considered $w_{max} = 0.05$.

We tested systems with various numbers of compute nodes and network links. Figure 15.3 displays the ratio between the throughput of graph-structured computation and that of the corresponding master–slave computation. Link density represents the number of edges in the system and is normalized as $|E|/[|V| \cdot (|V| - 1)/2]$. Each data point in Figure 15.3 is an average over 100 randomly generated graphs. Figure 15.3 illustrates the advantages of the graph-structured computation. When network links exist among the compute nodes, graph-structured computation is always better (w.r.t. throughput) than master–slave computation.

Recently, tree-structured computation has received a lot of attention. Various algorithms have been developed to utilize tree-structured systems. These system are

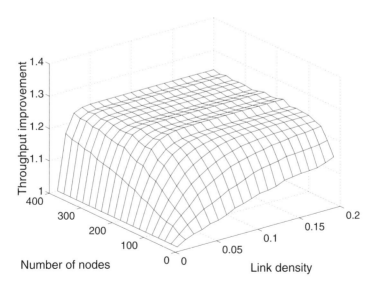

Figure 15.3   Comparison between graph-structured computation and master–slave computation. The Z-axis shows the relative throughput of graph-structured computation over master–slave computation.

easy to use because the routing is simple. However, most real systems, especially large-scale systems connected via the Internet, are connected through an arbitrary network rather than a tree. In this section, as can be expected, we show that a graph-structured system can achieve a higher throughput than a tree-structured system. More importantly, we show that the proposed resource allocation for graph-structured systems can be implemented very efficiently.

The next set of simulations compare the performance of graph-structured systems with tree-structured systems. We simulated two cases. In Case 1, we first randomly generate a graph-structured system. A graph is represented by its adjacency matrix A, where each nonzero entry a_{ij} represents the bandwidth of the corresponding link l_{ij}. If $a_{ij} = 0$, then link (V_i, V_j) does not exist. The graph is generated as follows. Initially, all entries in A are set to 0. Then a set of entries is randomly selected. Each selected entry is assigned a value that is uniformly distributed between 0 and 1. Given such a graph-structured system, we compare its performance against that of one of its spanning trees. Searching for the spanning tree that has the highest system throughput among all the spanning trees is critical to the system performance. However, to the best of our knowledge, we are not aware of any efficient algorithms to solve this problem. In our experiments, we use a breadth-first search (BFS) tree. Intuitively, a BFS tree attempts to find the shortest path for every node to communicate with the root node.

In Case 2, a tree-structured system is first constructed such that for every nonleaf node in the tree, its number of children is randomly chosen between 1 and 5. Given such a tree-structured system, we compare its performance against that of a graph-structured system that is constructed by randomly adding links to the nodes in the tree (until the required number of links are added). We limit the number of children for the nodes so that the tree can have multiple levels. We also evaluated the performance of single-level trees. We observed similar performance improvement. The results are omitted here due to space limitations.

In both Case 1 and Case 2, l_{ij}, c_i^{in}, and c_i^{out} are uniformly distributed between 0 and 1. We used $w_{max} = 0.05$ and $w_{max} = 0.1$, which represent an average computation/communication ratio of 20 and 10, respectively. The simulation results are shown in Table 15.1 and Table 15.2, where n is the number of nodes in the system. Data in the tables show the ratio of the throughput of the graph-structured system to the throughput of the corresponding tree-structured system. Each reported datum is an average over 50 randomly generated systems. As can be seen from these results, utilizing communication links in a general graph-structured system can significantly improve the system throughput.

The random adjacency matrices of the above simulated systems have uniform distribution. However, empirical studies [7] have shown that the Internet topologies exhibit power laws (e.g., out-degree vs. rank, number of nodes vs. out-degree, number of node pairs within a neighborhood vs. neighborhood size in hops). The next set of simulations studies the performance of the proposed graph-structured computation in systems with power-law distributed topologies. We generate the graph representation of the systems using Brite, which is a tool developed in [15] that generates networks with power law characteristics. For this set of simulations, the values of l_{ij}, c_i^{in}, and

Table 15.1   Comparison of graph-structured and tree-structured systems

	$w_{max} = 0.05$			
Link density	0.04	0.08	0.12	0.16
$n = 20$	1.15	2.42	2.38	2.70
$n = 40$	2.05	2.75	2.64	2.31
$n = 60$	2.32	2.53	1.78	1.74
$n = 80$	2.96	1.66	1.59	1.44
	$w_{max} = 0.1$			
Link density	0.04	0.08	0.12	0.16
$n = 20$	1.41	1.49	1.82	2.02
$n = 40$	1.65	2.19	1.48	1.52
$n = 60$	1.83	1.89	1.67	1.09
$n = 80$	2.13	1.33	1.58	1.06

Note: A graph is first generated and a tree is obtained by performing a breadth-first search.

c_i^{out} are uniformly distributed between 0 and 1; w_i is uniformly distributed between 0 and 0.05. Systems with 20 nodes (300 such systems in total) and systems with 80 nodes (300 such systems in total) were simulated. We compare the throughput of such graph-structured systems against their BFS trees. The simulation results are presented in Figure 15.4, where the results are sorted in the increasing order of the throughput of tree-structured computation. It can be seen that graph-structured systems can significantly improve the system throughput for power-law distributed systems.

Given a heterogeneous system, the optimal resource allocation can be determined (offline) by using the ENF representation. The next set of simulations show

Table 15.2   Comparison of graph-structured and tree-structured systems

	$w_{max} = 0.05$			
Link density	0.04	0.08	0.12	0.16
$n = 20$	1.22	1.29	1.32	1.49
$n = 40$	1.31	1.74	1.97	1.54
$n = 60$	1.38	1.26	1.60	1.60
$n = 80$	1.46	1.64	1.36	1.48
	$w_{max} = 0.1$			
Link density	0.04	0.08	0.12	0.16
$n = 20$	1.10	1.41	1.51	1.43
$n = 40$	1.27	1.11	1.30	1.46
$n = 60$	1.43	1.73	1.40	1.43
$n = 80$	1.40	1.26	1.27	1.44

Note: A tree is first generated and the graph is obtained by randomly adding links to the nodes in the tree.

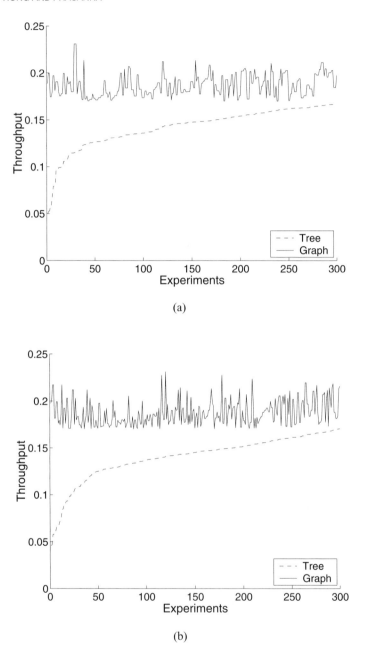

Figure 15.4   Comparison of graph-structured computation and tree-structured computation when the systems exhibit power-law characteristics. (a) Number of nodes = 20. (b) Number of nodes = 80.

that a simple protocol can approximate the optimal resource allocation and lead to good performance.

Each node in the system maintains a task buffer. Initially, the task buffer at the root node contains all the tasks to be executed by the system. All other task buffers are empty. The term valid successor (predecessor) is defined as follows. Given a graph G, node V_j is a valid successor (predecessor) of V_i if V_j is a neighbor of V_i and the optimal resource allocation calculated through the ENF representation shows a positive data flow from $V_i(V_j)$ to $V_j(V_i)$. For every node $V_i \in V$, its valid successors are assigned priorities according to the optimal resource allocation: the higher the data flow from V_i to V_j, the higher the priority of V_j. Its valid predecessors are also assigned priorities according to the optimal resource allocation: the higher the data flow from V_k to V_i, the higher the priority of V_k. For $\forall \, V_i \in V$, the following routine is executed:

1. If the task buffer at V_i is not empty and V_i is not computing any task, then V_i removes one task from the task buffer and computes the task.

2. If the task buffer at V_i is empty, then V_i requests one task from its valid predecessor with the highest priority. If the request is denied, V_i keeps sending the request to the next valid predecessor with a lower priority in a round-robin fashion until the request is satisfied.

3. When V_i receives a task request from one of its valid successors, the request is acknowledged if the task buffer at V_i is not empty and the current outgoing data flow rate on V_i does not exceed c_i^{out}, otherwise the request is denied. When multiple requests are received simultaneously, the request from the valid successor with a higher priority is processed first. To answer a request, V_i removes a task from its task buffer and sends it to the node that sent the request.

In order to demonstrate the effectiveness of the above protocol, we compare it against a greedy protocol, in which node V_i sends a task request to a randomly chosen neighbor when the task buffer at V_i becomes empty. When multiple requests are received simultaneously, the request from the neighbor with the highest computing power is processed first. This protocol represents the first-come-first-served approach, in which a compute node gets a task whenever it becomes free. Hence, the more powerful a compute node is, the greater the number of tasks assigned to it. No resource selection is performed and all compute nodes are considered as possible workers.

We simulated systems with various numbers of nodes and links. The graphs were generated as in Case 1 of the first set of experiments. w_{max} was set to 0.1. We initialized the root node with 1000 tasks. Figure 15.5 compares the throughput of the two protocols. The reported throughput is calculated as the number of tasks computed in one unit of time (1000/overall execution time), and has been normalized to the maximum throughput calculated (offline) by using the ENF representation. As can be seen, although neither protocol achieves the maximum possible throughput, the proposed protocol improves the system throughput by up to 41%.

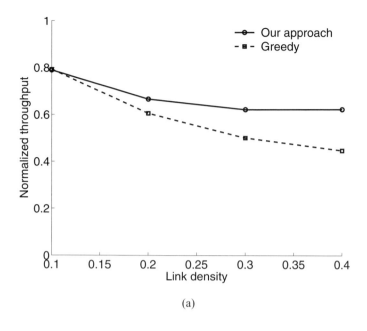

(a)

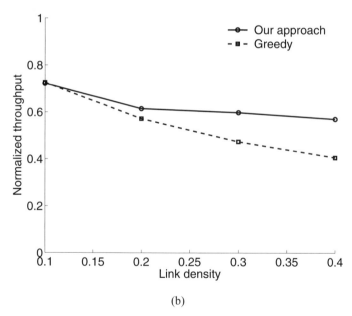

(b)

Figure 15.5 Comparison of the performance of the proposed protocol and the greedy protocol. (a) Number of nodes = 60. (b) Number of nodes = 80.

15.6 CONCLUSION

In this chapter, we studied the problem of computing a large set of equal-sized inde-pendent tasks on a heterogeneous computing system. We proposed to model the system as an undirected graph. In order to maximize the system throughput, we de-veloped a linear programming and an extended network flow (ENF) representation. Maximum-flow/minimum-cut algorithms are used to solve the proposed problem. The effectiveness of the graph-structured computation paradigm and our system throughput maximization approach were verified through simulations.

Future work needs to consider other operation scenarios of the compute nodes and communication links. For example, communications may not be overlapped with computation, communications may be half-duplex, or a compute node may not communicate with multiple nodes concurrently. These scenarios, along with the one that we have discussed in this chapter, can model a wide range of compute/communication resources. Another direction is to consider tasks with dif-ferent characteristics. For example, there may be m ($m > 1$) types of tasks such that a task of type i requires D_i units of data and requires W_i units of computation. In this chapter, we focused on the bandwidth when modeling the network links. It has been pointed out in [13] that in a distributed heterogeneous system, network latency is another factor that affects the performance of the system. Future studies should con-sider the impact of network latencies.

ACKNOWLEDGMENT

The work presented in this chapter was supported by the National Science Founda-tion under award No. ACI-0204046 and an equipment grant from Intel Corporation.

REFERENCES

1. C. Banino, O. Beaumont, A. Legrand, and Y. Robert, Scheduling Strategies for Master-slave Tasking on Heterogeneous Processor Grids, in *PARA '02: International Conference on Applied Parallel Computing,* LNCS 2367, pp. 423–432, Springer-Verlag, 2002.

2. O. Beaumont, A. Legrand, Y. Robert, L. Carter, and J. Ferrante, Bandwidth-Centric Al-location of Independent Tasks on Heterogeneous Platforms, in *International Parallel and Distributed Processing Symposium (IPDPS),* April 2002.

3. T. D. Braun, H. J. Siegel, and N. Beck, A Comparison of Eleven Static Heuristics for Mapping a Class of Independent Tasks onto Heterogeneous Distributed Computing Sys-tems, *Journal of Parallel and Distributed Computing, 61,* 810–837, 2001.

4. D. Collins and A. George, Parallel and Sequential Job Scheduling in Heterogeneous Clusters: A Simulation Study using Software in the Loop, *Simulation, 77*(6), 169–184, December 2001.

5. T. H. Cormen, C. E. Leiserson, and R. L. Rivest, *Introduction to Algorithms,* MIT Press, 1992.

6. Distributed.net. http://www.distributed.net.

7. M. Faloutsos, P. Faloutsos, and C. Faloutsos, On Power-law Relationships of the Internet Topology, in *ACM SIGCOMM,* pp. 251–262, 1999.

8. E. Heymann, M. A. Senar, E. Luque, and M. Livny, Evaluation of an Adaptive Scheduling Strategy for Master-Worker Applications on Clusters of Workstations, in *7th Internation Conference on High Performance Computing (HiPC 2000),* December 2000.

9. B. Hong and V. K. Prasanna, Distributed Adaptive Task Allocation in Heterogeneous Computing Environments to Maximize Throughput, in *18th International Parallel and Distributed Processing Symposium (IPDPS '04),* April 2004.

10. O. Ibarra and C. Kim, Heuristic Algorithms for Scheduling Independent Tasks on Non-identical Processors, *Journal of the ACM, 24*(2), 280–289, 1977.

11. E. Korpela, D. Werthimer, D. Anderson, J. Cobb, and M. Lebofsky, SETI@home-Massively Distributed Computing for SETI, *Computing in Science and Engineering,* January 2001.

12. S. M. Larson, C. D. Snow, M. Shirts, and V. S. Pande, Folding@Home and Genome@Home: Using Distributed Computing to Tackle Previously Intractable Problems, in *Computational Biology, Computational Genomics, R. Grant (Ed.),* Horizon Press, 2002.

13. C. Lee, C. DeMatteis, J. Stepanek, and J. Wang, Cluster Performance and the Implications for Distributed, HeterogeneousGrid Performance, in *9th Heterogeneous Computing Workshop,* May 2000.

14. M. Maheswaran, S. Ali, H. J. Siegel, D. Hensgen, and R. F. Freund, Dynamic Mapping of a Class of Independent Tasks onto Heterogeneous Computing Systems, *Journal of Parallel and Distributed Computing, 59*(2), 107–131, 1999.

15. A. Medina, I. Matta, and J. Byers, On the Origin of Power Laws in Internet Topologies, *ACM Computer Communication Review, 30*(2), 18–28, April 2000.

16. R. V. Nieuwpoort, T. Kielmann, and H. E. Bal, Efficient Load Balancing for Wide-area Divide-and-Conquer Applications, in *Proceedings of Eighth ACM SIGPLAN Symposium on Principles and Practice of Parallel Programming (PPoPP '01),* pp. 34–43, 2001.

17. G. Shao, F. Berman, and R. Wolski, Master/Slave Computing on the Grid, in *9th Heterogeneous Computing Workshop,* May 2000.

18. D. Thain, T. Tannenbaum, and M. Livny, Condor and the Grid, in F. Berman, A.J.G. Hey, and G. Fox (Eds.)*, Grid Computing: Making The Global Infrastructure a Reality,* Wiley, 2003.

19. B. Veeravalli and G. Barlas, Scheduling Divisible Loads with Processor Release Times and Finite Buffer Capacity Constraints in Bus Networks, Special Issue on Divisible Load Scheduling, *Cluster Computing, 6*(1), 63–74, January 2003.

20. J. B. Weissman, Scheduling Multi-Component Applications in Heterogeneous Wide-area Networks, in *Heterogeneous Computing Workshop, International Parallel and Distributed Processing Symposium IPDPS,* May 2000.

## CHAPTER 16

Scheduling Algorithms with Bus Bandwidth Considerations for SMPs

CHRISTOS D. ANTONOPOULOS, DIMITRIOS S. NIKOLOPOULOS, and
THEODORE S. PAPATHEODOROU

16.1 INTRODUCTION

Small symmetric multiprocessors have dominated the server market and the high-performance computing field, either as stand-alone components, or as components for building scalable clustered systems. Technology has driven the cost of SMPs down enough to make them affordable for desktop computing. Future trends indicate that symmetric multiprocessing within chips will be a viable option for computing in the embedded-systems world as well.

This class of machines is praised for cost-effectiveness but, at the same time, it is criticized for limited scalability. A major architectural bottleneck of most SMPs is the internal bus, which is used to connect the processors and the peripherals to memory. Despite technological advances that drive the design of system-level interconnects to more scalable, switch-based solutions such as HyperTransport [4] and InfiniBand [5], the bandwidth of the internal interconnection network of SMPs is a dominant barrier for performance. The problem is more acute in low-cost, SMPs in which low-end, low-performance buses are used.

Although it has been known for a long time that the internal bus of an SMP is a major performance bottleneck, software for SMPs has taken only indirect approaches to address the problem. The goal has always been to optimize the programs for the memory hierarchy and improve cache locality. The same philosophy is followed in SMP operating systems for scheduling multiprogrammed workloads with time sharing. All SMP schedulers use cache-affinity links for each thread. The affinity links are exploited to bias the scheduler, so that each thread keeps running on the same processor. This helps threads build state in the caches without interference noise coming from other threads. Program optimizations for cache locality and cache-affinity scheduling reduce the bus bandwidth consumed by programs. Therefore, they may improve the "capacity" of an SMP in terms of the number of threads the SMP can run simultaneously without slowing them down. Unfortunately, if the bus of the SMP is saturated due to contention between threads, memory hierarchy optimizations and affinity scheduling do not remedy the problem.

This chapter presents a direct approach for coping with the bus bandwidth bottleneck of SMPs in the operating system. We motivate this approach with experiments that show the impact of bus saturation on the performance of multiprogrammed SMPs. In our experiments, we use applications with very diverse bus bandwidth requirements that have already been extensively optimized for the target memory hierarchy. The experiments show clearly that this impact can be severe. The slowdown of jobs caused by bus bandwidth limitations can be significantly higher than the slowdown caused by interference between jobs on processor caches. In some cases, the slowdown due to bus saturation is even higher than the slowdown the programs would experience if they were simply timeshared on a subset of the system processors.

In this chapter, we describe scheduling algorithms that address the problem directly. They select the applications to coexecute driven by the bandwidth requirements of their threads. Bus utilization information is collected from the performance-monitoring counters that are provided by all modern processors. The algorithms measure the bandwidth consumption of each job at run time. The goal is to find candidate threads for coscheduling on multiple processors, so that the average bus bandwidth requirements per thread are as close as possible to the available bus bandwidth per processor. In other words, the scheduling policies try to achieve optimal utilization of the bus during each quantum without either overcommiting it or wasting bus bandwidth.

In order to evaluate the performance of our policies, we experiment with heterogeneous workloads on multiprogrammed SMPs. The workloads consist of the applications of interest combined with two microbenchmarks: one that is bus bandwidth consuming and another that poses negligible overhead on the system bus. The new scheduling policies demonstrate an up to 68% improvement of system throughput. On average, the throughput rises by 26%.

The rest of this chapter is organized as follows. Section 16.2 discusses related work. In Section 16.3 we present an experimental evaluation of the impact of bus bandwidth saturation on system performance. In Section 16.4 we describe the new, bus-bandwidth-aware scheduling policies. Section 16.5 presents an experimental evaluation of the proposed algorithms in comparison with the standard Linux scheduler. Finally, section 16.6 concludes the chapter.

16.2 RELATED WORK

Processor scheduling policies for SMPs have been primarily driven by two factors: the processor requirements and the cache behavior of programs. Most existing SMP schedulers use time sharing with dynamic priorities and include an affinity mask or flag that biases the scheduler so that threads that have had enough time to build their state in the cache of one processor are consecutively scheduled repeatedly on the same processor. In these settings, parallel jobs can use all the processors of the system. Few SMP OSs use space-sharing algorithms that partition the processors between programs so that each program runs on a fixed or variable subset of the system processors. If multiple jobs, including one or more parallel ones, run at the same time, space sharing schedulers prevent parallel jobs from using all processors of the system.

The effectiveness of cache affinity scheduling depends on a number of factors [16, 19, 21]. The cache size and replacement policy have an obvious impact. The smaller the size of the cache, the more the performance penalty for programs which are timesharing the same processor. The degree of multiprogramming is also important. The higher the degree of multiprogramming, the less are the chances that affinity scheduling will improve cache performance. The time quantum of the scheduler also affects significantly the effectiveness of affinity scheduling. With long time quanta, threads may not be able to reuse data from the caches if processors are timeshared among multiple threads. On the other hand, with short time quanta, threads may not have enough time to build state on the caches.

Dynamic space sharing policies [11, 12, 20, 23] attempt to surpass the cache performance limitations by running parallel jobs on dedicated sets of processors, the size of which may vary at run time. These policies tend to improve the cache performance of parallel jobs by achieving better locality, since jobs tend to execute on isolated sets of processors. The drawback of these policies is that they limit the degree of parallelism that the application can exploit. It has been shown that in most practical cases, the positive effect of improving locality outweighs the negative effect of losing processors. Thus, space-sharing policies tend to improve the performance of parallel jobs on multiprogrammed platforms.

New scheduling algorithms based on the impact of cache sharing on the performance of coscheduled jobs on multithreaded processors and chip multiprocessors were proposed in [17, 18]. The common aspect of this work and the policies presented in this chapter is that both are using contention on a shared system resource as the driving factor for making informed scheduling decisions. However, these algorithms are based on analytical models of program behavior on malleable caches, whereas our policies are using information collected from the program at run time. Scheduling with online information overcomes the limitations of modeling program behavior offline, and makes the scheduling algorithm portable on real systems, regardless of workloads.

To the best of our knowledge, none of the already proposed job scheduling algorithms for SMPs is driven by the effects of sharing system resources other than caches and processors. In particular, none of the policies is driven by the impact of sharing the bus, or in general, the network that connects processors and memory. Furthermore, among the policies that focus on optimizing memory performance, none considers the available bandwidth between different levels of the memory hierarchy as a factor for guiding scheduling decisions.

Related work on job scheduling for multithreaded processors [1, 15] has shown that the performance of the scheduler is improved when the scheduler takes into account the interference between applications on shared hardware resources. More specifically, it has been shown that it is possible to achieve better performance from multiprogrammed workloads if the programs that are coscheduled on multiple processors during a time quantum meet certain criteria that indicate good symbiosis between the programs on specific system resources. For example, the scheduler could select to coschedule programs that achieve the least number of stall cycles on a shared functional unit of a multiple-issue processor, or achieve the highest utilization of instruction slots, or fit in RAM without incurring paging. These studies indicated the importance of sharing resources other than caches and processor time on the performance of job scheduling algorithms, but did not propose implementable scheduling algorithms driven by the observed utilization of specific resources.

Most modern microprocessors are equipped with performance monitoring counters. Designed primarily for analyzing the performance of programs at the architectural level, they provide the programmer with a powerful tool for tracking performance bottlenecks due to the interactions between the program and the hardware. These counters have been widely used for off-line performance analysis of applications either autonomously [7, 14, 24] or as the basis for building higher-level tools [3, 8]. N. Amato et al. define a performance prediction function that takes into account the memory hierarchy and contention effects [2]. The function is expressed in terms that can be attained using performance counters. The authors provide experimental evidence that it can be employed as a prediction tool by extrapolating performance counter measurements from small pilot executions. However, information attained from performance monitoring counters has never been used before to either affect scheduling decisions at run time on a real system, or drive run time program optimizations.

16.3 THE IMPLICATIONS OF BUS BANDWIDTH FOR APPLICATION PERFORMANCE

In this section, we present experimental results that quantify the impact of sharing the bus of an SMP between multiple jobs. The experimental investigation is relevant for all types of shared-memory architectures that share some level of the memory hierarchy, whether a cache or RAM. Besides SMPs, the analysis is also relevant for multithreading processors and chip multiprocessors.

For the experiments, we used extensively optimized applications and computational kernels from two suites: the NAS benchmarks [6] and the Splash-2 benchmarks [22]. The benchmarks were compiled using the 7.1 version of Intel Fortran and C/C++ OpenMP compilers. We used codes that are optimized for spatial and temporal cache locality in order to avoid any chances that the observed bandwidth consumption occurs due to poor implementation of the used codes. We show that, even with heavily optimized code, bus bandwidth consumption is a major limitation for achieving high performance.

Our experimental platform is a dedicated, four-processor SMP with Hyperthreaded Intel Xeon processors, clocked at 1.4 GHz. It is equipped with 1 GB of main memory and each processor has 256 kB of L2 cache. The front-side bus of the machine, namely the medium that connects processors to memory, runs at 400 MHz. The operating system is Linux and the kernel version is 2.4.20. The values of hardware counters are monitored using the Mikael Pettersson's performance counter driver for Linux and the accompanying run-time library [13]. Unfortunately, the driver does not currently support concurrent execution of two threads on the same hyperthreaded processor if both threads use performance monitoring counters. As a consequence, we had to disable hyperthreading on all processors.

The theoretical peak bandwidth of the bus is 3.2 GB/s. However, the maximum sustained bandwidth measured by the STREAM benchmark [10] is 1797 MB/s when requests are issued from all processors. The highest bus transactions rate sustained by STREAM is 29.5 transactions/μs, hence, approximately 64 bytes are transferred with each bus transaction.

We have conducted four sets of experiments. The first one measures the bandwidth consumed by each application, when executed alone using two processors. The other three experiment sets simulate a multiprogrammed execution. In the second set, two identical instances of an application are executed using two processors each.

In the third experiment set, one instance of the application, using two processors, runs together with two instances of a microbenchmark (BBMA). Each instance of the microbenchmark uses one processor. The microbenchmark accesses a two-dimensional array, the size of which is twice as much as the size of Xeon's L2 cache. The size of each line of the array is equal to the cache line size of Xeon. The microbenchmark performs column-wise writes on the array. More specifically, it writes the first element of all lines, then the second element, then the third element, and so on. The microbenchmark is programmed in C, so the array is stored in memory row-wise. As a consequence, each write causes the processor to fetch a new cache line from memory. By the time the next element of each line is to be written, the specific line has been evicted from the cache. As a result, the microbenchmark has an almost 0% cache hit rate for the elements of the array. It constantly performs back-to-back memory accesses and consumes a significant fraction of the available bus bandwidth. On average, it performs 23.6 bus transactions/μs.

The fourth experiment set is identical to the third one, except for the configuration of the microbenchmark. The microbenchmark (nBBMA) accesses the array row-wise, so spatial locality is maximized. Furthermore, the size of the array is half the size of Xeon's L2 cache. Therefore, excluding compulsory misses, the elements are constantly accessed from the cache and the cache hit rate of the microbenchmark approaches 100%. Its average bus transactions rate is 0.0037 transactions/μs.

Figure 16.1 depicts the bus bandwidth consumption of each application, measured as the number of bus transactions per microsecond. The reported bus transactions rate is the accumulated rate of transactions issued from two threads running on two different processors. The applications are sorted in increasing order of issued bus transactions rate. The bandwidth consumption varies from 0.48 to 23.31 bus transactions per microsecond. Considering that each transaction transfers 64 bytes, the applications consume no more than 1422.73 MB/s; therefore, the bus offers enough bandwidth to run these applications alone.

Figure 16.2 shows the accumulated number of transactions per microsecond when two instances of each application run simultaneously using two processors each. The cummulative bus transactions rate is further analyzed in the diagram to depict the

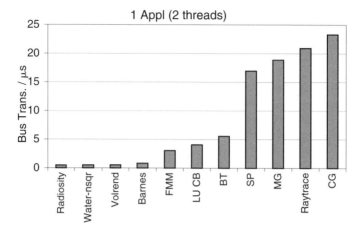

Figure 16.1   Bus transactions rate for the applications studied, when the applications are executed alone, using two processors.

contribution of each application instance. Both instances contribute, as expected, almost equally; however, the sustained bus transactions rate of each instance is generally lower than that of the stand-alone execution. The four applications with the highest bandwidth requirements (SP, MG, Raytrace, CG) push the system bus close to its capacity. Even in cases in which the cumulative bandwidth of two instances of these applications does not exceed the maximum sustained bus bandwidth, contention and arbitration contribute to bandwidth consumption and, eventually, bus saturation.

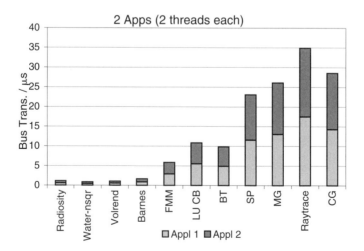

Figure 16.2   Cumulative bus transactions rate when two instances of each application are executed simultaneously, using two processors each.

It is worth noticing that four Raytrace threads yield a cumulative rate of 34.89 transactions/μs, which is higher than the transactions rate achieved by four concurrently executing threads of STREAM (29.5 transactions/μs). It has not been possible to reproduce this behavior with any other application or synthetic microbenchmark, even by varying the length of the data chunk transferred during each bus transaction.

Figure 16.3 shows the slowdown of the applications when two instances of each application are executed together using two processors each. Note that the two instances use different processors and there is no processor sharing. Theoretically, the applications should not be slowed down at all; however, in practice, there is slowdown due to contention between the applications on the bus. The results show that the applications with high bandwidth requirements suffer a 41% to 61% performance degradation.

Figures 16.4 and 16.5 illustrate the results from the experiments in which one parallel application competes with two copies of the BBMA microbenchmark that continuously streams data from memory without reusing it. These experiments isolate the impact of having applications run on an already saturated bus. Note that in Figure 16.4 the bus bandwidth consumed from the workload is very close to the limit of saturation, averaging 28.34 transactions/μs. Moreover, it is clear that the instances of the BBMA microbenchmark dominate the use of bus bandwidth. As a result, the available bandwidth for applications is often significantly lower compared with their bandwidth requirements that we measured during the standalone application execution. Memory-intensive applications suffer two- to almost three-fold slowdowns, despite the absence of any processor sharing. Even applications with moderate bus bandwidth requirements have slowdowns ranging between 2% and 55% (18% on average). The slowdown of LU CB is higher than expected. This can

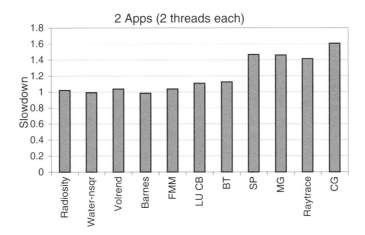

Figure 16.3 Slowdown of the applications when two instances of each application are executed simultaneously, using two processors each. The slowdown in the diagram is the arithmetic mean of the slowdown of the two instances.

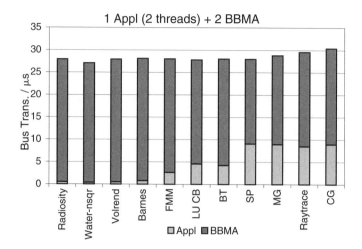

Figure 16.4 Cumulative bus transactions rate when one instance of each application, using two processors, is executed together with two instances of the BBMA microbenchmark that issues back-to-back memory accesses without reusing data from the cache.

be attributed to the fact that LU CB has a particularly high cache hit ratio (99.53% when executed with two threads). As a consequence, as soon as a working set has been built in the cache, the application tends to be very sensitive to thread migrations among processors. The same observation holds true for Water-nsqr.

Figures 16.6 and 16.7 depict the results from the concurrent execution of parallel applications, using two threads each, with two instances of the nBBMA mi-

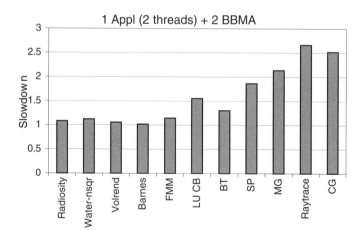

Figure 16.5 Slowdown of the applications when one instance of each application, using two processors, is executed together with two instances of the BBMA microbenchmark that issues back-to-back memory accesses without reusing data from the cache.

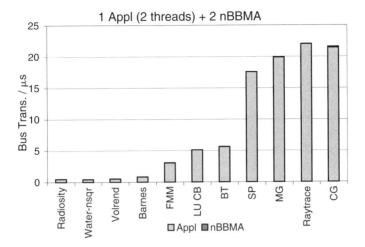

Figure 16.6 Cumulative bus transactions rate when one instance of each application, using two processors, is executed together with two instances of the nBBMA microbenchmark that reuses data from the cache and does not consume any bus bandwidth.

crobenchmark. The latter practically poses no overhead on the bus. It is clear that both the bus transactions rate and the execution time of applications are almost identical to those observed during the uniprogrammed execution. In fact, the contribution of nBBMA instances to the totaly consumed bandwidth is not even visible in Figure 16.6. This confirms that the slowdowns observed in the previously described experiments are not caused by lack of computational resources. Figures 16.6 and

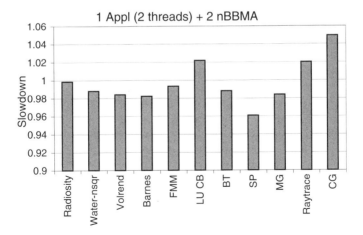

Figure 16.7 Slowdown of the applications when one instance of each application, using two processors, is executed together with two instances of the nBBMA microbenchmark that reuses data from the cache and does not consume any bus bandwidth.

16.7 also indicate that pairing high-bandwidth with low-bandwidth applications is a good way for the SMP scheduler to achieve higher throughput.

Figure 16.8 depicts the correlation between the reduction of the measured bus transactions rates of applications in all multiprogrammed executions and the corresponding slowdowns. All rate reductions and slowdowns have been calculated with respect to the stand-alone execution of the applications. The diagram also illustrates the regression line, fitted by applying the least squares algorithm on the (bus transactions rate reduction, slowdown) data points. Figure 16.8 indicates a close, almost linear relation between the limitation of the available bus bandwidth and the slowdown that applications are expected to suffer.

From the experimental data presented in this section, one can easily deduce that programs executing on an SMP may suffer significant performance degradation even if they are offered enough CPU and memory resources to run without sharing processors and caches and without causing swapping. These performance problems can be attributed to bus saturation. In some cases, the slowdowns exceed the slowdowns that would have been observed if the threads were simply time-shared on a single processor, instead of executing on different processors of a multiprocessor. Given the magnitude of these slowdowns, it is reasonable to search for scheduling policies that improve application and system performance by carefully managing bus bandwidth.

16.4   SCHEDULING POLICIES FOR PRESERVING BUS BANDWIDTH

We have implemented two new scheduling policies that schedule jobs on an SMP system taking into account the bus bandwidth the jobs consume. They are referred to as "latest quantum gang" (LQG) and "quanta window gang" (QWG). Both poli-

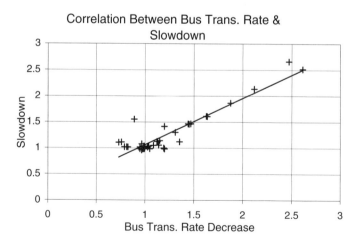

Figure 16.8   Correlation between the reduction of the bus transactions rate and the slowdown of applications in the multiprogrammed executions.

cies are gang-scheduling-like, in the sense that all threads of the same application are guaranteed to execute together. The scheduling quantum is fixed to a constant value. Applications coexisting in the system are conceptually organized as a list.

Table 16.1 outlines the pseudocode of LQG. At the end of each scheduling quantum, the scheduler updates the bus transactions rate statistics for all running jobs, using information provided by the applications. The bus transactions rate (BTR_{latest}) is calculated as the number of bus transactions caused by the application during the latest quantum, divided by the duration of the quantum. The previously running jobs are then transferred to the tail of the applications list.

Next, the policy initializes the available bus transactions rate ($ABTR$) for the next quantum to the system bus transactions rate ($SBTR$). $ABTR$ quantifies the available bus bandwidth for allocation at any time during the scheduling. $SBTR$ is a constant, characteristic of the system bus capacity. Its value is equal to the maximum bus transactions rate that does not saturate the bus.

Table 16.1 Pseudocode of LQG algorithm. The QWG algorithm is similar

---

Foreach running application

$$BTR_{latest} = \frac{Bus\ Transactions}{Quantum\ Length}$$

Enqueue the application at the tail of available applications.
$ABTR = SBTR$
Unallocated Processors = System Processors
Allocate processors to application at the head of available applications and dequeue it.
$ABTR = ABTR - BTR_{latest}$
Unallocated Processors − = Application Threads
While *Unallocated Processors* > 0

$$ABTR_{/proc} = \frac{ABTR}{Unallocated\ Processors}$$

Foreach available application
　　If *Application Threads* ≤ *Unallocated Processors*

$$Fitness = \frac{1000}{1 + |ABTR_{/proc} \times Application\ Threads - BTR_{latest}|}$$

If no application with *Application Threads* ≤ *Unallocated Processors* has been found
　　Scheduling has finished
Else
　　Allocate processors to the fittest application and dequeue it.
　　$ABTR = ABTR - BTR_{latest}$
　　Unallocated Processors − = Application Threads

Following this, the policy elects the applications that will execute during the next quantum. The application found at the head of the applications' list is allocated by default. This ensures that all applications will eventually have the chance to execute, independent of their bus bandwidth consumption characteristics. As a consequence, no job will suffer processor starvation.

Every time an application is selected for execution, its BTR_{latest} is subtracted from the available bus transactions rate ($ABTR$). Moreover, the scheduler calculates the available bus transaction rate per unallocated processor ($ABTR_{/proc}$) as

$$ABTR_{/proc} = \frac{ABTR}{Unallocated\ processors} \qquad (16.1)$$

As long as there are processors available, the scheduler traverses the applications list. For each application that fits in the available processors, a fitness value is calculated:

$$Fitness = \frac{1000}{1 + |ABTR_{/proc} \times Application\ Threads - BTR_{latest}|} \qquad (16.2)$$

Fitness is a metric of the proximity between the application's bus bandwidth requirements and the currently available bandwidth. The closer BTR_{latest} is to $ABTR_{/proc} \times Application\ Threads$, the fitter the application is for scheduling. The selection of this fitness metric favors an optimal exploitation of bus bandwidth. If processors have already been allocated to low-bandwidth applications, high-bandwidth ones become best candidates for the remaining processors. The reverse scenario holds true as well. The fitness metric behaves as expected even in cases when, due to the nature of the workload, bus saturation cannot be avoided. As soon as the bus gets overloaded, $ABTR_{/proc}$ turns negative and the application with the lowest BTR_{latest} becomes the fittest.

After each list traversal, the fittest application is selected to execute during the next quantum. If there are still unallocated processors, the $ABTR$ and $ABTR_{/proc}$ values are updated and a new list traversal is performed.

The QWG policy is quite similar to LQG. The sole difference is that instead of using the bus transactions rate of each application during the latest quantum, we calculate and use its bus transactions rate during a window of past quanta (BTR_{window}).

Using BTR_{window} instead of BTR_{latest} has the effect of smoothing sudden changes to the bus transactions caused by an application. This technique filters out sudden bursts with small duration, or bursts that can be attributed to random, external events such as cache state rebuild after a thread migration. However, at the same time, it reduces the responsiveness of the scheduling policy to true changes in the bus bandwidth requirements of applications. The selection of the window length must take this trade-off into account. Figure 16.9 illustrates the average bus transactions rate of Raytrace when windows of length 1 (no smoothing), 5, and 10 are used. When no filtering is applied, the bus transactions pattern is dominated by random variations of small duration. On the contrary, the use of a large window has the effect of distorting the observed pattern. The window used in QWG has been heuristically chosen to be

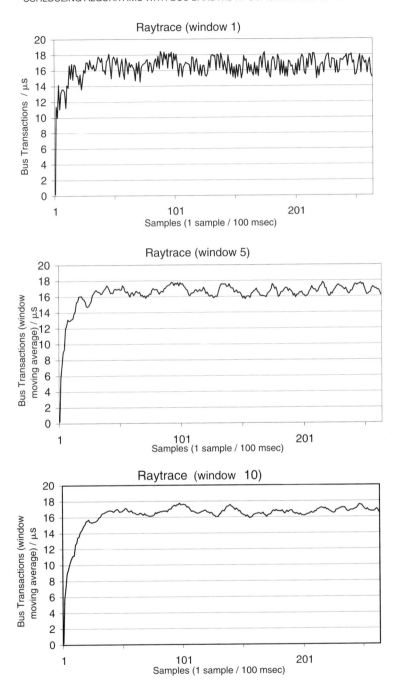

Figure 16.9   Bus transactions rate of Raytrace when a window of length 1 (top), 5 (middle), or 10 (bottom) is used. The reported rate is the average of the samples within the window. The hardware counters are sampled every 100 μs.

5 samples long. This window length limits the average distortion introduced by filtering within 5% of the observed transactions pattern for applications with irregular bus bandwidth requirements, such as Raytrace or LU. The use of a wider window would require techniques such as exponential reduction of the weight of older samples in order to achieve an acceptable policy responsiveness.

The use of a user-level CPU manager facilitates the design, testing, and comparison of scheduling policies without altering the OS kernel. We implemented a user-level CPU manager that executes as a server process on the target system. Its interface and functionality are similar to those of the NANOS CPU Manager [9].

Each application that wishes to use the new scheduling policies uses a standard UNIX socket to send a "connection" message to the CPU manager. The thread that contacted the CPU manager is the "application leader." The CPU manager responds to the message by creating a shared arena, that is, a shared memory page used as its primary communication medium with the application. It also informs the application how often the bus transactions rate information in the shared arena is expected to be updated. Moreover, the CPU manager adds the new application to a list of connected applications.

In order to ensure the timeliness of information provided from the applications, the bus transactions rate is updated twice per scheduling quantum. At each sampling point, the performance counters of all application threads are polled, their values are accumulated, and the result is written to the shared arena.

The applications are blocked/unblocked by the CPU manager according to the decisions of the effective scheduling policy. Blocking/unblocking of applications is achieved using standard unix signals. The CPU manager sends a signal to the "application leader," which, in turn, is responsible for forwarding the signal to the application threads. In order to avoid side effects from possible inversion ofn the order in which block/unblock signals are sent and received, a thread blocks only if the number of received block signals exceeds the corresponding number of unblock signals. Such an inversion is quite probable, especially if the time interval between consecutive blocks and unblocks is narrow.

A run-time library that accompanies the CPU manager offers all the necessary functionality for the cooperation between the CPU manager and applications. The modifications required to the source code of applications are limited to the addition of calls for connection and disconnection and to the interception of thread creation and destruction.

The overhead introduced by the CPU manager to the execution time of the applications it controls is usually negligible. In the worst-case scenario, namely when multiple identical copies of applications with low bus bandwidth requirements are coexecuted, it may rise up to 4.5%.

16.5 EXPERIMENTAL EVALUATION

We have evaluated the effectiveness of our policies using three sets of heterogeneous workloads. Each experiment set is executed both on top of the standard Linux scheduler and with one of the new policies, using the CPU manager. All workloads have a multiprogramming degree equal to two. In other words, the concurrently active threads are twice as many as the available physical processors. The scheduling quantum of the CPU manager is 200 ms, twice the quantum of the Linux scheduler. We have experimented with a quantum of 100 ms, which resulted to an excessive number of context switches. This is probably due to the lack of synchronization between the OS scheduler and the CPU manager, which in turn results in conflicting scheduling decisions at the user and kernel levels. Using a larger scheduling quantum eliminates this problem. In any case, we have verified that the duration of the CPU manager quantum does not have any measurable effect on the cache performance of the controlled applications.

In the first set, two instances of the target application, requesting two processors each, are executed together with four instances of the BBMA microbenchmark. This set evaluates the effectiveness of our policies on an already saturated bus. Figure 16.10 illustrates the improvement each policy introduces in the average turnaround time of applications in comparison with the execution on top of the standard Linux scheduler. Applications are sorted in increasing order of issued bus transactions rate in the uniprogrammed execution (as in Figure 16.1). LQG achieves improvements ranging from 4% to 68% (41% on average). The improvements introduced by QWG vary between 2% and 53%, with an average of 31%.

When executed with the standard Linux scheduler, applications with high bandwidth requirements may be coscheduled with instances of the BBMA microbenchmarks, resulting in bus bandwidth starvation. Our policies avoid this scenario. Applications with lower bandwidth requirements may be scheduled with instances of the BBMA microbenchmarks. However, even in this case, our policies ensure, due to the gang-like scheduling, that at least two low-bandwidth threads will run togeth-

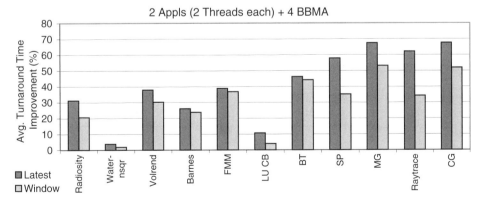

Figure 16.10 Performance improvement (%) of the workloads when two instances of each application (using two processors each) are executed simultaneously with four instances of the BBMA microbenchmark. The reported values are the improvement in the arithmetic mean of the execution times of both application instances.

er, in contrast to the Linux scheduler, which may execute one low-bandwidth thread with three instances of BBMA.

The second set of workloads consists of two instances of the target application—requesting two processors each—and four instances of the nBBMA microbench-mark. This experiment demonstrates the functionality of the proposed policies when low-bandwidth jobs are available in the system. Figure 16.11 depicts the performance gains attained by the new scheduling policies.

LQG achieves up to 60% higher performance; however, three applications slow down. The most severe case is that of Raytrace (19% slowdown). A detailed analysis of Raytrace revealed a highly irregular bus transactions pattern. The sensitivity of LQG to sudden changes in bandwidth consumption has probably led to this problematic behavior. Moreover, from Figure 16.1 one can deduce that running two threads of Raytrace together—which is the case, due to the gang-like nature of our policies—may alone drive the bus close to saturation. LU CB and Water-nsqr also suffer minimal slowdowns due to their high sensitivity to thread migrations among processors. On average, LQG improved workload turnaround times by 13%. QWG turned out to be much more stable. It improved workload turnaround times by up to 64%. Raytrace slows down once again, however, this time by only 1%. The average performance improvement is now 21%.

In this experiment set, our scheduling policies tend to pair bandwidth-consuming applications with instances of the nBBMA microbenchmark. As a consequence, the available bus bandwidth for demanding applications is higher. Even low-bandwidth applications seem to benefit from our algorithms. The new policies avoid executing two instances of the applications together in the presence of nBBMA microbenchmarks. Despite the fact that running two instances of low-bandwidth applications together does not saturate the bus, performance problems may occur due to contention among application threads for the possession of the

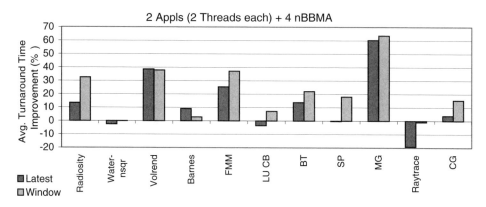

Figure 16.11 Performance improvement (%) of the workloads when two instances of each application (using two processors each) are executed simultaneously with four instances of the nBBMA microbenchmark. The reported values are the improvement in the arithmetic mean of the execution times of both application instances.

bus. Note that only one processor can transfer data over the shared bus at any given time snapshot.

The third experiment set combines two instances of the target application, requesting two processors each, with two instances of the BBMA and two instances of the nBBMA microbenchmark. Such workloads simulate execution environments in which the applications of interest coexist with more and less bus-bandwidth-consuming ones. The performance improvements of the new scheduling policies over the standard Linux scheduler are depicted in Figure 16.12.

LQG improves the average turnaround time of applications in the workloads by up to 50%. LU is the only application that experiences a 7% performance deterioration. The average performance improvement is 26%. The maximum and average improvement achieved by QWG are 47% and 25%, respectively. Two applications, namely, Water-nsqr and LU, suffer minimal slowdowns of 2% and 5%.

In summary, for the purposes of this experimental evaluation we used applications with a variety of bus bandwidth demands. All three experiment sets benefit significantly from the new scheduling policies. Both policies attain average performance gains of 26%. The scheduling algorithms are robust for both high-bandwidth and low-bandwidth applications. As expected, however, QWG proves to be much more stable than LQG. It performs well even in cases in which the latter exhibits problematic behavior due to sudden, short-term changes in the bandwidth consumption of applications.

16.6   CONCLUSIONS

Symmetric multiprocessors are nowadays very popular in the area of high-performance computing, both as stand-alone systems and as building blocks for computa-

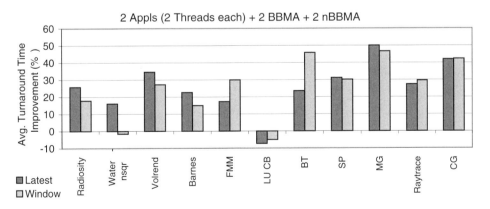

Figure 16.12   Performance improvement (%) of the workloads when two instances of each application (using two processors each) are executed simultaneously with two instances of the BBMA and two instances of the nBBMA microbenchmark. The reported values are the improvement in the arithmetic mean of the execution times of both application instances.

tional clusters. The main reason for this is that they offer a very competitive performance/price ratio in comparison with other architectures. However, the limited bandwidth of the bus that connects processors to memory has adverse effects on the scalability of SMPs. Although this problem is well known, neither user- nor system-level software are optimized to minimize these effects.

In this chapter, we presented experimental results that indicate that bus saturation is reflected in an almost up to three-fold decrease in the performance of bus-bandwidth-consuming applications. Even less demanding applications suffer slowdowns ranging between 2% and 55%.

Motivated by this observation, we introduced two scheduling policies that take into account the bus bandwidth requirements of applications. Both policies have been implemented in the context of a user-level CPU manager. The information required to drive policy decisions is provided by the performance-monitoring counters present in all modern processors. To the best of our knowledge, these counters have never before been used to improve application performance at run time. LQG uses the bus transactions rate of applications during the latest quantum, whereas QWG uses bus transactions rate calculated over a window of quanta. At any scheduling point, both policies try to schedule the application with the bus transactions rate per thread that best matches the available bus transactions rate per unallocated processor in the system.

In order to evaluate the performance of our policies, we have executed three sets of workloads. In the first set, applications of interest coexisted with highly bus-demanding microbenchmarks. The second set consisted of the applications of interest and microbenchmarks that pose no overhead on the bus. In the third set, applications executed in an environment composed of both highly demanding and nondemanding microbenchmarks. Both policies attained an average 26% performance improvement over the native Linux scheduler. Moreover, QWG has been much more stable than LQG. It maintained good performance even in corner cases in which LQG proved to be oversensitive to application peculiarities.

We plan to continue our study in the following directions. First, we plan to derive analytic or empirical models of the effect of sharing resources other than the CPU, including the bus, caches, and main memory, on the performance of multiprogrammed SMPs. Using these models, we can reformulate the multiprocessor scheduling problem as a multiparametric optimization problem and derive practical model-driven scheduling algorithms. We plan to test our scheduler with I/O and network-intensive workloads which also stress the bus bandwidth. This can be done in the context of scientific applications or other classes of applications, such as Web servers and database servers. The policies can also be extended in the context of multithreading processors, where sharing occurs also at the level of internal processor resources, such as the functional units.

ACKNOWLEDGMENTS

The first author is supported by a grant from the Alexander S. Onassis public benefit foundation and the European Commission through the POP IST project (grant No.

IST200133071). The second author is supported by NSF grants ITR/ACI0312980 and CAREER/CCF0346867.

REFERENCES

1. G. Alverson, S. Kahan, R. Corry, C. McCann, and B. Smith, Scheduling on the Tera MTA, in *Proceedings of the First Workshop on Job Scheduling Strategies for Parallel Processing (JSSPP'95), LNCS Vol. 949*, pp. 19–44, Santa Barbara, CA, April 1995.

2. N. M. Amato, J. Perdue, A. Pietracaprina, G. Pucci, and M. Mathis, Predicting Performance on SMPs. A Case Study: The SGI Power Challenge, in *Proceedings of the International Parallel and Distributed Processing Symposium (IPDPS 2000)*, Cancun, Mexico, May 2000.

3. Intel Corporation, Intel Vtune Performance Analyzer, http://developer.intel.com/software/products/vtune, 2003.

4. HyperTransport Consortium, Meeting the I/O Bandwidth Challenge: How HyperTransport Technology Accelerates Performance in Key Applications, Technical report, http://www.hypertransport.org/, December 2002.

5. Infiniband Trade Association, Infiniband Architecture Specification, Release 1.1, Technical report, http://www.infinibandta.org, November 2002.

6. H. Jin, M. Frumkin, and J. Yan, The OpenMP Implementation of NAS Parallel Benchmarks and its Performance, Technical Report NAS99011, NASA Ames Research Center, 1999.

7. K. Keeton, D. A. Patterson, Y. Q. He, R. C. Raphael, and W. E. Baker, Performance Characterization of a Quad Pentium Pro SMP Using OLTP Workloads, *ACM SIGARCH Computer Architecture News, Proceedings of the 25th Annual International Symposium on Computer Architecture (ISCA 98), 26*(3), April 1998.

8. K. London, J. Dongarra, S. Moore, P. Mucci, K. Seymour, and T. Spencer, Enduser Tools for Application Performance Analysis, Using Hardware Counters, in *Proceedings of the 15th International Conference on Parallel and Distributed Computing Systems (PDCS 2001)*, Dallas, August 2001.

9. X. Martorell, J. Corbalan, D. S. Nikolopoulos, N. Navarro, E. D. Polychronopoulos, T. S. Papatheodorou, and J. Labarta, A Tool to Schedule Parallel Applications on Multiprocessors, in *Proceedings of the 6th IEEE Workshop on Job Scheduling Strategies for Parallel Processing (JSSPP'2000)*, pp. 87–112, LNCS, May 2000.

10. J. D. McCalpin, Memory Bandwidth and Machine Balance in Current High Performance Computers, *Technical Committee on Computer Architecture (TCCA) Newsletter,* December 1995.

11. C. McCann, R. Vaswani, and J. Zahorjan, A Dynamic Processor Allocation Policy for Multiprogrammed Shared Memory Multiprocessors, *ACM Transactions on Computer Systems, 11*(2), 146–178, May 1993.

12. T. Nguyen, R. Vaswani, and J. Zahorjan, Maximizing Speedup through Self-Tuning Processor Allocation, in *Proceedings of the 10th IEEE International Parallel Processing Symposium (IPPS'96)*, pp. 463–468, Honolulu, HI, April 1996.

13. M. Pettersson, Perfctr Performance Counters Driver for Linux/x86 Systems, http://www.csd.uu.se/~mikpe/linux/perfctr.

14. A. Singhal and A. J. Goldberg, Architectural Support for Performance Tuning: A Case Study on the SPARCcenter 2000, *ACM SIGARCH Computer Architecture News, Proceedings of the 21st Annual International Symposium on Computer Architecture (ISCA 94), 22*(2), April 1994.

15. A. Snavely and D. Tullsen, Symbiotic Job Scheduling for a Simultaneous Multithreading Processor, in *Proceedings of the 9th International Conference on Architectural Support for Programming Languages and Operating Systems (ASPLOS'IX),* pp. 234–244, Cambridge, MA, November 2000.

16. M. Squillante and E. Lazowska, Using Processor-Cache Affinity Information in Shared-Memory Multiprocessor Scheduling, *IEEE Transactions on Parallel and Distributed Systems, 4*(2), 131–143, February 1993.

17. G. Suh, S. Devadas, and L. Rudloph, Analytical Cache Models with Applications to Cache Partitioning, in *Proceedings of the 15th ACM International Conference on Supercomputing (ICS'01),* pp. 1–12, Sorrento, Italy, June 2001.

18. G. Suh, L. Rudolph, and S. Devadas, Effects of Memory Performance on Parallel Job Scheduling, in *Proceedings of the 8th Workshop on Job Scheduling Strategies for Parallel Processing (JSSPP'02),* pp. 116–132, Edinburgh, June 2002.

19. J. Torrellas, A. Tucker, and A. Gupta, Evaluating the Performance of Cache-Affinity Scheduling in Shared-Memory Multiprocessors, *Journal of Parallel and Distributed Computing, 24*(2), 139–151, February 1995.

20. A. Tucker and A. Gupta. Process Control and Scheduling Issues for Multiprogrammed Shared-Memory Multiprocessors, in *Proceedings of the 12th ACM Symposium on Operating Systems Principles (SOSP'89),* pp. 159–166, Litchfield Park, AZ, December 1989.

21. R. Vaswani and J. Zahorjan, The Implications of Cache Affinity on Processor Scheduling for Multiprogrammed Shared Memory Multiprocessors, in *Proceedings of the 13th ACM Symposium on Operating System Principles (SOSP'91),* pp. 26–40, Pacific Grove, CA, October 1991.

22. S. C. Woo, M. O., E. Torrie, J. P. Singh, and A. Gupta, The Splash-2 programs: Characterization and Methodological Considerations, in *Proceedings of the 22nd Annual International Symposium on Computer Architecture (ISCA'95),* pp. 24–36, June 1995.

23. K. Yue and D. Lilja, An Effective Processor Allocation Strategy for Multiprogrammed Shared-Memory Multiprocessors, *IEEE Transactions on Parallel and Distributed Systems, 8*(12), 1246–1258, December 1997.

24. M. Zagha, B. Larson, S. Turner, and M. Itzkowitz, Performance Analysis Using the MIPS R10000 Performance Counters, in *Proceedings of the SuperComputing 1996 Conference (SC96),* Pittsburgh, November 1996.

## CHAPTER 17

Toward Performance Guarantee of Dynamic Task Scheduling of a Parameter-Sweep Application onto a Computational Grid

NORIYUKI FUJIMOTO and KENICHI HAGIHARA

17.1 INTRODUCTION

Public-resource computing [2], such as that the project SETI@home [2] has been carrying out, is the computing that is performed with donated computer cycles from computers in homes and offices in order to perform large-scale computation faster. Public-resource computing is one form of grid computing. In public-resource computing, the original users also use their computers for their own purposes, so, their use may dramatically impact the performance of each grid resource. This chapter refers to a set of computers distributed over the Internet and participating in public-resource computing as a computational grid (or simply a grid).

This chapter addresses task scheduling of a single-parameter-sweep application onto a computational grid. A parameter-sweep application is an application structured as a set of multiple "experiments," each of which is executed with a distinct set of parameters [3]. There are many important parameter-sweep application areas, including bioinformatics, operations research, data mining, business model simulation, massive searches, Monte Carlo simulations, network simulation, electronic CAD, ecological modeling, fractals calculations, and image manipulation [1, 14]. Such an application consists of a set of independent tasks such that each task corresponds to computation for a set of parameters. In a grid, communication delays are large. So, for achieving high performance, it is necessary that the granularity of an application on a grid be coarse grained.[1] Hence, we assume that an application consists of coarse-grained tasks. For example, each SETI@home task takes 3.9 trillion

---

[1]In this chapter, coarse-grain means that the execution time of every task is much longer than the communication delay required by the task. So, for a coarse-grained parameter-sweep application, communication delays are negligible in spite of large communication delay over the Internet.

High-Performance Computing: Paradigm and Infrastructure. Edited by L. T. Yang and M. Guo   **333**
Copyright © 2006 John Wiley & Sons, Inc.

floating-point operations, or about 10 hours on a 500 MHz Pentium II, yet involves only a 350 kB download and 1 kB upload [2]. Therefore, for the purpose of scheduling a single-parameter-sweep application, a computational grid can be modeled as a heterogeneous parallel machine such that processor speed unpredictably varies over time and communication delays are negligible.

The most common objective function of task scheduling problems (both for a grid and for a nongrid parallel machine) is makespan. Minimum makespan scheduling of independent tasks onto an identical parallel machine is the static and restricted version of the dynamic grid scheduling problem tackled in this chapter and is known to be strongly $\mathcal{NP}$-hard [5]. So, for grid scheduling, a makespan optimal schedule cannot be found in polynomial time unless $\mathcal{P} = \mathcal{NP}$. Moreover, on a grid, makespan of a nonoptimal schedule may be much longer than the optimal makespan because the computing power of a grid varies over time. For example, consider an optimal schedule with makespan OPT. If a grid is suddenly slowed down at time OPT and the slow speed situation continues for a long period, then the makespan of the second optimal schedule is far from OPT. So, if the criterion of a schedule is makespan, there is no approximation algorithm in general for scheduling onto a grid.

First, this chapter proposes a novel criterion of a schedule for a grid. The proposed criterion is called total processor cycle consumption (TPCC, for short), which is the total number of instructions the grid could compute from the starting time of executing the schedule to the completion time. TPCC represents the total computing power consumed by a parameter-sweep application. Next, we present a $(1 + \{m[\log_e(m-1)+1]/n\}\mu)$-approximation algorithm, called RR (list scheduling with round-robin order replication), for scheduling n independent coarse-grained tasks onto a grid with m processors where μ is the unevenness of the lengths of given n tasks. The formal definition of μ is given in Section 17.2.2. RR does not use any prediction information on the performance of underlying resources. This result implies that, regardless how the speed of each processor varies over time, the consumed computing power can be limited within $(1 + \{m[\log_e(m-1)+1]/n\}\mu)$ times the optimal one in such a case. This is not trivial because makespan cannot be limited even in the case.

The remainder of this chapter is organized as follows. First, Section 17.2 defines the grid scheduling model used in this chapter. Next, Section 17.3 surveys related works. Then, Section 17.4 shows the proposed algorithm RR and some properties of RR. Last, Section 17.5 proves the performance guarantee of RR.

17.2   A GRID SCHEDULING MODEL

17.2.1   A Performance Model

The length of a task is the number of instructions in the task. The speed of a processor is the number of instructions computed per unit time. A grid is heterogeneous, so processors in a grid have various speeds by nature. In addition, the speed of each processor varies over time due to the load imposed by the original users in public-resource computing. That is, the speed of each processor is the spare computing power of the processor that is not used by the original users and is dedicated to a grid. Let $s_{p,t}$ be the speed of processor p during time interval $[t, t + 1)$ where t is a nonnegative integer. Without loss of generality, we assume that the speed of each processor does not vary during time interval $[t, t + 1)$ for every t by adopting enough short time as the unit time. We also assume that we cannot know the value of any $s_{p,t}$ in advance. $s_{p,t}$ may be zero if the load imposed by the original users is very heavy or the processor is powered off. For simplicity, processor addition, processor deletion, and any failure are not considered in this chapter. Figure 17.1(a) shows an example of a set of tasks. Figure 17.1(b) shows an example of processor speed distribution.

17.2.2 Unevenness of the Lengths of a Set of Tasks

Formally, this chapter defines the unevenness of the lengths of a set of tasks as follows. Let T be a set of the n tasks. Let $\bar{L}$ be the average length of all the tasks in T. Let L_{max} be the maximum length of all the tasks in T. Then, the unevenness of the lengths of T is defined as $L_{max}/\bar{L}$ because of Theorem 1 in Section 17.5. For example, the unevenness of the lengths of the set of tasks in Figure 17.1(a) is $10/[(9 + 4 + 10 + \cdots + 4)/20] \approx 1.942$. If all the tasks have the same length, then the unevenness is one. Since it follows that $L_{max} \geq \bar{L}$, unevenness of the lengths of any set of tasks is at least one.

17.2.3 A Schedule

Let T be a set of n independent tasks. Let m be the number of processors in a computational grid. We define a schedule of T as follows. A schedule S of T onto a grid with m processors is a finite set of triples $\langle v, p, t \rangle$ which satisfies the following rules R1 and R2, where $v \in T$, p $(1 \leq p \leq m)$ is the index of a processor, and t is the starting time of task v. A triple $\langle v, p, t \rangle \in S$ means that the processor p computes the task v with length L between time t and time $t + d$ where d is defined so that the number of instructions computed by the processor p during the time interval $[t, t + d)$ is exactly L. We call $t + d$ the completion time of the task v. Note that starting time and completion time of a task are not necessarily integral.

> R1—For each $v \in T$, there is at least one triple $\langle v, p, t \rangle \in S$.
> R2—There are no two triples $\langle v, p, t \rangle, \langle v', p, t' \rangle \in S$ with $t \leq t' < t + d$ where $t + d$ is the completion time of v.

Informally, the above rules can be stated as follows. The rule $R1$ enforces each task v to be executed at least once. The rule $R2$ says that a processor can execute at most one task at any given time. A triple $\langle v, p, t \rangle \in S$ is called the task instance of v. Note that $R1$ permits a task to be assigned to more than one processor. Such a task has more than one task instance. Assigning a task to more than one processor is called task replication.

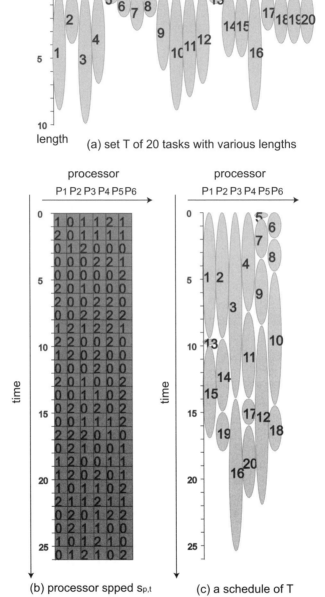

(a) set T of 20 tasks with various lengths

(b) processor spped $s_{p,t}$

(c) a schedule of T

Figure 17.1   The proposed grid scheduling model.

17.2.4 Criteria of a Schedule

17.2.4.1 Makespan The makespan of schedule S is the maximum completion time of all the task instances in S. For example, Figure 17.1(c) shows a schedule of T, $\{\langle v_1, P_1, 0 \rangle, \langle v_2, P_2, 0 \rangle, \cdots, \langle v_6, P_6, 0 \rangle, \langle v_7, P_5, 1/2 \rangle, \langle v_8, P_6, 2 \rangle, \cdots, \langle v_{20}, P_4, 16 \rangle\}$. The makespan of the schedule is $51/2$.

17.2.4.1 TPCC Let T be a set of n independent tasks. Let S be a schedule of T onto a grid with m processors. Let M be the makespan of S. Let $s_{p,t}$ be the speed of processor p during the time interval $[t, t+1)$. Then, the TPCC of S is defined as $\sum_{p=1}^{m} \sum_{t=0}^{\lfloor M \rfloor - 1} s_{p,t} + \sum_{p=1}^{m} (M - \lfloor M \rfloor) s_{p, \lfloor M \rfloor}$. For example, TPCC of the schedule in Figure 17.1(c) is $21 + 22 + 18 + 27 + 20 + 24 + \frac{1}{2}(0 + 1 + 2 + 1 + 0 + 2) = 135$.

The criterion means the total computing power dedicated to the parameter sweep application. The longer makespan is, the larger TPCC is. Conversely, the larger TPCC is, the longer makespan is. That is, every schedule with good TPCC is also a schedule with good makespan. The goodness of the makespan seems to be reasonable for the dedicated computing power, that is, the corresponding TPCC . This implies that a good algorithm for minimum TPCC grid scheduling is effective also for minimum makespan grid scheduling. In this sense, the criterion is meaningful.

17.2.5 A Grid Scheduling Problem

This chapter addresses the following grid scheduling problem:

- Instance: A set T of n independent tasks, a number m of processors, unpredictable speed $s_{p,t}$ of processor p during the time interval $[t, t+1)$ for each p and t
- Solution: A schedule S of T on a grid with m processors
- Measure: Either makespan or the TPCC $\sum_{p=1}^{m} \sum_{t=0}^{\lfloor M \rfloor - 1} s_{p,t} + \sum_{p=1}^{m} (M - \lfloor M \rfloor) s_{p, \lfloor M \rfloor}$ of S, where M is the makespan of S

A makespan optimal schedule is a schedule with the smallest makespan among all the schedules. An TPCC optimal schedule is a schedule with the smallest TPCC among all the schedules. Note that the set of makespan optimal schedules is the same as the set of TPCC optimal schedules.

17.3 RELATED WORKS

This section summarizes known results on complexity, heuristic algorithms, optimal algorithms, and approximation algorithms for scheduling independent coarse-grained tasks onto a homogeneous parallel machine, a heterogeneous parallel machine, or a grid. First, Section 17.3.1 introduces a brief notation to describe various scheduling problems. Next, Section 17.3.2 summarizes known results in the case of invariable processor speed. In this case, many results are known. Then, Section

17.3.3 summarizes several known results in the case of variable processor speed. In this case, all the known results are heuristic algorithms, that is, algorithms without performance guarantees.

17.3.1 Problem Description

For describing problems, the shorthand notation slightly extended from one in the literature [8] is used. Problems are described by three fields (e.g., $P|p_j = 1|C_{max}$ where | is a delimiter): the left field represents the machine environment, the middle field describes constraints, and the right field describes the objective function criterion.

Possible machine environments in the left field include P, P_m, Q, and Q; s_{jk}. Notation P indicates that m identical parallel processors are available, where m is part of the problem instance. Notation P_m indicates that m identical parallel processors are available. Notation Q indicates m parallel processors with integer speed ratios, where m is part of the problem instance. Notation Q_m indicates m parallel processors with integer speed ratios. Notation Q; s_{jk} indicates Q such that processor speed unpredictably varies over time.

Possible constraints in the middle field include ones on task processing times. Notation $p_j = 1$ indicates that all the tasks have unit processing times. Notation unpredictable p_j indicates that every task processing time cannot be known in advance. If the middle field has no constraints, then it means there are independent tasks with various lengths.

Possible criteria in the right field include C_{max} and Σs_{jk}. Notation C_{max} indicates that the criterion is the makespan of a schedule. Notation Σs_{jk} indicates that the criterion is the TPCC of a schedule.

Using this notation, the problem tackled in this chapter is represented as Q; $s_{jk}||\Sigma s_{jk}$.

17.3.2 The Case of Invariable Processor Speed

Let n be the number of tasks. Let m be the number of processors. Let PTAS be the class of problems that admit a polynomial-time approximation scheme [16]. Let FPTAS be the class of problems that admit a fully polynomial-time approximation scheme [16]. Then, the following results are known:

- $P||C_{max}$ is strongly $\mathcal{NP}$-hard [5].
- $P_2||C_{max}$ is $\mathcal{NP}$-hard [13].
- $P||C_{max}$ is approximable within a factor of $(\frac{4}{3} - \frac{1}{3m})$ [7].
- $P||C_{max}$ is approximable within a factor of $(1 + \varepsilon)$ in $O[(n/\varepsilon)^{1/\varepsilon^2}]$ time for any $\varepsilon > 0$ [10]. ($P||C_{max}$ is in PTAS.)
- $P||C_{max}$ is approximable within a factor of $(6/5 + 2^{-k})$ in $O[n(k + \log n)]$ time where k is every positive integer [10].
- $P||C_{max}$ is approximable within a factor of $(7/6 + 2^{-k})$ in $O[n(km^4 + \log n)]$ time where k is every positive integer [10].

- $P_m||C_{max}$ is approximable within a factor of $(1 + \varepsilon)$ in $O(n/\varepsilon)$ time for any $\varepsilon > 0$ [12]. ($P_m||C_{max}$ is in FPTAS.)
- $P|p_j = 1|C_{max}$ is trivial. The optimal makespan is $\lceil n/m \rceil$.
- $P|$unpredictable $p_j|C_{max}$ is approximable within a factor of $(2 - 1/m)$ [6].
- $P|$unpredictable $p_j|C_{max}$ is approximable within a factor of $(2 - 1/m - \varepsilon_m)$ where ε_m is some positive real depending only on m [4].
- $Q|p_j = 1|C_{max}$ can be solved in $O(n^2)$ time [8].
- $Q_2||C_{max}$ is approximable within a factor of $(1 + \varepsilon)$ in $O(n^2/\varepsilon)$ time for any $\varepsilon > 0$ [12]. ($Q_2||C_{max}$ is in FPTAS.)
- $Q||C_{max}$ is approximable within a factor of $(1 + \varepsilon)$ in $O[(\log m + \log(3/\varepsilon)](n + 8/\varepsilon^2)m \cdot n^{3+40/\varepsilon^2})$ time for any $0 < \varepsilon \le 1$ [11]. ($Q||C_{max}$ is in PTAS.)

17.3.3 The Case of Variable Processor Speed

- For $Q; s_{jk}||C_{max}$, some heuristic algorithms without task replication are known [1, 3, 9, 15].
- For $Q; s_{jk}||C_{max}$, some heuristic algorithms with task replication are known [2, 14].

17.4 THE PROPOSED ALGORITHM RR

Dynamic scheduling algorithm RR realizes approximation using task replication and task kill operations. RR replicates some tasks and kills them, except ones that returned the result earlier than any other task instance. This chapter assumes that the overhead of a kill operation is negligible because each task is coarse grained.

In the following, RR is illustrated. First of all, a data structure called a ring is defined. Then, using a ring of tasks, RR is described.

A ring of tasks is a data structure that manages a set of tasks. The tasks in a ring have a total order such that no task has the same order as any other task. A ring has a head that points to a task in the ring. The task pointed to by the head is called the current task. The next task in a ring is defined as follows. If the current task is the task with the highest order in the ring, then the next task in the ring is the task with the lowest order in the ring. Otherwise, the next task in a ring is the task with the minimum order of the tasks with higher order than the current task. A head can be moved so that the head points to the next task. Hence, using a head, the tasks in a ring can be scanned in the round-robin fashion. An arbitrary task in a ring can be removed. If the current task is removed, then a head is moved so that the next task is pointed to. Figure 17.2 shows the concept of a ring.

RR runs as follows.[2] At the beginning of the dynamic scheduling by RR, every

---

[2]In the following, we assume, without loss of generality, that no two tasks complete at the same time. RR can deal with the simultaneous completion as if it occurred in some order. Even in the case in which the simultaneous completion occurs, all the properties, lemmata, and theorems follow just as is.

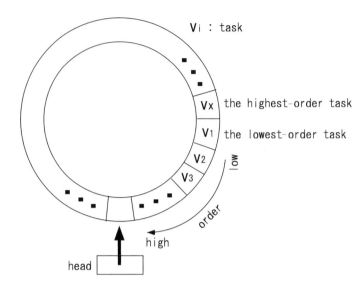

V_i : task

V_x the highest-order task

V_1 the lowest-order task

low

order

high

head

Figure 17.2 A ring of tasks.

processor is assigned exactly one task. If some of the assigned tasks are completed, then RR receives the result of the task and assigns one of yet unassigned tasks to the processor. RR repeats this process until all the tasks are assigned. At this point in time, exactly m tasks remain uncompleted. RR manages these m tasks using a ring of tasks. Then, RR repeats the following process until all the remaining m results are received. If the task instance of some task v is completed on processor p, then RR receives the result of v from p, kills all the task instances of v running on processors except p, removes v from the ring, selects task u in the ring in round-robin fashion, and replicates the task u onto the processor p.

The following is a pseudocode of RR:

Algorithm RR
Input: A set V of tasks, a number m of processors
/* Note that RR refer to neither processor speeds nor task lengths. */
Output: A dynamic schedule of V onto m processors
begin
    Let Q be a queue of tasks.
    Enqueue all the tasks in V to Q.
    Dequeue first m tasks in Q and assign them to processors one by one.
    repeat
        Wait some processor for returning a result.
        Dequeue the first task in Q and assign it to the free processor.
    until $Q = \emptyset$
    Let U be a set of all the uncompleted tasks.
    /* Note that $|U| = m$. */

Let R be a ring of all the tasks in U.
/* The total order of the tasks in R may be fixed arbitrarily. */
/* The head of R may be initialized to point to any task. */
repeat
    Wait some processor for returning a result.
    Kill all the task instances of the completed task.
    Remove the completed task from R.
    if $R \neq \emptyset$ ***then begin***
        while a free processor exists ***do begin***
            Assign to the free processor the current task of R.
            Move the head of R.
        end
    end
    until $R = \emptyset$
end

The original of task v is the task instance that is assigned earliest of all the task instances of v. The other task instances of v are called the replicas of v. Notice that the original of every task v is unique in a schedule generated by RR. Figure 17.3(c) shows a schedule that RR generates from 20 tasks $\{v_1, v_2, \cdots, v_{20}\}$ for six processors $\{P_1, P_2, \cdots, P_6\}$ in the case in which the queue Q is initialized $\langle v_1, v_2, \cdots, v_{20}\rangle$ and the ring R is initialized $\{v_{12}, v_{15}, v_{16}, v_{18}, v_{19}, v_{20}\}$ with the total order $v_{12} < v_{15} < v_{16} < v_{18} < v_{19} < v_{20}$, where $x < y$ means that task x has lower order than task y. In Figure 17.3(c), a solid (vs. dotted) line represents that the task instance is the original (vs. a replica). An ellipse (vs. a rectangle) represents that the task instance is completed (vs. killed because one of the other task instances completes earlier than the task instance). As for v_{12}, the replica completes later than the original. On the other hand, as for v_{16} and v_{20}, the replica completes earlier than the original.

In the following, some properties of RR are described. These properties are used in Section 17.5 in order to prove the performance guarantee of RR.

Since we assume coarse-grained tasks, the overhead of dynamic scheduling by RR is negligible, so the following property follows.

Property 1 From the starting time of a schedule to the completion time, RR never makes processors idle.

For example, the schedule in Figure 17.3(c) has no idle time interval. The kth last task is the task such that the order of completion is k from last.[3] Note that the kth last tasks is not necessarily the same as the task such that the order of scheduling is k from last because processors may have different speeds. Clearly, RR has the following property.

---

[3]In the case that some tasks complete at the same time, such tasks have the same order. For example, both v_{18} and v_{19} in Figure 17.3(c) are fourth last tasks. v_{15} in Figure 17.3(c) is the sixth last task, not the fifth last task.

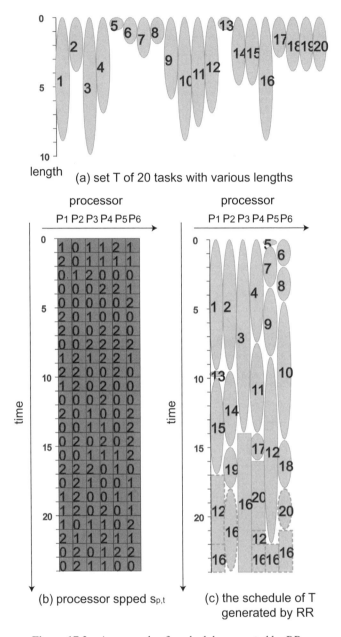

Figure 17.3   An example of a schedule generated by RR.

Property 2   For every k ($m \leq k \leq n$), RR never replicates the kth last task.

For example, consider the schedule in Figure 17.3(c). In this case, $n = 20$ and $m = 6$. The first last task is v_{16}. The second last task is v_{12}. The third last task is v_{20}. A fourth last task is v_{19}. Another fourth last task is v_{18}. So the tasks, except these five tasks, are never replicated.

The instance group of task v at time t is a set of the task instances of v that are being executed at time t. For example, consider the schedule in Figure 17.3(c). In the following, $\overline{v_i}$ (vs. $\underline{v_i}$) ($i \in \{1, 2, \cdots, 20\}$) represents that the task instance is the original (vs. a replica) of v_i. The instance group of task v_1 at time 2 is $\{\overline{v_1}$ on $P_1\}$. The instance group of task v_{20} at time 20 is $\{\overline{v_{20}}$ on $P_4, \underline{v_{20}}$ on $P_6\}$. The instance group of task v_{12} at time 21 is $\{\overline{v_{12}}$ on $P_5, \underline{v_{12}}$ on $P_1, \underline{v_{12}}$ on $P_4\}$. The size of an instance group is the number of the original and the replicas in the instance group. Then, RR has the following property.

Property 3   Let t be any time during executing a schedule. Then, the difference of the size between every pair of instance groups at time t is at most one.

Proof   Property 2 implies that, before the completion time t of the mth last task, Property 3 clearly follows. Assume that Property 3 follows at some time t' at and after the time t. Then, possible situations at the time t' are the following, where s is some positive integer:

- Case A: The size of every instance group is s.
- Case B: Some groups have size ($s + 1$), and the other groups have size s.

Let t'' be the earliest completion time of a task after t'. Let u be the completed task. Let I (vs. $\mathcal{J}$) be the set of the instance groups at time t' with size s (vs. $s + 1$) except the instance group of u. Then, at time t'', RR kills all the remaining task instances of u and increases the number of replicas of the tasks that are not completed until time t''. Regardless of the size of the instance group of u, first of all, RR increases by one replicas of the tasks of which the instance group is in I. If free processors remain after the size of every instance group in I is increased by one, then RR increases by one replicas of the tasks of which the instance group is in $\mathcal{J}$. If free processors still remain after the size of every instance group in $\mathcal{J}$ is increased by one, then RR increases by one replicas of the tasks of which the instance group is in I. RR repeats the above increment process until free processors run out. So, Property 3 follows also at time t''. Hence, by induction, Property 3 follows at any time.   ∎

For example, consider the schedule in Figure 17.3(c). The instance groups at time 5 are $\{\{\overline{v_1}$ on $P_1\}, \{\overline{v_2}$ on $P_2\}, \{\overline{v_3}$ on $P_3\}, \{\overline{v_4}$ on $P_4\}, \{\overline{v_9}$ on $P_5\}, \{\overline{v_{10}}$ on $P_6\}\}$. The instance groups at time 20 are $\{\{\overline{v_{12}}$ on $P_5, \underline{v_{12}}$ on $P_1\}, \{\overline{v_{16}}$ on $P_3, \underline{v_{16}}$ on $P_2\}, \{\overline{v_{20}}$ on $P_4, \underline{v_{20}}$ on $P_6\}\}$.

17.5 THE PERFORMANCE GUARANTEE OF THE PROPOSED ALGORITHM

This section gives a proof that RR is a $(1 + \{m[\log_e(m-1)+1]/n\}\mu)$-approximation algorithm. For this purpose, some lemmata are proved.

Consider scheduling n tasks onto a grid with m processors. Let L_k be the length of the kth last task. Let OPT be the optimal makespan. Since the grid must perform $\sum_{k=1}^{n} L_k$ instructions until time OPT, the following lemmata follow.

Lemma 1 The optimal TPCC is at least $\sum_{k=1}^{n} L_k$.

Lemma 2 Let $f(x)$ be the number of replicas of the xth last task ($x \in \{1, 2, \cdots, m-1\}$). Then, $f(x)$ satisfies the following inequality:

$$f(x) \leq \left\lceil \frac{m-x}{x} \right\rceil$$

Proof Let v be the xth last task. At and after the original of v is allocated onto a processor, the number of replicas of v monotonously increases over time until the completion of v. So, just before the completion of v, the number of replicas of v is the maximum.

Just before the completion of the xth last task, m task instances of exactly x tasks are being executed. These m task instances include exactly x originals. Hence, from Property 3, the lemma follows. ∎

For example, consider the schedule in Figure 17.3(c). The first last task v_{16} has six task instances. The second last task v_{12} has three task instances. The third last task v_{20} has two task instances.

From the harmonic series, the following fact is well known, where γ is Euler's constant ($\gamma \approx 0.5772156$):

$$\lim_{n \to \infty} \sum_{k=1}^{n} \frac{1}{k} = \log_e n + \gamma$$

Let $d(x) = \sum_{k=1}^{x} \frac{1}{k} - (\log_e x + \gamma)$. $d(x)$ is a monotonicall decreasing function. As x grows, $d(x)$ converges to zero. Since $d(1) = 1 - \gamma$, the following lemma follows:

Lemma 3 The harmonic series $\sum_{k=1}^{n} \frac{1}{k}$ is at most $(\log_e n + 1)$.

This lemma is used in the proof of the following lemma. Let L_{max} be $\max\{L_k | k \in \{1, 2, \cdots, n\}\}$.

Lemma 4 The TPCC consumed by all the replicas in a schedule generated by RR is at most $[m \log_e(m-1) + m]L_{max}$.

Proof From Lemma 2, the TPCC r is represented as follows:

$$r = \sum_{x=1}^{\min(n,m-1)} L_x f(x) \le L_{max} \sum_{x=1}^{m-1} \left\lceil \frac{m-x}{x} \right\rceil$$

$$< L_{max} \sum_{x=1}^{m-1} \left(\frac{m-x}{x} + 1 \right)$$

$$= L_{max} \sum_{x=1}^{m-1} \frac{m}{x}$$

Hence, from Lemma 3, we have:

$$r < (m \log_e(m-1) + m)L_{max}$$

∎

Theorem 1   The TPCC of a schedule generated by RR is at most $[1 + (m(\log_e(m-1) + 1)\mu/n]$ times the optimal TPCC, where μ is the unevenness of the lengths of given n tasks.

Proof From Lemma 4, every schedule S generated by RR performs at most

$$\sum_{k=1}^{n} L_k + (m \log_e(m-1) + m)L_{max}$$

instructions. In addition, from Property 1, S has no idle time interval. So, from Lemma 1, the approximation ratio of RR is at most

$$\frac{\sum_{k=1}^{n} L_k + (m \log_e(m-1) + m)L_{max}}{\sum_{k=1}^{n} L_k} = 1 + \frac{(m \log_e(m-1) + m)L_{max}}{n\bar{L}}$$

where $\bar{L} = (\sum_{k=1}^{n} L_k)/n$. So, from the definition of μ, the theorem follows. ∎

From Theorem 1, the approximation ratio of RR is inversely proportional to the number of tasks. So, if the number of processors and the unevenness of the lengths of given tasks are fixed, then the approximation ratio of RR decreases suddenly with an increase in the number of tasks. Table 17.1 through Table 17.3 show some values of approximation ratios of the proposed algorithm RR. It turns out that RR generates almost optimal schedules in cases in which the number of tasks is sufficiently larger than the number of processors.

Table 17.1 Approximation ratios of the proposed algorithm RR (in the case in which $\mu = 1$)

# of tasks	# of processors					
	4	8	16	32	64	128
1000	1.00839	1.02357	1.05933	1.14189	1.32916	1.74806
2000	1.00420	1.01178	1.02966	1.07094	1.16458	1.37403
3000	1.00280	1.00786	1.01978	1.04730	1.10972	1.24935
4000	1.00210	1.00589	1.01483	1.03547	1.08229	1.18701
5000	1.00168	1.00471	1.01187	1.02838	1.06583	1.14961
6000	1.00140	1.00393	1.00989	1.02365	1.05486	1.12468
7000	1.00120	1.00337	1.00848	1.02027	1.04702	1.10687
8000	1.00105	1.00295	1.00742	1.01774	1.04115	1.09351
9000	1.00093	1.00262	1.00659	1.01577	1.03657	1.08312
10000	1.00084	1.00236	1.00593	1.01419	1.03292	1.07481

Table 17.2 Approximation ratios of the proposed algorithm RR (in the case in which $\mu = 1.5$)

# of tasks	# of processors					
	4	8	16	32	64	128
1000	1.01259	1.03535	1.08899	1.21283	1.49374	2.12208
2000	1.00630	1.01768	1.04450	1.10642	1.24687	1.56104
3000	1.00420	1.01178	1.02966	1.07094	1.16458	1.37403
4000	1.00315	1.00884	1.02225	1.05321	1.12344	1.28052
5000	1.00252	1.00707	1.01780	1.04257	1.09875	1.22442
6000	1.00210	1.00589	1.01483	1.03547	1.08229	1.18701
7000	1.00180	1.00505	1.01271	1.03040	1.07053	1.16030
8000	1.00157	1.00442	1.01112	1.02660	1.06172	1.14026
9000	1.00140	1.00393	1.00989	1.02365	1.05486	1.12468
10000	1.00126	1.00354	1.00890	1.02128	1.04937	1.11221

Table 17.3 Approximation ratios of the proposed algorithm RR (in the case in which $\mu = 2$)

# of tasks	# of processors					
	4	8	16	32	64	128
1000	1.01679	1.04713	1.11866	1.28378	1.65832	2.49611
2000	1.00839	1.02357	1.05933	1.14189	1.32916	1.74806
3000	1.00560	1.01571	1.03955	1.09459	1.21944	1.49870
4000	1.00420	1.01178	1.02966	1.07094	1.16458	1.37403
5000	1.00336	1.00943	1.02373	1.05676	1.13166	1.29922
6000	1.00280	1.00786	1.01978	1.04730	1.10972	1.24935
7000	1.00240	1.00673	1.01695	1.04054	1.09405	1.21373
8000	1.00210	1.00589	1.01483	1.03547	1.08229	1.18701
9000	1.00187	1.00524	1.01318	1.03153	1.07315	1.16623
10000	1.00168	1.00471	1.01187	1.02838	1.06583	1.14961

17.6   CONCLUSION

This chapter has shown that minimum processor cycle scheduling is approximable within a factor of $(1 + \{m[\log_e(m-1) + 1]/n\}\mu)$ without using any kind of prediction information in the case of independent coarse-grained tasks. This result implies a nontrivial result so that, in such a case, wasteful use of dedicated computing power can be limited without any prediction information on the performance of underlying resources, regardless how the speed of each processor varies over time.

ACKNOWLEDGMENTS

This research was supported in part by Grant-in-Aid for Scientific Research on Priority Areas (16016262) from the Ministry of Education, Culture, Sports, Science, and Technology of Japan and also in part by Grant-in-Aid for Young Scientists (B)(14780213) from the Japan Society for the Promotion of Science.

REFERENCES

1. D. Abramson, J. Giddy, and L. Kotler, High performance parametric modeling with Nimrod/G: Killer application for the global grid? in *International Parallel and Distributed Processing Symposium (IPDPS)*, pp. 520–528, 2000.

2. D. P. Anderson, J. Cobb, E. Korpela, M. Lebofsky, and D.Werthimer, SETI@home: An experiment in public-resource computing. *Communications of the ACM, 45*(11), 56–61, 2002.

3. H. Casanova, A. Legrand, D. Zagorodnov, and F. Berman, Heuristics for scheduling parameter sweep applications in grid environments, in *9th Heterogeneous Computing Workshop (HCW)*, pp. 349–363, 2000.

4. G. Galambos and G. J. Woeginger, An on-line scheduling heuristic with better worst case ratio than Graham's list scheduling, *SIAM Journal on Computing, 22*(2), 349–355, 1993.

5. M. R. Garey and D. S. Johnson, Strong NP-completeness results: Motivation, examples, and implications, *Journal of the ACM, 25*(3), 499–508, 1978.

6. R. L. Graham, Bounds for certain multiprocessing anomalies, *Bell System Technical Journal, 45,* 1563–1581, 1966.

7. R. L. Graham, Bounds on multiprocessing timing anomalies, *SIAM Journal on Applied Mathematics, 17,* 416–429, 1969.

8. R. L. Graham, E. L. Lawler, J. K. Lenstra, and A. H. G. Rinnooy Kan, Optimization and approximation in deterministic sequencing and scheduling: A survey. *Annals of Discrete Mathematics, 5,* 287–326, 1979.

9. E. Heymann, M. A. Senar, E. Luque, and M. Livny, Adaptive scheduling for master-worker applications on the computational grid, in *1st IEEE/ACM International Workshop on Grid Computing (GRID)*, pp. 214–227, 2000.

10. D. S. Hochbaum and D. B. Shmoys, Using dual approximation algorithms for scheduling problems: Theoretical and practical results, *Journal of the ACM, 34,* 144–162, 1987.

11. D. S. Hochbaum and D. B. Shmoys, A polynomial approximation scheme for machine scheduling on uniform processors: Using dual approximation approach, *SIAM Journal on Computing, 17,* 539–551, 1988.

12. E. Horowitz and S. K. Sahni, Exact and approximate algorithms for scheduling nonidentical processors, *Journal of the ACM, 23,* 317–327, 1976.

13. J. K. Lenstra, A. H. G. Rinnooy Kan, and P. Brucker, Complexity of machine scheduling problems, *Annals of Discrete Machines, 1,* 343–362, 1977.

14. D. Paranhos, W. Cirne, and F. Brasileiro, Trading cycles for information: Using replication to schedule bag-of-tasks applications on computational grids, in *International Conference on Parallel and Distributed Computing (Euro-Par),* pp. 169–180, 2003.

15. G. Shao, F. Berman, and R. Wolski, Master/slave computing on the grid, in *9th Heterogeneous Computing Workshop (HCW),* pp. 3–16, 2000.

16. V. V. Vazirani, *Approximation Algorithms,* Springer-Verlag, 2001.

■■■■■■ **CHAPTER 18**

Performance Study of Reliability Maximization and Turnaround Minimization with GA-Based Task Allocation in DCS

DEO PRAKASH VIDYARTHI, ANIL KUMAR TRIPATHI, BIPLAB KUMER SARKER, KIRTI RANI, and LAURENCE T. YANG

Genetic algorithms (GAs) have emerged as successful tools for optimization problems. In our earlier work, we proposed a task allocation (TA) model to maximize the reliability of distributed computing systems (DCSs) using genetic algorithms. Our objective in this chapter, is to use the same GA to minimize the turnaround time of the task submitted to the DCS and to compare the resultant allocation with the allocation in which reliability is maximized. Comparison of both the algorithms are made and illustrated by examples and appropriate comments.

18.1 INTRODUCTION

A distributed computing system, consisting of multiple computing nodes connected in some fashion, provides a platform for concurrent task execution. Task allocation models and algorithms have been discussed in the literature for a long time [3–7]. As such, the problem of task allocation is NP-hard and heuristic solutions are applied to it. Task allocation algorithms also suffer from inefficiency, as a number of constraints are imposed by the task and the distributed system [7].

A genetic algorithm is based on the Darwin's theory of survival of the fittest [8–9]. It emulates the behavior of reproduction in nature. The task allocation model in this chapter uses a simple genetic algorithm to minimize the turnaround time of the task submitted to the DCS for execution. How minimization of turnaround time affects the reliability of the system has been studied by comparing the results with the results obtained in the earlier model [2] in which the reliability with task allocation is maximized.

High-Performance Computing: Paradigm and Infrastructure. Edited by L. T. Yang and M. Guo   **349**

The next section discusses the essentials of genetic algorithms for task allocation. This section also deals with the fitness function used in this model as well as
the fitness function used in the reliability model [2]. In Section 18.3 the GA, in algorithmic form, for the current task allocation is presented. Section 18.4 contains illustrated examples for the purpose of comparison. The work concludes with a discussion of the comparisons.

18.2   GA FOR TASK ALLOCATION

A genetic algorithm emulates biological evolutionary theories to solve optimization
problems. A GA is comprised of a set of individual elements (the population) and a
set of biologically inspired operators defined over the population. According to
evolutionary theory, only the elements most suited for the purpose in a population
are likely to survive and generate offspring, thus transmitting their biological hered-
ity to new generations [8]. The beauty of the GA is that it is inherently parallel, so it
is useful for parallel implementation in DCS [10].

The chromosomes in a GA population typically take the form of bit strings. But
the chromosome can take some other form of string as well, such as letters, digits,
and integers. Each chromosome can be thought of as a point in the search space of
candidate solutions. The GA processes populations of chromosomes, successively
replacing one such population with another. The GA requires a fitness function that
assigns a score (fitness) to each chromosome in the current population. The fitness
of a chromosome depends on how well that chromosome solves the problem at
hand [9].

The fitness function in a genetic algorithm is the objective function to be optimized. It is used to evaluate the search nodes; thus, it controls the GA [6]. As the
GA is based on the notion of the survival of the fittest, the better the fitness value,
the greater is the chance to survive. The simplest form of GA involves three types
of operators: selection, crossover, and mutation [9].

18.2.1   The Fitness Function

The fitness function in our problem is the turnaround time of the task submitted to
the DCS for execution. The turnaround time of the task is computed as follows.

The modules of the task allocated on the different nodes will be executed in parallel and, thus, the node taking the maximum time will furnish the turnaround time,
as all other nodes, taking less time, will complete the execution within the execution time of the task that takes maximum time. This time includes the time for the
actual execution and the time that it takes for communication with other modules
allocated on other computing nodes. The modules allocated on the same node will
incur zero communication. Different modules of the task may take varying times on
the different computing nodes of the DCS. The objective of this model is to minimize this time computed by the above method:

$$\text{Turnaround } (TA) = \text{Max}\left[\sum_{i=1}^{n}(e_{ij} \times x_{ij} + \sum_{\substack{k=1\\k\neq j}}^{p}\sum_{l=1}^{n} c_{il} \times x_{ij} \times x_{lk})\right] \quad \text{for all } j = p \quad (18.1)$$

Note that in the model the distance between the processing nodes are not taken into account.

18.2.2 Reliability Expression

The reliability of a DCS (which is always better than a uniprocessor system, as failure of some processors does not bring the system to a grinding halt) during the mission in which task T is allocated by the assignment X can be expressed as [11]

$$R(T, X) = \prod_{k=1}^{n} R_k(T, X) \prod_{lpq} R_{pq}(T, X) \quad (18.2)$$

where $R_k(T, X)$ is the reliability of the processing node P_k and $R_{pq}(T, X)$ is the reliability of the link l_{pq} (connecting node P_p and P_q). This is the probability that P_k and l_{pq} are operational for time T under assignment X.

$$R_k(T, X) = \exp\left(-\lambda_k \sum_{i=1}^{m} x_{ik} e_{ik}\right) \quad (18.3)$$

$$R_{pq}(T, X) = \exp\left(-\lambda_{pq} \sum_{j=1}^{m}\sum_{i\neq j}^{m} c_{ij} x_{ip} x_{jq}/W_{pq}\right) \quad (18.4)$$

where λ_k and λ_{pq} are failure rates of the processing node P_k and link l_{pq}, respectively, e_{ik} is the execution time of module m_i on node P_k, c_{ij} is the communication (in bytes) between m_i and m_j, W_{pq} is transmission rate of link l_{pq}, and x_{ik} is the element of the assignment matrix X, that is,

$$x_{ik} = \begin{cases} 1 & \text{if module } m_i \text{ is assigned to } P_k \\ 0 & \text{otherwise} \end{cases}$$

The reliability expression (18.2) is used in [2] to maximize the reliability of the DCS with allocation.

18.3 THE ALGORITHM

A genetic algorithm makes use of some fitness function to identify candidate solutions of the next generation. In this work, Equation (18.1) is used as the fitness function for TA minimization. The following are the various parts of the GA-based task allocation algorithm.

Initial Schedule( )
{
1. Compute height for each module in the task graph.
2. Keep modules of the same height (h) in the same group G(h).
3. Assign the modules of the same height from the same group G(h) onto the different processors. If some modules are unassigned, again assign it from the first processors in the same order. The assignment is to satisfy the system constraints.
4. Assign the modules of the G(h+1) in the same order of the Processors as in Step 3.
}

Many populations are generated by applying the Initial_Schedule() and changing the order of the processors.

Crossover( )
{
Two modules of different height are chosen for a crossover site in a generated population, and the portion of the strings is swapped.
}
// Length of strings should not change

Mutation( )
{
Randomly alter 0 to 1 and 1 to 0 by keeping number of 0 and 1 same.
}
// The probability of mutation is much less as it is an escape for premature convergence.

Reproduction( )
{
Use the fitness function of Equation (18.1). Choose the few best strings (with good fitness values).
}

Apply Crossover(), Mutation() and Reproduction() repeatedly, unless the solution converges.

18.4   ILLUSTRATIVE EXAMPLES

A few examples are given here that consider the turnaround time as the fitness function [Equation (18.1)]. The failure rates of the processors and links are in the range of 0.0001 to 0.0045 for the calculation of reliability of DCS with allocation. The ob-

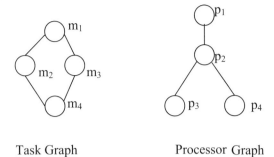

Task Graph   Processor Graph

Figure 18.1.

jective is to minimize the turnaround time of a task. Reliability corresponding to the minimum allocation is also computed. With software that uses the same GA to maximize reliability, reliability is computed for the same example. The results are shown in Tables 8-1–8.5.

18.4.1 Case 1

The task graph consisting of four modules TG (m_1, m_2, m_3, m_4) and the processor graph consisting of four nodes PG (p_1, p_2, p_3, p_4) are shown below in Figure 18.1. The corresponding execution time matrix and communication matrix for T_1 are given in Figure 18.6.

18.4.2 Case 2

This case is for the task graph of Figure 18.1 and the processor graph of Figure 18.2. Relevant matrices are shown for T_2 in Figure 18.6.

Table 18.1

Allocation without load balancing:
  $p_1 \leftarrow m_2, p_2 \leftarrow$ nil, $p_3 \leftarrow m_4, p_4 \leftarrow m_1, m_3$
  Turnaround time = 14 units
  Number of iterations = 2
  Reliability of the allocation = 0.992627
Allocation with load balancing of maximum modules 2:
  Same as above
Allocation to maximize reliability:
  $p_1 \leftarrow$ nil, $p_2 \leftarrow m_1, m_2, m_4, p_3 \leftarrow m_3, p_4 \leftarrow$ nil
  Reliability of the allocation = 0.997503
  Number of iterations = 2
  Turnaround time = 20 unit

---

p_1 ◯————◯ p_2

Figure 18.2.

Table 18.2

Allocation without load balancing:
$\quad p_1 \leftarrow m_1, m_3, p_2 \leftarrow m_2, m_4, p_3 \leftarrow$ nil, $p_4 \leftarrow$ nil
Turnaround time = 13 units
Number of iterations = 2
Reliability of the allocation = 0.987124
Allocation with load balancing of maximum modules 2:
$\quad$ Same as above.
Allocation to maximize reliability:
$\quad p_1 \leftarrow$ nil, $p_2 \leftarrow m_1, m_2, m_3, m_4, p_3 \leftarrow$ nil, $p_4 \leftarrow$ nil
Reliability of the allocation = 0.997953
Number of iterations = 3
Turnaround time = 18 units

18.4.3 Case 3

This case is for a task graph T_3 of three modules and a processor graph of three nodes shown in Figure 18.3. The execution time matrix and communication matrices are shown in Figure 18.6.

18.4.4 Case 4

This case is for a task graph T_4 of five modules and a processor graph of three nodes as shown in Figure 18.4. The matrices are shown in Figure 18.6.

18.4.5 Case 5

Finally, this case is for a task graph T5 consisting of seven modules and a processor graph of four nodes shown in Figure 18.5. The corresponding matrices are shown in Figure 18.6.

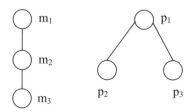

Figure 18.3.

Table 18.3

Allocation without load balancing:
  $p_1 \leftarrow$ nil, $p_2 \leftarrow m_3$, $p_3 \leftarrow m_1$, m_2
  Turnaround time = 31 units
  Number of iterations = 6
  Reliability of the allocation = 0.986561
Allocation with load balancing of maximum modules 2:
  Same as above.
Allocation with load balancing of maximum modules 1:
  $p_1 \leftarrow m_1$, $p_2 \leftarrow m_2$, $p_3 \leftarrow m_3$
  Turnaround time = 22 units
  Number of iterations = 2
  Reliability of the allocation = 0.985969
Allocation to maximize reliability:
  $p_1 \leftarrow$ nil, $p_2 \leftarrow$ nil, $p_3 \leftarrow m_1$, m_2, m_3
  Reliability of the allocation = 0.998361
  Number of iterations = 2
  Turnaround time = 4 units

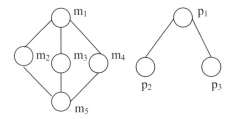

Figure 18.4.

Table 18.4

Allocation without load balancing:
  $p_1 \leftarrow m_5$, $p_2 \leftarrow m_3$, $p_3 \leftarrow m_1$, m_2, m_4
  Turnaround time = 11 units
  Number of iterations = 3
  Reliability of the allocation = 0.986561
Allocation with load balancing of maximum modules 2:
  $p_1 \leftarrow m_5$, $p_2 \leftarrow m_3$, m_4, $p_3 \leftarrow m_1$, m_2
  Turnaround time = 10 units
  Number of iterations = 3
  Reliability of the allocation = 0.985969
Allocation to maximize reliability:
  $p_1 \leftarrow$ nil, $p_2 \leftarrow m_1$, m_2, m_4, m_5, $p_3 \leftarrow m_3$
  Reliability of the allocation = 0.997304
  Number of iterations = 2
  Turnaround time = 21 units

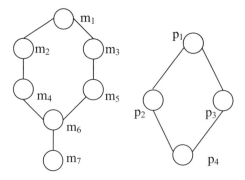

Figure 18.5.

Table 18.5

Allocation without load balancing:

$p_1 \leftarrow m_2, m_4, m_6, p_2 \leftarrow m_7, p_3 \leftarrow$ nil, $p_4 \leftarrow m_1, m_3, m_5$
Turnaround time = 15 units
Number of iterations = 2
Reliability of the allocation = 0.987320

Allocation with load balancing of maximum modules 2:

$p_1 \leftarrow m_4, m_7, p_2 \leftarrow m_2, m_6, p_3 \leftarrow m_3, m_5, p_4 \leftarrow m_1$
Turnaround time = 10 units
Number of iterations = 2
Reliability of the allocation = 0.987421

Allocation to maximize reliability:

$p_1 \leftarrow m_2, m_4 - m_6, p_2 \leftarrow m_1, p_3 \leftarrow m_3, p_4 \leftarrow$ nil
Reliability of the allocation = 0.993521
Number of iterations = 4
time = 23 units

18.5 DISCUSSIONS AND CONCLUSION

The distributed computing system considered here is heterogeneous, that is, different processing nodes of the DCS may take varying times for the execution of the modules (shown in the execution time matrixes in Figure 18.6). Some nodes are not even capable of executing certain modules so the time taken by the modules on those nodes is shown as ∞. The objective here is to minimize the turnaround time of the given task using the simple GA. Furthermore, the allocation is compared with that of [2] in which the same GA is used to maximize the reliability of the DCS with allocation. The reliability of the allocation corresponding to "minimum turnaround" and the "turnaround corresponding to maximum reliability" are also computed for effective comparison. We are able to get certain useful and expected results on the line that conforms to our idea of task allocation.

	p_1	p_2	p_3	p_4
m_1	5	3	∞	4
m_2	3	4	5	6
m_3	4	∞	2	5
m_4	3	4	5	2

Execution Time Matrix of T_1

	m_1	m_2	m_3	m_4
m_1	0	2	3	1
m_2	2	0	2	0
m_3	3	2	0	3
m_4	2	0	3	0

IMC (InterModule Communication) Matrix of

	p_1	p_2
m_1	1	1
m_2	3	5
m_3	∞	4
m_4	2	6

Execution Time Matrix of T_2

	m_1	m_2	m_3	m_4
m_1	0	8	13	11
m_2	8	0	6	7
m_3	13	6	0	12
m_4	11	7	12	0

IMC Matrix of T_2

	p_1	p_2	p_3
m_1	8	∞	1
m_2	10	6	2
m_3	9	10	1

Execution Time Matrix of T_3

	m_1	m_2	m_3
m_1	0	0	6
m_2	0	0	15
m_3	6	15	0

IMC Matrix of T_3

	p_1	p_2	p_3
m_1	5	3	∞
m_2	3	4	5
m_3	4	∞	2
m_4	3	4	5
m_5	4	5	3

Execution Time Matrix of T_4

	m_1	m_2	m_3	m_4	m_5
m_1	0	2	3	1	0
m_2	2	0	0	0	2
m_3	3	0	0	0	1
m_4	1	0	0	0	2
m_5	0	2	2	1	0

IMC Matrix of T_4

	p_1	p_2	p_3	p_4
m_1	5	3	∞	6
m_2	3	4	5	8
m_3	4	∞	2	5
m_4	3	4	5	4
m_5	5	2	3	∞
m_6	3	6	2	8
m_7	4	∞	5	6

Execution Time Matrix of T_5

	m_1	m_2	m_3	m_4	m_5	m_6	m_7
m_1	0	2	3	0	0	0	0
m_2	2	0	0	3	0	0	0
m_3	3	0	0	0	3	0	0
m_4	0	4	0	0	0	3	0
m_5	0	0	3	0	0	4	0
m_6	0	0	0	3	2	0	5
m_7	0	0	0	0	0	3	0

IMC Matrix of T_5

Figure 18.6   Execution and communication time matrices.

In the first case, the minimum turnaround is found to be 14 units and the reliability corresponding to this allocation is slightly less than the maximum possible reliability obtained in [2] for this example. The turnaround corresponding to maximum reliability is 20 units, which is more than the minimum turnaround (14 units). The result in second case is almost the same.

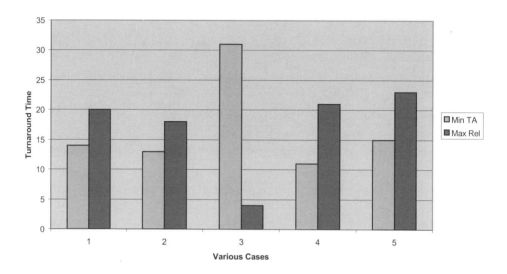

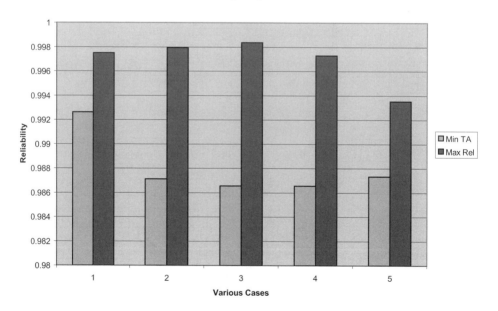

Figure 18.7. Comparison of turnaround time.

In the third case, while computing turnaround when load balancing is introduced, with one module maximum on each node, turnaround time is reduced, though little reliability is sacrificed. Furthermore, in this case, while maximizing reliability, all the modules are assigned to the same node because of much lower execution time on that node, as evident from the execution-time table. So the computation of turnaround time does not consider the communication time for these modules (as they are allocated on the same node) and, thus, the turnaround time is minimum.

Two more cases are considered by increasing the number of modules in the task. Reliability decreases when turnaround time is minimized. With the introduction of the load balancing factor, better turnaround is achieved at the cost of reliability. The results are depicted in Figure 18.7.

Considering the above cases, it is found that when turnaround time is minimized, the reliability of the DCS suffers a little. Also evident is the fact that introducing the load balancing factor produces better turnaround time for the task but results in reduced reliability. The effect is almost the same for the number of cases considered here, so it can be generalized. It can be concluded that as unless the reliability factor is absolutely essential, the consideration of minimum turnaround time as the objective (as is required in many cases) produces better task allocation in terms of reliability.

REFERENCES

1. Z. Michalewicz, *Genetic Algorithms + Data Structures = Evolution Programs,* Springer-Verlag, 1992.

2. D. P. Vidyarthi and A. K. Triapthi, Maximizing Reliability of Distributed Computing System with Task Allocation Using Simple Genetic Algorithm, *Journal of Systems Architecture, 47,* 549–554, 2001.

3. C. C. Shen and W. H. Tsai, A Graph Matching Approach to Optimal Task Assignment in Distributed Computing System Using a Minimax Criterion, *IEEE Transactions on Computers, C-34*(1), 197–203, 1985.

4. S. Kartik, C. S. Ram Murthy, Task Allocation Algorithms for Maximizing Reliability of Distributed Computing Systems, *IEEE Transactions on Computers, 46*(6), 719, June 1997.

5. S. M. Shatz, J. P. Wang, and M. Goto, Task Allocation for Maximizing Reliability of Distributed Computing Systems, *IEEE Transactions on Computers, 41*(9), 1156–1168, Sept. 1992.

6. A. K. Tripathi, D. P. Vidyarthi, and A. N. Mantri, A Genetic Task Allocation Algorithm for Distributed Computing System Incorporating Problem Specific Knowledge, *International Journal of High Speed Computing, 8*(4), 363–370, 1996.

7. D. P. Vidyarthi and A. K. Tripathi, Precedence Constrained Task Allocation in Distributed Computing System, *International Journal of High Speed Computing, 8,* 1, 47–55, 1996.

8. M. Sriniwas and L. M. Patnaik, Genetic Algorithms: A Survey, *IEEE Computer, 27*(6), 44–52, 1994.

9. M. Mitchell, *An introduction to Genetic Algorithms,* Prentice Hall of India, 1998.

10. D. P. Vidyarthi and A. K. Tripathi, Exploiting Parallelism in Genetic Task Allocation Algorithms, *International Journal of Information and Computing Science, 4*(1), 22–26, June 2001.

11. D. P. Vidyarthi and A. K. Tripathi, Studies on Reliability with Task Allocation of Redundant Distributed Systems, *IETE Journal of Research, 44*(6), 279–285, Nov.–Dec., 1998.

## CHAPTER 19

Toward Fast and Efficient Compile-Time Task Scheduling in Heterogeneous Computing Systems

TAREK HAGRAS and JAN JANEČEK

19.1 INTRODUCTION

Recent developments in high-speed digital communication have made it possible to connect a number of distributed machines with different capabilities in order to provide a powerful computing platform called a heterogeneous computing system [1]. Heterogeneous computing systems have gained importance due to the fact that a single parallel architecture may not be adequate for exploiting all available program parallelism. In some cases, heterogeneous computing systems have been able to produce high performance at lower cost than a single large machine in executing parallel program tasks [2]. However, the performance of parallel program execution on such platforms is highly dependent on the scheduling of the parallel program tasks onto these machines [3, 4].

The main objective of the scheduling mechanism is to assign multiple interacting program tasks onto machines and to order their execution so that precedence requirements are satisfied and minimum overall completion time is achieved. When the characteristics of the parallel program in terms of task execution times, task dependencies, and amount of communicated data are known a priori, scheduling can be accomplished during the compile time and the parallel program can be represented by the directed acyclic graph (DAG) [5, 6]. For the general form of compile-time task scheduling, the nodes of the DAG represent the parallel program tasks and the edges represent the intertask data dependencies. Each node is labeled by the computation cost (the expected computation time) of the task and each edge is labeled by the communication cost (the expected communication time) between tasks.

Early compile-time scheduling research made simplifying assumptions about the architecture of parallel programs and target computing systems, such as uniform task weights, zero edge weights, and availability of an unbounded number of computing machines. However, with some of these assumptions the scheduling problem has been proven to be NP-complete [3–5], except for a few restricted cases. Even in two simple cases, such as scheduling tasks with uniform weights to a bounded number of machines and scheduling tasks with weights equal to one or two units to two machines, the scheduling problem is still NP-complete. Only in three cases do there exist optimal polynomial-time algorithms. These cases are: scheduling tree-structure task graphs with uniform computation costs on a bounded number of machines, scheduling a task graph with a uniform computation cost to two machines, and scheduling an interval-ordered task graph with uniform task weights to a bounded number of machines [7]. In all these three cases, the communication cost among the tasks of the parallel program is assumed to be zero.

Due to the intractability of the NP-completeness of the scheduling problem, heuristics can be used to obtain a suboptimal schedule rather than parsing all possible schedules. In general, the compile-time task-scheduling problem has been extensively studied, and various heuristics have been proposed in the literature. Two of the main categories of compile-time task-scheduling heuristics are list scheduling and task duplication [3, 5]. List scheduling combines reasonable performance with reasonable complexity. Task duplication heuristics have better performance but higher complexity. List scheduling basically consists of two phases: a task prioritization phase, in which a certain priority is computed and is assigned to each node of the DAG, and a machine assignment phase, in which each task (in order of its priority) is assigned to the machine that minimizes a predefined cost function [8–12]. The basic idea of task duplication is to try to duplicate the parents of the current selected task onto the selected machine or onto another machine (or other machines), aiming to reduce or optimize the task start or finish time. The main weakness of duplication-based algorithms is their high complexity and that they mainly target an unbounded number of computing machines [13–16].

This chapter presents a compile-time task-scheduling algorithm based on list scheduling and task duplication. The algorithm is called the Heterogeneous Critical Tasks Reverse Duplicator (HCTRD). The algorithm works for a bounded number of heterogeneous machines interconnected by different speed links, and aims to introduce a lower-bound complexity task selection heuristic and a near-lower-bound complexity/duplication-based mechanism. The remainder of the chapter is organized as follows. The next section introduces the compile-time scheduling problem in a heterogeneous environment and provides definitions of some parameters utilized in the algorithm. The HCTRD scheduling algorithm is presented in the third section. The fourth section contains a brief overview of other frequently used heterogeneous scheduling algorithms that we apply for performance comparison. A performance evaluation, based on a large number of randomly generated application graphs and two real-world applications, is presented in the fifth section.

19.2 PROBLEM DEFINITION

This section presents the model of the application used for compile-time scheduling, the model of the heterogeneous computing environments, and the scheduling objective.

The application can be represented by a directed acyclic graph $G(V, W, E, C)$, as shown in Figure 19.1, where:

V is the set of v nodes, and each node $v_i \in V$ represents an application task, which is a sequence of instructions that must be executed serially on the same machine.

W is a $v \times p$ computation costs matrix in which each $w_{i,j}$ gives the estimated time to execute task v_i on machine p_j.

E is the set of communication edges. The directed edge $e_{i,j}$ joins nodes v_i and v_j, where node v_i is called the parent node and node v_j is called the child node. This also implies that v_j cannot start until v_i finishes and sends its data to v_j.

C is the set of communication costs, and edge $e_{i,j}$ has a communication cost $c_{i,j} \in C$.

A task without any parent is called an entry task and a task without any child is called an exit task. If there is more than one exit (entry) task, they may be connected to a zero-cost pseudoexit (entry) task with zero-cost edges, which do not affect the schedule.

The heterogeneous system model is a set P of p heterogeneous machines (processors) connected in a fully connected topology. It is also assumed that:

- Any machine (processor) can execute the task and communicate with other machines at the same time.
- Once a machine (processor) has started task execution, it continues without interruption, and after completing the execution it immediately sends the output data to all children tasks in parallel.

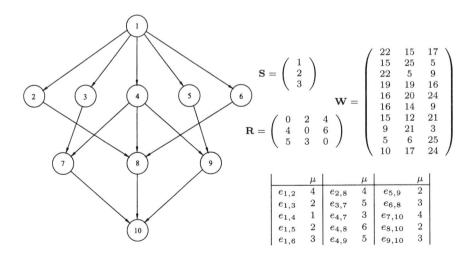

Figure 19.1 Heterogeneous systems application graph.

The communication costs per transferred byte between any two machines are stored in matrix R of size $p \times p$. The communication startup costs of the machines are given in a p-dimensional vector S. The communication cost of edge $e_{i,j}$ for transferring μ bytes data from task v_i (scheduled on p_m) to task v_j (scheduled on p_n) is defined as:

$$c_{i,j} = S_m + R_{m,n} \cdot \mu_{i,j}$$

where:

S_m is p_m communication startup cost (in seconds)

$\mu_{i,j}$ is the amount of data transmitted from task v_i to task v_j (in bytes)

$R_{m,n}$ is the communication cost per transferred byte from p_m to p_n (in sec/byte)

The average earliest start time $AEST(v_i)$ of v_i can be computed recursively by traversing the DAG downward starting from the entry task v_{entry}:

$$AEST(v_i) = \max_{v_m \in prnt(v_i)} \{AEST(v_m) + \overline{w_m} + \overline{c_{m,i}}\}$$

where $prnt(v_i)$ is the set of immediate parents of v_i and $AEST(v_{entry}) = 0$.

The average latest start time $ALST(v_i)$ of v_i can be computed recursively by traversing the DAG upward starting from the exit task v_{exit}:

$$ALST(v_i) = \min_{v_m \in chld(v_i)} \{ALST(v_m) - \overline{c_{i,m}}\} - \overline{w_i}$$

where $chld(v_i)$ is the set of immediate children of v_i and $ALST(v_{exit}) = AEST(v_{exit})$.

The average execution cost can be computed as follows:

$$\overline{w_i} = \sum_{j=1}^{p} \frac{w_{i,j}}{p}$$

and the average communication cost can be computed as follows:

$$\overline{c_{i,j}} = \overline{S} + \overline{R} \cdot \mu_{i,j}$$

where $\overline{S}$ is the average communication startup cost over all machines and $\overline{R}$ is the average communication cost per transferred byte over all machines.

The main objective of the scheduling process is to determine the assignment of tasks of a given application to a given machine (processor) set P such that the scheduling length (makespan) is minimized satisfying all precedence constraints.

19.3 THE SUGGESTED ALGORITHM

This section presents the suggested algorithm. The algorithm is called the Heterogeneous Critical Tasks Reverse Duplicator (HCTRD) and is based on list scheduling and task duplication. It works for a bounded number of heterogeneous machines and aims to achieve high performance and low complexity. The algorithm consists of two phases. The first phase is the listing phase, which is a lower-bound complexity-listing mechanism. The second phase is the machine assignment phase, which is a fast and near-lower-bound complexity-duplication mechanism. The suggested listed mechanisms have been presented with one of the selecting methodologies in [10].

19.3.1 Listing Mechanism

In contrast to the classical prioritization of list scheduling, this section presents a listing mechanism to build the list. The main idea of the suggested listing mechanism (Figure 19.2) comes from the fact that delaying a critical task (CT) will delay its child critical task. A CT is defined as the task that has zero difference between its *AEST* and *ALST*. Based on this fact, the mechanism tries to add the CTs (starting from the entry task and ending at the exit task) to the list (L) as early as possible. To achieve this goal, the mechanism should add the unlisted parents of each CT to L before adding the CT itself.

Selecting the CTs to be added to L as early as possible divides the application graph into a set of unlisted parent trees. The root of each parent tree is a CT. The simplest and most direct method to add the CT parent tree to L is to check the CT parents in depth first, starting from the CT itself, and to add a parent to L if it does not have any unlisted parents. Different selection methodologies are used in adding the CT parents, such as task maximum out-degree, highest average static level, and smallest *ALST*. The smallest *ALST* methodology is selected to be the parent listing method for the main mechanism since it has the best performance.

The algorithm starts with an empty listing queue L and an auxiliary stack S that contains the CTs pushed in decreasing order of their *ALST*s, that is, the entry task is on the top of S [$top(S)$]. Consequently, $top(S)$ is examined. If $top(S)$ has unlisted parents (i.e., has parents not in L), then the parent with the smallest *ALST* is pushed on the stack. Otherwise, $top(S)$ is popped and enqueued into L. The DAG in Figure 19.1 has four CTs, which are (v_1, v_3, v_7, and v_{10}). The listing trace is given in Table 19.1. The parent trees and the order of all tasks in L are as shown in Figure 19.3

---

traverse the graph downward and compute *AEST* for each task,
traverse the graph upward and compute *ALST* for each task,
push CTs on the stack S in reverse order of their *ALST*,
    while S is not empty **do**
        if there are unlisted parents of $top(S)$
        then
            push the parent with the smallest *ALST* on S
        else
            pop the $top(S)$ and enqueue it to L

Figure 19.2 The listing heuristic.

Table 19.1   Listing trace of the suggested heuristic

Step	$top(s)$	Checked parents	Pushed on S	Popped from S
1	1	—	—	1
2	3	—	—	3
3	7	4	4	—
4	4	—	—	4
5	7	—	—	7
6	10	8, 9	9	—
7	9	5	5	—
8	5	—	—	5
9	9	—	—	9
10	10	8	8	—
11	8	2, 6	2	—
12	2	—	—	2
13	8	6	6	—
14	6	—	—	6
15	8	—	—	8
16	10	—	—	10

19.3.2   Duplication Mechanism

This section presents the suggested duplication mechanism (Figure 19.4) that is used for the machine assignment phase. Basically, the task-duplication algorithms try to duplicate the parent tree or some selected parents of the current selected task to an unbounded number of machines. The goal of this duplication is to minimize or optimize the starting time of the duplicated parents in order to select the machine

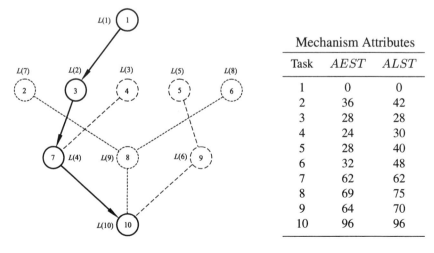

Task	$AEST$	$ALST$
1	0	0
2	36	42
3	28	28
4	24	30
5	28	40
6	32	48
7	62	62
8	69	75
9	64	70
10	96	96

Mechanism Attributes

Figure 19.3   Parent trees and task order.

while not the end of L **do**
    dequeue v_i from L
    for each machine p_q in the machine set P **do**
        compute $TFT(v_i, p_q)$
    select the machine p_m that minimizes TFT of v_i
    select v_{cp} and v_{cp2} of v_i
    if the duplication condition is satisfied
        if $TST(v_{cp}, p_m) \leq RT(p_m)$
            duplicate v_{cp} on p_m at $RT(p_m)$
            $RT(p_m) = RT(p_m) + w_{cp,m}$
        else
            duplicate v_{cp} on p_m at $TST(v_{cp}, p_m)$
            $RT(p_m) = TFT(v_{cp}, p_m)$
        if $DAT(v_{cp2}, p_m) > RT(p_m)$
            assign v_i to p_m at $DAT(v_{cp2}, p_m)$
            $RT(p_m) = DAT(v_{cp2}, p_m) + w_{i,m}$
        else
            assign v_i to p_m at $RT(p_m)$
            $RT(p_m) = RT(p_m) + w_{i,m}$
    else
        assign task v_i to p_m at $TST(v_i, p_m)$
        $RT(p_m) = TFT(v_i, p_m)$

Figure 19.4   The duplication mechanism.

that minimizes the starting time of the selected task. This big number of duplications increases the algorithm complexity while optimality is still far from being achieved. It is also impractical to consider an unbounded number of machines as a target computation environment.

In contrast to the basic idea for general duplication algorithms, the suggested mechanism selects the machine then checks for duplication. Instead of examining one task at each step, the mechanism examines one task and one parent, which does not increase the complexity of the basic noninsertion-based machine assignment mechanism. The main ideas of the suggested duplication mechanism are to:

1. Select the machine that minimizes the finish time of the current selected task.
2. Examine the idle time left by the selected task on the selected machine for duplicating one selected parent.
3. Confirm this duplication if it will reduce the starting time of the current selected task.

The following six definitions should be given to clarify the suggested mechanism.

Definition 1. The Task Finish Time on a machine (*TFT*) is defined as:

$$TFT(v_i, p_q) = \max_{v_n \in prnt(v_i)} \{RT(p_q), FT(v_n) + k.c_{n,i}\} + w_{i,q}$$

where:
$prnt(v_i)$ is the set of immediate parents of v_i
$RT(p_q)$ is the time when p_q is available
$FT(v_n)$ is the finish time of the scheduled parent v_n
$k = 1$ if the machine assigned to parent v_n is not p_q and, $k = 0$ otherwise

Definition 2. The Task Start Time on a machine (*TST*) is defined as:

$$TST(v_i, p_q) = TFT(v_i, p_q) - w_{i,q}$$

Definition 3. The Duplication Time Slot (*DST*) is defined as:

$$DTS(v_i, p_m) = TST(v_i, p_m) - RT(p_m)$$

Definition 4. The Critical Parent (*CP*) is the parent v_{cp} (scheduled on p_q) of v_i (tentatively scheduled on p_m) whose data arrival time at v_i is the latest.

Definition 5. $DAT(v_{cp2}, p_m)$ is the data arrival time of the *second* critical parent v_{cp2} on p_m.

Definition 6. The duplication condition is:

$$DTS(v_i, p_m) > w_{cp,m} \quad \text{and} \quad TFT(v_{cp}, p_m) < TST(v_i, p_m)$$

The machine assignment trace preserving the communication heterogeneity of the application graph in Figure 19.1 using the list generated by the suggested listing mechanism is shown in Table 19.2. The second and third columns indicate the selected task and machine in each step, the fourth column indicates the critical parent task, the fifth column indicates whether the duplication condition is satisfied, and the last column indicates the finish time before and after duplication. The resulting assignment is presented in Figure 19.5, where the gray tasks are the duplicated tasks.

19.3.3 Algorithm Complexity Analysis

Complexity is usually expressed in terms of the number of tasks v, the number of edges e, and the number of machines p:

- The complexity of computing the *AEST* and *ALST* of all tasks is $O(e + v)$.
- The complexity of listing all unlisted parent trees is $O(e + v)$.
- The complexity of assigning all tasks to p machines using the duplication mechanism or nonduplication is $O(pv^2)$.

Table 19.2 Machine assignment trace of the suggested duplication mechanism

Step	Select v	Select p	CP	Duplications condition satisfied?	Finish time Before duplication	After duplication
1	1	2	—	—	15	15
2	3	2	1	no	20	20
3	4	2	1	no	39	39
4	7	2	3	no	51	51
5	5	1	1	yes	41	38
6	9	2	5	no	57	57
7	2	3	1	yes	46	22
8	6	3	1	no	47	47
9	8	1	4	yes	74	71
10	10	1	9	no	81	81

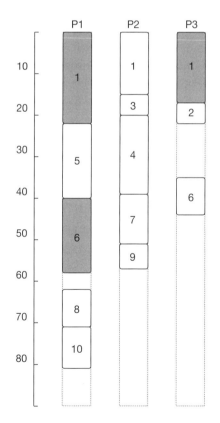

Figure 19.5 Scheduling of Figure 19.1 application graph preserving communication heterogeneity.

The total algorithm complexity is $O(e + v) + O(pv^2)$. Taking into account that e is $O(v^2)$, the total algorithm complexity is $O(pv^2)$.

19.4   HETEROGENEOUS SYSTEMS SCHEDULING HEURISTICS

This section briefly overviews the list-scheduling algorithms that we will use for a comparison with HCTRD. These algorithms are: Fast Load Balancing (FLB-f) [11], Heterogeneous Earliest Finish Time (HEFT) [12], and Critical Path on a Processor (CPOP) [12].

19.4.1   Fast Load Balancing (FLB-f) Algorithm

The FLB-f algorithm [11] utilizes a list called the ready list, which contains all ready tasks to be scheduled at each step. The ready task is defined as the task that has all its parents scheduled. In each step, the execution finish time for each ready task in the ready list is computed in all machines and the task–machine pair that minimizes the earliest execution finish time is selected. The complexity of the FLB-f algorithm is $O(vlogv + e)$.

19.4.2   Heterogeneous Earliest Finish Time (HEFT) Algorithm

The HEFT algorithm [12] has two phases. The first is a task prioritizing phase, in which the upward rank attribute is computed for each task and a task list is generated by sorting the tasks in decreasing order of the upward rank. The second phase is the machine assignment phase, in which tasks are selected in order of their priorities and are assigned to the best machine that minimizes the task finish time in an insertion-based manner. The complexity of the HEFT algorithm is $O(pv^3)$

19.4.3   Critical Path on a Processor (CPOP) Algorithm

The CPOP algorithm [12] has two phases: task prioritizing and machine assignment. In the task prioritizing phase, two attributes are used: the upward and downward ranks. Each task is labeled with the sum of upward and downward ranks. A priority queue is used to maintain the ready tasks at a given instant (initially, it contains the entry task). At any instant, the ready task with the highest priority is selected for machine assignment. In the machine assignment phase, the critical path machine is defined as the machine that minimizes the cumulative computation cost of the tasks on the critical path. If the selected task is on the critical path, it is assigned to the critical path machine; otherwise, it is assigned to a machine that minimizes the finishing execution time of the task. The complexity of the CPOP algorithm is $O(pv^2)$.

19.5   EXPERIMENTAL RESULTS AND DISCUSSION

This section presents a performance comparison of the HCTRD algorithm with the algorithms presented above. For this purpose, we consider two sets of graphs as the workload: random generated application graphs, and graphs that represent some numerical real-world problems. Several metrics were used for the performance evaluation. To be able to compare it with the other algorithm, homogeneous communication links are assumed and the average communication cost is considered as the communication cost. Finally, the performance of the different selection methods suggested to select the unlisted parents is examined. Also, the performance of the suggested duplication mechanism will be compared with the existing machine assignment mechanisms.

19.5.1 Comparison Metrics

The comparisons of the algorithms are based on the following metrics.

19.5.1.1 Makespan   The makespan, or scheduling length, is defined as:

$$makespan = FT(v_{exit})$$

where: $FT(v_{exit})$ is the finishing time of the scheduled exit task.

19.5.1.2 Scheduling Length Ratio (SLR)   The main performance measure is the makespan. Since a large set of application graphs with different properties is used, it is necessary to normalize the schedule length to the lower bound, which is called the Schedule Length Ratio (SLR). The SLR is defined as:

$$SLR = \frac{makespan}{\sum\limits_{v_i \in CP} \min_{p_j \in P} \{w_{i,j}\}}$$

The denominator is the sum of the minimum computation costs of the tasks on a critical path *CP*. The *SLR* of a graph cannot be less than one, since the denominator is the lower bound. We utilized average *SLR* values over a number of generated task graphs in our experiments.

19.5.1.3 Quality of Schedule   This is the percentage number of times that an algorithm produced a better (B), equal (E), or worse (W) schedule compared to every other algorithm in an experiment.

19.5.2 Random Graph Generator

The random graph generator was implemented to generate application graphs with various characteristics. The generator requires the following input parameters:

- Number of tasks in graph v
- Graph levels *GL*
- Heterogeneity factor β, where w_i is generated randomly for each task and (using a randomly selected β from β set for each p_j) $w_{i,j} = \beta \cdot w_i \ \forall v_i$ on p_j

- Communication to computation ratio *CCR*, which is defined as the ratio of the average communication cost $(\frac{1}{e}\sum_{i=1}^{v}\sum_{j=1}^{v}\overline{c_{i,j}})$ to the average computation cost $(\frac{1}{v}\sum_{i=1}^{v}\overline{w_i})$

In all experiments, only graphs with a single entry and a single exit node were considered. The input parameters were restricted to the following values:

$v \in \{20, 40, 60, 80, 100, 120\}$

$0.2v \le GL \le 0.8v$

$\beta \in \{0.5, 1.0, 2.0\}$

$CCR \in \{0.5, 1.0, 2.0\}$

19.5.3   Performance Results

The performances of the algorithms were compared with respect to graph size and with respect to the number of available machines.

Sixteen (16) heterogeneous machines were used in the performance evaluation with respect to graph size. The average *SLR* values for each set of 10,000 application graphs (with a selected v and random *GL*, β, and *CCR*) are shown in Figure 19.6. The quality of the schedules was as shown in Table 19.3.

The number of available machines used in the second experiment is $p \in \{4, 8, 16, 32\}$. For each number of available machines, a set of 3000 application graphs was generated for each $v = \{40, 80, 120\}$. The CCR, GL and β were selected randomly from the above CCR, GL, and β sets for each graph. The average SLR for the 9000 generated graphs for each number of available machines was as shown in Figure 19.7. The quality of the schedules was as shown in Table 19.4.

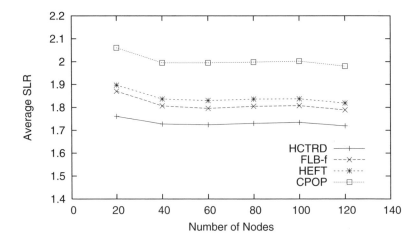

Figure 19.6   Average SLR of random generated graphs with respect to graph size.

19.5.4 Applications

In addition to random-generated application graphs, the performance of the suggested algorithm was examined in the basis of two real-world applications: Gaussian elimination and Laplace equation.

19.5.4.1 Gaussian Elimination   The structure of the application graph is defined in Gaussian elimination. The number of tasks v, and the number of graph levels GL depends on matrix size m. In the performance evaluation with respect to ma-

Table 19.3 Schedule quality of random generated graphs with respect to graph size

		FLB-f	HEFT	CPOP
HCTRD	B	76.39%	85.92%	95.7%
	E	3.24%	2.99%	1.96%
	W	20.38%	11.1%	2.27%

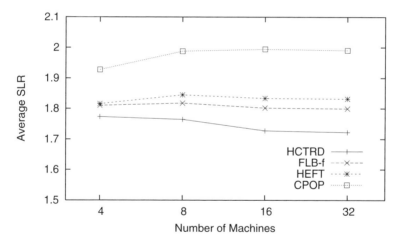

Figure 19.7 Average SLR of random generated graphs with respect to number of available machines.

Table 19.4 Schedule quality of random generated graphs with respect to number of available machines

		FLB-f	HEFT	CPOP
HCTRD	B	74.49%	83.61%	94.61%
	E	2.25%	1.8%	1.23%
	W	23.26%	14.59%	4.16%

trix size, only *CCR* and β were selected randomly for each *m*, and 16 heterogeneous machines were used as a target computing system. Figure 19.8 presents the average SLR of 1000 generated graphs for each matrix size $m \in \{4, 8, 16\}$, and the quality of the schedules was as shown in Table 19.5.

The number of available machines used in the second experiment is $p \in \{4, 8, 16, 32\}$. For each number of available machines, a set of 500 application graphs was generated for each $m \in \{8, 16\}$. The CCR, GL and β were selected randomly from the above CCR, GL, and β sets for each graph. The average SLR for 1000 generated graphs for each number of available machines was as shown in Figure 19.9. The quality of the schedules was as shown in Table 19.6.

19.5.4.2 *Laplace Equation*
The structure of the Laplace equation is also defined in terms of v and *GL*. In the performance evaluation with respect to graph size, only *CCR* and β were selected randomly for each v, and 16 heterogeneous machines were used as a target computing system. Figure 19.10 presents the average SLR of 1000 graphs generated for each $v \in \{16, 32, 64, 100\}$, and Table 19.7 presents the quality of the schedules.

The number of available machines used in the second experiment is $p \in \{4, 8, 16, 32\}$. For each number of available machines, a set of 500 application graphs

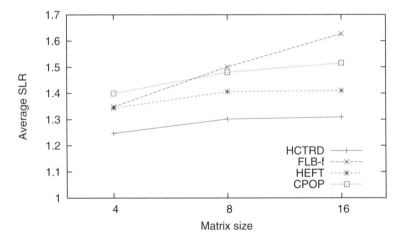

Figure 19.8 Average SLR of Gaussian elimination with respect to graph size.

Table 19.5 Schedule quality of Gaussian elimination with respect to graph size

		FLB-f	HEFT	CPOP
HCTRD	B	91.83%	83.27%	90.13%
	E	5.03%	12.53%	6.6%
	W	3.13%	4.2%	3.27%

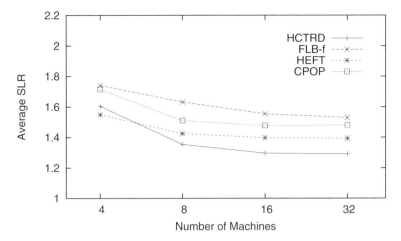

Figure 19.9   Average SLR of Gaussian elimination with respect to number of available machines.

Table 19.6   Schedule quality of Gaussian elimination with respect to number of available machines

		FLB-f	HEFT	CPOP
HCTRD	B	94.65%	75.38%	92.25%
	E	0.13%	2.75%	0.78%
	W	5.23%	21.88%	6.98%

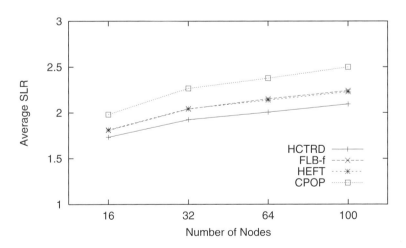

Figure 19.10   Average SLR of the Laplace equation with respect to CCR.

was generated for each $v \in \{36, 100\}$ using a random selection of CCR and β from the above sets for each graph. The average SLR for 1000 generated graphs for each number of available machines was as shown in Figure 19.11. The quality of the schedules was as shown in Table 19.8

19.5.5 Performance of Parents-Selection Methods

The suggested listing mechanism has four methods for selecting the unlisted parents of a critical task. These methods are:

Table 19.7   Schedule quality of the Laplace equation with respect to graph size

		FLB-f	HEFT	CPOP
HCTRD	B	77.43%	77.58%	91.93%
	E	1.98%	3.1%	1.78%
	W	20.6%	19.33%	6.3%

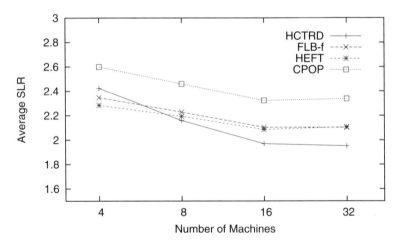

Figure 19.11   Average SLR of the Laplace equation with respect to number of available machines.

Table 19.8   Schedule quality of the Laplace equation with respect to number of available machines

		FLB-f	HEFT	CPOP
HCTRD	B	68.18%	63.55%	89.98%
	E	0.95%	1.03%	0.43%
	W	30.88%	35.43%	9.6%

1. Select parents in post order, depth first or simply the parent with the Lower Index (*LI*).
2. Select the parent with the smallest *ALST* (*sALST*).
3. Select the parent with the maximum *Out Degree* (*mOD*).
4. Select the parent with the highest Average Static Level (*hASL*), where the ASL can be computed recursively by traversing the DAG upward starting from the exit task v_{exit}:

$$ASL(v_i) = \overline{w_i} + \max_{v_m \in chld(v_i)} \{ASL(v_m)\},$$

where $chld(v_i)$ is the set of immediate children of v_i and $ASL(v_{exit}) = \overline{w_{exit}}$.

The random-generated-graphs experiment was used to examine the performance of the four suggested methods of unlisted parents selection with respect to graph size and with respect to number of available machines. Figure 19.12 and Figure 19.13 show the average *SLR* with respect to graph size and with respect to number of available machines, respectively.

19.5.6 Performance of the Machine Assignment Mechanism

This section examines the performance of the suggested duplication mechanism (RD) for machine assignment compared with the existing machine assignment mechanisms. Two machine assignment mechanisms have been presented in the literature: noninsertion-based (NI) with complexity $O(pv^2)$ and insertion-based (IB) with complexity $O(pv^3)$. The noninsertion-based mechanism tries to minimize the start or finish time of a task by considering only the ready time of a machine,

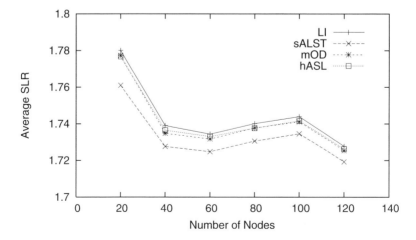

Figure 19.12 Average SLR of selection methods with respect to CCR.

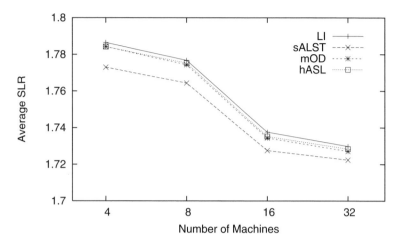

Figure 19.13 Average SLR of selection methods with respect to number of available machines.

whereas insertion based mechanism considers the idle time left by the previous assigned tasks in addition to the machine ready time.

The performance of the mechanisms was examined using randomly generated graphs with various characteristics. The same number of generated graphs with the same characteristics as in the random-generated-graphs experiment are used. A modified version of MCP [8] is used to generate L for each generated graph. Table 19.9 and Table 19.10 show the percentage of better schedules for each mechanism

Table 19.9 Schedules with better quality of machine assignment mechanisms with respect to graph size

	RD	IB	NI
RD		90.98%	93.93%
IB	3.72%		49%
NI	0.85%	5.32%	

Table 19.10 Schedules with better quality of machine assignment mechanisms with respect to number of available machines

	RD	IB	NI
RD		91.17%	95.44%
IB	5.06%		53.03%
NI	0.97%	5.61%	

in comparison with the other mechanisms with respect to graph size and with respect to number of available machines, respectively.

19.5.7   Summary and Discussion of Experimental Results

The performance of the suggested algorithm was examined in comparison with the most recent algorithms. Three types of application graphs were used: random-generated graphs, Gaussian elimination, and Laplace equation. A huge number of graphs with various characteristics were generated for each application. The performance of the examined algorithms was measured with respect to graph size and number of available machines. Mainly, the suggested algorithm outperformed all other algorithms in terms of the performance and complexity. Only in one case, when the number of available machines was small (four machines), did the HEFT algorithm perform better. Four selection methods of unlisted parents selection were examined: *sALST*, *mOD*, *hASL*, and *LI*. *sALST* has the best performance, *mOD* and *hASL* have almost the same performance, and *LI* has the lowest performance of all. The duplication mechanism (RD) outperformed all other machine assignment mechanisms.

19.6   CONCLUSION

In this chapter, we presented the HCTRD algorithm for scheduling tasks onto a bounded number of heterogeneous machines. The algorithm handles both computation and communication heterogeneity. The algorithm suggested a lower-bound complexity listing mechanism instead of the classical prioritization phase. A near-lower-bound complexity duplication mechanism is also suggested for machine assignment. Based on the experimental study using a large set of randomly generated application graphs with various characteristics and application graphs of real-world problems (such as Gaussian elimination, and Laplace equation), HCTRD outperformed the other algorithms in terms of performance and complexity. In conclusion, simple schedulers should be used in compiling parallel application programs. It would be better to use, for example, two simple scheduling algorithms and to select the better schedule in real compilers.

REFERENCES

1. J. G. Webster, Heterogeneous Distributed Computing, *Encyclopedia of Electrical and Electronics Engineering,* Vol. 8, pp. 679–690, 1999.

2. D. Feitelson, L. Rudolph, U. Schwiegelshohm, K. Sevcik, and P. Wong, Theory and Practice in Parallel Job Scheduling, in *Job Scheduling Strategies for Parallel Processing,* Springer LNCS 949, pp. 337–360, 1995.

3. J. Liou and M. Palis, A Comparison of General Approaches to Multiprocessor Scheduling, in *Proceedings of International Parallel Processing Symposium,* pp. 152–156, 1997.

4. A. Khan, C. McCreary, and M. Jones, A Comparison of Multiprocessor Scheduling Heuristics, *ICPP, 2,* 243–250, 1994.

5. Y. Kwok and I. Ahmad, A Comparison of Task-Duplication-Based Algorithms for Scheduling Parallel Programs to Message-Passing Systems, in *Proceedings of International Symposium of High-Performance Computing Systems (HPCS'97),* pp. 39–50, 1997.

6. T. Braun, H. Siegel, N. Beck, L. Bni, M. Maheswaran, A. Reuther, J. Robertson, M. Theys, B. Yao, D. Hensgen, and R. Freund, A Comparison Study of Static Mapping Heuristics for a Class of Meta-tasks on Heterogeneous Computing Systems, in *Heterogeneous Computing Workshop,* pp. 15–29, 1999.

7. Y. Kwok and I. Ahmad, Benchmarking and Comparison of the Task Graph Scheduling Algorithms, *Journal of Parallel and Distributed Computing, 59,* 3, 381–422, 1999.

8. W. Min-You and D. Gajski, Hypertool: A Programming Aid for Message-Passing Systems, *IEEE Transactions on Parallel and Distributed Systems, 1*(3), 330–343, 1990.

9. G. Sih and E. Lee, A Compile-Time Scheduling Heuristic for Interconnection-Constrained Heterogeneous Processor Architectures, *IEEE Transactions on Parallel Distributed Systems, 4,* 2, 175–187, 1993.

10. T. Hagras and J. Janecek, A Simple Scheduling Heuristic for Heterogeneous Computing Environments, in *IEEE Proceedings of Second International Symposium on Parallel and Distributed Computing (ISPDC'03),* pp. 104–110, October 2003.

11. A. Radulescu and A. van Gemund, Fast and Effective Task Scheduling in Heterogeneous Systems, in *9th Heterogeneous Computing Workshop,* pp. 229–238, 2000.

12. H. Topcuoglu, S. Hariri, and W. Min-You, Performance-Effective and Low-Complexity Task Scheduling for Heterogeneous Computing, *IEEE Transactions on Parallel and Distributed Systems, 13,* 3, 260–274, 2002.

13. S. Darbha and D. Agrawal, A Fast and Scalable Scheduling Algorithm for Distributed Memory systems, in *Proceedings of Symposium on Parallel and Distributed Processing,* pp. 60–63, 1995.

14. I. Ahmed and Y. Kwork, A New Approach to Scheduling Parallel Program Using Task Duplication, in *International Conference on Parallel Processing,* Vol. 2, pp. 47–51, 1994.

15. H. Chen, B. Shirazi, and J. Marquis, Performance Evaluation of a Novel Scheduling Method: Linear Clustering with Task Duplication, in *Proceedings of International Conference on Parallel and Distributed Systems,* pp. 270–275, 1993.

16. G. Park, B. Shirazi, and J. Marquis, DFRN: A New Approach for Duplication Based Scheduling for Distributed Memory Multiprocessor System, in *Proceedings of International Conference, Parallel Processing,* pp. 157–166, 1997.

## CHAPTER 20

An On-Line Approach for Classifying and Extracting Application Behavior in Linux

LUCIANO JOSÉ SENGER, RODRIGO FERNANDES DE MELLO,
MARCOS JOSÉ SANTANA, REGINA HELENA CARLUCCI SANTANA,
and LAURENCE TIANRUO YANG

20.1 INTRODUCTION

Technological evolution has allowed distributed systems, which are grouped on autonomous computers linked by distinct networks, to support a variety of workloads, including parallel, sequential, and interactive jobs [2]. When used to support parallel applications (i.e., computing applications composed of a communicating task group), distributed computers are treated as distributed processing elements (PEs) and compose a distributed memory MIMD (multiple instruction, multiple data) parallel architecture [21]. One of the challenges in such systems is to develop load balancing algorithms that assign the tasks of parallel applications to processing elements.

The load balancing algorithms are responsible for the decision making related to the process or task scheduling in a certain environment. This scheduling aims to distribute, in an equal way, the occupation of the available computing resources, consequently increasing the application performance [7, 12, 16, 32, 34, 37, 48, 61]. This distribution should be compatible with the capacity of each resource in the environment in order to avoid overload of some resources and idleness of the remaining ones.

The load balancing algorithms are composed of the following policies:

1. Transference policy that identifies the computers that send and receive processes. After this identification is done, the sender and receiver computers synchronize themselves for the process transference. The senders, also known as servers, are overloaded computers. The receivers are idle ones.

High-Performance Computing: Paradigm and Infrastructure. Edited by L. T. Yang and M. Guo   **381**
Copyright © 2006 John Wiley & Sons, Inc.

2. Selection policy that is responsible for deciding which processes should be transferred. The transference or migration aims to redistribute the load on a certain environment.

3. Location policy that aims to find the best process-receiving computer for the best sending one, or vice-versa. The best sender is defined as the most overloaded computer in the system. The best receiver is defined as the idlest one.

4. Information policy that defines what information is used and how it is used to characterize a single load index for the computers. This index is used by the location policy to find the senders and receivers. The policy set composes the decision-making process of the load balancing algorithms, which are essentially focused on the choice of efficient load indexes.

Efficient load indexes use the information on the resource occupation in the system. Following this line of thought, work has been proposed for data acquisition, information generation, and analysis [15, 23]. However, this work does not present on-line techniques for the obtainment of information that allows information usage with low intrusion and little influence on the computing system performance.

Motivated by the data acquisition and information generation that allow decision making by load balancing algorithms, this chapter presents a knowledge acquisition model that allows Linux process classification in accordance with the resources' usage behavior. This model uses an artificial self-organizing neural network architecture and specialized algorithms for the labeling and creation of a transition-state diagram. This model implementation in the Linux kernel allows the monitoring and classification of any process being executed in the system. The main objective is to use this classification on the selection and transference policies of load balancing algorithms, with the aim of analyzing the impacts on the process migration based on their resources's occupation features. The text is organized in the following sections. Section 20.2 discusses related works. Section 20.3 deals with the information acquisition of processes being executed in the Linux system. Section 20.4 presents the knowledge acquisition model, with a description of the neural architecture, labeling algorithm, and implementation of the model in the Linux kernel. The results obtained by the model utilization are described in Section 20.5. The evaluation of the model intrusion with regard to system performance is presented on Section 20.6. In Section 20.7, final considerations of this work are made.

20.2 RELATED WORK

Several works have been undertaken in the load balancing area, of which we highlight the ones by Zhou and Ferrari [61], Shivaratri et al. [48] and Mello et al. [35, 36]. Other works have been undertaken, but they do not seem to represent relevant contributions to the improvement of process global performance [1, 15, 18, 19, 25, 28, 29, 30, 33, 39, 40, 41, 42, 43, 44, 51, 53, 58, 59, 60, 62]. Zhou and Ferrari [61] evaluated five load balancing algorithms initiated by the server, that is, the most overloaded computer. The evaluated algorithms were the following: Disted, Global,

Central, Random, and Lowest. It was concluded that all of them increase performance when compared to an environment with no load balancing at all. Out of the analyzed algorithms, Lowest showed the highest performance as it generates on-demand messages for the process transference, which results in less overload on the communication links. Thus, Lowest provides the system with an incremental increase, as the number of messages generated in the environment does not depend on the number of computers.

Shivaratri et al. [48] analyzed the algorithms initiated by the receptor and by the server (symmetrically initiated, adaptive symmetrically initiated, and adaptive initiated). They concluded that algorithms initiated by the receptor show a higher performance than the ones initiated by the server, such as Lowest. In addition, it was observed that the highest-performance algorithm was the stable, symmetrically initiated one that preserves a history of the load information in the system and makes decisions on the process transference based on this information.

Later on, Mello et al. [35] developed a new load balancing algorithm named TLBA (Tree Load Balancing Algorithm), which, on simulations and through a prototype, has showed performance gains when compared to the stable, symmetrically initiated algorithm. These results use the decrease in the process execution time as well as in the number of messages to synchronize historical information on the environment resources occupation.

The adoption of techniques that use historical information for load balancing [35, 36, 48] has motivated the development of this work, which, through a knowledge basis, aims to extract and classify the process behavior. The process behavior is used as decision-making support by the selection and location policies.

Nowadays, the historical information used by the selection and location policies are used to define the load indexes on the environment. These indexes allow the quantification of the process occupation and the impacts that the transference of such processes may cause to the computer that emits or receives them. In addition, they do not allow the prediction of performance gains of all processes executed in the environment.

Work related to the extraction of features and acquisition of knowledge on parallel applications may be applied to the selection and transference policies of the load balancing algorithms. Devarakonda and Iyer [15] present a statistical approach for predicting CPU time, file I/O, and memory requirements of a program. For this purpose, the authors use statistical clustering (k-means algorithm) and a Markovian model to identify high-density regions of programs' resource usage. Feitelson et al. [17] observe that repeated runs of the same application tend to have similar patterns of resource usage and that much information related to the application behavior can be discovered without explicit user cooperation. A historical application profiler is presented by Gibbons [23]. This profiler is used to classify parallel applications in categories based on static templates composed of attributes such as user (who submits the application), executable name, and selected scheduler queue. These templates are used to group applications and to generate average run times and other statistical values of each created group. These derived values are used for run-time prediction of parallel applications. Smith et al. [50] review this profiler work, presenting a technique to derive predictions for run times of parallel applications from the run times of similar applications previously executed, using search techniques to dynamically determine which application characteristics (i.e., templates) yield the best definition of similarity. Silva and Scherson [49] investigate the use of runtime measurements to improve job scheduling. The authors use Bayesian estimators and fuzzy logic to construct a model to classify the application and improve gang scheduling decisions. Arpacci-Dusseau et al. [3] propose a gang scheduling scheme that uses the information gathered by execution of parallel applications. This information is employed to improve a gang scheduling coordination scheme. Corbalan et al. [13] put forward a hypothesis that scheduling software must make decisions about the number of resources assigned to the application, based not only on the user request but also on the information provided by execution of applications, aiming at guaranteeing efficient resource usage. The authors use this information and explore the malleability of the application to consider improvements in gang scheduling strategies. Previous works use knowledge of each parallel submitted application, but they do not present a consistent organization for storing acquired knowledge for future use. Moreover, the obtained knowledge is not easily expanded. This is not desirable when it is important to update knowledge at the arrival of new information. By analyzing the literature, it can be seen that the research concerning these characteristics and knowledge extraction are directed at specific scheduling policies, evidencing the need for defining and implementing the organization of automatic knowledge acquisition, which would be useful for different load balancing algorithms.

20.3   INFORMATION ACQUISITION

The instrumentation is carried out through the addition of a data structure to the process table of the Linux operating system. On Linux, the process table is defined in the source file `include/linux/sched.h`, through a data structure `task struct`. The structure that implements the process table has fields for the storage of process information such as status, memory usage, credentials (user and group), resource utilization limits, semaphores, used file system, and open files [6].

The new added structure is called `accounting_struct` and its fields are counters associated with each process. The variable added to the process table, from the `accounting_struct` type, is called `acct`. Such counters store the number of reading or writing operations on files or on the communication network, as well as the quantity of information involved in each operation. In network operations, there are specific counters for the TCP and UDP protocols. These protocols are monitored by the fact that message passing environments, such as the PVM [5] and the MPI [38], use them in the communication among processes that make up a parallel application. In addition, such protocols are an actual pattern for the communication among processes in the Linux environment. The created counters are shown in Table 20.1.

This counter updating is always made through the process that executes any of the monitored functions. For instance, if a process executes the reading of a certain

Table 20.1 Structure `accounting_struct` added to the Linux process table

Counter	Stored information
io_calls_read	Quantity of reading operations on file
io_bytes_read	Quantity of bytes transferred on file reading
io_calls_write	Quantity of writing operations on file
io_bytes_write	Quantity of bytes transferred on file writing
tcp_calls_read	Quantity of reading operations on *sockets* TCP
tcp_calls_write	Quantity of writing operations on *sockets* TCP
tcp_bytes_read	Quantity of bytes transferred (readings) on *sockets* TCP
tcp_bytes_write	Quantity of bytes transferred (writings) on *sockets* TCP
udp_calls_read	Quantity of reading operations on *sockets* UDP
udp_calls_write	Quantity of writing operations on *sockets* UDP
udp_bytes_read	Quantity of transferred bytes (readings) on *sockets* UDP
udp_bytes_write	Quantity of bytes transferred (writings) on *sockets* UDP
last_utime	Instant of the latest counter reading

file, the counters `io_calls_read` and `io_bytes_read` are updated. Table 20.2 illustrates the files of the kernel source code that were modified to perform the system instrumentation required for the updating of the structure counters account.

The counters have their values set at zero at the time the process is created. In the Linux system, the `clone` and `fork` system calls are used for process creation. Such calls create a copy (child process) exactly equal to the original process (parent process), so that all other processes in the system are organized in a tree format structure [52]. Internally, such calls invoke the kernel routine `do_fork()`. This routine is directly responsible for the creation of a process, by copying the data segment of the parent process and adjusting the values of the registers. The `do_fork()` routine is located on the source file `kernel/fork.c`. This routine is modified to mark as zero the counters' value at process creation. This initialization is important so that the subsequent readings of these counters will not obtain incoherent values.

In the system kernel, the pointer `current` is the reference for the current process that is requesting services of the kernel. This pointer makes reference to the function `get_current()`, located on the `include/asm/current.h` file, which sends back a pointer to the `task_struct` structure. In the instrumentation of the system kernel, this pointer is frequently referred to as the updating and collection of the counter values are added to the process table.

Table 20.2 Kernel source files modified for the instrumentation

Source file	Description
include/linux/sched.h	Data structure of the process table
kernel/fork.c	Processes creation
mm/filemap.c	Reading and writing on file descriptors
net/socket.c	Reading and writing on *sockets*

The reading routines in files are instrumented through the alteration on the source file `mm/filemap.c`. In this file, the following modifications have been made:

- The function `generic_file_read()` is modified to register the reading operations in the file counters `io_calls_read` and `io_bytes_read`.
- The function `generic_file_write()` is modified to register the writing in the files counters `io_calls_write` and `io_bytes_write`.

The access points to the TCP/IP protocols are implemented in the code stored in the file `net/socket.c`. In this file, the following modifications have been made:

- The function `sock_read()` is modified to register the reading operations in *sockets* TCP in the counters `tcp_calls_read` and `tcp_bytes_read`.
- The function `sock write()` is modified to register the writing operations in *sockets* TCP in the counters `tcp_calls_write` and `tcp_bytes_write`.
- The function `sys_recvfrom()` is modified to register the reading operations in *sockets* UDP in the counters `udp_calls_read` and `udp_bytes_read`.
- The function `sys_sendto()` is modified to register the reading operations in *sockets* UDP in the counters `udp_calls_read` and `udp_bytes_read`.
- The function `sock_readv_writev()` is modified to register the reading and bytes transferred in TCP sockets, when the `readv()` and `writev()` system calls are invoked by Linux processes.

20.4 LINUX PROCESS CLASSIFICATION MODEL

The knowledge acquisition aimed at the classification of Linux process behavior is conducted through the utilization of an artificial self-organizing neural network architecture [45, 46, 47]. In neural networks, the processing is inspired by the functioning of biological neural structures and carried out by a set of processing units distributed and interconnected through synaptic links [26]. Artificial neural networks have the ability of obtaining knowledge from a set of examples and generalizing it, thus allowing the construction of prediction and classification models that work in a manner similar to the way the brain functions.

The network architecture defines the way the processing units are organized. Of the different architectures, self-organizing and nonsupervised architectures have been successfully used on nonlabeled data classification tasks. Nonsupervised learning means that the network is able to learn with nonlabeled input patterns, that is, without using an external supervising mechanism, just opposite to the networks with supervised learning, where the network receives a training set composed of input and output pairs. Biological systems such as vision and hearing use nonsupervised learning [14]. In this kind of learning, the network has the ability to create internal representations to codify entries through a set of output or representational units. This kind of learning usually uses architectures composed of an input layer, an output layer, or representation and a set of connections or weights within these layers. In this kind of formation, the input layer accomplishes the initial processing of the input set and the output layer is responsible for the data representation, through the creation of classes, where each class describes (codifies) a subset of the input patterns. It is usual in such architectures that the implementation of the learning process is through competition, in which the units of the output layer compete among themselves to store the input pattern. The winning representation unit is chosen to represent the input pattern and then its respective weights are modified (adapted).

The ART-2A [11] architecture is used to classify the processes. The ART (Adaptive Resonance Theory) neural network family is composed of self-organizing and nonsupervised architectures that learn through stable representation codes in response to an arbitrary sequence of input patterns [9, 10]. The ability of the ART-2A network family differs from the other self-organizing architectures as it allows the user to control the degree of similarity among the patterns grouped at the same representation unit. This control allows the network to be sensitive to the differences existing in the input patterns and to be able to generate more or less classes in response to this control. Moreover, the learning in the network's ART is continuous: the network adapts itself to the incoming data, creating new processing units to learn the patterns, when required. Out of the different versions of network ART, ART-2A is notable as it allows the quick learning of the input patterns represented by continuous values. Because of its attractive features, such as noise filtering and good computing and classification performance, the neural ART network family has been used in several domains, such as to recognize Chinese characters [22], interpretation of data originated with nuclear reactor sensors [31, 56, 57], image processing [55], detection of land mines [20], treatment of satellite images [8], and robotic sensorial control [4].

The ART 2A network architecture is composed of two main components: the attention and orientation systems (Figure 20.1). The attention system is provided with

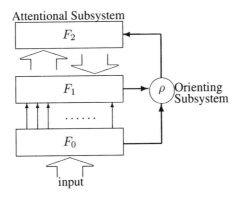

Figure 20.1   ART 2A neural network basic architecture.

an F_0 preprocessing layer, an F_1 input representation layer, and a F_2 class representation layer. The input and representation layers are interconnected through a set of adaptive weights called bottom-up ($F_1 \rightarrow F_2$) and top-down ($F_2 \rightarrow F_1$). The path from the neuron ith of layer F_1 to the neuron jth of the layer F_2 is represented by w_{ij}. Likewise, the jth neuron of layer F_2 is connected to ith neuron of layer F_1 through the adaptive weight w_{ji}. These weights multiply the signals that are sent among the neuron layers and are responsible for the storage of the knowledge obtained by the network. The interactions between the layers F_1 and F_2 are controlled by the orientation system, which uses a ρ vigilance parameter, and the way by which the weights are updated to obtain knowledge of the input patterns is defined by the training algorithm.

20.4.1   Training Algorithm

The ART-2A dynamics are determined by the $\rho \in [0, 1]$ vigilance parameter and the $\beta \in [0, 1]$ learning rate. Initially, the output layer F_2 does not have any class. In our classification model, the input pattern I^0 is composed of a set of attributes associated with the process to be classified (see Table 20.1). The ART-2A training algorithm is composed of the following stages: preprocessing, activation, search, resonance or reset, and adaptation.

20.4.1.1 *Preprocessing*   This phase performs input normalization operations I^0:

$$I = \aleph\{F_0[\aleph(I^0)]\} \tag{20.1}$$

where and F_0 describe the following operations:

$$\aleph(x) \equiv \frac{x}{\|x\|} \equiv \frac{x}{\sqrt{\sum_{i=0}^{m} x^2}}, \qquad F_0(x) = \begin{cases} x & \text{if } x > \theta \\ 0 & \text{otherwise} \end{cases} \tag{20.2}$$

Such operations perform Euclidean normalization and noise filtering. The noise filtering, through the θ parameter, only makes sense if the main features of the input patterns, which lead to the creation of different classes, are represented *exclusively* on the highest values of the input components.

20.4.1.2 *Activation*   This phase is responsible for sending out the incoming signals to the neurons of the representation layer F_2:

$$T_j = \begin{cases} I w_{ij} & \text{if } j \text{ indexes a committed prototype} \\ \alpha \Sigma_j I_j & \text{otherwise} \end{cases} \tag{20.3}$$

where T_j corresponds to the jth neuron activation on the F_2 layer. Initially, all the neurons are marked as uncommitted and become committed when their weights are adapted to learn a certain input pattern. The α choice parameter defines the maximum depth of search for a fitting cluster. With $\alpha = 0$, the value used in this work, all committed prototypes are checked before an uncommitted prototype is chosen as winner.

20.4.1.3 Search This phase is responsible for finding a candidate neuron to store the current pattern. The network competitive learning indicates that the most activated neuron is the one chosen as the candidate to represent the input pattern:

$$T_J = max \ \{T_j : \text{for all } F_2 \text{ nodes}\} \tag{20.4}$$

20.4.1.4 Resonance or reset After selecting the most activated neuron, the reset condition is tested:

$$y_J > \rho \tag{20.5}$$

If the inequality is real, the candidate neuron is chosen to store the pattern and the adaptation stage is initiated (resonance). If not, the winning neuron is inhibited and the searching stage is repeated (reset).

20.4.1.5 Adaptation This stage describes how the pattern will be learned by the network. It comprehends the updating of the network weights for the J winning neuron, which, then, becomes committed:

$$w_{Ji}^{new} = \begin{cases} \aleph[\beta\aleph\Psi + (1-\beta)w_{Ji}^{old}] & \text{if } j \text{ indexes a committed prototype} \\ I & \text{otherwise} \end{cases} \tag{20.6}$$

$$\Psi_i \equiv \begin{cases} I_i & \text{if } w_{Ji}^{old} > \theta \\ 0 & 0 \text{ otherwise} \end{cases} \tag{20.7}$$

Table 20.3 illustrates the examples of values for the ART-2A network parameters. The ρ vigilance value defines the quantity of classes that will be created by the network. The ρ value forms a circular decision boundary with a radius of $2(1-\rho)$ around the weight vector of each category [27]. With $\rho = 0$, all input patterns are

Table 20.1   ART-2A main parameters

Parameter	Description	Value example
m	Number of input units	7
n	Maximum number of representation units	15
θ	Noise suppression parameter	$\theta = \dfrac{1}{\sqrt{m}}$
β	Learning rate	$\beta = 0.7$
ρ	Vigilance parameter	$\rho = 0.9$

grouped at the same class. With $\rho = 1$, a class is created for each input pattern presented to the network. The β learning rate defines the adaptation speed of the prototypes in response to the input patterns. The ART-2A should not be used with $\beta \cong 1$, as the prototypes tend to jump among the input patterns associated with a class instead of converging to the patterns' average.

Each committed neuron of the F_2 layer defines a similar pattern group. The committed neuron set defines the classification generated by the network for the submitted values. As the input patterns over the process behavior are not previously labeled, it is required that an algorithm define a label to represent each class created by the network.

20.4.2 Labeling Algorithm

The labeling algorithm is built in accordance with the idea that the ART-2A network weights resemble the input patterns that have been learned by a certain neuron of the F_2 layer. The ART-2A network weights are also called prototypes because they define the direction for the data grouping. The data normalization operations performed by the ART network allow all the vectors to be canonically normalized. Thus, only the angle formed among the prototypes is preserved. If the process monitoring values are initially normalized (see Equation 20.2), such values do not differ too much in their magnitude. In addition, according to the rule for updating the ART network weights (see Equation 20.7), the prototypes are also normalized. Thus, each attribute contribution can be obtained, based on its value in the weight vector. Such value represents the attribute significance for the local grouping chosen by the network.

After the data grouping is performed by the ART-2A network, a label is added to each neuron of the F_2 layer. For this purpose, a significance matrix is defined, which is composed of a SV_{ij} significance value set [54]. The significance matrix supports the decision about which components of the input vector are significant to label each committed neuron of the F_2 layer. The significance values are obtained directly from the ART-2A network weights, where the number of columns of the significance matrix is equal to the number of committed neurons of the F_2 layer, which represent the obtained classes, and the number of lines is equal to the number of components of the input vector. For instance, a $SM = (SV_{ij})^{7 \times 4}$ significance matrix is obtained through a network that has four classes to represent a process described by an input vector with $m = 7$ components.

The labeling algorithm is illustrated by Algorithm 1 (see below). In order to detect the most important attributes to describe the class, the significance values of the attributes are normalized in relation to the sum of the total significance values of a certain class, that is, the sum of the elements of the column. After such normalization is done, the column values are arranged in a decreasing manner and the accumulated frequency of the significance values is calculated. For labeling the class, the set of the more significant attributes is selected until the accumulated frequency sum does not exceed a certain χ threshold. By the end of the algorithm execution, there will be a C set of more relevant attributes for each category created by the network to label the class.

Algorithm 1   Labeling of the Classes Obtained by the ART-2A Network

---

1: defines the threshold value χ (p.e. $\chi = 55\%$) e m (input vector dimension)
2: create the significance matrix, one column for each class created by the ART-2A network
3: **for** each column created on the significance matrix **do**
4:      sum the significance values of each attribute
5:      normalize the significance values based on the sum
6:      calculate the distribution of the accumulated frequency
7:      arrange in a decreasing order the column attributes
8:      $sum := 0$
9:      $i := 1$
10:     $C :=$
11:     **while** ($sum \leq \chi$) **and** ($i \leq m$) **do**
12:         add the $attribute_i$ to the C set
13:         add the $attribute_i$ accumulated frequency to the sum variable
14:         $i := i + 1$
15:     **end while**
16:     label the class based on the attributes contained on C set
17: **end for**

20.4.3   Classification Model Implementation

The knowledge acquisition model is implemented in the kernel of the Linux operating system.[1] This allows the classification impact on the system performance to be reduced and any process being executed can be monitored and classified in a simple and trustful manner. The Table 20.4 describes the kernel files in the Linux system that were modified to accommodate the ART-2A implementation.

In `/include/linux/lbs.h` the source file are defined: the `struct TArt2` structure and the function prototypes that handle such structure. The ART-2A network algorithm is implemented in the `fs/proc/array.c` source file. The implementation follows the routines for the network creation and training of each monitored process. The network is created for the whole monitored process through the access to the `/proc/pid/status` file of `procfs`, where `pid` corresponds to the monitored process identifier. For each process, it is defined a fixed-size buffer. The counter values associated with the process, which form an input pattern in the network, are inserted at each access to the `/proc/pid/status` file, at the last position of the buffer. This buffer is submitted a constant number of times to the ART-2A network, each time the file `status` is accessed. The buffer circular structure and the submission repetition to the neural network guarantee that the network learning is stable and the classification model behavior stronger with respect to noise.

---

[1]The kernel files of Linux in our classification model may be found at the following Internet address: `http://www.icmc.usp.br/~mello/outr.html`.

Table 20.1   Kernel source files modified for the ART-2A network implementation

Source file	Description
include/linux/lbs.h	Network routines function prototypes
fs/proc/array.c	Network routines implementation
kernel/exit.c	Linux processes exit

The labeling algorithm is applied after the ART-2A network training. A transition state diagram is created for each process after the network training. This diagram identifies the process behavior related to the usage states of the identified resources, the transition order, and the frequency with which these states were visited during the process execution.

The classification by the neural network and the labeling algorithm are protected by a critical region, implemented through a semaphore. Thus, it is assured that each request to the monitoring file is processed until it is completed.

20.5   RESULTS

The knowledge acquisition model has been successfully employed in a miscellaneous sets of parallel applications [45–47]. The results obtained with the utilization of the classification model on the kernel applications and compact applications of the package NAS are described on here. The package NAS was defined through the evaluation of the actual parallel applications in the fluid dynamic area of the NASA Ames Research Center. The benchmark sets of the package are arranged into two groups: parallel kernels and compact applications. The parallel kernel benchmarks used are:

- *Embarrassing Parallel* (EP). This benchmark generates Gaussian random deviations based on a specific scheme and tabulates the pairs. It provides an estimate of the upper achievable limits for floating point performance, without significant interprocessor communication.
- *Multigrid* (MG). This benchmark solves four interactions of a V-cycle multigrid algorithm to obtain an approximate u solution to the discrete Poisson problem $\nabla^2 u = v$ on a $256 \times 256 \times 256$ grid. It requires highly structured long-distance communication and tests on both short and long-distance data communication.
- *Conjugate Gradient* (CG). The inverse-power method is used to compute an approximation of the smallest eigenvalue of a large, sparse, symmetric, positive definite matrix. This benchmark is typical of unstructured grid computations in which it tests irregular long-distance communication, employing unstructured matrix vector multiplication.

- *Integer Sort* (IS). A large integer sort. This benchmark performs a sorting operation that is important in particle method codes and tests both integer computation speed and communication performance.

The compact applications are based on the general operations in CFD and use three methods to solve the equations:

- *Lower–Upper Symmetric Gauss–Seidel* (LU). Solves a finite difference discretization of the three-dimensional Navier–Stokes equations through a block-lower-triangular, block-upper-triangular approximate factorization of the original difference scheme.
- *Scalar Pentadiagonal* (SP). Solves multiple independent systems of nondiagonally dominant scalar pentadiagonal equations using a $N \times N \times N$ grid size.
- *Block Tridiagonal* (BT). Solves multiple independent systems of nondiagonally dominant block tridiagonal equations. SP and BT are very similar, but differ in their communication-to-computation ratio.

In order to illustrate the classification that may be obtained with the classification model, executions of the *SP* compact application are considered. The *SP* application is executed taking into account three workloads: *W*, *A*, and *B*. The difference among these workloads is the size of the considered problem, which is equal to $36 \times 36 \times 36$ for the problem size *W*, $64 \times 64 \times 64$ for the problem size *A*, and $102 \times 102 \times 102$ for the problem size *B*.

The Table 20.5 illustrates the ART-2A prototypes obtained with the classification and the significance matrix of each attribute considered at the *W* workload. In this case, the class is created by the network and the labeling algorithm has identified two attributes (Table 20.6), *tcp read* and *tcp write,* to label the identified class.

The prototypes created for the *A* and *B* workloads after the ART-2A training are illustrated on Tables 20.7, 20.8, and 20.9. Three additional classes are created for these workloads. Such classes reflect the application behavior change regarding the resources usage. With increase in workload, the processing time spent is higher and

Table 20.5   ART-2A prototypes for the *SP* application with problem size *W*

Attribute	Class (*k*) k_1	Significance matrix (%), *SM* k_1
1	0.0470	3.24
2	0.0000	0.00
3	0.0000	0.00
4	0.7801	53.72
5	0.6250	43.04
6	0.0000	0.00
7	0.0000	0.00

Table 20.6   Selected attributes for labelling the classes obtained for the application *SP* (load *W*)

Classes	Attributes	Description	Frequency (%)
k_1	4.5	Communication intensive	100.00

a better status segregation checked by the parallel application is observed. The plasticity of the ART-2A network may also be noted: the prototypes of the created states (classes) are updated and only the probabilities of the states-transition diagram are altered, according to the change on the application workload.

In addition to the classification, the model allows the on-line creation of the process-state-transition diagram. The value p_{ij}, which describes the probability transition of a state i for a state j, is estimated based on the following equation [15]:

$$p_{ij} = \frac{\text{observed number of transitions from state } i \text{ to state } j}{\text{observed number of transitions from state } i} \tag{20.8}$$

The state-transition diagrams for the *SP* application are illustrated in Figures 20.2, 20.3, and 20.4. Each utilization state of certain resources is represented by a circle and the transition among states is indicated by a right arrow. Such circles represent the neurons (classes) created on the F_2 representation layer of the ART-2A network. The right arrows have a percent value that indicates the transitions probability among the states.

20.6   EVALUATION OF THE MODEL INTRUSION ON THE SYSTEM PERFORMANCE

Benchmark executions are taken into account to measure the impact of the classification model on system performance. The benchmarks are executed 30 times and their average execution times are collected. The sampling intervals used for the in-

Table 20.7   ART-2A prototypes for the *SP* application with *A* and *B* problem sizes

Attribute	Classes (k)				Significance matrix (%)			
	k_1	k_2	k_3	k_4	k_1	k_2	k_3	k_4
1	0.047	0.066	1.000	0.117	3.24	6.20	100.00	10.54
2	0.000	0.000	0.000	0.000	0.00	0.00	0.00	0.00
3	0.000	0.000	0.000	0.000	0.00	0.00	0.00	0.00
4	0.780	0.998	0.000	0.000	53.72	93.80	0.00	0.00
5	0.624	0.000	0.000	0.993	43.04	0.00	0.00	89.45
6	0.000	0.000	0.000	0.000	0.00	0.00	0.00	0.00
7	0.000	0.000	0.000	0.000	0.00	0.00	0.00	0.00

Figure 20.2   States diagram for the *SP* application (problem size *W*).

formation collection and for the network classification are equal to 250, 500, and 1000 milliseconds. A sampling interval equal to 250 milliseconds, for instance, indicates that at each second of the execution time it will send four samples of its behavior to the ART-2A network. Lower sampling intervals allow a lower granulation analysis of the process behavior, although they impose delays on the process response times.

The performance metric used is the *slowdown*. This measure corresponds to the execution time of a certain application at a T_b busy system normalized by the execution time on a T_i idle system:

$$Slowdown = \frac{T_b}{T_i} \tag{20.9}$$

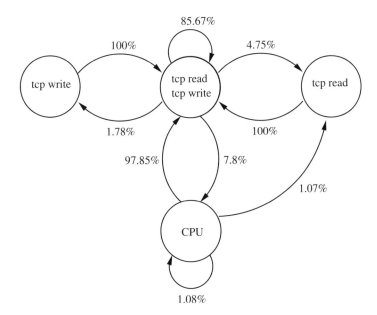

Figure 20.3   States diagram for the *SP* application (problem size *A*).

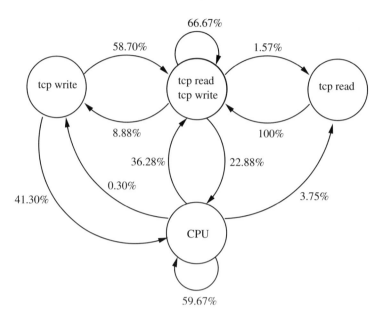

Figure 20.4   States diagram for the *SP* application (problem size *B*).

The busy system is the operating system kernel after the implementation of the neural network. The idle system is the operational system kernel that has not been modified. Thus, a *slowdown* value equal to 1.01 indicates that the classification implementation imposes a delay equal to 1% at the response time of the considered application.

The results of the intrusion analysis of the ART-2A implementation on the system performance are described on Table 20.10. A low impact of applications' response time is observed. On average, there is a delay of 2%, 1%, and 0.7%, respectively, for the sampling intervals of 250, 500, and 1000 milliseconds. As foreseen, this indicates that the less frequent the sampling, the lower the impact on the application response time. Such behavior is due to the fact that the less frequent the sampling, the lower the data quantity sent to the classification algorithm. Although higher sampling intervals tend to reduce the impact on system performance, a lower

Table 20.8   Attributes selected to label the classes obtained for the application *SP* (problem size *A*)

Class	Attributes	Description	Frequency (%)
k_1	4.5	Communication intensive	87.33
k_2	4	Communication intensive	4.22
k_3	1	CPU bound	6.89
k_4	5	Communication intensive	1.56

Table 20.9 Attributes selected to label the classes obtained for the application *SP*
(problem size *B*)

Class	Attributes	Description	Frequency (%)
k_1	4.5	Communication intensive	55.87
k_2	4	Communication intensive	2.31
k_3	1	CPU bound	36.75
k_4	5	Communication intensive	5.07

value of application behavior may depreciate the classification quality. It has been observed [45–47] that sampling intervals from around 250 to 500 are adequate for a representative set of parallel applications.

20.7 CONCLUSIONS

One of the greatest challenges to distributed computing systems is process scheduling aimed at optimizing load balances, leading to good resource usage and a higher application performance. The load balance quality is proportionally increased to the precise level of the information and processes being executed. Motivated by information obtainment, this paper presents an on-line model for the acquisition, classification, and extraction of the process behavior.

The information acquisition is done through the instrumentation of the kernel routines, which eliminates the need for alterations and the recompilations of the user applications required to be monitored. This information is submitted to the ART-2A neural network architecture, which extracts and classifies the process behavior. As showed by the experiments, this architecture offers high-performance computing and good results on classification, as well as stability and plasticity. After completing this stage, the labeling of the created classes is done, as well as the transition-state diagram.

With this model, the process behavior and the change of states of the resources usage can be obtained, with low intrusion on system performance. These contributions are attractive for several situations where a detailed knowledge of the system workload is required.

Table 20.10 Values of *slowdown* observed

Benchmark	bt	cg	ep	is	lu	mg	sp
$T_o = 250$ ms	1.00641	1.01813	1.00543	1.07795	1.01821	1.00604	1.00833
General average				1.02007			
$T_o = 500$ ms	1.00439	1.00408	1.00513	1.07131	1.00098	1.00335	1.00241
General average				1.01309			
$T_o = 1$ s	1.00342	1.00337	1.00417	1.02877	1.00516	1.00031	1.00396
General average				1.00702			

ACKNOWLEDGMENTS

The authors thank CAPES and Fapesp Brazilian Foundations (under process number 04/02411-9).

REFERENCES

1. Y. Amir, An opportunity cost approach for job assignment in a scalable computing cluster, *IEEE Transactions on Parallel and Distributed Systems, 11*(7), 760–768, July 2000.

2. T. Anderson, D. Culler, and D. Patterson, A case for NOW (networks of workstations), *IEEE Micro, 15*(1), 54–64, 1995.

3. A. C. Arpaci-Dusseau, D. E. Culler, and M. Mainwaring, Scheduling with implicit information in distributed systems, in *Proceedings of ACM SIGMETRICS' 98,* pp. 233–248, August 1998.

4. I. Bachelder,A.Waxman, and M. Seibert, Aneural system formobile robot visual place learning and recognition, in *Proceedings of the 5th Annual Symposium on Combinatorial Pattern Matching,* vol. 807, pp. 198–212, Berlin, 1993. Springer-Verlag.

5. A. Beguelin, A. Gueist, J. Dongarra, W. Jiang, R. Manchek, and V. Sunderam, *PVM: Parallel Virtual Machine: User's Guide and tutorial for Networked Parallel Computing,* MIT Press, 1994.

6. D. P. Bovet and M. Cesati, *Understanding the Linux Kernel,* O'Reilly, October 2000.

7. R. Buyya, *High Performance Cluster Computing—Architecture and Systems,* vol. 1, Prentice-Hall, 1999.

8. G. A. Carpenter, M. N. Gjaja, S. Gopal, and C. E. Woodcock, ART neural networks for remote sensing: Vegetation classification from Lansat TM and terrain data, *IEEE Transactions on Geoscience and Remote Sensing, 35*(2), 308–325, March 1997.

9. G. A. Carpenter and S. Grossberg, The ART of adaptive pattern recognition by a self-organizing neural network, *Computer,* (21), 77–88, 1988.

10. G. A. Carpenter and S. Grossberg, ART 2: Self-organization of stable category recognition codes for analog input patterns, *Applied Optics, 26*(23), 4919–4930, 1989.

11. G. A. Carpenter, S. Grossberg, and D. B. Rosen, ART 2-A: An adaptive resonance algorithm for rapid category learning and recognition, *Neural Networks, 4,* 4934–504, 1991.

12. T. L. Casavant and J. G. Kuhl, A Taxonomy of scheduling in general-purpose distributed computing systems, *IEEE Transactions on Software Engineering, 14*(2), 141–154, February 1988.

13. J. Corbalan, X. Martorell, and J. Labarta, improving gang scheduling through job performance analysis and malleability, in *International Conference on Supercomputing,* pp. 303–311, Sorrento, Italy, June 2001.

14. A. de P. Braga, T. B. Ludermir, and A. C. P. L. F. Carvalho, *Redes Neurais Artificiais: Teoria e Aplicações,* LTC, 2000.

15. M. V. Devarakonda and R. K. Iyer, Predictability of process resource usage: A measurement-based study on UNIX, *IEEE Transactions on Software Engineering, 15*(12), 1579–1586, 1989.

16. L. G. Fagundes, R. F. Mello, and C. E. Moron, An environment for generating applications involving remote manipulation of parallel machines, in *IEEE 7TH International*

Workshop on Parallel and Distributed Real-Time Systems (WPDRTS/99), Puerto Rico, Apr. 1999.

17. D. G. Feitelson, L. Rudolph, U. Schwiegelshohn, K. C. Sevcik, and P. Wong, Theory and practice in parallel job scheduling, in *Job Scheduling Strategies for Parallel Processing,* pp. 1–34. Springer-Verlag, 1997.

18. D. Ferguson, Y. Yemini, and C. Nikolau, Microeconomic algorithms for load balancing in distributed computer systems, in *VII International Conference on Distributed Computer Systems,* pp. 491–499, 1988.

19. S. M. Figueira and F. Berman, A slowdown model for applications executing on time-shared clusters of workstations, *IEEE Transactions on Parallel and Distributed Systems, 12*(6), 653–670, June 2001.

20. A. Filippidis, L. C. Jain, and P. Lozo, Degree of familiarity ART2 in knowledgebased landmine detection, *IEEE Transactions on Neural Networks, 10*(1), 186– 193, January 1999.

21. M. J. Flynn and K. W. Rudd, Parallel architectures, *ACMComputing Surveys, 28*(1), 68–70, 1996.

22. K. Gan and K. Lua, Chinese character classification using adaptive resonance network, *Pattern Recognition, 25,* 877–888, 1992.

23. R. Gibbons, A historical application profiler for use by parallel schedulers, in *Job Scheduling Strategies for Parallel Processing,* pp. 58–77. Springer-Verlage, 1997.

24. R. C. Gonzalez and R. E. Woods, *Processamento de Imagens Digitais,* Edgard Blücher, 2000.

25. K. K. Goswami, M. Devarakonda, and R. K. Iyer, Prediction-based dynamic load-sharing heuristics, *IEEE Transactions on Parallel and Distributed Systems, 4*(6), 638–648, June 1993.

26. S. Haykin, *Neural Networks—A Compreensive Foundation,* Prentice-Hall, 1994.

27. J. He, A.-H. Tan, and C.-L. Tan, Modified Art 2A growing network capable of generating a fixed number of nodes, *IEEE Transactions on Neural Networks, 15*(3), 728–737, 2004.

28. R. L. Henderson, Job scheduling under the portable batch system, in *Job Scheduling Strategies for Parallel Processing (IPPS·95),* pp. 280–94, Apr. 1995.

29. T. Hsu, Task allocation on a network of processors, *IEEE Transactions on Computers, 49*(12), 1339–1353, 2000.

30. C. Hui and S. T. Chanson, Hydrodynamic load balancing, *IEEE Transactions on Parallel and Distributed Systems, 10*(11), 1118–1137, Nov. 1999.

31. S. Keyvan and L. C. Rabelo, Sensor signal analysis by neural networks for surveillance in nuclear reactors, *IEEE Transactions on Nuclear Science, 39*(2), Apr. 1992.

32. P. Krueger and M. Livny, The diverse objectives of distributed scheduling policies, in *Seventh International Conference Distributed Computing Systems,* pp. 242–249, *IEEE Computer Science Press, 1987.*

33. P. K. K. Loh, How network topology affects dynamic load balancing, *IEEE Parallel & Distributed Technology, 4*(3), 25–35, 1996.

34. R. F. Mello, L. C. Trevelin, M. S. Paiva, and L. T. Yang, Comparative study of the server-initiated lowest algorithm using a load balancing index based on the process behavior for heterogeneous environment, in *Networks, Software Tools and Applications,* Kluwer, 2004.

35. R. F. Mello, L. C. Trevelin, M. S. Paiva, and L. T. Yang, Comparative analysis of the prototype and the simulator of a new load balancing algorithm for heterogeneous computing environments, in *International Journal Of High Performance Computing And Networking,* 2004.

36. R. F. Mello, L. C. Trevelin, M. S. Paiva, and L. T. Yang, Comparative study of the server-initiated lowest algorithm using a load balancing index based on the process behavior for heterogeneous environment, in *Networks, Software Tools and Applications,* Kluwer, 2004.

37. R. R. Mello and C. E. Moron, Análise dos mecanismos de tempo real em java, in *Workshop De Tempo Real do XVII Sinpósio Brasileiro de Redes De Computadores,* vol. 1, pp. 43–50, Salvador, Bahia, Brazil, May 1999.

38. Message Passing Interface Forum, *MPI-2: Extensions to the Message Passing Interface,* July 1997.

39. M. Mitzenmacher, How useful is old information? *IEEE Transactions on Parallel and Distributed Systems, 11*(1), 6–20, Jan. 2000.

40. M. Mitzenmacher, The power of two choices in randomized load balancing, *IEEE Transactions on Parallel and Distributed Systems, 12*(10), 1094–1104, Oct. 2001.

41. M. Neeracher, *Scheduling for Heterogeneous Opportunistic Workstation Clusters,* PhD thesis, Swiss Federal Institute of Technology, Zurich, 1999.

42. L. M. Ni, C. Xu, and T. B. Gendreau, A distributed drafting algorithm for load balancing, *IEEE Transactions on Software Engineering, 11*(10), 1153–1161, 1985.

43. M. A. Palis, J. Liou, and D. S. L. Wei, Task clustering and scheduling for distributed memory parallel architectures, *IEEE Transactions on Parallel and Distributed Systems, 7*(1), 46–55, Jan. 1996.

44. J. Ryou and J. S. K. Wong, A task migration algorithm for load balancing in a distributed system, in *XXII Annual Hawaii International Conference on System Sciences,* pp. 1041–1048, Jan. 1989.

45. L. J. Senger, M. J. Santana, and R. H. C. Santana, Uma nova abordagem para a aquisição de conhecimento sobre o comportamento de aplicações paralelas na utilização de recursos, in *Proceedings of WORKCOMP,* pp. 79–85, São José dos Campos, São Paulo, Brazil, October 2002.

46. L. J. Senger, M. J. Santana, and R. H. C. Santana, A new approach fo acquiring knowledge of resource usage in parallel applications, in *Proceedings of International Symposium on Performance Evaluation of Computer and Telecommunication Systems (SPECTS'2003),* pp. 607–614, 2003.

47. L. J. Senger, M. J. Santana, and R. H. C. Santana, Using runtime measurements and historical traces for acquiring knowledge in parallel applications, in *International Conference on Computational Science (ICCS).* Springer-Verlag, 2004.

48. N. G. Shivaratri, P. Krueger, and M. Singhal, Load distributing for locally distributed systems, *IEEE Computer, 25*(12), 33–44, 1992.

49. F. A. B. D. Silva and I. D. Scherson, Improving parallel job scheduling using runtime measurements, in D. G. Feitelson and L. Rudolph (Eds.), *Job Scheduling Strategies for Parallel Processing,* pp. 18–38. Springer-Verlag, 2000.

50. W. Smith, I. T. Foster, and V. E. Taylor, Predicting application run times using historical information, *LNCS J459,* 122–142, 1998.

51. T. T. Y. Suen and J. S. K. Wong, Efficient task migration algorithm for distributed systems, *IEEE Transactions on Parallel and Distributed Systems, 3*(4), 488–499, 1992.

52. A. S. Tanenbaum, *Modern Operating Systems*. Prentice-Hall, 1992.

53. M. Tiemeyer and J. S. K. Wong, A task migration algorithm for heterogeneous distributed computing systems, *The Journal of Systems and Software, 41*(3), 175–188, 1998.

54. A. Ultsch, Self-organising neural networks for monitoring and knowledge acquisition of a chemical process, in *Proceedings of ICANN-93,* pp. 864–867, 1993.

55. N. Vlajic and H. C. Card, Vector quantization of images using modified adaptive resonance algorithm for hierarchical clustering, *IEEE Transactions on Neural Networks, 12*(5), September 2001.

56. J. R. Whiteley and J. F. Davis, Qualitative interpretation of sensor patterns, *IEEE Expert, 8,* 54–63, 1993.

57. James R. Whiteley and James F. Davis, Observations and problems applying ART2 for dynamic sensor pattern interpretation, *IEEE Transactions on Systems, Man and Cybernetics-Part A: Systems and Humans, 26*(4), 423–437, 1996.

58. M. H. Willebeek-Lemair and A. P. Reeves, Strategies for dynamic load balancing on highly parallel computers, *IEEE Transactions on Parallel and Distributed Systems, 4*(9), 979–993, Sept. 1993.

59. M. Wu, On runtime parallel scheduling for processor load balancing, *IEEE Transactions on Parallel and Distributed Systems, 8*(2), 173–186, Feb. 1997.

60. Y. Zhang, Impact of workload and system parameters on next generation cluster schedulingmechanisms, *IEEE Transactions on Parallel and Distributed Systems, 12*(9), 967–985, Sep. 2001.

61. S. Zhou and D. Ferrari, An experimental study of load balancing performance, Technical Report UCB/CSD 87/336, PROGRES Report N.o 86.8, Computer Science Division (EECS), University of California, Berkeley, Jan. 1987.

62. A. Y. Zomaya and Y. TEH, Observations on using genetic algorithms for dynamic load-balancing, *IEEE Transactions on Parallel and Distributed Systems, 12*(9), 899–911, Sept. 2001.

## CHAPTER 21

Peer-to-Peer Grid Computing and a .NET-Based Alchemi Framework

AKSHAY LUTHER, RAJKUMAR BUYYA, RAJIV RANJAN, and SRIKUMAR VENUGOPAL

21.1 INTRODUCTION

The idea of metacomputing [2] is very promising as it enables the use of a network of many independent computers as if they were one large parallel machine or virtual supercomputer at a fraction of the cost of traditional supercomputers. Although traditional virtual machines (e.g., clusters) have been designed for local area networks, the exponential growth in Internet connectivity allows this concept to be applied on a much larger scale. This, coupled with the fact that desktop PCs (personal computers) in corporate and home environments are heavily underutilized—typically only one-tenth of processing power is used—has given rise to interest in harnessing these unused CPU cycles of desktop PCs connected over the Internet [20]. This new paradigm has been dubbed peer-to-peer (P2P) computing [18], and more recently called enterprise desktop grid computing [17].

Although the notion of desktop grid computing is simple enough, the practical realization of a peer-to-peer grid poses a number of challenges. Some of the key issues include: heterogeneity, resource management, failure management, reliability, application composition, scheduling, and security [13]. Furthermore, for wide-scale adoption, desktop grid computing infrastructure must also leverage the power of Windows-class machines since the vast majority of desktop computers run variants of the Windows operating system.

However, there is a distinct lack of service-oriented architecture-based grid computing software in this area. To overcome this limitation, we have developed a Windows-based desktop grid computing framework called Alchemi, implemented on the Microsoft .NET Platform. The Microsoft .NET Framework is the state-of-the-art development platform for Windows and offers a number of features that can be leveraged for enabling a computational desktop grid environment on Windows-class machines.

High-Performance Computing: Paradigm and Infrastructure. Edited by L. T. Yang and M. Guo **403**
Copyright © 2006 John Wiley & Sons, Inc.

Alchemi was conceived with the aim of making grid construction and development of grid software as easy as possible without sacrificing flexibility, scalability, reliability, and extensibility. The key features supported by Alchemi are:

- Internet-based clustering [21, 22] of Windows-based desktop computers
- Dedicated or non-dedicated (voluntary) execution by individual nodes
- Object-oriented grid application programming model (fine-grained abstraction)
- File-based grid job model (coarse-grained abstraction) for grid-enabling legacy applications
- Web services interface supporting the job model for interoperability with custom grid middleware, for example, for creating a global, cross-platform grid environment via a custom resource broker component

The rest of the chapter is organized as follows. Section 21.2 presents background information on P2P and grid computing and Section 21.3 discusses the basic architecture of an enterprise desktop grid system along with middleware design considerations. Section 21.4 introduces desktop grids and discusses issues that must be addressed by a desktop grid. Section 21.4 briefly presents various enterprise grid systems along with their comparison to our Alchemi middleware. Section 21.5 presents the Alchemi desktop grid computing framework and describes its architecture, application composition models, and features with respect to the requirements of a desktop grid solution. Section 21.6 deals with system implementation and presents the lifecycle of an Alchemi-enabled grid application, demonstrating its execution model. Section 21.6 presents the results of an evaluation of Alchemi as a platform for execution of applications written using the Alchemi API. It also evaluates the use of Alchemi nodes as part of a global grid alongside Unix-class grid nodes running Globus software. Finally, we conclude the chapter with a discussion of work planned for the future.

21.2 BACKGROUND

In the early 1970s, when computers were first linked by networks, the idea of harnessing unused CPU cycles was born [34]. A few early experiments with distributed computing—including a pair of programs called Creeper and Reaper—ran on the Internet's predecessor, the ARPAnet. In 1973, the Xerox Palo Alto Research Center (PARC) installed the first Ethernet network and the first fully fledged distributed computing effort was underway. Scientists at PARC developed a program called "worm" that routinely cruised about 100 Ethernet-connected computers. They envisioned their worm migrating from one machine to another, harnessing idle resources for beneficial purposes. The worm would roam throughout the PARC network, replicating itself in each machine's memory. Each worm used idle resources to perform a computation and had the ability to reproduce and transmit clones to other nodes of the network. With the worms, developers distributed graphic images and shared computations for rendering realistic computer graphics.

Since 1990, with the maturation and ubiquity of the Internet and Web technologies, along with the availability of powerful computers and system area networks as commodity components, distributed computing scaled to a new global level. The availability of powerful PCs, workstations, and high-speed networks (e.g., Gigabit Ethernet) as commodity components has lead to the emergence of clusters [35] serving the needs of high-performance computing (HPC) users. The ubiquity of the Internet and Web technologies along with the availability of many low-cost and high-performance commodity clusters within many organizations has prompted the exploration of aggregating distributed resources for solving large-scale problems of multiinstitutional interest. This has led to the emergence of computational grids and P2P networks for sharing distributed resources. The grid community is generally focused on aggregation of distributed high-end machines such as clusters, whereas the P2P community is looking into sharing low-end systems such as PCs connected to the Internet for sharing computing power (e.g., SETI@Home) and content (e.g., exchanging music files via Napster and Gnuetella networks). Given the number of projects and forums [36, 37] started all over the world in early 2000, it is clear that the interest in the research, development, and deployment of Grid and P2P computing technologies, tools, and applications is rapidly growing.

21.3 DESKTOP GRID MIDDLEWARE CONSIDERATIONS

Figure 21.1 shows the architecture of a basic desktop grid computing system. Typically, users utilize the APIs and tools to interact with a particular grid middleware to develop grid applications. When they submit grid applications for processing, units of work are submitted to a central controller component that co-ordinates and manages the execution of these work units on the worker nodes under its control. There are a number of considerations that must be addressed for such a system to work effectively.

Security Barriers—Resource Connectivity Behind Firewalls. Worker nodes and user nodes must be able to connect to the central controller over the Internet (or local network) and the presence of firewalls and/or NAT servers must not affect the deployment of a desktop grid.

Unobtrusiveness—No Impact on Running User Applications. The execution of grid applications by worker nodes must not affect running user programs.

Programmability—Computationally Intensive Independent Work Units. As desktop grid systems span across the high latency of the Internet environment, applications with a high ratio of computation to communication time are suitable for deployment and are, thus, typically embarrassingly parallel.

Reliability—Failure Management. The unreliable nature of Internet connections also means that such systems must be able to tolerate connectivity disruption or faults and recover from them gracefully. In addition, data loss must be minimized in the event of a system crash or failure.

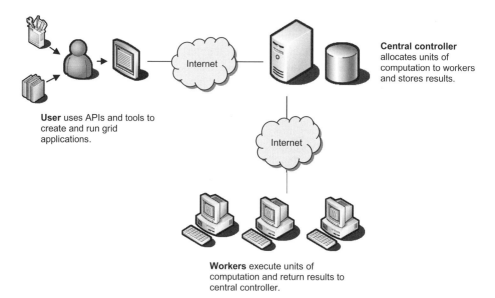

Central controller allocates units of computation to workers and stores results.

User uses APIs and tools to create and run grid applications.

Workers execute units of computation and return results to central controller.

Figure 21.1 Architecture of a basic desktop grid.

Scalability—Handling Large Users and Participants. Desktop grid systems must be designed to support the participation of a large number of anonymous or approved contributors ranging from hundreds to millions. In addition, the system must support a number of simultaneous users and their applications.

Security—Protecting Both Contributors and Consumers. Finally, the Internet is an insecure environment and strict security measures are imperative. Specifically, users and their programs must only be able to perform authorized activities on the grid resources. In addition, users/consumers must be safeguarded against malicious attacks or worker nodes.

21.4 REPRESENTATIVE DESKTOP GRID SYSTEMS

In addition to its implementation based on a service-oriented architecture using state-of-the-art technologies, Alchemi has a number of distinguishing features when compared to related systems. Table 21.1 shows a comparison between Alchemi and some related systems such as Condor, SETI@home, Entropia, GridMP, and XtermWeb.

Alchemi is a .NET-based framework that provides the runtime machinery and programming environment required to construct desktop grids and develop grid applications. It allows flexible application composition by supporting an object-oriented application-programming model in addition to a file-based job model. Cross-platform support is provided via a Web services interface and a flexible ex-

Table 20.1 Comparison of Alchemi and some related desktop grid systems

Property	Alchemi	System				
		Condor	SETI@home	Entropia	XtermWeb	Grid MP
Architecture	Hierarchical	Hierarchical	Centralized	Centralized	Centralized	Centralized
Web services interface for cross-platform integration	Yes	No	No	No	No	Yes
Implementation technologies	C#, Web . Services, & NET Framework	C	C++, Win32	C++, Win32	Java, Linux	C++, Win32
Multi-clustering	Yes	Yes	No	No	No	Yes
Global grid brokering mechanism	Yes (via Gridbus Broker)	Yes (via Condor-G)	No	No	No	No
Thread programming model	Yes	No	No	No	No	No
Level of integration of application, programming, and runtime environment	Low (general purpose)	Low (general purpose)	High (single-purpose, single-application environment)	Low (general purpose)	Low (general purpose)	Low (general purpose)

ecution model supports dedicated and nondedicated (voluntary) execution by grid nodes.

The Condor [19] system was developed by the University of Wisconsin at Madison. It can be used to manage a cluster of dedicated or nondedicated compute nodes. In addition, unique mechanisms enable Condor to effectively harness wasted CPU power from otherwise idle desktop workstations. Condor provides a job queuing mechanism, scheduling policy, workflow scheduler, priority scheme, resource monitoring, and resource management. Users submit their serial or parallel jobs to Condor, and Condor places them into a queue, chooses when and where to run the jobs based upon a policy, carefully monitors their progress, and ultimately informs the user upon completion. It can handle both Windows and UNIX class resources in its resource pool. Recently, Condor has been extended (see Condor-G [38]) to support the inclusion of Grid resources within a Condor pool.

The Search for Extraterrestrial Intelligence (SETI) project [9, 14], named SETI@Home, based at the University of California at Berkeley is aimed at doing good science in such a way that it engages and excites the general public. It developed a desktop grid system that harnesses hundreds and thousands of PCs across the Internet to process a massive amount of astronomy data captured daily by the Arecibo telescope in Puerto Rico. Its worker software runs as a screen saver on contributor computers. It is designed to work on heterogeneous computers running Windows, Mac, and variants of UNIX operating systems. Unlike other desktop systems, the worker module is designed as application-specific software as it supports processing of astronomy application data only.

Entropia [17] facilitates a Windows desktop grid system by aggregating the raw desktop resources into a single logical resource. Its core architecture is centralized—a central job manager administers various desktop clients. The node manager provides a centralized interface to manage all of the clients on the Entropia grid, which is accessible from anywhere on the enterprise network.

XtermWeb [16] is a P2P [15, 18] system developed at the University of Paris-Sud, France. It implements three distinct entities—the coordinator, the workers, and the clients—to create a so-called XtermWeb network. Clients are software instances available for any user to submit tasks to the XtermWeb network. They submit tasks to the coordinator, providing binaries and optional parameter files, and permit the end user to retrieve results. Finally, the workers are software parts spread among volunteer hosts to compute tasks.

The Grid MP (MP) [23] was developed by United Devices, whose expertise is mainly in the recruitment of key developers of SETI@Home and Distributed.Net enterprise grid systems. Like other systems, it supports harnessing and aggregation of computer resources available on their corporate network. It basically has a centralized architecture, in which a Grid MP service acting as a manager accepts jobs from the user and schedules them on the resources having predeployed Grid MP agents. The Grid MP agents can be deployed on clusters, workstations, or desktop computers. Grid MP agents receive jobs and execute them on resources, advertise their resource capabilities on Grid MP services, and return results to the Grid MP services for subsequent collection by the user.

21.5 ALCHEMI DESKTOP GRID FRAMEWORK

Alchemi's layered architecture for a desktop grid computing environment is shown in Figure 21.2. Alchemi follows the master–worker parallel computing paradigm [31], in which a central component dispatches independent units of parallel execution to workers and manages them. In Alchemi, this unit of parallel execution is termed a "grid thread" and contains the instructions to be executed on a grid node, whereas the central component is termed the "Manager."

A "grid application" consists of a number of related grid threads. Grid applications and grid threads are exposed to the application developer as .NET classes or objects via the Alchemi .NET API. When an application written using this API is executed, grid thread objects are submitted to the Alchemi Manager for execution by the grid. Alternatively, file-based jobs (with related jobs comprising a task) can be created using an XML representation to grid enable legacy applications for which precompiled executables exist. Jobs can be submitted via the Alchemi Console Interface or Cross-Platform Manager Web service interface, which, in turn,

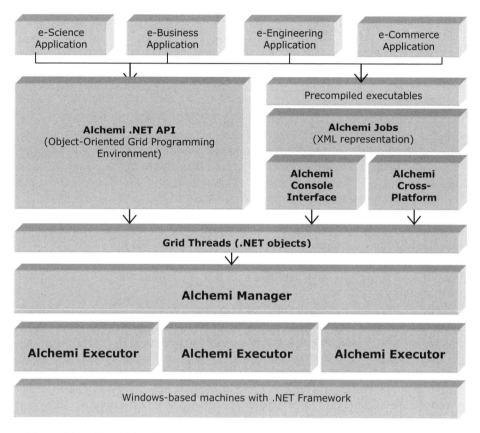

Figure 21.2 The Alchemi layered architecture for a desktop grid computing environment.

convert them into the grid threads before submitting then to the Manager for execution by the grid.

21.5.1 Application Models

Alchemi supports functional as well as data parallelism. Both are supported by each of the two models for parallel application composition—the grid thread model and the grid job model.

21.5.1.1 Grid Thread Model Minimizing the entry barrier to writing applications for a grid environment is one of Alchemi's key goals. This goal is served by an object-oriented programming environment via the Alchemi .NET API, which can be used to write grid applications in any .NET-supported language.

The atomic unit of independent parallel execution is a grid thread; many grid threads comprise a grid application (hereafter, "applications" and "threads" can be taken to mean grid applications and grid threads, respectively, unless stated otherwise). The two central classes in the Alchemi .NET API are `GThread` and `GApplication`, representing a grid thread and grid application, respectively. There are essentially two parts to an Alchemi grid application. Each is centered on one of these classes:

1. "Remote code": code to be executed remotely, that is, on the grid (a grid thread and its dependencies)
2. "Local code": code to be executed locally (code responsible for creating and executing grid threads)

A concrete grid thread is implemented by writing a class that derives from `GThread`, overriding the `void Start()` method, and marking the class with the `Serializable` attribute. Code to be executed remotely is defined in the implementation of the overridden `void Start()` method.

The application itself (local code) creates instances of the custom grid thread, executes them on the grid, and consumes each thread's results. It makes use of an instance of the `GApplication` class, which represents a grid application. The modules (.EXE or .DLL files) containing the implementation of this `GThread`-derived class and any other dependency types that not part of the .NET Framework must be included in the `Manifest` of the `GApplication` instance. Instances of the `GThread`-derived class are asynchronously executed on the grid by adding them to the grid application. Upon completion of each thread, a "thread finish" event is fired and a method subscribing to this event can consume the thread's results. Other events such as "application finish" and "thread failed" can also be subscribed to. Thus, the programmatic abstraction of the grid in this manner allows the application developer to concentrate on the application itself without worrying about "plumbing" details.

Appendix A shows the entire code listing of a sample application for multiplying pairs of integers.

21.5.1.2 Grid Job Model

Traditional grid implementations have offered a high-level abstraction of the "virtual machine," in which the smallest unit of parallel execution is a process. In this model, a work unit is typically described by specifying a command, input files, and output files. In Alchemi, such a work unit is termed a "job" and many jobs constitute a "task."

Although writing software for the "grid job" model involves dealing with files, an approach that can be complicated and inflexible, Alchemi's architecture supports it by:

- Grid-enabling existing applications
- Providing interoperability with grid middleware that can leverage Alchemi via the Cross Platform Manager Web service

Tasks and their constituent jobs are represented as XML files conforming to the Alchemi task and job schemas. Figure 21.3 shows a sample task representation

```
<task>
  <manifest>
    <embedded_file name="Reverse.exe" location="Reverse.exe" />
  </manifest>

  <job id="0">
    <input>
      <embedded_file name="input1.txt" location="input1.txt" />
    </input>
    <work run_command="Reverse.exe input1.txt > result1.txt" />
    <output>
      <embedded_file name="result1.txt"/>
    </output>
  </job>

 <job id="1">
    <input>
      <embedded_file name="input2.txt" location="input2.txt" />
    </input>
    <work run_command="Reverse input2.txt > result2.txt" />
    <output>
      <embedded_file name="result2.txt"/>
    </output>
  </job>
</task>
```

Figure 21.3   Sample XML-based task representation.

that contains two jobs to execute the `Reverse.exe` program against two input files.

Before submitting the task to the Manager, references to the "embedded" files are resolved and the files themselves are embedded into the task XML file as Base64-encoded text data. When finished jobs are retrieved from the Manager, the Base64-encoded contents of the "embedded" files are decoded and written to disk.

It should be noted that tasks and jobs are represented internally as grid applications and grid threads, respectively. Thus, any discussion that applies to "grid applications" and "grid threads" applies to "grid tasks" and "grid jobs" as well.

21.5.2   Distributed Components

Four types of nodes (or hosts) take part in desktop grid construction and application execution (see Figure 21.4). An Alchemi desktop grid is constructed by deploying a Manager node and deploying one or more Executor nodes configured to connect to the Manager. One or more Users can execute their applications on the cluster by connecting to the Manager. An optional component, the Cross-Platform Manager, provides a Web service interface to custom grid middleware. The operation of the Manager, Executor, User, and Cross-Platform Manager nodes is described below.

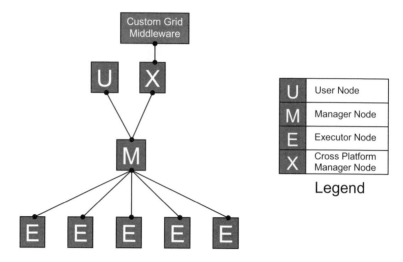

Figure 21.4   Distributed components and their relationships.

21.5.2.1 Manager   The Manager provides services associated with managing execution of grid applications and their constituent threads. Executors register themselves with the Manager, which in turn monitors their status. Threads received from the User are placed in a pool and scheduled to be executed on the various available Executors. A priority for each thread can be explicitly specified when it is created or submitted. Threads are scheduled on a Priority and First-Come–First-Served (FCFS) basis, in that order. The Executors return completed threads to the Manager; they are subsequently collected by the respective Users. A scheduling API is provided that allows custom schedulers to be written.

The Manager employs a role-based security model for authentication and authorization of secure activities. A list of permissions representing activities that need to be secured is maintained within the Manager. A list of groups (roles) is also maintained, each containing a set of permissions. For any activity that needs to be authorized, the user or program must supply credentials in a form of a user name and password and the Manager only authorizes the activity if the user belongs to a group that contains the particular permission.

As discussed previously, failure management plays a key role in the effectiveness of a desktop grid. Executors are constantly monitored and threads running on disconnected Executors are rescheduled. Additionally, all data is immediately written to disk so that in the event of a crash, the Manager can be restarted into the precrash state.

21.5.2.2 Executor   The Executor accepts threads from the Manager and executes them. An Executor can be configured to be dedicated, meaning the resource is centrally managed by the Manager, or nondedicated, meaning that the resource is managed on a volunteer basis via a screen saver or explicitly by the user. For nondedicated execution, there is one-way communication between the Executor and the Manager. In this case, the resource that the Executor resides on is managed on a volunteer basis since it requests threads to execute from the Manager. When two-way communication is possible and dedicated execution is desired, the Executor exposes an interface so that the Manager may communicate with it directly. In this case, the Manager explicitly instructs the Executor to execute threads, resulting in centralized management of the resource on which the Executor resides. Thus, Alchemi's execution model provides the dual benefit of:

- Flexible resource management—centralized management with dedicated execution versus decentralized management with nondedicated execution
- Flexible deployment under network constraints—the component can be deployment as nondedicated when two-way communication is not desired or not possible (e.g., when it is behind a firewall or NAT/proxy server)

Thus, dedicated execution is more suitable when the Manager and Executor are on the same local area network, whereas nondedicated execution is more appropriate when the Manager and Executor are to be connected over the Internet.

Threads are executed in a "sandbox" environment defined by the user. The CAS (code access security) feature of .NET are used to execute all threads with the *AlchemiGridThread* permission set, which can be specified to a fine-grained level by the user as part of the .NET *Local Security Policy.*

All grid threads run in the background with the lowest priority. Thus, any user programs are unaffected since they have higher priority access to the CPU over grid threads.

21.5.2.3 User Grid applications are executed on the User node. The API abstracts the implementation of the grid from the user and is responsible for performing a variety of services on the user's behalf, such as submitting an application and its constituent threads for execution, notifying the user of finished threads, and providing results and notifying the user of failed threads along with error details.

21.5.2.4 Cross-Platform Manager The Cross-Platform Manager is a Web services interface that exposes a portion of the functionality of the Manager in order to enable Alchemi to manage the execution of grid jobs (as opposed to grid applications utilizing the Alchemi grid thread model). Jobs submitted to the Cross-Platform Manager are translated into a form that is accepted by the Manager (i.e., grid threads), which are then scheduled and executed as normal in the fashion described above. In addition to support for the grid enabling of legacy applications, the Cross-Platform Manager allows custom grid middleware to interoperate with and leverage Alchemi on any platform that supports Web services.

21.5.3 Security

Security plays a key role in an insecure environment such as the Internet. Two aspects of security addressed by Alchemi are: (1) allow users to perform authorized operations whether they are system related or resource related operations, and (2) allow authorized or nonauthorized users to contribute resources.

The problem of allowing users to only perform activities they are authorized to do is addressed using the role-based authorization model. All security-sensitive activities on the Manager are protected in this manner. The Manager can be configured to support anonymous or nonanonymous Executors. Figure 21.5 shows the operation of various Alchemi components to enforce security as indicated below.

0   The Alchemi administrator configures user, group and permission data in addition to allowing anonymous/nonanonymous Executors.

1   A user or program connects to the Manager, supplies security credentials, and requests a particular activity.

2, 3, 4   The Manager authenticates the user and authorizes the user for the activity. This process is skipped if anonymous Executors are allowed.

Information about permission, groups, and users is maintained in the Alchemi database in the *prm, grp,* and *usr* tables, respectively. Figure 21.6 shows the relationships between these tables.

Each activity on the Manager is associated with a particular permission. The following permissions are defined:

• *ExecuteThread* (activities related to thread execution, e.g., getting a thread to execute and returning its results)

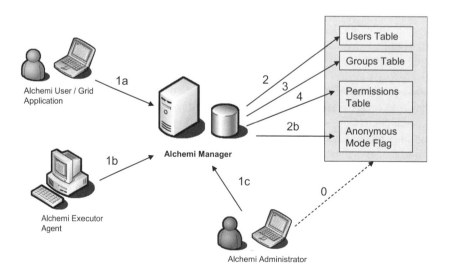

Figure 21.5   Role-based security in Alchemi.

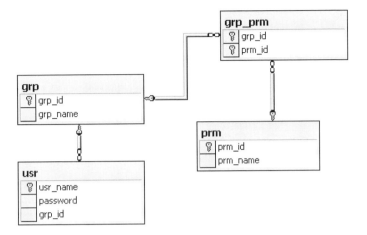

Figure 21.6   Relationships between security-related database tables.

- *ManageOwnApp* (activities related to the ownership of a particular application, e.g., creating an application and getting its finished threads)
- *ManageAllApps* (activities related to the ownership of all applications in the system, e.g., getting a list of all applications along with statistics)
- *ManageUsers* (activites related to user management, e.g., adding users, changing passwords, and changing group membership)

Users belong to a particular group, with each group containing a set of permissions. The following groups are defined:

- *Users (ManageOwnApp)*
- *Executors (ExecuteThread)*
- *Administrators (ManageOwnApp, ManageAllApps, ExecuteThread, ManageUsers)*

For any activity that needs to be authorized, the user or program must supply credentials in a form of a user name and password and the Manager only authorizes the activity if the user belongs to a group that contains the particular permission. Figure 21.7 shows the process of authentication and authorization.

The second aspect of security that Alchemi addresses is the protection of the machine hosting the Executor from malicious code. This is solved by the creation of a "sandbox" environment in which the Executor runs grid threads. This environment can be defined by the user. The CAS (code access security) feature of .NET is used to execute all threads with the *AlchemiGridThread* permission set, which can be specified to a fine-grained level by the user as part of the .NET *Local Security Policy.*

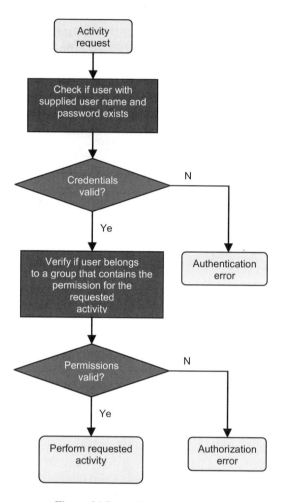

Figure 21.7   Authorization flow.

21.6   ALCHEMI DESIGN AND IMPLEMENTATION

Figures 21.8 and 21.9 provide an overview of the implementation by way of a deployment diagram and class diagram (showing only the main classes, without attributes or operations), respectively.

21.6.1   Overview

The .NET Framework offers two mechanisms for execution across application domains—remoting and Web services (application domains are the unit of isolation for a .NET application and can reside on different network hosts).

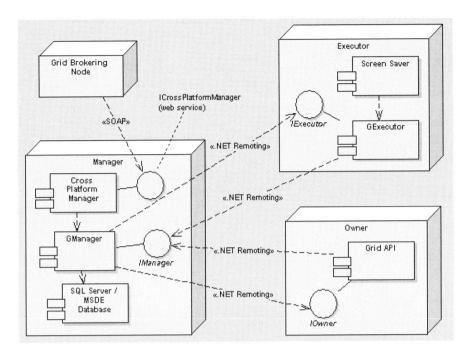

Figure 21.8   Alchemi architecture and interaction between its components.

.NET Remoting allows a .NET object to be "remoted" and expose its functionality across application domains. Remoting is used for communication between the four Alchemi distributed grid components as it allows low-level interaction transparently between .NET objects with low overhead (remote objects are configured to use binary encoding for messaging).

Web services were considered briefly for this purpose, but were decided against due to the relatively higher overheads involved with XML-encoded messages, the inherent inflexibility of the HTTP protocol for the requirements at hand, and the fact that each component would be required to be configured with a Web services container (Web server). However, Web services are used for the Cross-Platform Manager's public interface since cross-platform interoperability was the primary requirement in this regard.

The objects remoted using .NET Remoting within the four distributed components of Alchemi, the Manager, Executor, Owner, and Cross-Platform Manager, are instances of `GManager`, `GExecutor`, `GApplication`, and `CrossPlatform-Manager`, respectively.

It should be noted that classes are named with respect to their roles vis-à-vis a grid application. This discussion, therefore, refers to an "Owner" node synonymously with a "User" node, since the node from which the grid application is being submitted can be considered to "own" the application.

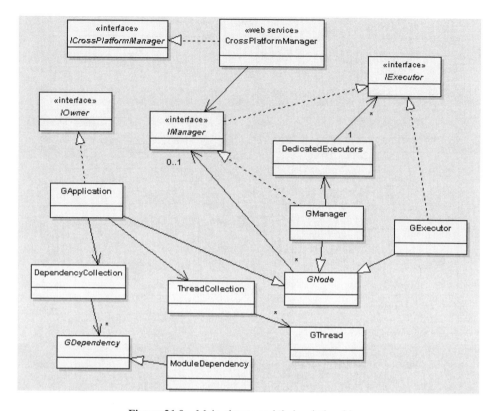

Figure 21.9   Main classes and their relationships.

The prefix "I" is used in type names to denote an interface, whereas "G" is used to denote a "grid node" class. GManager, and GExecutor, GApplication derive from the GNode class, which implements generic functionality for remoting the object itself and connecting to a remote Manager via the IManager interface.

The Manager executable initializes an instance of the GManager class, which is always remoted and exposes a public interface, IManager. The Executor executable creates an instance of the GExecutor class. For nondedicated execution, there is one-way communication between the Executor and the Manager. Where two-way communication is possible and dedicated execution is desired, GExecutor is remoted and exposes the IExecutor interface so that the Manager may communicate with it directly. The Executor installation provides an option to install a screen saver, which initiates nondedicated execution when activated by the operating system.

The GApplication object in Alchemi API communicates with the Manager in a similar fashion to GExecutor. Although two-way communication is currently not used in the implementation, the architecture caters for this by way of the IOwner interface.

The Cross-Platform Manager Web service is a thin wrapper around GManager and uses applications and threads internally to represent tasks and jobs (the GJob

class derives from `GThread`) via the public `ICrossPlatformManager` interface.

21.6.2 Grid Application Lifecycle

To develop and execute a grid application, the developer creates a custom grid
thread class that derives from the abstract `GThread` class. An instance of the
`GApplication` object is created and any dependencies required by the application are added to its `DependencyCollection`. Instances of the `GThread`-de-
rived class are then added to the `GApplication`'s `ThreadCollection`.

The lifecycle of a grid application is shown in Figures 21.10 and 21.11, showing
simplified interactions between the Owner and Executor nodes, respectively, and
the Manager.

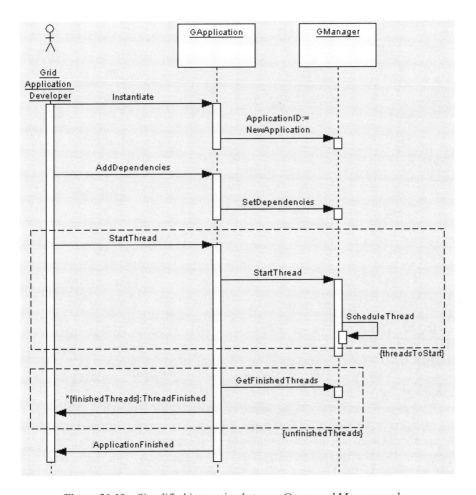

Figure 21.10   Simplified interaction between Owner and Manager nodes.

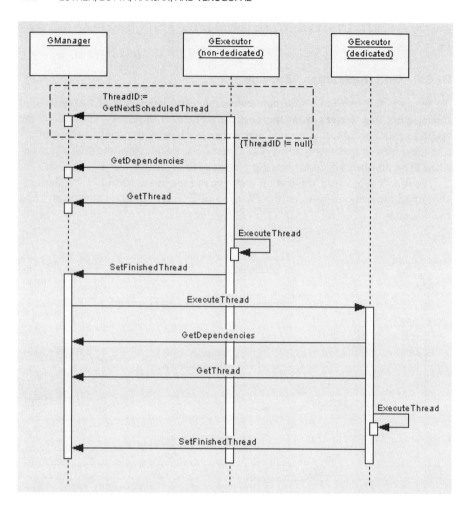

Figure 21.11   Simplified interaction between Executor and Manager nodes.

The GApplication serializes and sends relevant data to the Manager, where it is written to disk and threads are scheduled. Application and thread state is maintained in a SQL Server/MSDE database. Nondedicated executors poll for threads to execute until one is available. Dedicated executors are directly provided a thread to execute by the Manager.

Threads are executed in .NET application domains, with one application domain for each grid application. If an application domain does not exist that corresponds to the grid application that the thread belongs to, one is created by requesting, desterilizing, and dynamically loading the application's dependencies. The thread object itself is then desterilized, started within the application domain, and returned to the Manager on completion.

After sending threads to the Manager for execution, the `GApplication` polls the Manager for finished threads. A user-defined `GThreadFinish` delegate is called to signify each thread's completion, and once all threads have finished, a user-defined `GApplicationFinish` delegate is called up.

21.7   ALCHEMI PERFORMANCE EVALUATION

In this section, first we demonstrate the suitability of Alchemi to support the execution of applications created using the Alchemi Grid Threads interface on a stand-alone desktop grid. Next, we treat an Alchemi desktop setup as one of the Grid nodes within a global grid environment and use its job model and Web services interface to submit jobs for processing on it. This will be carried our by a grid resource broker, which has the ability to interoperate with different low-level grid middleware and schedule applications on distributed grid nodes.

21.7.1   Stand-Alone Alchemi Desktop Grid

21.7.1.1   Testbed   The testbed is an Alchemi cluster consisting of six Executors (Pentium III 1.7 GHz desktop machines with 512 MB physical memory running Windows 2000 Professional). One of these machines is additionally designated as a Manager.

21.7.1.2   Test Application and Methodology   The test application is the computation of the value of π to n decimal digits. The algorithm used allows the computation of the pth digit without knowing the previous digits [29]. The application utilizes the Alchemi grid thread model. The test was performed for a range of workloads (calculating 1000, 1200, 1400, 1600, 1800, 2000, and 2200 digits of π), each with one to six Executors enabled. The workload was sliced into a number of threads, each to calculate 50 digits of π, with the number of threads varying proportionally with the total number of digits to be calculated. Execution time was measured as the elapsed clock time for the test program to complete on the Owner node.

21.7.1.3   Results   Figure 21.12 shows a plot between thread size (the number of decimal places to which π is calculated to) and total time (in seconds taken by the all threads to complete execution) with varying numbers of Executors enabled.

At a low workload (1000 digits), there is little difference between the total execution time with different quantities of Executors. This is explained by the fact that the total overhead (network latency and miscellaneous overheads involved in managing a distributed execution environment) is in a relatively high proportion to the actual total computation time. However, as the workload is increased, there is a near-proportional difference when higher numbers of executors are used. For example, for 2200 digits, the execution time with six executors (84 seconds) is nearly one-fifth of that with one executor (428 seconds). This is explained by the fact that

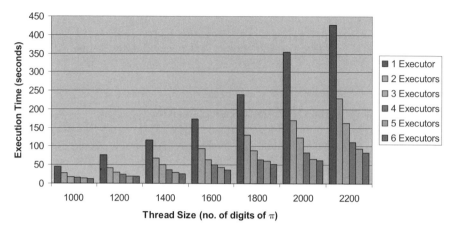

Figure 21.12   A plot of thread size versus execution time on a standalone Alchemi cluster.

for higher workloads, the total overhead is in relatively lower proportion to the actual total computation time.

21.7.2   Alchemi as Node of a Cross-Platform Global Grid

21.7.2.1   Testbed   A global grid was used for evaluating Alchemi as a potential low-level grid middleware with the Gridbus Grid Service Broker managing global grid resources (see Figure 21.13). The Windows Desktop Grid node is grid-enabled using Alchemi middleware, whereas other nodes running Linux OS are grid-enabled using Globus middleware (Globus 2.4) [7]. The Gridbus Broker developed in Java was running on Linux PC loaded with JVM (Java Virtual Machine), Globus, and Alchemi Client Side Interfaces. For details on testbed setup and software confirgration see Figure 21.13 and Table 21.1. The Gridbus resource-brokering mechanism obtains the users' application requirements and evaluates the suitability of various resources. It then schedules the jobs to various resources in order to satisfy those requirements.

21.7.2.2   Test Application and Methodology   For the purpose of evaluation, we used an application that calculates mathematical functions based on the values of two input parameters. The first parameter, X, is an input to a mathematical function and the second parameter, Y, indicates the expected calculation complexity in minutes plus a random deviation value between 0 to 120 seconds. This creates an illusion of small variation in execution time of different parametric jobs similar to a real application. A plan file modeling this application as a parameter sweep application using the Nimrod-G parameter specification language [12] is shown in Figure 21.14. The first part defines parameters and the second part defines the task that is to be performed for each job. As the parameter X varies from values 1 to 100 in step 1, this parameter specification (plan file) would create 100 jobs with input values from 1 to 100.

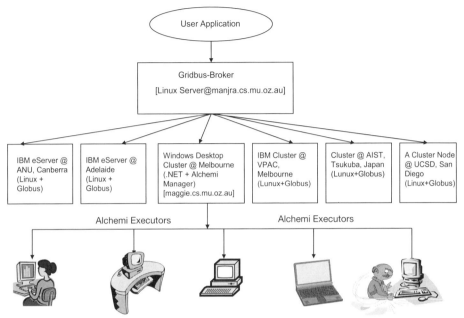

Figure 21.13   Testbed setup and software configuration.

21.7.2.3   Results   The results of the experiment shown in Figure 21.15 show the number of jobs completed on different Grid resources at different times. The parameter calc.$OS directs the broker to select appropriate executables based a target grid resource architecture. For example, if the target resource is Windows/Intel, it selects calc.exe and copies it to the grid node before its execution. This demon-

Table 21.1   Grid resources and jobs processed

Resource	Location	Configuration	Grid middleware	Jobs completed
maggie.cs.mu.oz.au [Windows cluster]	University of Melbourne	6 × Intel Pentium IV 1.7 GHz	Alchemi	21
quidam.ucsd.edu [Linux cluster]	University of California, San Diego	1 × AMD Athlon XP 2100+	Globus	16
belle.anu.edu.au [Linux cluster]	Australian National University	4 × Intel Xeon 2	Globus	22
koume.hpcc.jp [Linux cluster]	AIST, Japan	4 × Intel Xeon 2	Globus	18
brecca-2.vpac.org [Linux cluster]	VPAC, Melbourne	4 × Intel Xeon 2	Globus	23

```
#Parameter definition
parameter X integer range from 1 to 100 step 1;
parameter Y integer default 1;
#Task definition
task main
        #Copy necessary executables depending on node type
        copy calc.$OS node:calc
        #Execute program with parameter values on remote node
        node:execute ./calc $X $Y
        #Copy results file to use home node with jobname as extension
        copy node:output ./output.$jobname
endtask
```

Figure 21.14   Parametric job specification.

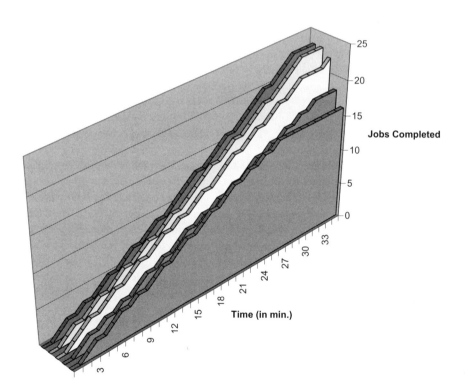

Figure 21.15   A plot of the number of jobs completed on different resources versus the time.

strates the feasibility of utilizing Windows-based Alchemi resources along with other Unix-class resources running Globus.

21.8 SUMMARY AND FUTURE WORK

We have discussed a .NET-based grid computing framework that provides the run-time machinery and object-oriented programming environment needed to easily construct desktop grids and develop grid applications. Its integration into the global cross-platform grid has been made possible via support for execution of grid jobs via a Web services interface and the use of a broker component.

We plan to extend Alchemi to a number of areas. First, support for additional functionality via the API, including inter-thread communication, is planned. Second, we are working on support for multiclustering with peer-to-peer communication between managers. Third, we plan to support utility-based resource allocation policies driven by economic, quality-of-service, and service-level agreements. Fourth, we are investigating strategies for adherence to OGSI (Open Grid Services Infrastucture) standards by extending the current Alchemi job management interface. This is likely to be achieved by its integration with .NET-based, low-level grid middleware implementations (e.g., University of Virginia's OGSI.NET [33]) that conform to grid standards such as OGSI [25, 32]. Finally, we plan to provide data grid capabilities to enable resource providers to share their data resources in addition to computational resources.

ACKNOWLEDGMENT AND AVAILABILITY

The work described in this chapter was carried as part of the Gridbus Project and is supported through the University of Melbourne Linkage Seed and the Australian Research Council Discovery Project grants. Alchemi software and its documentation can be downloaded from the following web site: http://www.alchemi.net.

REFERENCES

1. I. Foster and C. Kesselman (Eds.), *The Grid: Blueprint for a Future Computing Infrastructure,* Morgan Kaufmann Publishers, 1999.
2. L. Smarr and C. Catlett, Metacomputing, *Communications of the ACM Magazine, 35,* 6, 44–52, June 1992.
3. Microsoft Corporation, .NET Framework Home, http://msdn.microsoft.com/netframework/ (accessed November 2003).
4. P. Obermeyer and J. Hawkins, *Microsoft .NET Remoting: A Technical Overview,* http://msdn.microsoft.com/library/en-us/dndotnet/html/hawkremoting.asp (accessed November 2003).

5. Microsoft Corp., Web Services Development Center, http://msdn.microsoft.com/web-services/ (accessed November 2003).

6. D. H. Bailey, J. Borwein, P. B. Borwein, and S. Plouffe, The quest for Pi, Math. *Intelligencer, 19,* 50–57, 1997.

7. I. Foster and C. Kesselman, Globus: A Metacomputing Infrastructure Toolkit, *International Journal of Supercomputer Applications, 11*(2), 115–128, 1997.

8. I. Foster, C. Kesselman, and S. Tuecke, The Anatomy of the Grid: Enabling Scalable Virtual Organizations, *International Journal of Supercomputer Applications, 15*(3), 2001.

9. D. Anderson, J. Cobb, E. Korpela, M. Lebofsky, and D. Werthimer, SETI@home: An Experiment in Public-Resource Computing, *Communications of the ACM, 45,* 11, November 2002.

10. Y. Amir, B. Awerbuch, and R. S. Borgstrom, The Java Market: Transforming the Internet into a Metacomputer, *Technical Report CNDS-98-1,* Johns Hopkins University, 1998.

11. P. Cappello, B. Christiansen, M. F. Ionescu, M. O. Neary, K. E. Schauser, and D. Wu, Javelin: Internet-Based Parallel Computing Using Java, in *Proceedings of the 1997 ACM Workshop on Java for Science and Engineering Computation,* June 1997.

12. R. Buyya, D. Abramson, and J. Giddy, Nimrod/G: An Architecture for a Resource Management and Scheduling System in a Global Computational Grid, in *Proceedings of 4th International Conference on High Performance Computing in Asia-Pacific Region (HPC Asia 2000),* Beijing, China, 2000.

13. R. Buyya, *Economic-based Distributed Resource Management and Scheduling for Grid Computing,* Ph.D. Thesis, Monash University Australia, April 2002.

14. W. T. Sullivan, D. Werthimer, S. Bowyer, J. Cobb, and D. Gedye, D. Anderson, A new major SETI Project Based on Project Serendip Data and 100,000 Personal Computers, in *Proceedings of the 5th International Conference on Bioastronomy,* 1997.

15. B. J. Wilson, *JXTA,* New Riders Publishing, 2002.

16. C. Germain, V. Neri, G. Fedak, and F. Cappello, XtremWeb: Building an experimental platform for Global Computing, in *Proceedings of the 1st IEEE/ACM International Workshop on Grid Computing (Grid 2000),* Bangalore, India, Dec. 2000.

17. A. Chien, B. Calder, S. Elbert, and K. Bhatia, Entropia: Architecture and Performance of an Enterprise Desktop Grid System, *Journal of Parallel and Distributed Computing, 63,* 5, May 2003.

18. A. Oram (Ed.), *Peer-to-Peer: Harnessing the Power of Disruptive Technologies,* O'Reilly Press, 2001.

19. M. Litzkow, M. Livny, and M. Mutka, Condor—A Hunter of Idle Workstations, in *Proceedings of the 8th International Conference of Distributed Computing Systems (ICDCS 1988),* January 1988, San Jose, CA, IEEE Computer Science Press, 1988.

20. M. Mutka and M. Livny, The Available Capacity of a Privately Owned Workstation Environment, *Journal of Performance Evaluation, 12,* 4, 269–284, July 1991.

21. N. Nisan, S. London, O. Regev, and N. Camiel, Globally Distributed Computation over the Internet: The POPCORN Project, in *International Conference on Distributed Computing Systems (ICDCS'98),* May 26–29, 1998, Amsterdam, The Netherlands, IEEE Computer Science Press, 1998.

22. Y. Aridor, M. Factor, and A. Teperman, cJVM: a Single System Image of a JVM on a

Cluster, in *Proceedings of the 29th International Conference on Parallel Processing (ICPP 99),* September 1999, Fukushima, Japan, IEEE Computer Society Press.

23. Intel Corporation, United Devices' Grid MP on Intel Architecture, http://www.ud.com/ rescenter/files/wp_intel_ud.pdf (accessed November 2003).

24. Ardaiz O. and Touch J., Web Service Deployment Using the Xbone, in *Proceedings of Spanish Symposium on Distributed Systems,* SEID 2000.

25. I. Foster, C. Kesselman, J. Nick, and S. Tuecke, *The Physiology of the Grid: An Open Grid Services Architecture for Distributed Systems Integration,* Technical Report, Argonne National Lab, USA, January 2002.

26. P. Cauldwell, R. Chawla, V. Chopra, G. Damschen, C. Dix, T. Hong, F. Norton, U. Ogbuji, G. Olander, M. A. Richman, K. Saunders, and Z. Zaev, *Professional XML Web Services,* Wrox Press, 2001.

27. E. O'Tuathail and M. Rose, Using the Simple Object Access Protocol (SOAP) in Blocks Extensible Exchange Protocol (BEEP), in *IETF RFC 3288,* June 2002.

28. E. Christensen, F. Curbera, G. Meredith, and S. Weerawarana, Web Services Description Language (WSDL) 1.1.W3C Note 15, 2001. www.w3.org/TR/wsdl.

29. World Wide Web Consortium, *XML Schema Part 0:Primer: W3C Recommendation,* May 2001.

30. F. Bellard, Computation of the n'th Digit of pi in Any Base in O(n^2), http://fabrice.bellard.free.fr/pi/pi_n2/pi_n2.html (accessed June 2003).

31. C. Kruskal and A. Weiss, Allocating Independent Subtasks on Parallel Processors, *IEEE Transactions on Software Engineering, 11,* 1001–1016, 1984.

32. Global Grid Forum (GGF), *Open Grid Services Infrastructure (OGSI) Specification 1.0,* https://forge.gridforum.org/projects/ogsi-wg (accessed January 2004).

33. G. Wasson, N. Beekwilder, and M. Humphrey, OGSI.NET: An OGSI-Compliant Hosting Container for the .NET Framework, University of Virginia, USA, 2003. http:// www.cs.virginia.edu/~humphrey/GCG/ogsi.net.html (accessed Jan 2004).

34. United Devices, The History of Distributed Computing, http://www.ud.com/company/ dc/history.htm, October 9, 2001.

35. R. Buyya (Ed.), *High Performance Cluster Computing,* Vols. 1 and 2, Prentice-Hall–PTR, 1999.

36. M. Baker, R. Buyya, and D. Laforenza, Grids and Grid Technologies for Wide-Area Distributed Computing, *International Journal of Software: Practice and Experience (SPE), 32,* 15, 1437–1466, December 2002.

37. R. Buyya (Ed.), Grid Computing Info Centre, http://www.gridcomputing.com/, Accessed on June 2004.

38. J. Frey, T. Tannenbaum, I. Foster, M. Livny, and S. Tuecke, Condor-G: A Computation Management Agent for Multi-Institutional Grids, in *Proceedings of the Tenth IEEE Symposium on High Performance Distributed Computing (HPDC10),* San Francisco, August 7–9, 2001.

APPENDIX A—SAMPLE APPLICATION EMPLOYING THE GRID THREAD MODEL

```
using System;
using Alchemi.Core;
namespace Alchemi.Examples.Tutorial
{
    [Serializable]
    public class MultiplierThread : GThread
    {
        private int _A, _B, _Result;

        public int Result
        {
            get { return _Result; }
        }

        public MultiplierThread(int a, int b)
        {
            _A = a;
            _B = b;
        }

        public override void Start()
        {
            if (Id == 0) { int x = 5/Id; } // divide by zero
            _Result = _A * _B;
        }
    }

    class MultiplierApplication
    {
        static GApplication ga;

        [STAThread]
        static void Main(string[] args)
        {
            Console.WriteLine("[enter] to start grid application ...");
            Console.ReadLine();

            // create grid application
            ga = new GApplication(new GConnection("localhost", 9099));

            // add GridThread module (this executable) as a dependency
            ga.Manifest.Add(new ModuleDependency(typeof(MultiplierThread).Module));

            // create and add 10 threads to the application
            for (int i=0; i<10; i++)
            {
                // create thread
                MultiplierThread thread = new MultiplierThread(i, i+1);

                // add thread to application
                ga.Threads.Add(thread);
```

```
        }

        // subscribe to events
        ga.ThreadFinish += new GThreadFinish(ThreadFinished);
        ga.ThreadFailed += new GThreadFailed(ThreadFailed);
        ga.ApplicationFinish += new GApplicationFinish(ApplicationFinished);
        // start application
        ga.Start();

        Console.ReadLine();
    }

    static void ThreadFinished(GThread th)
    {
        // cast GThread back to MultiplierThread
        MultiplierThread thread = (MultiplierThread) th;

        Console.WriteLine(
            "thread # {0} finished with result '{1}'",
            thread.Id,
            thread.Result);
    }

    static void ThreadFailed(GThread th, Exception e)
    {
        Console.WriteLine(
            "thread # {0} finished with error '{1}'",
            th.Id,
            e.Message);
    }

    static void ApplicationFinished()
    {
        Console.WriteLine("\napplication finished");
        Console.WriteLine("\n[enter] to continue ...");
    }
    }
}
```

## CHAPTER 22

Global Grids and Software Toolkits: A Study of Four Grid Middleware Technologies

PARVIN ASADZADEH, RAJKUMAR BUYYA, CHUN LING KEI,
DEEPA NAYAR, and SRIKUMAR VENUGOPAL

A grid is an infrastructure that involves the integrated and collaborative use of computers, networks, databases, and scientific instruments owned and managed by multiple organizations. Grid applications often involve large amounts of data and/or computing resources that require secure resource sharing across organizational boundaries. This makes grid application management and deployment a complex undertaking. Grid middlewares provide users with seamless computing ability and uniform access to resources in the heterogeneous grid environment. Several software toolkits and systems have been developed, most of which are results of academic research projects all over the world. This chapter will focus on four of these middlewares-UNICORE, Globus, Legion, and Gridbus. It also presents our implementation of a resource broker for UNICORE as this functionality was not supported in it. A comparison of these systems on the basis of the architecture, implementation model, and several other features is included.

22.1 INTRODUCTION

The last decade has seen a substantial increase in commodity computer (PCs) and network performance, mainly as a result of faster hardware and more sophisticated software. These commodity technologies have been used to develop low-cost, high-performance computing systems, popularly called clusters, to solve resource-intensive problems in a number of application domains [1]. However, there are number of problems in the fields of science, engineering, and business that are not tractable using the current generation of high-performance computers. In fact, due to their size and complexity, these problems are often resource (computational and data) intensive and they also need to work collaboratively with distributed interdisciplinary application models and components. Consequently, such applications require a variety of resources that are not available in a single organization.

High-Performance Computing: Paradigm and Infrastructure. Edited by L. T. Yang and M. Guo **431**

The ubiquity of the Internet and Web as well as the availability of powerful computers and high-speed wide-area networking technologies as low-cost commodity components is rapidly changing the computing landscape and society. These technology opportunities have prompted the possibility of harnessing wide-area distributed resources for solving large-scale problems, leading to what is popularly known as grid computing [2]. The term "grid" is chosen as an analogy to the electrical power grid that provides consistent, pervasive, dependable, transparent access to electric power irrespective of its source. The level of analogy that exists between electrical and computational power grids is discussed in [3].

Grids enable the sharing, exchange, discovery, selection, and aggregation of geographically Internet-wide distributed heterogeneous resources such as computers, databases, visualization devices, and scientific instruments. Accordingly, they have been proposed as the next-generation computing platform and global cyber-infrastructure for solving large-scale problems in science, engineering, and business. Unlike traditional parallel and distributed systems, Grids address issues such as security, uniform access, dynamic discovery, dynamic aggregation, and quality of services. A number of prototype applications have been developed and scheduling experiments have been carried out within grids[4–8]. The results of these efforts demonstrate that the grid computing paradigm holds much promise. Furthermore, grids have the potential to allow the sharing of scientific instruments such as particle accelerators (CERN Large Hadron Collider [9]), the Australian radio telescope [10], and synchrotrons [11] that have been commissioned as national/international infrastructures due to the high cost of ownership and to support on-demand and real-time processing and analysis of data generated by them. Such a capability will radically enhance the possibilities for scientific and technological research and innovation, industrial and business management, application software service delivery, commercial activities, and so on.

A high-level view of activities involved within a seamless, integrated computational and collaborative grid environment is shown in Figure 22.1. The end users interact with the grid resource broker that performs resource discovery, scheduling, and the processing of application jobs on the distributed grid resources. In order to provide users with a seamless computing environment, the grid middleware systems need to solve several challenges originating from the inherent features of the grid [12]. One of the main challenges is the heterogeneity in grid environments, which results from the multiplicity of heterogeneous resources and the vast range of technologies encompassed by the grid. Another challenge involves the multiple administrative domains and autonomy issues because of geographically distributed grid resources across multiple administrative domains owned by different organizations. Other challenges include scalability (the problem of performance degradation as the size of grids increases) and the dynamicity/adaptability (the problem of resource failure is high). Middleware systems must tailor their behavior dynamically and use the available resources and services efficiently and effectively.

A tremendous amount of effort has been spent in the design and implementation of middleware software for enabling computational grids. Several of these software

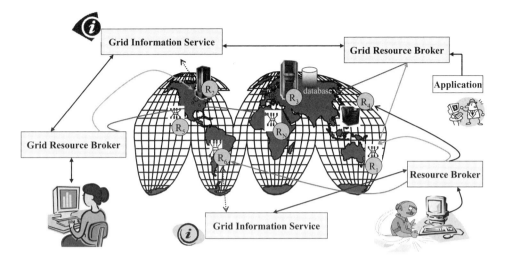

Figure 22.1 A world-wide grid computing environment.

packages have been successfully deployed and it is now possible to build grids beyond the boundaries of a single local area network. Examples of grid middleware are UNICORE (UNiform Interface to COmputing REsources) [13], Globus [13], Legion [16], and Gridbus [17]. These middleware systems aim to provide a grid-computing infrastructure in which users link to computer resources without knowing where the computing cycles are generated.

The remainder of this chapter provides an insight into the different grid middleware systems existing today, followed by the comparison of these systems, and also casts some light on the different projects using the abovementioned middleware.

22.2 OVERVIEW OF GRID MIDDLEWARE SYSTEMS

Figure 22.2 shows the hardware and software stack within a typical Grid architecture. It consists of four layers: fabric, core middleware, user-level middleware, and applications and portals layers.

The grid fabric level consists of distributed resources such as computers, networks, storage devices, and scientific instruments. The computational resources represent multiple architectures such as clusters, supercomputers, servers, and ordinary PCs that run a variety of operating systems (such as UNIX variants or Windows). Scientific instruments such as telescopes and sensor networks provide real-time data that can be transmitted directly to computational sites or stored in a database.

Core grid middleware offers services such as remote process management, coal-location of resources, storage access, information registration and discovery, security, and aspects of quality of service (QoS) such as resource reservation and trading.

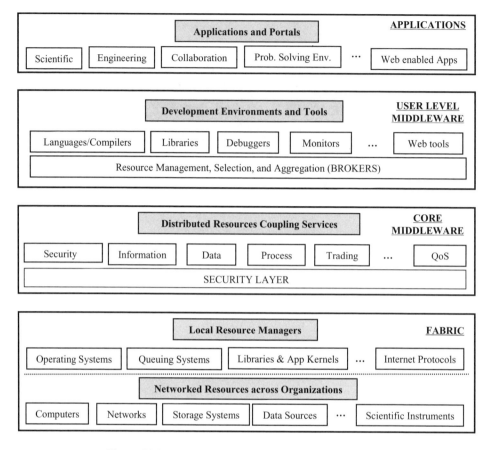

Figure 22.2 A Layered grid architecture and components.

These services abstract the complexity and heterogeneity of the fabric level by providing a consistent method for accessing distributed resources.

User-level grid middleware utilizes the interfaces provided by the low-level middleware to provide higher-level abstractions and services. These include application development environments, programming tools, and resource brokers for managing resources and scheduling application tasks for execution on global resources.

Grid applications and portals are typically developed using grid-enabled languages and utilities such as HPC++ or MPI. An example application, such as parameter simulation or a grand-challenge problem, would require computational power and access to remote datasets, and may need to interact with scientific instruments. Grid portals offer Web-enabled application services, with which users can submit and collect results for their jobs on remote resources through the Web.

The middleware surveyed in this chapter extends across one or more of the levels above the grid fabric layer of this generic stack. A short description for each of them is provided in Table 22.1.

Table 22.1 Grid middleware systems

Name	Description	Remarks	Website
UNICORE	Vertically integrated Java-based grid computing environment that provides a seamless and secure access to distributed resources.	Project funded by the German Ministry for Education and Research with cooperation between ZAM, Deutscher, etc.	http://www.unicore.org
Globus	Open-source software toolkit that facilitates construction of computational grids and grid-based applications across corporate, institutional, and geographic boundaries without sacrificing local autonomy.	R&D project conducted by the "Globus Alliance," which includes Argonne National Laboratory, Information Sciences Institute, and others.	http://www.globus.org
Legion	Vertically integrated object-based metasystem that helps in combining a large number of independently administered heterogeneous hosts, storage systems, databases legacy codes, and user objects distributed over wide-area networks into a single, object-based metacomputer that accommodates high degrees of flexibility and site autonomy.	A R&D project at the University of Virginia. The software developed by this project is commercialized through a new company called Avaki	http://legion.virginia.edu
Gridbus	Open-source software toolkit that extensively leverages related software technologies and provides an abstraction layer to hide idiosyncracies of heterogeneous resources and low-level middleware technologies from application developers. It focuses on realization of utility computing and market-oriented computing models scaling from clusters to grids and to peer-to-peer computing systems.	A research and innovation project led by the University of Melbourne GRIDS Lab with support from the Australian Research Council.	http://www.gridbus.org/

22.3   UNICORE

UNICORE [13] is a vertically integrated grid computing environment that facilitates the following:

- A seamless, secure, and intuitive access to resources in a distributed environment. For end users.
- Solid authentication mechanisms integrated into their administration procedures, reduced training effort and support requirements. For grid sites.
- Easy relocation of computer jobs to different platforms. For both end users and grid sites.

UNICORE follows a three-tier architecture, which is shown in Figure 22.3 (drawn with ideas from [14]). It consists of a client that runs on a Java-enabled user workstation or a PC, a gateway, and multiple instances of Network Job Supervisors (NJS) that execute on dedicated, securely configured servers; multiple instances of Target System Interfaces (TSI) executing on different nodes provide interfaces to underlying local resource management systems such as operating systems and the batch subsystems. From an end user's point of view, UNICORE is a client–server system based on a three-tier model:

1. User tier. The user is running the UNICORE Client on a local workstation or PC.
2. Server tier. On the top level, each participating computer center defines one or several UNICORE Grid sites (Usites) that clients can connect to.

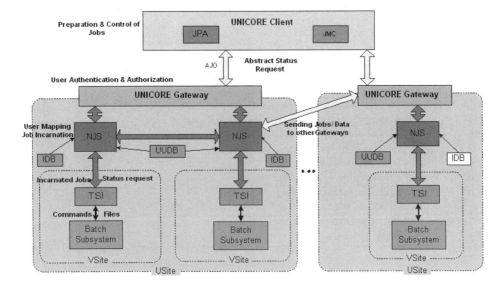

Figure 22.3   The UNICORE architecture.

3. Target system tier. A Usite offers access to computing or data resources. They are organized as one or several virtual sites (Vsites) that can represent the execution and/or storage systems at the computer centers.

The UNICORE client interface consists of two components: JPA (job preparation agent) and JMC (job monitor component). Jobs are constructed using JPA and the status and results of the jobs can be obtained through the JMC. The jobs or status requests and the results are formulated in an abstract form using the abstract job oObject (AJO) Java classes. The client connects to a UNICORE Usite gateway and submits the jobs through AJOs.

The UNICORE Gateway is the single entry point for all UNICORE connections into a Usite. It provides an Internet address and a port that users can use to connect to the gateway using SSL.

A UNICORE Vsite is made up of two components: the NJS (network job supervisor) and the TSI (target system interface). The NJS server manages all submitted UNICORE jobs and performs user authorization by looking for a mapping of the user certificate to a valid login in the UUDB (UNICORE user database). NJS also deals with the incarnation of jobs from the AJO definition into the appropriate concrete command sequences for a given target execution system, based on specifications in the incarnation database (IDB). UNICORE TSI accepts incarnated job components from the NJS, and passes them to the local batch systems for execution.

UNICORE's features and functions can be summarized as follows:

1. **User driven job creation and submission.** A graphical interface assists the user in creating complex and interdependent jobs that can be executed on any UNICORE site without job definition changes.

2. **Job management.** The job management system provides user with full control over jobs and data.

3. **Data management.** During the creation of a job, the user can specify which datasets have to be imported into or exported from the USpace (set of all files that are available to a UNICORE job), and also which datasets have to be transferred to a different USpace. UNICORE performs all data movement at run time, without user intervention.

4. **Application support.** Since scientists and engineers use specific scientific applications, the user interface is built in pluggable manner in order to extend it with plug-ins that allow them to prepare specific application input.

5. **Flow control.** A user job can be described as a set of one or more directed acyclic graphs.

6. **Single sign-on.** UNICORE provides a single sign-on through X.509V3 certificates.

7. **Support for legacy jobs.** UNICORE supports traditional batch processing by allowing users to include their old job scripts as part of a UNICORE job.

8. **Resource management.** Users select the target system and specify the required resources. The UNICORE client verifies the correctness of jobs and alerts users to correct errors immediately.

The major grid tools and application projects making use of UNICORE as their low-level middleware include: EuroGrid [18] and their applications—BioGrid [19], MeteoGrid, and CAEGrid—Grid Interoperability Project (GRIP)[20], OpenMol-Grid [19], and Japanese NAREGI (National Research Grid Initiative) [22].

22.3.1 Overview of Job Creation, Submission, and Execution in UNICORE Middleware

The UNICORE client assists in creating, manipulating and managing complex interdependent multisystem jobs, multisite jobs, synchronization of jobs, and movement of data between systems, sites, and storage spaces. The client creates an abstract job object (AJO) represented as a serialized Java Object or in XML format. The UNICORE Server (NJS) performs

- Incarnation of the AJO into target-system-specific actions
- Synchronization of actions (work flow)
- Transfers of jobs and data between user workstations, target systems, and other sites
- Monitoring of status

The two main areas of UNICORE are: (1) seamless specification of some work to be done at a remote site and (2) transmission of the specification, results and related data. The seamless specification in UNICORE is dealt with by a collection of Java classes known loosely as the AJO (abstract job object) and the transmission is defined in the UNICORE protocol layer (UPL). The UPL is designed as a protocol that transmits data regardless of its form. The classes concerned with the UPL are included in the org.unicore.package and the org.unicore.upl package, with some auxiliary functions from the org.unicore.utility package.

The main packages for the AJO are org.unicore.ajo, org.unicore.outcome, org.unicore.resources, and org.unicore.idiomatic. The AJO is how a UNICORE client application such as a job preparation agent (JPA) or job monitor controller (JMC), can specify the work that a UNICORE user wants to do to a UNICORE server (NJS). One aim of the AJO is to allow seamless specification of jobs that can be retargeted to different computer sites just by changing the address; the specification of the work remains the same, regardless of differing site policies, different executables and options, different authorisation policies, and so on. The mapping of the seamless specification to the actual site values, known as incarnation in UNICORE, is done at run time by the NJS at the target site.

The atom of execution in UNICORE is an abstract job. NJSs execute abstract jobs for users. An abstract job contains one or more subtasks. The subtasks are abstract actions and define simple actions, such as fetch files, compile, and execute.

Abstract jobs are also abstract actions and so can be contained within a parent abstract job.

When an NJS starts executing an abstract job, it creates a directory on a file system for the abstract job. This directory is known as the abstract job's Uspace. All files used by the child abstract actions are assumed to be in the Uspace. Most abstract actions do not have direct access to a site's file system (Xspace). Any files used by abstract actions has to be imported to the Uspace before they are used and any files that have to be saved have to be explicitly saved from the Uspace. The available ways to save a file are to export it, return it with the AJO's results, or to spool it to a semipermanent holding area. The Uspace is deleted when the AJO finishes execution.

The child abstract actions of an abstract job are kept in a directed acyclic graph (DAG) that defines the order of execution. Successor abstract actions start execution when all their predecessor abstract actions have finished execution successfully. Lf an abstract action fails in execution, then none of its successor abstract actions are executed.

The results of executing abstract actions are known as outcomes. Outcomes consist of the stdout and stderr produced by an executable, logging and status information from the NJS, and/or representations of the results returned by the abstract action. Each type of abstract action is matched by a type of outcome.

The core classes for the definition of work are the subclasses of org.unicore.ajo.AbstractTask. These define work that will be performed by the target system, outside of the NJS, and so define tasks such as execute, link, compile, and various file manipulations. These tasks can request resources such as the number of processors, amount of memory, time, and also any external software packages they require. A client can ask the site for a description of the supported resources and so only request resources that are available.

The other major grouping of abstract actions is based on those that can manipulate other abstract actions, for example, return current status, return results, kill and so on.

The UNICORE object hierarchy is shown below:

- AbstractAction: Parent class of all UNICORE actions
- ActionGroup: Container for UNICORE actions
- AbstractJob: ActionGroup that can run remotely
- RepeatGroup: Actions in a loop
- AbstractTask: A computational action, for example, copy file
- AbstractService: A service action, for example, kill job.
- ConditionalAction: If–then–else for actions

ActionGroup contains a DAG of AbstractActions that shows dependencies between actions (nodes) that define control flow. Actions in the DAG can be any subtype of AbstractAction. An action starts when all it predecessors are "DONE." The following subclasses of DONE are used for control.

- SUCCESSFUL: The AbstractAction completed without error.
- NOT_SUCCESSFUL: The AbstractAction failed.
- NEVER_RUN: A predecessor of the AbstractAction failed.
- NEVER_TAKEN: The AbstractAction is on the not taken branch of a conditional action.

The work flow constructs in UNICORE allow:

- Automating complex multisite, multisystem chains of jobs
- Run computational experiments like parameter studies
- Use all features of UNICORE, like security and seamlessness

22.4 GLOBUS

The Globus project provides an open-source software toolkit [13] that can be used to build computational grids and grid-based applications. It allows sharing of computing power, databases, and other tools securely online across corporate, institutional, and geographic boundaries without sacrificing local autonomy. The core services, interfaces, and protocols in the Globus Toolkit allow users to access remote resources seamlessly while simultaneously preserving local control over who can use resources and when. The Globus architecture, shown in Figure 22.4, has three main groups of services accessible through a security layer. These groups are resource management, data management, and information services.

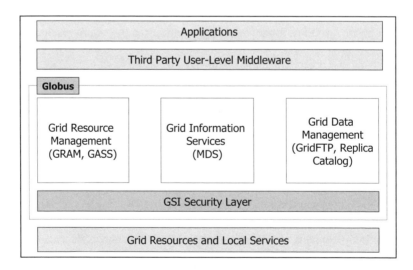

Figure 22.4 The Globus architecture.

The local-services layer contains the operating-system services, network services like TCP/IP, cluster scheduling services provided by Load Leveler, job submission, query of queues, and so on. The higher layers of the Globus model enable the integration of multiple or heterogeneous clusters. The core services layer contains the Globus Toolkit building blocks for security, job submission, data management, and resource information management. The high-level services and tools layer contains tools that integrate the lower level services or implement missing functionality.

22.4.1 GSI Security Layer

The grid security infrastructure (GSI) [23] provides methods for authentication of grid users and secure communication. It is based on SSL (secure sockets layer), PKI (public key infrastructure), and X.509 certificate architecture. The GSI provides services, protocols, and libraries to achieve the following aims for grid security:

- Single sign-on for using grid services through user certificates
- Resource authentication through host certificates
- Data encryption
- Authorization
- Delegation of authority and trust through proxies and certificate chains of trust for certificate authorities (CAs)

Users gain access to resources by having their grid certificate subjects mapped to an account on the remote machine by its system administrators. This also requires that the CA that signed the user certificate be trusted by the remote system. Access permissions have to be enforced in the traditional UNIX manner through restrictions on the remote user account.

CAs are also a part of realizing the notion of virtual organizations (VOs) [54]. VOs are vertical collaborations, and a user who has a certificate signed by the CA of the VO gains access to the resources authenticated by the same CA. VOs can cooperate between themselves by recognizing each others' CAs so that users can access resources between collaborations. These mechanisms are used in many grid testbeds. Depending on the structure of the testbed and the tools used, the users may gain access automatically to the resources or may have to contact the system administrators individually to ensure access.

Most services require mutual authentication before carrying out their functions. This guarantees repudiation and data security on both sides. However, the current state of GSI tools makes it more likely that some users may share the usage of a single certificate to gain access to higher number of resources or that they may be mapped to the same account on the remote machine. This may raise serious questions about the authenticated users and the confidentiality of user data on the remote machine. Production testbeds have policies in place to restrict this behavior but there is still some way to go before these are restricted at the middleware level.

22.4.2 Resource Management

The resource management package enables resource allocation through job submission, staging of executable files, job monitoring, and result gathering. The components of Globus within this package are:

Globus Resource Allocation Manager (GRAM). GRAM [24] provides remote execution capability and reports status for the course of the execution. A client requests a job submission from the gatekeeper daemon on the remote host. The gatekeeper daemon checks to see if the client is authorized (i.e., the client certificate is in order and there is a mapping of the certificate subject to any account on the system). Once authentication is over, the gatekeeper starts a job manager that initiates and monitors the job execution. Job managers are created depending on the local scheduler on that system. GRAM interfaces to various local schedulers such as Portable Batch System (PBS), Load Sharing Facility (LSF), and LoadLeveler. The job details are specified through the Globus Resource Specification Language (RSL), which is a part of GRAM. RSL provides syntax consisting of attribute–value pairs for describing resources required for a job, including the minimum memory and the number of CPUs.

Globus Access to Secondary Storage (GASS). GASS [27] is a file-access mechanism that allows applications to prefetch and open remote files and write them back. GASS is used for staging-in input files and executables for a job and for retrieving output once it is done. It is also used to access the standard output and error streams of the job. GASS uses secure HTTP-based streams to channel the data and has GSI-enabled functions to enforce access permissions for both data and storage.

22.4.3 Information Services

The information services package provides static and dynamic properties of the nodes that are connected to the grid. The Globus component within this package is called Monitoring and Discovery Service (MDS) [25].

MDS provides support for publishing and querying of resource information. Within MDS, schema define classes that represent various properties of the system. MDS has a three-tier structure at the bottom of which are information providers (IPs) that gather data about resource properties and status and translate them into the format defined by the object classes. The Grid Resource Information Service (GRIS) forms the second tier and is a daemon that runs on a single resource. GRIS responds to queries about the resource properties and updates its cache at intervals defined by the time to live by querying the relevant IPs. At the topmost level, the GIIS (Grid Information Index Service) indexes the resource information provided by other GRISs and GIISs that are registered with it.

The GRIS and GIIS run on the Lightweight Directory Access Protocol (LDAP) back end in which the information is represented as a hierarchy of entries, each entry consisting of 0 or more attribute–value pairs. The standard set of IPs provide data on CPU type, system architecture, number of processors, and memory available, among others.

22.4.4 Data Management

The data management package provides utilities and libraries for transmitting, storing, and managing massive datasets that are part and parcel of many scientific computing applications [26]. The elements of this package are:

> **GridFTP.** An extension of the standard FTP protocol that provides secure, efficient, and reliable data movements in grid environments. In addition to standard FTP functions, GridFTP provides GSI support for authenticated data transfer, third-party transfer invocation, and striped, parallel, and partial data transfer support.
>
> **Replica Location and Management.** This component supports multiple locations for the same file throughout the grid. Using the replica management functions, a file can be registered with the replica location service (RLS) and its replicas can be created and deleted. Within a RLS, a file is identified by its logical file name (LFN) and is registered within a logical collection. The record for a file points to its physical locations. This information is available from the RLS upon querying.

The major Grid tools and application projects making use of Globus as their low-level middleware include: AppLeS [28], Ninf [30], Nimrod-G [29], NASA IPG[36], Condor-G [31], Gridbus Broker [32], UK eScience Project [33], GriPhyN [35], and EU Data Grid [34].

22.5 LEGION

Legion [16] is a middleware system that combines very large numbers of independently administered heterogeneous hosts, storage systems, databases legacy codes, and user objects distributed over wide-area networks into a single coherent computing platform. Legion provides the means to group these scattered components together into a single, object-based metacomputer that accommodates high degrees of flexibility and site autonomy.

Figure 22.5 shows the architecture for Legion middleware. It is structured as a system of distributed "objects"—active processes that communicate using a uniform remote method invocation service. All hardware and software resources in a grid system will be represented by Legion objects. Legion's fundamental object models are described using an interface description language (IDL), and are compiled and linked to implementations in a given language. This approach enables component interoperability between multiple programming languages and heterogeneous execution platforms. Since all elements in the system are objects, they can

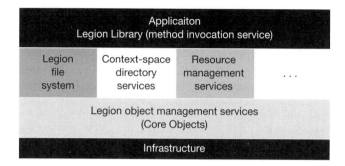

Figure 22.5   Legion architecture.

communicate with one another regardless of location, heterogeneity, or implementation details, thereby addressing problems of encapsulation and interoperability.

A "class object" is used to define and manage its corresponding Legion object. Class objects are given system-level responsibility; they control the creation of new instances, scheduling execution, and activating and deactivating instances, and provide information about their current location to client objects that wish to communicate with the instances. In other words, classes are act as managers and policy makers of the system. Metaclasses are used to describe the classes' instances.

Legion defines a set of core object types that support basic system services, such as naming and binding, object creation, activation, deactivation, and deletion. These objects provide the mechanisms that help classes to implement policies appropriate for their instances. Legion also allows users to define and build their own class objects. Some core objects are:

- **Host objects:** represent processors in Legion
- **Vault objects:** represent persistent storage
- **Context objects:** map context names to LOIDs (Legion object identifiers)
- **Binding agents:** LOIDs to LOAs (Legion object address)
- **Implementation object:** maintained as an executable file that a host object can execute when it receives a request to activate or create an object

Host objects provide a uniform interface to object (task) creation, and vault objects provide a uniform storage allocation interface, even though there may be many different implementations of each of these. Also, these objects naturally act as resource guardians and policy makers.

A three-level naming system is used in Legion. Human-readable strings, called "context names," which allow users to take advantage of a wide range of possible resources, are at the highest level. Context objects map the context names to LOIDs (Legion object identifiers) that form the next level. LOIDs are location independent and, hence, are insufficient for communication; therefore, LOIDs are transformed into LOAs (Legion object addresses) for communication. A LOA is a physical address (or set of addresses in the case of a replicated object) that contains sufficient information to allow other objects to communicate with the object.

The major grid tools and testbeds that make use of Legion as their low-level middleware include: NPACI Testbed [42], Nimrod-L [41], and NCBioGrid [40]. Additionally, it has been used in the study of axially symmetric steady flow [39] and protein folding [38] applications.

22.6 GRIDBUS

The Gridbus Project [17] is an open-source, multiinstitutional project led by the GRIDS Lab at the University of Melbourne. It is engaged in the design and development of service-oriented cluster and grid middleware technologies to support eScience and eBusiness applications. It extensively leverages related software technologies and provides an abstraction layer to hide idiosyncrasies of heterogeneous resources and low-level middleware technologies from application developers. In addition, it extensively focuses on realization of utility computing model scaling from clusters to grids and to peer-to-peer computing systems. It uses economic models [43] in efficient management of shared resources and promotes commoditization of their services. Thus, it enhances the tradability of grid services and manages efficiently the supply and demand for resources.

Gridbus supports commoditization of grid services at various levels:

- Raw resource level (e.g., selling CPU cycles and storage resources)
- Application level (e.g., molecular docking operations for drug design applications [7])
- Aggregated services (e.g., brokering and reselling of services across multiple domains)

The idea of a computational economy helps in creating a service-oriented computing architecture in which service providers offer paid services associated with a particular application, and users, based on their requirements, would optimize by selecting the services they require and can afford within their budget. Gridbus emphasizes the end-to-end quality of services driven by computational economy at various levels—clusters, peer-to-peer (P2P) networks, and the grid—for the management of distributed computational, data, and application services.

Figure 22.6 shows a layered architecture depicting the Gridbus components in conjunction with other middleware technologies—Globus and Unicore—that have been discussed before and Alchemi, which is discussed in detail in the next chapter, although we briefly present it here for completeness.

Gridbus provides software technologies that spread across the following categories:

- Enterprise grid infrastructure (Alchemi)
- Cluster economy and resource allocation (Libra)

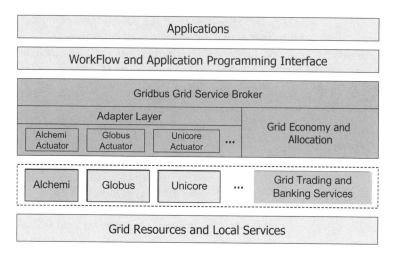

Figure 22.6 The Gridbus architecture.

- Grid economy and virtual enterprise (Grid Market Directory, Compute Power Market)
- Grid trading and accounting services (GridBank)
- Grid resource brokering and Scheduling (Gridbus Broker)
- Grid workflow management (Gridbus Workflow Engine)
- Grid application programming interface (Visual Parametric Modeller)
- Grid portals (GMonitor, Gridscape)
- Grid simulation (GridSim)

22.6.1 Alchemi

Though scientific computing facilities have been heavy users of Unix-class OSes, the vast majority of computing infrastructure within enterprises is still based on Microsoft Windows. Alchemi was developed to address the need within enterprises for a desktop grid solution that utilizes the unused computational capacity represented by the vast number of PCs and workstation running Windows within an organization. Alchemi is implemented on top of the Microsoft .NET Framework and provides the runtime machinery for constructing and managing desktop grids. It also provides an object-oriented programming model along with Web service interfaces that enable its services to be accessed from any programming environment that supports SOAP-XML abstraction.

22.6.2 Libra

Libra is a cluster scheduling system that guarantees a certain share of the system resources to a user job such that the job is completed by the deadline specified by the user, provided he has the requisite budget for it. Jobs whose output is required immediately require a higher budget than those with a more relaxed deadline. Thus, Libra delivers utility value to the cluster users and increases their satisfaction by creating realistic expectations for the job turnaround times.

22.6.3 Market Mechanisms for Computational Economy

Grid Market Directory (GMD) is a registry service with which service providers can register themselves and publish the services they are providing, and consumers can query to obtain the service that meets their requirements. Some of the attributes of a service are its access point, input mechanism, and the cost involved in using it.

Compute Power Market (CPM) is a market-based resource management and scheduling system developed over the JXTA platform. It enables trading of idle computational power over P2P networks. The CPM components that represent markets, consumers, and providers are Market Server, Market Resource Agent, and Market Resource Broker (MRB). It supports various economic models for resource trading and matching service consumers and providers, and allows plugging in of different scheduling mechanisms.

22.6.4 Accounting and Trading Services

GridBank is a grid-wide accounting and micropayment service that provides a secure infrastructure for grid service consumers (GSCs) to pay grid service providers (GSPs) for the usage of their services. The consumer is charged on the basis of resource usage records maintained by the provider and service charges that have been agreed upon by both parties beforehand. GridBank can also be used as an authentication and authorization mechanism, thereby ensuring access to resources to only those consumers with the requisite credit in their accounts.

22.6.5 Resource Broker

The Gridbus Resource Broker provides an abstraction to the complexity of grids by ensuring transparent access to computational and data resources for executing a job on a grid. It uses user requirements to create a set of jobs; discover resources; schedule, execute, and monitor the jobs; and retrieve their output once they are finished. The broker supports a declarative and dynamic parametric programming model for creating grid applications.

The Gridbus Resource Broker has the capability to locate and retrieve the required data from multiple data sources and to redirect the output to storage from which it can be retrieved by processes downstream. It has the ability to select the best data repositories from multiple sites based on availability of files and quality of data transfer.

22.6.6 Web Portals

G-monitor is a Web portal for monitoring and steering computations on global grids. G-monitor interfaces with resource brokers such as Gridbus Broker and Nimrod-G and uses their services to initiate and monitor application execution. It provides the user with up-to-date information about the progress of the execution at the individual job level and at the overall experiment level. At the end of the execution, the user can collect the output files through G-monitor.

To manage and monitor Grid testbeds, the Gridbus Project has created a testbed portal and generation tool called Gridscape. Gridscape generates interactive and dynamic portals that enable users to view the status of the resources within the testbed and easily add new resources when required. It is also possible to customize the portal to reflect the unique identity of the organization managing the testbed.

22.6.7 Simulation and Modeling

The GridSim toolkit provides facilities for the modeling and simulation of resources and network connectivity with different capabilities, configurations, and domains. It supports primitives for application composition, information services for resource discovery, and interfaces for assigning application tasks to resources and managing their execution. It also provides a visual modeler interface for creating users and resources. These features can be used to simulate parallel and distributed scheduling systems such as resource brokers or grid schedulers for evaluating performance of scheduling algorithms or heuristics.

The major grid tools and application projects making use of Gridbus components within their middleware include: ePhysics Portal [52], Australian Virtual Observatory [51], Belle Analysis Data Grid [50], Global Data Intensive Grid Collaboration [49], NeuroGrid [48], Natural Language Engineering on the Grid [53], HydroGrid [46], and Amsterdam Private Grid [47].

22.7 IMPLEMENTATION OF UNICORE ADAPTOR FOR GRIDBUS BROKER

As a complete integrated system, Legion provides its own grid broker that facilitates management, selection, and aggregation of resources and scheduling of applications for execution on global resources, whereas Globus and UNICORE do not provide their own. Globus has a number of third-party grid broker implementations such as Nimrod-G, Gridbus Broker, and Condor-G, but UNICORE does not have such an add-on service. The absence of brokerage services in UNICORE motivates the need for porting a grid resource broker to UNICORE. An extension of Gridbus Broker and the implementation of adaptor for UNICORE middleware is described in this section.

The scheduler in Gridbus has a platform-independent view of the nodes and is concerned only with their performance. Therefore, it is possible for the broker to operate across different middleware. Gridbus Broker is already capable of operating on resources that are grid-enabled, using Globus and Alchemi middleware. Similarly, Gridbus Broker can be designed to work with UNICORE middleware by extending the ComputeServer, JobWrapper, JobMonitor, and JobOutput classes in Gridbus. The main components in the implementation of Gridbus Broker on UNICORE is shown in Figure 22.7 and in the UML Diagram in Figure 22.8.

22.7.1   UnicoreComputeServer

The ComputeServer object in Gridbus Broker is responsible for describing nodes in a system. By extending the ComputeServer class for UNICORE, the attributes of nodes that are grid enabled by UNICORE can be described in UnicoreCompute-Server.

In order to establish access to resources, first we need to create an identity that is used for AJO execution:

```
Identity identity = new Identity( new File(<keystore>), <password>);
```

The created identity is then used to set up a SSL connection to the gateway and to establish a link to the Vsite.

```
Reference reference = new Reference.SSL(<gateway_address>, identity);
VsiteTh vsite = new VsiteTh(reference, <Vsite name>);
```

Since the information is extracted from the command line directly, no checking is required by the gateway. Dynamic applications can only accept some gateway

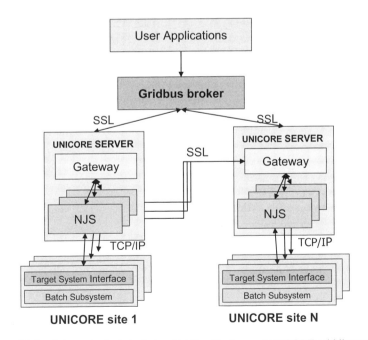

Figure 22.7   Schematic for interfacing Gridbus Broker on UNICORE middleware.

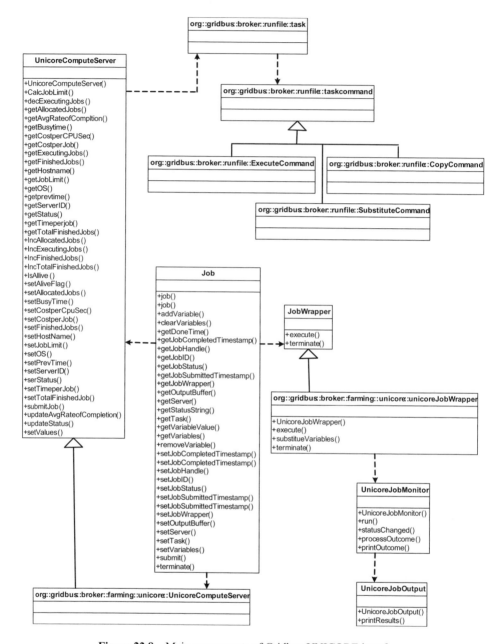

Figure 22.8   Main components of Gridbus-UNICORE interface.

addresses and then present the list of Vsites and ports to the user. Resources could also be fetched from the Vsites by using the VsiteManager that provides a global view of all the known Vsites.

22.7.2 UnicoreJobWrapper

The main function of this object is to convert the job specified by Gridbus Broker through an XML-based parameter sweep specification (xPSS) document to a format that is understandable by the ComputeServer running UNICORE middleware. In an xPSS document, there are three commands, namely, SUBSTITUTE, COPY, and EXECUTE. For the COPY command, we need to copy the files required for the execution of the AJO from the client machine to the remote machine and copy the resulting files back to the local machine.

In the first case, the required files are first put into IncarnateFiles, which creates files in the Uspace from data contained in the instance. This is provided as an alternative way of transferring files to Uspaces. In this case, the bytes of the files are placed in the AJO and, therefore, this method is only practical for small files. Large files should be streamed. Finally, files are put into a portfolio that is transferred along with the AJO to be executed.

22.7.2.1 Method 1

```
MakePortfolio mp1= new MakePortfolio ();
File file=new File(<file_name>);
FileInputStream fin=new FileInputStream(file);
byte[] file_contents= new byte[(int) file.length()];
fin.read(file_contents);
IncarnateFiles inf1 = new IncarnateFiles("Required Files");
inf1.addFile(<file_name>,file_contents);
mp1.addFile(<file_name>);
```

22.7.2.2 Method 2

```
Portfolio portfolio = new Portfolio();
PortfolioTh files = new PortfolioTh(portfolio, <java.io.File[] Files>);
```

In Method 2, the resulting files in the remote machine are added to the job outcome, which is transferred to the local machine. This is done because all the files in the Uspace are deleted at the end of AJO execution.

Step 1: Let the NJS know about the files (make a Portfolio):

```
MakePortfolio mp2 = new MakePortfolio()
mp2.addFile(<result file name in Upsace>);
```

Step 2: Save files:

```
CopyPortfolioToOutcome cpto = new CopyPortfolioToOutcome ();
cpto.setTarget(mp2.getPortfolio().getId());
```

For the EXECUTE command, the executable in the plan file is converted into a script and an `ExecuteScriptTask` is created which is included in the AJO:

```
String the_script = "date\n";
the_script += "hostname\n";
inf.addFile("script",the_script.getBytes());


MakePortfolio mp = new MakePortfolio("AJO Example");
mp.addFile("script");


ExecuteScriptTask est = new ExecuteScriptTask("AJO Example Task");
est.setScriptType(ScriptType.CSH);
est.setExecutable(mp.getPortfolio());
```

Finally, the AJO is created by adding the components and their dependencies and is submitted to the remote machine using the `job_manager.consign-Synchronous` method in the com.fujitsu.arcon.servlet.JobManager class within the Arcon client library:

```
AbstractJob ajo = new AbstractJob("AJO Example");
ajo.addDependency(inf,mp);
ajo.addDependency(inf1,mp1);
ajo.addDependency(mp,est);
ajo.addDependency(est, mp2);
ajo.addDependency(mp2,cpto);
outcome = JobManager.consignSynchronous(ajo,vsite);
```

The UnicoreJobWrapper also starts the UnicoreJobMonitor thread, which is responsible for monitoring the status of the job execution.

22.7.3   UnicoreJobMonitor

The UnicoreMonitor is used to monitor the execution of the job and display the detailed status information during the execution. The status information includes information related to all AbstractActions and AbstractTasks involved such as MakePortfolio and ExecuteScriptTask. It is also responsible for terminating the job in case of job failure or job completion.

22.7.4   UnicoreJobOutput

As the name suggests, UnicoreJobOutput is used to get back the results of the job. It displays the contents of the standard output and standard error files from the computeServer on the local machine. If other result files are produced as a result of the job execution, UnicoreJobOutput renames these files in "filename.jobid" format and saves them in the local directory. The outcome is fetched from the client side using the `Job_manager.getOutcome` function of the JobManager.

Thus, all the result files are written to local storage if the AJO is successfully completed:

```
Collection c = outcome.getFilesMapping().get(cpto.getId());
Iterator i = c.iterator();
while (i.hasNext())
{
        File f = (File)i.next();
        System.out.println("\n\nRESULT FILE:
          "+f.getCanonicalPath()+"\nCONTENTS\n");
        BufferedReader reader = new BufferedReader(new FileReader(f));
        String line;
        while((line = reader.readLine()) != null)
        {System.out.println(line);}
}
```

22.8   COMPARISON OF MIDDLEWARE SYSTEMS

Figure 22.9 compares the surveyed middleware on the basis of the services provided across the grid architecture stack. UNICORE and Legion are vertically integrated and tightly coupled. They provide both server and client components. Globus follows a "bag-of-services" approach and provides a rich set of basic tools that can be used selectively to construct grid systems. For example, although Gridbus has its own independent low-level middleware, its broker has been designed to operate with Globus. The Gridbus component set, though spread across the stack, is not integrated as tightly as UNICORE and Legion and the components can be used completely independent of each other.

A comparison of the various middleware systems based on their architecture, implementation model, and category, is given in Table 22.2. Another comparison between Globus and Legion can be found in [37].

In addition to the above comparison, the middleware systems can be compared on the basis of resource management, data management, communication methods, and security. Globus and Legion provide broker services, whereas UNICORE and

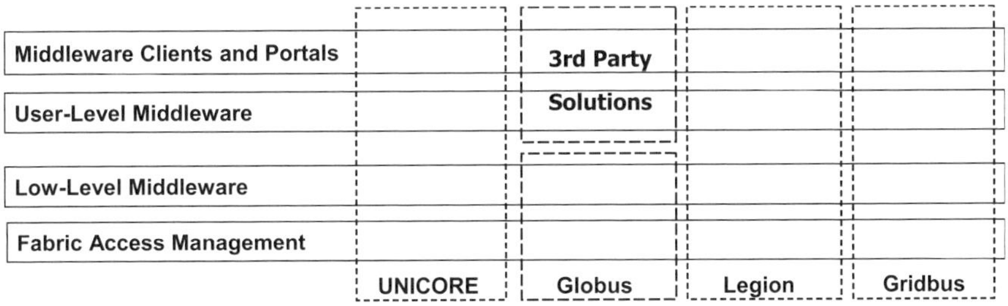

Figure 22.9   Comparison of UNICORE, Globus, Legion, and Gridbus.

Table 22.2 Comparison of grid middleware systems

	Middleware			
Property	UNICORE	Globus	Legion	Gridbus
Focus	High-level programming models	Low-level services	High-level programming models	Abstractions and market models
Category	Mainly uniform job submission and monitoring	Generic computational	Generic computational	Generic computational
Architecture	Vertical multitiered system	Layered and modular toolkit	Vertically integrated system	Layered component and utility model
Implementation model	Abstract job object	Hourglass model at system level	Object-oriented metasystem	Hourglass model at user level
Implementation technologies	Java	C and Java	C++	C, Java, C#, and Perl
Runtime platform	Unix	Unix	Unix	Unix and Windows with .NET (Alchemi)
Programming environment	Workflow environment	Replacement libraries for Unix and C libraries. Special MPI library (MPICH-G), CoG (commodity grid) kits in Java, Python, CORBA, Matlab, Java Server Pages, Perl, and Web services	Legion application programming interfaces (API). Command line utilities	Broker Java API XML-based parameter-sweep language. Grid thread model via Alchemi
Distribution model	Open source	Open source	Not open source. Commercial version available	Open source
Some users and applications	EuroGrid [18], Grid Interoperability Project (GRIP) [20], OpenMolGrid [19], and Japanese NAREGI [22].	AppLeS [28], Ninf [30], Nimrod-G [29], NASA IPG [36], Condor-G [31], Gridbus Broker [32], UK eScience Project [33], GriPhyN [35], and EU Data Grid [34]	NPACI Testbed [42], Nimrod-L [41], and NCBioGrid [40]. Additionally, it has been used in the study of axially symmetric steady flow [39] and protein folding [38] applications.	ePhysics Portal [52], Belle Analysis Data Grid [50], NeuroGrid [48], Natural Language Engineering [53], HydroGrid [46], and Amsterdam Private Grid [47]

Alchemi do not provide brokering of user requests. In the case of Alchemi, Gridbus Broker fulfills the role of grid brokering. The Globus communications module is based on the Nexus communication library and UNICORE's communication methods are based on AJO model and do not support synchronous message passing. Legion supports a variation of RMI for communication through LOIDs. UNICORE security is based on the Secure Socket Layer (SSL) protocol and X.509V3-type certificates. Globus provides security services through GSI, which is again based on SSL and X.509 certificates. In Gridbus's Alchemi middleware, security services are leveraged from the powerful toolset in the Microsoft .NET framework. Other Gridbus components extensively leverage security services provided by Globus GSI.

22.9 SUMMARY

There has been considerable research aimed at the development of grid middleware systems and most of these systems have been successfully applied in other grid-related projects and applications. The Globus Toolkit is one of the most widely used low-level grid middleware systems in use today. It provides key services such as resource access, data management, and security infrastructure. UNICORE is a Java-based grid computing system that is being used in projects including EUROGRID and GRIP. Gridbus toolkit extensively leverages related software technologies and provides an abstraction layer to hide idiosyncrasies of heterogeneous resources and low-level middleware technologies from application developers. It focuses on realization of utility computing models scaling from clusters to grids and to peer-to-peer computing systems. Legion is an object-based middleware system implemented in projects like Boeing's R&D project.

The comparison of grid middleware systems has shown that there is considerable overlap between their functionality. The main difference has been found to be in their architecture or implementation model. An examination of UNICORE's features shows that it does not provide brokerage services that manage or schedule computations across global resources. This shortcoming motivated us to port the Gridbus Resource Broker to the UNICORE environment.

ACKNOWLEDGMENT

We would like to thank Sven van den Berghe from Fujitsu Laboratories of Europe for his valuable technical guidance during the creation of the Gridbus Broker adaptor for UNICORE environments.

REFERENCES

1. R. Buyya (Ed.), *High Performance Cluster Computing,* Prentice-Hall, 1999.
2. I. Foster and C. Kesselman (Eds.), *The Grid: Blueprint for a Future Computing Infrastructure,* Morgan Kaufmann Publishers, 1999.

3. M. Chetty and R. Buyya, Weaving Computational Grids: How Analogous Are They with Electrical Grids?, *Computing in Science and Engineering (CiSE), 4,* 4, 61–71, July–August 2002.

4. M. D. Brown et al., *The International Grid (iGrid): Empowering Global Research Community Networking Using High Performance International Internet Services,* http://www.globus.org/research/papers.html, April 1999.

5. S. Smallen et al., Combining Workstations and Supercomputers to Support Grid Applications: The Parallel Tomography Experience, in *9th Heterogenous Computing Workshop (HCW 2000, IPDPS),* Mexico, April, 2000.

6. SC 2000 Net Challenge, http://www.npaci.edu/sc2000/netchallenge.html.

7. R. Buyya, K. Branson, J. Giddy, and D. Abramson, The Virtual Laboratory: A Toolset for Utilising the World-Wide Grid to Design Drugs, in *2nd IEEE International Symposium on Cluster Computing and the Grid (CCGrid 2002),* 21–24 May 2002, Berlin, Germany.

8. iGrid 2002, International Exhibition on Grid Applications, http://www.igrid2002.org.

9. CERN LHC Computing Grid Project, http://lhcgrid.web.cern.ch/LHCgrid/.

10. Australia Telescope National Facility, http://www.atnf.csiro.au/.

11. Australian Synchrotron Project, http://www.synchrotron.vic.gov.au.

12. M. Baker, R. Buyya, and D. Laforenza, Grids and Grid Technologies for Wide-Area Distributed Computing, *International Journal of Software: Practice and Experience (SPE), 32,* 15, 1437–1466, December 2002.

13. J. Almond and D. Snelling, UNICORE: Uniform Access to Supercomputing as an Element of Electronic Commerce, *Future Generation Computer Systems 613,* 1–10, 1999.

14. M. Romberg, The UNICORE Architecture: Seamless Access To Distributed Resources, in *Proceedings of the Eighth International Symposium on High Performance Distributed Computing,* Redondo Beach, CA, 1999.

15. I. Foster and C. Kesselman, Globus: A Metacomputing Infrastructure Toolkit, *International Journal of Supercomputer Applications, 11*(2), 115–128, 1997.

16. A. Grimshaw and W. Wulf, The Legion Vision of a Worldwide Virtual Computer, *Communications of the ACM* 40(1), 1997.

17. R. Buyya and S. Venugopal, The Gridbus Toolkit for Service Oriented Grid and Utility Computing: An Overview and Status Report, in *Proceedings of the First IEEE International Workshop on Grid Economics and Business Models* (GECON 2004), April 23, 2004, Seoul, Korea, pp. 19–36, IEEE Press.

18. The EuroGrid Project, http://www.eurogrid.org/.

19. P. Bala, J. Pytlinski, and M. Nazaruk, BioGRID—An European Grid for Molecular Viology, in *Proceedings of 11th IEEE International Symposium on High Performance Distributed Computing* (HPDC-11), Edinburgh, UK, 2002.

20. R. Menday and P. Wieder, GRIP: The Evolution of UNICORE towards a Service-Oriented Grid, Presented at Cracow Grid Workshop, October 27–29, 2003, Cracow Poland.

21. Open Computing Grid for Molecular Science and Engineering (OpenMolGRID), http://www.openmolgrid.org/.

22. NAREGI Project, http://www.naregi.org/.

23. I. Foster, C. Kesselman, G. Tsudik, and S. Tuecke, A Security Architecture for Computational Grids, in *Proceedings of 5th ACM Conference on Computer and Communications Security,* San Francisco, CA.

24. K. Czajkowski, I. Foster, N. Karonis, C. Kesselman, S. Martin, W. Smith, and S. Tuecke, *A Resource Management Architecture for Metacomputing Systems, in* Proceedings of IPPS/SPDP '98 Workshop on Job Scheduling Strategies for Parallel Processing, Orlando, FL, 1998.

25. S. Fitzgerald, I. Foster, C. Kesselman, G. von Laszewski, W. Smith, and S. Tuecke, A Directory Service for Configuring High-Performance Distributed Computations, in Proceedings of 6th IEEE Symposium on High-Performance Distributed Computing, Portland, OR, 1997.

26. B. Allcock, J. Bester, J. Bresnahan, A. Chervenak, I. Foster, C. Kesselman, S. Meder, V. Nefedova, D. Quesnel, and S. Tuecke, Secure, Efficient Data Transport and Replica Management for High-Performance Data-Intensive Computing, Presented at IEEE Mass Storage Conference, San Diego, CA, 2001.

27. J. Bester, I. Foster, C. Kesselman, J. Tedesco, and S. Tuecke, GASS: A Data Movement and Access Service for Wide Area Computing Systems, Presented at Sixth Workshop on I/O in Parallel and Distributed Systems, Atlanta, GA, USA, May 5, 1999.

28. F. Berman and R. Wolski, The AppLeS Project: A Status Report, Presented at 8th NEC Research Symposium, Berlin, Germany, May 1997

29. D. Abramson, J. Giddy, and L. Kotler, High Performance Parametric Modeling with Nimrod/G: Killer Application for the Global Grid?, in *Proceedings of the International Parallel and Distributed Processing Symposium* (IPDPS 2000), May 1–5, 2000, Cancun, Mexico, IEEE Computer Science Press, 2000.

30. M.Sato, H. Nakada, S. Sekiguchi, S. Matsuoka, U. Nagashima, and H. Takagi, Ninf: A Network Based Information Library for Global World-Wide Computing Infrastructure, in *Proceedings of the International Conference on High Performance Computing and Networking Europe* (HPCN Europe), Vienna, Austria, April 28–30, 1997.

31. J. Frey, T. Tannenbaum, I. Foster, M. Livny, and S. Tuecke, Condor-G: A Computation Management Agent for Multi-Institutional Grids, in *Proceedings of the Tenth IEEE Symposium on High Performance Distributed Computing* (HPDC10) San Francisco, CA, August 7–9, 2001.

32. S. Venugopal, R. Buyya, and L. Winton, A Grid Service Broker for Scheduling Distributed Data-Oriented Applications on Global Grids, Technical Report, GRIDS-TR-2004-1, Grid Computing and Distributed Systems Laboratory, University of Melbourne, Australia, February 2004.

33. T. Hey and A. E. Trefethen, The UK e-Science Core Programme and the Grid, *Future Generation Computer Systems, 18,* 8, 1017–1031, 2002.

34. W. Hoschek, J. Jaen-Martinez, A. Samar, H. Stockinger, and K. Stockinger, Data Management in an International Data Grid Project, in *Proceedings of the First IEEE/ACM International Workshop on Grid Computing,* India, 2000, Springer-Verlag.

35. Grid Physics Network, (GriPhyN).http://www.griphyn.org/ (accessed Jun 2004).

36. W. Johnston, D. Gannon, and B. Nitzberg, Grids as Production Computing Environments: The Engineering Aspects of NASA's Information Power Grid, In *Proceedings of Eighth IEEE International Symposium on High Performance Distributed Computing,* Redondo Beach, CA, 1999.

37. M. Baker and G. Fox, *Metacomputing: Harnessing Informal Supercomputers,* in R. Buyya (Ed.), High Performance Cluster Computing, Prentice Hall, 1999.

38. A. Natrajan, M. Crowley, N. Wilkins-Diehr, M. Humphrey, A. D. Fox, A. Grimshaw,

and C. L. Brooks III, Studying Protein Folding on the Grid: Experiences Using CHARMM on NPACI Resources under Legion, in *Proceedings of the 10th International Symposium on High Performance Distributed Computing* (HPDC-10), August 7–9, 2001.

39. N. Beekwilder and A. Grimshaw, *Parallelization of an Axially Symmetric Steady Flow Program,* CS Technical Report CS-98-10, University of Virginia, May 29, 1998.

40. NC-BioGrid, http://www.ncbiogrid.org/.

41. D. Abramson, Nimrod on Legion Middleware, http://www.dstc.edu.au/Research/activesheets-ov.html.

42. A. Grimshaw, *A Worldwide Virtual Computer for an Advancing Legion of Applications,* NPACI, http://www.npaci.edu/enVision/v15.2/legion.html.

43. R. Buyya, *Economic-based Distributed Resource Management and Scheduling for Grid Computing,* PhD Thesis, Monash University, Melbourne, Australia, April 12, 2002.

44. A. Luther, R. Buyya, R. Ranjan, and S. Venugopal, Alchemi: A .NET-based Grid Computing Framework and Its Integration into Global Grids, http://www.gridbus.org/papers/Alchemi.pdf.

45. R. Buyya, D. Abramson, and J. Giddy, An Economy Driven Resource Management Architecture for Global Computational Power Grids, in *The 2000 International Conference on Parallel and Distributed Processing Techniques and Applications (PDPTA 2000),* Las Vegas, NV, June 26–29, 2000.

46. J. Rahman and G. Davis, TIME and DIME: Supporting Natural Resource Modelling with .NET and Alchemi, CSIRO, http://alchemi.net/projects.html.

47. A. Warmenhoven, *Amsterdam PrivateGrid,* The Netherlands, http://www.private-grid.nl/.

48. R. Buyya, S. Date, Y. Mizuno-Matsumoto, S. Venugopal, and D. Abramson, Composition of Distributed Brain Activity Analysis and Its On-Demand Deployment on Global Grids, in *New Frontiers in High-Performance Computing: Proceedings of the 10th International Conference on High Performance Computing (HiPC 2003) Workshops* (Dec. 17, 2003, Hyderabad, India), Elite Publishing House, New Delhi, India.

49. R. Buyya et. al, Global Data Intensive Grid Collaboration, in *HPC Challenge Proposal and Demonstration, IEEE/ACM Supercomputing Conference* (SC 2003), Nov. 2003, http://www.gridbus.org/sc2003/.

50. BADG Project, *Belle Analysis Data Grid,* http://epp.ph.unimelb.edu.au/epp/grid/badg/.

51. Australian Virtual Observatory (Aus-VO), http://www.aus-vo.org/.

52. B. Beeson, S. Melnikoff, S. Venugopal, and D. Barnes, *A Portal for Grid-enabled Physics,* Australian Virtual Observatory, http://www.aus-vo.org/.

53. B. Hughes, S. Venugopal, R. Buyya, *Grid-based Indexing of a Newswire Corpus,* Technical Report, GRIDS-TR-2004-4, Grid Computing and Distributed Systems Laboratory, University of Melbourne, Australia, June/July 2004.

54. I. Foster, C. Kesselman, and S. Tuecke, The Anatomy of the Grid: Enabling Scalable Virtual Organizations, *International Journal of High Performance Computing Applications, 15,* 200–222, 2001.

## CHAPTER 23

High-Performance Computing on Clusters: The Distributed JVM Approach

WENZHANG ZHU, WEIJIAN FANG, CHO-LI WANG, and FRANCIS C. M. LAU

A distributed Java virtual machine (DJVM) is a clusterwide virtual machine that supports parallel execution of a multithreaded Java application on clusters, as if it were executed on a single machine but with improved computation power. The DJVM hides the physical boundaries between the cluster nodes and allows parallely executed Java threads to access all cluster resources through a unified interface. It is a more user-friendly parallel environment than many other existing parallel languages [8] or libraries for parallel programming such as MPI [13], CORBA [16], and Java RMI [7]. The DJVM research is valuable for high-performance computing as Java has become the dominant language for building server-side applications such as enterprise information systems, Web services, and large-scale grid computing systems, due to its platform independency and built-in multithreading support at the language level.

This chapter addresses the realization of a distributed Java virtual machine, named JESSICA2, on clusters. Section 23.1 describes Java, Java Virtual Machine, and the main programming paradigms using Java for high-performance computing. We then focus our study on the newly emerging distributed JVM research in Section 23.2. In Section 23.3, we introduce our JESSICA2 Distributed JVM. Section 23.4 gives the performance analysis of JESSICA2. Related work is given in Section 23.5. Section 23.6 concludes this chapter.

23.1 BACKGROUND

23.1.1 Java

Java [11] is a popular, general object-oriented programming language. Java supports concurrency through its multithreading framework. A Java program can have simultaneous control flows (threads), and all the threads share a common memory space. To avoid the competition among threads, Java includes a set of synchronization primitives based on the classic monitor paradigm. The synchronized keyword is used for declaring a critical section in Java source code.

Java objects can be regarded as monitors. Each object has a header containing a lock. A lock is acquired on entry to a synchronized method or block, and is released on exit. The lock is also associated with a wait queue. The class java.lang.Object provides three additional methods to control the wait queue within the synchronized methods or blocks, that is, wait, notify, and notifyAll. The method wait causes the current thread to wait in the queue until another thread invokes the notify method or the notifyAll method, which wake up a single thread or all the threads waiting for this object, respectively.

Each Java object consists of data and methods. The object has associated with it a pointer to a virtual method table. The table stores the pointers to their methods. When a class is loaded into a Java virtual machine (JVM), the class method table will be filled with pointers to the entries of the methods. When an object is created, its method table pointer will point to its class method table.

The heap is the shared memory space for Java threads to store the created objects. The heap stores all the master copies of objects. Each thread has a local working memory to keep the copies of objects loaded from the heap that it needs to access. When the thread starts execution, it operates on the data in its local working memory.

23.1.2   Java Virtual Machine

Unlike most of other programming languages, a Java source program is usually not directly compiled into native code running on the specific hardware platform. Instead, the Java compiler will translate the Java source program into a machine-independent binary code called the bytecode. The bytecode consists of a collection of class files, each corresponding to a Java class. A JVM is then used to load and execute the compiled Java bytecode. The bytecode is then interpreted or translated by the JVM execution engine. The JVM provides the run-time environment for the execution of the Java bytecode. Once a JVM is designed on a specific computer architecture, the computer can execute any Java program distributed in bytecode format without recompilation of source code.

The JVM is a stack-oriented and multithreaded virtual machine. Figure 23.1 illustrates the architecture of a JVM. Inside a JVM, each thread has a run-time data structure called a Java stack to hold the program counter (PC) and the local variables. The threads create Java objects in the centralized garbage-collected heap and refer to the objects using object references in the Java stack. All the created objects are visible to all the threads.

The execution engine is the processor of the JVM. The earlier JVMs execute Java bytecode by interpretation. The method entries of the object are set to the call to the interpreter with the method id as the argument. The interpreter creates the

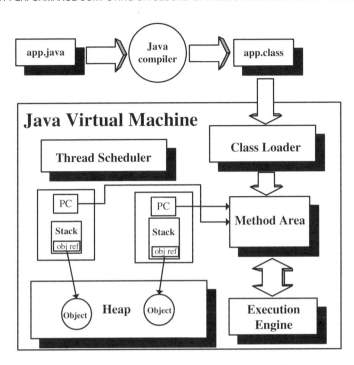

Figure 23.1   The architecture of a Java virtual machine.

data structures for the Java method and try to simulate the semantics of bytecode in-structions by operating on these data structures in a big loop.

The interpreter is simple to implement. However, such interpretation is slow be-cause it cannot efficiently use the machine registers for computation. And it cannot cache the previously computed results such as the constant offset to an object. To boost the Java execution performance, the concept of just-in-time (JIT) compilation is introduced.

A JIT compiler compiles Java methods on demand. The method pointers in the virtual method table will be set to the JIT compiler. The first time each method is called up, the JIT compiler is invoked to compile the method. The method pointer then points to the compiled native code so that future calls to the method will jump to the native code directly. As the time for JIT compilation is charged to the execu-tion time of Java program, the JIT compiler requires lightweight compilation tech-niques. Usually, a JIT compiler can improve the performance of a Java application by a factor of one.

23.1.3   Programming Paradigms for Parallel Java Computing

Several programming paradigms exist for the parallelization of applications. Gener-ally, we have three major paradigms, namely, data parallel, message passing, and shared memory. To support these paradigms in Java, many libraries and run-time systems have been proposed since Java was created in 1995.

23.1.3.1 *Data Parallel*

The data-parallel paradigm applies the same operation on different datasets residing on different cluster nodes.

One example to support the data-parallel programming paradigm is the HPJava language [8]. It extends ordinary Java with some shorthand syntax for describing how arrays are distributed across processes. HPJava has no explicit interfaces for communication among processes. The communication among processes is handled transparently by the HPJava compiler.

The shortcoming of HPJava is that Java programmers need to master HPJava's specific syntax in order to exploit data parallelism and leverage the cluster-computing capability. However, due to the high portability of Java, HPJava could be favored by those who are familiar with the data-parallel paradigm and are willing to try Java.

23.1.3.2 *Message Passing*

Message passing is probably the most common paradigm for parallel programming on the clusters. In this paradigm, the programmers write explicit code to send and receive messages for the communication and coordination among different processes in a parallel application. Besides the famous Socket interface to support TCP/IP communication, Java programmers can also use some additional high-level message passing mechanisms such as Message Passing Interface (MPI), the Java Remote Method Invocation (RMI) [7], and Common Object Request Broker Architecture (COBRA) [16].

MPI is a widely accepted interface standard for communication. One implementation of MPI on Java is the mpiJava [4] library. It enables the communication of Java programs by introducing a new class called MPI. Using mpiJava, the programmers need to handle data communication explicitly, which usually is a complicated and error-prone task.

Java RMI is similar to the remote procedure call—it enables a Java program to invoke methods of an object in another JVM. RMI applications use the client/server model. A RMI server application creates some objects, and publishes them for the remote RMI clients to invoke methods on these objects. RMI provides the mechanism by which the server and the client can communicate.

CORBA is an open, vendor-independent architecture for interfacing different applications over networks. Java also provides an interface description language (IDL) to enable the interaction between Java programs and the CORBAcompliant distributed applications widely deployed on the Internet. The shortcoming of COBRA is that it is difficult for programmers to master.

23.1.3.3 *Shared Memory*

The shared memory paradigm assumes a shared memory space among the cooperative computation tasks. The multithreading feature of Java fits this paradigm well in a single-node environment. However, the current standard JVM can only achieve limited parallelism of multithreaded programs even though the machine on which it runs is an SMP machine.

23.2 DISTRIBUTED JVM

A DJVM is a clusterwide virtual machine that supports the parallel execution of threads inside a multithreaded Java application with singlesystem image (SSI) illusion on clusters. In this way, the multithreaded Java application runs on a cluster as if it were running on a single machine with improved computation power. As a result, DJVM supports the shared memory programming paradigm. Several approaches have been proposed for developing the distributed JVM [2, 3, 14, 25]. In this chapter, we focus our study on the research of distributed JVM in the following sections. Such research is valuable for high-performance computing. Java provides a highly portable language environment and a simple thread model; thus, a DJVM can provide a more portable and more user-friendly parallel environment than many other existing parallel languages or libraries for parallel programming, as discussed in Section 23.1.3.

23.2.1 Design Issues

Building a DJVM on a cluster poses a number of challenges:

- *Java thread scheduling.* The thread scheduler basically decides which thread will grasp the CPU and switches thread contexts inside the virtual machine. The scheduling of Java threads on clusters requires a nontrivial design of the virtual machine's kernel, so that the Java threads can be transparently deployed on different cluster nodes and run in parallel efficiently. Inefficient scheduling can lead the system to an imbalanced state, which results in poor execution performance. It is, therefore, desirable to provide mechanisms for load balancing in a DJVM.
- *Distributed shared heap.* The heap is the shared memory space for Java threads to store the created objects. The separation of memory spaces among cluster nodes conflicts with the shared memory view of Java threads. Such a shared memory abstraction should be reflected in a DJVM so that threads among different nodes can still share the Java objects. Efficient management of Java objects on clusters is critical to the reduction of communication overheads.
- *Execution engine.* The JVM execution engine is the processor of Java bytecode. To make a high-performance DJVM, it is necessary to have a fast execution engine. Therefore, the execution of Java threads in native code is a must. As the threads and heap are distributed, the execution engine needs to be extended to be "cluster-aware"; that is, it should be able to choose appropriate actions for local and remote objects.

23.2.2 Solutions

In our design for distributed thread scheduling, we do not choose the simple initial thread placement, which simply spawns a thread remotely upon thread creation as used in related projects [2, 3, 19]. Though it can achieve the efficient parallel execution for threads with balanced workload, it is not enough for a wide range of applications that exhibit significant imbalanced computation workloads among threads. To provide advanced support for load balancing, we seek a lightweight and transparent Java thread migration mechanism.

The design of the heap actually provides distributed shared object services, similar to what a multithreaded software DSM does, and there do exist a number of DJVMs [2, 14, 25] that are directly built on top of an unmodified software distributed shared memory (DSM). This approach simplifies the design and implementation of a DJVM as it only needs to call up the application programming interface (API) of the DSM to realize the heap. However, it is far from an efficient solution since such a layered design will impose significant overheads on the interactions between the JVM and the DSM due to the mismatch of the memory model of Java and that of the underlying DSM. Moreover, the run-time information at the JVM level, such as the object type information, cannot be easily channelled to the DSM. Also the off-the-shelf DSM is difficult to be extended for supporting other services like the SSI view of I/O objects. In our system, we instead use a built-in distributed shared object technique that realizes the JMM. This approach can make use of the run-time information inside the DJVM to reduce the object access overheads as it is tightly coupled with the DJVM kernel.

For the execution engine, we adopt the JIT compiler as the execution engine. A Java bytecode interpreter is relatively simple, yet it suffers from the slow Java execution in interpretative mode and thus may not be efficient enough for solving computation-intensive problems that are the main targets of a DJVM. Static compilers, as used in Hyperion [2] and Jackal [19], although they can achieve high-performance native execution of Java threads, usually miss the dynamic JVM functionalities such as loading new Java classes from remote machines during run-time. The mixed-mode execution engine, which was first introduced in Sun's hotspot compiler, is much more complex to be adopted in the DJVM design. Dynamic or JIT compilers were rarely considered or exploited in previous DJVM projects. The JIT compiler is relatively simpler than the full-fledged static compilers, but it can still achieve high execution performance. Therefore, we believe that it is the best choice for a DJVM.

23.3   JESSICA2 DISTRIBUTED JVM

23.3.1   Overview

The overall architecture of our DJVM JESSICA2 is shown in Figure 23.2. It runs in a cluster environment and consists of a collection of modified JVMs that run in different cluster nodes and communicate with each other using TCP connections.

The class files of the compiled multithreaded Java program can be directly run on JESSICA2 without any preprocessing. We call the node that starts the Java program the master node and the JVM running on it the master JVM. All the other nodes in the cluster are worker nodes, each running a worker JVM to participate in

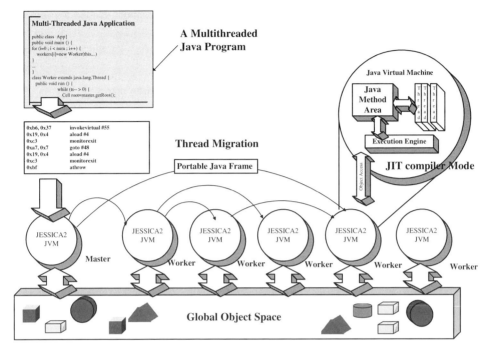

Figure 23.2   The JESSICA2 system overview.

the execution of a Java application. The worker JVMs can dynamically join the execution group. The Java thread can be dynamically scheduled by the thread scheduler to migrate during run time in order to help achieve a balanced system load throughout. Being transparent, the migration operation is done without explicit migration instructions inserted in the source program.

In a distributed JVM, the shared memory nature of Java threads calls for a global object space (GOS) that "virtualizes" a single Java object heap spanning the entire cluster to facilitate transparent object accesses. In the distributed JVM, each node can dynamically create new objects and manage them independently. The objects created at the remote nodes can be replicated to improve the access locality. Concurrent accesses on the copies of shared objects are also allowed, thus raising the issue of memory consistency. The memory consistency semantics of the GOS are defined based on the Java memory model (Chapter 8 of the JVM specification [12]).

There is no assumption of a shared file system in the implementation. The application class files can be duplicated in each node, or they can be stored only in the master node. In the latter case, when a worker JVM cannot find a class file locally, it will request the class bytecode from the master JVM on demand through network communication. The initialization of Java classes will be guaranteed to be done only once for all JVMs. When one worker JVM loads a class, the modified JVM class loader will first query the master JVM to check if it has been loaded and initialized. All such queries from different JVMs will be sequentialized. If the initialization of the class has been done, the worker JVM will fetch its static data and copy them into local static data area.

Our system does not rely on a single shared distributed file system such as NFS, nor is it restricted to a single IP address for all the nodes in the running cluster. The system has built the I/O redirection functionalities inside to enable the SSI view of the file I/O operations and the networking I/O operations.

The following sections discuss our implementation of JESSICA2 [20, 22, 23].

23.3.2 Global Object Space

We follow the Java memory model (JMM) to solve the memory consistency issue in GOS. We also incorporate several optimization techniques to further improve the performance of GOS by exploiting the run-time information inside JVM.

23.3.2.1 *Implementing the Java Memory Model*   According to the Java memory model, the synchronization operations in Java are used not only to guarantee exclusive access in the critical section, but also to maintain the consistency of objects among all threads that have performed synchronization operations on the same lock.

We follow the operations defined in the JVM specification to implement this memory model. Before a thread releases a lock, it must copy all assigned values in its private working memory back to the heap, which is shared by all threads. Before a thread acquires a lock, it must flush (invalidate) all variables in its working memory; later uses will load the values from the heap.

Figure 23.3 shows all the memory access operations in the GOS. In the JVM, connectivity exists between two Java objects if one object contains a reference to another. Based on the connectivity, we divide Java objects in the GOS into two categories: distributed-shared objects (DSOs) and node-local objects (NLOs). Distributed-shared objects are reachable from at least two threads in different cluster nodes in the distributed JVM, whereas node-local objects are reachable from only one cluster node. Distributed-shared objects can be distinguished from node-local objects (by default) at run time [21].

We adopt a home-based multiple writer cache coherence protocol to implement the Java memory model. Each shared object has a home from which all copies are derived and to which all writes (diffs) are propagated. The access events of a distributed-shared object comprise those on nonhome nodes and those on the home node. On nonhome nodes, after acquiring a lock, the first read should fault in the object from its home. All the subsequent reads or writes can be performed on the local copy. Before acquiring or releasing a lock, the locally performed writes should be identified using twin and diff techniques and sent to the home node. We call the object faultingin remote read, and the diff propagation remote write.

In order to facilitate some optimizations such as object home migration that will be discussed later, we also monitor the access operations on the home node. On the

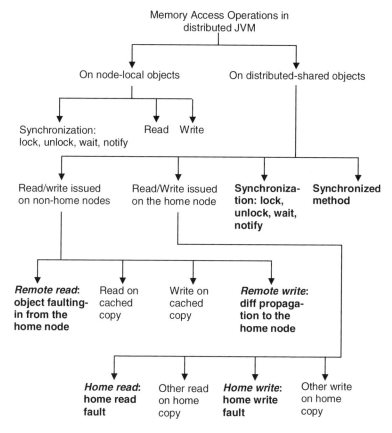

Figure 23.3 Memory access operations in GOS.

home node, the access state of the home copy will be set to invalid on acquiring a lock and to read only on releasing a lock. Home read fault and home write fault will be trapped. For both types of fault, the GOS does nothing more than set the object to the proper access state. We call the home read fault home read, and the home write fault home write.

All the synchronization operations performed on a distributed-shared object, such as lock, unlock, wait, and notify, influence the object access behavior, and are thus considered access events too. The synchronized method is treated as a special access event.

23.3.2.2 Optimizations
Since our GOS is a built-in component inside the distributed JVM, we are able to effectively calibrate the run-time memory access patterns and dynamically apply optimized cache coherence protocols to minimize consistency maintenance overhead. The optimization devices include an object home migration method that optimizes the single-writer access pattern, synchro-

nized method migration that allows the execution of a synchronized method to take place remotely at the home node of its locked object, and connectivity-based object pushing that uses object connectivity information to perform prefetching.

Object home migration. In a home-based cache coherence protocol, the home node of a DSO plays a special role among all nodes holding a copy. Accesses happening in the nonhome nodes will incur communication with the home node, whereas accesses in the home node can proceed at full speed.

Our GOS is able to determine a better location of the home of an object and perform object home migration accordingly. We choose to only apply object home migration to those DSOs exhibiting the single-writer access pattern, in which the object is only written by one node, to reduce home migration notices that are used to notify of the new home. In the situation of a multiple-writer pattern in which the object is written by multiple nodes, it does not matter which is the home node as long as the home node is one of the writing nodes.

In order to detect the single-writer access pattern, the GOS monitors all home accesses as well as nonhome accesses at the home node. To minimize the overhead in detecting the single-writer pattern, the GOS records consecutive writes that are from the same remote node and that are not interleaved by the writes from other nodes. We follow a heuristic that an object is in the single-writer pattern if the number of consecutive writes exceeds a predefined threshold.

Synchronized method migration. The execution of a synchronized method of a DSO not at its home will trigger multiple synchronization requests to the home node. For example, on entering and exiting the synchronized method, the invoking node will acquire and then release the lock of the synchronized object. Memory consistency maintenances are also involved according to Java memory model. Migrating a synchronized method of a DSO to its home node for execution will combine multiple roundtrip messages into one and reduce the overhead for maintaining memory consistency. While object shipping is the default behavior in the GOS, we apply method shipping, particularly to the execution of synchronized methods of DSOs.

Connectivity-based object pushing. Object pushing is a prefetching strategy which takes advantage of the object connectivity information to more accurately prestore the objects to be accessed by a remote thread, thereby minimizing the network delay in subsequent remote object accesses. Connectivity-based object pushing actually improves the reference locality. The producer–consumer pattern is one of the patterns that can be optimized by connectivity-based object pushing [21].

Object pushing is better than pull-based prefetching, which relies on the requesting node to specify explicitly which objects are to be pulled according to the object connectivity information. A fatal drawback of pull-based prefetching is that the connectivity information contained in an invalid object may be obsolete. Therefore, the prefetching accuracy is not guaranteed. Some unneeded objects, even garbage objects, may be prefetched, which will result in wasting communication bandwidth. On the contrary, object pushing gives more accurate prefetching results since the home node has the up-to-date copies of the objects and the connectivity information in the home node is always valid.

In our implementation, we rely on an optimal message length, which is the preferred aggregate size of objects to be delivered to the requesting node. Reachable objects from the requested object will be copied to the message buffer until the current message length is larger than the optimal message length. We use a breadth-first search algorithm to select the objects to be pushed.

23.3.3 Transparent Java Thread Migration

One of the unique features of our system is that we support the dynamic transparent migration of Java threads. This section describes our lightweight and efficient solution for thread migration in the context of JIT compiler.

Transparent thread migration has long been used as a load balancing mechanism to optimize the resource usage in distributed environments [10]. Such systems usually use the raw thread context (RTC) as the communication interface between the migration source node and target node. RTC usually includes the virtual memory space, thread execution stack, and hardware machine registers.

We adopt the bytecode-oriented thread context (BTC) to make the system more portable. The BTC consists of the identification of the Java thread, followed by a sequence of frames. Each frame contains the class name, the method signature and the activation record of the method. The activation record consists of bytecode program counter (PC), JVM operand stack pointer, operand stack variables, and the local variables, all encoded in a JVM-independent format.

In a JIT-enabled JVM, the JVM stack of a Java thread becomes the native stack and no longer remains bytecode-oriented. We solve the transformation of the RTC into the BTC directly inside the JIT compiler. Our solution is built on two main functions, stack capturing and stack restoration (see Figure 23.4). Stack capturing takes a snapshot of the RTC of a running Java thread and transforms the snapshot into an equivalent BTC. Stack restoration is to reestablish the RTC using the BTC. Such a process via an intermediate BTC takes advantage of the portability of the BTC.

23.3.3.1 Stack Capturing   To support the RTCBTC transformation, we perform just-in-time native code instrumentation inside the JIT compiler. We insert additional optimized native code in a method when it is first compiled. The instrumented code enables the running thread to manage its own context in a reflexive way. During execution, the thread maintains the execution trace of the Java thread in some lightweight run-time data structures. Figure 23.5 shows the workflow of the JIT compiler in our system.

In the instrumentation of JIT compiler, we limit the migration to take place at some specific points called migration points. We choose two types of points in our system. The first type (referred to as M-point) is the site that invokes a Java method. The second type (referred to as B-point) is the beginning of a bytecode basic block pointed to by a back edge, which is usually the header of a loop.

At such points, the instrumented native code is used to check the migration request and to spill the machine registers to the memory slots of the variables. For the

Raw Thread Context (RTC)

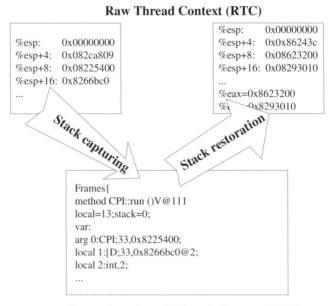

Bytecode-oriented Thread Context (BTC)

Figure 23.4   The thread stack transformation. The frame for method run() of class CPI is encoded in a text format in the BTC box.

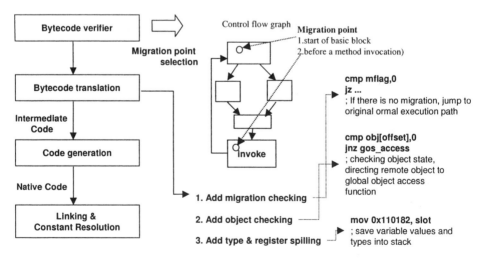

Figure 23.5   The working flow of the JIT compiler.

variable types, we use type spilling to store the variable types at the migration points. The type information of stack variables will be gathered at the time of byte-code verification. We use one single type to encode the reference type of stack variable, as we can identify the exact type of a Java object from the object reference. Therefore, we can compress one type into 4-bit data. Eight compressed types will be bound in a 32-bit machine word, and an instruction to store this word will be generated to spill the information to an appropriate location in the current method frame. For typical Java methods, only a few instructions are needed to spill the type information of stack variables in a method.

The Java frames in the stack are linked by the generated native code. The code only needs a few instructions to spill the previous Java frame stack pointer and previous machine stack pointer. Such an arrangement makes it possible to tell a Java frame from the internal JVM functions frames (we call them C frames). In our thread migration, we choose the consecutive Java frames to be migrated to the remote machine. Upon completion of such Java frames, the control will return back to the source machine to complete the C frame execution.

23.3.3.2 Stack Restoration   The restoration of the thread is done through the BTC-to-RTC transformation. The destination JVM, after accepting the thread context BTC in the JVM-independent text format, will create a new native thread. The newly created thread becomes the clone of the migrated thread in current JVM. The clone thread then brings back the calling sequence as described by the input context. In our system, we build a sequence of stack frames with the return addresses and the frame pointers properly linked together to simulate the method invocation. The local variable inside the frames will be initialized to the values according to the input thread context.

The stack restoration needs to recover the machine registers in the migration target node. Most previous approaches supporting thread stack restoration often build the stack by simulating the method invocation and use additional status variables to distinguish the restoring execution flow and the normal execution flow inside the methods [18]. This will result in large overheads because it needs to add such branching codes in all the methods. Instead, we directly build the thread stack and use recompilation techniques to get the mapping between the thread variables and the machine registers at all restoration points. Each mapping is then used by a generated code stub that will be executed before the restoration point to recover the machine registers. In our implementation, we allocate the code stubs inside the restored thread stack so that they will be freed automatically after execution.

23.3.3.3 Load Balancing Policy   We have integrated the load balancing policy in our current DJVM so that it is responsive to thread scheduling. The policy adopts a scheme similar to work stealing [6]. A lightly loaded JVM will try to acquire computation threads from other heavily loaded nodes periodically. The load information such as the CPU and memory usages is stored on the master node. All the worker JVMs do not directly contact each other for the exchange of workload information to save bandwidth. Instead, the lightly loaded node will post its advertisement on the master node, whereas the heavily loaded node will try to acquire the information from the master node. Subsequent thread migration operations will be negotiated between the lightly loaded node and the heavily loaded node.

The worker JVM maintains its own workload by querying the CPU and memory usage in the local/proc file system. The state transition in a worker JVM between heavy load and light load resembles the charging and discharging of electricity capacity. In the charging phase, the JVM will go in the direction of acquiring threads until some threshold is met. It will switch the state to heavy load after it stays at the state of heavy load for a time period. Then the discharging begins by migrating threads to lightly loaded nodes.

The master node will not be a bottleneck caused by the load information because only those worker nodes that have radical load changes (from heavy load state to light load state or vice versa) will send the messages to it.

23.4 PERFORMANCE ANALYSIS

Our distributed JVM, JESSICA2, is developed based on Kaffe open JVM 1.0.6 [24]. We run JESSICA2 on theHKUGideon 300 Linux cluster to evaluate the performance. Each cluster node consists of 2GHz Pentium 4 CPU, 512M RAM, and runs Linux kernel 2.4.14. The cluster is connected by a Foundry Fastiron 1500 Fast Ethernet switch.

The following benchmarks are used in our experiments.

- CPI calculates an approximation of π by evaluating the integral.
- ASP (all-shortest path) computes the shortest paths between any pair of nodes in a graph using a parallel version of Floyd's algorithm.
- TSP (Traveling Salesman Problem) finds the shortest route among a number of cities using a parallel branch-and-bind algorithm.
- Raytracer renders a three-dimensional scene by using the raytracing method.
- SOR (successive overrelaxation) performs red–black successive overrelaxation on a two-dimensional matrix for a number of iterations.
- Nbody simulates the motion of particles due to gravitational forces between each other over a number of simulation steps using the algorithm of Barnes and Hut.
- SPECjvm98 [9] is the benchmark suite used for testing JVM's performance.

23.4.1 Effects of Optimizations in GOS

In the experiments, all adaptations are disabled initially; we then enable the planned adaptations incrementally. Figure 23.6 shows the effects of adaptations on the execution time. We present the normalized execution time against different problem sizes.

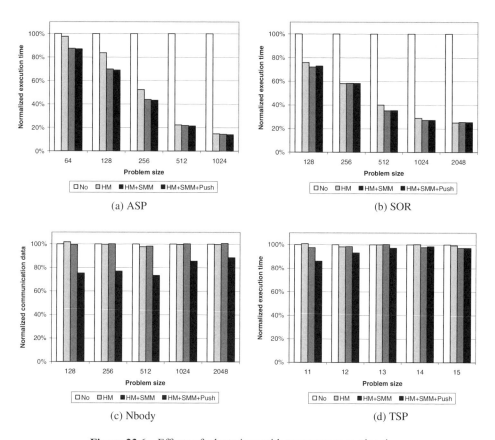

Figure 23.6   Effects of adaptations with respect to execution time.

Our application suite consists of four multithreaded Java programs, namely ASP, SOR, Nbody, and TSP. In ASP, we scale the size of the graph; in SOR, we scale the size of the two-dimensional matrix; in Nbody, we scale the number of the bodies; in TSP, we scale the number of the cities. All data are normalized to that when none of the adaptations are enabled. All tests run on 16 processors. In the legend, "No" denotes no adaptive protocol enabled, "HM" denotes object home migration, "SMM" denotes synchronized method migration, and "Push" denotes object pushing. All the application are running in the interpreter mode of JVM.

As can be seen in the figures, object home migration greatly improves the performance of ASP and SOR. In ASP and SOR, the data are in the two-dimensional matrices that are shared by all threads. In Java, a two-dimensional matrix is implemented as an array object whose elements are also array objects. Many of these array objects exhibit the single-writer access pattern after they are initialized. However, their original homes are not the writing nodes. Object home migration automatically makes the writing node the home node in order to reduce communication. We can see that object home migration dramatically reduces the execution time. Also, the effect of object home migration is amplified when the problem size is scaled up in ASP and SOR. In Nbody and TSP, the single-writer access pattern is insignificant and, therefore, the effect of object home migration obviously cannot be observed.

Synchronized method migration optimizes the execution of a synchronized method of a nonhome DSO. Although it does not reduce the communication volume, it reduces the number of messages significantly. We also observe in Figure 23.6(a) and (b) that synchronized method migration improves ASP's and SOR's overall performance to some extent, particularly when the problem size is small. ASP requires n barriers for all the threads in order to solve an n-node graph. The synchronization is quite heavy in ASP, so synchronized method migration has a more positive effect on ASP. When the problem size is scaled up, the communication-to-computation ratio decreases, thus the adaptation effect becomes not so evident. The synchronization overhead comprises not only the processing and transmission time, but also the waiting time. Sometimes the synchronization overhead is dominated by the waiting time, which cancels out the benefit from synchronized method migration. Nbody's synchronization uses synchronized block instead of synchronized method, and so synchronized method migration has no effect here. TSP's situation is similar to Nbody's.

Connectivity-based object pushing is a prefetching strategy that takes advantage of the object connectivity information to improve reference locality. Particularly, it improves the producer–consumer pattern greatly. Nbody is a typical application of the producer–consumer pattern. In Nbody, a quad tree is constructed by one thread and then accessed by all other threads in each iteration. The quad tree consists of a lot of small-sized objects. We can see that object pushing greatly reduces the execution time in Nbody, as seen from Figure 23.6(c). However, when the problem size is scaled up, the communication-to-computation ratio decreases; thus, the effect of object pushing decreases. Notice that there is relatively little communication in TSP, so the improvement on the total execution time due to this optimization is limited. Compared with Nbody and TSP, most DSOs in ASP and SOR are array objects, and object pushing is not performed on them to reduce the impact of pushing unneeded objects.

23.4.2 Thread Migration Overheads

We first test the space and time overheads charged to the execution of Java threads by the JIT compiler when enabling the migration mechanism. Then we measure the latency of one migration operation.

The time overheads are mainly due to the checking at the migration points, and the space overheads are mainly due to the instrumented native code. We do not require the benchmarks to be multithreaded in the test since the dynamic native code instrumentation will still function, even on single-threaded Java applications.

We use the SPECjvm98 benchmark in the test. The initial heap size was set to 48 MB. We compared the differences in time and space costs between enabling and disabling the migration checking at migration points. The measurements on all the benchmarks in SPECjvm98 were carried out 10 times and the values were then averaged.

Table 23.1 shows the test results. The space overheads are in terms of the average size of native code per bytecode instruction, that is, it is the blow-up of the native code compiled from the Java bytecode.

From the table, we can see that the average time overheads charged to the execution of Java thread with thread migration are about 2.21% and the overheads of generated native code are 15.68%. Both the time and space overheads are much smaller than the reported results from other static bytecode instrumentation approaches. For example, JavaGoX [17] reported that for four benchmark programs (Fibo, qsort, nqueen, and compress in SPECjvm98), the additional time overheads range from 14% to 56%, whereas the additional space costs range from 30% to 220%.

We also measured the overall latency of a migration operation using different multithreaded Java applications, including a latency test (LT) program, CPI, ASP, Nbody, and SOR. The latency measured includes the time from the point of stack capturing to the time when the thread has finished its stack restoration on the remote node and has sent back the acknowledgment. CPI only needs 2.68 ms to migrate and restore thread execution because it only needs to load one single frame and one Java class during the restoration. LT and ASP need about 5 ms to migrate a thread context consisting of one single frame and restore the context. Although they only have one single frame to restore, they both need to load two classes inside their frame contexts. For SOR, which migrates two frames, the time is about 8.5 ms. For NBody, which needs to load four classes in eight frames, it takes about 10.8 ms.

23.4.3 Application Benchmark

In this section, we report the performance of four multithreaded Java applications on JESSICA2. The applications are CPI, TSP, Raytracer, and Nbody.

Table 23.1 The execution overheads using SPECjvm98 benchmarks

Benchmarks	Time (seconds)		Space (native code/bytecode)	
	No migration	Migration	No migration	Migration
compress	11.31	11.39 (+0.71%)	6.89	7.58 (+10.01%)
jess	30.48	30.96 (+1.57%)	6.82	8.34 (+22.29%)
raytrace	24.47	24.68 (+0.86%)	7.47	8.49 (+13.65%)
db	35.49	36.69 (+3.38%)	7.01	7.63 (+8.84%)
javac	38.66	40.96 (+5.95%)	6.74	8.72 (+29.38%)
mpegaudio	28.07	29.28 (+4.31%)	7.97	8.53 (+7.03%)
mtrt	24.91	25.05 (+0.56%)	7.47	8.49 (+13.65%)
jack	37.78	37.90 (+0.32%)	6.95	8.38 (+20.58%)
Average		(+2.21%)		(+15.68%)

We run TSP with 14 cities, Raytracer within a 150×150 scene containing 64 spheres, and Nbody with 640 particles in 10 iterations. We show the speedups of CPI, TSP, Raytracer, and Nbody in Figure 23.7 by comparing the execution time of JESSICA2 against that of Kaffe 1.0.6 (in a single node) under the JIT compiler mode. From the figure, we can see nearly linear speedup in JESSICA2 for CPI, despite the fact that all the threads needed to run in the master JVM for 4% of the overall time at the very beginning. For the TSP and Raytracer, the speedup curves show about 50% to 60% of efficiency. Compared to the CPI program, the number of messages exchanged between nodes in TSP has been increased because the migrated threads have to access the shared job queue and to update the best route during the parallel execution, which will result in flushing of working memory in the worker threads. In Raytracer, the number of messages is small, as it is only necessary to transfer the scene data to the worker thread in the initial phase. The slowdown comes from the object checking in the modified JVM as the application accesses the object fields extensively in the inner loop to render the scene. But for the Nbody program, the speedup is only 1.5 for 8 nodes. The poor speedup is expected, which is due to the frequent communications between the worker threads and the master thread in computing the Barnes–Hut tree.

23.5   RELATED WORK

Our system was motivated by recent work on distributed JVM, particularly cJVM [3] and JESSICA [14]. However, these systems are mainly based on slow Java interpreters. Our work distinguishes itself from these projects in that we use JIT compilers for the construction of the DJVM. Besides the relationship to the distributed

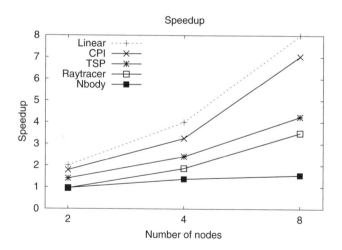

Figure 23.7   Speedup measurement of Java applications.

JVM, our system also relates to techniques of software distributed shared memory and computation migration. These techniques are exploited in our system in the context of JIT compilers.

23.5.1   Software Distributed Shared Memory

The software distributed shared memory (DSM) has been studied extensively during the past decade. Orca [5] is one object-based DSM that uses a combination of compile-time and run-time techniques to determine the placement of objects. Our GOS differs from Orca in that we provide the shared object abstraction supports at run time through the JVM JIT compiler.

TreadMarks is a page-based DSM [1] that adopts lazy release consistency protocols and allows multiple concurrent writers on the same page. Treadmarks uses the hardware pagefaulting support; therefore, it can eliminate the overheads of software checking on object status. One of the drawbacks, however, is that the page-based DSM will have the problem of false sharing if directly applied to an object-based language such as Java.

23.5.2   Computation Migration

Computation migration has been studied for many years. Process migration can be regarded as the ancestor of thread migration. Paper [15] reviews the field of process migration up to 1999. It provides detailed analysis on the benefits and drawbacks of process migration. The systems included in the paper range from user-level migration systems to kernel-level migration ones. Compared to the existing computation migration techniques, we try to solve the computation migration from the new perspective by introducing just-in-time compilation.

There are systems developed to support thread migration. Arachne [10] is one of such systems. It provides a portable user-level programming library that supports thread migration over a heterogeneous cluster. However, the thread migration is not transparent to the user as it requires that programs be written using special thread library or APIs.

There are related systems in the mobile computing area that support the mobility of Java threads. For example, JavaGoX [17] and and Brakes [18] use the static preprocessor to instrument Java bytecodes to support the migration of the Java thread. These systems do not address the distributed shared object issues.

23.5.3   Distributed JVM

cJVM [3] is a cluster-aware JVM that provides SSI of a traditional JVM running in cluster environments. The cJVM prototype was implemented by modifying the Sun JDK1.2 interpreter. cJVM does not support thread migration. It distributes the Java threads at the time of thread creation.

There are other DSM-based DJVM prototypes, for example, JESSICA [14] and Java/DSM [25]. Both systems are based on interpreters. JESSICA supports thread migration by modifying the Java interpreters. Java/DSM lacks supports for the location transparency of Java threads. It needs programmers' manual coding to place the threads on different cluster nodes.

Jackal [19] and Hyperion [2] adopt the static compilation approaches to compile the Java source code directly into native parallel code. The parallel code is linked to some object-based DSM library packages.

23.6 SUMMARY

Java is becoming an important vehicle for writing parallel programs due to its built-in concurrency support and high portability. To support high-performance Java computing on clusters, there exist three main paradigms: data parallel, message passing, and shared memory. The support for shared memory for Java inspires the new research on distributed JVM (DJVM), which aims to extend the single-node JVM to clusters for achieving high-performance multithreaded Java computing without the need for introducing new APIs. The multithreaded Java programs running on a DJVM is written in the usual manner. The underlying DJVM tries to hide all the physical machine boundaries for the Java application transparently.

This chapter focuses on the study of supporting shared memory paradigms on clusters using DJVM. We use our prototype system JESSICA2 as an example to discuss the design, implementation, and performance analysis of a DJVM. The design of a DJVM needs to provide a virtually shared heap for the Java threads inside one single application. Due to Java's memory model constraints, the existing consistency protocols of software distributed shared memory cannot match well with that of Java. Incorporating the distributed shared object support inside DJVM is worthy of the efforts for achieving the improved communication performance. Another important aspect of a DJVM is the scheduling of threads. We believe that a lightweight thread-migration mechanism can help balance the workload among cluster nodes especially for irregular multithreaded applications in which the workload cannot be simply estimated and equally partitioned among the threads.

ACKNOWLEDGMENTS

This research is supported by Hong Kong RGC Grant HKU7030/ 01E and HKU Large Equipment Grant 01021001.

REFERENCES

1. C. Amza, A. L. Cox, S. Dwarkadas, P. Keleher, H. Lu, R. Rajamony, W. Yu, and W. Zwaenepoel, Treadmarks: Shared Memory Computing on Networks of Workstations, *IEEE Computer, 29*(2), 18–28, February 1996.

2. G. Antoniu, L. Bougé, P. Hatcher, K. McGuigan, and R. Namyst, The Hyperion System: Compiling Multithreaded Java Bytecode for Distributed Execution, *Parallel Computing, 27*(10), 1279–1297, 2001.

3. Y. Aridor, M. Factor, and A. Teperman, cJVM: A Single System Image of a JVM on a Cluster, in *International Conference on Parallel Processing,* pp. 4–11, 1999.

4. M. Baker, B. Carpenter, G. Fox, and S. H. Koo, mpiJava: An Object-Oriented Java Interface to MPI, in *Workshop on Java for Parallel and Distributed Computing, IPPS/SPDP,* 1999.

5. H. E. Bal, R. Bhoedjang, R. Hofman, C. Jacobs, K. Langendoen, T. Rühl, and M. Frans Kaashoek, Performance Evaluation of the Orca Shared-Object System, *ACM Transactions on Computer Systems, 16*(1), 1–40, 1998.

6. R. Blumofe and C. Leiserson, Scheduling Multithreaded Computations by Work Stealing, in *Proceedings of the 35th Annual Symposium on Foundations of Computer Science,* pp. 356–368, November 1994.

7. F. Breg, S. Diwan, J. Villacis, J. Balasubramanian, E. Akman, and D. Gannon, Java RMI Performance and Object Model Interoperability: Experiments with Java/HPC++, *Concurrency: Practice and Experience, 10*(11–13), 941–955, 1998.

8. B. Carpenter, G. Zhang, G. Fox, X. Li, and Y. Wen, HPJava: Data Parallel Extensions to Java, *Concurrency: Practice and Experience, 10,* 873–877, 1998.

9. The Standard Performance Evaluation Corporation, SPEC JVM98 Benchmarks. http://www.spec.org/org/jvm98, 1998.

10. B. Dimitrov and V. Rego, Arachne: A Portable Threads System Supporting Migrant Threads on Heterogeneous Network Farms, *IEEE Transactions on Parallel and Distributed Systems, 9*(5), 1998.

11. J. Gosling, B. Joy, G. Steele, and G. Bracha, *The Java Language Specification Second Edition.* Addison-Wesley, 2000.

12. T. Lindholm and F. Yellin, *The Java™ Virtual Machine Specification,* 2nd ed., Addison Wesley, 1999.

13. Snir M., Otto S. W., Huss Lederman S., Walker D.W., and Dongarra J., *MPI—The Complete Reference,* The MIT Press, 1996.

14. Matchy J. M. C.-L. Wang, and F. C. M. Lau, JESSICA: Java Enabled Single System Image Computing Architecture, *Parallel and Distributed Computing, 60*(10), 1194–1222, October 2000.

15. D. S. Milojicic, F. Douglis, Y. Paindaveine, R. Wheeler, and S. Zhou, Process Migration, *ACM Computer Survey, 32*(3), 241–299, 2000.

16. R. Orfali and D. Harkey, *Client/Server Programming with JAVA and CORBA,* 2nd ed., Wiley, 1998.

17. T. Sakamoto, T. Sekiguchi, and A. Yonezawa, Bytecode Transformation for Portable Thread Migration in Java, in *Joint Symposium on Agent Systems and Applications/Mobile Agents,* pp. 16–28, 2000.

18. E. Truyen, B. Robben, B. Vanhaute, T. Coninx, W. Joosen, and P. Verbaeten, Portable Support for Transparent Thread Migration in Java, in *Joint Symposium on Agent Systems and Applications/Mobile Agents (ASA/MA),* pp. 29–43, 2000.

19. R. Veldema, R. F. H. Hofman, R. Bhoedjang, and H. E. Bal, Runtime Optimizations for a Java DSM Implementation, in *Java Grande,* pp. 153–162, 2001.

20. W. Fang, C.-L. Wang, and F. C. M. Lau, Efficient Global Object Space Support for Dis-

tributed JVM on Cluster, in *The 2002 International Conference on Parallel Processing (ICPP2002),* pp. 371–378, British Columbia, Canada, August 2002.

21. W. Fang, C.-L. Wang, and F. C. M. Lau, On the Design of Global Object Space for Efficient Multithreading Java Computing on Clusters, in *Parallel Computing, 29,* 1563–1587, 2003.

22. W. Zhu, C.-L. Wang, and F. C. M. Lau, JESSICA2: A Distributed Java Virtual Machine with Transparent Thread Migration Support, in *IEEE Fourth International Conference on Cluster Computing,* Chicago, September 2002.

23. W. Zhu, C.-L. Wang, and F. C. M. Lau, Lightweight Transparent Java Thread Migration for Distributed JVM, in *International Conference on Parallel Processing,* pp. 465–472, Kaohsiung, Taiwan, October 2003.

24. T. Wilkinson, Kaffe—A Free Virtual Machine to Run Java Code, http://www.kaffe.org/, 1998.

25. W. Yu and A. L. Cox, Java/DSM: A Platform for Heterogeneous Computing, *Concurrency: Practice and Experience, 9*(11), 1213–1224, 1997.

26. J.-D. Choi, M. Gupta, M. J. Serrano, V. C. Sreedhar, and S. P. Midkiff, Escape Analysis for Java, in *Proceedings of the Conference on Object-Oriented Programming Systems, Languages, and Applications (OOPSLA),* 1999.

Data Grids: Supporting Data-Intensive Applications in Wide Area Networks

XIAO QIN and HONG JIANG

24.1 INTRODUCTION

A grid is a collection of geographically dispersed computing resources, providing a large virtual computing system to users. The objective of a data grid system is two-fold. First, it integrates heterogeneous data archives stored in a large number of geographically distributed sites into a single virtual data management system. Second, it provides diverse services to fit the needs of high-performance distributed and data-intensive computing. There are four commonly used kinds of resources in grids: computation, storage, communications, and software. In what follows, we briefly introduce the storage resources.

Storage is viewed as the second most commonly used resource in a grid. The grid that presents an integrated view of storage is called a data grid. Memory, hard disks, and other permanent storage media are referred to as storage resources. In this study, we are particularly interested in secondary storage systems in grids, since secondary storage is 1000 times slower than main memory attached to a processor. Throughout this chapter, we only address the issues of data grids with respect to secondary storage. Many networked file systems, which exhibit security and reliability features, have been widely applied to data grids. These file systems include Network File System (NFS) [28], Distributed File System (DFS), Andrew File System (AFS) [19], General Parallel File System (GPFS), and Parallel Virtual File System (PVFS) [16, 44].

The amount of scientific data generated by simulations or collected from large-scale experiments is generally large, and such data tends to be geographically stored across wide-area networks for the sake of large-scale collaborations. The notion of a computational grid has been proposed for several years, mainly focusing on effective usage of global computational and network resources in a wide area network/Internet environment. However, the performance of a computational grid, in which the effective usage of storage resources is ignored, will be degraded substantially if the vast majority of applications running in the grid are data intensive. To overcome this problem, various techniques have been developed and incorporated into a so-called data grid infrastructure. In this chapter, we will take a close look at these techniques presented in the literature, and point out some open issues in data grid research.

The rest of the chapter is organized as follows. Section 24.2 reviews three major data grid services. In Section 24.3, techniques for achieving high performance in data grids are described in detail. Security issue in data grids is briefly reviewed in Section 24.4. Section 24.5 identifies several open issues, and discusses the potential solutions to the open problems. Finally, Section 24.6 concludes the chapter by summarizing the main open problems and preliminary solutions.

24.2   DATA GRID SERVICES

In this section, we focus on three essential services: metadata service, data access service, and performance measurement.

24.2.1   Metadata Services for Data Grid Systems

The metadata of a data grid system is the management information regarding the data grid. The metadata includes file instances, the contents of file instances, and a variety of storage systems in the data grid. The goal of metadata service is to facilitate an efficient means of naming, creating, and retrieving the metadata of the data grid [13]. There are two types of metadata: application metadata and fabric metadata. The former defines the logical structure of information represented by data files (e.g. XML [10]); the latter corresponds to information related to the characteristics of data grids.

Since a data grid consists of a large number of storage resources geographically dispersed over a large-scale distributed environment, an essential requirement of data grids is the capability of scaling up to accommodate a large number of users. Wahl et al. have proposed a so-called Lightweight Directory Access Protocol (LDAP) [41], which achieves a high scalability by applying a hierarchical naming structure along with rich data models. Fitzgerald et al. have developed a distributed directory service for general grid metadata, which is applied to represent the metadata of data grids [17]. Baru et al. proposed a metadata catalog (MCAT) for a storage resource broker [4]. MCAT not only distinguishes the logical name space from physical name space, but also provides the specification of a logical collection hierarchy, thereby achieving a high scalability. In addition, performance is improved in MCAT by introducing containers to aggregate small files.

Chervenak et al. recently developed a prototype Metadata Service (MCS) for data grids, in which metadata is classified into two categories: logical and physical file metadata [14]. A logical file name in this prototype represents a unique identifier for data content, whereas a physical file name denotes an identifier for physical content on the storage system. Unlike MCAT mentioned earlier, the services in MCS are dedicated to describing files, and the physical file properties are not covered by MCS. Whereas MCAT utilizes a proprietary data exchange format to communicate with storage resource broker servers, MCS employs XML interface [10] to communicate with clients.

24.2.2 Data Access Services for Data Grid Systems

Data stored and retrieved by a data grid may reside, by design, in different sites on different storage devices. For this reason, data grids have to provide a global view of data for applications running on the grids [13]. Data access services are required to be compatible with traditional file systems and, as a consequence, applications that are not originally designed for grid environments can run on a grid without complicated modifications.

Globus, serving as an infrastructure for grid computing, provides access to remote files through x-gass, ftp, or HTTP protocols [18]. White et al. have proposed the Legion I/O model that provides a remote access capability [42]. To allow end users to exploit context space and manipulate context structures, Legion also offers some command line utilities, which are similar to those in a Unix file system. Patten and Hawick have proposed a Distributed Active Resource Architecture (DARC) that enables the development of portable, extensible, and adaptive storage services optimized for end users' requirements [24].

24.2.3 Performance Measurement in a Data Grid

Since multiple resources may affect one another across time and space, performance problems (e.g., low throughput and high latency) might be imposed by a combination of resources. Thus, it is important and nontrival to diagnose performance problems in accordance with performance measurements provided by monitors. With a monitoring service in place, one can analyze the monitoring data from different points of view. The objective of the monitoring service is to observe performance bottlenecks, which are likely to occur in any components of the data grid.

Previous studies have demonstratively shown that monitoring at the application level is an effective approach to both performance analysis and application debugging [9, 39]. For example, Snodgrass has incorporated relational databases into a monitoring system to monitor complex systems [29].

GMA (grid monitoring architecture) embraces the key components of a grid monitoring system along with some essential interactions [38]. The data model used in the Network Weather Service [34] has been extended by Lee et al. to fulfill the special needs of monitoring data archives in grid environments [21]. More specifically, Lee et al. have proposed a relational monitoring data archive that is designed to efficiently handle high-volume streams of monitoring data [21].

24.3 HIGH-PERFORMANCE DATA GRID

We now turn our attention to the issues related to data replication, scheduling, and data movement, which must be addressed in order to achieve high performance and scalability in data grids.

24.3.1 Data Replication

There is a large body of work on data replication for distributed applications [11, 32, 35]. The existing techniques supporting data replication in data grids can be divided into four groups, namely, (1) architecture and management for data replication, (2) data replication placement, (3) data replication selection, and (4) data consistency.

24.3.1.1 Architecture of a Data Replication Service A general high-level architecture with four layers for data replication services of a data grid system is depicted in Figure 24.1 [13]. We describe each layer as follows:

1. The file transfer layer consists of file transfer protocols such as FTP, HTTP, and GridFTP [3]. Note that GridFTP is an extended version of FTP.
2. The replica catalogue [3] layer is leveraged to map logical file names to physical files.
3. The replica manager layer's functionalities include create, move, modify, and delete replicas in a data grid. Once a file is copied from one site to another by the replica manger layer and registered in the replica catalogue, the file can be retrieved by any application running on an arbitrary site in the grid.
4. The replica selection layer is responsible for choosing the most appropriate replica from those copies geographically dispersed across grids. The selections of replication policies largely depend on read and write accesses to data that can be classified into the three categories: read-only data, writable data with well-defined file ownership, and writable data with varying writers.

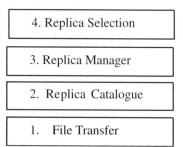

Figure 24.1 Architecture of a data replication service in a data grid system.

24.3.1.2 Data Replication Management   We first take a look at replication policies designed for read-only data. A pilot project called the Grid Data Management Pilot (GDMP) has been launched to develop a prototype for replication management within a data grid environment [27]. In the GDMP software, a secure replication of database files has been used, and a high-level replica catalog interface is implemented by using the native objectivity federation catalogue.

More broadly, replications can be optionally implemented at different levels of granularity, such as file level and object level [31]. Realizing that file replications in a data analysis application are potentially inefficient, Stockinger et al. have fully implemented object replication in a data grid prototype using Globus Data Grid tools [31].

Foster et al. recently developed a general framework that defines a parameterized set of basic mechanisms to create a variety of replica location services [15]. By configuring system parameters dynamically, one is able to tune system performance by means of considering the trade-off among reliability and communication overhead and storage update/access costs.

24.3.1.3 Data Replication Placement   In a recent study [25], several replication selection strategies for managing large datasets have been proposed and evaluated. Unlike static replications, dynamic replication approaches automatically add and delete replicas in accordance with changing workload, thereby sustaining high performance even in the face of diverse data access patterns [25].

24.3.1.4 Data Replication Selection   Once data replicas are generated and stored at multiple sites according to a variety of replication placement strategies discussed above, the performance of the data grid can be noticeably improved by choosing an optimized replica location for each data access. Replica selection is a high-level service that helps grid applications choose a replica based on system performance and data access features. Vazhkudai et al. [40] have designed and implemented a replica selection service that uses information with respect to replica location as well as the application's specific requirements to determine a replica among all replica alternatives.

24.3.1.5 Data Consistency in Data Grid Systems   The data replication techniques reviewed above mainly aim at maintaining replication for read-only files, thereby avoiding data consistency problems. In general, local consistency at each site is completely guaranteed by database management systems (DBMS), whereas global consistency in data grid systems needs to be maintained by a so-called grid consistency service.

There have been extensive studies of data consistency in distributed environments [33, 43]. The main target of the consistency model proposed by Sun et al. [33] is real-time cooperative editing systems that allow multiuser, physically dispersed people to view and edit a shared document at the same time over networks. To address the issue of grid data consistency maintenance, Düllmann et al. proposed a consistency service [23] that is supported by existing data grid services.

To maintain the basic consistency level, a replication operation must be manipulated as a database read transaction [23]. Thus, a read lock on a file has to be obtained before a site is ready to produce a new replica of the file. The site releases the read lock when the replica has been successfully duplicated. Likewise, the consistency service rests on write locks when update operations are issued on a set of replicas. All data replication techniques discussed above are summarized in Table 24.1.

24.3.2 Scheduling in Data Grid Systems

Previous research has shown that scheduling is a fundamental approach to achieving good performance for grid applications [1, 7, 30, 35]. However, these approaches do not take into account distributed data constraints.

Scheduling schemes designed for data-intensive jobs have generally been classified into two major categories: moving data to a job and moving a job to data. To reduce the frequency of remote data access and the amount of transferred data, data replication can be an optimization technique, as we discussed in Section 24.3.1.

Thain et al. developed a system in which execution sites band together into I/O communities [36]. Each I/O community comprises several CPUs and storage devices that provide storage and data retrieval services both for local and remote jobs. To enable jobs to declare constraints on storage devices within I/O communities, Thain et al. extended ClassAds [36] that are currently used in Condor system [22] to describe jobs' requirements in a distributed system. A single ClassAd is a list of attribute–value pairs in which value can be either atomic or complex expressions. Figure 24.2 illustrates three different kinds of ClassAds [36].

To minimize remote data access overheads, Basney et al. have invented a so-called execution domain framework to define an affinity between CPU and data resources in the grid [5]. By applying the framework to the Condor system, data-intensive jobs can be scheduled to run on CPUs that have access to required data.

Table 24.1 Summary of data replication techniques

Researchers	Granularity	Data type	Consistency	Technique
Samar et al. replication model	File	Read only	No[a]	Subscription and partial
Vazhkudai et al.	File	Read only	No	Replication selection
Stockinger et al.	File/object	Read only	No[b]	Object replication
Chervenak et al.	File	Read only	Yes[c]	Replication location service
Ranganathan	File	Read only	No	Replication placement et al.
Lamehamedi	File	Read only	No	Replication placement et al.
Mullmann et al.	File	Read/write	Yes	Consistency service
Sun et al.	String	Read/write	Yes	Three novel properties

[a]Producer decides when to publish new files.
[b]Consumer decides when to replicate objects.
[c]Relaxed consistency for metadata.

```
Type = "job"            Type = "machine"        Type = "storage"
TargetType = "machine"  TargetType = "job"      Name = "machine"
Cmd = "sim.exe"         Name = "raven"          HasCMSData = true
Owner = "thain"         Opsys = "linux"         CMSDataPath =
Requirements =          Requirements =                    "/cmsdata"
(Owner = "thain") &&      (Onwer = "thain")
NearestStorage.HasCMSData NearestStorage =
                          (Name="turkey")&&
                          (Type = "storage")
```

Figure 24.2   Examples of a job ClassAd, machine ClassAd, and storage ClassAd.

To gain an efficient execution of parameter sweep applications on the grid, Casanova et al. have studied four adaptive scheduling algorithms that consider distributed data storage [12]. The proposed algorithms are heuristic yet effective in environments where some computing nodes are best for some tasks but not for others. The key idea behind these scheduling algorithms is to judiciously place files for maximum reuse. These scheduling algorithms have been implemented in a user-level grid middleware, which centrally handles task scheduling.

Ranganathan and Foster have proposed a distributed scheduling framework in which each site consists of an external scheduler, a local scheduler, and a dataset scheduler [26]. The external scheduler of a site is responsible for dispatching the submitted jobs to an appropriate site, which can either be the one with the least load or the one in which required data have been staged. The functionality of the local scheduler is to decide the order in which jobs are executed at the site. The dataset scheduler makes decisions on when and where to replicate data.

24.3.3   Data Movement

In a computational grid, data movement mechanisms play an important role in achieving high system performance. This is driven by two requirements imposed by both grid applications and the data grid itself. First, applications need to access data that is not located at the site where the computation is performed. Second, replication services are responsible for managing replicas by means of copying and moving data through networks.

To fulfill the above two requirements, Bester et al. have proposed a data movement and access service called Global Access to Secondary Storage (GASS) [8]. The service not only incorporates data movement strategies that are geared for the common I/O patterns of grid applications, but also supports programmer management of data movement. The performance evaluation shows that GASS is an efficient approach to data movement in grid environments.

Thain et al. have developed a data movement system called Kangaroo, which improves reliability as well as throughput of grid applications by hiding network storage devices behind memory and disk buffers [37]. More specifically, the approach relies on Kangaroo's ability to overlap CPU and I/O processing intervals by using background processes to move data and handle errors.

24.4 SECURITY ISSUES

With the use of different machines in a grid, the issue of security, which has been provided by most existing data grids [13, 27, 42], becomes one of the prime concerns. In principle, traditional security techniques, such as encryption and access control, can be conservatively applied to a grid. For example, a user has to be authenticated and authorized before contacting any remote site.

Due to the limits, in what follows we only review two intriguing issues in security addressed in GDMP [27], namely, the main security issues of sensitivity of data and unauthorized use of network bandwidth to transfer huge files. Specifically, the security module of the GDMP server, based on the Globus Security Service (GSS) API, offers functions to acquire credentials, initiate context establishment on the client side and accept context requests on the server side, encrypting and decrypting messages, and client authorization. Consequently, the security module protects a site from any undesired file transfers and rejects any unauthorized requests.

24.5 OPEN ISSUES

Although a variety of techniques have been proposed to achieve high performance in data grids, there are still some open issues to be addressed. This section lists the open issues related to high-performance data grids.

24.5.1 Application Replication

Although some efforts have been made to replicate actual data accessed by grid applications, little attention has been paid to replicating frequently used grid applications across the grid. Once a scheduling scheme decides to move an application toward its data, a replication selection policy for applications can be developed to choose the most appropriate application copy in the grid. There are three reasons that motivate us to distinguish application code from actual data:

1. Foremost, an executable code of an application at one site might not be able to run on another site. One can straightforwardly tackle this problem by using a java-programming environment, which has become increasingly popular [2]. However, a large number of existing scientific applications have been developed in FORTRAN, C, or other programming languages. To solve this problem, one can have the source code moved to destination sites and obtain the executable code by compiling the source code at the destination sites.

2 The application replication techniques provide efficient support for a parallel–shared–nothing architecture. For example, a well-designed partition algorithm can be used to dynamically and effectively divide data among the processors at which the processing application has been staged to achieve maximum parallelism.

3. It is reasonably assumed that data can be stored at any site, provided that it has registered as a member of a data grid. Unfortunately, this assumption is not practical for applications since some sites might not be able to fulfill applications' hardware or/and software requirements.

To facilitate a parallel computing environment in computational grids, future work could be directed at studying an application replica service that includes application replica management and application selection. The application replica management would be designed to duplicate, remove, and update copies of application instances, as well as to maintain the consistency among the replicas. The application selection service would be devised to choose an optimized location at which an application replica has been stored to run the job.

24.5.2 Consistency Maintenance

In Section 24.3.1, we discussed the requirements of consistency maintenance imposed by scientific data and metadata. We believe that the proposed application replication services make the consistency maintenance even more complex. This is because in order to obtain high scalability, it is appealing to offer the services in a distributed fashion. In addition, a group of programmers are allowed to collaborate with one another to develop some large-scale applications in a grid environment, and grid applications are likely to be periodically upgraded.

We realize that from the summary of data replication techniques given in Table 24.1, most existing consistency models in data grids work well for read-only data, but much less attention has been devoted to the consistency issues for data that needs to be written multiple times. In a data grid environment, many datasets are multiply written in nature. When a group of programmers collaboratively develop a large-scale scientific application on the grid, some programmers might be working on the same source code, implying that the code not only needs to be written multiple times but also is likely to be written concurrently by several programmers. Therefore, it could be interesting to develop a relaxed consistency model to effectively handle the consistency problems in multiply-written data.

24.5.3 Asynchronized Data Movement

The impact of data movement on the performance of a local site is enormous, and this is especially true if the volume of transferred data is huge or data movements occur frequently. To alleviate such a burden resulting from data movements, future study could devise a new way of moving data without sacrificing the performance of applications running on local sites. In particular, a protocol could be designed to move asynchronized data if the load of source site and destination site are below a certain threshold. Compared with existing data movement approaches that treat synchronized and asynchronized data equally, our potential solution is expected to improve the performance of data grids when I/O and network load at each site are bursting in nature.

24.5.4   Prefetching Synchronized Data

We notice that data prefetching schemes for synchronized data have attracted little attention. We believe that data prefetching technique, which complements the new data movement approaches presented in Section 24.3.3, can optimize the performance of data grids in cases in which required data is moved to a remote site where its job resides.

By using ClassAd language to explicitly define applications' required files, a static prefetching scheme can make these files available before applications need to access them. As one of the possible future areas of study, a new prefetching algorithm that is able to dynamically predict files would be developed to establish correlations among files based on a statistic model. This new dynamic prefetching algorithm would actively provide grid applications with files by shipping required files in advance before applications are locally loading the files.

24.5.5   Data Replication

As can be seen from Table 24.1, the idea of replicating frequently accessed data on multiple sites has been eagerly pursued. The drawback of most existing replication techniques is that as the replication granularity is a file, a large file might be replicated even if only a small portion of the file is frequently accessed. This problem is analogous to false sharing in distributed shared memory systems. To provide a potential solution to tackle this problem, one could investigate a new data model in which the replication granularity could be dynamically adjusted according to benefits gained from replicas and overheads of generating replications.

Interestingly, there is no clear consensus on developing caching algorithms with efficient disk cache replacement policies in the context of data grids. As a result, there is a distinct need to study a caching algorithm in which files cached on local disks are viewed as temporary replicas. The main difference between cached files and regular replicas is that files in disk cache might be removed when disk cache is unable to accommodate newly arrived files.

24.6   CONCLUSIONS

We have reviewed a number of data grid services and various techniques for improving the performance of data grids. Additionally, the issue of security in data grids has been briefly discussed. Five open issues and possible future research directions are summarized below.

1. Although a significant amount of data grid research has been done on data replication, the idea of replicating frequently used grid applications across the grid has received little attention. One possible future area of research would be to develop a new application replica service that could be built on top of a data replication service.

2. It is noticed that most consistency models in existing data grids have not addressed consistency issues for multiply-written data. As one of the future directions, one can develop a relaxed consistency model to effectively handle the consistency problems for a number of common file access patterns, including multiply-written data.

3. There is a distinct need to study a new way of moving data at a time when both source and destination sites are lightly loaded, thereby achieving better performance in data grids without sacrificing the performance of applications running on local sites.

4. A fourth interesting future direction would be to design a new prefetching algorithm that could dynamically predicate files that are likely to be retrieved.

5. Last but not least, one of the possible future directions of research would be to study a file-caching algorithm with which the replication granularity of a new data model could be dynamically tuned in accordance with the benefits and overheads of generating replicas.

ACKNOWLEDGMENTS

This work was partially supported by a start-up research fund (103295) from the research and economic development office of the New Mexico Tech, an NSF grant (EPS-0091900), a Nebraska University Foundation grant (26-0511-0019), and a UNL Academic Program Priorities Grant.

REFERENCES

1. D. Abramson, J. Giddy, I. Foster, and L. Kotler, High Performance Parametric Modeling with Nimrod /G: Killer Application for the Global Grid, in *Proceedings of the International Parallel and Distributed Processing Symposium,* May, 2000.

2. J. Al-Jaroodi, N. Mohamed, H. Jiang, and D. Swanson, An Agent-Based Infrastructure for Parallel Java on Heterogeneous Clusters, in *Proceedings of 4th IEEE International Conference on Cluster Computing,* Chicago, Illinois, September (2002).

3. B. Allcock, J. Bester, J. Bresnahan, A. Chervenak, I. Foster, et. al., Efficient Data Transport and Replica Management for High-Performance Data-Intensive Computing, in *Proceedings 18th IEEE Symposium on Mass Storage Systems,* 2001.

4. C. Baru, R. Moore, A. Rajasekar, and M. Wan, The SDSC Storage Resource Broker, Proc of CASCON Conference, 1998.

5. J. Basney, M. Livny, and P. Mazzanti, Utilizing Widely Distributed Computational Resources Efficiently with Execution Domains, *Computer Physics Communications, 140,* 2001.

6. J. Basney, R. Raman, and M. Livny, High-throughput Monte Carlo, in *Proceedings of the Ninth SIAM Conference on Parallel Processing for Scientific Computing,* March 1999.

7. F. Berman, R. Wolski, S. Figueira, J. Schopf, and G. Shao, Application-Level Scheduling on Distributed Heterogeneous Networks, in *Proceedings of Supercomputing,* 1996.

8. J. Bester, I. Foster, C. Kesselman, J. Tedesco, and S. Tuecke, GASS: A Data Movement and Access Service for Wide Area Computing Systems, in *Proceedings of Sixth Workshop on I/O in Parallel and Distributed Systems,* May 5, 1999.

9. W. Bethel, B. Tierney, J. Lee, D. Gunter, and S. Lau, Using High-Speed WANs and Network Data Caches to Enable Remote and Distributed Visualization, in *Proceedings of the IEEE Supercomputing Conference,* 2002.

10. T. Bray, J. Paoli, and C. Sperberg-McQueen, The Extensible Markup Language (XML)1.0W3C Recommendation, World Wide Web Consortium, Feb. 1998.

11. L. Breslau, P. Cao, L, Fan, G. Phillips, and S. Shenker, Web Caching and Zipflike Distributions: Evidence and Implications, in *Proceedings of IEEE Infocom,* 1999.

12. H. Casanova, G. Obertelli, F. Berman, and R. Wolski, The AppLeS Parameter Sweep Template: User-Level Middleware for the Grid, in *Proceedings Supercomputing,* 2000.

13. A. Chervenak, I. Foster, C. Kesselman, C. Salisbury, and S. Tuecke, The Data Grid: Towards an Architecture for the Distributed Management and Analysis of Large Scientific Datasets, in *Proceedings of Network Storage Symposium,* 2000.

14. A. Chervenak, E. Deelman, C. Kesselman, L. Pearlman, and G. Singh, A Metadata Catalog Service for Data Intensive Applications, GriPhyN Technical Report, Information Science Institute, 2002.

15. A. Chervenak, E. Deelman, I. Foster, et al., Giggle: A Framework for Constructing Scalable Replica Location Services, in *Proceedings IEEE Supercompuing Conference,* 2002.

16. A. Ching, A. Choudhary, W. Liao, R. Ross, and W. Gropp, Noncontiguous I/O through PVFS, in *Proceedings of IEEE International Conference on Cluster Computing,* September, 2002.

17. S. Fitzgerald, I. Foster, C. Kessenlman, G. Laszewski, W. Smith, and S. Tuecke, A Directory Service for Configuring High-performance Distributed Computations, in *Proceedings 6th IEEE Symposiumon High-Performance Distributed Computing,* pp. 365–375, 1997.

18. I. Foster and C. Kesselman, Globus: A Metacomputing Infrastructure Toolkit, *International Journal of Supercomputer Applications, 11,* 2, 115–128, 1997.

19. J. Howard, M. Kazar, S. Menees, D. Nichols, M. Satyanarayanan, R. Sidebotham, and M. West, Scale and Performance in a Distributed File System, *ACM Transactions on Computer Systems, 6,* 1, 51–81, 1988.

20. H. Lamehamedi, B. Szymanski, Z. Shentu, and E. Deelman, Data Replication Strategies in Grid Environments, in *Proceedings Of the Fifth International Conference on Algorithms and Architectures for Parallel Processing,* 2002.

21. J. Lee, D. Gunter, M. Stoufer, and B. Tiemey, Monitoring Data Archives for Grid Environments, in *Proceedings Supercomputing,* 2002.

22. M. Litzkow, M. Livny, and M. Mutka, Condor—A Hunter of IdleWorkstations, in *Proceedings of the 8th International Conference on Distributed Computing Systems,* pp. 104–111, 1988.

23. D. Mullmann, W. Hosckek, J. Jaen-Martinez, and B. Segal, Models for Replica Synchronization and Consistency in Data Grid, in *Proceedings IEEE Symposium on High Performance on Distributed Computing,* 2001.

24. C. J. Patten and K. A. Hawick, Flexible High-performance Access to Distributed Storage Resources, in *Proceedings of High Performance Distributed Computing,* 2000.

25. K. Ranganathan and I. Foster, Identifying Dynamic Replication Strategies for a High-Performance Data Grid, in *Proceedings International Grid Computing Workshop,* Denver, November 2001.

26. K. Ranganathan and I. Foster, Decoupling Computation and Data Scheduling in Distributed Data-Intensive Applications, in *Proceedings of the 11th IEEE Symposium on High Performance Distributed Computing,* 2002.

27. A. Samar and H. Stockinger, Grid Data Management Pilot (GDMP): A Tool for Wide Area Replication, in *Proceedings of International Conference on Applied Informatics,* Feb. 2001.

28. R. Sandberg, D. Goldberg, S. Kleiman, D. Walsh, and B. Lyon, Design and Implementation of the Sun Network Filesystem, in *Proceedings of USENIX Conference,* Berkeley, 1985.

29. R. Snodgrass, A Relational Approach to Monitoring Complex System, *ACM Transactions on Computer Systems, 6,* 2, 157–196, 1988.

30. N. Spring and R. Wolski, Application level scheduling: Gene Sequence Library Comparison, in *Proceedings of ACM International Conference on Supercomputing,* 1998.

31. H. Stockinger, A. Samar, B. Allock, I. Foster, K. Holtman, and B. Tierney, File and Object Replication in Data Grids, in *Proceedings of IEEE Symposium on High Performance Distributed Computing,* 2001.

32. H. Stockinger, Distributed Database Management Systems and the Data Grid, *18th IEEE Symposium on Mass Storage Systems and 9th NASA Goddard Conference on Mass Storage Systems and Technologies,* San Diego, April 17–20, 2001.

33. C. Sun, X. Jia, Y. Zhang, Y. Yang, and D. Chen, Achieving Convergence, Causality-Preservation, and Intention-Preservation in Real-Time Cooperative Editing Systems, *ACM Transactions on Computer-Human Interaction, 5,* 1, 63–108, March, 1998.

34. M. Swany and R. Wolski, Representing Dynamic Performance Information in Grid Environments with Network Weather Service, in *Proceedings of the 2nd IEEE International Symposium on Cluster Computing and the Grid,* May 2002.

35. R. Tewari, M. Dahlin, H. Vin, and J. Kay, Design Considerations for Distributed Caching on the Internet, in *Proceedings of IEEE International Conference on Distributed Computing Systems,* 1999.

36. D. Thain, J. Bent, A. Arpaci-Dusseau, R. Arpaci-Dusseau, and M. Livny, Gathering at the Well: Creating Communities for Grid I/O, in *Proceedings Supercomputing,* 2001.

37. D. Thain, J. Basney, S. Son, and M. Livny, The Kangaroo Approach to Data Movement on theGrid, in *Proceedings of the 10th IEEE SymposiumonHigh Performance Distributed Computing,* 2001.

38. B. Tierney, R. Aydt, D. Gunter, W. Smith, V. Taylor, R. Wolski, and M. Swany, A Grid Monitoring Service Architecture, Global Grid Forum While Paper, 2001.

39. B. Tierney, W. Johnston, B. Crowley, G. Hoo, C. Brooks, and D. Gunter, The NetLogger Methodology for High Performance Distributed Systems Performance Analysis, in *Proceedings of IEEE High Performance Distributed Computing,* July, 1998.

40. S. Vazhkudai, S. Tuecke, and I. Foster, Replica Selection in the Global Data Grid, in *Proceedings of the International Workshop on Data Models and Databases on Clusters and the Grid,* 2001.

41. M. Wahl, T. Howes, and S. Kille, Lightweight Directory Access Protocol, RFC 2251, Internet Engineering Task Force, 1997.

42. B. White, A. S. Grimshaw, and A. Nguyen-Tuong, Grid-Based File Access: The Legion I/O Model, in *Proceedings of High Performance Distributed Computing,* 2000.

43. H. Yu and A. Vahdat, Design and Evaluation of a Conit-based Continuous Consistency Model for Replicated Services, *ACM Transactions on Computer Systems,* August, 2002.

44. Y. Zhu, H. Jiang, X. Qin, and D. Swanson, A Case Study of Parallel I/O for Biological Sequence Analysis on Linux Clusters, in *Proceedings of the 5th IEEE International Conference on Cluster Computing,* pp. 308–315, Hong Kong, Dec. 1–4, 2003.

## CHAPTER 25

Application I/O on a Parallel File System for Linux Clusters

DHEERAJ BHARDWAJ

Parallelism is the key to performance of large-scale scientific applications on any computer system manufactured today. A high level of I/O performance is necessary to make efficient use of parallel machines. The data involved in several large-scale applications can be more than a terabyte in size. Even if the computations can be performed in-core, the time required to read, distribute across the processors, and write the data is substantial. Often, I/O is the bottleneck in scientific application codes. Linux clusters are now common parallel computing platforms in the scientific community. In this article, we discuss how the effect of the "I/O bottleneck" can be mitigated by parallel I/O operations using ROMIO MPI-IO implementation over parallel virtual file systems (PVFSs) on Linux clusters. As an application example, a seismic imaging algorithm is shown to perform better with parallel I/O.

25.1 INTRODUCTION

Since the introduction of clusters in early 1990s, parallel processing has proven to be a viable solution for large-scale scientific and engineering problems to improve performance. With the change in demand, it has become very difficult to solve grand challenge applications on serial architecture machines to cope with increases in data volume. Nevertheless, nearly all grand challenge applications show inherent parallelism in physics or in the solution methodology. Indeed, parallel processing is the solution to the challenges. The I/O problems are also better solved with parallel processing and parallel I/O is needed for higher performance [1].

Linux clusters have matured as platforms for high-performance parallel computing. A critical but often ignored component of the cluster performance is the I/O system. Most of these cluster use Network File System (NFS) and MPI (Message Passing Interface) for parallel programming. One limitation of NFS is that the I/O nodes are driven by standard UNIX read and write calls, which are blocking requests. Several applications demand a great deal from the underlying storage sys-

High-Performance Computing: Paradigm and Infrastructure. Edited by L. T. Yang and M. Guo

tem and parallel I/O to meet large data-intensive requirements. Linux clusters have always lacked in I/O throughput compared to commercial parallel computers due to the unavailability of high-performance parallel file systems. Without such file systems, Linux clusters cannot perform well for large I/O-intensive applications. Parallel Virtual File System (PVFS) [2], which is available for Linux clusters, can be used to improve the I/O performance substantially.

Using the parallel processing concepts of clustering with efficient parallel I/O, several challenges such as terabytes of data, hundreds of gigaflop performance, and mathematically complex algorithms can be solved at a lower cost.

In this chapter, we study the standard Unix I/O and parallel I/O using MPI-IO functions of the ROMIO library on NFS and with PVFS support. Then we look at some of the data distribution strategies from the point of view scientific applications with an example of seismic Imaging [3].

With the rapid advancement in computational science, processing capabilities, memory size, multimedia capabilities, data-collection devices, and integration of enterprise data are providing enormous amounts of data ranging from hundreds of gigabytes to several terabytes. Many large-scale scientific applications such as seismic Imaging, life sciences, and high-energy physics typically need high-performance, scalable, reliable I/O performance for the processing of data ranging from a few terabytes to several terabytes.

Seismic imaging is an echo-reconstructive technique based on experiments in which a certain earth volume is illuminated by an explosive or vibratory source, and the energy backscattered by the inhomogeneties of the medium is recorded on the surface in digital form. The inhomogeneties act as reflecting surfaces that cause signal echoing. The echoes are then recorded at the surface and processed through a "computational lens" defined by a propagation model to yield an image of the inhomogeneties.

Applications such as Seismic Imaging demand a great deal from the underlying storage subsystem and parallel I/O to meet large data-intensive requirements. Any high-performance computing system expected to deliver the required performance needs a balanced architecture in interconnecting the CPU, memory, interprocessor communication, storage, and I/O.

25.2 APPLICATION I/O

Several applications such as high-energy physics and seismic imaging have shifted from being compute intensive to more I/O intensive in recent years. For example, more accurate and better resolution of geological subsurfaces requires larger data volumes for larger migration apertures, deeper images, larger offsets, and finer sampling. The improvements in data collection techniques have inundated the industry with huge amounts of data. A typical three-dimensional survey collects several terabytes of data. In order to analyze the changes in subsurface formations with time, four-dimensional surveys are common. Four-dimensional seismic surveys add one more dimension to the data volume. The digital data that needs to be processed before obtaining an interpretable image of the subsurface geological structures is enormous, amounting to hundreds of gigabytes or a few terabytes for three-dimensional acquisition. Geophysicists and geologists examine all this numerical input to formulate an initial or penultimate interpretation that will be passed perhaps 10 to 20 times through a major computer facility, and only after the complex numerical operations will the final sections be processed. Some of high-energy physics experiments are expected to collect petabytes of data per year. Parallel computers with efficient parallel I/O capabilities are essential to cope with this increase in data.

25.3 PARALLEL I/O SYSTEM SOFTWARE

This chapter is focused on the combined use of three I/O system software packages to provide both a convenient API and high-performance I/O access. The Parallel Virtual File System (PVFS), the ROMIO, MPI-IO implementation, and the interface for accessing the database together provide the I/O functionality needed by the scientific applications. Table 25.1 shows the organization of three components into a software stack with seismic imaging application at top level and PVFS at the lowest level.

25.3.1 Network File System (NFS)

NFS is arguably the most successful distributed application that has been produced. But the limitations on its robustness have set a limitation on the scalability of NFS. Because of the intrinsic unreliability of the NFS protocol, use of NFS is limited to a fairly small number of machines, geographically colocated and centrally administered. The ways NFS has dealt with partial failure have been to informally require a centralized resource manager (a system administrator) who can detect system failure, initiate resource reclamation, and ensure system consistency. But by introducing this central resource manager, one could argue that NFS is no longer a genuinely distributed application.

25.3.2 Parallel Virtual File System (PVFS)

The Parallel Virtual File System (PVFS) [2] is a parallel file system designed for Linux Clusters. PVFS provides high-speed access to file data for a parallel applica-

Table 25.1   I/O System software stack

HPC application
Database/File System
ROMIO/ROMIO with PVFS
NFS/PVFS

tion. It stripes file data across multiple disks in different nodes in a cluster. By spreading out file data in this manner, larger files can be created, potential bandwidth is increased, and network bottlenecks are minimized. A 64 bit interface is implemented as well, allowing large (more than 2 GB) files to be created and accessed. PVFS also supports the UNIX I/O interface and allows existing UNIX I/O programs to use PVFS files without recompiling.

PVFS is designed as a client–server system with multiple servers, called I/O daemons. These daemons typically run on separate nodes in the cluster, called I/O nodes, which have disk/RAID attached to them. Each PVFS file is striped across the disk on the I/O nodes. Application processes interact with PVFS via a client library. PVFS also has a manager daemon that handles only metadata operations such as permission checking for file creation, and open, close, and remove operations. This metadata manager does not participate in read and write operations. The clients, I/O daemons, and the manager need not be run on different machines. However, running them on different machines may result in higher performance.

PVFS currently uses TCP for all internal communication. As a result, it is not dependent on any particular message-passing library. Multiple user interfaces of PVFS are available. In addition to the traditional UNIX I/O interface, a multidimensional block interface has also been implemented for PVFS. ROMIO authors have also implemented hooks to allow their MPI-IO implementation to store files on PVFS.

25.3.3   ROMIO

ROMIO is a high-performance, portable implementation of MPI-IO [4, 5]. On Linux clusters, ROMIO can be configured to operate on top of both NFS and PVFS, providing applications using the MPI-IO interface direct access to NFS/PVFS file systems [2]. This allows applications to utilize this high-performance I/O option without constraining the application programmers to using the NFS/PVFS interface. Scientific applications require high-level interfaces for data storage that more easily map to the application data structure. ROMIO provides a standard interface on which a higher-level I/O interface may be built.

25.3.4   I/O Interface for Databases

Enormous amounts of seismic data require a database for proper data management. ROMIO provides an interface for MPI-IO to develop an API for accessing data from databases that can take advantage of the ROMIO/PVFS [6]. For example, Pro-C can be used for all kinds of RDBMS.

25.4   STANDARD UNIX AND PARALLEL I/O

Most file systems support only the regular Unix open and do not have collective open functions. MPI-IO (ROMIO) provides collective I/O functions, which must be called up by the processors that together open the file. Collective I/O has been shown to be a very important optimization in parallel I/O and can improve performance significantly [2]. This is because most file systems do not support shared file pointers.

For the purpose of implementing a data-parallel application on a parallel computer, we need to partition the input file across the processors. Figure 25.1 depicts the partitioning of the entire input file across the p processors.

We carried out experiments using the following four I/O approaches for data distribution across the participating processors in the parallel program:

1. UNIX I/O on NFS
2. Collective I/O (ROMIO) on NFS
3. UNIX I/O with PVFS support
4. Collective I/O (ROMIO) with PVFS support

In the case of UNIX I/O, a process with rank zero reads the input file using standard UNIX read, partitions it, and distributes it to other processors. Distribution is done using *MPI_Send* and processors with rank greater than zero receive their corresponding blocks by *MPI_Recv*. In collective I/O, all the processors open the file using the MPI-I/O (ROMIO) function *MPI_File_open* and read their required data blocks by moving the offset pointer to the beginning of their corresponding data block in the input file. This is done using the MPI-I/O (ROMIO) function *MPI_File_read_at.* In case of NFS, file is nfs mounted from the server to all the compute nodes. In the case of PVFS support, file is pvfs mounted the same as the NFS server to I/O nodes [7].

We have used a Linux cluster consisting of 16 nodes, each with CPU Intel PIV 1.8 GHz, 512 MB RAM, and 512 K cache. The interconnection network used for this cluster is 100 Mbps fast Ethernet. Red Hat 8.0 is the Linux version installed on this system.

In order to compare these approaches, first we fixed the size of the block needed by each processor for block sizes 10 MB, 20 MB, 40 MB, 60 MB, and 80 MB. In case of UNIX I/O, data is read by the master processor and sent to slaves. They receive the data, perform the required computations, and send it back to the master. The master receives the data and writes it on to the disk. For MPI IO, all participating processors read the data and write it back to the disk. Columns in Table 25.2 show the timings for fixed block size per CPU distributed across a number of

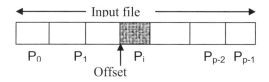

Figure 25.1   File view and its distribution across the p processors.

Table 25.2   I/O time for varying data sizes and number of CPUs

	Data size	10 MB	20 MB	40 MB	60 MB	80 MB
	# CPUs			Time (sec)		
UNIX I/O	2	6.44	20.04	178.54	398.52	666.76
NFS	4	12.28	84.74	326.75	736.51	1254.56
	8	23.52	230.48	640.41	1524.32	2245.12
	12	34.99	370.5	962.65	2291.12	3343.32
	16	45.42	524.58	1328.28	3188.16	4667.32
UNIX I/O	2	0.95	4.36	44.32	63.46	120.57
PVFS	4	2.57	12.93	76.44	103.84	205.24
	8	7.56	39.42	138.52	174.71	382.05
	12	11.54	68.45	215.64	280.78	574.56
	16	16.44	97.95	305.23	380.65	788.36
Collective I/O	2	3.62	20.87	108.85	230.41	362.53
NFS	4	6.82	50.69	239.42	463.42	746.68
	8	13.25	137.41	487.07	905.56	1442.56
	12	21.06	221.46	746.95	1360.46	2335.47
	16	28.58	313.34	1003.03	1882.73	3152.63
Collective I/O	2	0.63	3.61	30.61	63.46	97.18
PVFS	4	3.03	10.65	43.03	92.84	134.5
	8	4.1	25.56	74.37	162.54	229.34
	12	6.81	38.21	104.54	240.78	335.23
	16	9.86	54.86	142.64	323.23	455.23

processors.

Figures 25.2–25.5 show the I/O time for data of size 60 MB on each processor versus number of processors. Figure 25.2 shows that the I/O time difference in UNIX I/O and MPI I/O over NFS increases as the number of processors increases. It is evident that MPI-I/O performs better than UNIX I/O over NFS. Comparison of UNIX I/O on NFS and PVFS shows that UNIX I/O over PVFS performs better, as shown in Figure 25.3. Figure 25.4 clearly shows that MPI-IO with PVFS support provides better I/O time compared to UNIX-I/O with PVFS support as we increase the number of processors. Finally, we can conclude from Figure 25.5 that MPI-IO with PVFS support gives the best I/O performance for a fixed size of data on each CPU with the increase in number of processors.

The time required for standard Unix reading and distribution of the input data and the time required to read the data blocks by the processors concurrently (MPI I/O) using shared file pointers are functions of data size. Next, we fix the number of CPUs participating in the parallel execution and vary the data sizes on each CPU.

Figures 25.6–25.9 show the I/O time for 16 CPUs versus varying data sizes on each CPU. Figure 25.6 shows that the I/O time difference in UNIX I/O and MPI I/O over NFS increases as the size of the data increases. It is evident that MPI-I/O performs better than UNIX I/O over NFS. Comparison of UNIX I/O on NFS and PVFS

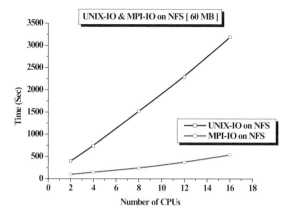

Figure 25.2 Graph showing the time required to read and write data of size 60 MB using UNIX I/O and MPI-IO on NFS versus number of CPUs.

shows that UNIX I/O over PVFS performs better, as shown in Figure 25.8.

Figure 25.7 clearly shows that MPI-IO with PVFS support provides better I/O time than UNIX-I/O with PVFS support as we increase the data size from 10 MB to 80 MB on each CPU. Finally, we can conclude from Figure 25.9 that MPI-IO with PVFS support gives the best I/O performance for a fixed number of CPUs with the increase in the size of the data.

Next, we studied the I/O for a data block that is required by all the processors. Figures 25.10 and 25.11 show the comparison between UNIX reading and broad-

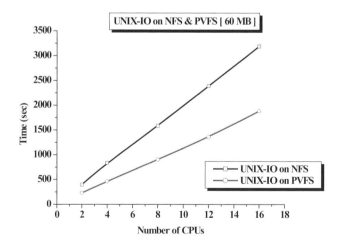

Figure 25.3 Graph showing the time required to read and write data of size 60 MB using UNIX I/O on NFS and with PVFS support versus number of CPUs.

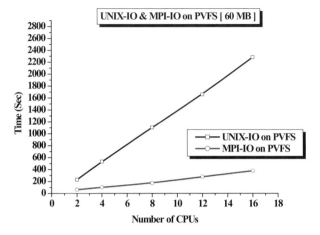

Figure 25.4 Graph showing the time required to read and write data of size 60 MB using UNIX I/O and MPI-IO with PVFS support versus number of CPUs.

casting of a fixed data size (80 MB), and concurrent read (MPI-IO) on NFS and PVFS support, respectively. The graphs in both figures show that the concurrent read (MPI-IO) performance is better in both cases.

Figure 25.12 compares concurrent reading using MPI-IO (ROMIO) functions on NFS and PVFS support for a fixed data size (80 MB). It shows that the difference in time increases with the increase in the number of processors. We can conclude from Figures 25.10–25.12 that for the data required by all the participating CPUs, MPI-IO

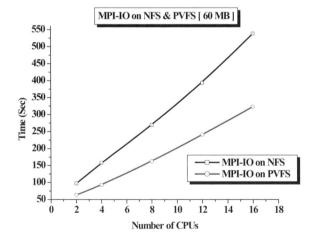

Figure 25.5 Graph showing the time required to read and write data of size 60 MB using MPI I/O on NFS and with PVFS support versus number of CPUs.

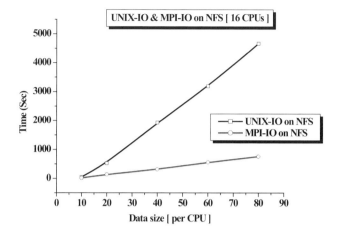

Figure 25.6 Graph showing the time required for reading and writing the data on 16 CPUs with standard Unix I/O and MPI I/O on NFS versus the varying data size per CPU.

with PVFS support provides the best performance as compared to other approaches.

25.5 EXAMPLE: SEISMIC IMAGING

Wave-equation-based seismic imaging methods are the standard in the industry as they provide finer geological details. Finite-difference methods are the most pre-

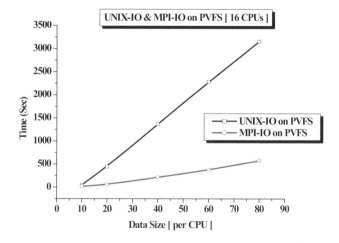

Figure 25.7 Graph showing the time required for reading and writing the data on 16 CPUs with standard Unix I/O and MPI I/O with PVFS versus the varying data size per CPU.

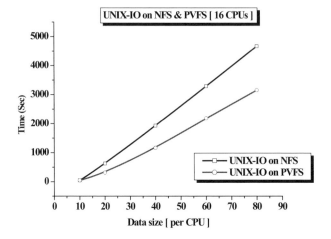

Figure 25.8 Graph showing the time required for reading and writing the data on 16 CPUs with UNIX I/O on NFS and with PVFS support versus the varying data size per CPU.

ferred methods for solving wave equations computationally. Finite-difference methods provide direct solution by solving partial differential equations with initial and boundary conditions.

The seismic imaging methods are comprised of two steps: a preprocessing phase (input phase) and migration phase. The initial input to the seismic imaging codes is a sequence of seismic traces, which are scattered across all the disk/RAID systems

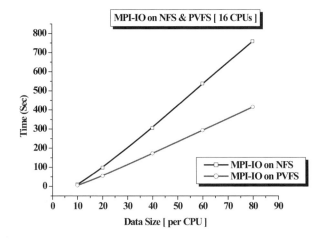

Figure 25.9 Graph showing the time required for reading and writing the data on 16 CPUs with MPI I/O (ROMIO) on NFS and with PVFS support versus the varying data size per CPU.

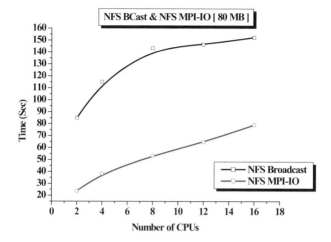

Figure 25.10 Graph showing comparison between UNIX reading and broadcasting of 80 MB of data, and reading using MPI-IO on NFS.

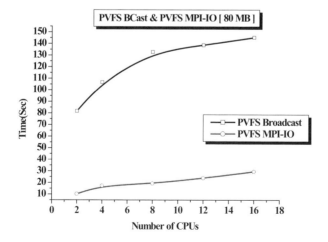

Figure 25.11 Graph showing comparison between UNIX reading and broadcasting of 80 MB of data, and reading using MPI-IO with PVFS support.

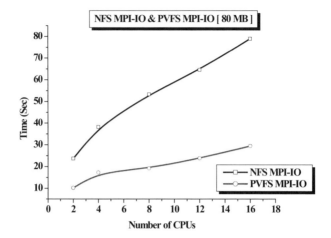

Figure 25.12   Graph showing comparison between concurrent reading of 80 MB of data with NFS and PVFS support.

in the I/O subsystem in a particular order, stored in the database. The traces must be read from the database, Fourier transformed, and redistributed to the appropriate processors for computations.

The migration phase is comprised of two steps: extrapolation and imaging. The extrapolation equation is a parabolic partial differential equation derived from the dispersion relations and solved by finite difference methods [8]:

$$k_z = \frac{\omega}{v}\left(\sqrt{1 - \left(\frac{vk_x}{\omega}\right)^2} + \sqrt{1 - \left(\frac{vk_y}{\omega}\right)^2} - 1\right) \qquad (25.1)$$

Where, x, y, and z are inline, crossline, and depth axes respectively, k_x, k_y, and k_z are the wavenumbers in x, y, and z directions, respectively; v is the velocity; and ω is the frequency. We approximate the square root terms by continued fraction expansion, Padé approximation, or any other optimization method. By inverse Fourier transforming in the x and z directions, we obtain the parabolic partial differential equation. At the imaging phase, extrapolated data is stacked in a particular fashion depending on the imaging condition for the algorithm used, and written on the disk.

25.5.1 I/O

Seismic data sets consisting of recorded pressure waves are usually very large, ranging from several gigabytes to terabytes. The computations can be done in-core, but the time required to read the initial seismic data, read the velocity models, and, finally, write the images is substantial. The type of initial data depends on the migration algorithms (poststack or prestack).

For poststack migration, data will be CMP stack data, stored as shown in the Fig-

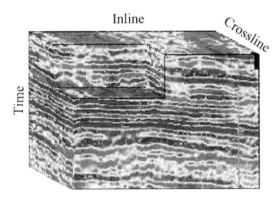

Figure 25.13   CMP stack data volume stored as inline planes.

ure 25.13, and can be accessed as inline planes. Thus, distribution of the data across the processors has to be over crosslines. A standard Unix I/O approach should strictly follow a master–slave programming paradigm. The master reads the data as inline planes and sends them to the processors by using *MPI_Send.* Parallel I/O uses a collective I/O operation with a shared file pointer for concurrent reading by all the participating processors.

For prestack migration, parallelization is done over the shots from the shot-gather data. In the standard Unix I/O case, the master reads the shots and sends them to respective slave processors. In the parallel I/O case, all processors get the shot data by concurrent reading.

The migration phase requires a velocity model as input. All the participating processors for migration need this velocity model. It is often the case when the velocity model is on a much smaller grid than the processing grid. In such cases, the velocity must be interpolated to the required grid. The velocity model has to be read plane by plane and broadcast to all the processors; each processor will interpolate it for the required grid and create a velocity model cube for migration. After the image is summed, all processors send their portion of image by a collective call to the processors with rank zero. These processors pass on their images to the I/O node(s) to be written onto the disk.

25.5.2   Performance Analysis of Seismic Migration

For implementing seismic migration algorithms, we looked at some of the data distribution strategies. If every processor has to read different blocks from datasets, then every processor can open and read the required dataset using a collective call of MPI-IO. This methodology is good for reading input pressure wavefield seismic data (stack or prestack). This is evident from Figure 25.9 and 25.12. But if every processor needs the same data, then the processor with rank zero should read it and broadcast it to other processors. This method is good for reading velocity depth

Table 25.3   Problem size for the dataset and the execution time on 64 processors

Size of FFT data	1.3 GB
Size of velocity model	1.2 GB
Total number of frequencies migrated	256
Number of processors	64
Total execution time with parallel I/O using ROMIO	7 hrs 44 mins
Total execution time with standard Unix I/O	9 hrs 20 mins

slices. Final imaging, in which all the partially imaged data have to be summed, should be done using a collective operation.

An experiment of poststack finite difference migration in the frequency–space domain was carried out on a real marine dataset. The data set used for testing was comprised of 950×665 CDPs. The inline spacing, crossline spacing, and depth step size were 25 m. The data was migrated for 480 depth steps. Fourier transformation was done outside the main migration code. Table 25.3 shows all the other parameters and the time required to migrate this dataset with 64 processors.

For the distribution of frequency data, a collective I/O approach has been used and velocity model has been read by the rank zero process and broadcast to all the processes. The results show an improvement of approximately 18% over the parallel I/O approach on standard Unix I/O.

25.6   DISCUSSION AND CONCLUSION

Most data-parallel scientific applications require reading, distributing of data across the processors, and writing, as mentioned in the seismic imaging example. NFS does not provide any functionality for parallel data accessing from/to storage systems, whereas PVFS helps in improving the I/O throughput by striping the data across the I/O nodes. The PVFS I/O daemons help in accessing the data in parallel.

The collective I/O approach using ROMIO has advantages over the standard UNIX I/O functions, which are blocking in nature. Thus, out of the four I/O approaches studied here, we can conclude that ROMIO with support on Linux clusters can improve overall application I/O throughputs substantially.

In this chapter it has been shown that how system software comprising PVFS, ROMIO, and API for Database can be used together to provide high-performance I/O for large-scale scientific algorithms on Linux clusters. In a Linux cluster, if there is more than one I/O nodes, it is advisable to distribute the dataset across the disks and assign the I/O to handle it, to increase the total disk-to-memory bandwidth.

In the seismic industry, where the amount of data that needs to be processed is often measured by the number of tapes, which amount to hundreds of gigabytes or even terabytes, the improvement in execution time by making efficient use of the I/O subsystem, and overlapping I/O with communications and computations, becomes increasingly apparent. A 10% to 20% improvement in runtime, especially for prestack migration, would amount to savings of millions of dollars of processing time. The above-mentioned results are a step in that direction.

REFERENCES

1. J. M. May, *Parallel I/O for High Performance Computing,* Morgan Kaufmann Publishers, 2001.
2. R. Thakur, and A. Choudhary, 1996, An extended two phase method for accessing sections of out-of-core arrays, *Scientific Programming, 5,* 301–317.
3. S. Phadke, D. Bhardwaj, and S. Yerneni, Wave equation based migration and modelling algorithms on parallel computers, in *Proceedings of SPG (Society of Petroleum Geophysicists), 2nd* Conference, pp. 55–59, 1998.
3. P. H. Carns, W. B. Ligon III, R. B. Ross, and R. Thakur, PVFS: A parallel file system for Linux Clusters. Proc. 4th Annual Linux Showcase and Conference, 317–327, 2000.
4. R. Thakur, E. Lusk, and W. Gropp, *User Guide for ROMIO: A High Performance, Portable MPI-IO Implementation,* TM No. 234, ANL, (USA), 1998.
5. R. Thakur, W. Gropp, E. Lusk, On implementing MPI-IO portably and with high performance, in *Proceedings of the Sixth Workshop on I/O in Parallel and Distributed Systems,* pp. 23–32, 1999.
6. R. Ross, D. Nurmi, A. Cheng, and M. Zingale, A case study in application I/O on Linux clusters, in *Proceedings of SC2001,* 2001.
7. H. Stern, *Managing NFS and NIS,* O'Reilly & Associates, Inc., 1991.
8. J. F. Claerbout, *Imaging the Earth's Interior,* Blackwell Scientific Publications, 1985.

## CHAPTER 26

One Teraflop Achieved with a Geographically Distributed Linux Cluster

PENG WANG, GEORGE TURNER, STEPHEN SIMMS, DAVE HART, MARY PAPAKHIAN, and CRAIG STEWART

26.1 INTRODUCTION

The Top 500 List [12] is the leading authority in evaluating computational performance of a supercomputer. The performance data of a listed system is obtained by running a portable high-performance benchmark called High Performance LINPACK (HPL)—an efficient parallel, dense linear system solver using LU factorization.

Systems on the Top 500 list are almost exclusively single site installations with the exception of Indiana University's AVIDD facility (Analysis and Visualization of Instrument-Driven Data) [2]. AVIDD is installed based on the existing high bandwidth I-light optical network infrastructure [6] to realize geographical distribution and disaster resilience. With appropriate tuning, we were able to achieve low latency communication among necessary components of the facility and realize 1.058 teraflop performance for LINPACK benchmark (57.4% of theoretical peak performance). It ranks 50th on the June 2003 Top 500 list.

In the next section, we describe the hardware and software setup of the AVIDD facility; in Section 26.3, the benchmarking result and system parameters are reported and examined after a detailed discussion of HPL's performance model; and in Section 26.4, as a conclusion, the cost and benefits of the distributed cluster building approach are discussed in terms of robustness and performance.

26.2 HARDWARE AND SOFTWARE SETUP

The AVIDD facility includes a suite of four distributed Linux clusters. Two identical clusters, each with 104 IBM x335 nodes with dual CPUs, form the core of this suite of clusters. One of these clusters is located in Indianapolis (AVIDD-I), the other in Bloomington (AVIDD-B), 84 kilometers (52 miles) apart. Each of the local clusters includes a Myrinet interconnect. In addition, one Force 10 E600TM switch on each side configured with 120 1000 Base-T ports provides Gigabit Ethernet connectivity to each of the AVIDD-B and AVIDD-I nodes. AVIDD-B and AVIDD-I are connected via dual 10 gigabit pipelines using the two Force 10 switches and two dedicated fibers of the I-light through a private network. The switches are configured with 10 Gbase-ER modules with optics capable of exceeding the 40 km 10 Gigabit Ethernet reach while remaining within the standards.

Each cluster has three head nodes, 97 compute nodes, and four storage nodes. All the nodes are equipped with dual 2.4 GHz Xeon processors with 512 MB L2 cache and 400 MHz FSB (front side bus). Hyper-threading is disabled at the BIOS level. All the nodes are installed with Redhat Linux 7.3 and kernel 2.4.18. Each node has 2.5 Gbyte of 266 MHz ECC DDR RAM.

For LINPACK benchmark, we use HPL 1.0 [5].

26.3   SYSTEM TUNING AND BENCHMARK RESULTS

Within this section, based on the performance model of HPL, we are going to discuss the impact of BLAS library and network communication on LINPACK performance. Furthermore, we are going to analyze HPL's communication pattern based on profiling results and the geographical distribution of the AVIDD cluster's effect on the performance based on benchmarking data using LAM over Gigabit Ethernet.

26.3.1   Performance Model of HPL

HPL is a SPMD parallel application to solve a dense linear system of N unknowns using LU factorization. When running, it distributes the $N \times N$ matrix evenly to memory of each node in the cluster. According to [5], its parallel efficiency can be estimated as:

$$E = \frac{T_{serial}}{PQT_{hpl}} = \frac{1}{1 + \dfrac{3\beta(3P + Q)}{4N\gamma_3} + \dfrac{3PQ\alpha((NB + 1)\log P + P)}{2N^2NB\gamma_3}} \tag{26.1}$$

assuming a linear communication model,

$$T_c = \alpha + \beta L \tag{26.2}$$

where $2N^3/3$ is the number of floating point operations needed in LU factorization and

$$T_{hpl} = \frac{2N^3}{3PQ\gamma_3} + \frac{\beta N^2(3P + Q)}{2PQ} + \frac{\alpha N[(NB + 1)\log P + P]}{NB} \tag{26.3}$$

The meanings of the symbols are described in Table 26.1.
Several observations can be made regarding the above performance model:

- It is appropriate for a homogeneous system, where matrix–matrix operations on all the processing units can be modeled using one single parameter γ_3, and MPI message passing time can be modeled using a linear model. Within a single cluster, this assumption certainly holds, irrespective of whether we use Gigabit Ethernet or Myrinet. In addition, we argue that the system including both AVIDD-B and AVIDD-I is suitable for this model since both clusters are identical and homogeneous, and any heterogeneity due to the network connection between Bloomington and Indianapolis is negligible based on experiments and tuning. We are going to illustrate this point further in the subsection discussing benchmarking results with Gigabit Ethernet.
- With everything else unchanged, increasing the problem size N will increase execution time but will improve LINPACK performance E.
- Using a good BLAS library will improve γ_3, thereby, reducing LINPACK execution time, T_{hpl}. From Equation 26.1, it is clear that as problem size N increases and other parameters remain constant, the second and third terms in the denominator are going to diminish and the performance E will be converging to $PQ\gamma_3$ as N goes to infinity, so having a high-performance BLAS library is critical to the overall system performance.
- Reducing α and β through network tuning could improve performance and reduce execution time.
- From Equation 26.1, it appears that a bigger NB or block size will yield better performance; however, cache effect is not taken into consideration in Equation 26.1. In addition, only the third term in the denominator contains NB, so its effect is limited. During testing, we found 200 to be an optimal value of NB for our system.

Table 26.1   Meanings of different symbols

T_C	The time spent to communicate a message of L double precision items between two given processors
α	The time to prepare a message for transmission on the interprocessor network
β	$L \times \beta$ indicates the time it takes for a length L message to traverse the interprocessor network
γ_3	Approximate floating point operations per second when the processor is performing matrix–matrix operations
NB	Block size. The coefficient matrix is logically partitioned into $NB \times NB$ blocks, and cyclically distributed to the process grid.
P, Q	Total $P \times Q$ processors
$T_{serial} = \dfrac{2N^3}{3\gamma_3}$	The time it takes a serial program to run
T_{hpl}	The time it takes HPL to run

With additional consideration of the memory constraint, we can obtain a rough estimate of the highest performance we could achieve with a given processor grid. Since each node contains approximately 2.5 GB of memory, there is an upper limit on problem size N given a $P \times Q$ processor grid:

$$8N^2 \leq 1.25PQ \times 10^9 \qquad (26.4)$$

Using Equations 26.1 and 26.4, an upper limit of overall system performance that is more realistic than $PQ\gamma_3$ can be obtained:

$$E < \cfrac{PQ}{\cfrac{1}{\gamma_3} + 2.078\beta \times 10^{-4} + \cfrac{9.6\alpha \times 10^{-9}(201 \times \log P + P)}{200}} \qquad (26.5)$$

The above formula is a better fit for a near-square processing grid. α and β can be determined by performing round-robin tests using a range of large message sizes (3000 doubles to 3 million doubles) that is typical in LINPACK panel broadcasting and applying the least squares fit on the resulting average "per-hop" time, that is, the time it takes a message of a given size to be sent from one process to another.

Based on the above discussion, our benchmarking strategy should be:

- Select an optimal BLAS library.
- Perform network tuning to reduce message passing latency and increase bandwidth.
- Use a problem size that fully makes use of the physical memory in the system while preventing swapping.

HPL offers many variants for various operations and users specify desired variants in its input file. An optimal set of parameters can be easily determined experimentally. Table 26.2 lists the parameter combination that we found optimum for our benchmarking.

26.3.2 BLAS Library

LINPACK benchmark mainly utilizes the DGEMM routine of the BLAS library, therefore, it is desirable that we pick a BLAS implementation that has the best performance in DGEMM. As shown in Figure 26.1, we compared the performance of ATLAS [1], the high-performance BLAS implementation by Kazushige Goto [4], and the generic BLAS library included in the LAPACK [9] distribution on one of the compute nodes of AVIDD. The comparison is done using the Blasbench program in the University of Tennessee llcbench [10] package. Both the ATLAS and the generic BLAS library were compiled using the Intel 7.1 compiler, and the Goto library is a precompiled dynamic linked library.

Based on Figure 26.1, we can see that the Goto library has the best performance in DGEMM so far. In the following benchmark runs, we used the Goto library as the BLAS implementation HPL links against.

Table 26.2   Optimum HPL parameters

*NB*s (block size)	200
Threshold	16.0
Number of panel facts	1
PFACTs (0 = left, 1 = Crout, 2 = right)	2
Number of recursive stopping criterion	1
NBMINs (≥ 1)	4
Number of panels in recursion	1
NDIVs	3
Number of recursive panel facts	1
RFACTs (0 = left, 1 = Crout, 2 = right)	2
Number of broadcast	1
BCASTs (0 = 1rg, 1 = 1rM, 2 = 2rg, 3 = 2rM, 4 = Lng, 5 = LnM)	1
Number of lookahead depths	1
DEPTHs (≥ 0)	0
SWAP (0 = bin-exch, 1 = long, 2 = mix)	2
Swapping threshold	64
L1 in (0 = transposed, 1 = no-transposed) form	0
U in (0 = transposed, 1 = no-transposed) form	0
Libration (0 = no, 1 = yes)	1
Memory alignment in double (> 0)	8

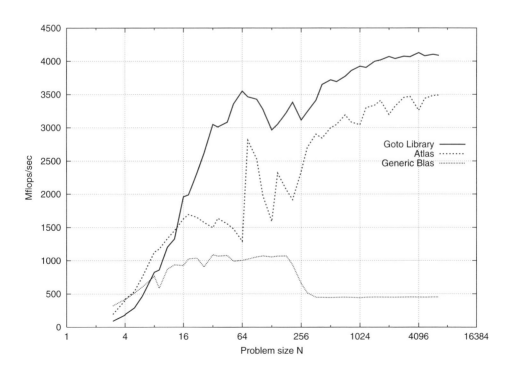

Figure 26.1   Performance comparison of DGEMM of different BLAS libraries.

26.3.3 Results Using Myrinet

We ran the LINPACK benchmark within a single cluster using MPICH over Myrinet at both Bloomington and Indianapolis. MPICH-GM 1.2.4.8 and Myrinet-GM 1.6.3 are used. Production services such as PBS and GPFS were shut down to free up memory before the benchmark runs, and problem sizes were chosen to achieve best performance while preventing swapping on individual nodes. Table 26.3 lists the results of three runs.

26.3.4 Results Using Gigabit Ethernet

HPL assumes a uniform communication pattern among all the processes. It is not aware of low-latency communication paths and takes advantage of that. With our distributed AVIDD-B and AVIDD-I clusters, communication latency within a cluster is lower than that of between the two clusters. We find that this communication latency difference could be tuned to be so small that HPL experiences little performance penalty. The Ethernet network interface cards we use are Broadcom BCM5703X 1000 base-T cards with driver version 2.2.27. They are capable of CPU task offloading by providing on-card segmentation and checksum. To improve communication bandwidth and reduce latency, both the NICs and the switches are jumbo-frame enabled to process 9000 bytes MTU. Force 10 FTOS v4.3.2.0 is used as switch firmware. LAM 6.6b2 is used in all our HPL runs over Gigabit Ethernet. Table 26.4 lists the broadcom driver parameters we adjusted.

To improve the networking performance of the Linux TCP/IP stack, we adjusted the Linux kernel sysctl variables [3] as shown in Table 26.5.

With above tuning, the communication latency between Bloomington and Indianapolis is comparable to that within a single cluster. In fact, the round-trip time of a 320 Kbytes MPI message is 3.2ms between two nodes in AVIDD-B, and 4.5 ms between one node in AVIDD-B and one node in AVIDD-I. Furthermore, for bigger messages, the cross-cluster message passing tends to have less impact on the round-trip time given the linear communication model in Equation 26.2. To further understand the communication characteristics of HPL 1.0 and verify that geographical distribution of the cluster incurs little performance penalty, we profiled two HPL runs using eight processors (processor grid of two by four) on problem size of 10,000, one on AVIDD-B only, the other spanning across both clusters (four

Table 26.3 Performance data of MPICH over Myrinet

Total Gflops	LINPACK problem size	% of Peak theoretical capacity	Number of CPUs	Total RAM	Date	Location
682.6	170000	68.4	208	260	3/10/2003	Bloomington, IN
682.5	170000	68.4	208	260	4/15/2003	Indianapolis, IN
614.4	150000	66.7	192	240	3/9/2003	Bloomington, IN

Table 26.4   Broadcom NIC firmware parameters

Variable name	Value
adaptive_coalesce	0
rx_coalesce_ticks	1
rx_max_coalesce_frames	1
tx_coalesce_ticks	1
tx_max_coalesce_frames	1
mtu	9000

processors on AVIDD-B and four processors on AVIDD-I), and compared their performance results. The run within AVIDD-B yields 18.33 Gflops, while the one involving both clusters yields 18.27 Gflops. Figures 26.2 and 26.3 show the side-by-side comparisons of complete and zoomed-in profiling results. The profiles on the top are from the run within AVIDD-B; the ones on the bottom are from the run involving both clusters. In the bottom profile, processes 0–3 are within AVIDD-B, whereas 4–7 are within AVIDD-I. From the profiles, we can see that themessages passed between clusters are between processes 0 and 4 and 1 and 5. These are panel updates sent among processes that are on the same process column (processes whose array data blocks reside on the same column). In this case, the length of the message is around several megabytes (changing from 8 MB to 2 MB). From Figure 26.3, for messages of this size, we can see that message-passing time between the clusters in the bottom profile is about the same as within the cluster in the top profile. This ensures that the geographical distribution of the processes has little impact on the performance.

However, we need to note that the link between Bloomington and Indianapolis has both higher bandwidth and higher latency than within a single cluster; therefore, it is more appropriate for passing large messages instead of lots of small messages. Since a lot of small messages (message lengths around 1 KB to 3 KB) are passed among processes on the same process row (processes whose array data blocks reside on the same row) during the panel factorization and updates, processes on the same process row should be kept within a single cluster (even better if they are on

Table 26.5   Adjusted Linux kernel parameters

Variable path	Value
/proc/sys/net/ipv4/tcp_timestamp	1
/proc/sys/net/ipv4/tcp_windows_scaling	1
/proc/sys/net/ipv4/tcp_sack	1
/proc/sys/net/core/wmem_max	8,388,608
/proc/sys/net/core/rmem_max	8,388,608
/proc/sys/net/ipv4/tcp_rmem	4096, 256,000, 4,194,304
/proc/sys/net/ipv4/tcp_wmem	4096, 256,000, 4,194,304

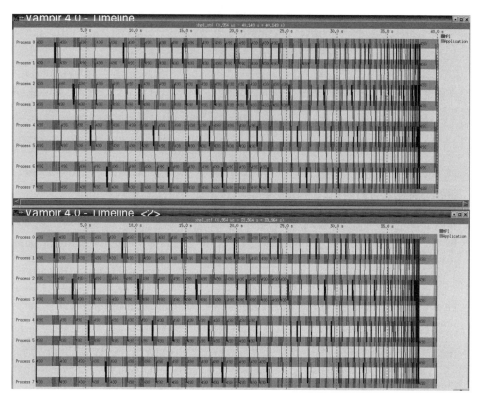

Figure 26.2 Side-by-side comparison of complete profiling results of two HPL runs with and without communication between Bloomington and Indianapolis.

the same node communicating via shared memory as in the previous two cases); otherwise, HPL performance will suffer. For the case of eight processes working on problem size of 10,000, when the processes on the same process row are arranged on different clusters using LAM's schema file, the overall HPL performance falls to 16.20 Gflops. Figure 26.4 shows the side-by-side comparison of profiling results between this case and the 18.27 Gflops case. It is obvious that the performance drop is due to the longer communication time between processes in the same process row during the panel factorization and updates. With the above tuning and appropriate arrangements of processes in the same process row, for larger scale tests, intercluster communication again incurs little performance penalty (compare rows 1 and 2 of Table 26.6). The benchmark run using 48 nodes of AVIDD-B and 48 nodes of AVIDD-I with a smaller problem size of 140,000 yields 563.6 Glops, which is within 2% of performance of running on 96 nodes within the Bloomington cluster with a bigger problem size. As a result, when running the benchmarks, we treat AVIDD-B and AVIDD-I as a single cluster. Table 26.6 lists the performance data of different runs.

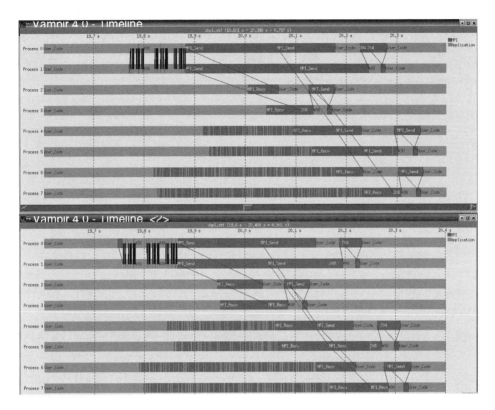

Figure 26.3   Zoomed in side-by-side comparison of profiling results of two HPL runs with and without communication between Bloomington and Indianapolis.

26.4   PERFORMANCE COSTS AND BENEFITS

Several conclusions can be drawn from the analysis in the previous sections:

- Although it is a common approach to evaluate LINPACK performance against the product of the number of processors in the system and the theoretical peak performance of each processor, realistically, LINPACK performance is further constrained by the BLAS performance on a processor; specifically, performance of the matrix and matrix products. Therefore, it is critical to use a high-performance BLAS library.
- Communication among processes on the same process row are both latency and bandwidth sensitive because both infrequent large messages (several megabytes and up) and frequent small messages (several kilobytes) are passed around, whereas communication among processes on the same process column is only bandwidth sensitive. For a geographically distributed cluster like AVIDD with plenty of bandwidth between AVIDD-B and

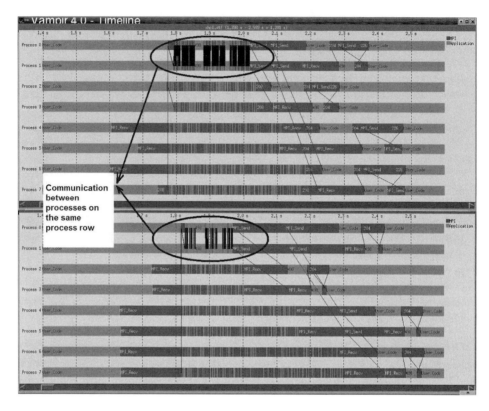

Figure 26.4   Performance impact of putting processes on the same row on different clusters.

Table 26.6   Performance data of LAM over Gigabit Ethernet

Total Gflops	LINPACK problem size	% of Peak theoretical capacity	Number of CPUs	Total RAM	Date	Location
563.6	140,000	61.2	192	240	4/19/2003	Indianapolis, IN and Bloomington, IN
575.0	150,000	62.4	192	240	4/21/2003	Bloomington, IN
580.8	160,000	63.0	192	240	4/19/2003	Indianapolis, IN and Bloomington, IN
1058	220,000	57.4	384	480	4/30/2003	Indianapolis, IN and Bloomington, IN

AVIDD-I, it is important to perform the benchmarking according to this communication pattern. We accomplish this by arranging processes on the same process row within a single cluster, and distribute array columns onto different clusters.

- Based on the communication pattern of LINPACK, it will be advantageous to use a MPI implementation that supports multiprotocol use; for example, use Myrinet within a single cluster and use Gigabit Ethernet between different clusters.

- Although the merits of grid-based computing [7] are in many ways clear, it is not often that there is an opportunity to consider the costs and benefits of this approach as compared to other possible approaches. In the case of the AVIDD facility, the use of private networks made it possible to evaluate the costs in terms of performance of a distributed approach. The cost in terms of performance was a decrease of approximately 9% (comparing the last row of Table 26.6 and last row of Table 26.3) in performance, on the HPL benchmark, based on the results we would have expected if the entire cluster had been in one location. However, we need to note that an application designed to be latency tolerant and teragrid scalable [11] will be more resilient when running on such distributed clusters. Moreover, the benefits of the distributed approach are several, and many of them have to do with physical facilities and resilience in the face of disasters. A distributed Linux cluster split between two locations reduced the impact on Indiana University's existing machine rooms in terms of electrical power and cooling. This was important given that neither of the two existing machine rooms had electrical power and cooling facilities sufficient to house the entire system and modifications to change that would have been extremely expensive. In addition, the distributed approach creates resilience in the face of a disaster striking one of the two machine rooms. If one machine room were destroyed, it would still be possible for the AVIDD system to provide services to researchers, albeit at half capacity. This is important given that Bloomington is on the edge of a tornado alley. There were important benefits to the distributed approach taken in the creation of the AVIDD Linux clusters. In terms of raw performance, there was a cost in performance as well, but the cost was modest. There are many other reasons for a grid-based approach to computing infrastructure, but even in a very simple installation where many of the potential benefits of grid computing did not apply, the grid approach has proven useful.

ACKNOWLEDGMENTS

This work has been funded in part by the National Science Foundation (NSF) under grant CDA-9601632 and the Indiana Genomics Initiative INGEN (INGEN). The Indiana Genomics Initiative of Indiana University is support in part by Lilly Endowment Inc.

REFERENCES

1. Automatically Tuned Linear Algebra Software homepage, http://www.netlib.org/atlas/.
2. AVIDD homepage, http://www.indiana.edu/ uits/rac/avidd.
3. Enabling High Performance Data Transfers, http://www.psc.edu/networking/perf tune. html.
4. High Performance BLAS library homepage, http://www.cs.utexas.edu/users/flame/goto.
5. High Performance LINPACK homepage, http://www.netlib.org/benchmark/hpl.
6. I-light homepage, http://www.i-light.org.
7. I. Foster and C.Kesselman, (Eds.), *The Grid: Blueprint for a New Computing Infrastructure,* Morgan-Kaufmann, 1998.
8. LAM MPI homepage, http://www.lam-mpi.org.
9. Linear Algebra PACKage homepage, http://www.netlib.org/lapack.
10. llcbench homepage, http://icl.cs.utk.edu/projects/llcbench/.
11. P. R. Woodward and S. Anderson, Scaling to the Teragrid by Latency Tolerant Application Design, in *PACI-DoE Workshop, Scaling to New Heights,* May 20, 2002.
12. The Top 500 List, http://www.top500.org.

## CHAPTER 27

A Grid-Based Distributed Simulation of Plasma Turbulence

BENIAMINO DI MARTINO, SALVATORE VENTICINQUE, SERGIO
BRIGUGLIO, GIULIANA FOGACCIA, and GREGORIO VLAD

Grid technology is widespread, but most grid-enabled applications just exploit shared storage resources rather than computational ones, or utilize static remote allocation mechanisms of grid platforms. In this chapter, the porting on a Globus-equipped platform of a hierarchically distributed, shared-memory parallel version of an application for particle-in-cell (PIC) simulation of plasma turbulence is described, based on the hierarchical integration of MPI and OpenMP, and originally developed for generic (nongrid) clusters of SMP nodes.

27.1 INTRODUCTION

Grid technology is becoming more and more widespread within the scientific community. Despite the original motivations behind many grid initiatives, that is, sharing and cooperatively using computational resources scattered through the globe in a transparent way with respect to their physical location, most grid-enabled applications just exploit shared storage resources rather than computational ones, or utilize static remote allocation mechanisms in order to transparently select and allocate sequential or parallel tasks, running, in any case, on a single grid node. Nowadays, most grid platforms are able to present computational and storage resources spread all over the world and managed by different entities as if they were a single, virtually homogeneous, parallel machine. Parallel tasks and applications could, at least in principle, be managed and executed over widespread, heterogeneous platforms.

Most of the existing grid platforms are built by using the Globus Toolkit, an open-source software toolkit developed by the Globus Alliance and many other groups all over the world [11]. The Globus environment includes MPICH-G [9], a complete implementation of MPI for heterogeneous, wide-area environments, based on MPICH [12]. Built on top of Globus_io and native MPI, MPICH-G allows communication among multiple machines connected across a wide-area network in order to couple them in a single execution.

The aim of this work is testing the viability of this approach on real, large-scale parallel applications by porting on a Globus-equipped platform a hierarchically distributed, shared-memory parallel version of an application for particle-in-cell (PIC) simulation of plasma turbulence, based on the hierarchical integration of MPI and OpenMP [2], originally developed for generic (nongrid) clusters of SMP nodes. Toward this aim, a cluster of SMP workstations has been configured as a distributed system of single-node SMP Globus machines, representing a lowest-order approximation of a more complex geographically distributed, heterogeneous grid.

The chapter proceeds as follows. In Section 27.2, we describe the internode workload decomposition strategy, adopted in the distributed-memory context, along with its MPI implementation. The integration of such internode strategy with the intranode (shared-memory) one, implemented by OpenMP, is discussed in Section 27.3. In Section 27.4, the testing platform is described and experimental results are provided. Final conclusions are discussed in the last section.

27.2 MPI IMPLEMENTATION OF THE INTERNODE DOMAIN DECOMPOSITION

Particle-in-cell simulation consists [1] in evolving the coordinates of a set of N_{part} particles in certain fluctuating fields computed (in terms of particle contributions) only at the points of a discrete spatial grid and then interpolated at each particle (continuous) position. Two main strategies have been developed for the workload decomposition related to porting PIC codes on parallel systems: the particle decomposition strategy [6] and the domain decomposition one [7, 10]. Domain decomposition consists in assigning different portions of the physical domain and the corresponding portions of the spatial grid to different processes, along with the particles that reside on them. Particle decomposition, instead, statically distributes the particle population among the processes, while assigning the whole domain (and the spatial grid) to each process. As a general fact, particle decomposition is very efficient and yields a perfect load balancing, at the expense of memory overheads. Conversely, the domain decomposition does not result in memory waste, while presenting particle migration between different portions of the domain, which causes communication overheads and the need for dynamic load balancing [4, 7].

Such workload decomposition strategies can be applied both to distributed-memory parallel systems [6, 7] and shared-memory ones [5]. They can also be combined, when porting a PIC code on a hierarchically distributed shared-memory system (e.g., a cluster of SMPs), in two-level strategies: a distributed-memory level decomposition (among the n_{node} computational nodes), and a shared-memory one (among the n_{proc} processors of each node).

In this chapter we consider the combination of the domain-decomposition strategy at the internode level (described in the present section) with the particle-decomposition strategy at the intranode level (cf. Section 27.3).

The typical structure of a PIC code for plasma particle simulation can be represented as follows. At each time step, the code

1. Computes the electromagnetic fields only at the N_{cell} points of a discrete spatial grid (field solver phase)
2. Interpolates the fields at the (continuous) particle positions in order to evolve particle phase–space coordinates (particle pushing phase)
3. Collects the particle contribution to the pressure field at the spatialgrid points to close the field equations (pressure computation phase).

We can schematically represent the structure of this time iteration by the following code excerpt:

```
call field_solver(pressure,field)
call pushing(field,x_part)
call compute_pressure(x_part,pressure)
```

Here, `pressure(1:n_cell)`, `field(1:n_cell)`, and `x_part(1: n_part)` (with n_cell = N_{cell} and n_part = N_{part}) represent pressure, electromagnetic-field, and particle-position arrays, respectively. In order to simplify the notation, we will refer, in the pseudocode excerpts, to a one-dimensional case; the experimental results reported in the following refer to a three-dimensional (3-D) application.

In implementing a parallel version of the code, according to the distributed-memory, domain-decomposition strategy, different portions of the physical domain and of the corresponding spatial grid are assigned to the n_{node} different nodes, along with the particles that reside on them. This approach yields benefits and problems that are complementary to those yielded by the particle-decomposition one [6]: on the one hand, the memory resources required for each node are approximately reduced by the number of nodes (n_part~ N_{part}/n_{node}, n_cell~ N_{cell}/n_{node}); an almost linear scaling of the attainable physical-space resolution (i.e., the maximum size of the spatial grid) with the number of nodes is then obtained. On the other hand, internode communication is required to update the fields at the boundary between two different portions of the domain, as well as to transfer those particles that migrate from one domain portion to another. Such a particle migration possibly determines a severe load unbalancing of the different processes, which then requires a dynamic rebalancing, at the expense of further computations and communications.

Three additional procedures then characterize the structure of the parallel code at each time step:

- The number of particles managed by a process has to be checked, in order to avoid excessive load unbalancing among the processes (if such an unbalancing is verified, the load-balancing procedure must be invoked).
- Particles that moved from one subdomain to another because of particle pushing must be transferred from the original process to the new one.

- The values of the pressure array at the boundaries between two neighbor subdomains must be corrected, because their local computation takes into account only those particles that belong to the subdomain, neglecting the contribution of neighbor subdomain particles.

Let us report here the schematic representation of the time iteration performed
by each process, before giving some detail on the implementation of such procedures:

```
    call field_solver(pressure,field)
    call check_loads(i_check,n_part,n_part_left_v,
&      n_part_right_v)
    if(i_check.eq.1)then
    call load_balancing(n_part_left_v,n_part_right_v,
&      n_cell_left,n_cell_right,n_part_left,n_part_right)
    n_cell_new=n_cell+n_cell_left+n_cell_right
    if(n_cell_new.gt.n_cell)then
     allocate(field_aux(n_cell))
     field_aux=field
     deallocate(field)
     allocate(field(n_cell_new))
     field(1:n_cell)=field_aux(1:n_cell)
     deallocate(field_aux)
    endif
    n_cell=max(n_cell,n_cell_new)
    n_cell_old=n_cell
    call send_receive_cells(field,x_part,
&      n_cell_left,n_cell_right,n_part_left,n_part_right)
    if(n_cell_new.lt.n_cell_old)then
     allocate(field_aux(n_cell_old))
     field_aux=field
     deallocate(field)
     allocate(field(n_cell_new))
     field(1:n_cell_new)=field_aux(1:n_cell_new)
     deallocate(field_aux)
    endif
    n_cell=n_cell_new
    n_part=n_part+n_part_left+n_part_right
   endif
   call pushing(field,x_part)
   call transfer_particles(x_part,n_part)
   allocate(pressure(n_cell))
   call compute_pressure(x_part,pressure)
   call correct_pressure(pressure)
```

In order to avoid continuous reallocation of particle arrays (here represented by x_part) because of the particle migration from one subdomain to another, we overdimension (e.g., +20%) such arrays with respect to the initial optimalbalance size, N_{part}/n_{node}. Fluctuations of n_part around this optimal size are allowed within a certain band of oscillation (e.g., ±10%). This band is defined in such a way to prevent, under normal conditions, index overflows and, at the same time, to avoid excessive load unbalancing. One of the processes (the MPI rank0 process) collects, in subroutine check_loads, the values related to the occupation level of the other processes and checks whether the band boundaries are exceeded on any process. If this is the case, the "virtual" number of particles (n_part_left_v, n_part_right_v) that each process should send to the neighbor processes to recover the optimal-balance level is calculated (negative values means that the process has to receive particles), and i_check is set equal to 1. Then, such information is scattered to the other processes. These communications are easily performed with MPI by means of the collective communication primitives MPI_Gather, MPI_Scatter, and MPI_Bcast. Load balancing is then performed as follows.

Particles are labeled (subroutine load_balancing) by each process according to their belonging to the units (e.g., the n_cell spatial-grid cells) of a finer subdivision of the corresponding subdomain. The portion of the subdomain (that is, the number of elementary units) the process has to release, along with the hosted particles, to neighbor subdomains in order to best approximate those virtual numbers (if positive) is then identified. Communication between neighbor processes allows each process to get the information related to the portion of the subdomain it has to receive (in the case of negative "virtual" numbers). Net transfer information is finally put into the variables n_cell_left, n_cell_right, n_part_left, and n_part_right. Series of MPI_Sendrecv are suited to a deadlock-free implementation of the above described communication pattern.

As each process could be requested, in principle, to host (almost) the whole domain, overdimensioning the spatial-grid arrays (pressure and field) would cause loss of the desired memory scalability (there would be, indeed, no distribution of the memory-storage loads related to such arrays). We then have to resort to dynamical allocation of the spatial-grid arrays, possibly using auxiliary backup arrays (field_aux), when their size is modified.

Portions of the array field now have to be exchanged between neighbor processes, along with the elements of the array x_part related to the particles residing in the corresponding cells. This is done in subroutine send_receive_cells by means of MPI_Send and MPI_Recv calls. The elements of the spatial-grid array to be sent are copied in suitable buffers, and the remaining elements are shifted, if needed, in order to be able to receive the new elements or to fill possible holes. After sending and/or receiving the buffers to/from the neighbor processes, the array field becomes densely filled in the range 1:n_cell_new. Analogously, the elements of x_part corresponding to particles to be transferred are identified on the basis of the labeling procedure performed in subroutine `load_balancing` and copied into auxiliary buffers; the residual array is then compacted in order to avoid the presence of "holes" in the particle-index space. Buffers sent by the neighbor processes can then be stored in the higher-index part of the `x_part` (remember that such an array is overdimensioned).

After rearranging the subdomain, subroutine pushing is executed, producing the new particle coordinates, `x_part`. Particles whose new position falls outside the original subdomain have to be transferred to a different process. This is done by subroutine `transfer_particles`. First, particles to be transferred are identified, and the corresponding elements of `x_part` are copied into an auxiliary buffer, ordered by the destination process; the remaining elements of `x_part` are compacted in order to fill holes. Each process sends to the other processes the corresponding chunks of the auxiliary buffer, and receives the new-particle coordinates in the higher-index portion of the array `x_part`. This is a typical all-to-all communication; the fact that the chunk size is different for each destination process makes the `MPI_Alltoallv` call up the tool of choice.

Finally, after reallocating the array `pressure`, subroutine compute pressure is called. Pressure values at the boundary of the subdomain are then corrected by exchanging the locally computed value with the neighbor process (subroutine `correct_pressure`) by means of `MPI_Send` and `MPI_Recv` calls. The true value is obtained by adding the two partial values. The array pressure can now be yielded to the subroutine `field_solver` for the next time iteration.

Note that, for the sake of simplicity, we referred, in the above description, to one-dimensional field arrays. In the real case, we have to represent field informations by means of multidimensional arrays. This requires us to use MPI-derived datatypes as arguments of MPI calls in order to communicate blocks of pages of such arrays.

27.3 INTEGRATION OF THE INTERNODE DOMAIN DECOMPOSITION WITH INTRANODE PARTICLE DECOMPOSITION STRATEGIES

The implementation of the particle decomposition strategy for a PIC code at the shared-memory level in a high-level parallel programming environment like Open-MP has been discussed in references [5] and [3]. We refer the reader to those papers for the details of such implementation. Let us just recall the main features of this intranode approach, keeping in mind the internode domain-decomposition context. It is easy to see that the particle-pushing loop is suited for trivial work distribution among different processors. The natural parallelization strategy for shared-memory architectures consists in distributing the work needed to update particle coordinates among different threads (and, then, processors), irrespective of the portion of the domain in which each particles resides. OpenMP allows for a straightforward implementation of this strategy: the `parallel do` directive can be used to distribute the loop iterations over the particles. With regard to the pressure loop, the computation for each update is split among the threads into partial computations, each of them involving only the contribution of the particles managed by the responsible thread; then the partial results are reduced into global ones. The easiest way to implement such a strategy consists in introducing an auxiliary array, `pressure_aux`, defined as a `private` variable with the same dimensions and extent as `pressure`. Each processor works on a separate copy of the array and there is no conflict between processors updating the same element of the array. At the end of the loop, however, each copy of `pressure_aux` contains only the partial pressure due to the particles managed by the owner processor. Each processor must then add its contribution, outside the loop, to the global, shared, array pressure in order to obtain the whole-node contribution; the `critical`directive can be used to perform such a sum. The corresponding code section then reads as follows:

```
       pressure(1:n_cell) = 0.
!$OMP parallel private(l,j_x,pressure_aux)
       pressure_aux(1:n_cell) = 0.
!$OMP do
       do l=1,n_part
        j_x = f_x(x_part(l))
        pressure_aux(j_x) = pressure_aux(j_x) + h(x_part(l))
       enddo
!$OMP end do
!$OMP critical (p_lock)
       pressure(:) = pressure(:) + pressure_aux(:)
!$OMP end critical (p_lock)
!$OMP end parallel
```

with f_x being the function that relates the (continuous) particle position to the cell index, and h the pressure-updating function that has associative and distributive properties with respect to the contributions given by every single particle. Note that this strategy, based on the introduction of an auxiliary array, makes the execution of the n_{part} iterations of the loop perfectly parallel. The serial portion of the computation is limited to the reduction of the different copies of `pressure_aux` into `pressure`.

The integration of the internode domain-decomposition strategy with the intranode particledecomposition one does not present any relevant problem. The only fact that should be noted is that, although the identification of particles to be transferred from one subdomain to the others can be performed, in subroutine `transfer_particles`, in a parallel fashion, race conditions can occur in updating the counters related to such migrating particles and their destination subdomains. Also, the updating has then to be protected within `critical` sections.

27.4 THE MPICH-G2 IMPLEMENTATION

In this section, we want to compare the parallel porting of the described PIC application on a "classical" hierarchically distributed shared-memory architecture by simple integration of MPI and OpenMP [2] and the parallel porting of the same application to a grid environment. The system used as testbed for this comparison is the Cygnus cluster of the Parsec Laboratory at the Second University of Naples. This is a Linux cluster with four SMP nodes equipped with two Pentium Xeon 1 GHz, 512 MB RAM and a 40 GB hard drive, and a dualPentium Xeon 3.2 GHz front end.

Although the parallel porting on the "classical" architecture can be performed quite easily by resorting to the Argonne MPICH implementation of MPI (Gropp and Lusk, [12]), a large effort is necessary to build up and configure a Grid programming environment in order to support the vendor's compiler and facilities. The most important among these facilities is represented by the Globus Toolkit, an open-source software toolkit developed by the Globus Alliance and many other groups all over the world, widely used for building grids [11]. The Globus environment includes MPICH-G [9], a complete implementation of MPI for heterogeneous, wide-area environments, based on MPICH. Built on top of Globus io and native MPI, MPICH-G allows communication among multiple machines connected across a wide-area network in order to couple them in a single execution. It uses Globus io services in order to convert data in messages sent between machines of different architectures, and selects TCP for wide-area messaging and vendor-supplied MPI for cluster-of-workstations messaging. Existing parallel programs written for MPICH can be executed over the Globus infrastructure just after recompilation.

MPICH-G has recently been completely rewritten, giving rise to an upgraded version, MPICH-G2 [14], with greatly improved performance. Although the communication functionality of MPICH is based on a communication device having a common abstract device interface (ADI), MPICH-G2 uses a new device named globus2. As MPICH-G2 does not support shared-memory communication, in order to exploit the shared-memory and multithreading features of our architecture, we integrate, also in the grid-porting framework, the MPI facility with OpenMP support provided by the Intel compiler.

For the experiments we report in this section, we have installed on our system the ROCKS LINUX distribution supported by NPACI and Globus Toolkit 2.0, integrated with MPCH-G2 v. 1.5.2. Building and installing the GT2 implementation of the Globus Toolkit along with the Intel compiler, needed to exploit the OpenMP resource for SMP programming, did not prove to be a trivial task.

We considered three different configurations of the system:

1. A classic configuration: the SMP cluster, with no Globus environment
2. A single Globus machine configuration, with four two-way nodes
3. A set of Globus machines configuration, each equipped with a single two-way node

The first of such configurations will represent the reference case of a parallel porting of the PIC application on a hierarchically distributed shared-memory architecture [2]. The application is executed by using MPICH built with the ch_p4 device. The second configuration uses a front end as a single Globus node for the submission of a single MPIch_p4 job on the four-node machine. It corresponds to the entry-level exploitation of the grid facilities for scientific computing: the assignment of a parallel job to a single, remote Globus-parallel machine. In the third configuration, each of the four nodes hosts a Globus gatekeeper, which is able to run MPICH-G2 jobs. The MPICH-G2 request, submitted from the front-end node, spreads one process per Globus node. This configuration is the most ambitious one in the present investigation, as it allows us to test the effective capability of the grid environment in supporting distributed (not just remote) computation.

Table 27.1 shows, for the classic-configuration experiment, the elapsed time for the different phases of a single iteration (time step in Section 27.2) of our application. The results corresponding to cases with different numbers of nodes and/or processors per node are reported. Here and in the following, we consider a moderate-size case, with a 3-D spatial grid of $128 \times 32 \times 16$ points and $128 \times 32 \times 16 \times 16$ particles.

Figure 27.1 shows the corresponding speedup values measured with respect to the whole single iteration. It can be seen that the parallel porting obtained with integration of MPI and OpenMP is very efficient, as noted in reference [2]. The experiments performed with the system configured as a single Globus machine yield, as expected, very close figures for the single-iteration speedup values. We also observe, however, in the whole simulation elapsed time, a contribution related to the time needed to process the request submitted from the front end. Such a contribution is contained in 8–10 sec, with no significant dependence on the simulation size or the number of nodes effectively used by the single Globus machine. The results obtained with the set of Globus machines configuration are reported, for the single-iteration time and speedup values in Table 27.2 and Figure 27..2, respectively. The qualitative features observed with the previous configurations (efficient use of the SMP architecture by means of OpenMP and drop in efficiency in the less symmetric cases) are obtained also in this case.

From a quantitative point of view, the efficiency of this grid parallel porting is still fairly good, though it has to be stressed that we are dealing with a rather ideal grid (no geographical spreading, no network problems). Similarly to the single Globus machine case, an offset is revealed in the elapsed whole-simulation time, related to the submission of the request from the front end to each gatekeeper, as well as to starting all the processes and, later on, releasing the reserved resources. As be-

Table 27.1 Elapsed times (in seconds) for 3-D skeleton-code implementation at different pairs n_{node}/n_{proc} for the classic configuration

	1/1	1/2	2/1	2/2	3/1	3/2	4/1	4/2
Load balancing $\times 10^{-2}$	0.000	0.001	7.50	13.22	18.27	30.14	10	16.14
Pushing	2.379	0.978	1.763	0.721	0.744	0.298	0.558	0.224
Compute pressure	1.967	1.043	0.905	0.479	0.577	0.309	0.526	0.223
Correct pressure $\times 10^{-2}$	0.007	0.007	1.15	0.943	0.999	0.975	0.783	0.52
Transfer particles	0.225	0.130	0.134	0.084	0.112	0.078	0.093	0.069

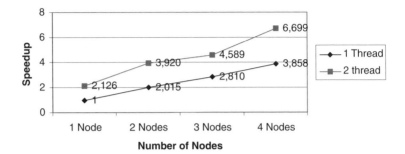

Figure 27.1 Speedup for the classical configuration.

fore, the offset does not show any relevant dependence on the simulation size. In this case, however, it increases with the number n_G of Globus machines, as is shown in Figure 27.3. Note that, for realistic simulations (thousands of iterations and much larger number of particles and spatial-grid points), such offset would be in fact negligible, if not too large sets of Globus machines (and not too large numbers of nodes per machine) are considered.

Finally, we check how worthwhile is the effort aimed to allow the integration of OpenMp and MPICH-G2 (through resorting to the Intel compiler) in this set of Globus machines configuration. Instead of exploiting the SMP facility, we can execute two MPI processes on each node. For this eight-MPICH-G2 process case, we get a speedup of 6.07%, compared with the value (6.44) obtained in the OpenMP case.

27.5 CONCLUSIONS

In this chapter we have addressed the issue of distributing parallel computation among the Globus machines of a grid environment. The case of a scientific application—namely, a particle-in-cell one—has been considered. A cluster of workstation was configured as a distributed system of four single-node SMP Globus machines, as a lowest-order approximation of a more complex geographically distributed, heterogeneous grid. Installing the MPICH-G2 library and the Intel Fortran compiler on

Table 27.2 Elapsed times (in seconds) for 3-D skeleton-code implementation at different pairs n_{node}/n_{proc} for the set of Globus machines configuration

	1/1	1/2	2/1	2/2	3/1	3/2	4/1	4/2
Load balancing × 10^{-2}	0.002	1.55	7.57	13.50	17.08	29.98	98.05	15.99
Pushing	2.376	1.11	1.114	0.525	0.749	0.342	0.556	0.255
Compute pressure	1.967	1.062	0.902	0.478	0.582	0.307	0.426	0.222
Correct pressure × 10^{-2}	0.008	0.007	1.51	0.96	1.09	0.70	0.95	0.40
Transfer particles	4.567	2.31	2.27	1.238	1.617	1.032	1.18	0.709

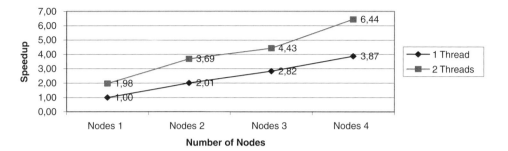

Figure 27.2   Speedup for the set of Globus machines configuration.

the cluster allowed us to port a parallel version of the application, based on the hierarchical integration of MPI and OpenMP, originally developed for generic (nongrid) clusters of SMP nodes. We were then able to compare the performances obtained in the grid environment with those obtained with the simple cluster of SMP nodes (same hardware). We found that the parallelization efficiency is slightly reduced, though maintained at a fairly high level.

Though the integration of the Globus toolkit and the Intel compiler was not a straightforward task, the related effort is a valuable one, as the Intel compiler allows us to use the OpenMP facility and to fully exploit the SMP architecture of each node. Replacing OpenMP programming with the execution of as many MPI processes as the processors owned by each node yields indeed lower efficiency values.

Finally, the time offsets due to the submission of the request to the gatekeepers, to the activation of the processes, and to releasing of the resources, though scaling with the number of Globus machines, appear to be negligible in comparison to realistic-simulation elapsed times.

These conclusions are partly affected, of course, by the almost-ideal character of the grid environment considered (close, homogeneous, dedicated nodes). Real grid

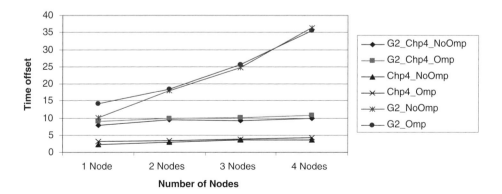

Figure 27.3   The time offset versus the number of Globus nodes.

porting of the same application, which will be the subject of future work, could be much less efficient. Nonetheless, such a porting, whose feasibility we have here demonstrated, would maintain its value with respect to the task of increasing memory resources and, then, the achievable simulation size.

REFERENCES

1. C. K. Birdsall and A. B. Langdon, *Plasma Physics via Computer Simulation,* McGraw-Hill, New York, 1985.

2. S. Briguglio, B. Di Martino, G. Fogaccia, and G. Vlad, Hierarchical MPI+OpenMP Implementation of Parallel PIC Applications on Clusters of Symmetric MultiProcessors, in *Lecture Notes in Computer Science,* vol. 2840, pp. 180–187. Springer-Verlag, 2003.

3. S. Briguglio, B. Di Martino, and G. Vlad, Workload Decomposition Strategies for Hierarchical DistributedShared Memory Parallel Systems and their Implementation with Integration of High Level Parallel Languages, *Concurrency and Computation: Practice and Experience, 14,* 11, 933–956, 2002.

4. G. Cybenko, Dynamic Load Balancing for Distributed Memory Multiprocessors, *Journal of Parallel and Distributed Computing, 7,* 279–391, 1989.

5. B. Di Martino, S. Briguglio, G. Vlad, and G. Fogaccia, Workload Decomposition Strategies for Shared Memory Parallel Systems with OpenMP, *Scientific Programming, 9,* 23, 109–122, 2001.

6. B. Di Martino, S. Briguglio, G. Vlad, and P. Sguazzero, Parallel PIC Plasma Simulation through Particle Decomposition Techniques, *Parallel Computing, 27,* 3, 295–314, 2001.

7. R. D. Ferraro, P. Liewer, and V. K. Decyk, Dynamic Load Balancing for a 2D Concurrent Plasma PIC Code, *Journal of Computational Physics, 109,* 329–341, 1993.

8. I. Foster, (2001). The anatomy of the Grid: Enabling scalable virtual organizations. *Lecture Notes in Computer Science 2150*

9. I. Foster and N. Karonis, A Grid-Enabled MPI: Message Passing in Heterogeneous Distributed Computing Systems, in *Proceedings of SC'98,* 1998.

10. G. C.Fox, M. Johnson, G. Lyzenga, S. Otto, J. Salmon, and D. Walker, *Solving Problems on Concurrent Processors,* Prentice Hall, Englewood Cliffs, New Jersey, 1988.

11. I. Foster and C. Kesselman, Globus: A Metacomputing Infrastructure Toolkit, *International Journal of Supercomputer Applications, 11*(2), 115–128, 1997.

12. B. Gropp, R. Lusk, T. Skjellum, and N. Doss, Portable MPI Model Implementation, Argonne National Laboratory, July 1994.

13. Message Passing Interface Forum, MPI: A Message Passing Interface Standard, *International Journal of Supercomputer Application, 8*(3/4), 165–416, 1994.

14. N. Karonis, B. Toonen, and I. Foster, MPICH-G2: A GridEnabled Implementation of the Message Passing Interface, *Journal of Parallel and Distributed Computing, 63*(5), 551–563, May 2003.

15. OpenMP Architecture Review Board, OpenMP Fortran Application Program Interface, ver. 1.0, October 1997.

16. V. Sunderam, J. Dongarra, A. Geist, and R Manchek, The PVM Concurrent Computing System: Evolution, Experiences and Trends, *Parallel Computing, 20,* 4, 531–547, April 1994.

## CHAPTER 28

Evidence-Aware Trust Model for Dynamic Services

ALI SHAIKH ALI, OMER F. RANA, and RASHID J. AL-ALI

28.1 MOTIVATION FOR EVALUATING TRUST

The service-oriented architectures generally, and Web Services in particular, facilitate novel forms of communication between individuals and organizations, thus supporting new flexible work patterns and making organizational boundaries more permeable. In general, this increases the physical and cultural distances both within and between organizations choosing to work together, as the use of a service-oriented approach necessitates delegating control (and reliance on the results generated) to a third party. Hence, this lack of presence and visibility within organizational transactions, resulting from the use of services, may lead to a feeling of distrust and vulnerability. At the same time, the increase in physical distance is a key opportunity for the deployment of new services, and the availability of additional marketplaces within which services can be deployed and shared. For these reasons, a significant number of users have started to realize the importance of "trust" management for supporting business and scientific interactions electronically in service-oriented architectures.

Trust can be viewed from two different perspectives: that of the service provider, and that of the service consumer. From the service provider perspective, trust has always been considered as a security issue. Hence, the main focus is on authenticating and authorizing users to utilize the provider resources. From the consumer perspective, trust is considered as a predictability issue addressing questions such as "which service provider is truly reliable to deliver this service?" and "how much credence should I give to what this provider says about this service?" The predictability concern is also related to whether a given consumer is likely to receive the same result from a given provider on a subsequent invocation of a service. Answers to such concerns may be used by a service consumer to select between multiple providers offering the same "kind" of service, or to choose a service provider based on nonfunctional criteria associated with a service (such as performance, cost, etc.). Such nonfunctional criteria are important when a consumer needs to op-

High-Performance Computing: Paradigm and Infrastructure. Edited by L. T. Yang and M. Guo **535**

timize its use of a collection of services over a particular time interval. This is particularly relevant in the context of grid computing, in which resources need to be scheduled across multiple application users. Grid computing also introduces predictability concerns, as results generated by a service provider (for a particular service request) must be repeatable. As control needs to be delegated to a third-party provider (generally managed by a different administrator), it is even more important that some mechanism to gauge repeatability be provided.

There has been a significant debate recently about the role of Web Services technologies to support grid computing. The grid computing community has primarily been driven by the need to share computational and data resources (geographically distributed) in some coordinated fashion. A consequence of this has been the development of middleware, the most often mentioned of which is the Globus Toolkit [15], which provide a number of predefined packages integrated into one system. These packages enable job submission to remote machines, data transfers in parallel, and secure access (via certificates) to authenticate users, etc. Recently, these packages have been converted into a collection of services, with interfaces defined in a Grid Services Specification Language [6] using some specialist tags not supported in the Web Services Description Language (WSDL). These services are provided in the Open Grid Services Infrastructure [1] and are based on a more abstract architecture called the Open Grid Services Architecture. This specification also provides additional management functionality above and beyond the services provided in the previous version of Globus, such as "Softstate" (Leasing) and "Factory" for creating services). To develop a grid service, it is necessary to [2]:

1. Write a WSDL `PortType` definition, using OGSA types (or define new ones). This is achieved by using a `Service Data Elements` extension (which makes grid services incompatible with WSDL).
2. Write a WSDL binding definition, identifying ways in which one could connect to the service, for example, using SOAP/HTTP or TCP/IP.
3. Write a WSDL service definition based on the `PortTypes` supported by the service and identified in step (1) above.
4. Implement a factory by extending the `FactorySkeleton` provided, to indicate how new instances of a service are to be created.
5. The factory must be configured with various options available, such as schemas supported.
6. Implement the functionality of the service, by extending the `ServiceSkeleton` class. If an existing code (legacy code) is to be used in some way, then the "delegation" mechanism should be used. When used in this mode, the factory returns a skeleton instance in step (4) above
7. Implement code for the client that must interact with the service

Much of the functionality in OGSI was provided to complement that available in Web services at the time. OGSI, therefore, provided the additional set of services (and mechanisms) that would enable one to make use of distributed computing (data and processor) resources. With the recent changes in Web Services standards (such as the emergence of WSX specifications, such as WS-Context, WS-Addressing, WS-Notification, WS-Transactions, etc.), has come the realization that much of the functionality in OGSI can be achieved via Web services. The WSGAF (Web Services-Grid Application Framework) [3] was aimed at supporting such an alternative. This has led to current work on the Web Services Resource Framework (WSRF) [4], which aims to utilize standard Web Services technologies, rather than attempting to extend them (as undertaken in OGSI). The WSRF specification makes a distinction between a "resource" and a "service," essentially in that a resource (a logical entity) can be stateful, whereas a service is stateless. In some ways, the ideas expressed in this standard are similar to those of WS-Context [5], albeit WS-Context is primarily aimed at supporting workflow and service aggregation, and does not indicate any ideas of state persistence or notification. Overall, WSRF is the recognition that grid computing may be useful to a wider community if it fully utilizes existing Web services standards and provides additional functionality as a collection of services that make use of these standards.

In the context of grid computing, we can, therefore, assign trust for both infrastructure services (such as a job or data manager service) and application services (such as a Bioinformatics or a numerical optimization service). Determining how trust must be aggregated across these two sets of services is explored in [18].

28.2 SERVICE TRUST—WHAT IS IT?

A survey of existent approaches to trust management in electronic transactions is provided. We start by providing some preliminary definitions dealing with the communication model found in Web Services, and then explain the properties a trust model needs to provide.

28.2.1 The Communication Model

A registry service plays an important part in recording and managing trust. Hence, as data about services is recorded within a registry service, a trust value for each service is also recorded. Often, two classes of architectures may be considered in this context, based on the existence of a central or a distributed registry to support the calculation of trust. It is now necessary that all transactions that occur between consumers and providers be monitored by a central trusted authority. This trust authority needs to update the trust value associated with a service in a central registry.

The autonomy of entities providing and using services implies that an entity may defect in the course of a transaction. Defection in this instance corresponds to an entity not delivering a preagreed service or not meeting a set of predefined nonfunctional criteria associated with a service (such as response time). The defection is reported to the central trust authority, which in turn modifies the trust value that this authority has on the defecting entity. Consumers and providers can also retrieve the trust values of other entities from the central authority.

Alternatively, when a distributed registry system is being used, the trust values are also distributed. Each entity must now maintain its own trust values, which represent the "local" trust an entity has in another, based on past interactions. In order to retrieve trust values about other entities, each entity uses its own trust value stored locally, or asks other entities with which it interacts about their opinion or recommendations. Requests for such recommendations are equivalent to an entity sending a query to retrieve local trust values held by another entity. The autonomy of the entities also implies that a recommendation returned as a result of such a query may be inaccurate. Therefore, before taking a recommendation into account, the recipient has to assess the truthfulness of the recommendation.

We assume for the rest of the chapter that no entity acts against its own interest. This assumption is rather natural and allows us to avoid dealing with situations in which a dishonest entity (an entity not following the trust model) breaks some of the underlying rules by adopting a behavior that can be detrimental to itself. We also suppose that entities are able to send authenticated messages. This means that the recipient of a message knows which entity sent it. For authentication purposes, it is, therefore, necessary to support a persistent identifier to label entities. We assume the existence of a naming scheme that allocates such identifiers. We also assume that trust is evaluated for transactions rather than general interactions. This abstraction is not a limitation but rather a point of view on interactions, since most interactions can be modeled by transactions. Collaborations can be viewed as a group of transactions, one for each collaborator.

28.2.2 Trust Definition

The notion of trust has been defined in many ways, based on the particular perspective being considered and the particular domain of interest of the researcher. Computer science researchers tend to agree with the definition provided by Gambetta [7] or McKnight and Chervany [8]. Gambetta defines trust as: "a particular level of the subjective probability with which an entity will perform a particular action, both before [we] can monitor such action and in a context in which it affects [our] own action." Gambetta's definition of trust places emphasis on the term "subjective expectation" rather than "subjective probability" to emphasize the point that trust is a summary statistic that an entity has toward another based on a number of previous encounters between them. On the other hand, McKnight and Chervany define trust as: "the extent to which one party is willing to depend on somebody, or something, in a given situation with a feeling of relative security, even though negative consequences are possible."

McKnight and Chervany's definition focuses on the subjective nature of trust by relating this to an entity's willingness and relative security. The aspect of dependence is implicitly complemented by uncertainty through possibility, and by risk through negative consequences. The definition also places emphasis on the term "situation," which enables this definition to be adapted to most needs, and thus be general enough to be used in uncertain and changing environments. Based on these, we derive a simple definition for trust which can be applied to online transactions as the measurable subjective expectation an entity (consumer or provider) has about another entity's future behavior, in a given situation, based on the history of their encounters for a specified period, and within a specified context.

According to this definition, therefore:

1. Trust is context specific. If entity A trusts entity B for financial data, this does not mean that B trusts A for medical (or other kinds of) data.

2. Trust is time dependent. If A trusts B to a certain degree today, it does not mean that A will trust B to the same extent in the future.

3. Trust is based on prior experiences. Prior experiences do not have to be directly between A and B, that is, A could ask a third trusted party for its recommendation about B.

4. Trust is specific to a particular situation. These situational factors that affect the trust relationship include:
   - The nature of the task being considered
   - How much prior knowledge the entity has about the other partner involved
   - How much shared background or experience entities have that causes them to trust another entity as a consequence

28.2.3 Service Provider Trust

The current approach that service providers use for validating access to their service interface is user authentication. User authentication is a common technique found in many types of applications, and is also commonly used in grid computing. The approach is simple: each user for the system is assigned a unique username. Access to resources or functionality associated with that username is protected by knowledge of a specific password. The ubiquity of user authentication systems is beneficial for Web Services because most users are already comfortable with this security technique.

Applying user authentication security to Web Services is also undertaken in a similar way—each Web method call requires two additional parameters, username and password. Each time a Web method is called up, the first action taken will be to check that the username exists in the database. The second step is to ensure that the password provided matches the password for the specified username. If both of these checks pass, then operation of the Web method continues normally. If either of these checks fails, the Web method needs to provide some sort of error message to the calling function. Hence, either authentication can be made once and some state information recorded to ensure that the user can connect without username/password authentication in subsequent interactions, or authentication is made for each operation called up.

A common variation to this technique is to require just a user identification code, typically a globally unique identifier (GUID). In this case, the Web method call accepts one parameter, UserID, in addition to its standard parameters. This approach is usually just as effective as using a username/password combination because

GUIDs are very hard to duplicate. An example of this technique is the `authToken` used in the Universal Description, Discovery and Integration (UDDI) [16] registry to authenticate users for publishing service descriptions into the registry.

Although such approaches are commonly used because of their simplicity, there have been many concerns about them in recent years. These approaches not only cause overheads for administrators by maintaining databases for storing user-name/password combinations, but also limit exposing the functionally of Web Services to the registered users only. The idea here is that service providers know who these users are and, hence, trust them. However, in an open system such as the Internet, we need an approach that enables the interaction with anonymous users, who may not have access to predefined certificates or be allocated a user-name/password.

An early approach for trusting anonymous users was achieved by the use of digital certificates. Digital certificates are small pieces of software installed on user machines that verify the user's identity. This verification is done through a third party that creates a unique certificate for every user machine using industry standard encryption. The certificate is then passed along when the user requests a Web Service. The Web Service checks for the presence of the digital certificate and reacts accordingly. In the context of grid computing, the GSI [9] provides a client-certificate-based approach to authenticating users/systems, based on a globally unique name called a distinguished name (DN) which is based on the X.500 directory service naming convention. An example DN could be "C=UK, O=eScience, OU=Cardiff, L=WeSC, CN=firstname.lastname." The DN can be used to obtain a certificate from a trusted third party. It is also possible to create a delegation chain, whereby trusted certificate authorities can be grouped into some hierarchy. A request to verify the credentials of a particular user then follows the chain until the request reaches the topmost level in the hierarchy (if verification cannot be undertaken at lower levels in the hierarchy).

Digital certificates can be obtained in several ways: a service can issue a self-signed certificate on its own, or can request it from a trusted certificate authority (CA). The choice between the two approaches depends on the purpose of using the certificate. If the purpose of the certificate is for personal needs, it is sufficient to use self-signed certificate. If the purpose of the certificate is to use it universally, the certificate signed by a CA is required. The level of recognition of these certificates depends on the CAs themselves. The `thawte.com` site, for example, issues a certificate after confirming the email address of the certificate requester. A more recognized certificate can be obtained, for example, from `Verisign.com`, who requires the provision of notarized documents to prove the user's identity. Hence, the greater the range of external services that will recognize a certificate, the greater will be the trust level given to a user that has the certificate. Grid computing CAs have also been established to allow scientific users to share services with each other. In some instances, such certificates have a limited lifetime, allowing a client to access a remote service for a particular time period. Lifetime-limited certificates are particularly useful when a service provider may change its configuration often. The encryption technology used in digital certificates is based on the Public-Key Infrastructure (PKI). PKI is a security architecture that has been introduced to provide an increased level of confidence for exchanging information over an increasingly insecure Internet. It offers certainty of the quality of information sent and received electronically, certainty of the source and destination of that information, assurance of the time and timing of that information (providing the source of time is known), and certainty of the privacy of that information.

An important benefit of user authentication using digital certificates or the traditional approaches of username/password combination is the option of creating more complex authorization schemes. Hence, authentication is the process of proving a user identity, and authorization is the process of identifying resources accessible by that user. Since each Web method has to authenticate the specific user making the request, it is possible to create a complex authorization scheme in which users are authorized to use only a portion of the available Web methods. The traditional authorization approach is, after authenticating the user, each Web method makes one additional check to determine if the authenticated user should be allowed to access the given Web method using an access control list.

The Privilege Management Infrastructure (PMI) [10] has been designed for the purpose of providing authorization after user authentication has been completed. PMI allocates roles to different users based on the context in which they access a particular set of resources, and confirms or denies whether the access. X.5091, published by the International Telecommunication Union Telecommunication sector (ITUT), is the first publication to standardize fully the certificate mechanism in PMI. The primary data structure in PMI is an attribute certificate (AC), which binds a set of attributes to its holder. These attributes are used to describe the various privileges that the issuer has bestowed upon the holder.

In this respect, a public key certificate can be seen to be a specialization of a more general AC. The entity that signs a public key certificate digitally is called a certification authority (CA), and the entity that signs an AC is called an attribute authority (AA). Examples of attributes and issuers might be: a numerical service being offered by a research group, the role of a monitoring entity assigned by an application manager or file access permissions issued by a file's owner. The root of trust of a PKI is sometimes called the root CA, whereas the root of trust of the PMI is called the source of authority (SOA). CAs may have subordinate CAs that they trust and to which they delegate the powers of authentication and certification (the delegation chain mentioned above). Similarly, SOAs may delegate their powers of authorization to subordinate AAs. If a user needs to have his or her signing key revoked, a CA will issue a certificate revocation list. Similarly, if a user needs to have authorization permissions revoked, an AA will issue an attribute certificate revocation list.

28.2.4 Service Consumer Trust

The main interest of service consumers is to select services that they believe to be trustworthy and dependable. There are many approaches for constructing trust relations introduced in the literature. We categorise these approaches as follows.

28.2.4.1 *Collaborative Trust*

The basic idea of collaborative trust, or "network of friends" as it is often referred to, is to build on the assumption that if entity A does not have a trust relationship with entity B, then A asks entities that it interacts with (especially those that it trusts) about their opinions or recommendations about B. Then A usually weighs these opinions based on the trust that A places on entities that returned these opinions. A system that uses collaborative trust to retrieve the trust value of an entity is usually called a recommendation-based reputation system. The system usually consists of entities that may enter into transactions with other entities at any time. Each transaction occurs between a pair of entities. The autonomy of each entity implies that an entity may defect in the course of a transaction. Take, for example, two entities, a service consumer and a service provider, who negotiate on delivering a particular service based on some performance criteria associated with the service, and establish a service level agreement (SLA) that contains the agreed upon values (or ranges) associated with these performance criteria. It is possible that the service provider will not meet these preagreed performance criteria and thereby be assumed to have defected on the initial contract/SLA.

The most often quoted example of such a transitive trust system is EigenTrust [11], a trust management system for peer-to-peer systems. In EigenTrust, each peer i is given a unique global trust value that reflects the trust that the whole system puts in i based on past download experience. The system computes the global trust value of a peer i by computing the left principle eigenvector of a matrix, where each eigenvector encodes the normalized local trust values of all the peers in the network that had transaction with i. The local trust values of any peer toward i is then the average number of satisfactory transactions it had with i. Peers use these global values to choose the peers from whom they download and, hence, they effectively identify malicious peers and isolate them from the network. This mechanism of rating peers is also found in the popular music sharing system KaZaA.com, which enables each peer to rate others via a $\{+1, 0, -1\}$ value depending on whether the download from the other peer was "useful," "neutral," or "not useful," respectively. Usefulness is related to issues such as the popularity of the file downloaded and the size of the file.

28.2.4.2 *Rule-Based Mechanisms*

The general concept associated with this approach is to derive rules to determine whose recommendation must be trusted. Abdul-Rahman and Hailes [12] propose a model for the deployment of rules in virtual communities to allow agents to decide which others agents' opinion they trust more. In this way, agents are able to progressively tune their understanding based on the outcomes of previous interactions. For this model, the trustworthiness of agents is determined based on the agent's collected statistics on (1) direct experiences and (2) recommendations from other agents. Agents do not maintain a database of specific trust statements in the form of *A trusts B with respect to context c*. Instead, at any given time, the trustworthiness of a particular agent is obtained by summarizing the relevant subset of recorded experiences.

28.2.4.3 *Transfer of Importance*

The basic idea of this approach is that if entity A has a reference to entity B, then a portion of A's importance is passed to B.

A well-known reputation system that follows this approach is PageRank [13], the main ranking system for Web pages performed by the popular Google.com search engine. The basic idea of PageRank is that the page rank (PR) of each page depends on the PR of the pages pointing to it. A page has a high PR value if there are many pages pointing to it, or if there are some pages pointing to it that have a high PR value. To bootstrap the system, a page is given a high PR if it has a high volume of traffic generated to it. PR is, therefore, primarily determined by the popularity of a page, and not its content. The PR algorithm represents the structure of the Web as a matrix, and PR value as a vector. The PR vector is derived by computing the matrix–vector multiplication. This vector forms the principal eigenvector of the matrix and has to be normalized frequently. That means it is difficult to directly use these algorithms to rank large graphs representing page cross-references, due to the computational complexity associated with the approach.

28.2.4.4 *Evidence-Aware Reputation Systems*   The basic idea of this approach is the use of a nonrepudiation protocol, such as one that necessitates the issuing of "receipts" after a transaction has completed. Consider a transaction taking place between two entities. During the transaction, the provider submits a document to the consumer. In turn, the consumer generates a receipt that is sent back to the provider. In this context, the receipt represents evidence. If the consumer defames the provider by stating the service has not been delivered, the provider should be able to refute the defamation by showing the receipt. One of the advantages of this approach is self-recommendation. For example, if the consumer goes offline immediately after handing over the receipt, the provider may selfrecommend by stating that it has behaved well during a transaction with the consumer. Such selfrecommendation should be provable, especially if the receipt is sent as a basis for this. The FreeHaven.net project is an example of a system for using receipts in online transactions.

28.2.4.5 *Measuring the Expertise Similarity*   This approach is based on measuring the similarity between the types of services being offered within a given context. It requires the maintenance of some type of user profile that enables such similarity to be calculated. Several multiagent systems have been developed to serve this purpose. Agents in these systems act on behalf of particular application users, maintaining profiles or routing questions to other agents. These agents use profile similarity as a criterion for finding possible partners. It is not only important to detect which agents posses the adequate expertise for solving a problem, but is also crucial to assess the extent of the expertise of these agents. The trust and reputation for experts is usually assessed as a function of the quality of the agents' response to knowledge requests coming from other members of the community.

28.2.5 Limitations of Current Approaches

The approaches mentioned above, apart from the evidence-aware reputation system, are generally based on plausibility consideration. Plausibility consideration, which is contingent upon prior beliefs, fails to provide an effective mechanism for establishing a network of trust between interacting participants. Plausibility considerations imply that trust is established based on recommendations provided by others, and not on any particular evidence that has been gathered (with actual data backing up this evidence, such as receipts). Obreiter [14] and others point out the limitations of plausibility consideration as follows:

1. The system assumes that the recommendation from a trusted entity is always correct (trustworthy).
2. The recommendations from newcomers are considered trusted, as there is no firsthand experience with the recommendee and the recommendation behavior of the recommender is unknown.
3. The plausibility consideration may be infeasible due to the lack of background information, although the recommendation might be correct.
4. Recommendations can only be credibly passed on by commonly trusted entities. If the system lacks such entities, the recommender is solely in charge of the dissemination of the issued recommendation.
5. The system lacks a formal method for the defamed entity to appeal and defend itself which may lead to (6).
6. There may be doubts about the effectiveness of the reputation system.

In this context, effectiveness refers to the pruning of untruthful recommendations, and to the subsequent dissemination of these recommendations. If there are doubts about the effectiveness of such pruning, the entities will lack incentive for good behavior.

28.3 EVIDENCE-AWARE TRUST MODEL

In considering the limitations of plausibility consideration, we discussed demand for an alternative model for trust. In this section, we introduce a model that allows for the verifiability of recommendations.

Before proposing and discussing the model, we illustrate the key terms in an introductory example. Let us assume that entity A wants to use a signal processing service provided by B, in a context of a particular application. A sends a request to B and attempts to negotiate parameters associated with the delivery of the service, for example, performance terms such as response time, latency, and throughput. As a result, entities A and B establish a service level agreement (SLA) that contains the values for the agreed terms. A sends the SLA to an independent trusted monitoring service that is responsible for monitoring the service execution. A can now invoke the service, and B must ensure that the service is executed based on the agreed upon SLA. After the service invocation, the monitoring service sends a status report to both A and B that can be used to confirm if the parameters agreed upon in the SLA have been violated during the service execution. If the SLA was not violated, A

sends a receipt, containing the report from the monitoring service, to a trusted third party responsible for verifying transactions and assigning trust values to services. If A's receipt says that the SLA was not violated, then the trust degree of B's service is increased. Any subsequent interactions of the service provided by B will now see the updated value of trust associated with B.

28.4   THE SYSTEM LIFE CYCLE

We identify three phases for computing the service reputation: the reputation interrogation phase, the SLA negotiation phase, and the trust verification phase, as described below.

28.4.1   The Reputation Interrogation Phase (RIP)

In the reputation interrogation phase, a service consumer is responsible for integrating the trust value associated with a particular service. In our model, we extend the Web Services UDDI registry to support service discovery based on service trust. The extension provides a user with the capability to encode the trust values as properties associated with a service. Therefore, users request UDDIe [17] (the extended UDDI registry) for the reputation matrices of given services. This registry service is identified as rUDDI in Figure 28.1.

28.4.2   The SLA Negotiation Phase

We assume that service providers and consumers negotiate, prior to invocation, a service level agreement (SLA) that defines the required service metrics as a set of terms and rules. For our purpose, we define an SLA as a set of terms and a set of rules that are required for service delivery to be successful and are agreed upon *a priori*. The rules specify the 'policy' to determine how the SLA is to be validated. An SLA is formally defined as: a contract between two entities that contains a set of assertions R (specified as a set of relationships or rules) and a set of terms T and their associated values v, hence $SLA = [R, (T, v)]$.

The SLA elements are required to be measurable and quantifiable, and may have some interdependencies among them. The values associated with particular terms may either be literal (a single number or string) or ranges. Hence, a term $t_i \in T$ may have a value v_i, where $(0 < v_i < 10)$. The assertions R specify a set of relationships that may be recursively applied to the terms T. An SLA is generally established between two entities. SLAs that exist for a group (i.e., a single service provider holding an SLA for a group of clients) are equivalent to multiple SLAs in our system. Example SLAs are

$$SLA_1 = [>, (CPU, 10)]$$

$$SLA_2 = \{AND, [>, (CPU, 10)], [<, (latency, 5)]\}$$

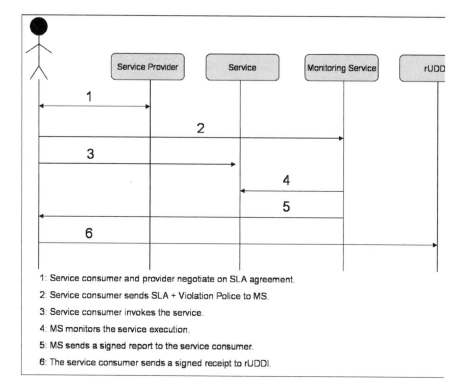

1: Service consumer and provider negotiate on SLA agreement.
2: Service consumer sends SLA + Violation Police to MS.
3: Service consumer invokes the service.
4: MS monitors the service execution.
5: MS sends a signed report to the service consumer.
6: The service consumer sends a signed receipt to rUDDI.

Figure 28.1   A Sequence diagram showing the interaction between the components.

SLA_1 indicates that for this contract to be valid, the provider agrees to provide more than 10 units (or percentage) of CPU time. SLA_2 is composed of an *AND* between multiple terms, stating that the provider agrees to offer more than 10% of CPU and less than 5 units of latency to a client. SLA_2 also demonstrates the recursive mechanism for specifying the contract. Essentially, inner terms, such as [*latency*, 5] from SLA_2, must be evaluated first, followed by the expression that aggregates these terms (this is the *AND* relation in SLA_2). The measurability and quantifiability of the elements mean that at any instance during the service invocation, the elements can be verified by a monitoring service. Having established the SLA, the service consumer defines a violation policy that contains the rules that identify actions that need to be taken if an SLA violation is detected. We define a violation policy as:

Definition (Violation Policy). A violation policy is an assertion A, where A is a set of rules that defines an SLA violation. We also identify two types of violation: full SLA violation and partial SLA violation.

Definition (SLA Full Violation). Full violation occurs if any relation $r_i \in R$ is violated.

Definition (SLA Partial Violation). A partial violation occurs if a maximum of m relations, for each $r_j \in R$, are violated. The value of m can either be literal, indicating a maximum number of rule violations, or may indicate a particular subset of terms from the initial SLA.

The violation policy is attached to the SLA and sent to a monitoring service. The monitoring service is a trusted third party similar to the hosting Web server. You can trust the Web server for delivering the Web pages upon request but you cannot trust the Web pages themselves. During the service invocation, the monitoring service performs an SLA check. This check also includes a verification to see if the service is being executed based on the SLA terms and rules. Accordingly, a report to the service consumer and provider is returned. The report contains the result of the SLA check and the signature of the monitoring service. An SLA also has the following properties:

1. SLA_i is atomic, that is, all R must be verified (or verifiable) to determine its status. The complexity of these relationships can vary from simple Boolean functions (such as AND, OR) to userdefined functions.
2. SLA_i is satisfiable, that is, it must be either true or false. This suggests that all R (for the full violation case), or a predefined subset (for the partial violation case) in the SLA must be either true or false. An evaluation of false during a service session implies a violation. Only attributes that can be dynamically monitored can become false during the execution of a service.
3. SLA_i is consistent, that is, terms and relationships must not contradict each other. Two relationships over the same set of terms cannot be both true and false at a particular time t.

28.4.3 The Trust Verification Phase (TVP)

Having received a report from the monitoring service, the service consumer issues a receipt describing the service's behavior. A receipt is evidence that describes the behavior of a specific entity. A receipt contains a set of terms T and their values that were actually observed during the execution of a service. The exact calculation of these values (either as summary statistics or via other mechanisms) needs to be agreed upon by the service consumer and provider. The receipt must contain the following elements:

- Transaction ID—the ID of the transaction.
- SLA Check—the report generated by the monitoring service. The SLA check is signed by the monitoring service.
- Time Stamp—the time when the receipt is issued.
- Service IDs—the unique ID of the service consumer and provider.

The receipt is sent to the rUDDI registry manager, which checks the SLA of the receipt and accordingly modifies the reputation metric of the involved service. The

```
<receipt>
    <transactionID>....</transactionID>
    <SLA_check>... <SLA_check>
    <time_stamp>..</time_stamp>
    <userIDcertificate>...</userIDcertificate>
</receipt>
```

Figure 28.2   An example of a receipt.

receipt provides evidence of whether the SLA has been violated or not, and may be archived by the service provider.

28.5 CONCLUSION

A survey of approaches to trust management in electronic services is presented. The key aim is to identify mechanisms for supporting issues of trust and reputation, and, in particular, outline how these mechanisms are relevant to grid computing. Limitations, namely, the issue of plausibility considerations, of existing approaches are outlined, and, to overcome these, a new approach based on the use of "evidence" is presented. Such an evidence-aware approach is not averse to the use of trust recommendations, but is likely to be more reliable, as it provides a qualitative assessment of the actual past execution of a particular service.

The key concept in our approach is the definition of a service level agreement (SLA) and the availability of specialist monitoring services that quantify terms within this agreement. The accuracy and frequency of measurement are important and form the basis for evaluating whether service providers are able meet their obligations defined in the SLA. Many existing grid projects, such as the U.S. Tera-Grid and the European EGEE, are beginning to make use of such SLAs. It has also been recognized that SLAs are essential to support production-level services on the grid infrastructure.

REFERENCES

1. Open Grid Services Infrastructure (OGSI) Version 1.0 (draft), Global Grid Forum Open Grid Services Infrastructure WG 5, April 2003.
2. T. Sandholm and J. Gawor, Grid Services Development Framework Design. Available as http://www.globus.org/ogsa/releases/TechPreview/ogsadf.pdf.
3. S. Parastatidis, Web Services Grid Application Framework. Available at http://www.neresc.ac.uk/ws-gaf/documents.html, October 2003.
4. S. Tuecke, Web Services Resource Framework. Available at http://www.globus.org/wsrf/, January 2004.
5. OASIS Technical Committee, Web Services Composite Application Framework. Presentation available at www.oasis-open.org/committees/download.php/4477/WS-CAF%20cut%20down.ppt.

6. S. Tuecke, K. Czajkowski, I. Foster, J. Frey, S. Graham, C. Kesselman, T. Maguire, T. Sandholm, P. Vanderbilt, and D. Snelling, Open Grid Services Infrastructure (OGSI) Version 1.0, Global Grid Forum Draft Recommendation, June 27, 2003. Available at http://www.globus.org/research/papers/Final_OGSI Specification_V1.0.pdf.

7. D. Gambetta, *Trust: Making and Breaking Cooperative Relations,* Oxford: Basil Black-well, 1998.

8. D. H. McKnight and N. L. Chervany, The Meaning of Trust, Technical Report, MISRC Working Paper Series 9604, University of Minnesota, Management Information Systems Research Center, 1996. Available at http://www.misrc.umn.edu/wpaper/wp96-04.htm.

9. Argonne National Laboratory/Globus project, Grid Security Infrastructure (GSI). Available at http://www.globus.org/security/. Last viewed June 2004.

10. D. W. Chadwick and A. Otenko, The PERMIS X.509 Role Based Privilege Management Infrastructure, in *Proceedings of 7th ACM Symposium on Access Control Models and Technologies,* 2002.

11. S. D. Kamvar, M. T. Schlosser, and H. Garcia-Molina, The EigenTrust Algorithm for Reputation Management in P2P Networks, in *Proceedings of the 12th International World Wide Web Conference,* 2003

12. A. Abdul-Rahman and S. Hailes, Supporting Trust in Virtual Communities, in *Proceedings of Hawaii International Conference on System Sciences (HICSS) 33,* Maui, Hawaii, 4–7 January 2000. Available at http://citeseer.nj.nec.com/235466.html. Last viewed June 2004.

13. L. Page, S. Brin, R. Motwani, and T. Winograd, The PageRank Citation Ranking: Bringing Order to the Web, Technical Report SIDL-WP-1999-0120, Stanford Digital Library Technologies Project, 1999. Available at http://dbpubs.stanford.edu:8090/pub/1999-66. Last viewed June 2004.

14. P. Obreiter, Case for Evidence-Aware Distributed Reputation Systems—Overcoming the Limitations of Plausibility Considerations, in *Proceedings of the 4th International Workshop on Cooperative Information Agents,* 2000

15. Argonne National Laboratory, The Globus Project. Available at http://www.globus.org/. Last viewed June 2004.

16. OASIS, Universal Description, Discovery and Integration (UDDI) Specifications—Advancing Web Services Discovery Standard. Available at http://www.uddi.org/specification.html. Last viewed June 2004.

17. A. Shaikh Ali, O. Rana, R. Al-Ali, and D. Walker, UDDIe: An Extended Registry for Web Services, in *Proceedings of the Workshop on Service-oriented Computing: Models, Architectures and Applications,* at IEEE SAINT Conference, January 2003.

18. S. Majithia, A. Shaikhali, O. Rana, and D. Walker, Reputation-based Semantic Grid Service Discovery, in *Proceedings of Emerging Technologies for Next Generation Grid Workshop,* at 13th IEEE WETICE Conference, Modena, Italy, June 2004.

## CHAPTER 29

Resource Discovery in Peer-to-Peer Infrastructure

HUNG-CHANG HSIAO and CHUNG-TA KING

29.1 INTRODUCTION

The ubiquitous Internet has interconnected an enormous amount of computing and storage devices. Resources on these devices, such as storage and CPU cycles, are often underutilized. Aggregating their resources through a network enables large-scale services and computations that are either impossible or too expensive to attempt with centralized resources. This aggregation calls for an Internet-scaled distributed system, and the rapid advances in recent peer-to-peer (P2P) computing can be viewed as a response to that call.

In a P2P system, peer nodes contribute portions of their resources to the community. They are treated as functionally identical. There is no distinct role of clients or servers—a peer node can act as a client, a server, and a router. Nodes may come from different administrative domains; this often implies no centralized management and administration. Peers may dynamically join or leave the system. Examples of P2P systems include Freenet [7], Gnutella [22], Napster [24], and SETI@home [29].

P2P systems can be generally categorized into unstructured and structured architectures. Unstructured P2P systems such as Napster, Freenet, and Gnutella allow peer nodes to interconnect freely and do not impose any structure on the managed resources. Napster relies on centralized index servers for matching queries, which may create performance bottlenecks and single points of failure. Gnutella and Freenet employ a pure distributed architecture and rely on a certain kind of message flooding to search for resources of interest. For example, Gnutella adopts a breadth-first approach to flood the requests, whereas Freenet uses a depth-first approach. To prevent the high cost of flooding the entire network, both systems use a time-to-live (TTL) value to limit the scope of a search.

Structured P2P systems, such as CAN [26], Chord [31], Pastry [27], Tapestry [33], and Tornado [20], manage the peer nodes with a logical structure. For example, CAN is based on a multidimensional torus, whereas Chord, Pastry, Tapestry, and Tornado adopt a hypercube-like structure with a ring threading through all the nodes

High-Performance Computing: Paradigm and Infrastructure. Edited by L. T. Yang and M. Guo

[17]. Underlying these node structures is the concept of distributed hash tables (DHT). In essence, structured P2P systems impose one or more distributed hash tables over all the peer nodes. Every peer node and every published object[1] will receive a hash value. With all the peers numbered in the hash space, a peer can then link to other peers according to the node structure defined by the P2P system. An object with the hash key k will be managed by the peer node whose hash key is the closest to k. To look for that object, the request message is routed through the peer nodes according to the node structure of the P2P system. On top of such a communication substrate, other services can be deployed, for example, service discovery [3, 18], multicast communication [6], information retrieval [19, 32], and file sharing [12, 23, 28].

Structured P2P systems offer controllable management on peer nodes and resources. They can guarantee that the query messages are forwarded to the managing peer nodes in bounded time. However, the hash scheme limits the search capability of the system to exact matches. Other forms of searches, such as partial matches or range searches, will require manipulation of the hash functions, which usually is complex and ad hoc. On the other hand, unstructured P2P systems are quite flexible in retrieving stored information due to their flooding nature in query processing. The problem is that since there is no structure maintained among the peers, search requests issued from different nodes might consult different sets of peers in the systems. This, consequently, results in different query results. It is also possible that the same search query issued by the same node at different times will result in different answers. This is because the neighboring nodes may change with time. Thus, the search in unstructured P2P systems is not quality guaranteed.

Peers in P2P systems handle their connectivity using an end-to-end communication protocol, such as the TCP/IP protocol. The resultant node structure of the P2P system can be viewed as forming a virtual network on top of the physical network. Such a virtual network is denoted as an overlay network. Figure 29.1 illustrates an example of an overlay network comprised of eight end nodes. These nodes are structured as a logical ring.

The purpose of this chapter is to give an overview of P2P systems with an emphasis on their supports for resource discovery. The remainder of this chapter is structured as follows. We review the design requirements of a P2P resource discovery system in Section 29.2. Section 29.3 introduces two unstructured P2P systems. Representative structured P2P systems are surveyed in Section 29.4. We next consider how to support more complex resource discovery in structured P2P systems in Section 29.5. Finally, we conclude this chapter in Section 29.6.

29.2 DESIGN REQUIREMENTS

Aggregating dynamic resources over a large-scale network in a decentralized manner presents challenging issues that are not encountered in centralized or client–server

[1]An object is either the resource itself or a description of the resource so that it can be found. We will use the terms, "objects" and "resources" interchangeably in this chapter. In other P2P research, objects may refer to data items such as MP3 files.

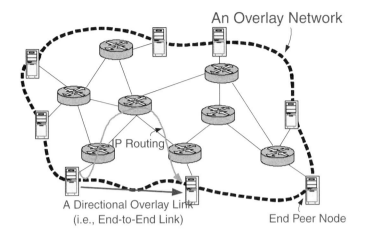

Figure 29.1   An example of an overlay network.

systems. Most importantly, the resources may not be reliable, may freely join and leave the network, and may be from different administrative domains. Thus, designing a P2P resource discovery system should meet the following requirements:

- *Fault resilience.* Resources exploited on the Internet may be highly volatile. For instance, the aggregated resources may be attacked and become unavailable, or they may be linked to the Internet through intermittent wireless links. A P2P system must accommodate such unstable resources and tolerate possible faults.
- *Self-administration.* A P2P system often admits nodes from different administrative domains and allows them to dynamically join and leave the system. Each node should manage its connectivity to the system and help other nodes to perform their requests without a centralized control.
- *Load distribution.* To prevent performance bottlenecks, a P2P system has to distribute the system load as evenly as possible, according to the node capability. If objects need to be published as in structured P2P systems, they should be allocated to the nodes evenly. Peer nodes should handle requests evenly, perhaps through caching or replication.
- *Data availability.* Since nodes may dynamically leave the system, objects maintained by those nodes might not be available. To guarantee that objects are accessible at any time, a P2P system should provide high data availability, often through replication.
- *Scalability.* The entire state of the system should be distributed to the nodes so as to achieve scalability. The amount of partial states maintained by each node should not scale to the system size.
- *Performance.* A P2P system should serve data access requests promptly. The response time should not be influenced significantly by the number of requests and the system size.

There are other issues that a P2P resource discovery system needs to consider, for example, security and incentive, but we will not consider them in this chapter. A P2P system should be secure since nodes coming from different administrative domains may not be trusted. A malicious node may peek at objects in the infrastructure and alter them. A P2P system not only needs to provide encryption for objects by its owner, but also needs to make sure that the communication is secure. A P2P system should also encourage the participating peers to open their resources for sharing instead of consuming only others' resources. This may involve certain kinds of payment or sharing mechanisms.

29.3 UNSTRUCTURED P2P SYSTEMS

Unstructured P2P systems allow peer nodes to interconnect freely and do not impose any structure on the node structures. The objects are stored and managed by their owner or hosting peers. Therefore, unstructured P2P systems are very flexible and dynamic. Their feasibility for internet-scaled applications has been verified in real tests such as music swapping. We review two representative systems, Gnutella and Freenet, in this section.

29.3.1 Gnutella

Gnutella is a "search" protocol. The Gnutella protocol (version 0.6) [22] specifies how a node connects to an unstructured P2P system running Gnutella and how a node searches for objects. Objects that are stored in a Gnutella node are retrieved via a certain transport protocol, HTTP. In the following, we will briefly discuss how a node joins a Gnutella system and how a search is performed.

When a node x intends to join a Gnutella network, it first links to one of the default Gnutella nodes (called the host caches) using the CONNECT message. It then issues a PING message to the connected host cache to receive a number of PONG messages. A PONG message is comprised of the IP address and port number of a potentially active Gnutella node. Based on the received PONG message, x can create connections to those active Gnutella nodes using CONNECT messages.

When a Gnutella node y receives a PING message, it immediately replies with a number of selected PONG messages maintained in its local pong caches. Note that each connection maintained by a node possesses a pong cache, which maintains about 10 PONG messages received from the corresponding connection. The replied PONG message may also be chosen from the pong cache of another connection that is not the one that received the PING message.

After replying with the PONG messages, node y also redirects the PING message to each of the nodes that have a direct connection to it, except the originating node. The nodes that have direct connections to a node are the "neighbors" of that node, and a node maintains only a limited number of such neighbors. When an active neighbor of y receives a redirected PING message, it performs similar operations. Since each message in Gnutella is tagged with a TTL value (usually 7) and the value is decremented by 1 after each hop, these `PING` and `PONG` messages will be dropped when their TTL value reaches 0.

Conceptually, a Gnutella node creates a limited search horizon that is a circle with a radius of 7. Processing a search request (in the `QUERY` messages) is similar to forwarding a `PING` message. A node searches requested objects in its search horizon. When there are matching objects, it replies a `QUERYHIT` message containing its IP address, port number, and information of the matched objects. The `QUERYHIT` message is then sent to the requesting node along the reverse path of the corresponding `QUERY` message. Since several nodes may provide the requested objects, the requesting node can select a node to retrieve the object via the HTTP protocol.

Gnutella can support complex searches. A requester specifies the conditions to match, for example, the key features of the resources to be found, and issues query requests with these conditions into the system. Those objects that meet the specified conditions, which appear in the peers within the requester search scope, will be returned to the requester. In Gnutella, there is no mapping between objects and peers. Note that the Gnutella protocol defines how a peer sends `QUERYHIT`/`PONG` messages in response to `QUERY`/`PING` messages, and also defines how a peer forwards `QUERY` and `PING` messages upon receiving them from one of its neighbors. However, Gnutella does not explicitly define how peers are interconnected with each other. Thus, this does not exclude the possibility of using a structured P2P network as an "underlay" to interconnect the peer nodes in a Gnutella network. However, this requires more investigation.

29.3.2 Freenet

Freenet [7] is an anonymous file sharing system that allows objects to be published, replicated, and retrieved while maintaining the anonymity of data producers and consumers. We will not address the anonymity issue, though.

In Freenet, every peer and every object will receive a hash key, but the objects are not published and stored to specific nodes in the system. The storage space contributed by each node consists of a set of entries. Each entry records the content of a cached object and the associated hashing key. Direct links to data sources may be added, which serve as shortcuts. The storage is managed as an LRU cache.

To access an object, a requesting node examines its local storage first. If such an object can be found locally, the data is returned immediately. Otherwise, the request will be forwarded to the node that is in its shortcut list and has a hash key numerically closest to the requested key. The next node also does the same, and so on. If any node reached has cached a copy of the requested object, it returns the object along the reversed path to the requesting node. The intermediate nodes along the routing path also replicate the replied object, together with the address of the source node. As a result, frequently requested objects will be widely replicated in Freenet. Replication not only improves search latencies but also clusters objects with similar key values into the nodes. This gives hints for directional searches to nodes that more probably can serve the request.

If, on the other hand, the request message passes through the nodes without discovering the requested object and its TTL limit is reached, a failure message will be returned back to the requesting node. Note that this may occur even if the requested object is in the network but out of the TTL range. There is no guarantee that a stored object will always be discovered. This is a common problem in unstructured P2P systems.

To publish an object, the request is passed through nodes in a way similar to that in read. If the TTL limit is reached while there is no identical key found in the route, a reply is returned back to the requesting node, indicating no duplication of key value. A second message carrying the object is then propagated through the established route, and all the nodes along the path cache a copy of the object.

29.3.3 Optimizations

A number of recent studies [8–11, 21, 25, 30] aim at improving the search performance for unstructured P2P systems. In [25], a node x accepts a node y as its neighbor according to some "preferences." The preferences may include a node's capability (e.g., the network bandwidth, the processor speed, and memory size), the network delay between x and y, or whether y can provide desirable results for most queries issued by x.

In [10, 11, 21, 30], unstructured P2P systems are designed to exploit the similarity of contents. A node in these systems constructs its local index by collecting indices from other nodes. The index maintained by a node provides hints for forwarding a query to nodes that may provide the requested object. The index comprises a mapping from objects (or querying keywords) to peer nodes. In [10], the nodes that appear in the routing index of a node are its neighbors in the overlay. On the other hand, in [11, 21, 30] a node may include any node in its index. Thus, this requires that every node broadcast a summary of its stored objects [11] or maintain relevant peers that are associated with each of its queries [21, 30].

Note that a node in a Gnutella network maintains connections to its neighbors. Upon receiving a query request, a node forwards the request to its neighbors directly. However, a node in unstructured P2P systems using the above-mentioned optimization techniques (e.g., [10, 11, 21, 30]) does not maintain a direct connection with the nodes in its local index. Hence, when an inquiry node chooses a preferred node from its local index, it needs to additionally create a costly TCP/IP connection to that node before sending its query request. In other words, a query in these systems needs to dynamically create connections to an unstructured overlay network.

Unstructured P2P systems with multiple overlays are also proposed. An overlay represents a collection of nodes that share similar objects, and the size of each overlay may not be identical. A node may participate in several overlays and maintain a number of connections to each overlay. The study in [8] uses probabilistic analysis to show that multiple overlays, with each devoted to a particular "kind" of object, can improve the search performance considerably. Additionally, rare items can be rapidly discovered by consulting the corresponding overlay, because the size of the overlay is much smaller. A similar study [9] using a real dataset also reaches the same conclusion.

Among unstructured P2P systems with multiple overlays, YAPPERS [14] partitions a Gnutella network into k equal partitions, where k is the number of neighbors of a node. Each partition is a Gnutella network and hosts a similar amount of objects. YAPPERS ensures that each partition is connected, and by creating links among partitions, the entire overlay is connected.

29.3.4 Discussion

Gnutella and Freenet do not explicitly maintain routing paths between any two nodes. Lacking such a routing facility, they are more useful for searching designated objects, that is, both are search networks. Gnutella implements a breadth-first search (BFS) mechanism, whereas Freenet adopts a depth-first search (DFS) mechanism. Both Gnutella and Freenet can support complex searches. Freenet uses replication to improve search latency and cluster objects for directional search. The negative side is the extra storage space needed for replicas. Clearly, Gnutella and Freent do not guarantee that an object in the network can always be discovered. They also do not ensure the performance bound of a search. Although there are many proposals to enhance the search performance, there is still no guarantee on search quality.

Unstructured P2P systems are the first-generation P2P systems that were originally proposed for search and, thus, information sharing (file sharing). Thus, they did not conform to the design requirements mentioned in Section 29.2. The second-generation P2P systems, those with structured P2P overlays based on DHTs, have a more generic overlay infrastructure that can benefit from applications such as multicast communication [6], file sharing [12, 28], and distributed file systems [23]. DHT-based overlays, thus, encompass those design requirements to not only provide a robust and efficient lookup substrate, but further serve as a routing infrastructure for end peers.

29.4 STRUCTURED P2P SYSTEMS

A structured P2P resource discovery system implements a P2P object locating and routing protocol (simply denoted as the structured P2P protocol) through a logical node structure. A structured P2P system provides application programming interfaces (APIs) such as JOIN, PUT, and GET for applications to access the system. A peer node x first calculates its hash key [i.e., $H(x)$] on joining the P2P network [via JOIN($H(x)$)]. The key may be generated by using information specific to x, such as the machine name, the IP address, and port number. Similarly, an object d is also associated with a hash key [i.e., $H(d)$] on its publication [i.e., PUT($H(d)$, d)] or retrieval [i.e., GET($H(d)$)]. The key may be generated using information specific to d, such as the file name, the metadata description, and content. Note that the hash functions (H) used to name a peer and an object are identical.

In the following, we present some representative systems.

29.4.1   Example Systems

CAN [26] maintains an n-dimensional hash space via n hashing functions. Each node has a unique coordinate and is responsible for a subspace in the n-dimensional hash space. For example, consider a 2-dimensional CAN, where a node p with the coordinate (a, b) is responsible for the hash space in the X-axis from x_1 to x_2 and from y_1 to y_2 in the Y-axis, where $x_1 \le a < x_2$ and $y_1 \le b < y_2$. A CAN node needs only to maintain links to four neighboring nodes in the coordinate space. A message will be forwarded toward its destination by greedily forwarding to the node whose coordinate is numerically closest to the destination's.

Pastry [27] and Tapestry [33] maintain only a 1-dimensional hash space but use a richer node structure. Again, each node has a unique hash key, which can be represented as $x_1 x_2 x_3 \ldots x_n$, where $0 \le x_i < b$, $i = 1, 2, 3, \ldots, n$ and b is a predefined constant. A node p with the key $x_1 x_2 x_3 \ldots x_n$ maintains the links to a set of peer nodes. The nodes are partitioned into neighbor sets such that the nodes in the jth ($j \ge 1$) neighbor set have the same prefix $x_1 x_2 x_3 \ldots x_{j-1} y_j y_{j+1} \ldots y_n$, for all $y_j \in \{0, 1, 2, \ldots, b-1\} - \{x_j\}$, in the keys. Suppose we want to send a message to the destination node $q = y_1 y_2 y_3 \ldots y_n$ from the source node $p = x_1 x_2 x_3 \ldots x_n$. The node p first sends the message to its neighbor (say $r = y_1 y_2 y_3 \ldots y_k x_{k+1} \ldots x_n$) with the longest prefix as q. Upon receiving the message, r performs similar operations.

Obviously, a node maintains $O(n)$ entries in its neighbor sets, where each entry takes $O(\log N)$ bits (N is the total number of nodes in the system). Consider an example with $b = 2$ and $n = 4$. Suppose the source with the key 0010 (denoted node 0010) sends a message to the destination 1101. The message may first visit the neighbor node whose key has the same first prefix. Let it be node 1011. Then node 1011 may forward the message to its neighbor node 1111, which has the same digit value in the second prefix as the destination. The message may then go through node 1100 and finally reach the destination node 1101.

Chord [31] and Tornado [20] also embed peer nodes with a one-dimensional hash space. The nodes are organized as a ring. A successor of a given hash key x is defined as the node whose hash key immediately follows x. For example, consider a Chord or Tornado system whose hash space is from 0 to 7. Suppose that the system has five nodes with the keys 0, 1, 2, 3, and 6. The successors of nodes 1, 2, and 6 are nodes 2, 3, and 0, respectively, in a clockwise fashion. For performance, in Chord or Tornado, each node i relies on a set of fingers (successors are special fingers) to help forward a message it received. The fingers are those nodes with the keys that are smaller than and closest to $i + 2^k \bmod 2^m$, where $k = 0, 1, 2, \ldots, m-1$ and the hash space has a size of 2^m (Tornado relaxes this definition, which will be discussed later). Basically, when a node receives a message destined for node x, it will simply forward the message to one of its fingers whose hash key is smaller than and closest to x. Clearly, a node only requires to maintain $O(m)$ entries for its fingers.

29.4.2   Routing and Joining Process

Before describing the joining process of a node, the components that are used by a DHT-based P2P protocol are defined first:

- *distance(x, y)*. Given two keys x and y, the *distance()* function defines the distance in the hash space between x and y. For example, Chord and Tornado use the numerical difference in a clockwise fashion to estimate the distance between x and y.
- $\phi(x, y)$. Given two keys x and y, the ϕ operator defines the operator to calculate the distance between x and y. For example, Chord and Tornado define the ϕ operator as the minus.
- *forward(x, k, y)*. A node x receiving a packet with the designated hash key y uses the *forward()* function to forward the packet to the next node, whose hash key is k.
- *neighbor(x)*. The *neighbor set* of node x is denoted as *neighbor(x)*. An element of *neighbor(x)* is typically a pair of <a, a's network attachment point>, where a is the key of a neighbor peer having a transport connection with node x. The network attach point can be the IP address and/or port number of a neighbor node. The neighbor set of node x contains a set of nodes that have a direct connection to node x. The direct connection can be any transport connection such as a TCP/IP link or a UDP link.
- *construct(x, l, y)*. When node y newly joins a P2P system, it calls up the *construct()* function to establish its neighbor set based on the list l received from node x.

Two major operations of a P2P protocol are *route()* and *join()*, where PUT and GET highly rely on the *route()* operation and *join()* is the core operation for JOIN. To design a routing algorithm, it is important to consider performance as well as correctness. Performance determines whether a P2P community is operated in an efficient way. Correctness ensures that a P2P system is strongly connected.

The *route()* algorithm is presented as follows:

```
01 // a node x sends a message towards a node with the key closest to the
      designated value y
02 route(x, y) begin
03    while (true)
04       // choose a node with the key k from the local neighbor set
05       if (k ∈ neighbor(x) and distance(k, y) <² distance(x, y))
06          forwarding(x, k, y);
07          x = k;
08       else
09          // inform the application that node x has the key closest to y
10          return x;
11 end.
12
13 // calculate the distance between given hash keys x and y
```

---

[2]The < operator is defined on the ϕ operator.

14 *distance*(*x*, *y*) **begin**
15   **return** $\phi(x, y)$;
16 **end.**

Conceptually, a message routed toward a given hash key *d* is moved along nodes with hash keys closer[3] and closer to *d*. To guarantee the correct function of a P2P protocol, each node *x* should maintain a partial set of neighbors that have the hash keys closest to *x*. The number of this partial set can be constant in order to reduce the overhead of protocol maintenance. Chord, Pastry, Tapestry, and Tornado all follow this strategy. We will call such a partial set the closest-neighbor set. The closest neighbor set of node *x* is a subset of *neighbor*(*x*) and links the peers in a ring.

Note that in Line 5 of algorithm *route*(), the selection of the "best" *k* is based on the goals that the routing protocol wants to achieve. For example, if the routing latency is the major concern, *x* can select its neighbor *k* that not only can reduce the distance to the destination but is the geographically closest to *x*. The flexibility of choosing a neighbor to help forward a message is called route selection [5, 17, 20]. If the number of routing hops is the primary design consideration, the route selection can choose a neighbor that can reduce the maximum distance in the hash space. In this way, systems such as Chord and Tornado can guarantee that the maximum number of hops between any two nodes is $O(\log N)$ [17, 20].

The node joining algorithm is illustrated below.

01 // a node *x* issues a joining request
02 *join*(*x*) **begin**
03   // randomly select a node *w* via an out-of-band mechanism
04   Let node *w* be randomly selected from the system;
05   **while** (true)
06   // choose a node *k* in the neighbor set of the node *w*
07   **if** (*k* ∈ *neighbor*(*w*) and *distance*(*k*, *x*) < *distance*(*w*, *x*))
08   *forward*(*w*, *k*, *x*);
09   // let *l* be a node list prepared by node *w*
10   Let *l* ⊆ *neighbor*(*w*);
11   *construct*(*w*, *l*, *x*);
12   *w* = *k*;
13 **end.**

Its operations are similar to those in the routing algorithm. When a node newly joins the system, it first locates an active peer to help with the join operation by using an out-of-band mechanism. The active peer then issues a node joining message that includes the key [i.e., *x* in algorithm *join*()] of the joining node. The algorithm *route*() will forward the message hop by hop to the node whose key is the closest to *x*. One advantage of this joining process is that the message not only introduces the

[3]Each P2P routing protocol has its definition of closeness. In Chord and Tornado, the key closeness is according to the numerical difference.

joining node to those nodes visited, but also requests their recommendation of their neighbors to the joining node. This helps the joining node to construct its neighbor set and improve the quality of the neighbor sets of the visited nodes. Second, since the joining process uses the joining node's key as the destination key, this helps the newly joining node construct its closest-neighbor set.

Note that the joining node can determine its neighbor set by estimating the actual network distance to those neighbors recommended by the relaying nodes. The flexibility of selecting a neighbor is called proximity neighbor selection [5, 17, 20]. Chord, Pastry, Tapestry, and Tornado support proximity neighbor selection to construct a topology-aware P2P system that matches the topology of the real network. Note also that in algorithm $join()$, the neighbor set of a joining node depends on those nodes visited (Line 7) and the recommended list provided by the visited nodes (Line 10).

In Chord, Pastry, Tapestry, and Tornado, the set $neighbor(x) - \{x\text{'s closest}$ neighbor set} is called the routing table. The routing table and the closest-neighbor set respectively have a size of $O(\log N)^2$ and $O(k \times \log N)$ bits, where k is a constant. Since detecting the failure of a neighboring peer relies on periodically sending PING/PONG messages, maintaining neighbors in a routing table and a closest-neighbor set take $O(\log N)$ and k PING/PONG messages per period, respectively. If the probing traffic is a design consideration, a node can use a longer probing period for neighbors in the routing table while using a shorter period for neighbors in the closest-neighbor set.

Studies [13, 17, 20] show that proximity neighbor selection is better than route selection in terms of the delay stretch. The delay stretch from a source node x to a destination node y in an overlay network is defined as

$$\frac{D(x, y)}{d(x, y)} \tag{29.1}$$

where $D(x, y)$ denotes the delay perceived by routing from x to y using algorithm $route()$, and $d(x, y)$ is the IP delay from x to y. An intuitive explanation is that proximity neighbor selection exploits network locality in choosing neighbors. Routing a message can be accomplished by asking a geographically nearby node to help forward, except perhaps the last hop. The last hop has a delay equal to the average IP delay since there is very limited selection for the next neighbor. In contrast, a node implementing route selection does not check geographical proximity in maintaining its neighbors. When forwarding a message, the next neighbor may be distant physically, which results in a longer delay stretch. Another interesting result from those studies shows that proximity neighbor selection has a delay stretch of nearly 3, no matter what the system size is. This conforms to the theoretical study by Gavoille and Gengler [16].

29.4.3 Discussion

Table 29.1 summarizes the main features of representative structured P2P systems, Chord, Pastry, Tapestry, and Tornado. For fair comparison, Pastry/Tapestry have

Table 29.1 Comparison of performance and overhead of Chord/Tornado, Pastry/Tapestry, and CAN

	Neighbor set size	Path length	Number of routing tables	Route selection	Local convergence
Chord/Tornado	$O(\log N)^2 + O(\log N)$	$O(\log N)$	$O(\Pi_{i=1}^{\log N} 2^i)$	$O(\log N)$	Yes
Pastry/Tapestry[a]	$O(\log N)^2 + O(\log N)$	$O(\log N)$	$O(\Pi_{i=1}^{\log N} 2^i)$	$O(1)$	Yes
CAN[b]	$O(\log N)^2$	$O(\log N)$	$O(1)$	$O(\log N)$	No

[a]Pastry and Tapestry have the base value $b = 2$.
[b]CAN implements a $\log N$-dimensional coordinate space.
Note: The total number of nodes is N.

the base value 2 and CAN implements a $\log N$-dimensional coordinate space. In this way, each system requires a node routing table of $O(\log N)^2$ bits. As mentioned above, Chord, Pastry, Tapestry, and Tornado maintain a ring structure among peers. Each node thus needs additional storage space for maintaining its closest-neighbor set. However, the overhead is only $O(\log N)$ bits.

The path length in Table 29.1 denotes the maximum number of hops required for routing a message between any pair of source and destination nodes. Basically, every DHT-based system has a path length of $O(\log N)$.

The number of routing tables indicates how many routing tables a node can have [17], where a routing table comprises $\log N$ entries. For example, in Chord and Tornado, the routing table of a node x maintains the neighbors that "can" have keys closest to $x + 2^0, x + 2^1, x + 2^2, \ldots, x + 2^{m-1}$, respectively, if $N = 2^m$ (the modulo notation is ignored). Particularly, Tornado relaxes the neighbor definition of Chord, which allows node x to choose its ith neighbor whose key is within the hash space $(x + 2^{i-1}, x + 2^i]$, where $i = 1, 2, \ldots, m - 1$. If $i = 0$, the neighbor is selected from the hash space $(x, x + 2^0]$. Clearly, such a selection flexibility allows a node to have $O(\Pi_{i=1}^{\log N} 2^i)$ routing tables. Similarly, a Pastry or Tapestry node can also have $O(\Pi_{i=1}^{\log N} 2^i)$ routing tables. In contrast, a node in CAN only maintains the $O(1)$ routing table. This implies that CAN cannot exploit the real network locality. Note that this is based on the assumption that the key of a peer node is randomly chosen.[4]

The flexibility of selecting routing tables is critical to a DHT-based P2P system if the delay stretch is a major design concern. Such flexibility allows a node to find those geographically nearby nodes as its neighbors.

As mentioned above, the route selection is defined as the flexibility of selecting a neighbor to help forward a message. Chord and Tornado both allows route selection. More specifically, in Chord and Tornado, node x can choose those neighbors whose keys do not exceed the destination key in the circular hash space. Node x thus has $O(\log N)$ neighbors to help forward a message. CAN also allows a node to request one of its $O(\log N)$ neighbors to help forward themessage. In contrast, in

---

[4]It is possible that a node will choose its network coordinate as its key if a network coordinate system is available. In this way, CAN is constructed based on real network locality. However, this may introduce load imbalance since the keys of the nodes may not be uniformly distributed. Some nodes may need to host a larger hash space.

Pastry and Tapestry, node $x = x_1x_2x_3 \ldots x_{j-1}p_jp_{j+1} \ldots p_n$ needs to forward a message to its neighbor $y = x_1x_2x_3 \ldots x_{j-1}x_jq_{j+1}q_{j+2} \ldots q_n$ such that y can at least correct one digit for the destination key $x_1x_2x_3 \ldots x_{j-1}x_jr_{j+1}r_{j+2} \ldots r_n$. If y does not exist, x asks a node in its closest-neighbor set to help forward the message, that is, traverse the ring structure. As a result, a Pastry or Tapestry node has $O(1)$ route selection only. Note that route selection is one of the bases for the resilience of a DHT-based overlay.

Local convergence was first identified in [6]. When two nearby nodes x and y send messages to the same location, their messages may converge at some common node z. Consider Chord or Tornado. A node can choose its log Nth neighbor from $(2^{m-2}, 2^{m-1}]$ candidates. It is very possible that two nearby nodes choose the same node as their log Nth neighbor [17]. DHT-based overlays that exhibit local convergence include Chord, Pastry, Tapestry, and Tornado. Interestingly, Pastry exploits local convergence by asking a joining peer to perform expanded ring search in order to participate in the system. This allows a Pastry node to efficiently discover a geographically nearby node within its local domain. When such a peer is discovered, it helps the joining node to join the system. It can also recommend its neighbors to the joining node. Since the recommended neighbors are close to that peer physically, that peer is close to the joining node physically. Thus, those recommended neighbors are also geographically close to the joining peer.

Local convergence is an important property of a structured overlay. Using the above example, we can see that if the DHT-based overlay is used as a content delivery infrastructure, the convergence point then plays as a proxy node, which can deliver cached contents to a nearby node.

29.4.4 Revisiting Design Requirements

Table 29.2 revisits the design requirements of a P2P system mentioned in Section 29.2. The related techniques for fulfilling such requirements are also illustrated. For fault resilience, a DHT-based P2P protocol can exploit the redundant routing paths. A node can also maintain a closest-neighbor set to ensure that the system is strongly connected. For self-administration, a peer node can periodically refresh its neigh-

Table 29.2 The design requirements of a DHT-based P2P protocol and related techniques

Requirements	Techniques
Fault resilience	Exploit flexibility in route selection; maintain closest neighbor sets
Self-administration	Periodically update routing tables and closest neighbor sets
Load distribution	Rely on a uniform hash to name nodes and objects
Data availability	Replicate k copies of an object to k closest nodes
Scalability	Maintain $O(\log N)$ neighbors
Performance	A route takes $O(\log N)$ hops; exploit real network locality with proximity neighbor selection

bor set. This not only updates the node with the up-to-date system state, but also informs other nodes of its aliveness. Load balance in the system relies on the uniform and random hash function.

For data availability, a published object with the hash key x can be replicated to k different nodes whose hash keys are closest to x. This can be simply achieved by utilizing the ring structure [12, 28]. Note that a request (e.g., PUT and GET) accessing an object with key x will be processed by the node whose hash key is the closest to x. If this node failed, the requester can still discover another copy in a node whose hash key is "currently" closest to x. For scalability and performance, a DHT-based P2P protocol can efficiently manage a per-node neighbor set with an $O(\log N)^2$-bit memory overhead while transmitting a message in $O(\log N)$ hops.

29.5   ADVANCED RESOURCE DISCOVERY FOR STRUCTURED P2P SYSTEMS

Structured P2P overlays offer several desirable features. First, they provide directional routing. A lookup request in most proposed overlays takes log N hops and messages. In contrast, Gnutella-like unstructured P2P systems often rely on flooding, which generates large network traffic. Second, a lookup request can be resolved with high probability and the associated cost is predictable. On the other hand, unstructured overlays cannot discover a requested object if this object is out of the search scope. Even if the requested objects can be discovered, the cost is unpredictable. Third, results of a search are deterministic in structured overlays. In unstructured overlays, different peers may receive different results when issuing the same search request.

The problem with DHT-based P2P resource discovery systems is that the hashing scheme does not exploit any semantics in the inputs and mainly supports exact matches. Even a one-character difference in the input will produce vast different hashing output values. In this section, we discuss how structured P2P systems can support advanced searches in resource discovery—searches based on keywords, attribute-value pairs, and range.

29.5.1   Keyword Search

Suppose we want to search for all papers with the keyword "distributed processing." In a DHT-based P2P system, this is done by first obtaining the hash key of "distributed processing," and then storing all such papers in a peer node whose node key is the closest to that hash key. This creates several problems. First, if there are many papers on "distributed processing," then the hosting peer node will be overloaded. Second, if a paper on "distributed processing" can also be characterized as being on "computer architecture," then we have to decide which keyword to use to publish the paper. This then precludes the use of the other keyword to find the paper, unless we duplicate the paper to both sites. Third, we cannot issue a search with multiple keywords, such as <"distributed processing", "computer architecture">, and find all papers that match this query. It is even difficult to find papers characterized by <"distributed processing," "computer architecture," "something else">.

One solution is to build multiple suboverlays on top of the structured overlay. Each suboverlay handles objects that are characterized by the same keyword. To search with multiple keywords, the corresponding suboverlays are consulted and each returns objects that match a specific keyword. The inquirer then examines the received objects and filters out those that do not match all the specified keywords. Clearly, this approach will result in a large amount of traffic in transmitting objects that do not fully match the specified keywords. Besides, if the number of keywords in the system is large, this approach requires a huge number of overlays. A node that participates in k overlays will require k times the overhead to maintain these suboverlays.

Meteorograph [19] and PeerSearch [32] are enhanced structured P2P systems that support keyword searches. They are based on the vector space model [4].

29.5.1.1 *Vector Space Model*

In the vector space model, given a set of objects $S = \{t_1, t_2, t_3, \ldots, t_n\}$, a set of keywords $K = \{k_1, k_2, k_3, \ldots, k_m\}$, and the associated weights $W = \{w_1, w_2, w_3, \ldots, w_m\}$, each object t_i in S can be represented as a vector $\vec{d_i} = [v_1, v_2, v_3, \ldots, v_m]$, where $v_i = w_i$ ($1 \leq j \leq m$) if k_i can characterize d_i; $v_i = 0$ otherwise. Thus, the set $M = \{\vec{d_1}, \vec{d_2}, \vec{d_3}, \ldots, \vec{d_n}\}$ can be used to represent S.

Given a query vector $\vec{q} = [q_1, q_2, q_3, \ldots, q_m]$ to search for a set of similar objects U from S, we can apply the dot product (denoted by •) to $\vec{q}$ and each $\vec{d_i}$ in S, obtaining the result $r = \vec{q} \bullet \vec{d_i}$. The angle θ between $\vec{q}$ and $\vec{d_i}$ is calculated by $\theta = \cos^{-1}(r)$. Note that $0° \leq \theta \leq 180°$. Cosine is thus a one-to-one and onto function, and the inverse function, $\cos^{-1}$, exists. The value θ can then be used to evaluate whether the two vectors are similar. If θ is smaller than a predefined threshold τ, we say that $\vec{q}$ and $\vec{d_i}$ are similar and thus d_i must be in the set of U. Other similarity measurements are possible, for instance, finding ten most similar objects to a query from S.

29.5.1.2 *Meteorograph*

Meteorograph utilizes the ring structure in DHT-based P2P systems, such as Chord, Pastry, Tapestry, and Tornado. It logically maintains a set of nodes in a half circle over a two-dimensional X–Y space. Each object (denoted by the vector $\vec{d}$) in Meteorograph is represented as an angle λ with respect to the axis $Y = 0$ by $\lambda = \cos^{-1}(\vec{d} \bullet \vec{x})$. The vector $\vec{x}$ is the projection vector of $\vec{d}$ in the vector space M. Similar objects in S will have nearly identical angle λ and will thus be "published" in vicinity of the half circle (i.e., the nearby nodes). To retrieve a set of objects by the given query vector, Meteorograph calculates the angle between the query vector and the unity $\vec{1}$. Then it locates the node (or a set of nearby nodes) in the circle to retrieve those objects closely matching the query.

Absolute Angle. Given a vector $\vec{d} = [d_1, d_2, d_3, \ldots, d_m]$ in an m-dimensional space M, we define the absolute angle, θ, as

$$\theta = \sqrt{\frac{\theta_1^2 + \theta_2^2 + \theta_3^2 + \ldots + \theta_m^2}{m}} \tag{29.2}$$

where θ_i is the angle between $\vec{d}$ and the unit vector $I_i = [0_1, \ldots, 0_{i-1}, 1_i, 0_{i+1}, \ldots, 0^m]$, for $1 \leq i \leq m$. Note that $0° \leq \theta \leq 180°$. The angle θ_i is calculated as

$$\theta_i = \cos^{-1}\left(\frac{\vec{d} \bullet \vec{d}_{proj(i)}}{|\vec{d}||\vec{d}_{proj(i)}|}\right) \tag{29.3}$$

where $\vec{d}_{proj(i)} = [d_{1i}, d_{2i}, d_{3i}, \ldots, d_{mi}]$ is the projection vector of $\vec{d}$ onto the subspace spanned by I_i. Let $|\vec{d}| = \sqrt{\sum_{i=1}^{m} d_i^2}$ and $|\vec{d}_{proj(i)}| = \sqrt{\sum_{k=1}^{m} d_{ki}^2}$. Then, $\vec{d} \bullet \vec{d}_{proj(i)} = \sum_{k=1}^{m} d_i d_{ki}$, where $\vec{d}_{proj(i)}$ is

$$\vec{d}_{proj(i)} = \left(\vec{d} \bullet \frac{I_i}{|I_i|}\right)\frac{I_i}{|I_i|} \tag{29.4}$$

Using the vector space model, objects with similar vector representations have nearly identical absolute angles. Meteorograph exploits this property to publish similar objects to logically nearby nodes in Tornado.

Naming. Given a vector $\vec{v} = [v_1, v_2, v_3, \ldots, v_m]$ that represents a query or an object, Meteorograph computes its absolute angle θ_v using Equation 29.2. The corresponding hash key, h_v of $\vec{v}$ in Tornado is then calculated as follows

$$h_v = \left\lceil \left(\frac{\theta_v}{\pi}\right) \times R \right\rceil \tag{29.5}$$

where R is the size of the hash space.

From Equations 29.3 and 29.4, $\vec{v}$'s projection vector in the subspace spanned by I_i is $\vec{v}_{proj(i)} = [0_1, 0_2, \ldots, 0_{i-1}, v_i, 0_{i+1}, \ldots, 0_m]$, for $1 \leq i \leq m$. Thus, Equation 29.5 can be further simplified as

$$h_v = \left\lceil \left(\frac{\left(\sum_{i=1}^{m}\left(\cos^{-1}\left(\frac{v^2_{i}}{\sqrt{A}v_i}\right)\right)\frac{1}{m}\right)^{1/2}}{\pi}\right) \times R \right\rceil \tag{29.6}$$

where $A = \sum_{i=1}^{m} v_i^2$.

Publishing and Retrieving. To publish an object represented by the vector $\vec{p}$, Meteorograph performs the following steps:

- Step 1: Resolve the object's hash key h_v via Equation 29.6.
- Step 2: Publish the object to a node x with the hash key closest to h_v.
- Step 3: If x cannot satisfy the publishing request due to a shortage in its storage space, x replaces the least alike object with the published object h_v. Node x then asks its closest neighbor to help store the replaced object. That neighbor then performs similar operations. Note that the originating node of

the publishing request can specify a "hop count" value to constrain the maximum number of neighbors visited. If the publishing request can be accomplished within the specified hop count, the publishing is successful. Otherwise, the originating node informs the application of the failure of publishing.

To search for objects that match the given keywords, the issuing node simply calculates the hash key representing the query vector $\vec{q}$. Then, it forwards the search request to node x whose hash key is the closest to the hash key of $\vec{q}$. Depending on the "amount" of objects requested, x can simply look up its local index to retrieve the requested objects. If x cannot fulfill the designated amount, it consults its closest neighbors to further process the query. Since objects that are more alike will replace dissimilar ones, the most similar objects must be stored in a node or a set of close nodes. Meteorograph exploits this aggregation feature and combines it with the ring structure of DHT-based P2P systems. It can thus discover the most similar k objects for a given key.

A naive structured overlay names each participating peer by a uniform hash function. It publishes an object to a peer whose hash key is the closest to the key representing that object. If the distribution of the hash keys of objects is uniform, each peer will host about the same amount of objects. However, if some keywords are particularly popular, the distribution of the objects may be biased toward some particular peers. This causes unbalanced load in the peer nodes and renders the hash-addressing space underutilized. Meteorograph has considered load balance; see [19].

29.5.1.3 PeerSearch   Another interesting system for keyword searches in the structured P2P system CAN is PeerSearch [32]. PeerSearch also follows the vector space model. Since CAN organizes peers as a multidimensional coordinate space, an object represented by a vector $\vec{v}$ can simply be mapped to a point in the coordinate space maintained by CAN. To look up objects that have the designated keywords, PeerSearch routes the lookup request to a peer responsible for the subspace that covers the query vector. In order to collect sufficient objects, the peer can perform expanded ring search, broadcasting the lookup requests to its neighbors. The neighbors then perform similar operations. PeerSearch suggests that using a CAN with a 300-dimensional coordinate space is appropriate.

Unfortunately, PeerSearch cannot be directly applied to DHT-based systems with a ring structure, such as Chord, Pastry, Tapestry, and Tornado. These P2P systems do not maintain a multidimensional coordinate space.

29.5.2 Search by Attribute-Value Pairs

29.5.2.1 INS/Twine   Resources in INS/Twine [3] are described with hierarchies of attribute-value pairs called AVTree. An example of an AVTree description of a resource is as follows:

```
<res>camera
     <man>ACompany</man>
     <model>Amodel</model>
</res>
<subject>traffic</subject>
```

INS/Twine supports prefix-matched queries. For example, the above resource description will match the query `<res>camera<man>Acompany</man> </res>` or the query `<res>camera<res>`. This implies that a user needs to know the "structures" of the descriptions of resources in order to specify his query.

INS/Twine extracts the prefix subsequences of an AVTree. A subsequence is called a strand. Consider the following AVTree:

```
<res>camera
     <man>ACompany</man>
</res>
```

The strands that can be extracted are as follows:

h_1 = `<res></res>`
h_2 = `<res>camera</res>`
h_3 = `<res>camera<man></man></res>`
h_4 = `<res>camera<man>Acompany</man></res>`

The strands are then published to a DHT-based P2P system. In INS/Twine, only the longest strand (i.e., h_4) is resolved, rather than looking up individual strands (i.e., h_1, h_2, h_3, and h_4). Since resources installed in the system are named using the same stand-splitting mechanism, the queried stand and the preinstalled strands can be matched in a peer node. Clearly, If a resource has n attribute-value pairs, INS/Twine extracts $2n$ stands from that resources. This then takes $2n$ PUT operations to publish to the P2P system.

29.5.2.2 *Neuron*   Neuron [18] chooses a free-form expression for naming a resource. Each resource is characterized by a tuple of ($name, e_1, e_2, e_3, \ldots, e_n$), where *name* is the resource name and $e_i = (attribute_i = value_i)$ indicates the associated attribute-value pair. With such a naming scheme, the application developers need not know the naming structure of the resources, as does INS/Twine. Of course, Neuron can accept the INS/Twine's hierarchical naming scheme, by splitting the AVTree structure into a Neuron tuple. Consider the example of a color display in room 734 of the EECS building. This resource can be characterized as (LCD Display, color depth = 65536, resolution = 1024 × 768, room = 734, building = EECS).

Neuron is suitable for describing resources that have only few numbers of resource descriptions. Therefore, to publish a resource description, Neuron enumerates all possible ordered tuples and then stores them in the DHT-based P2P system.

If a resource description contains n elements in a tuple, Neuron will generate all $n!$ tuples and perform $n!$ PUT operations. This cost gives the advantage of free-form resource expression.

29.5.2.3 Discussion   The study in [3] investigated two data sets from Netlib and privately collected MP3 files. They conclude that the average number of attribute-value pairs in the two data sets is 6.5 and 4.4, respectively. Another study [15] investigated two empirical data sets: BibFinder and NetBib. They showed that 57% of users only use a single attribute (i.e., author) to index BibFinder and 77% of users query BibFinder using two attributes (i.e., author and title). Users querying NetBib show similar results: queries for a given author, title, and date of publication are more than 95% of the total query requests. Both findings [3, 15] lead to the following interesting results. (1) The number of attribute-value pairs to describe a resource is very low. (2) If there exist hot attributes, publishing a resource description can use only those hot attributes. This can further reduce the number of strands (in INS/Twine) or tuples (in Neuron) to characterize a resource. Encouragingly, when taking the hot attributes into consideration, the study [15] shows that the "flat" designs like Neuron can provide better performance than the hierarchy approach in terms of query delay and network traffic.

29.5.3 Range Search

Suppose that a user wants to discover machines that are equipped with an X86 processor and are running the Linux operating system. The processor is operated in clocks between 1 and 2.5 Ghz, which has 128 to 2048 Mbytes of memory. The user may want to issue a query as follows:

```
<spec>Machine
     <model> X86 </model>
     <cpu> > 1 Ghz && < 2.5 Ghz </cpu>
     <os> Linux </os>
     <memory> > 128 Mbytes && < 2048 Mbytes</memory>
</spec>
```

The above query combines keyword (i.e., "X86" and "Linux") and range search (i.e., the clock speed and memory size).

A range search searches with an integer attribute in the range $[i, j]$, where i and j are known in advance and $i < j$. Consider a DHT-based system with a ring structure, for example, Chord, Pastry, Tapestry, and Tornado. To publish a resource that has an integer attribute of value x ($i \leq x \leq j$), the resource description is first published using the hash key $\lceil (R/j - i) \times (x - i) \rceil$. Given a query with the same attribute in the range $[a, b]$, where $i \leq a < b \leq j$, the lookup request using the hash key $\lceil (R/j - i) \times (a + b)/2 \rceil$ is issued. The message will be sent to a node responsible for the attribute values in $(a + b)/2$. The node can simply return those matched resource descriptions to the requester and broadcast the lookup to its two adjacent neighbors in the ring.

Note that the matched resource descriptions may be piggybacked later when the search request reaches the end of matched range. A node receiving the lookup requests checks whether the range values can meet the designated search range and replies with those resource descriptions that meet the designated range. Otherwise, the search is complete. Clearly, a range query request is forwarded along the ring, clockwise and counterclockwise.

However, the above search mechanism cannot be directly applied to CAN, because CAN does not maintain a ring structure among peers. The study [1] shows that CAN can be embedded with a ring structure using a space filling cure, for example, the Hilbert curve. For further reading, refer to [2].

29.6 SUMMARY

In this chapter, we have reviewed two types of P2P resource discovery systems, namely, unstructured and structured P2P systems. Unstructured P2P overlays do not impose any structure on the interconnection of the participating nodes. A peer can choose any other peer as its neighbor. Unstructured P2P overlays use broadcasting with a limited scope to discover resources. They can support complex searches but cannot guarantee the performance bound and the quality of search results.

Structured P2P systems include CAN, Chord, Pastry, Tapestry, and Tornado. They use hash functions to name the peer nodes and the resources to be published. With the hash keys, it is then possible to interconnect the peers with a logical structure. A resource is published to a peer with the closest hash key. We discuss how to perform routing and joining operations in a structured P2P overlay. With hashing, structured P2P systems only support exact matches in resource discovery. We discuss how a structured P2P system can be enhanced to support searches by keyword, attribute-value pairs, and range.

REFERENCES

1. A. Andrzejak and Z. Xu, Scalable, efficient range queries for grid information services, in *Proceedings of the International Conference on Peer-to-Peer Computing,* pp. 33–40, IEEE Computer Society, September 2002.

2. T. Asano, D. Ranjan, T. Roos, E. Welzl, and P. Widmayer, Space-filling curves and their use in the design of geometric data structures, *Theoretical Computer Science, 181*(1), 3–15, July 1997.

3. M. Balazinska, H. Balakrishnan, and David Karger, Ins/twine: A scalable peer-to-peer architecture for intentional resource discovery, in *International Conference on Pervasive Computing.* Springer-Verlag, August 2002.

4. M. W. Berry, Z. Drmac, and E. R. Jessup, Matrices, vector spaces, and information retrieval, *SIAM Review, 41*(2), 335–362, 1999.

5. M. Castro, P. Druschel, Y. C. Hu, and A. Rowstron, Exploiting network proximity in distributed hash tables, in *International Workshop on Future Directions in Distributed Computing,* pp. 52–55, June 2002.

6. M. Castro, P. Druschel, A.-M. Kermarrec, and A. Rowstron, Scalable application-level anycast for highly dynamic groups, *Lecture Notes in Computer Science, 2816,* 47–57, September 2003.

7. I. Clarke, S. G. Miller, T. W. Hong, O. Sandberg, and B. Wiley, Protecting free expression online with freenet, *IEEE Internet Computing, 6*(1), 40–49, January/February 2002.

8. E. Cohen, A. Fiat, and H. Kaplan, A case for associative peer to peer overlays, *ACM SIGCOMM Computer Communication Review, 33*(1), 95–100, January 2003.

9. A. Crespo and H. Garcia-Molina, Semantic overlay networks, Technical Report 2003-75, Stanford University, May 2003.

10. A. Crespo and H. Garcia-Molina, Routing indices for peer-to-peer systems, in *Proceedings of the International Conference of Distributed Computing Systems,* pp. 23–32, IEEE Computer Society, July 2002.

11. F. M. Cuenca-Acuna and T. D. Nguyen, Text-based content search and retrieval in ad hoc p2p communities, *Lecture Notes In Computer Science,* 220–234, May 2002.

12. F. Dabek, M. F. Kaashoek, David Karger, R. Morris, and I. Stoica, Wide-area cooperative storage with cfs, in *Proceedings of the Symposium on Operating Systems Principles,* pp. 202–215, ACM Press, October 2001.

13. F. Dabek, J. Li, E. Sit, F. Kaashoek, R. Morris, and C. Blake, Designing a dht for low latency and high throughput, in *Proceedings of the Symposium on Networked Systems Design and Implementation,* March 2004.

14. P. Ganesan, Q. Sun, and Hector Garcia-Molina, Yappers: A peer-to-peer lookup service over arbitrary topology, in *Proceedings of IEEE INFOCOM,* pp. 1250–1260, April 2003.

15. L. Garces-Erice, P. A. Felber, E. W. Biersack, G. Urvoy-Keller, and K. W. Ross, Data indexing in peer-to-peer dht networks, in *Proceedings of the International Conference on Distributed Computing Systems,* IEEE Computer Society, March 2004.

16. C. Gavoille and M. Gengler, Space-efficiency of routing schemes of stretch factor three, *Journal of Parallel and Distributed Computing, 61*(5), 679–687, May 2001.

17. K. Gummadi, R. Gummadi, S. Gribble, S. Ratnasamy, and S. Shenker and I. Stoica, The impact of dht routing geometry on resilience and proximity, in *Proceedings of the International Conference on Applications, Technologies, Architectures, and Protocols for Computer Communications,* pp. 381–394, ACM Press, August 2003.

18. H.-C. Hsiao and C.-T. King, Neuron: A wide-area service discovery infrastructure, in *Proceedings of the International Conference on Parallel Processing,* pp. 455–462, IEEE Computer Society, August 2002.

19. H.-C. Hsiao and C.-T. King, Similarity discovery in structured peer-to-peer overlays, in *Proceedings of the International Conference on Parallel Processing,* pp. 636–644, IEEE Computer Society, October 2003.

20. H.-C. Hsiao and C.-T. King, Tornado: A capability-aware peer-to-peer storage overlay, *Journal of Parallel and Distributed Computing, 64*(6), 747–758, June 2004.

21. V. Kalogeraki, D. Gunopulos, and D. Zeinalipour-Yazti, A local search mechanism for peer-to-peer networks, in *Proceedings of the International Conference on Information and Knowledge Management,* pp. 300–307, ACM Press, November 2002.

22. T. Klingberg and R. Manfredi, The gnutella 0.6 protocol draft. http://rfcgnutella.source-forge.net/.

23. J. Kubiatowicz, D. Bindel, Y. Chen, P. Eaton, D. Geels, R. Gummadi, S. Rhea, H. Weatherspoon, W. Weimer, C. Wells, and B. Zhao, Oceanstore: An architecture for

global-scale persistent storage, in *Proceedings of the International Conference on Architectural Support for Programming Languages and Operating Systems,* pp. 190–201, ACM Press, November 2000.

24. Napster, http://www.napster.com/.

25. M. K. Ramanathan, V. Kalogeraki, and J. Pruyne, Finding good peers in peer-to-peer networks, in *Proceedings of the International Parallel and Distributed Processing Symposium,* IEEE Computer Society, April 2002.

26. S. Ratnasamy, P. Francis, M. Handley, R. Karp, and S. Shenker, A scalable content-addressable network, in *Proceedings of the International Conference on Applications, Technologies, Architectures, and Protocols for Computer Communications,* pp. 161–172, ACM Press, August 2001.

27. A. Rowstron and P. Druschel, Pastry: Scalable, distributed object location and routing for large-scale peer-to-peer systems, *Lecture Notes in Computer Science, 2218,* 161–172, November 2001.

28. A. Rowstron and P. Druschel, Storage management and caching in past, a large-scale, persistent peer-to-peer storage utility, in *Proceedings of the Symposium on Operating Systems Principles,* pp. 188–201, ACM Press, October 2001.

29. SETI@home, http://setiathome.ssl.berkeley.edu/.

30. K. Sripanidkulchai, B. Maggs, and H. Zhang, Efficient content location using interest-based locality in peer-to-peer systems, in *Proceedings of IEEE INFOCOM,* pp. 2166–2176, April 2003.

31. I. Stoica, R. Morris, D. Karger, M. F. Kaashoek, and H. Balakrishnan, Chord: A scalable peer-to-peer lookup service for internet applications, in *Proceedings of the International Conference on Applications, Technologies, Architectures, and Protocols for Computer Communications,* pp. 149–160, ACM Press, August 2001.

32. C. Tang, Z. Xu, and S. Dwarkadas, Peer-to-peer information retrieval using self-organizing semantic overlay networks, in *Proceedings of the International Conference on Applications, Technologies, Architectures, and Protocols for Computer Communications,* pp. 175–186, ACM Press, August 2003.

33. B. Y. Zhao, L. Huang, J. Stribling, S. C. Rhea, A. D. Joseph, and J. D. Kubiatowicz, Tapestry: A resilient global-scale overlay for service deployment, *IEEE Journal on Selected Areas in Communications, 22*(1), 41–53, January 2004.

## CHAPTER 30

Hybrid Periodical Flooding in Unstructured Peer-to-Peer Networks

YUNHAO LIU, LI XIAO, LIONEL M. NI, and ZHENYUN ZHUANG

Blind flooding is a popular search mechanism used in current commercial peer-to-peer (P2P) systems because of its simplicity. However, blind flooding among peers or super-peers causes large volume of unnecessary traffic, although the response time is short. Some improved statistics-based search mechanisms can reduce the traffic volume but also significantly shrink the query coverage range. In some search mechanisms, not all peers may be reachable, creating the so-called partial coverage problem. Aiming at alleviating the partial coverage problem and reducing the unnecessary traffic, we propose an efficient and adaptive search mechanism, hybrid periodical flooding (HPF). HPF retains the advantages of statistics-based search mechanisms, alleviates the partial coverage problem, and provides the flexibility to adaptively adjust different parameters to meet different performance requirements. The effectiveness of HPF is demonstrated through simulation studies.

30.1 INTRODUCTION

In an unstructured P2P system, such as Gnutella [3] and KaZaA [4], file placement is random, with no correlation with the network topology [29]. Unstructured P2P systems are most commonly used in today's Internet. In an unstructured P2P system, when a source peer needs to query an object, it sends a query to its neighbors. If a peer receiving the query cannot provide the requested object, it may relay the query to its own neighbors. If the peer receiving the query can provide the requested object, a response message will be sent back to the source peer along the inverse of the query path. The most popular query operation in use, such as used by Gnutella and KaZaA (among supernodes), is to blindly "flood" a query to the network. A query is broadcast and rebroadcast until a certain criterion is satisfied. This mechanism ensures that the query will be "flooded" to as many peers as possible within a short period of time in a P2P overlay network. However, flooding also causes a lot of network traffic, most of which is unnecessary. The study in [21] shows that P2P traffic contributes the largest portion of the Internet traffic based on measurements on three popular P2P systems, FastTrack (including KaZaA and Grokster) [1], Gnutella, and DirectConnect. The inefficient blind flooding search technique causes the unstructured P2P systems to be far from scalable [19].

To avoid the large volume of unnecessary traffic incurred by flooding-based search, many efforts have been made to improve search algorithms for unstructured P2P systems [5, 8, 11, 14, 16–18, 20, 21, 23, 27, 29]. One typical approach is statistics based, in which instead of flooding to all immediate overlay neighbors, a peer selects only a subset of its neighbors to query, based on some statistical information of some metrics and heuristic algorithms. When handling a query message (either relayed from its neighbor or originated from itself) in a statistics-based search algorithm, the peer determines the subset of its logical neighbors to relay the query message to. Statistics-based search mechanisms may significantly reduce the traffic volume but may also reduce the query coverage range so that a query may traverse a longer path to be satisfied or cannot be satisfied. In some search mechanisms, not all peers may be reachable, creating the so-called partial coverage problem. Our objective is to try to alleviate the partial coverage problem and reduce unnecessary traffic.

In this chapter, Section 30.2 will give an overview and classification of known search mechanisms. The concept of our proposed periodical flooding method will be introduced in Section 30.3. Based on periodical flooding and weighted metrics in selecting relay neighbors, the hybrid periodical flooding (HPF) method is detailed in Section 30.3. The proposed HPF can improve the efficiency of blind flooding by retaining the advantages of statistics-based search mechanisms and by alleviating the partial coverage problem. Section 30.4 describes our simulation method and the performance metrics. Performance evaluation of our proposed HPF method against other search methods is described in Section 30.5. Section 30.6 concludes the chapter.

30.2 SEARCH MECHANISMS

In unstructured P2P systems, the placement of objects is loosely controlled and each peer has no hint as to where the intended objects are stored. Without having the global knowledge of the dynamic overlay network and the locations of target peers, a source peer has to send a query message to explore as many peers as possible in the overlay network. A well-designed search mechanism should seek to optimize both efficiency and quality of service (QoS). Efficiency focuses on better utilizing resources, such as bandwidth and processing power, whereas QoS focuses on user-perceived qualities, such as number of returned results and response time. In unstructured P2P systems, the QoS of a search mechanism generally depends on the number of peers being explored (queried), response time, and traffic overhead. If more peers can be queried by a certain query, it is more likely that the requested object can be found. In order to avoid having query messages flowing around the network forever, each query message has a TTL (time to live: the number of times a query will be forwarded) field. A TTL value is set to limit the search depth of a query. Each time a peer receives a query, the TTL value is decremented by one. The peer will stop relaying the query if the TTL becomes zero. A query message will also be dropped if the query message has visited the peer before. Note that the query messages are application-level messages in an overlay network.

In statistics-based search mechanisms, a peer selects a subset of its neighbors to relay the query to, based on some statistical information of some metrics and heuristic algorithms. Based on the number of selected logical query neighbors and the criteria for selecting logical query neighbors, the statistics-based search algorithms in unstructured P2P systems can be roughly classified into two types: uniformed selection of relay neighbors and weighted selection of relay neighbors.

30.2.1 Uniformed Selection of Relay Neighbors

In this approach, all logical neighbors are equally treated when selected to relay the query message.

30.2.1.1 Blind Flooding   The blind flooding mechanism relays the query message to all its logical neighbors, except the incoming peer. This mechanism is also referred to as breadth-first search (BFS) and is used among peers in Gnutella or among superpeers in KaZaA. For each query, each node records the neighbors that relay the query to it. Thereby, on each link, at most two query messages can be sent across it. For an overlay network with m peers and average n neighbors per peer, the total traffic caused by a query is mn if the value of TTL is no less than the diameter of the overlay network. Note that in a typical P2P system, the value of m (more than millions) is much greater than n (less than tens) [21]. In this approach, the source peer can reach its target peer (object) through a shortest path. However, the overhead of blind flooding is very large since flooding generates large amount of unnecessary traffic, wasting bandwidth and processing resources. The simplicity of blind flooding makes it very popular in practice.

30.2.1.2 Depth-First Search (DFS)   Instead of sending queries to all the neighbors, a peer just randomly selects a single neighbor to relay the query message when the TTL value is not zero and waits for the response. This search mechanism is referred to as depth-first search (DFS) and is used in Freenet [2]. DFS can terminate in a timely fashion when the required object has been found, thus avoiding sending out too many unnecessary queries. In DFS, the value of TTL should be set sufficiently large to increase the probability of locating the object. The maximum number of peers that a query message will visit is TTL. Thus, setting a proper TTL value is a key issue to determine the search quality. The response time could be unbearably large due to the nature of its sequential search process. Because of the random selection of relay neighbors, it is possible that an object can be found only with difficulty.

30.2.1.3 k-Walker   In the k-walker query algorithm proposed in [16], a query is sent to k different walkers (relay neighbors) from the source peer. For a peer in each walker, it just randomly selects one neighbor to relay the query to. For each walker, the query processing is done sequentially. For k walkers with up to TTL steps, each query can reach up to $k \times$ TTL peers in the P2P network. We can view the k-walker search mechanism as a multiple of DFS. It has been shown that the k-walker mechanism creates less traffic than the BFS and provides shorter response time than the DFS. However, k-walker suffers from limited query coverage range due to the random nature of selecting query neighbors.

30.2.2   Weighted Selection of Relay Neighbors

Instead of randomly selecting relay neighbors, some mechanisms have been proposed to select relay neighbors more subjectively so that neighbors who are most likely to return the requested results are selected. Some statistical information is collected based on some metrics when selecting relay neighbors. Possible metrics include delay of the link to the corresponding neighbor, the processing time of the neighbor, the computing power, the cost (if possible), the amount of shared data, and the number of neighbors.

30.2.2.1   Directed BFS (DBFS)   Each peer maintains statistical information based on some metrics, such as the number of results received from neighbors from previous queries or the latency of the connection with that neighbor [29]. A peer selects a subset of the neighbors to send its query to based on some heuristics, such as selecting the neighbors that have returned the largest number of results from previous queries or selecting the neighbors that have the smallest latency.

30.2.2.2   Routing Indices (RI)   The concept of routing indices was proposed in [10]. Each peer keeps a local RI that is a detailed summary of indices, such as the number of files on different topics of interests along each path. When a peer receives a query, it forwards the query to the neighbor that has the largest number of files under a particular topic, rather than selecting relay neighbors at random or flooding to all neighbors.

Some weighted-selection search mechanisms have demonstrated performance improvement compared with uninformed-selection search mechanisms. However, weighted-selection search mechanisms suffer from the partial coverage problem to be illustrated in Section 30.2.4.

30.2.3   Other Approaches

In addition to the aforementioned search policies, there are other techniques that may be used to improve search performance. For example, a peer can cache query responses in the hope that subsequent queries can be satisfied quickly by the cached indices or responses [22, 26, 28, 29]. Peers can also be clustered based on different criteria, such as similar interests [22], location information [12, 13, 15, 17, 18, 21, 25], and associative rules [9]. Our proposed statistics-based technique can be used to complement these techniques.

30.2.4 Partial Coverage Problem

Statistics-based search algorithms indeed can reduce network traffic. For example, compared with blind flooding, DBFS can reduce the aggregate processing and bandwidth cost by about 28% and 38%, respectively, with a 40% increase in the response time [29]. However, our study will show that statistics-based search mechanisms may leave a large percentage of the peers unreachable no matter how large the TTL value is set. We call this phenomenon the partial coverage problem. This problem is illustrated in Figure 30.1(a). The number by an edge is the latency between two logical nodes and the number in each node is the number of shared files on that peer. Suppose the size of a selected neighbor subset is one and the metric used to select the neighbor is based on the number of shared files. We consider the scenario in which the query source is A, which has four neighbors (B, C, D, E). It will only send its query to C since C has the largest number of shared files (170). Similarly, C selects D, which has the largest number of shared files in all C's neighbors (B, D, F, G) to relay A's query. Then, D selects A in the same way, which leads to a loop query path: $A \rightarrow C \rightarrow D \rightarrow A$. Thus, only three nodes are queried in the whole query process whereas all other nodes are invisible from the query source A. If we change the metric to be the smallest latency, the problem still exists because another loop is formed from source A: $A \rightarrow C \rightarrow B \rightarrow A$. It is very possible that the query cannot be satisfied in the loop. This problem can be less serious when the size of the query subset increases, which will be discussed in Section 30.3.

Many statistics-based search approaches use only one metric to collect statistical information to select relay neighbors, which does not always lead to an optimal search path. Figure 30.1(b) shows an example in which A is still the source node. When the search metric is the volume of shared data, the query path would be $A \rightarrow D \rightarrow E$, along which the query will check 250 files in 200 units of time. But, obviously, if the query path is $A \rightarrow C \rightarrow G \rightarrow F \rightarrow H$, the query can check 500 files in 20 units of time. The first path selected using one search metric is not as good as the second one.

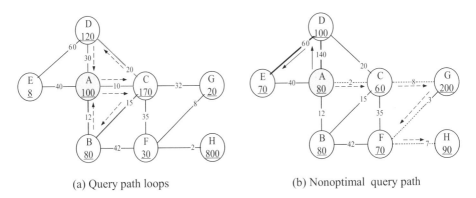

(a) Query path loops   (b) Nonoptimal query path

Figure 30.1   The partial coverage problem.

30.3   HYBRID PERIODICAL FLOODING

In order to effectively reduce the traffic incurred by flooding-based search and alleviate the partial coverage problem, we propose hybrid periodical flooding (HPF). Before discussing HPF, we first define periodical flooding.

30.3.1   Periodical Flooding (PF)

We notice that in all the existing statistics-based search techniques, the number of relay neighbors, h, does not change at all peers along the query path. In the case of blind flooding, the phenomenon exhibits traffic explosion. The concept of periodical flooding tries to control the number of relay neighbors based on the TTL value along the query path. More specifically, given a peer with n logical neighbors and the current value of TTL, the number of relay neighbors, h, is defined by $h = f(n, TTL)$. Thus, in blind flooding (BFS), we have $h = f_{BFS}(n, TTL) = n$. In DFS, we have $h = f_{DFS}(n, TTL) = 1$.

The function $h = f(n, TTL)$ can be viewed as a periodical function that changes as TTL changes. We call a search mechanism using a periodical function periodic flooding (PF), in which the query mechanism is divided into several phases that are periodically repeated. We call the number of different repeated phases a cycle, C. All existing statistics-based search techniques, have a cycle of $C = 1$, and so are special cases of PF. We can ask the following questions in order to design an efficient search mechanism. Under what conditions does a search mechanism with $C = 1$ behave better than a search mechanism with $C > 1$? What is the optimal value of C in terms of a desired performance metric under different underlying physical network topologies? For a given C, what is the optimal number of relay neighbors? One example of PF functions with $C = 2$ is shown below:

$$f(n, TTL) = \begin{cases} \left\lceil \dfrac{1}{2} n \right\rceil, & \text{if } TTL \text{ is odd} \\[3mm] \left\lceil \dfrac{1}{3} n \right\rceil, & \text{if } TTL \text{ is even} \end{cases}$$

We compare BFS and the example PF in Figure 30.2. Suppose peer O initiates a query. Blind flooding (BFS) is employed in Figure 30.2(a), where the query is sent or forwarded 36 times to reach all the nodes. We use thin connections to represent the links on which the query traverses once and thick connections to represent the links on which the query traverses twice. We have explained that for each query, each peer records the neighbors that forward the query to it. Thereby, on each link, at most two query messages can be sent across it. When a link is traversed twice, unnecessary traffic is incurred. For example, one of the messages from A to B and from B to A is unnecessary. These redundant messages are shown in Figure 30.2(a) using dotted arrows.

Figure 30.2(b) illustrates the query process of the example PF. Peer O has four neighbors and has $TTL = 7$. We randomly select relay neighbors. Peer O will select

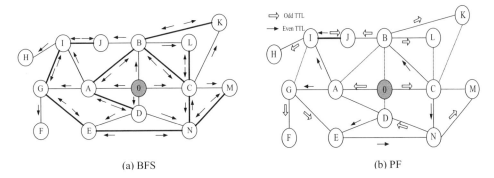

(a) BFS   (b) PF

Figure 30.2   Comparison between BFS and PF.

two nodes (that is $n/2 = 2$ since $TTL = 7$, that is, odd), peers A and C, as relay neighbors. Peer A has five neighbors. It will select two neighbors (G and I) to relay the query initiated from peer O since $TTL = 6$ and $h = \lceil n/3 \rceil, = 2$. Similarly, peer C relays the query to peer B and N ($TTL = 6$ and $h = \lceil n/3 \rceil, = 2$). Although the redundancy problem still exists in PF (such as the traffic from B to J and from I to J), it is significantly reduced compared with that of BFS.

Table 30.1 compares the redundancy degree of both PF and BFS. It presents the query messages relayed to new peers. For example, in BFS, peers with $TTL = 5$ relay the query to 15 peers, but only two of the 15 peers receive the query first time. In PF, peers with $TTL = 5$ relay the query to nine peers, of which eight are first-time receivers. That means for peers with $TTL = 5$, BFS sends 7.5 queries to one new queried peer on average, whereas PF only sends 1.12 queries to one new queried peer on average. An efficient mechanism should query more peers using fewer messages. Thus, PF is much more efficient than BFS in terms of traffic volume.

30.3.2   Hybrid Periodical Flooding

30.3.2.1 *HPF Overview*   After determining the number of relay neighbors (h), a peer decides which h nodes should be selected. A simple approach called

Table 30.1   PF and Blind Flooding

	TTL	Query Msg	New peers	Msg per peer
BFS	7	4	4	1.00
	6	17	8	2.12
	5	15	2	7.50
PF	7	2	2	1.00
	6	4	4	1.00
	5	9	8	1.12

random periodical flooding (RPF) selects h relay neighbors at random. Selecting relay neighbors more objectively may result in better performance. For example, we may use the shared data volume as a metric to select query neighbors if we find that peers with more shared data are more likely to satisfy queries. By selecting the neighbors with larger amounts of shard data, a query is more likely to succeed in fewer hops than that of random selection. We may also use the latency between the peer and its neighbors as a metric to select neighbors. In this case, for a given TTL value, a query will experience a shorter delay. If we consider multiple metrics in relay neighbor selection, the search mechanism is expected to have better performance. This motivates us to propose hybrid periodical flooding (HPF), in which the number of relay neighbors can be changed periodically based on a periodical function and the relay neighbors are selected based on multiple metrics in a hybrid way.

HPF differs from RPF in that RPF selects relay neighbors randomly, and differs from DBFS in that DBFS only uses one metric to select relay neighbors. HPF selects neighbors based on multiple metrics and provides flexibility to justify different parameters to improve overall performance. Let h denote the expected number of relay neighbors, which is given by $h = h_1 + h_2 + \ldots + h_t$, where t is the number of metrics used in relay neighbor selection and h_i is the number of relay neighbors selected by metric i.

30.3.2.2 Metrics

There are many metrics that may be used to select relay neighbors, such as communication cost, bandwidth, number of returned results from the neighbor, average number of hops from the neighbor to peers who responded to the previous queries, and so on. These metrics may have different weights in a system with different query access patterns or different performance requirements. For example, we may give higher weights to some metrics that are more sensitive to the performance in a specific system. We have $\sum_{i=1}^{t} w_i = 1$, where w_i is the weight assigned to metric i ($1 \leq i \leq t$). To alleviate the partial coverage problem, we select relay neighbors in a hybrid way. We select h_i neighbors using metric i, where h_i is determined by $h_i = \lceil h \times w_i \rceil$. Let S_i denote the set of neighbors selected based on the metric i. The complete set of relay neighbors is $S = \bigcup_{i=1}^{t} S_i$, where $h_i = |S_i|$. Note that a neighbor may be selected by more than one metric. Thus, the actual number of relay neighbors selected may be less than h.

30.3.2.3 Termination of Search Queries

A query process is terminated when a preset *TTL* value has been decreased to zero. Choosing an appropriate *TTL* value is very difficult. A large *TTL* may cause higher traffic volume, whereas a small *TTL* may not respond with enough query results. Furthermore, there are no mutual feedbacks between the source peer and the peers who forward or respond the query. Thus it is hard for peers to know when to stop forwarding the query before the *TTL* value is reduced to zero.

Iterative deepening [29] is a method that attempts to address this problem in some degree. In iterative deepening, a policy P is used to control the search mechanism, which provides a sequence of *TTLs* so that a query is flooded from a very small *TTL*, and if necessary, to gradually enlarge the scope. For example, one policy can be $P = \{a, b, c\}$, where P has three iterations. A query starts to be flooded with $TTL = a$. If the query cannot be satisfied, it will be flooded with $TTL = b - a$ from all peers that are a hops away from the source peer. Similarly, if the query still cannot be satisfied, it will be flooded with $TTL = c - b$ from all peers that are b hops away from the source peer. In this policy, c is the maximal length of a query path. Iterative Deepening is a good mechanism in the sense that it alleviates the process time of middle nodes between iterations.

In HPF, we use this policy to terminate the successful queries without incurring too much unnecessary traffic. Since the combination is quite straightforward and the performance of iterative deepening has been evaluated in [29], this policy will not be reevaluated in this chapter.

30.4   SIMULATION METHODOLOGY

We use simulation to evaluate the performance of RPF and HPF and analyze the effects of the parameters.

30.4.1   Topology Generation

Two types of topologies, physical topology and logical topology, have to be generated in our simulation. The physical topology should represent the real topology with Internet characteristics. The logical topology represents the overlay P2P topology built on top of the physical topology. All P2P nodes are in the node subset of the physical topology. The communication cost between two logical neighbors is calculated based on the physical shortest path between this pair of nodes. To simulate the performance of different search mechanisms in a more realistic environment, the two topologies must accurately reflect the topological properties of real networks in each layer.

Previous studies have shown that both large-scale Internet physical topologies [24] and P2P overlay topologies exhibit small-world and power-law properties. The power law describes the node degree, whereas small-world properties govern characteristics of the path length and clustering coefficient [7]. Studies [20] have found that the topologies generated using the AS model have small-world and power-law properties. BRITE [6] is a topology generation tool that provides the option to generate topologies based on the AS Model. Using BRITE, we generate 10 physical topologies each with 10,000 nodes. The logical topologies are generated with the number of peers ranging from 1000 to 5000. The average number of edges of each node ranges from 6 to 20.

30.4.2   Simulation Setup

The total network traffic incurred by queries and average response time of all queries are two major metrics that we use to evaluate the efficiency of a search mechanism. High traffic volume will limit system scalability and long response time is intolerable for users. Network administrators care more about how much network bandwidth is consumed by a P2P system, whereas users care more about the response time of queries, which is viewed as a part of the QoS of the system.

In our simulation, we consider two metrics with the same weight to select relay neighbors in HPF. In practice, more metrics could be used for neighbor selection. The two metrics are the communication cost (metric 1) that is the distance between a peer and its neighbor, and the shared number of files (metric 2) on each node. Based on the first metric, a peer will select the neighbors with the lowest communication costs. Based on the second metric, a peer will select the neighbors with the larger amount of shared data.

For each given search criterion, we distribute 100 files satisfying the search on the peers in a generated P2P topology. That means there are totally 100 possible results for a specific query in the whole P2P network. The distribution of the 100 files on the network is random. For each peer, we generate a number from 1 to 1000 as the number of shared files in this peer. Based on the second metric in selecting relay neighbors, a neighbor with more shared files is more likely to return a response than a neighbor with fewer shared files.

30.5   PERFORMANCE EVALUATION

In this section, we present simulation results to show the effectiveness of HPF compared with DBFS and BFS.

30.5.1   Partial Coverage Problem

Based on [10, 29], statistics-based search mechanisms are more efficient and incur less traffic to the Internet compared with blind flooding. However, statistics-based search mechanisms suffer from partial coverage problem as we discussed in Section 30.2.4. We quantitatively illustrate the partial coverage problem in this section.

We first illustrate the case in which only one relay neighbor is selected to send/forward a query ($h = 1$) based on the number of shared files in neighbors. We set *TTL* at infinity. Figure 30.3 shows the node distribution versus the number of peers being queried, which is defined as coverage size. For example, queries initiated from 8% of peers can only reach 10 other peers. Most of peers can only push their queries to 10 to 30 other peers. This means that loops are formed and only a very small number of peers can be reached for any queries. Note that the overlay network has 1000 nodes and the physical network has 10,000 nodes. Figure 30.4 illustrates the node distribution versus the coverage size, where $h = 2$ and $TTL = $ infinity. The coverage size is about 400 peers on average, which is still a small number in a P2P network.

Figure 30.5 shows node distribution versus coverage size when we use network latency as the metric to select relay neighbors. Again, we see the partial coverage

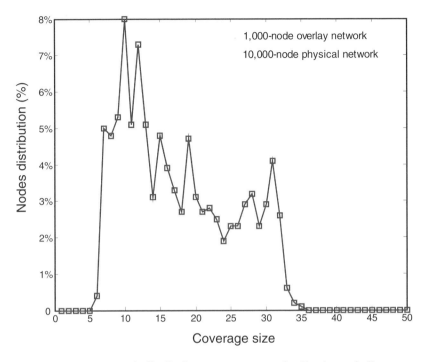

Figure 30.3   Node distribution versus coverage size ($h = 1$, metric 2).

problem. The partial coverage problem will disappear when $h = n$, which is the case of blind flooding. We did the same group of simulations on different topologies using different metrics. The results are quite consistent. Figure 30.6 shows the percentage of covered peers to total peers versus the number of relay neighbors ($h = 1$, 2, $n/5$, $n/4$, $n/3$, $n/2$, and $\sqrt{n}$). The percentage of coverage is larger for a larger h. A larger h means a smaller chance for all reached peers to form a loop.

30.5.2   Performance of Random PF

We have evaluated network traffic and average response time of RPF that selects relay neighbors at random. We can use many different periodical flooding functions to determine the number of relay neighbors. These functions should not be overly complicated. We have tried tens of periodical flooding functions with different C.

Figures 30.7 and 30.8 show the normalized network traffic cost and normalized average response time versus the required number of response results. The traffic and average response time always perform in opposite ways. If a search mechanism causes low traffic, it will suffer from high response time and vice versa. RPF is designed to provide an opportunity to have a trade-off between total traffic and average response time, thus obtaining a better overall search performance. We may expect a search mechanism to reduce a large amount of traffic by increasing response

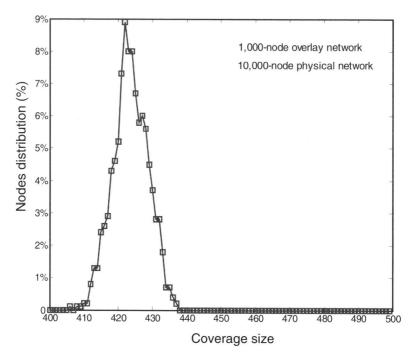

Figure 30.4 Node distribution versus coverage size ($h = 2$, metric 2).

time a little or vice versa. How to quantitatively measure the overall performance based on the tradeoff is an issue.

It is hard to find the best search mechanism. We define p to measure the overall performance, where $p = \lambda_C$ *traffic* $+ \lambda_R$ *time*; *traffic* and *time* are normalized values of total network traffic and average response time, λ_C and λ_R are the weight parameters for network traffic and response time, and $\lambda_C + \lambda_R = 1$. We seek an asymptotically periodical flooding function $f_a(n, TTL)$ such that p can be minimal or close to minimal. If a system places more emphasis on low network traffic, we can set $\lambda_C > \lambda_R$; otherwise, we can set $\lambda_C < \lambda_R$ for a system placing more emphasis on quick response time.

Based on different topologies with different numbers of average connections and different values of λ_C and λ_R, the functions of $f_a(n, TTL)$ may be derived differently. In our simulation of HPF, the average number of edge connections is 10. We choose $\lambda_C = 0.6$ and $\lambda_R = 0.4$. Thus, the corresponding period function is derived as:

$$f(n, TTL) = \begin{cases} \left\lceil \dfrac{1}{2} n \right\rceil, & \text{if } TTL \text{ is odd} \\[2mm] \left\lceil \dfrac{1}{4} n \right\rceil, & \text{if } TTL \text{ is even} \end{cases}$$

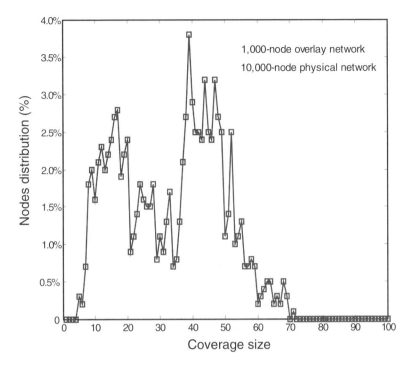

Figure 30.5   Node distribution versus coverage size ($h = 1$, metric 1).

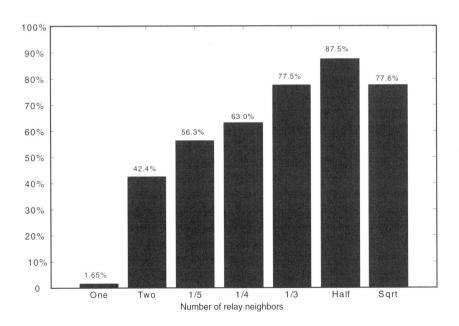

Figure 30.6   Percentage of coverage versus the number of relay neighbors.

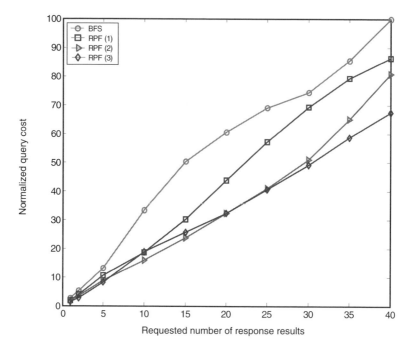

Figure 30.7 Normalized traffic of RPF.

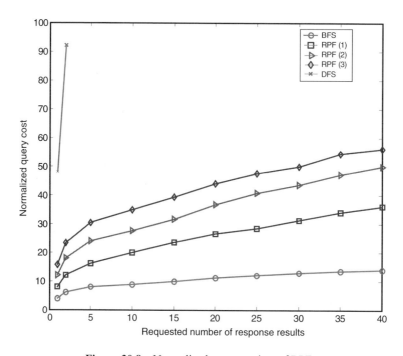

Figure 30.8 Normalized response time of RPF.

30.5.3 Effectiveness of HPF

HPF selects relay neighbors based on multiple metrics in a hybrid way. We use communication cost and the volume of shared data as two metrics to select relay neighbors.

Based on the simulation over 10,000 queries, Figure 30.9 shows the normalized network traffic versus the required number of response results of four different search mechanisms: BFS, RPF, DBFS, and HPF. DBFS reduces the network traffic by about 30–50% compared with BFS. HPF outperforms DBFS by up to 20%. Figure 30.10 compares the normalized response time of four different search mechanisms over 10,000 queries versus the required number of response results. HPF performs the best compared with RPF and DBFS, but is still worse than BFS. DBFS selects relay neighbors who have the largest volume of shared files. Each query may get more results by reaching fewer peers. HPF needs to query more peers to obtain the same amount of results as DBFS but much less than BFS and RPF. That is because we use multiple metrics instead of a single metric used in DBFS, expecting to obtain better overall performance, which is shown in Figures 30.9 and 30.10.

30.5.4 Alleviating the Partial Coverage Problem

HPF can effectively address the partial coverage problem discussed in Section 30.2.4. Figure 30.11 shows the percentage of queried peers as *TTL* increases. BFS

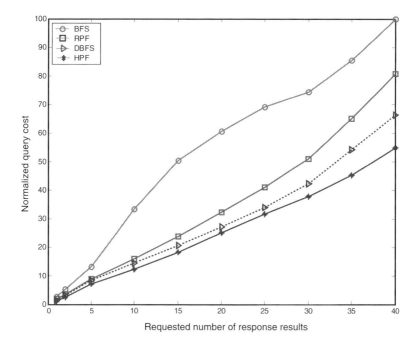

Figure 30.9 Normalized traffic comparison.

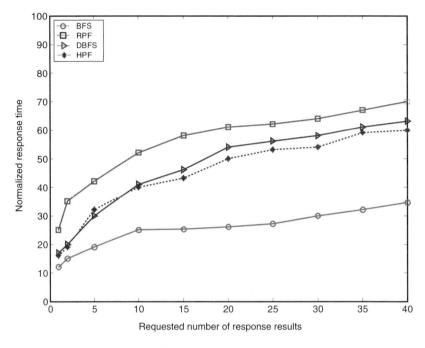

Figure 30.10 Normalized response time comparison.

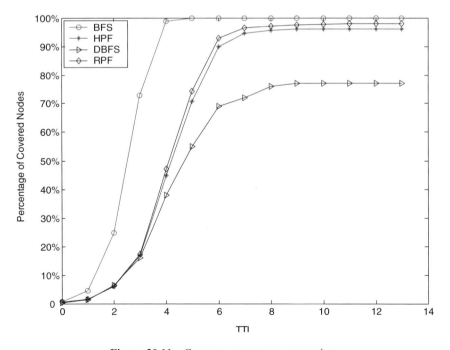

Figure 30.11 Coverage percentage comparison.

can quickly cover 100% peers, whereas DBFS can only cover up to 77% peers in our simulation because of the partial coverage problem. DBFS still covers only around 77% when the value of *TTL* is set to infinity in our simulation. However, HPF and RPF can cover more than 96% peers as *TTL* is increased to 10.

Figure 30.12 compares the peer coverage size of DBFS and HPF. In DBFS, most nodes can cover 760–780 peers out of 1000 nodes. The coverage size is increased to 950–970 in HPF.

30.6 CONCLUSION

In this chapter, we have proposed an efficient and adaptive search mechanism called hybrid periodical flooding. HPF improves the efficiency of blind flooding by retaining the advantages of statistics-based search mechanisms and by alleviating the partial coverage problem. We summarize our contributions as follows:

- Analyzed the current search mechanisms used in and proposed for unstructured P2P networks.
- Qualitatively and quantitatively analyzed the partial coverage problem caused by statistics-based search mechanisms, such as DBFS.

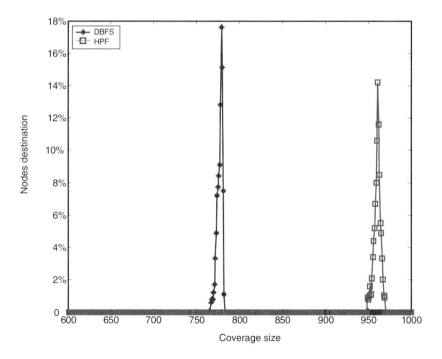

Figure 30.12 Partial coverage comparison.

- Proposed use of a periodical flooding function to define the number of relay neighbors, which can be adaptively changed. This is the first technique used in HPF.
- Proposed to use multiple metrics to select relay neighbors to obtain better overall performance or adaptively meet different performance requirements, which is the second technique used in HPF.

We have shown the performance of HPF using two metrics to select relay neighbors. HPF provides the flexibility to use more metrics and allows the application to define multiple metrics and give them different weights, the algorithm is thereby more flexible in practice to meet different performance requirements.

REFERENCES

1. Fasttrack, http://www.fasttrack.nu.
2. Freenet, http://freenet.sourceforge.net.
3. Gnutella, http://gnutella.wego.com/.
4. KaZaA, http://www.kazaa.com.
5. B. Bhattacharjee, S. Chawathe, V. Gopalakrishnan, P. Keleher, and B. Silaghi, Efficient Peer-to-peer Searches Using Result-caching, in *Proceedings of the 2nd International Workshop on Peer-to-Peer Systems (IPTPS),* 2003.
6. BRITE, http://www.cs.bu.edu/brite/.
7. T. Bu and D. Towsley, On Distinguishing between Internet Power Law Topology Generators, in *Proceedings of IEEE INFOCOM,* 2002.
8. Y. Chawathe, S. Ratnasamy, L. Breslau, N. Lanham, and S. Shenker, Making Gnutella-like P2P Systems Scalable, in *Proceedings of ACM SIGCOMM,* 2003.
9. E. Cohen, H. Kaplan, and A. Fiat, Associative Search in Peer-to-peer Networks: Harnessing Latent Semantics, in *Proceedings of IEEE INFOCOM,* 2003.
10. A. Crespo and H. Garcia-Molina, Routing Indices for Peer-to-peer Systems, in *Proceedings of 28th Conference on Distributed Computing Systems,* 2002.
11. S. Jiang, L. Guo, and X. Zhang, LightFlood: An Efficient Flooding Scheme for File Search in Unstructured Peer-to-Peer Systems, in *Proceedings of International Conferenece on Parallel Processing (ICPP),* 2003.
12. B. Krishnamurthy and J. Wang, Automated Traffic Classification for Application-Specific Peering, in *Proceedings of ACM SIGCOMM Internet Measurement Workshop,* 2002.
13. Y. Liu, X. Liu, L. Xiao, L. M. Ni, and X. Zhang, Location-Aware Topology Matching in Unstructured P2P Systems, in *Proceedings of IEEE INFOCOM,* 2004.
14. Y. Liu, L. Xiao, and L. M. Ni, Building a Scalable Bipartite P2P Overlay Network, in *Proceedings of 18th International Parallel and Distributed Processing Symposium (IPDPS),* 2004.
15. Y. Liu, Z. Zhuang, L. Xiao, and L. M. Ni, A Distributed Approach to Solving Overlay Mismatch Problem, in *Proceedings of the 24th International Conference on Distributed Computing Systems (ICDCS),* 2004.

16. Q. Lv, P. Cao, E. Cohen, K. Li, and S. Shenker, Search and Replication in Unstructured Peer-to-peer Networks, in *Proceedings of the 16th ACM International Conference on Supercomputing,* 2002.

17. S. Ratnasamy, M. Handley, R. Karp, and S. Shenker, Topologically-Aware Overlay Construction and Server Selection, in *Proceedings of IEEE INFOCOM,* 2002.

18. M. Ripeanu, A. Iamnitchi, and I. Foster, Mapping the Gnutella Network, *IEEE Internet Computing,* 2002.

19. Ritter, Why Gnutella Can't Scale. No, Really, http://www.tch.org/gnutella.html.

20. S. Saroiu, P. Gummadi, and S. Gribble, A Measurement Study of Peer-to-Peer File Sharing Systems, in *Proceedings of Multimedia Computing and Networking (MMCN),* 2002.

21. S. Sen and J. Wang, Analyzing Peer-to-peer Traffic Across Large Networks, in *Proceedings of ACM SIGCOMM Internet Measurement Workshop,* 2002.

22. K. Sripanidkulchai, B. Maggs, and H. Zhang, Efficient Content Location Using Interest-Based Locality in Peer-to-Peer Systems, in *Proceedings of IEEE INFOCOM,* 2003.

23. T. Stading, P. Maniatis, and M. Baker, Peer-to-peer Caching Schemes to Address Flash Crowds, in *Proceedings of the 1st International Workshop on Peer-to-Peer Systems (IPTPS),* 2002.

24. H. Tangmunarunkit, R. Govindan, S. Jamin, S. Shenker, and W. Willinger, Network Topology Generators: Degree-Based vs. Structural, in *Proceedings of ACM SIGCOMM,* 2002.

25. M. Waldvogel and R. Rinaldi, Efficient Topology-aware Overlay Network, in *Proceedings of ACM HotNets,* 2002.

26. C. Wang, L. Xiao, Y. Liu, and P. Zheng, Distributed Caching and Adaptive Search in Multilayer P2P Networks, in *Proceedings of the 24th International Conference on Distributed Computing Systems (ICDCS),* 2004.

27. Z. Xu, C. Tang, and Z. Zhang, Building Topology-aware Overlays Using Global Soft-state, in *Proceedings of the 23rd International Conference on Distributed Computing Systems (ICDCS),* 2003.

28. B. Yang and H. Garcia-Molina, Designing a super-peer network, in *Proceedings of the 19th International Conference on Data Engineering (ICDE),* Bangalore, India, March 2003.

29. B. Yang and H. Garcia-Molina, Efficient Search in Peer-to-peer Networks, in *Proceedings of the 22nd International Conference on Distributed Computing Systems (ICDCS),* 2002.

## CHAPTER 31

HIERAS: A DHT Based Hierarchical P2P Routing Algorithm

ZHIYONG XU, YIMING HU, and LAXMI BHUYAN

31.1 INTRODUCTION

In peer-to-peer (P2P) systems [6, 7, 9, 11], a routing request is the process of searching the location information of a specific file or object. It is the most frequently executed operation and has a major influence on the overall system performance. In distributed hash table (DHT) based systems such as CAN [13], Pastry [15, 16], Chord [17], and Tapestry [20], each peer is given a unique identifier called nodeid, and each file is associated with a key called fileid, using collision-free hash functions. Routing information of the files is stored in DHTs. A routing procedure is accomplished by consulting the DHTs on several peers. At each routing hop, the message is sent to a peer whose nodeid is numerically closer to the request key and a routing request is guaranteed to be finished within a small number of routing hops [normally $\log(N)$, N is the total number of peers]. Most of these systems only try to minimize the number of routing hops. In a large-scale P2P system in which peers are spread all over the world, the network link latencies between two peers vary widely. Two nodes may be connected by a high-speed Ethernet, or separated by a slow dial-up link. As a result, many of these algorithms cannot achieve the best routing performance in terms of routing latencies.

This problem is caused by the negligence of peers' topological characteristics. In most DHT algorithms, routing tables are created according to the peers' logical characteristics but not the topological properties. In this chapter, we propose a new DHT-based routing algorithm, HIERAS, to improve P2P routing performance by combining hierarchical structures with existing DHT-based routing algorithms.

31.2 HIERARCHICAL P2P ARCHITECTURE

HIERAS distinguishes itself from other DHT algorithms with the introduction of the hierarchical structure. In this section, we describe HIERAS' design in detail.

High-Performance Computing: Paradigm and Infrastructure. Edited by L. T. Yang and M. Guo

31.2.1 Hierarchical P2P Layers

Most DHT algorithms view the whole system as a single flat space (e.g., a single P2P ring). HIERAS, on the other hand, uses a hierarchical structure to improve DHT performance. In HIERAS, many P2P rings coexist in different layers. A P2P ring is a self-organized and relatively independent unit that contains a subset of peers. The members in a P2P ring are equally important and take equal responsibilities for the workloads within this ring. In each P2P layer, all the peers are grouped into several disjointed P2P rings. There is only one ring in the highest layer that contains all the peers. A peer must belong to a P2P ring in each layer. We organize P2P rings in such a way that the lower the layer, the topologically closer are the nodes within a P2P ring in this layer. A simple illustration of a two-layer HIERAS system is shown in Figure 31.1. It contains three layer-2 P2P rings: P1, P2, and P3. P is the layer-1 (biggest) P2P ring that contains all three layer-2 rings. Node A is a member of P3 and Node B is a member of P1. Both of them are members of P as well. Every node in the system belongs to P and one of three layer-2 rings.

A routing procedure starts by searching a fileid in a ring in the lowest layer first, using an existing DHT routing algorithm within this ring. If routing cannot be completed within this ring, it moves up to a higher-layer P2P ring and may eventually reach the highest-layer. By using this strategy, a large portion of routing hops previously executed in the global P2P ring are now replaced by hops in lower-level rings, which are topologically close and have short latencies. As a result, the routing overheads can be reduced significantly. A detailed discussion of the routing algorithm will be presented later.

31.2.2 Distributed Binning Scheme

An important issue in HIERAS is how to create the P2P rings and determine to which rings a new node should be added, accroding to the topology information of

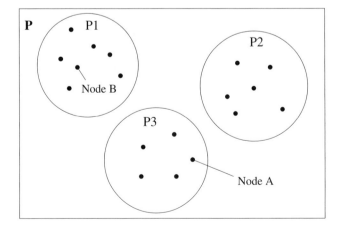

Figure 31.1   Overview of a two-layer HIERAS system.

the node. A simple and relatively accurate topology measurement mechanism is the distributed binning scheme proposed by Ratnasamy et al. [12]. In this scheme, a well-known set of machines is chosen as the landmark nodes. All nodes in the system partition themselves into disjoint bins such that nodes that fall within a given bin are relatively closer to each other in terms of network link latency. Although the network latency measurement method (ping) is not very accurate since it is affected by many uncertain factors, it is adequate for HIERAS, thus we use it for ring creation. Our simulation results show that this mechanism is sufficient for the HIERAS algorithm to achieve good performance.

Table 31.1 shows six sample nodes—A, B, C, D, E, and F—in a two-layer HIERAS system with the measured network link latencies to four landmark nodes, L1, L2, L3, and L4. We divide the range of possible latencies into three levels: level 0 for latencies in [0, 20], level 1 for latencies in [20, 100], and level 2 for latencies higher than 100. The order information is created according to the measured latencies to the four landmark nodes L1, L2, L3, and L4, and this information is used for layer-2 P2P ring decision. For example, Node A's landmark order is 1012. Nodes C and D have the same order, 2200, and they are in the same layer-2 ring, "2200." All the other nodes belong to different layer-2 rings.

31.2.3 Landmark Nodes

We use a well-known set of landmark machines spread across the Internet as suggested by Ratnasamy et al. [12]. In case of a landmark node failure, newly added nodes are binned using the surviving landmarks, whereas previous binned nodes only need to drop the failed landmark(s) from their order information. This solution may degrade the overall performance, however. We can also use multiple geographically close nodes as one logical landmark node to tolerate node failures.

31.2.4 Hierarchy Depth

The hierarchy depth also has great influence on HIERAS efficiency. As the hierarchy depth increases, more routing hops previously taken in the higher-layer rings will be replaced by hops in lower-layer rings, resulting in better routing performance. However, with an increased hierarchy depth, each node must maintain more

Table 31.1 Sample nodes in a two-layer HIERAS System with four landmark nodes

Node	Dist-L1	Dist-L2	Dist-L3	Dist-L4	Order
A	25 ms	5 ms	30 ms	100 ms	1012
B	40 ms	18 ms	12 ms	200 ms	1002
C	100 ms	180 ms	5 ms	10 ms	2200
D	160 ms	220 ms	8 ms	20 ms	2200
E	45 ms	10 ms	100 ms	5 ms	1020
F	20 ms	140 ms	50 ms	40 ms	0211

routing information and more P2P rings will be created, so the maintenance overhead will increase. In our simulation, we found that two to three layers are sufficient to achieve good routing performance without introducing significant overhead. Deeper hierarchy results in diminishing returns in routing performance.

31.3 SYSTEM DESIGN

HIERAS is a multilayer DHT-based P2P routing algorithm. Like other DHT algorithms, all the peers in a HIERAS system form a P2P overlay network on the Internet. However, HIERAS contains many other P2P overlay networks (P2P rings) in different layers inside this overall P2P network. Each P2P ring contains a subset of all system peers. These rings are organized in a scheme such that the lower the layer of a ring, the smaller the average link latency between two peers inside it. In HIERAS, a routing procedure is first executed in the lowest-layer P2P ring that the request originator is located in. If the routing procedure cannot be completed within this layer, it moves up and may eventually reach the highest (biggest) P2P ring. A large portion of the routing hops in HIERAS are taken in lower-layer P2P rings, which have relatively smaller network link latencies. Thus, overall lower routing latency is achieved. In this section, we describe the detailed design of a HIERAS algorithm.

31.3.1 Data Structures

In HIERAS, each node or file is given a unique identifier generated by a collision-free algorithm such as SHA-1, similar to other DHT-based systems.

All the current DHT based routing algorithms such as Chord have well-organized data structures and efficient routing schemes. HIERAS focuses on improving the efficiency of current DHT-based routing algorithms by utilizing peers' topological characteristics. Instead of reinventing a new set of algorithms, we chose to build HIERAS on top of an existing DHT routing scheme. In each layer, it uses the underlying routing algorithm to perform routing tasks. In the rest of this chapter, we use Chord as the underlying routing algorithm for its simplicity. However, it is easy to extend the design to other DHT algorithms such as CAN.

HIERAS' routing data structures can be easily created by adding a hierarchical structure on top of the underlying DHT algorithm. For example, in Chord, each node has a finger table with (at most) k entries (if the identifier length is k bit), the ith entry in node N's finger table contains the nodeid and IP address of the first node, S, that succeeds N by at least 2^{i-1} on the name space. It is denoted by $N.finger[i].node$. A peer can be added into a node's finger table if it satisfies the numerical requirements for that entry [17]. This Chord finger table is used as the highest-layer finger table in HIERAS without any modification.

Besides this highest-layer finger table, each node in HIERAS creates $m - 1$ (m is the hierarchy depth) other finger tables in lower-layer P2P rings it belongs to. For a node to generate a lower-layer finger table, only the peers within its corresponding P2P ring can be chosen and put into this finger table. A simple illustration is shown in Table 31.2. The sample system is a two-layer HIERAS system with three landmark nodes, L1, L2, and L3; all the nodeids are created on a 2^8 name space. Table 31.2 shows the finger tables on a sample node with the nodeid 121; its second-layer P2P ring is "012." In the highest-layer finger table, the successor nodes can be chosen from all system peers. For example, the layer-1 successor node in the range [122, 123] is a peer chosen from all system peers; its nodeid is 124 and it belongs to the layer-2 P2P ring "001." Whereas in the second-layer finger table, the layer-2 successor nodes can only be chosen from the peers inside the same P2P ring as node 121, which is "012." For example, the successor node in the range [122, 123] is the node whose nodeid is 143; it also belongs to layer-2 P2P ring "012."

Besides the data structures inherited from the underlying DHT algorithms, in HIERAS, we use a landmark table to maintain landmark nodes information. It simply records the IP addresses of all the landmark nodes. Ring tables are used to maintain information on different P2P rings. Each ring has a ringname that is defined by the landmark order information such as "012." A ringid is generated by using the collision-free algorithm on the ringname. A ring table is stored on the node whose nodeid is the numerically closest to its ringid. It records four nodes inside the ring: the node with the smallest nodeid, the node with the second-smallest nodeid, the node with the largest nodeid, and the node with the second-largest nodeid. The ring table is duplicated on several nodes for fault tolerance. The node that stores the ring table periodically checks the status of these nodes. In case of a node failure, a new routing procedure is performed to add a new node to the table.

31.3.2 Routing Algorithm

HIERAS uses a hierarchical routing mechanism. In an m-layer HIERAS system, a routing procedure has m loops. In the first loop, the routing procedure starts from the lowest P2P ring that the request originator belongs to, using the finger table in this ring. The routing procedure inside this ring continues until the routing message has

Table 31.2 Node 121 ("012") finger tables in a two-layer HIERAS system

Start	Intervals	Layer-1 successor	Layer 2 successor
122	[122,123)	124 ("001")	143 ("012")
123	[123,125)	124 ("001")	143 ("012")
125	[125,129)	131 ("011")	143 ("012")
129	[129,137)	131 ("011")	143 ("012")
137	[137,153)	139 ("022")	143 ("012")
153	[153,185)	158 ("012")	158 ("012")
185	[185,249)	192 ("001")	212 ("012")
249	[249,121)	253 ("012")	253 ("012")

been forwarded to a peer whose nodeid is the numerically closest to the requested key than any other peers in this ring, or until the message reaches the destination node.

If the routing procedure cannot be completed in the current layer, the message is forwarded to the upper layer and the same operation is repeated. The only difference is the use of a different finger table. As the routing procedure continues, more peers are included and the message is forwarded closer to the destination node. In the last loop, the routing procedure is executed on the largest P2P ring that includes all system peers, so the routing procedure definitely will end at the destination node. After the message arrives at the destination node, the node returns the location information of the requested file to the originator and the routing procedure finishes. Predecessor and successor lists can be used to accelerate the process.

Clearly, in HIERAS, the same underlying DHT routing algorithm is used continuously in different layer rings with the corresponding finger tables. Though we use Chord here as an example, it is easy to adopt other algorithms. For example, if we use CAN as the underlying algorithm, the whole coordinate space can be divided multiple times in different layers. We therefore can create multilayer neighbor sets accordingly and use these neighbor sets in different loops during a routing procedure. The pseudocode of HIERAS' routing algorithm is shown in Figure 31.2.

Compared to existing DHT-based algorithms, such a hierarchical scheme has several advantages. First, it preserves the scalability property of the current algo-

```
// n is the start node
// m is the hierarchy depth,
// key is the requested key
// finish, 0: routing not finish, 1: routing finish
n.hieras_routing(key)
   layer=m;
   n'=n;
   finish=0;
   while(finish!=1)
       n'=n'.hieras_underlying_routing(layer,key,finish);
       layer=layer-1;
   return n';

n'.hieras_underlying_routing(layer,key,finish)
   current_finger_table=finger_table[layer];
   n'=n'.underlying_routing_algorithm
       (current_finger_table,key);
   if(n' is the destination)
       // using mechanism in underlying algorithm
       finish=1;
   return n':
```

Figure 31.2   The pseudocode of the HIERAS routing algorithm.

rithms—a routing procedure definitely finishes within O (log N) steps. Although it takes several loops, it has the same trend as the underlying algorithm—the routing message keeps moving toward the destination node by reducing the distance by nearly half each time. Second, it greatly reduces the actual routing latency, since many routing hops now take place in lower-level rings in which nodes are topologically close. Third, by using an existing DHT routing algorithm as the underlying algorithm, we greatly reduce the design complexity of HIERAS and can take advantages of the nice features of the underlying DHT design such as fault tolerance, load balance, and caching schemes.

31.3.3   Node Operations

In HIERAS, when a new node n joins the system, it first sends a message to another node n' in the DHT (just like in other DHT algorithms). Node n' replies with the information of landmark nodes. Node n fills its landmark table, and decides on the distance between itself and the landmark nodes. It then uses the distributed binning scheme to determine the suitable P2P rings it should join.

In the following steps, it must create routing data structures such as finger tables in each layer. First, it creates the highest-layer finger table; the mechanism used in Chord can be introduced without modification. Because node n already knows one nearby node n' in the system, it can learn its fingers by asking node n' to look them up in the whole P2P overlay network. The detailed process is described in [17]. Second, it needs to create finger tables in lower layers. To create the finger table in a specific ring, node n must know at least one node p in that ring. This is done as follows: node n calculates the ringid of this ring and sends a ring table request message to node c, which stores the ring table of this ring using the highest-layer finger table. This particular routing procedure is not a multilayer process. Rather, it is just an ordinary Chord routing procedure. As c receives this message, it sends a response to node n with the stored ring table, then node n knows several nodes in that ring. To create its own finger table of this ring, node n sends a finger table creation request to a node p inside this ring with its own nodeid. Node p modifies its corresponding finger table to coordinate the arrival of the new node and create the finger table for node n using the same mechanism as in the highest layer except that, this time, the routing only occurs within this ring. After p generates the finger table of n, it sends it back to n. Node n is successfully joined to this specific ring. n then compares its nodeid with the nodeids in the ring table, and if it should replace one of them (larger than the second-largest nodeid or smaller than the second-smallest nodeid), it sends a ring table modification message back to node c and c modifies the ring table accordingly. In an m-layer HIERAS system, this procedure will repeat m times. After that, all the finger tables of the newly added node n are created. Node n joins system successfully.

In a P2P system, a node may leave the system or fail silently. As in Chord, the key to handling node failure is maintaining correct successor pointers. HIERAS can use the same strategy except that a node must keep a "successor list" of its r nearest successors in each layer.

31.3.4 Cost Analysis

The routing performance gain in HIERAS comes at the cost of extra overhead. In Chord, each node only needs to maintain one finger table, whereas in HIERAS, each node must maintain multiple finger tables, which increases the system maintenance overhead. HIERAS has multiple "successor lists," whereas Chord only has one. Also, HIERAS needs more operations such as calculating ring information and requesting the ring table when a node joins the system. However, in the case of a small hierarchy depth like 2 or 3, the cost is affordable. The space occupied by multilayer finger tables is only hundreds or thousands of bytes. Normally, the number of nodes in the lower-layer finger table is smaller than that in the higher-layer finger table (as described in Table 31.2). Moreover, the nodes in lower-layer rings are topologically closer to each other, so the cost of keeping the content of their finger tables up to date is much smaller compared to those in higher layers.

31.4 PERFORMANCE EVALUATION

We conducted trace-driven simulation experiments to evaluate HIERAS' routing performance. First, we describe the network models, workload traces, and routing algorithms used in our simulation. Then we present our simulation results.

31.4.1 Simulation Environment

We chose the GT-ITM Transit-Stub (TS model) as the primary network topology model. TS is an internetwork topology model proposed by Zegura et al. [18]. In our simulation, the delays of the intratransit domain links, the stub-transit links, and the intra-stub domain links were set to 100, 20, and 5 ms respectively.[1] Besides TS, Inet [8] and BRITE [10] models were also used for comparison purposes.

In our simulations, we varied the number of system nodes from 1000 to 10,000 in all simulated networks, except in Inet, where the minimal number of nodes is 3000. We used Chord as the underlying DHT algorithm in HIERAS and we compared the routing performance of the original Chord design with HIERAS. We used a two-layer configuration for HIERAS in all simulations except in Section 31.4.5 when evaluating the effects of hierarchy depth.

31.4.2 Routing Costs

The primary goal of HIERAS is to reduce the routing cost in current DHT algorithms. In this simulation, we compare the routing performance of HIERAS with that of Chord. HIERAS uses a four landmark nodes configuration. In each experiment, we simulated 100,000 randomly generated routing requests.

Figure 31.3 shows the comparison of results measured with the traditional metric of "average number of routing hops." Both the HIERAS and Chord algorithms

---

[1]We also used other distributions but our conclusion does not change.

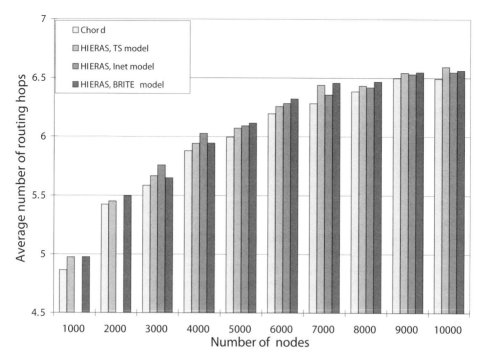

Figure 31.3 HIERAS and chord routing performance comparison (routing hops).

have good scalability: as the network size increases from 1000 nodes to 10,000 nodes, the average number of routing hops only increases around 32%. HIERAS performs slightly worse than Chord, as HIERAS has a slight larger average number of routing hops. However, the difference is very small, between 0.78% to 3.40%.

Figures 31.4, 31.5, and 31.6 compare the average routing latencies of HIERAS and Chord. Although HIERAS has higher average numbers of routing hops than Chord, it has much smaller latencies in all experiments. For the TS model, the average routing latency in HIERAS is only 51.8% of that in Chord. For the Inet and BRITE models, the average latency is 53.4% and 62.5% of that in Chord, respectively. Clearly, the average link latency per hop in HIERAS is much smaller than that in Chord; therefore, the routing cost is greatly recduced. We will show this in the following simulations.

31.4.3 Routing Cost Distribution

To better understand the effects of using hierarchical structures in HIERAS, we analyzed the routing cost distributions shown in Figures 31.7 and 31.8. The data were collected from 100,000 randomly generated routing requests on a 10,000 node TS network.

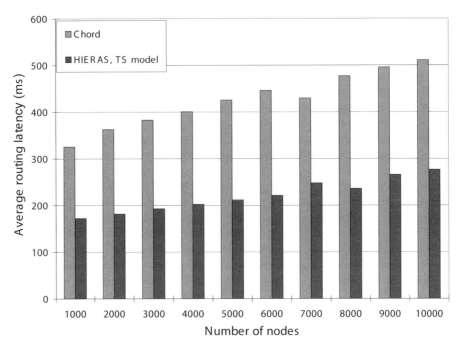

Figure 31.4 HIERAS and chord routing performance comparison (average latency, TS model).

The probability density function (PDF) distribution curves of the average number of routing hops in Chord and HIERAS are nearly coherent. However, as shown in the third distribution curve, in HIERAS, only 1.9 hops per request were taken in the higher layer; the rest of the 71% routing hops were executed on the lower-layer P2P rings.

Figure 31.8 also shows the measured cumulative density function (CDF) distribution curves of the average routing latency in Chord and HIERAS algorithms. The average routing latency in Chord is 511 ms, whereas in HIERAS it is only 276 ms, roughly a 50% improvement.

The performance improvement comes from moving a large number of routing hops from the higher-layer P2P ring to the lower-layer rings. As a result, the number of requests finishing with a small routing latency in HIERAS is much more than that in Chord. In this simulation, the average link delay in the higher-layer ring is 79 ms, whereas in the lower-layer rings it is only 35% of that (28 ms). In HIERAS, although routing hops taken on the lower layer occupy 71% of all routing hops, the network latency in the lower layer only occupies 47% of the overall routing latency. Note that the delay difference ratio between higher and lower levels is only 2.85 in our simulated networks. We can expect an even larger link latency difference to exist between local area networks (LANs) and wide area networks (WANs) in real

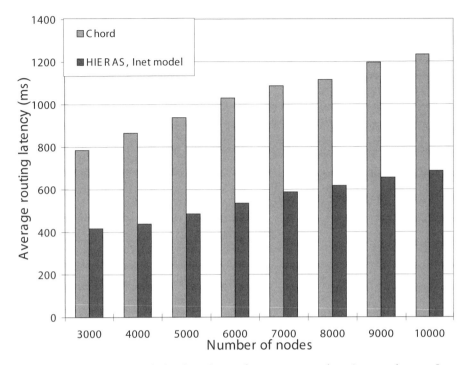

Figure 31.5 HIERAS and chord routing performance comparison (average latency, Inet model).

world. Therefore, we expect that HIERAS can achieve even better performance improvement.

31.4.4 Landmark Nodes Effects

The previous experiments used only four landmark nodes for HIERAS. To study the effects of the number of landmark nodes, we conducted another set of experiments on a 10,000 node TS network using 100,000 randomly generated routing requests. We varied the number of landmark nodes from 2 to 12 and obtained the results shown in Figure 31.9.

The number of landmark nodes has almost no effect on the average number of routing hops. On the other hand, as the number of landmark nodes increases from 2 to 8, the average number of routing hops taken on the lower-layer P2P rings decreases sharply. Further increasing the number of landmark nodes beyond 8 does not result in much improvement. The intuition behind this fact is straightforward. As the number of landmark nodes increases, the number of P2P rings also rises. The average number of peers in each ring decreases; hence, the routing hops taken on the lower layer decrease.

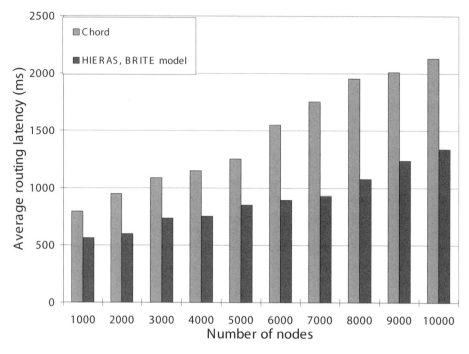

Figure 31.6 HIERAS and chord routing performance comparison (average latency, BRITE model).

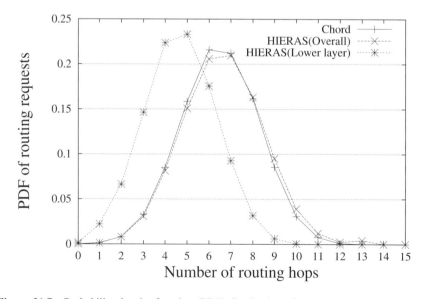

Figure 31.7 Probability density function (PDF) distribution of the number of routing hops.

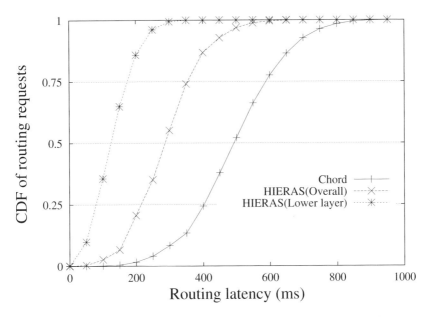

Figure 31.8   Cumulative density function (CDF) distribution of the routing latency.

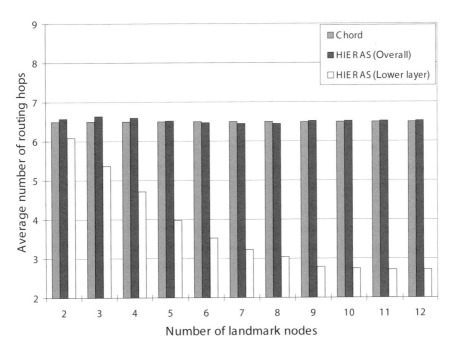

Figure 31.9   Comparing average number of routing hops with different number of land-mark nodes in the HIERAS algorithm, TS model.

Figure 31.10 compares the average routing latencies. If the number of lardmark nodes is too small, say less than four, HIERAS cannot obtain optimal performance since the system cannot generate enough lower-layer P2P rings to group adjacent nodes inside. With an 8-landmark nodes configuration, however, HIERAS achieves the highest performance: the average routing latency is only 43% of that in Chord. Further increasing the number of lardmark nodes does not result in better performance.

31.4.5   Hierarchy Depth Effect

We evaluated the effects of hierarchy depth in this simulation. We changed the hierarchy depth from 2 to 4. The number of nodes in the simulated TS network varied from 5000 to 10,000. Six landmark nodes were used. The results are shown in Figures 31.11 and 31.12. The average number of routing hops in HIERAS increases very slightly as the hierarchy depth increases. Even in a four-layer HIERAS system, the average number of routing hops is only 0.29% to 1.65% larger than in a two-layer system. On the other hand, the average routing latency decreases as the depth increases. For example, increasing the depth from two layer to three layer results in average routing latency reduction of between 9.64% and 16.15%. Further increasing the depth from three layer to four layer results in diminishing returns. For example, the average latency reduction in this case is only between 2.12% and 5.42%, and the latency actually increases for a 7000 node net-

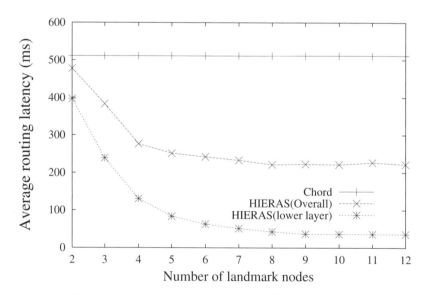

Figure 31.10   Comparing average routing latency with different number of landmark nodes in the HIERAS algorithm, TS model.

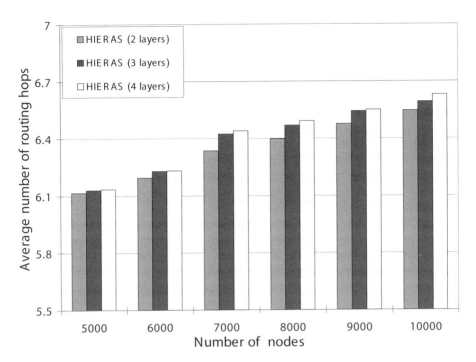

Figure 31.11 HIERAS performance with different hierarchy depths (average number of hops), TS model.

work. The increased depth also brings more system maintenance overhead. Overall, a two- or three-layer HIERAS system is the optimal configuration.

31.5 RELATED WORKS

Chord [5, 17], CAN [13], Pastry [16], and Tapestry [20] are all based on distributed hash tables. Chord and CAN are relatively simple and easy to manage, with little consideration of the network topological characteristics. As a result, they can achieve the minimal average number of routing hops but not the real minimum routing latency. In fact, in most cases, a route chosen by these algorithms is not the shortest path measured by link latency, as discussed in Section 31.1. HIERAS is simpler and easier to manage than Pastry, and it can greatly improve routing efficiency for other DHT-based algorithms such as Chord.

Ratnasamy et al. [12] pointed out that P2P or other large-scale network applications could potentially benefit from some level of knowledge about the relative proximity between its participating nodes. They suggested allocating the topologically adjacent peers with congruent identifiers together, and they applied this idea to CAN with good results. HIERAS has a similar objective and also utilizes nodes' topological properties to improve P2P routing performance. We use their distributed binning

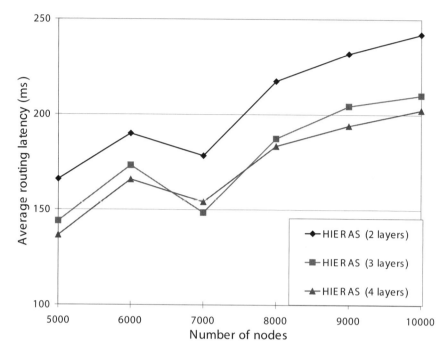

Figure 31.12   HIERAS performance with different hierarchy depths (average latency), TS model.

scheme to create P2P rings. However, HIERAS differs from their work in two aspects. First, the routing procedures in their method still occur in a one-dimensional name space, whereas in HIERAS, routing becomes a multilevel procedure. Second, they created a topologically sensitive CAN network by modifying the identifier generation mechanism, which makes the coordinate space no longer uniformly populated. In HIERAS, we keep the original system architecture and build the HIERAS system on top of it. The underlying network architecture is untouched.

Rhea and Kubiatowicz [14] used probabilistic location and routing schemes to enhance P2P location mechanisms in the case where a replica for the queried data exists close to the client. They used different approaches to reduce the routing overhead of P2P systems. Zhang et al. [19] used a small-world model to improve the performance of Freenet [4], a non-DHT-based P2P system.

Opus [2] chooses m hosts within an N-node peer-to-peer system ($m \ll n$) to increase the system availability, survivability, and performance. It also uses a hierarchical method to solve the scalability problem. However, in Opus, the m selected hosts are more important than other hosts. In HIERAS, each node takes equal responsibility. Also, Opus's algorithm to determine the m-sized subset is more complex.

Harvest Cache [1, 3] is a proxy-cache architecture that creates a hierarchical cache organization and helps in distributing load from hot spots. In Harvest Cache, the roles of clients and servers in each level are strictly separated, so it is still a traditional client/server system. On the contrary, in HIERAS, in every P2P ring, the role and responsibility of each node is the same. By introducing the hierarchical structure into the current DHT-based routing algorithms, HIERAS achieves significant routing performance improvement.

31.6 SUMMARY

We propose a new DHT-based P2P routing algorithm called HIERAS. Besides the biggest P2P ring, which includes all the nodes in the system, HIERAS creates many small P2P rings in different layers by grouping topologically adjacent nodes together. A node belongs to several different layer P2P rings simultaneously. Within each P2P ring, the members have equal responsibilities for workloads. A routing procedure is executed in lower-layer P2P rings before it increases, and might eventually reach the global P2P ring if necessary. By taking a large portion of routing hops in lower-layer P2P rings, which have smaller link latencies between any two nodes inside these rings, HIERAS greatly reduces the P2P routing cost. From the simulation results, we can draw the following conclusions:

1. Hierarchical structure does not conflict with P2P architectures. By combing hierarchy with DHT, an efficient routing algorithm with lower average routing latency is obtained for structured P2P systems.
2. Network topology information can be exploited to improve P2P system performance.
3. Hierarchical structures can improve the routing performance of current DHT routing algorithms that do not take network topology into account.
4. The number of landmark nodes and the hierarchy depth have a great influence on HIERAS efficiency.

ACKNOWLEDGMENTS

This work was supported in part by the National Science Foundation Career Award CCR-9984852, and Ohio Board of Regents. Juan Li provided many suggestions during the writing of this chapter.

REFERENCES

1. C. M. Bowman, P. B. Danzig, D. R. Hardy, U. Manber, and M. F. Schwartz, The Harvest information discovery and access system, *Computer Networks and ISDN Systems,* *28*(1–2), 119–125, 1995.
2. R. Braynard, D. Kostic, A. Rodriguez, J. Chase, and A. Vahdat, Opus: An overlay peer utility service, in *Fifth IEEE Conference on Open Architectures and Network Programming (OPENARCH),* pp. 167–178, June 2002.
3. A. Chankhunthod, P. B. Danzig, C. Neerdaels, M. F. Schwartz, and K. J. Worrell, A hi-

erarchical internet object cache, in *USENIX Annual Technical Conference,* pp. 153–164, 1996.

4. I. Clarke, O. Sandberg, B. Wiley, and T. W. Hong, Freenet: A distributed anonymous information storage and retrieval system, in *Workshop on Design Issues in Anonymity and Unobservability,* Berkeley, CA, pp. 46–66, July 2000.

5. F. Dabek, E. Brunskill, M. F. Kaashoek, D. Karger, R. Morris, I. Stoica, and H. Balakrishnan, Building peer-to-peer systems with Chord, a distributed lookup service, in *8th IEEE Workshop on Hot Topics in Operating Systems (HotOS),* Schloss Elmau, Germany, pp. 195–206, May 2001.

6. Edonkey, http://www.edonkey2000.net/.

7. Gnutella, http://www.gnutella.wego.com.

8. C. Jin, Q. Chen, and S. Jamin, Inet: Internet topology generator, Report CSETR443- 00, Department of EECS, University of Michigan, 2000.

9. KaZaA, http://www.kazaa.com/.

10. A. Medina, A. Lakhina, I. Matta, and J. Byers, Brite: An approach to universal topology generation, in *Proceedings of the International Workshop on Modeling, Analysis and Simulation of Computer and Telecommunications Systems (MASCOTS'01),* Cincinnati, OH, Aug. 2001.

11. Napster, http://www.napster.com.

12. S. Ratnasamy, M. Handley, R. Karp, and S. Shenker, Topologically-aware overlay construction and server selection, in *Proceedings of IEEE INFOCOM'02,* New York, June 2002.

13. S. Ratnasamy, P. Francis, M. Handley, R. Karp, and S. Shenker, A scalable content addressable network, Technical Report, TR-00-010, UC Berkeley, CA, 2000.

14. S. Rhea and J. Kubiatowicz, Probabilistic location and routing, in *Proceedings of IEEE INFOCOM'02,* New York, June 2002.

15. A. Rowstron and P. Druschel, Storage management and caching in PAST, a large-scale, persistent peer-to-peer storage utility, in *Proceedings of the 18th ACM Symposium on Operating Systems Principles (SOSP),* Banff, Alberta, Canada, pp. 188–201, Oct. 2001.

16. A. I. T. Rowstron and P. Druschel, Pastry: Scalable, decentralized object location, and routing for large-scale peer-to-peer systems, in *Proceedings of the 18th IFIP/ACM International Conference on Distributed Systems Platforms (Middleware),* Heidelberg, Germany, pp. 329–350, Nov. 2001.

17. I. Stoica, R. Morris, D. Karger, M. Kaashoek, and H. Balakrishnan, Chord: A scalable peer-to-peer lookup service for internet applications, Technical Report TR-819, MIT, Mar. 2001.

18. E. W. Zegura, K. L. Calvert, and S. Bhattacharjee, How to model an internetwork, in *Proceedings of the IEEE Conference on Computer Communication,* San Francisco, CA, pp. 594–602, Mar. 1996.

19. H. Zhang, A. Goel, and R. Govindan, Using the small-world model to improve freenet performance, in *Proceedings of IEEE INFOCOM'02,* New York, June 2002.

20. B. Zhao, J. Kubiatowicz, and A. Joseph, Tapestry: An infrastructure for faulttolerant widearea location and routing, Technical Report UCB/CSD-01-1141, UC Berkeley, 2001.

## CHAPTER 32

Flexible and Scalable Group Communication Model for Peer-to-Peer Systems

TOMOYA ENOKIDO and MAKOTO TAKIZAWA

32.1 INTRODUCTION

In peer-to-peer (P2P) systems [1], multiple peer processes are cooperating with each other. Multiple peer processes first establish a group and then exchange messages with each other [2, 4, 6, 7, 8, 12, 13, 10, 14, 15, 16]. Group communication supports basic communication mechanisms to realize cooperation of multiple peer processes. There are group protocols that support the causally ordered and atomic delivery of messages [2, 6, 7, 8, 10, 13, 16]. A group protocol is realized by protocol functions: coordination, multicast/broadcast, receipt confirmation, detection and retransmission of messages lost, ordering of messages received, and membership management. There are multiple ways to realize each function, for example, selective retransmitting of messages lost [5] and centralized and distributed coordinations. Here, a class of each function defines a way to implement the function.

The complexity and efficiency of implementation of group protocols depends on what types and quality of service (QoS) are supported by the underlying network. Messages sent by a process may be lost and unexpectedly delayed due to congestion and faults in the network. Thus, QoS parameters like bandwidth, delay time, and loss ratio are dynamically changed, especially in a P2P system. The higher the level of communication function supported, the larger the computation and communication overheads are. Hence, the system has to have classes of functions necessary and sufficient to support required service by making use of the underlying network service.

A communication architecture that supports a group of multiple processes that satisfy application requirements in change of network service is discussed in [16]. However, a protocol cannot be dynamically changed each time QoS supported by the underlying network is changed. In addition, each process in a group has to use

High-Performance Computing: Paradigm and Infrastructure. Edited by L. T. Yang and M. Guo

the same protocol functions. It is not easy to change protocol functions in all the processes since a large number of processes are cooperating and some computers like personal computers and mobile computers are not always working well.

In this chapter, we discuss an autonomic architecture for a group communication protocol that can support QoS required by applications even if QoS supported by the underlying network is changed. A protocol module is composed of classes of protocol functions. Each protocol module is realized in an autonomous agent. An agent autonomously changes classes, that is, implements each group protocol function depending on network QoS monitored. An agent might take different classes of protocol functions from other agents but is consistent with the other agents. We discuss what combinations of protocol function classes are consistent. If a group is too large for each agent to perceive QoS supported by other agents and manage the group membership, the group is decomposed into views making the group scalable. Each agent has a view that is a subset of agents to which the agent can directly send messages. In each view, messages are exchanged by using the view's own consistent protocol functions.

In Section 32.2, we describe a system model. In Section 32.3, we present classes of protocol functions. In Section 32.4, we present an agent-based group protocol. In Section 32.5, we discuss how to change retransmission functions.

32.2 GROUP OF AGENTS

32.2.1 Autonomic Group Agent

A group of multiple application processes $A_1, \ldots, A_n$ ($n \geq 2$) are cooperating by taking usage of group communication service. The group communication service is supported by cooperation of multiple peer autonomous group (AG) agents $p_1, \ldots, p_n$ (Figure 32.1). For simplicity, "agent" means an AG agent. The underlying network supports a pair of agents with basic communication service that is characterized by quality of service (QoS) parameters: delay time (msec), message loss ratio (%), and bandwidth (bps).

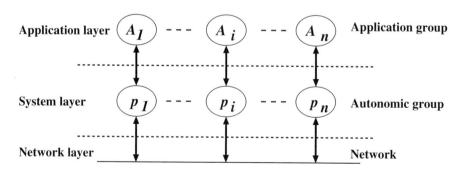

Figure 32.1 System model.

A group protocol is realized in a collection of protocol functions: transmission, confirmation, retransmission, ordering of messages, detection of messages lost, coordination schemes, and membership management. There are multiple ways to implement each protocol function. A class of a protocol function means a way to implement the protocol function. The classes are stored in a protocol class base (CB_i) of each agent p_i (Figure 32.2). Each agent p_i autonomously takes one class for each protocol function from CB_i, which can support an application with necessary and sufficient QoS by making use of QoS supported by the underlying network. Each agent p_i monitors the underlying network and stores QoS information of the underlying network in a QoS base (QB_i) of the agent p_i. If enough QoS cannot be supported or too much QoS is supported for the application, the agent p_i reconstructs a combination of protocol function classes that are consistent with the other agents by selecting a class for each protocol function in the class base CB_i. Here, each agent negotiates with other agents to reach a consensus on which class to take for each protocol function. In this chapter, we discuss how an agent autonomously changes classes of protocol functions with respect to change of QoS monitored.

32.2.2 Views

A group G is composed of multiple agents $p_1, \ldots, p_n$ ($n > 1$). An agent is an autonomous peer process that supports an application process with group communication service by exchanging messages with other agents. In a group G including a larger number of agents, it is not easy for each agent to maintain the membership of the group G. Each agent p_i has a view $V(p_i)$ that is a subset of the group G to which the agent p_i can deliver messages directly or indirectly. For every pair of agents p_i and p_j, p_i is in $V(p_j)$ if p_j is in $V(p_i)$. Each agent p_i maintains the membership of its view $V(p_i)$. A view can be a collection of agents interconnected in a local network.

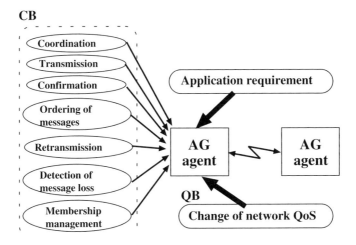

Figure 32.2 Autonomic group protocol.

A pair of different views V_1 and V_2 may include a common gateway agent p_k (Figure 32.3). A collection of gateway agents that are interconnected in a trunk network is also a view V_3. If an agent p_i belongs to only one view, p_i is a leaf agent. An agent p_i that takes a message m from an application process A_i and sends the message m is an original sender agent of the message m. If an agent p_j delivers a message m to an application process, the agent p_j is an original destination agent of the message m. If an agent p_k forwards a message m to another agent in a same view V, p_k is a routing agent. Let $src(m)$ be an original source agent and $dst(m)$ be a set of original destination agents. A local sender and destination agents of a message m are agents that send and receive m in a view, respectively.

A view V including all the agents in a group G is referred to as being complete. A global view is a complete view in a group G. If $V \subset G$, V is partial.

32.3 FUNCTIONS OF GROUP PROTOCOL

We discuss what classes exist for each protocol function. There are protocol functions, coordination of agents, message transmission, receipt confirmation, retransmission, detection of message loss, ordering of messages, and membership management.

There are centralized and distributed classes to coordinate the cooperation of agents in a view. In centralized control, there is one centralized controller in a view V. On the other hand, each agent can make a decision on correct receipt of a message among multiple destination agents, delivery order of messages received, and group membership by itself in the distributed control class.

There are centralized, direct, and indirect classes to multicast a message to multiple agents in a view (Figure 32.4). In centralized transmission, an agent first sends a message to a forwarder agent and then the forwarder agent forwards the message to all the destination agents in a view [Figure 32.4(a)]. The forwarder agent plays a role of a centralized controller. In direct transmission, each agent not only sends a message directly to each destination agent but also receives messages from other sender agents in a view V [Figure 32.4(b)]. In indirect transmission, a message is

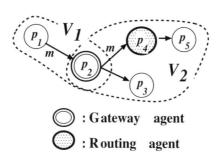

⬭ : Gateway agent

⬭ : Routing agent

Figure 32.3 Group views.

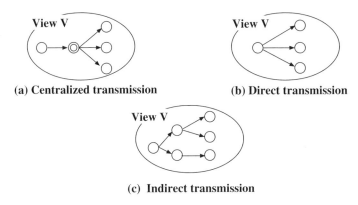

(a) Centralized transmission   (b) Direct transmission

(c) Indirect transmission

Figure 32.4 Transmission classes.

first sent to some agent in a view V. The agent forwards the message to another agent and finally delivers the message to the destination agents in the view V [Figure 32.4(c)]. Tree routing [3] is an example.

There are centralized, direct, indirect, and distributed classes to confirm receipt of a message in a view V. In centralized confirmation of message receipt, every agent sends a receipt confirmation message to one confirmation agent in a view V. After receiving confirmation messages from all the destination agents, the destination agent sends a receipt confirmation to the local sender agent [Figure 32.5(a)]. In the direct confirmation, each destination agent p_i in the view V sends a receipt confirmation of a message m to the local sender agent p_j, which first sends the message m in the view V [Figure 32.5(b)]. In the indirect confirmation, a receipt confirma-

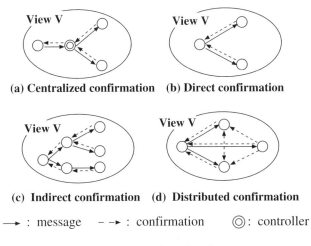

(a) Centralized confirmation   (b) Direct confirmation

(c) Indirect confirmation   (d) Distributed confirmation

⟶ : message   - -▸ : confirmation   ◎ : controller

Figure 32.5 Confirmation classes.

tion of a message m is sent back to a local sender agent p_i in a view V by each agent p_j that has received the message m from the local sender agent p_i [Figure 32.5(c)]. In the distributed confirmation, each agent that has received a message m sends a receipt confirmation of the message m to all the other agents in the same view [10] [Figure 32.5(d)].

A group of multiple agents exchange messages in the network. A message m_1 causally precedes another message m_2 $(m_1 \rightarrow m_2)$ if and only if (iff) a sending event m_1 happens before a sending event m_2 [7]. A message m_1 is causally concurrent with another message m_2 $(m_1 \parallel m_2)$ if neither $m_1 \rightarrow m_2$ nor $m_2 \rightarrow m_1$. A common destination agent of messages m_1 and m_2 is required to deliver m_1 before m_2 if m_1 causally precedes m_2 $(m_1 \rightarrow m_2)$. Real-time clocks with NTP (network time protocol) [9] and logical clocks like the linear clock [7] and vector clock [8] are used to causally deliver messages.

There are sender and destination classes to retransmit messages lost with respect to which agent retransmits the messages (Figure 32.6). Suppose an agent p_j sends a message m to other agents but one destination agent p_i fails to receive the message m. An agent that loses a message is referred to as a faulty agent. In sender retransmission, the local sender agent p_j that first sent the message m in the view V retransmits m to the faulty destination agent p_i. In destination retransmission, one or more than one destination agent in the view V that have safely received the message m forwards m to the agent p_i which fails to receive m [Figure 32.6(b)]. In the distributed confirmation, each agent can know if every other destination agent safely receives a message m. A distination agent p_k can retransmit the message m to a faulty destination agent p_i if p_k had received no confirmation from p_i.

There are centralized and distributed classes for managing the membership. In the centralized class, one membership manager communicates with all the member agents to obtain their states. In the distributed one, each agent obtains the states of the other agents by communicating with other agents.

A centralized system provides centralized coordination, transmission, and confirmation. There is one controller that forwards messages to destination agents and confirms receipt of messages. Most traditional distributed systems like teleconference systems and Amoeba [11] take the centralized approach. A system with distributed coordination, transmission, and centralized confirmation systems is called

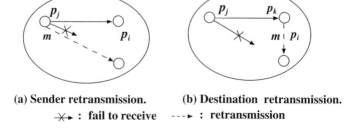

(a) Sender retransmission.   (b) Destination retransmission.

$\times\!\!\!\!\rightarrow$: fail to receive $--\!\!\rightarrow$: retransmission

Figure 32.6   Retransmission classes.

decentralized. ISIS [2] takes the decentralized approach. Takizawa et al. [10] take a fully distributed approach, in which coordination, transmission, and confirmation are distributed.

32.4 AUTONOMIC GROUP PROTOCOL

32.4.1 Local Protocol Instance

In this chapter, we consider protocol, coordination (C), transmission (T), confirmation (CF), and retransmission (R) functions of all the functions discussed. They are the most significant in the design and implement of a group protocol. Let $\mathbf{F}$ be a set of the significant protocol functions, $\mathbf{F} = \{C, T, CF, R\}$. For each protocol function F in the protocol functions set $\mathbf{F}$, let $Cl(F)$ be a set of classes to implement the protocol function F. Table 32.1 shows possible classes for the protocol functions. For example, $Cl(C) = \{C, D\}$ since there are centralized (C) and distributed (D) ways to coordinate agents.

We rewrite the protocol functions set $\mathbf{F}$ to be in a tuple $\langle F_1, F_2, F_3, F_4 \rangle$ of protocol functions where each element F_i shows a protocol function, that is, $\langle F_1, F_2, F_3, F_4 \rangle = \langle C, T, CF, R \rangle$. A tuple $\langle c_1, c_2, c_3, c_4 \rangle \in Cl(F_1) \times Cl(F_2) \times Cl(F_3) \times Cl(F_4)$ is referred to as a protocol instance. Each agent takes a protocol instance $C = \langle c_1, c_2, c_3, c_4 \rangle$, that is, a class c_i is taken from $Cl(F_i)$ for each protocol function F_i ($i = 1, 2, 3, 4$).

As discussed in the preceding section, the destination retransmission class can be taken with the distributed confirmation class but not with the centralized one. A protocol instance $\langle c_1, c_2, c_3, c_4 \rangle$ is consistent iff an agent taking the protocol instance can work with other agents which take the same protocol instance to support group communication service. If an agent takes an inconsistent protocol instance, the agent cannot work. Thus, some protocol instances of the classes are consistent. An agent can take only a consistent protocol instance. A protocol profile is a consistent protocol instance. Table 32.2 summarizes possible protocol profiles. A protocol profile signature "$c_1 c_2 c_3 c_4$" denotes a protocol profile $\langle c_1, c_2, c_3, c_4 \rangle$. For example, a signature $DDDirS$ shows a protocol profile $\langle D, D, Dir, S \rangle$, which is composed of distributed control (Dis), direct transmission (D), direct confirmation (Dir), and sender retransmission (S) classes. If every agent takes the same protocol profile, a group of the agents can support group communication service. Let $PF(1)$, $PF(2)$, $PF(3)$, $PF(4)$, $PF(5)$, $PF(6)$, and $PF(7)$ show the protocol profiles $CCCenS$, $DDDirS$, $DDDisS$, $DDDisD$, $DIIndS$, $DIDisS$, and $DIDisD$, respectively, which are

Table 32.1 Protocol classes

Function f	Protocol classes $Cl(f)$
C	$\{C(\text{centralized}), D(\text{distributed})\}$
CF	$\{Cen(\text{centralized}), Dir(\text{direct}), Ind(\text{indirect}), Dis(\text{distributed})\}$
T	$\{C(\text{centralized}), D(\text{direct}), I(\text{indirect})\}$
R	$\{S(\text{sender}), D(\text{destination})\}$

Table 32.2   Protocol profiles

Control	Transmission	Confirmation	Retransmission	Signature
Centralized	Centralized	Centralized	Sender	CCCenS
Distributed	Direct	Direct	Sender	DDDirS
		Distributed	Sender	DDDisS
			Destination	DDDisD
	Indirect	Direct	Sender	DIDirS
		Indirect	Sender	DIIndS
		Distributed	Sender	DIDisS
			Destination	DIDisD

shown in Table 32.2. Let **P** be a collection of possible protocol profiles $\{PF(i) \mid i = 1, \ldots, 7\}$. Each agent p_i takes one protocol profile in the protocol profiles set **P**.

32.4.2 Global Protocol Instance

Suppose autonomous group (AG) agents $p_1, \ldots, p_n$ are in a view V of a group G. Let C_i be a protocol profile, that is, consistent protocol instance $\langle c_{i1}, \ldots, c_{i4} \rangle$ ($\in$ **P**), which is taken by an agent p_i. A global protocol instance C for a view $V = \{p_1, \ldots, p_n\}$ is a tuple $\langle C_1, \ldots, C_n \rangle$, where each element C_i is a protocol profile which an agent p_i takes ($i = 1, \ldots, n$). Here, each C_i is referred to as a local protocol instance of an agent p_i ($i = 1, \ldots, n$). In traditional protocols, every agent is required to take the same local consistent protocol instance, that is, $C_1 = \cdots = C_n$ ($\in$ **P**). Hence, if some agent p_i would like to exchange a class c_{ik} of a protocol function F_k with another class c'_{ik}, all the agents have to be synchronized to reach a consensus on a new protocol instance. If a consensus is reached, every agent exchanges the class c_{ik} with c'_{ik} and then the agents cooperate to support group communication service. However, it takes time to reach a consensus and change protocol profiles in every agent. A global protocol instance $C = \langle C_1, \ldots, C_n \rangle$ is complete if $C_1 = \cdots = C_n$. If $C_i \neq C_j$ for some pair of agents p_i and p_j, C is incomplete. C is consistent if a collection of agents of which each agent p_k takes a protocol profile C_k ($k = 1, \ldots, n$) can support group communication service. It is trivial that a complete global protocol instance is consistent from the definition.

We discuss which global protocol instances are consistent. A global protocol instance satisfying the following property is not consistent.

Property. A global protocol instance $C = \langle C_1, \ldots, C_n \rangle$ of a view V is not consistent if V includes more than three agents and C satisfies one of the following conditions:

1. At least one agent in V takes the protocol profile $CCCenS$ and the global protocol instance C is not complete.

2. At least one agent takes an indirect transmission class in V and at least one other agent takes a direct confirmation class in V.

In this chapter, we discuss a group protocol in which agents $p_1, \ldots, p_n$ in a view can take an incomplete but consistent global protocol instance $C = \langle C_1, \ldots, C_n \rangle$. First, suppose that a global protocol instance $C = \langle C_1, \ldots, C_m \rangle$ is complete and some agent p_i exchanges a local protocol instance C_i with another one C_i'. We discuss whether or not a global protocol instance $\langle C_1, \ldots, C_{i-1}, C_i', C_{i+1}, \ldots, C_n \rangle$ is consistent, that is, all the agents $p_1, \ldots, p_n$ can support group communication service through the cooperation even if $C_i' \neq C_j$ for some agent p_j.

We introduce a notation α_I for $I \in 2^{\{1, \ldots, 7\}}$ to show a global protocol instance. First, let α_i indicate a global protocol profile in which all the agents take the same local protocol profile $PF(i)$ for $i = 1, \ldots, 7$. For example, α_2 shows that all the agents take $PF(2) = DDDirS$. For $I = i_1 \cdots i_l$ ($i_h < i_k$ ($h < k$), $l \leq 7$), α_I shows a global protocol instance in which each agent takes one of the local protocol profiles $PF(i_1), \ldots, PF(i_l)$ and each protocol profile $PF(i_k)$ is taken by at least one agent ($k = 1, \ldots, l$). For example, α_{23} means a global protocol instance in which every agent takes a protocol profile $PF(2) = DDDirS$ or $PF(3) = DDDisS$ and each of $PF(2)$ and $PF(3)$ is taken by at least one agent. Suppose every agent takes a global protocol instance α_I. Here, if an agent p_k changes a protocol profile to another protocol profile $PF(i)$ where $i \notin I$, a global protocol instance is changed to α_{Ii}.

Definition. A global protocol instance α_I can be transitted to another global protocol instance α_J ($\alpha_I \rightarrow \alpha_J$) iff α_I and α_J are consistent and one of the following conditions hold:

1. $I = J$.
2. If $J = Ii$, an agent taking $PF(k)$, where $k \in I$ autonomously takes $PF(i)$ ($i \neq k$) and another agent still takes $PF(k)$.
3. If $I = Jj$, only one agent takes $PF(j)$ in α_I and takes $PF(k)$ where $k \in I$.
4. For some global protocol instance α_K, $\alpha_I \rightarrow \alpha_K$, and $\alpha_K \rightarrow \alpha_J$.
5. $\alpha_J \rightarrow \alpha_I$.

The transition relation "$\rightarrow$" among global protocol instances is reflexive, symmetric, and transitive. Figure 32.7 shows a Hasse diagram in which a node shows a consistent global protocol instance and a directed edge from a node α_I to another α_J indicates a transition relation "$\alpha_I \rightarrow \alpha_J$". For example, $\alpha_2 \rightarrow \alpha_{24}$ since an agent can autonomously change a local protocol profile $PF(2) = DDDirS$ to $PF(4) = DDDisD$. A global protocol instance α_1 means that every agent takes the protocol profile $PF(1) = CCCenS$. α_1 cannot be transitted according to the property. α_{234} shows that each agent takes $PF(2) = DDDirS$, $PF(3) = DDDisS$, and $PF(4) = DDDisD$, which is direct transmission. $PF(5)$, $PF(6)$, and $PF(7)$ are using indirect transmission. Thus, α_{234} cannot be transitted.

In change of network QoS and application requirement, each agent autonomously changes the protocol profile. For example, suppose an agent p_3 belongs to a pair of views V_1 and V_2 (Figure 32.8). In the view V_1 where all of the agents take $PF(2)$

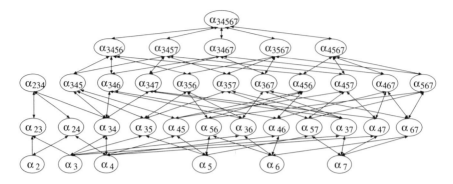

Figure 32.7 Hasse diagram.

= *DDDirS*, an agent p_1 sends a message m to all the other agents. On receipt of the message m, an agent p_3 with the protocol profile *DDDirS* forwards the message m to the other agents p_5 and p_6, which belong to another view V_2 with $PF(4)$ = *DDDisD*. Here, the agent p_3 can receive the receipt confirmation of the message m from a pair of agents p_5 and p_6 in the view V_2. In addition, the agent p_3 sends back the receipt confirmation of the message m to the original sender agent p_1. Here, the original sender agent p_1 can receive the receipt confirmation from all the destination agents in the view V_1. Therefore, the agent p_3 does not need to change the protocol profile since the agent p_3 can forward the message m to another agent in the view V_2 by using the current protocol profile $PF(2)$.

32.5   RETRANSMISSION

We discuss how an agent can autonomously change the retransmission classes in a group as an example.

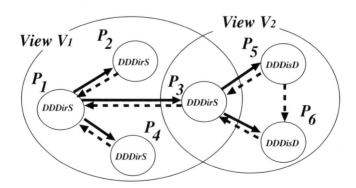

Figure 32.8   Change of profiles.

32.5.1 Cost Model

Suppose there are three agents p_s, p_t, and p_u in a view V. An agent p_s sends a message m to a pair of agents p_t and p_u. Then, p_t receives m while p_u fails to receive m. Let d_{st} be delay time between agents p_s and p_t (msec), f_{st} show the probability that a message is lost, and b_{st} indicate bandwidth [bps]. Let $|m|$ show the size of a message m (bit).

First, let us consider the sender retransmission. It takes $(2d_{su}+ |m|/b_{su})$ (msec) to detect that a message m is lost after an agent p_s sends the message m. Then, p_s retransmits m to p_u. Here, the message m may be lost again. The expected time ST_{su} and number SN_{su} of messages to be transmitted to deliver a message m to a faulty destination p_u are given as $ST_{su} = (2d_{su} + |m|/b_{su})/(1 - f_{su})$ and $SN_{su} = 1/(1 - f_{su})$.

In the destination retransmission, some destination agent p_t forwards the message m to p_u (Figure 32.9). The expected time DT_{ut} and number DN_{su} of messages to be transmitted to deliver a message m to p_u are given as follows:

1. $DT_{su} = (d_{su} + |m|/b_{su} + d_{ut}) + (2d_{ut} + |m|/b_{ut})/(1 - f_{ut})$ if $d_{st} \leq d_{su} + d_{ut}$, $(d_{st} + |m|/b_{st}) + (2d_{ut} + |m|/b_{ut})/(1 - f_{ut})$ otherwise.
2. $DN_{su} = 1 + 1/(1 - f_{ut})$.

If $ST_{su} > DT_{su}$, the destination agent p_t can forward the message m to the faulty agent p_u because the message m can be delivered earlier.

An agent p_t obtains delay time d_{ut}, bandwidth b_{ut}, and message loss probability f_{ut} for each agent p_u in the QoS base (QB_t) by periodically exchanging QoS information messages with all the agents in a view. If the agent p_t receives QoS information b_{su}, d_{su}, and f_{su} for p_u from p_s, $Q_{su} := \langle b_{su}, d_{su}, f_{su} \rangle$ in QB_t for $u = 1, \ldots, n$.

35.5.2 Change of Retransmission Class

Suppose an agent p_s sends a message m and every agent p_t takes the sender retransmission class, local protocol profile $C_t = \langle \cdots, S \rangle$. As shown in Figure 32.9, an agent p_u fails to receive the message m. According to the change of QoS supported by the underlying network, the sender agent p_s makes a decision to exchange the retransmission class with the destination one, say, an agent p_t forwards m to p_u. However, p_t still takes the sender retransmission. Here, no agent forwards m to p_u.

Next, suppose all agents are taking the destination retransmission class. Here, QoS supported by the network is changed and an agent p_t decides to take the sender retransmission class. However, no agent forwards a message m to p_u since the sender p_s still takes the destination retransmission class. In order to prevent these silent situations, we use the following protocol:

1. A sender agent p_s sends a message m to all the destination agents. Every destination agent sends receipt confirmation not only to the sender agent p_s but also to the other destination agents (Figure 32.9).

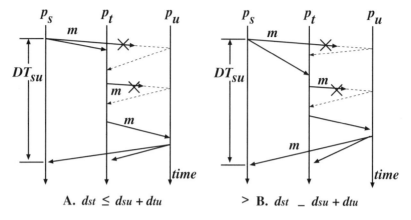

Figure 32.9   Destination retransmission.

2. If an agent p_t detects that a destination p_u has not received m, the agent p_t selects a retransmission class that p_t considers to be best based on the QoS information Q.

   2.1   If p_t is a destination agent and changes a retransmission class, p_t forwards m to p_u and sends *Retx* message to the sender p_s.

   2.2   If p_t is a sender of a message m and takes the sender retransmission class, p_t retransmits m to p_u. If p_t takes a destination retransmission class, p_t waits for *Retx* message from a destination. If p_t does not receive *Retx*, p_t retransmits m to p_u.

In the protocol, it is straightforward for the following property to hold:

Theorem. At least one agent forwards a message m to an agent that fails to receive the message m in the protocol.

32.5.3   Evaluation

We evaluate the autonomic group protocol (AGP) in terms of delivery time of a lost message. We make the following assumptions in this evaluation.

1. $d_{st} = d_{ts}$ for every pair of p_s and p_t.
2. The protocol processing time of every process is the same.
3. No confirmation message is lost.

Let us consider a view V of three agents p_s, p_t, and p_u in which each agent takes a profile *DDDisS*, that is, distributed control, direct transmission, distributed confirmation, and sender retransmission. Here, suppose that an agent p_s sends a message m

to a pair of agents p_t and p_u. Then, p_t receives m but p_u fails to receive m. After the sender p_s and destination p_t detect that p_u fails to receive m, p_s and p_t autonomously select the retransmission class based on the QoS information in the QoS base QB_t. Here, we evaluate time to deliver a message m to a faulty agent p_u. In the view V, we assume $b_{st} = b_{su} = b_{ut} = 10$ (Mbps), $f_{st} = f_{su}$, and $f_{ut} = 0$ (%). Figure 32.10 shows an agent graph for the new V, where each node denotes an agent and each edge shows a communication channel between agents. The labels indicate delay time.

First, we consider a case $d_{su} \geq d_{st} + d_{ut}$. There are further cases: $d_{st} = d_{ut}$ (Figure 32.10 A.1), $d_{st} > d_{ut}$ (Figure 32.10 A.2), and $d_{st} < d_{ut}$ (Figure 32.10 A.3). Figure 32.11 shows the expected time DT_{ut} for three cases. In Figure 32.11 the horizontal axis shows a message loss probability of f_{su} and f_{ut}. For case of Figure 32.10 A.2, $DT_{su} < ST_{su}$. For case of Figure 32.10 A.1, $DT_{su} < ST_{su}$ if $f_{su} > 15\%$ and $f_{ut} > 15\%$. For the case of Figure 32.10 A.3, $DT_{su} < ST_{su}$ if $f_{su} > 50\%$ and $f_{ut} > 50\%$.

Next, we consider a case $d_{su} \leq d_{st} + d_{ut}$. There are the following cases (Figure 32.10):

a. $d_{st} > d_{su}$ and $d_{st} > d_{ut}$: $d_{su} = d_{ut}$ (B.1), $d_{su} > d_{ut}$ (B.2), and $d_{su} < d_{ut}$ (B.3).
b. $d_{ut} > d_{su}$ and $d_{ut} > d_{st}$: $d_{su} = d_{st}$ (C.1), $d_{su} > d_{st}$ (C.2), and $d_{su} < d_{st}$ (C.3).

The expected time DT_{ut} (Figure 32.10 B and 32.10 C) is shown for these six cases in Figures 32.12 and 32.13. For Figure 32.10 B.1 and B.3, $DT_{su} > ST_{su}$. For

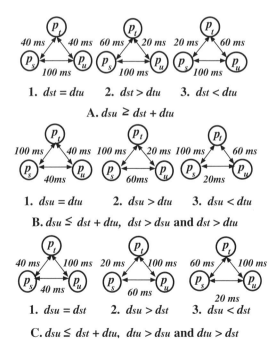

Figure 32.10 AG agent graph.

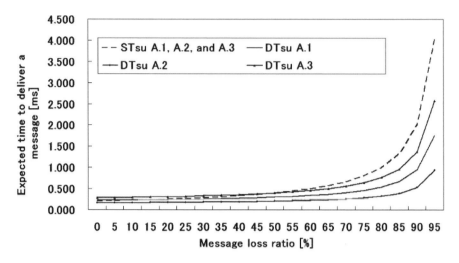

Figure 32.11 $d_{su} \geq d_{st} + d_{ut}$.

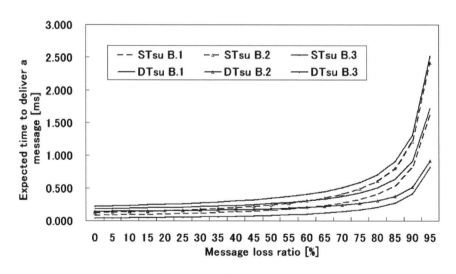

Figure 32.12 $d_{su} \leq d_{st} + d_{ut}$, $d_{st} > d_{su}$, and $d_{st} > d_{ut}$.

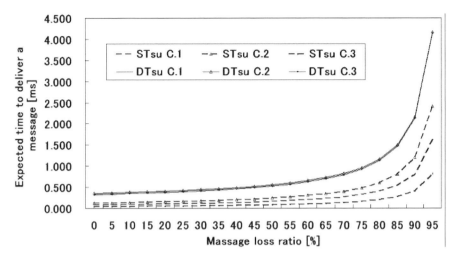

Figure 32.13 $d_{su} \leq d_{st} + d_{ut}$, $d_{ut} > d_{su}$, and $d_{ut} > d_{st}$.

Figure 32.10 B.2, $DT_{su} < ST_{su}$ if $f_{su} > 20\%$ and $f_{ut} > 20\%$. For Figure 32.10 C, $DT_{su} > ST_{su}$.

32.6 CONCLUDING REMARKS

In this chapter, we discussed an agent-based protocol to support distributed applications with autonomic group service in change of network and application QoS. We made clear what classes of functions are to be realized in group communication protocols. Every agent autonomously changes a class of each protocol function, which may not be the same as but are consistent with the other agents in a group. We discussed how to support applications with the autonomic group service by changing retransmission classes as an example. We showed which retransmission class can be adopted for types of network configuration. We also discussed other aspects of scalable groups and how to synchronize different types of clocks.

REFERENCES

1. P. E. Agre, P2P and the promise of internet equality, *Communication of the ACM, 46*(2), 39–42, 2003.

2. K. Birman, A. Schiper, and P. Stephenson, Lightweight causal and atomic group multicast, *ACM Transactions on Computer Systems, 9*(3), 272–290, 1991.

3. S. Deering, Host groups: A multicast extension to the internet protocol, *RFC 966,* 1985.

4. T. Enokido and M. Takizawa, Autonomic group communication protocol, *Journal of Interconnection Networks (JOIN), 4*(3), 309–328, 2003.

5. M. F. Kaashoek, and A. S. Tanenbaum, An evaluation of the amoeba group communication system, in *Proceedings of IEEE the 16th International Conference on Distributed Computing Systems (ICDCS16)*, pp. 436–447, 1996.

6. S. Kawanami, T. Enokido, and M. Takizawa, Heterogeneous groups to causally ordered delivery, in *Proceedings of the 6th ICDCS International Workshop on Multimedia Network Systems and Applications (MNSA'2004)*, pp. 70–75, 2004.

7. L. Lamport, Time, clocks, and the ordering of events in a distributed system, *CACM, 21*(7), 558–565, 1978.

8. F. Mattern, Virtual time and global states of distributed systems, *Parallel and Distributed Algorithms*, pp. 215–226, 1989.

9. D. L. Mills, Network time protocol, *RFC 1305*, 1992.

10. A. Nakamura and M. Takizawa, Reliable broadcast protocol for selectively ordering PDUs, in *Proceedings of IEEE the 11th InternationalConference on Distributed Computing Systems (ICDCS11)*, pp. 239–246, 1991.

11. C. Steketee, W. P. Zhu, and P. Moseley, Implementation of process migration in amoeba, in *Proceedings of IEEE the 14th International Conference on Distributed Computing Systems (ICDCS14)*, pp. 194–201, 1994.

12. K. Taguchi and M. Takizawa, Twolayered protocol for a largescale group of processes, *Journal of Information Science and Engineering (JISE), 19*(3), 451–465, 2003.

13. K. Taguchi T. Enokido and M. Takizawa, Hierarchical protocol for broadcasttype group communication, in *Proceedings of the ICPP Workshop on Applications of Ad Hoc Networks (AANET 2003)*, pp. 21–28, 2003.

14. T. Tojo T. Enokido and M. Takizawa, Notification-based qos control protocol for group communication, *Journal of Interconnection Networks (JOIN), 4*(2), 211–225, 2003.

15. T. Tojo T. Enokido and M. Takizawa, Notification-based qos control protocol for multimedia group, in *Proceedings of IEEE the 24th International Conference on Distributed Computing Systems (ICDCS2004)*, pp. 644–651, 2004.

16. R. van Renesse, K. P. Birman, and S. Maffeis, Horus: A flexible group communication system, *CACM, 39*(4), 76–83, 1996.

## CHAPTER 33

Study of Cache-Enhanced, Dynamic, Movement-Based Location-Management Schemes for 3G Cellular Networks

KRISHNA PRIYA PATURY, YI PAN, XIAOLA LIN, YANG XIAO, and JIE LI

Mobility management is important for both 2G personal communications services (PCS) networks and 3G cellular networks. This research outlined here aims at implementing the gateway location register (GLR) concept in 3G cellular networks by employing a caching location strategy at the location registers for certain classes of users meeting certain call and mobility criteria. Results obtained without any cache are compared with those from the three cases in which a cache is applied only at the GLR, only at the visitor location register (VLR), and at both. Our study indicates when a cache is preferred in 3G cellular networks.

33.1 INTRODUCTION

Location management [1–8] keeps track of the mobile terminals (MTs) moving from one place to another, and consists of two major operations: location update and paging. Location update is a process that keeps track of locations of MTs that are not engaged in conversation. Paging is a search process by which the system searches for the MT by sending polling signals to cells in the paging area (PA), which includes one or more cells.

In cellular networks, the service area is divided into location areas (LAs), Each LA consists of many cells. Each cell has a base station and multiple MTs. Groups of several such cells are connected to a mobile switching center (MSC). MSCs are connected with PSTN. In 2G cellular networks, the two-tier mobility databases, home location register (HLR) and visitor location register (VLR), are utilized to support location management.

Location management schemes can be broadly classified into static or dynamic location schemes. In a static scheme, the size of a PA is fixed and is equal to the

LA. In dynamic location management, the size of a PA is determined dynamically according to the changes in mobility and calling patterns of mobile terminals. There are basically three kinds of dynamic schemes: time-based [1], distance-based [2], and movement-based [3-6], of which movement-based location management is the most practical approach [3]. A cache location strategy was proposed for the 2G cellular networks in [7].

The gateway location register (GLR) within the 3G cellular UMTS core network was proposed in [8], as well as in some related work [5–6, 9]. The GLR is the node between the VLR and/or SGSN and the HLR. It handles location management of roaming MTs in a visited network without involving the HLR in every change of LAs. Therefore, the signaling traffic between the visited and home mobile systems will be reduced and the location updating and handling of user profile data across network boundaries is optimized. The GLR is located in the visited network. It stores the roamer's information and handles location management within the network. Interface between the HLR and the GLR is the same as that between the HLR and VLR, as the presence of the GLR is invisible from the home network.

In this chapter, we propose a caching location strategy for 3G cellular networks when the GLR is deployed. Results obtained without any cache are compared with those from the three cases when a cache is applied only at the GLR, only at the VLR, and at both. Our study indicates when a cache is preferred in 3G cellular networks.

33.2 LOCATION MANAGEMENT WITH AND WITHOUT CACHE

Based on our papers [5–6], we first introduce location management for 3G cellular networks in Section 33.1. Then we introduce a cache scheme based on [7] in Section 33.2.

33.2.1 Movement-based Location Management in 3G Cellular Networks

Figure 33.1 shows the simplified network architecture for 3G cellular networks with GLR deployment at the edge of the visited networks. A GLR contains roaming MTs' profile and location information. At the first location update procedure under the GLR, the subscriber profile information is downloaded from the HLR to the GLR. Figure 33.1 shows the basic architecture as far as the location management databases are concerned in this chapter. The entire service area (SA) would be handled by the HLR with the help of a number of GLRs that, in turn, have a number of VLRs under them. Each VLR is under the control of an MSC, which would be covering the area of a number of base stations (BSs), each of which services a geographically area called a cell.

The GLR handles update location messages from VLRs. This helps in the minimization of the costly internetwork signaling for location management, as the entire procedure is invisible from the home network. The profile information is kept in the GLR until a cancel location message is received from the HLR. The relationship be-

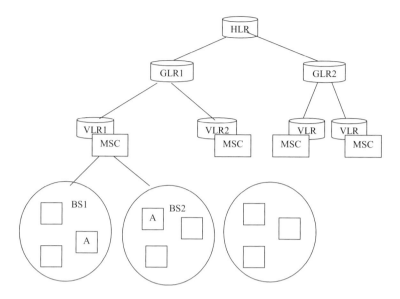

Figure 33.1   The structure of the 3G cellular network.

tween the GLR and the HLR in 3G cellular networks is the same as that between the VLR and the HLR in the 2G wireless cellular systems (such as GSM) in terms of signaling traffic for location management.

There are three kinds of location updates in 3G cellular networks: HLR location updates, GLR location updates, and VLR location updates. All of these, together with paging procedures, will incur a significant amount of cost such as wireless bandwidth and processing power at the mobile terminals, and the BSs, and in mobility databases.

The service area is divided into gateway location areas (G-LAs), with each G-LA consisting of a number of LA's, which, in turn, are groups of cells. A paging area (PA) includes a number of cells within an LA, and its size is variable. To make things simple, we assume that the cellular network is a homogeneous hexagonal cell configuration, in which all the cells have the same shape (hexagonal) and the same size. The ring concept for the movement-based location-management scheme is that the cell that is under consideration is treated as the center cell (Ring-0) and the Ring-1 includes all six cells around the center cell, and so on. Hence it is easy to see that Ring-r has six cells and that Ring-0 has only one cell, where $r = 0, 1, 2 \ldots$.

An HLR location update is performed when an MT crosses the boundary of a G-LA. A GLR location update, on the other hand, is performed when an MT crosses the boundary of an LA. A VLR location update is performed when an MT completes d movements between cells, where d is the movement threshold. A HLR location update involves the updating of both the GLR and the VLR, whereas a GLR location update involves only the VLR update. It is important to note that a PA is the area within the LA, where the last VLR location update is performed and the circle area with the diameter $d - 1$ and the center where the last VLR location update happens.

33.2.2   Per-User Caching

A per-user caching technique for 2G cellular networks is discussed in [7]. The per-user caching scheme reduces the network signaling and database processing loads of the basic strategies in exchange for increased CPU processing and memory costs. The call-to-mobility ratio (CMR) of a user is defined as the average number of calls to a user per unit time, divided by the average number of times the user changes registration areas per unit time [7]. Local CMR (LCMR) is defined as the average number of calls to a user from a given originating switch per unit time, divided by the average number of times the user changes registration areas per unit time [7]. For each user, the amount of savings due to caching is a function of the probability that the cached pointer correctly points to the user's location, and increases with the user's LCMR [7]. The caching threshold is parameterized with respect to costs of traversing signaling network elements and network databases and can be used as a guide to select the subset of users to whom caching should be applied.

A related issue is that of cache size and management. In practice it is likely that the monetary cost of deploying a cache may limit its size. In that case, cache entries may not be maintained for some users; selecting these users carefully is important to maximize the benefits of caching. The cache-hit-ratio threshold cannot necessarily be used to determine which users have cache entries, since it may be useful to maintain cache entries for some users even though their hit ratios have temporarily fallen below the threshold. A simple policy that has been found to be effective in computer systems is the least recently used (LRU) policy, in which cache entries that have been least recently used are discarded.

33.3   THE CACHE-ENHANCED LOCATION MANAGEMENT SCHEME

With the existing location management method, the access to the HLR and the associated volume of signaling has been increasing explosively with the increase in the number of roaming users. This is because the inter-SA cost is much higher than the intra-SA cost. For example, if an MT locates far away from its HLR, the inter-SA will increase a lot with existing location management schemes. In 3G networks, Gateway location register (GLR) is introduced to solve the roaming problem. Though some argue that most current PCS networks are mostly 2G cellular networks, the focus of this chapter is to improvise the existing 3G strategy for a particular set of users, as the future of all wireless networks is definitely 3G.

Inspired by Ravi Jain's work on the caching strategy to reduce the network impacts of PCS and cellular networks [7], an improved movement-based location management scheme is introduced for 3G cellular networks.

Based on the experimental results obtained in [7], it is observed that under very conservative assumptions, caching requires a relatively high LCMR (25–50 for every 1000 calls) to be beneficial. But, in practice, they could be significantly lowered (say LCMR > 5). In this chapter, we run a simulation for a case in which caching is applied only for users who have LCMR $\geq$ 5 by keeping track of the number of times an MT gets a call from the same caller. All these results are then compared and tabulated to get the percentage benefit of caching over the rest.

Four basic schemes/cases will be considered here and dealt with in detail: the standard 3G without any additional cache, with a cache at the VLR, with a cache at the GLR, and with cache at both.

33.3.1 Caching Schemes

33.3.1.1 At the VLR This scheme is similar to the standard 3G scheme without cache. The only difference is that an additional cache is placed at the VLR to keep track of those MTs that are very frequently called by the users under that particular VLR. It is quite a common practice that a certain set of users keeps calling a particular set of users more frequently than others. It is reasonable to keep a cache at the local database of that MT so that the next time a call needs to be made, the cache is checked for the address of the called MT. If there is a cache hit, a lot cost is saved, as the lengthy procedure of going through the call delivery process need not be followed.

33.3.1.2 At the GLR This scheme is similar to the one described above except that the cache is placed at the GLR instead of at the VLR. In most cases, it is beneficial to place a cache at the GLR instead of the VLR for a number of reasons, though the difference might not be too much depending on the calling patterns of the users. One situation in which this is true is as follows. A calls X a number of times. X is under GLR2, say, and A under GLR1, VLR1. Since A frequently calls X, an entry is made in the cache at the GLR1. Now suppose a user C under VLR2, GLR1 needs to make a call to X. He/she would have to go through the entire procedure if the cache were at the VLR since an entry for X has not yet been made in VLR2. However if the cache were at the GLR, C could have had a cache hit. Also if A had moved to VLR2 during the process, it would have a cache miss, as the entry is not available in VLR2 for X.

33.3.1.3 At Both the VLR and the GLR Keeping all this in mind, it might seem a better idea to keep a cache at both the VLR and the GLR to get the maximum benefit. The question, however, would be if the extra memory would be worth the gain in performance. The answer for this could be observed from the experimental results provided in Section 33.5.

33.3.2 The Location Update Scheme in Detail

The MT detects that it has entered a new RA and sends a location update message to the MSC through the base station. In this chapter, we consider a one-to-one relation between the VLR and MSC, with each MSC controlling a number of base stations. Hence, every MSC controls one VLR area and has a number of BSs. A location update occurs either if the MT crosses "*d*" cell boundaries since the last update, where *d* is the threshold value, or the MT moves out current LA. There are two basic possibilities while performing location updates in 3G.

Case 1: When an MT moves from LA to LA (as shown in Figure 33.2)

1. (This first step is deleted according to Fig. 33.1.) If the MT moves into a new area (LA) covered by the MSC, the MSC updates its associated VLR, indicating that the MT is residing in its area.
2. The MSC sends a location registration message to the GLR (assuming that the information has already been dumped into this GLR when it moved under this GLR).
3. The GLR sends a registration cancellation message to the old MSC.
4. The old MSC deletes the record of the MT in its associated VLR and sends a cancellation acknowledgement message to the GLR.
5. The GLR updates its record indicating the current serving MSC of the MT and sends a registration acknowledgement message to the new MSC.

Case 2: When an MT moves from G-LA to G-LA (as shown in Figure 33.3)

1. When the MT moves into a new area covered by the MSC, the MSC updates its associated VLR, indicating that the MT is residing in its area.
2. The MSC sends a location registration message to the new GLR.
3. When the GLR detects that the MT is not yet registered under it, it asks the HLR to insert the MT's subscription information.

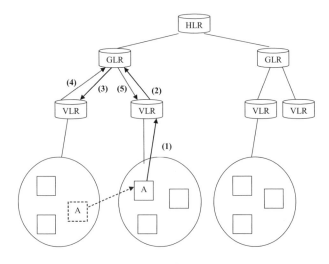

Figure 33.2   The flow of control for the location update case 1.

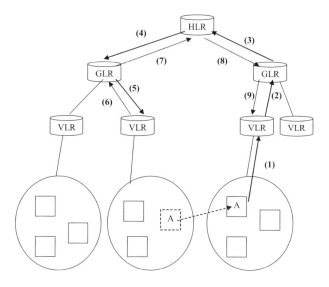

Figure 33.3 The flow of control for the location update case 2.

4. The HLR sends a registration cancellation message to the old GLR.
5. The old GLR sends a registration cancellation message to the old MSC.
6. The old MSC deletes the record of the MT in its associated VLR and sends a cancellation acknowledgement message to the old GLR.
7. The old GLR deletes the record of the MT and sends a cancellation acknowledgement message to the HLR.
8. The HLR then inserts all the subscription information of the MT into the new GLR.
9. The new GLR updates its record indicating the current serving MSC of the MT and sends a registration acknowledgement message to the new MSC.

33.3.3 Paging Scheme

The shortest distance first (SDF) partitioning scheme with paging delay is used as our paging strategy. When a location request arrives, the network pages the cells within a distance d from the last registered cell, where d is the threshold value.

Depending on the maximum paging delay allowed and movement threshold value, the paging area of the MT is divided into subareas. The network will search from inside to outside. For example, if we use hexagonal configuration, maximum paging delay equals three and movement threshold value also equals three.

The following are the cases considered in call delivery.

Case 1. As soon as an MT initiates a call, the base station forwards the call initiation signal to the MSC and the MSC searches for the called MT's id within its VLR (paging is performed here).

If there is a cache hit (the called MT is within the same VLR as the calling MT), then the MSC determines the cell location of the called MT and assign it a temporary location directory number (TLDN). A direct connection can then be made. If there is no cache hit, the MSC searches to see if the mobile id exists in the cache in the VLR.

If there is an entry for the callee, a direct connection using the TLDN is attempted. If a connection could not be made (which means it is a cache miss and the callee had moved), then the location information is retrieved using the rest of the procedure (as in Cases 2 and 3) and the cache entry is updated at the end of both the VLR and the GLR.

If there is no entry for the callee, the location information is retrieved using the rest of the procedure (as in Cases 2 and 3). The callee threshold is checked with the calling MT and if it meets/crosses the threshold value, an entry is made for it in the cache and at its GLR as well.

Case 2. If the called MT is within the same GLR as the calling MT, the location request is forwarded to the GLR. The GLR then pages for the mobile id within its G-LA.

If it is found that it requests the called MSC for its location, the called MSC then assigns a TLDN to the called MT and forwards this to the GLR. The GLR then forwards this TLDN to the calling MSC. The connection is then established between the two terminals.

If no request is made, the GLR searches to see if the mobile id exists in the cache in the GLR. If there is an entry for the callee, a direct connection using the TLDN is attempted. If a connection could not be made (which means it is a cache miss and the callee had moved), then the location information is retrieved using the rest of the procedure (as in Case 3) and the cache entry is updated at the end of the GLR.

Alternatively, the location information is retrieved using the rest of the procedure (as in Case 3). The callee threshold is checked with the calling MT and if it meets/crosses the threshold value, an entry is made for it in the cache at the GLR if it already does not have one.

Case 3. When both the MTs are within the same the HLR (but different GLRs) or even different HLRs, the procedure is same as when both the MT's are within the same the HLR. The location request is routed to an STP, which determines the HLR of the called MT from its mobile identification number, by a table look-up procedure called the GTT (Global Title Translation). The location request message is then forwarded to the HLR. The HLR of the called MT then sends a location request message to the concerned GLR. The GLR forwards the request to MSC serving the called MT. Paging is performed here. The MSC determines the cell location of the called MT and assign it a Temporary Location Directory Number (TLDN). The MSC then sends this TLDN to the GLR. The GLR forwards the TLDN to the HLR of the called MSC. The HLR of the called MSC then acknowledges the request by the GLR of the callee and sends it the TLDN. The GLR forwards the same to the calling MSC. The calling MSC then sets up a connection with the called MSC using TLDN.

Figure 33.4 shows the flow of control for call delivery when the called MT is not within the same GLR (Case 3). The sequence of corresponding operations is as follows.

(1) An MT initiates a call and the base station forwards the call initiation signal to the MSC. (2) The MSC sends a location request message the GLR. (3) The location request is forward to the HLR of the called MT (identified by the GTT). (4) The HLR of the called MT then sends a location request message to the concerned GLR. (5) The GLR forwards the request to MSC serving the called MT. Paging is performed here. (6) The MSC determines the cell location of the called MT and assign it a Temporary Location Directory Number (TLDN). The MSC then sends this TLDN to the GLR. (7) The GLR forwards the TLDN to the HLR of the called MSC. (8) The HLR of the called MSC then acknowledges the request by the GLR of the callee and sends it the TLDN. (9) The GLR forwards the same to the calling MSC. (10) The calling MSC then sets up a connection with the called MSC using TLDN.

33.4 SIMULATION RESULTS AND ANALYSIS

In order to study the performance of the location management schemes, we have set up a system to simulate the 3G cellular network. Network topology and corresponding teletraffic models are selected for the targeted network. An object-oriented discrete-event simulator is also described in this section.

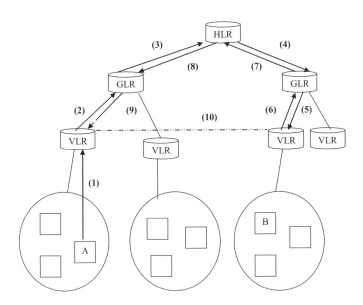

Figure 33.4   The flow of control for call delivery when the called MT is not within the same G-LA. (Case 3).

33.4.1 Simulation Setup

For the purposes of this study, we have chosen following target network. We assume that the cellular network is partitioned into cells of the same size. We use the hexagon as the cell configuration. The network consists of the following components:

- Two home location registers (HLRs). The area served by HLR is called service area (SA). The two SAs are numbered as SA1 and SA2 and are adjacent.
- Each HLR has two gateway location registers (GLRs). The area served by GLR is called the gateway location area (G-LA).
- Each GLR has two visitor location registers (VLRs). The area served by VLR is called location area (LA).
- Each VLR has 61 base stations (BSs).
- Each BS serves four mobile terminals (MTs).
- There are two SAs, two G-LAs, four LAs, 488 BSs and 1952 MTs.

The residence time represents the amount of time the MT stays in a location before moving somewhere else. We assume a geometric (exponential) cell-residence-time distribution in our study. The distribution is assumed to be independent and identically distributed for all cells. We assume that each MT resides in a cell for a time period, then moves to one of its neighbors with equal probability. The Poisson process and exponential process are used to describe the incoming call arrivals and the service time of a phone call, respectively. The simulation time is set to 60,000.

The first experiment is conducted to compare the total location management cost of four schemes: Scheme 1 (Standard 3G without any cache), Scheme 2 (with cache at the VLR alone), Scheme 3 (with cache at the GLR alone), and Scheme 4 (with cache at the VLR and the GLR). The second experiment studies the effect of cache size on the improved cache-based location management scheme. The experiments are discussed in detail in the following section.

33.4.2 Experiment 1: Comparison of the Four Schemes of Location Management

In this section, we will compare four schemes of location management: standard 3G, 3G with cache at the VLR, 3G with cache at the GLR, and 3G with cache at both the VLR and the GLR. The total cost, paging cost, and update cost are compared separately.

For all the schemes, the default threshold value is used. The default value may not give the best result but it is sufficient for our study.

Table 33.1 shows the total location management cost of the four schemes under different CMRs. Figure 33.5 plots the total cost of each scheme with CMR.

From Table 33.1 and Figure 33.5, we can see that, generally, the cases in which a cache has been employed give much better performance than the standard scheme.

Table 33.1   Total location management cost for the four schemes

Item	Data : Comparison of the four schemes by total location management cost						
Target CMR	0.01	0.1	0.5	1.0	2.0	4.0	6.0
Actual CMR	0.013	0.104	0.504	1.004	2.004	4.004	6.0061
# successful calls	2018	15,121	73,706	146,677	293,500	586,685	880,047
# dropped calls	5689	45,536	221,504	441,385	880,447	1,758,385	2,637,668
Total # calls	7707	60,657	295,210	588,062	1,173,947	2,345,070	3,517,715
# migrations	587,641	587,641	587,640	587,641	587,640	587,640	587,640
Cost: Case 1 (standard 3G)	1,385,760	1,717,096	3,197,154	5,035,379	8,733,333	16,105,155	23,478,675
Cost: Case 2 (cache at VLR)	1,384,676	1,688,448	3,040,974	4,721,485	8,096,007	14,828,380	21,559,094
Cost: Case 3 (cache at GLR)	1,385,714	1,709,209	3,063,273	4,734,045	8,076,420	14,745,718	21,424,369
Cost: Case 4 (cache at GLR,VLR)	1,384,678	1,685,357	2,946,335	4,480,756	7,551,658	13,686,281	19,803,478

When the CMR is small, (0.1), the cost produced by Case 3 is a little higher than that of Case 2 (cache at VLR).

However, as the CMR increases the cache at the GLR proves to be more useful than the cache at the VLRs. This is because the cache at the GLR would keep in track all of the frequently called MTs in its cache and, hence, another MT that needs to call one of these would be making use of this cache, which is not the case for cache at the VLR.

When the CMR becomes larger, the paging cost will become higher and more significant. So with bigger CMR, the improved schemes become superior to the standard scheme; when CMR is 6.0, the total location cost of movement-based scheme is 18.5% less than the total of standard scheme. This steadily increases when the network or CMR become larger (the savings will be significant).

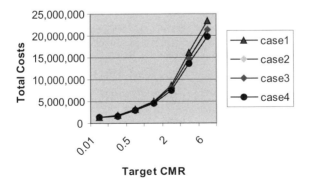

Figure 33.5   Comparison of four location management schemes.

Figure 33.5 shows the comparison of the costs in the four schemes with increase in CMR. It can be seen that for most cases the cache at the GLR is a little more beneficial than cache at the VLR, and cache at both is the most effective, especially for high CMR values.

Table 33.2 and Figure 33.6 show the paging cost for the four location management schemes. In general, the paging cost of the standard scheme is larger than the cache-enhanced schemes. The difference is magnified when the CMR becomes larger. This is because with the cache enhanced schemes, the network needs to page part of the LA only in the case when there is cache miss, whereas with standard scheme, the LA area will be paged for the incoming call for all cases.

33.4.3   Experiment 2: The Effect of Cache Size on the Improved Movement-Based Location-Management Scheme

The improved movement-based scheme is superior to the standard scheme in terms of performance. In this section, we will explore the effects of difference of cache size on the improved scheme.

The same program is run for different values of the cache size, keeping all other values constant. The experiment is done in two parts: the first deals with the cache at the VLR and the second on the cache at the GLR.

In the improved scheme, a cache is maintained at the VLR and GLR both separately and together, and the gain is observed. A cache is maintained at the VLR for all those MTs that are frequently called by the MTs under that particular VLR if they meet a certain threshold value. In this section, we will study the effect of cache size at the VLR on the total cost or, in fact, the paging cost, since the update cost would remain the same.

Table 33.2   Total paging cost for the four schemes

Item	Data: Comparison of all the four schemes by total location paging cost						
Target CMR	0.01	0.1	0.5	1.0	2.0	4.0	6.0
Actual CMR	0.013	0.104	0.504	1.004	2.004	4.004	6.0061
# successful calls	2018	15,121	73,706	146,677	293,500	586,685	880,047
# dropped calls	5689	45,536	221,504	441,385	880,447	1,758,385	2,637,668
Total # calls	7707	60,657	295,210	588,062	1,173,947	2,345,070	3,517,715
# migrations	587,641	587,641	587,640	587,641	587,640	587,640	587,640
Cost: Case 1 (standard 3G)	54,679	386,015	1,866,076	3,704,298	7,402,252	14,774,077	22,147,597
Cost: Case 2 (cache at VLR)	53,595	357,367	1,709,896	3,390,404	6,764,929	13,497,302	20,228,016
Cost: Case 3 (cache at GLR)	54,633	378,128	1,732,195	3,402,964	6,745,342	13,414,640	20,093,291
Cost: Case 4 (cache at GLR&VLR)	53,597	354,276	1,615,257	3,149,675	6,220,580	12,355,203	18,472,400

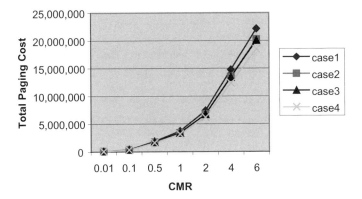

Figure 33.6 Comparison of paging cost for the four schemes.

It can be seen from Figure 33.7 that the update cost remains the same as the cache size increases, as the change in cache size does not affect the update costs. It is, however, observed that the paging cost decreases considerably as the cache size is increased. In fact, there is a linear relation between the two.

In the improved scheme, a cache is maintained at the VLR and GLR both separately and together, and the gain is observed. A cache is maintained at the GLR for all those MTs that are frequently called by the MTs under that particular GLR if they meet a certain threshold value. In this section, we study the effect of cache size at the VLR on the total cost or, in fact, the paging cost since the update cost would remain the same. The results are tabulated in Tables 33.3 and 33.4.

It can be seen from Figure 33.8 that the update cost remains the same as the cache size increases, as the change in cache size does not affect the update costs. It is, however, observed that the paging cost decreases considerably as the cache size is increased. In fact there is a linear relation between the two. On comparison with

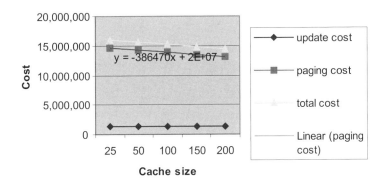

Figure 33.7 Effect of different sizes of cache at the VLR on the total cost.

Table 33.3 Effect of cache size at VLR on the Total Cost

Item					
Cache size @ VLR	25	50	100	150	200
Total update cost	1,331,078	1,331,078	1,331,078	1,331,078	1,331,078
Total paging cost	14,574,946	14,363,400	13,924,187	13,497,302	13,075,645
Total LM\cost	15,906,024	15,694,478	15,255,265	14,828,380	14,406,723

Data: Cache size at VLR—impact on the improved scheme. CMR constant at 4.0 (0.02/0.005). Actual CMR = 4.004. Total # of Calls = 2345070. Total # of Migrations = 587640.

Table 33.4 Effect of cache size at GLR on the total cost

Item					
Cache size@ GLR	50	100	150	200	300
Total update cost	1,331,078	1,331,078	1,331,078	1,331,078	1,331,078
Total paging cost	14,311,700	13,858,795	13,414,640	12,960,075	12,058,208
Total LM\cost	15,642,778	15,189,873	14,745,718	14,291,153	13,389,286

Data: Cache size at VLR—Impact on the Improved scheme. CMR constant at 4.0 (0.02/0.005). Actual CMR = 4.004. Total # of Calls = 2345070. Total # of Migrations = 587640.

the Figure 33.6, it can be seen that the effect is seen more on the cache at the GLR than the one at the VLR (from the equations).

33.5 CONCLUSION

Four schemes have been implemented in this chapter: standard 3G, standard 3G with cache at VLR, standard 3G with cache at the GLR, and standard 3G with cache at both GLRs and VLRs. The new schemes not only retain all the benefits of 3G systems but a significant gain in performance is also obtained for a particular set of users who have certain calling and mobility patterns. The cache-enhanced 3G schemes are the main contributions of our work.

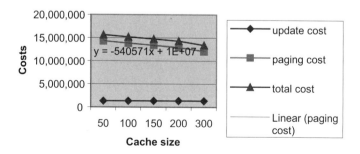

Figure 33.8 Effect of different sizes of cache at the GLR on total cost.

In summary, the cache-enhanced location management schemes provide better performance than movement-based scheme in terms of location management cost. Of the three cache-enhanced schemes explored, it is found that having a cache both at GLR and VLR would be most effective, no matter how small the cache size is. It is also observed that the cache is even more useful when the CMR gets high. In fact, both are directly proportional.

REFERENCES

1. C. Rose, Minimizing the Average Cost of Paging and Registration: A Timer-Based Method, *ACM/Baltzer Journal of Wireless Networks, 2,* 2, 109–16, June 1996.

2. B. Liang and Z. J. Haas, Predictive Distance-Based Mobility Management for PCS Networks, in *Proceedings of IEEE INFOCOM'99,* 1999.

3. I. F. Akyildiz, J. S. M. Ho, and Y-B. Lin, Movement-Based Location Update and Selective Paging for PCS Networks, *IEEE/ACM Transactions on Networking, 4,* 4, 629–638, August 1996.

4. J. Li, Y. Pan, and X. Jia, Analysis of Dynamic Location Management for PCS Networks, *IEEE Transactions on Vehicular Technology, 51,* 5, 1109–1119, September 2002.

5. Y. Xiao, Y. Pan, and J. Li, Movement-based Location Management for 3G Cellular Networks, in *Proceedings of IEEE Globecom 2003,* pp. 4101–4105, 2003.

6. Y. Xiao, Y. Pan, and J. Li, Design and Analysis of Location Management for 3G Cellular Networks, *IEEE Transactions on Parallel and Distributed Systems, 15,* 4, 339–349, April 2004.

7. R. Jain, Y.-B. Lin, C.Lo, and S. Mohan, A Caching Strategy to Reduce Network Impacts of PCS, in *Wireless Communication and Mobile Computing,* 2002.

8. Third Generation Partnership Project, Technical Specification Group Services and Systems Aspects; Network Architecture (Release 5), 2000–12, 2000.

9. Y. Xiao, Hierarchical Mobility Database Overflow Control, *Wireless Communications and Mobile Computing, 3,* 3, 329–343, May 2003.

## CHAPTER 34

Maximizing Multicast Lifetime in Wireless Ad Hoc Networks

GUOFENG DENG and SANDEEP K. S. GUPTA

34.1 INTRODUCTION

Wireless ad hoc networks (WANETs), which can consist of any handheld device with a transceiver (e.g., PDAs and laptops), are designed for applications such as disaster rescue and military applications, in which traditional infrastructure-based cell networks do not exist or cannot exist. Moreover, recent advances in micro-electromechanical systems (MEMS) technology, wireless communications, and digital electronics have enabled the development of low-cost, low-power, multi-functional sensor nodes that are small in size and communicate untethered over short distances [16]. However, most of these devices, including both sensors and regular-size devices, are driven by batteries with finite capacity. Not only it is inconvenient to recharge batteries while in operation, but also in sensor networks, which are based on collaborative efforts of a large number of sensors, it is impractical to collect all sensors to recharge the batteries.

Due to the limitation of available energy in the battery-driven devices in WANETs, the longevity of the network is of prime concern. This chapter mainly considers the problem of maximizing the lifetimes of WANETs when multicast traffic dominates. Multicast is an efficient method to disseminate data to a group of destinations. It is the basis of most group communications, which are important applications in WANETs. Most implementations of multicast are tree based; data traverse multicast tree links from the root to all destinations. A tree established for each source is a source-based multicast tree, which is rooted at the source and spans the group of destinations. Problems discussed in this chapter have one source and, therefore, multicast information is delivered to the group of destinations through a single or combination of multiple source-based multicast trees. In the case of multiple sources, one option is that sources share a tree structure, which is referred to as a group-shared multicast tree or core-based tree. To multicast data, each source is first required to transmit data to the core, which is the root of the shared tree. Then, the core forwards them to all destinations through the tree, as if it were the source of the data. The application of a group-shared tree inevitably leads to traffic concentration on the shared tree and, in turn, fast energy depletion at the nodes in the tree. From this perspective, a group-shared tree is not preferred when network lifetime is of concern. Alternatively, multiple source-based multicast trees could be constructed, each of which is rooted at a single source. Thus, it is possible that some nodes are common nodes for several trees. The problem of maximizing lifetime in this scenario is complicated and beyond the discussion in this chapter.

Besides multicast lifetime, some other objectives motivated by limited energy in WANETs have been addressed. The one closely relevant is energy-efficient multicast routing, whose target is to maintain a multicast connection from the source to a group of destinations with minimum total energy consumption by all nodes. This problem has been studied intensively in the past few years and many topology control and power-aware techniques have been developed to address the issue of limited energy [5–7]. A wireless node is able to arbitrarily choose the transmission power level at which its transceiver transmits packets. The value of transmission power, in reality, is proportional to the transmission range, a scope within which the signal is legible to the receiver. Furthermore, due to the broadcast nature of the wireless medium, every node located within a node's transmission range can receive packets from that node. This phenomenon is the so-called wireless multicast advantage (WMA). Therefore, each node can determine the set of possible one-hop-away neighbors by adjusting its transmission power. Adjustment of the transmission power in wireless nodes to create a desirable optimized topology is called topology control [1].

The problem of constructing a multicast tree with minimum total energy consumption has been proven to be NP-complete [15]. An energy-efficient multicast tree, however, cannot guarantee an optimum lifetime. Approaches tackling energy constraints in unicast routing in WANETs have one of two different targets. Similar to energy-efficient multicast algorithms, the performance objective of energy-efficient unicast routing is to minimize the total consumed energy per unit flow, that is, to find a path from the source to the destination in which the sum of energy consumption is minimized [2]. A maximum lifetime unicast algorithm considers the problem of maximizing the time to network partition [2–4, 8]. Results of unicast routing are not directly applicable to multicast problems due to the different traffic pattern between unicast and multicast routing, which is one to one versus one to many. But unicast is a special case of multicast in which only one destination exists.

This chapter is organized as follows. We first introduce energy consumption model in WANETs as background. This is followed by definitions of maximum multicast lifetime routing. In the fourth section, we present solutions to the problem of maximizing multicast lifetime using a single tree (MMLS). Then, an approach is discussed in which multiple multicast trees are allowed, that is, maximizing multicast lifetime using multiple trees (MMLM). We briefly summarize this chapter in the last section and discuss some open research issues.

34.2   ENERGY CONSUMPTION MODEL IN WANETs

As in traditional networks, nodes in WANETs consume energy for processing internal data and simply for being "on" in an idle mode. But the main factor, which constitutes the energy consumption of a wireless node, is the power required to transmit and receive data. Node i can communicate directly with node j if the transmission power from i exceeds some threshold value p_{ij}. In reality, $p_{ij} \propto d_{ij}^{\alpha}$, where d_{ij} is the Euclidean distance between nodes i and j, and exponent α, $2 \leq \alpha \leq 4$, models the decay of the radio signal in the intervening medium [18]. p_{ij} captures the cost of the link from node i to node j. For simplicity, we assume symmetric links, that is, $p_{ij} = p_{ji}$ for any nodes i and j. Therefore, the power required at node i in order to communicate with node j can be expressed as

$$p_i = \begin{cases} p_{ij} & \text{if } i \text{ is the source node} \\ p_{ij} + p_R & \text{otherwise} \end{cases} \tag{34.1}$$

where p_R is power used for reception. The source does not receive data from other nodes and, therefore, no reception cost is involved in a source node. Actually, as will be seen later, the approaches are valid, even if the reception cost is not considered except for some minor differences in results. For simplicity, we choose to only consider power used to transmit data in our energy consumption model.

Moreover, the unit of power mentioned above is joules per unit time, say, second. The energy consumed in each node is directly related to the volume of data transmitted and/or received, especially when power consumed for being simply "on" is negligible compared with that for data transmission and reception. Two units, which are joules per second and joules per bit of data (or joules per packet), can be related to each other by a constant transmission rate C in bits per second (or packets per second). Therefore, they are equivalent. However, to avoid confusion, e_i is used as the transmission power of node i, e_{ij} as the cost of the link from node i to node j, and e_R as the power used for reception, all of which are in joules per bit. Clearly, $e_i = p_i/C$, $e_{ij} = p_{ij}/C$ and $e_R = p_R/C$. From this point of view, the two units could be used interchangeably. Furthermore, lifetime or duration of multicast tree(s) and wireless node(s) can be described in either time, say, seconds, or volume of data, say, bits, for the same reason.

Any node, say, i, is assumed to be able to control its transmission range by choosing an appropriate transmission power level p_i. Basically, p_i could be any value satisfying $p_{min} \leq p_i \leq p_{max}$, where p_{min} is the minimum transmission power required to send a packet to an arbitrarily nearby node, and p_{max} is the maximum transmission power in a wireless node. $p_i = 0$ means that node i decides not to transmit packets to any other nodes. If we define node j as a neighbor of node i when node j can successfully receive packets from node i directly, the neighborhood relationship is irreversible. It is possible that node i can hear node j but node j cannot receive packets from node i because of different transmission power at nodes i and j. So, the connectivity of the wireless network depends on the transmission power levels at all nodes, which is referred to as a power assignment.

The wireless multicast advantage (WMA) is due to the broadcast nature of the wireless medium. For example, in Figure 34.1, node s is transmitting data to nodes a and b. The minimum power required at node s is $\max\{p_{sa}, p_{sb}\}$ instead of $p_{sa} + p_{sb}$. From another point of view, node s transmits data at a power level sufficient for the farthest neighbor to receive it, but to the rest of its neighbors that are closer free of charge of energy. It is safe to say that WMA has enabled the design to achieve energy efficiency as well as extended network lifetime.

For a node in a multicast tree, specifically, the power required at this node depends on the farthest child it has:

$$e_i(T_k) = \max_{j \in V_i(T_k)} e_{ij} \tag{34.2}$$

where $e_i(T_k)$ stands for transmission power required at node i in multicast tree T_k, and $V_i(T_k)$ is the set of children of node i in tree T_k. Unless stated otherwise, algorithms presented in this chapter are off-line algorithms based on global knowledge of the network deployment. We assume that once a multicast tree is constructed, it will be used for a comparatively long time before any structure modification. Also, because nodes in the network are assumed to be reliable and static, overhead for multicast tree maintenance is negligible.

So far, we have introduced power consumption by a node in WANETs. Due to WMA, both energy and bandwidth in wireless communications are conserved. On the other hand, it leads to increased levels of interference and collision. To focus on the discussion of network lifetime, we assume some reliable protocols at the Medium Access Control (MAC) layer; energy consumed for reliable transmission at the MAC layer is not considered in this chapter.

34.3 DEFINITIONS OF MAXIMUM MULTICAST LIFETIME

The lifetime of an individual node can be defined as a continuous amount of time during which the node is operational until the first failure due to battery depletion or, equivalently, the number of bits of data a node can transmit at certain transmission power. Lifetime of node i, denoted by L_i, is determined by both its battery capacity, R_i (joule or millijoule), and the transmission power required at that node:

$$L_i = \frac{R_i}{e_i} \tag{34.3}$$

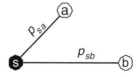

Figure 34.1   Wireless multicast advantage.

Furthermore, link longevity is defined as the maximum number of bits that the source of a link can transmit to the node at the other end of the link. We denote longevity of link i to j by L_{ij}:

$$L_{ij} = \frac{R_i}{e_{ij}} \tag{34.4}$$

Notice that $L_{ij} \neq L_{ji}$ if $R_i \neq R_j$.

Then, what is the relationship between longevity of a node and that of each link starting from it? Since a node is always transmitting data to reach its farthest neighbor, the lifetime of this node is determined by the smallest link longevity originating from it:

$$L_i = \frac{R_i}{e_i} \quad \text{(according to Equation 34.3)}$$

$$= \frac{R_i}{\max_j e_{ij}} \quad \text{(according to Equation 34.2)}$$

$$= \min_j \frac{R_i}{e_{ij}}$$

$$= \min_j L_{ij} \quad \text{(according to Equation 34.4)}$$

where j is any neighbor of node i. By Equation (34.3), the lifetime of node i in multicast tree T_k can be expressed as

$$L_i(T_k) = \frac{R_i}{e_i(T_k)} \tag{34.5}$$

This means that in order to maintain a tree connection, the transmission power at each node in the tree must be at least the maximum power required to communicate with its farthest child:

$$L_i(T_k) = \frac{R_i}{\max_{j \in V_i(T_k)} e_{ij}} \tag{34.6}$$

A leaf node has an infinite lifetime because of its zero transmission power.

A tree is an acyclic structure. Any node failure will result in at least one tree link failure and hence, disconnect the tree. So, a (multicast) tree gets disconnected even if a single node dies. Consequently, the lifetime of a multicast tree is same as the lifetime of the bottleneck node, the node in the tree with the shortest lifetime among all the tree nodes.

Definition 1: Lifetime of a single multicast tree   In the scenario in which one multicast tree is used throughout the multicast session, the lifetime of this tree is the time until the first node dies due to power depletion. We denote lifetime of multicast tree T_k by $L(T_k)$ such that

$$L(T_k) = \min_{i \in V(T_k)} L_i(T_k) \tag{34.7}$$

where $V(T_k)$ is set of nodes in tree T_k. Then, by substituting $L_i(T_k)$ in Equation (34.5), we get

$$L(T_k) = \min_{i \in V(T_k)} \frac{R_i}{e_i(T_k)} \tag{34.8}$$

For example, Figure 34.2(a) shows the network deployment with the cost of each link specified. Node s is the source and nodes a, b, and c are destinations, all of which have an identical initial energy level of 200 units. In the multicast tree in Figure 34.2(b), transmission power at nodes s, a, b, and c is 1.0, 0.8, 1.7, and 0 unit, respectively. In the multicast tree in Figure 34.2(c), the values are 1.0, 2.0, 0, and 0 unit, respectively. Node a in Figure 34.2(c) transmits packets at a power of 2.0 unit in order to reach its farthest child c, but can multicast data to nodes b and c at the same time. According to Definition 1, the multicast tree in Figure 34.2(b) has a lifetime of 118 bits and the multicast tree in Figure 34.2(c) 100 bits with nodes b and c being bottleneck nodes, respectively.

For a given network deployment, the problem of maximizing multicast lifetime of the network using a single tree (MMLS) is to find a multicast tree that has the highest lifetime among all viable multicast trees connecting the given source and destinations:

$$MMLS = \max_k \min_{i \in V(T_k)} \frac{R_i}{e_i(T_k)} \tag{34.9}$$

where T_k is any viable multicast tree.

When a tree is used throughout the multicast session, the intermediate nodes in the multicast tree consume their energy quickly, especially the bottleneck. The tree dies when the bottleneck exhausts its battery. In many situations, multiple multicast trees can be used alternately to increase the multicast lifetime of the network. For

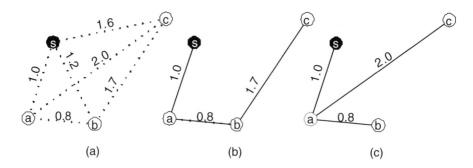

Figure 34.2 Network deployment and sample multicast trees.

instance, in the example drawn in Figure 34.2, the multicast tree in Figure 34.2(b) has a lifetime of 118 bits and the multicast tree in Figure 34.2(c) 100 bits. If the trees in Figure 34.2(b) and Figure 34.2(c) are used one after another, for example, the tree in Figure 34.2(b) is used to transmit 80 bits of data and then the multicast session is continued through the tree in Figure 34.2(c), the session will eventually die. After 80 bits are transmitted in the multicast tree in Figure 34.2(b), the residual energy at nodes s, a, b, and c is 120, 136, 64, and 200 units, respectively. This means that 68 bits of data can be delivered with the residual energy until the failure of first node, that is, node a. As a result, a total of 148 bits of data are sent from node s to nodes a, b, and c. Instead, if we to choose the multicast tree in Figure 34.2(b) for 100 bits and then switch to the tree in Figure 34.2(c) to multicast as much data as possible, a multicast lifetime of 160 bits can be achieved.

Multicast lifetime can be increased by using multiple trees alternately because the system is able to balance energy consumption at wireless nodes. The idea is that in each multicast tree, there are one or more nodes whose transmission power is comparatively higher than others. The bottleneck is one of these nodes. If multiple trees exist such that nodes with higher energy cost in each tree are different or, in other words, each node in the network is not costly all the time, it is possible to find a combination of these trees that is capable of extending the time until the first node dies.

We know the lifetime of a single multicast tree is determined by the distribution of initial energy and power consumed at each node. For multiple multicast trees, however, the lifetime is affected by the set of multicast trees and duration of each tree used as well, which is shown in the preceding example.

Definition 2: Switching schedule   In a multicast session, several multicast trees are used alternately to deliver data from a given source to a group of destinations. A switching schedule describes the duration of each multicast tree that will be used during the multicast session such that energy available at each node in the network can be enough for all transmissions described in the switching schedule, and after the execution of the entire switching schedule, the residual energy at each node can support no more multicast tasks.[1]

Formally, a switching schedule SP can be expressed as a bituple set of (t, d), where t is a multicast tree and $d > 0$ is the time that multicast tree t will be used. $t_i \neq t_j$ for any elements (t_i, d_i), $(t_j, d_j) \in SP$, $i \neq j$.

Definition 3: Multicast lifetime of multiple trees   Given several multicast trees and a switching schedule, the lifetime of these trees is the sum of the duration of each multicast tree in the switching schedule. If L stands for the multicast lifetime using switching schedule SP, then

$$L = \sum_{(t_i, d_i) \in SP} d_i \qquad (34.10)$$

---

[1]According to our assumption, only the duration of each tree has an effect on the multicast lifetime; the sequence does not.

For instance, two switching schedules appearing in the previous example are {(tree (b), 80 bits), (tree (c), 68 bits)} and {(tree (b), 100 bits), (tree (c), 60 bits)}, respectively. Therefore, lifetime is 148 bits and 160 bits, respectively.

The task of maximizing the multicast lifetime of the network using multiple trees (MMLM) is actually to find a switching schedule that maximizes the network life-time. In other words, besides choosing an appropriate set of multicast trees, the duration of each tree has to be optimized.

Broadcast is a special case of multicast, in which all nodes except the source are destinations. So, the above definitions are directly applicable to broadcast applications. So far, the definitions of multicast lifetime have been provided. We will look at the differences between two related designs, energy-efficient and maximum-lifetime multicast routing, based on these definitions. The idea of energy-efficient algorithms is to minimize the total energy consumption by all nodes in the multicast tree. Due to wireless multicast's advantage, a wireless node can communicate with all nodes within its transmission range with a transmission power required to reach its farthest one-hop-away neighbor. To reach an even farther node, the sender can transmit packets at higher power or one of its neighbors can forward the packets for the sender. Among these two options, the first is preferred if the increment of the transmission power at that node is smaller than the transmissionpower required at the forwarder. Generally, the objective of energy efficiency leads to higher energy consumption at a subset of nodes and lower consumption at others. We know that for a node with fixed battery capacity, however, the higher the transmission power, the shorter the lifetime. Therefore, minimum total energy consumption cannot guarantee maximum multicast lifetime. Figure 34.3(a) illustrates an example deployment of wireless ad hoc networks consisting of three nodes and with link cost specified. Among these nodes, node s is the source, and both nodes a and b are receivers. We assume that all three nodes have same initial energy, say, 200 units. Figures 34.3(b) and 34.3(c) are two multicast trees connecting the source and destinations. Actually, the tree in Figure 34.3(b) is a multicast tree with minimum total energy consumption by all nodes and the tree in Figure 34.3(c) is the one with maximum lifetime. Specifically, transmission power at nodes s, a, and b is 4, 0, and 0 units, respectively, in Figure 34.3(b) and 2, 3, and 0 units in Figure 34.3(c). Total power consumption is 4 units $(4 + 0 + 0)$ in Figure 34.3(b) and 5 units $(2 + 3 + 0)$ in Figure 34.3(c), whereas lifetime is 40 bits with node s being the bottleneck and 200/3, a little more than 66 bits, with bottleneck node a, respectively. The result in this example is that the tree in Figure 34.3(c) has a better lifetime than tree Figure 34.3(b), although it consumes more energy as a whole.

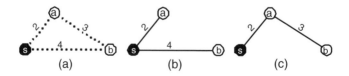

Figure 34.3 Network deployment and sample multicast trees.

34.4 MAXIMUM MULTICAST LIFETIME OF THE NETWORK USING A SINGLE TREE (MMLS)

The MMLS problem naturally leads to a max–min optimization problem because the minimum time at which the first node failure occurs needs to be maximized [10]. In this section, we first prove that MMLS is solvable within polynomial time under both identical and nonidentical battery capacity situations. Then, the solution in a special case, which is maximum broadcast lifetime of the network using a single tree (MBLS), is presented. Approaches discussed in the first two subsections are centralized solutions. A distributed algorithm, L-REMiT [9], will be introduced briefly at the end of this section.

34.4.1 MMLS

We know that battery capacity together with transmission power assignment determines node lifetime, and further affects the lifetime of the multicast tree, as shown in Equations (34.5) and (34.8). In the case of same type of battery at each node, the problem of MMLS is reduced to finding a multicast tree, whose highest transmission power is minimized. That is, if $R_1 = R_2 = \cdots = R^*$, then

$$MMLS = \max_k \min_{i \in V(T_k)} \frac{R^*}{e_i(T_k)} = \frac{R^*}{\min_k \max_{i \in V(T_k)} e_i(T_k)} \qquad (34.11)$$

A straightforward method is to enumerate all possible multicast trees connecting the given source and destinations and then choose the tree whose highest transmission power is smallest among all trees. The lifetime of this tree is an answer to MMLS. However, this simple method is not desirable because of poor efficiency. According to the Cayley formula [14], the number of spanning trees of a complete graph K_n is n^{n-2} for any $n \geq 2$. So, the above method has an exponential time complexity.

Is there a solution with better complexity? The answer is, yes. Referring to Equation (34.8), if $R_1 = R_2 = \cdots = R^*$, we have

$$L(T_k) = \min_{i \in V(T_k)} \frac{R^*}{e_i(T_k)} = \frac{R^*}{\max_{i \in V(T_k)} e_i(T_k)}$$

This means that under the situation of identical battery capacity, the lifetime of multicast tree is determined by the largest transmission power in the tree. Suppose that in multicast tree T_k, the highest transmission power is $e(T_k)$. For any node i in tree T_k, its transmission power satisfies $e_i(T_k) \leq e(T_k)$. By increasing $e_i(T_k)$ to $e(T_k)$, the lifetime of the multicast tree is not changed although the lifetime of node i is decreased. So, we can increase power consumed at each node to $e(T_k)$ if possible without affecting lifetime of the tree. The idea is to assign the same transmission power to each node in the network and search for the lowest power such that a multicast tree can be constructed spanning the given source and destinations [15].

The network is modeled as a unidirectional graph $G = (V, E)$, where V is the set of nodes and E is the set of available links, that is $E = \{(i, j)|e_{ij} \leq e_i\}$. When each node in the network is assigned the same transmission power p, E is denoted by E_p and $E = E_p = \{(i, j)|e_{ij} \leq p\}$. It is straightforward that $E_p \subseteq E_q$ if $p \leq q$. To construct corresponding E_p for given network deployment, the only thing that needs to be done is to compare the link cost between each node pair to the assigned power. Furthermore, we know that in a connected graph, the basic tree-growing scheme [14] is able to generate a multicast tree spanning all the nodes. So, there exists such a tree as long as the source and all the receivers are in a single connected graph. The following algorithm is used to incrementally construct a connected subgraph starting from the given source, say, node s, when E is available.

Connected-Subgraph-Construction (E, s):

```
C = {s};
N = V/C;
for each node i in C
    for each node j in N
    {
        if (i, j) ∈ E
        {
            C = C + {j};
            N = N − {j};
        }
    }
return C;
```

Return value C from the algorithm Connected-Subgraph-Construction is a connected subgraph including the source s. All destinations are connected to node s directly or indirectly as long as they are included in C. The procedure for solving MMLS in the scenario of identical battery power is summarized in the following algorithm, which is based on the ideas by Lloyd et al. [15].

Minimum-Transmission-Power-Search:

```
Sort all possible transmission power levels;
While (true)
{
    p = smallest possible transmission power that has not been tried so far;
    Calculate Ep;
    C = Connected-Subgraph-Construction (Ep, s);
    If (the set of destinations ⊆ C) break;
}
return p;
```

After minimum transmission power p is returned successfully from the preceding algorithm, MMLS can be computed easily by dividing R over p. If C is a connected subgraph corresponding to the minimum transmission power p, any multicast tree built through the tree-growing scheme based on C has a lifetime of MMLS. The multicast tree may include some unrelated nodes that are not multicast nodes (either the source or one of the destinations) and none of their descendants is a multicast node. These nodes will be removed by pruning. The structure of the multicast tree with maximum lifetime may not be unique.

Now, we consider the complexity of this searching algorithm.[2] Since e_{ij} is known for any nodes i and j, to calculate E_p, n^2 comparisons are needed, where n is the total number of nodes in the network. The number of steps to construct a connected subgraph will be less than $O(n^2)$, as per the Connected-Subgraph-Construction algorithm. So, for each possible transmission power value, $O(n^2)$ steps are required to check the feasibility. For each node, there are not more than $n-1$ possible transmission power levels because there is at most one new power value for each neighbor. This does not include the possibility that a node could choose not to forward any data, that is zero transmission power. These add up to at most n possibilities. Then, for all n nodes in the network, there are n^2 different transmission power levels at most. As a result, the total running time to find the optimized maximum lifetime is $O(n^4)$, that is, it is polynomial. The above minimum power search algorithm can be optimized by sorting the $O(n^2)$ candidate solution values and using binary search to determine the smallest value such that the given source and destinations are connected [15]. In this situation, the running time is reduced to $O(n^2 \log n)$.

The above approach is able to solve MMLS in the scenario of identical battery capacity, where the lifetime of a multicast tree is determined by the highest transmission power in the tree. In more general situations, where batteries are not identical, the node with highest transmission power may not be the bottleneck. To search for the maximum lifetime, longevity of each node is used instead of transmission power. Each node is assigned the same lifetime and the transmission power is adjusted according to its initial energy. For example, if l is a candidate lifetime, which is intuitively the lifetime of the possible multicast tree for node i with initial energy R_i, node i must choose its transmission power e_i to be $\min\{R_i/l, p_{max}\}$. Based on the transmission power at each node, link set E is calculated. Similar to the situation of identical battery, the number of possible node lifetime is at most n^2. The following Maximum-Lifetime-Search algorithm is a variation of the algorithm of Minimum-Transmit-Power-Search and, therefore, has same running time. As opposed to Minimum-Transmit-Power-Search algorithm, this algorithm returns MMLS directly.

Maximum-Lifetime-Search:
   Sort all possible node lifetime:
   While (true)
   {
      l = the highest link longevity that has not been tried so far;
      Calculate $e_i = R_i/l$ for each node i;

---

[2]Similar complexity analysis appeared in [15].

Calculate $E = \{(i, j)|e_{ij} \le e_i\}$
C = Connected-Subgraph-Construction (E, s);
If (the set of destinations $\subseteq C$) break;
}
return l;

34.4.2 MBLS

So far, we have shown that MMLS is solvable by using enumeration within polynomial time. Now, we are going to introduce approaches to a special case problem,
which is maximum broadcast lifetime of the network using a single tree (MBLS).
Similarly, the solutions are divided into two cases: identical and nonidentical battery capacity.

A minimum spanning tree (MST) is a tree containing each vertex in the graph
such that the sum of the edges' weights is minimum. It has been proven to be the
tree minimizing maximum power consumption as well [10]. In the case of identical
battery capacity, according to Equation (34.11), MST is a globally optimal solution
to MBLS. Further, a hybrid algorithm, which applies both the Borvka algorithm and
the Prim algorithm, is developed to solve the minimum spanning tree problem in
$O(m \log \log n)$ time, where m is the number of edges and n is the number of nodes
[19]. This is faster than $O(n^2 \log n)$, the time complexity of the enumerating

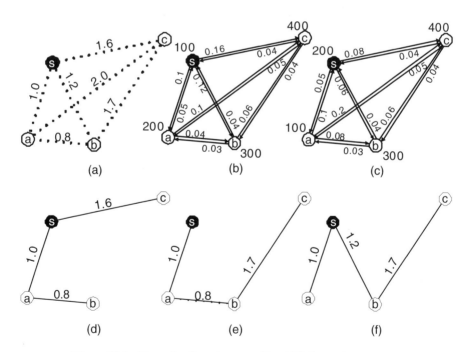

Figure 34.4   Example of maximum multicast lifetime using one tree.

method, since $m \leq n(n - 1)$. One example is depicted in Figure 34.4(a) and Figure 34.4(d). Figure 34.4(a) is network deployment with link cost specified and the tree in Figure 34.4(d) is an MST generated through the Prim algorithm [14]. If an identical battery capacity of 200 units is assumed, the MBLS of the network in Figure 34.4(a) will be 125 bits, with node s being the bottleneck.

MST could also be applied to solve the MBLS problem when batteries are non-identical, where the network is modeled as a directed graph instead, and the weight of each link is no longer transmission power, but the inverse of link longevity [12]. Then, an MST is built based on the directed graph and the resulting MST is referred to as a DMST (directed MST). DMST minimizes the maximum inverse of link longevity and, in turn, maximizes the minimum link longevity. Therefore, DMST is a globally optimal broadcast tree with maximum broadcast lifetime.

Here is an example. The deployment and link costs are shown in Figure 34.4(a). Figure 34.4(b) shows initial energy available at each node, specifically, 100, 200, 300, and 400 units at nodes s, a, b, and c, respectively. The inverse of each link longevity is also specified in Figure 34.4(b). The tree in Figure 34.4(e) is a DMST generated from the network in Figure 34.4(b) through the Prim algorithm. Then, MBLS in this scenario is 100 bits, with node s dying first. Another example with the same deployment but different initial energy at each node is provided in Figure 34.4(c) to illustrate the effects of distribution of battery capacity. In this network, nodes s, a, b, and c have 200, 100, 300, and 400 units of energy, respectively. The tree in Figure 34.4(f) is the DMST constructed from Figure 34.4(c) and it is different from the broadcast tree in Figure 34.4(e). MBLS of the network in Figure 34.4(c) is 176 bits until node b's depletion of energy.

34.4.3 A Distributed MMLS Algorithm: L-REMiT

Above discussion presents centralized approaches to the MMLS problem in WANETs. L-REMiT [9], a refinement-based distributed algorithm, is introduced as follows.

Basically, L-REMiT formulates the task of extending the lifetime of a multicast tree as extending the lifetime of bottlenecks in the tree. By reassigning the farthest children to other nodes, the bottleneck is able to reduce its transmission power and, in turn, increase its lifetime. The rationale behind L-REMiT is that a multicast tree remains connected after a node switches its parent to a nondescendant node if the node itself, its original parent, and the possible new parent are all in the multicast tree. Further, the two nodes, the parent before and after the switch, are the only nodes whose lifetimes are affected. Therefore, the lifetime of the multicast tree will be increased as long as the lifetime of the former parent, which is the bottleneck, is increased, and, at the same time, the updated lifetime of the new parent is greater than the lifetime of the original multicast tree.

L-REMiT works as follows. All nodes run a distributed algorithm, say, the algorithm proposed by Gallager et al. [20], to build an MST at the beginning. Then, refinement steps are conducted on the initial spanning tree in rounds coordinated by the source. In each round, a bottleneck is chosen in a bottom-up manner from the leaf nodes to the source. After the bottleneck gets the L-REMiT token from the source, it switches its farthest child to another node in the tree if the lifetime of the tree will be increased. Otherwise or after the refinement, the bottleneck passes the token back to the source using the reverse tree path from itself to the source. The procedure stops when no further improvement can be found. As the last step, pruning is conducted to remove all the nodes that are not needed to cover all the multicast group nodes.

34.5   MAXIMUM MULTICAST LIFETIME OF THE NETWORK USING MULTIPLE TREES (MMLM)

In the previous section, we studied the approaches to maximum lifetime when one multicast tree is used throughout multicast session. This is also referred to as static power assignment [11]. In a static power assignment, one result is inevitable: only a subset of nodes fails due to battery exhaustion while there is still some energy remaining at other nodes. Especially, residual energy at the leaf nodes is barely touched. This part of energy is actually wasted. In this section, approaches to extend multicast lifetime by making use of all available energy are discussed.

34.5.1   MMLM

The problem of maximum multicast lifetime of a network using multiple trees (MMLM) is also called the dynamic assignment problem [11] because the transmission power at each node is allowed to change dynamically in order to switch from one multicast tree to another. We have seen an example of multiple multicast trees being used alternately earlier in this chapter. Recall the conclusion we reached earlier: solving the MMLM problem is equivalent to finding a collection of multicast trees connecting the source and destinations, along with the corresponding duration of each tree, which we refer to as an appropriate switching schedule.

We first introduce a solution based on linear programming (LP), which is an efficient mathematical tool used to solve maximum or minimum linear functions subject to linear constraints [13]. The authors in [11] have come with a similar approach. If the MMLM problem can be transformed to a linear function and corresponding linear constraints, LP is capable of solving the problem. The following expression shows one possible transform:

$$
\begin{aligned}
&\max CX \\
&\text{s.t. } AX \le R \text{ and } X \ge 0 \\
&\text{where } C = [1, 1, \ldots, 1], \\
&X = [x_1, x_2, \ldots, x_m]^T, \\
&A = [a_{i,j}]_{n \times m}, \\
&\text{and } R = [R_1, R_2, \ldots, R_n]
\end{aligned} \tag{34.12}
$$

In this linear program, the objective is to maximize total execution time, that is, the lifetime. Suppose there are n nodes in the network and m viable multicast trees,

x_i stands for execution time of tree T_i, A is power assignment matrix, and element $a_{i,j}$ is transmission power of node i in tree T_j. the Since network deployment is given, all viable multicast trees could be enumerated. Actually, matrix A is a description of these multicast trees. R_i is the battery capacity in node i. The constraints $AX \leq R$ mean that the sum of energy consumed by every node in each tree will not exceed its initial energy. Apparently, execution time in each tree should not be less than 0. The objective function and constraints are then fed to any mathematical tool that is capable of solving linear programs, for example, Matlab [21]. Finally, MMLM is computed by summing up x_i.

A numerical example is provided to illustrate how LP finds optimal solutions. Network deployment is given in Figure 34.5(a). Node s is the source and nodes a, b, and c are receivers. Each node has an identical battery capacity of 200 units. To make the example more realistic, we assume reception cost to be 0.1 units. Matlab [21] is used as the linear program optimization tool.

As a result, MMLM of the network in Figure 34.5(a) is 188 packets and the detailed switching schedule can be seen in Table 34.1. Notice that in Figure 34.5, only

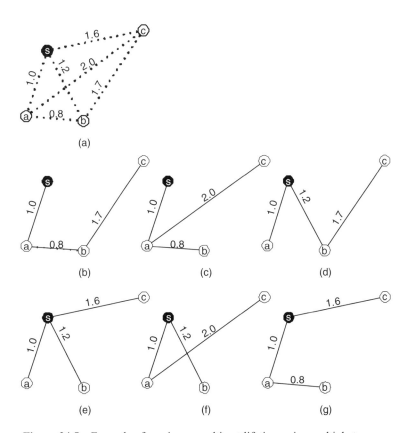

Figure 34.5   Example of maximum multicast lifetime using multiple trees.

Table 34.1   Optimal switching schedule in
the example

Multicast tree	Duration
Figure 34.5(b)	55 bits
Figure 34.5(c)	75 bits
Figure 34.5(d)	58 bits

a subset of all possible multicast trees is shown, among which multicast trees in Figure 34.5(b), Figure 34.5(c), and Figure 34.5(d) appear in the LP result. Multicast trees in Figure 34.5(e), Figure 34.5(f), and Figure 34.5(g) are drawn here for comparison. The tree in Figure 34.5(g) is actually an MST generated through the Prim algorithm. From the results reached in the previous section, we know that in a single-tree situation, MST is a tree that has the maximum lifetime, which is 125 bits. Compared with MMLS, MMLM performs about 50% better in this scenario.

We have shown that LP is capable of dealing with the MMLM problem when all the multicast trees are given. Although LP can solve the max/min problem efficiently even for some comparatively large number of constraints, it is not desirable to apply LP in the above manner. This is because the time complexity to enumerate all possible multicast trees is exponential. It has been proven that the quantized version of MMLM problem is NP-hard [11].

34.5.2   Some Heuristic Solutions

The problem of MMLM is hard because of NP-hardness. Up to now, only very few results have appeared in the literature. Now, we are going to introduce two algorithms aimed at extending lifetime by applying the idea of multiple multicast trees.

One algorithm developed by Floréen et al. [11] utilizes LP in a way similar to the method presented earlier in this section. To avoid exponential complexity, the algorithm generated fixed number of multicast trees. All these trees are built randomly. To conserve energy, these trees are optimal in the sense that transmission power at each node is minimized such that any reduction will lead to tree partition. Based on these trees, LP is used to achieve optimal solutions. The problem with this algorithm is that it is hard to choose an appropriate number of multicast trees. Besides, randomly generated multicast trees cannot guarantee an optimal solution.

Another algorithm by Sheu et al. [17] is a probabilistic solution. It is different from the idea of dynamic assignment presented earlier in this section and the above algorithm because this algorithm does not work toward a specific switching schedule. It is actually a probabilistic flooding algorithm. A node determines its transmission power or whether or not to forward the packet randomly only after a packet is received. The decision is made based on local information, such as its residual energy level, number of neighbors, and average residual energy of neighbors. The nodes with less energy will have lower probability to broadcast than those with more energy. The low-energy nodes are inhibited from forwarding in order to balance the residual energy at each node and, in turn, extend the lifetime of the networks. The problems with this algorithm include no guarantee of data reception by destinations and nonoptimal result.

34.6 SUMMARY

In this chapter, we have discussed approaches to both MMLS and MMLM problems. Solutions to MMLS and its special case problem, which is MBLS, have been explained and proven to have polynomial time complexity. Although multicast lifetime could be extended by using a switching schedule with multiple trees, the problem of MMLM is hard due to its NP-hardness. We will end our discussion by introducing some observed impacts of various parameters on network lifetime performance with multiple multicast trees through simulation by Kang et al. [12]: the achievable gain in network lifetime is about twice the optimal network lifetime using a single tree; when the switching interval is below a certain threshold, no further gain in lifetime is observed; the network lifetime using multiple trees increases linearly as a function of network density, which is mainly due to increase in the available energy pool of the network, that is, total energy at all nodes.

ACKNOWLEDGMENTS

Special thanks to Bin Wang and Tridib Mukherjee of Arizona State University for valuable suggestions and discussions. This work is supported in part by NSF grants ANI-0123980 and ANI-0196156.

REFERENCES

1. R. Ramanathan and R. Rosales-hain, Topology Control of Multihop Wireless Networks using Transmit Power Adjustment, in *IEEE Proceedings of INFOCOM,* Tel-Aviv, Israel (2000).

2. S. Singh, M. Woo, and C. S. Raghavendra, Power-Aware Routing in Mobile Ad Hoc Networks, in *Proceedings of Fourth Annual ACM/IEEE International Conference on Mobile Computing and Networking,* Dallas, TX , Oct.1998, pp. 181–190.

3. J.-H. Chang and L. Tassiulas, Routing for Maximum system Lifetime in Wireless Ad-hoc Networks, in *Proceedings of 37th Annual Allerton Conference on Communication, Control, and Computing,* September 1999.

4. J.-H. Chang and L. Tassiulas, Energy Conserving Routing in Wireless Ad-hoc Networks, in *IEEE Proceedings of INFOCOM,* 2000.

5. J. E. Wieselthier, G. D. Nguyen, and A. Ephremides, On the Construction of Energy-Efficient Broadcast and Multicast Tree in Wireless Networks, in *IEEE Proceedings of INFOCOM,* 2000.

6. M. Cagalj, J. P. Hubaux, and C. Enz, Minimum-Energy Broadcast in All Wireless Networks: NP-Completeness and Distribution Issues, in *ACM Proceedings of MOBICOM*, 2002.

7. B. Wang and S. K. S. Gupta, S-REMiT: A Distributed Algorithm for Source-Based Energy Efficient Multicasting in Wireless Ad Hoc Networks, in *Proceedings of IEEE 2003 Global Communications Conference (GLOBECOM)*, San Francisco, CA, December 2003.

8. A. Sankar and Z. Liu, Maximum Lifetime Routing in Wireless Ad-hoc Networks, in *IEEE Proceedings of INFOCOM*, 2004.

9. B. Wang and S. K. S. Gupta, On Maximizing Lifetime of Multicast Trees in Wireless Ad Hoc Networks, in *Proceedings of the 2003 International Conference on Parallel Processing (ICPP'03)*.

10. I. Kang and R. Poovendran, Maximizing Static Network Lifetime of Wireless Broadcast Adhoc Networks, in *Communications, 2003. ICC '03. IEEE International Conference on Communications*, Volume: 3, 11–15 May 2003, pp. 2256–2261.

11. P. Floréen, P. Kaski, J. Kohonen, and P. Orponen, Multicast Time Maximization in Energy Constrained Wireless Networks, in *DIALM-POMC'03*, September 19, 2003, San Diego, CA.

12. I. Kang and R. Poovendran, Maximizing Network Lifetime of Broadcasting over Wireless Stationary Adhoc Networks, in *UWEETR-2003-0002, UWEE Technical Report Series*.

13. R. B. Darst, *Introduction to Linear Programming–Applications and Extensions*, Marcel Dekker, 1990.

14. J. Gross and J. Yellen, *Graph Theory and Its Applications*, CRC Press, 1998.

15. E. L. Lloyd, R. Liu, and M. V. Marathe, Algorithm Aspects of Topology Control Problems for Ad Hoc Networks, in *MOBIHOC'02*, June 9–11, 2002, EPFL, Lausanne, Switzerland.

16. I. F. Akyildiz, W. Su, Y. Sankarasubramaniam, and E. Cayirci, Wireless Sensor Networks: a Survey, *Computer Networks, 38*, 393–422, 2002.

17. J.-P. Sheu, Y.-C. Chang, and H.-P. Tsai, Power-Balance Broadcast in Wireless Mobile Ad Hoc Networks, in *The Fifth European Wireless Conference*, February 24–27, 2004, Barcelona, Spain.

18. T. S. Rappaport, *Wireless Communications: Principles and Practice*, Prentice-Hall, 1996.

19. B. Y. Wu and K.-M. Chao, *Spanning Trees and Optimization Problems*, Chapman & Hall/CRC, 2004.

20. R. Gallager, P. A. Humblet, and P. M. Spira, A Distributed Algorithm for Minimum Weight Spanning Trees, *ACM Transactions Programming Language & Systems, 5*(1), 66–77, Jan. 1983.

21. www.mathworks.com.

## CHAPTER 35

A QoS-Aware Scheduling Algorithm for Bluetooth Scatternets

YOUNG MAN KIM, TEN H. LAI, and ANISH ARORA

35.1   INTRODUCTION

Bluetooth [1] is a new radio interface standard that provides a means to interconnect mobile electronic devices to personal area ad hoc network (PAN). The devices include cell phones, laptops, headphones, GPS navigators, palm pilots, beep-
ers, and portable scanners, in addition to access points to the Internet, sensors, and
actuators. When users walk into a new environment like a conference room, business office, hospital, or home, they might want to quickly become aware of what
services are provided in it and how to use them; for example, to exchange real-
time multimedia data, to browse web pages, to control room temperature, or adjust the lighting.

Thus, a PAN infrastructure based on Bluetooth should provide many different
communication services [2] such as Internet access, real-time monitoring and control over sensors and actuators, and multimedia stream service.

Bluetooth is a short-range radio technology operating in the unlicensed ISM (In-
dustrial-Scientific-Medical) band at 2.45 GHz. A frequency hop transceiver is applied to combat interference and fading. Two or more nodes sharing the same channel form a piconet, in which one unit acts as a master and the other units (up to
seven) act as slaves. Within a piconet, the channel is shared using a slotted time-
division duplex (TDD) scheme. The master polls the slaves to exchange data. A
scatternet is established by linking several piconets together in an ad-hoc fashion to
yield a global wireless ad-hoc network in a restricted space. A bridge in a scatternet
delivers interpiconet messages between two neighboring piconets. Since each piconet operates in a unique frequency sequence determined by its own master, a
bridge should know the exact instant of polling from each master in advance for an
efficient data exchange. The master can schedule, in any order, the communication
between it and the pure slaves.

Different applications and protocols place different demands on the link. For example, a file transfer application may want to move data reliably; it doesn't matter

if the link is bursty. On the other hand, an application transferring compressed video or audio streams may want a link that is not bursty, and may be able to miss some data as long as the delay and jitter are not too high. Sensor and control data are another class of traffic in which data should arrive at the destination within a fixed time and message loss rate should be minimized. To meet this requirement, the Bluetooth specification provides a quality of service (QoS) configuration. It allows the properties of links to be configured according to the requirements of higher-layer applications or protocols. In particular, Bluetooth LMP commands are used to configure the poll interval to provide QoS service to the higher layer. However, QoS implementation in scatternets is not described in the specification. Moreover, in scatternets, bridge schedule affects directly the fundamental QoS properties: the bandwidth, delay, and jitter.

As far as we know of Bluetooth research activities until now, there has been no trial to study QoS-aware scatternet scheduling. In this chapter, we study scatternet scheduling with QoS together by presenting two versions of QoS-aware scheduling algorithms: a perfect algorithm for a bipartite scatternet, and a distributed, local algorithm for a general scatternet. Then, we show that both algorithms are perfect over tree scatternets. Finally, we provide the QoS analysis about the schedule generated by the algorithms.

The scheduling problem for multihop packet radio networks has been extensively studied [3, 4, 5]. Most of these studies concentrate on finding fair, conflict-free algorithms that minimize the required number of slots using graph theory. However, none of these algorithms is applicable in a Bluetooth scatternet [6, 7]. The scheduling problem here is augmented by the need to coordinate the presence of bridges such that timing mismatches are avoided. Also, the slot boundaries of different piconets do not match in general; this is called phase difference. The Bluetooth scatternet scheduling problem, that minimizes assigned time slots for a given link loads is NP-complete [6, 8] even if there is at most one link between each pair of nodes, all link requirements are equal, the phase difference is ignored, and the scheduling is executed in a central processor that has all the information in advance.

Several heuristic algorithms are proposed in literature [6, 9, 10, 11]. Johansson et al. [6] present a distributed-time-slot scheduling algorithm. Rácz et al. [10] propose a random algorithm in which a set of time slots are assigned at random locations along the time line of each link and, if necessary, empty slots between two consecutively assigned slots are dynamically allotted for the same link. Johansson et al. [11] propose a new Bluetooth mode, JUMP, in which a communication window is dynamically determined. Golmie et al. [9] consider radio interference effects and present an interference-aware scheduling method.

The remaining part of the chapter is organized as follows. In the next section, perfect assignment problem for a bipartite scatternet is defined with a set of notations, followed by a QoS-aware perfect scatternet scheduling algorithm for bipartite scatternets in Section 35.3. In Section 35.4, we propose a distributed, local version of the QoS-aware scheduling algorithm. In Section 35.5, first, the bandwidth allocation of both algorithms against bipartite scatternet are evaluated by simulation. Then, we analyze QoS properties, bandwidth, delay, and jittering of the schedule produced by the algorithm and show that delay and jitter of the schedule are bounded. Finally, the jittering simulation result is presented. We conclude with some future research topics in Section 35.6.

35.2 PERFECT SCHEDULING PROBLEM FOR BIPARTITE SCATTERNETS

We distinguish between four types of nodes in a scatternet: pure masters, pure slaves, master bridges, and slave bridges. A pure master or slave is a master or a slave that belongs to one exclusive piconet. Thus, scatternets need the existence of bridges that connect multiple piconets. A master bridge has two roles: it acts as the master in one piconet and the slave in the other piconet(s). A slave bridge always operates as the slave in each piconet. Let M_p be the set of all pure masters, M_b, the set of all master bridges, S_p the set of pure slaves, and S_b the set of all slave bridges. These four sets are pairwise disjoint. Also, for convenience, let $M = M_p \cup M_b$ and $S = S_p \cup S_b$. We represent the topology of a scatternet with an adjacency matrix $A(M, S \cup M_b)$ such that $A(i, j) = 1$, where $i \in M$ and $j \in S \cup M_b$, if j is an active slave of i. Each row in A describes the structure of a piconet and, thus, has at most seven nonzero entries. Each column of A shows the piconet interconnection structure at a slave or master bridge.

A scatternet is said to be bipartite if it contains no master bridges (i.e., $M_b = \emptyset$). Figure 35.1 depicts a bipartite scatternet consisting of eight pure masters and nine slaves. A general or nonbipartite scatternet is one that contains at least one master bridge.

In Bluetooth, the time line is divided into slots, each 625 μs long. Basic communication between a master and its slaves consists of two consecutive slots, the first

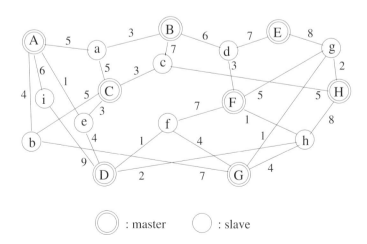

Figure 35.1   A bipartite graph with eight masters and nine slaves.

one for polling and the next for response. Thus, a couple of slots compose a basic unit of internodal communication. From now on, we use the term "slot" to actually represent two consecutive slots.

In a scatternet, each link is associated with a load or bandwidth request, which is expressed in terms of slots. Thus, for $i \in M$ and $j \in S \cup M_b$, $L(i, j)$ denotes the number of slots that link (i, j) requires in each frame of 2^n slots. L, defined on $M \times (S \cup M_b)$, is referred to as a load matrix, which indicates the load of each link on the scatternet.

Given a load matrix $L(M, S \cup M_b)$, let $L(i, *) = \Sigma_j L(i, j)$, and $L(*, j) = \Sigma_i L(i, j)$. For a pure master $i \in M_p$, the total load on i is $L(i, *)$. Similarly, the total load on a pure slave or slave bridge $j \in S$ is $L(*, j)$. However, the total load on a master bridge $x \in M_b$ is $L(x, *) + L(*, x)$. The total load of a node x in the load matrix L is denoted as $T(L, x)$. Notice that, for a master or slave x in a bipartite scatternet, $T(L, x)$ is equal to $L(x, *)$ or $L(*, x)$, respectively. Figure 35.2 shows load matrix L and total load of node $x \in M \cup S$, $T(L, x)$, on the scatternet of Figure 35.1.

A feasible load matrix L must satisfy, at minimum, the constraint $T(L, x) \leq 2^n$ for all nodes x. For example, load matrix L in Figure 35.2 is feasible in the case of $n \geq 4$. It is, however, not clear whether this condition is sufficient for a load matrix to be feasible.

A schedule F for a scatternet over a period of 2^n slots is a function $F(i, j, k), i \in M$, $j \in M_b \cap S, k \in [0 \dots 2^n - 1]$, where $F(i, j, k) = 1$ if link (i, j) is allocated at slot k; $F(i, j, k) = 0$, otherwise. $F(i, j, *)$ gives the schedule of link (i, j) over a time period of 2^n slots, whereas $F(*, *, k)$ depicts the slot assignment over the whole scatternet at time k. Scheduled load $S(x, k)$ of node x at slot k denotes total loads of node x in slot assignment $F(*, *, k)$. For a pure master $i \in M_p$, scheduled load $S(i, k)$ is $\Sigma_j F(i, j, k)$. Similarly, the scheduled load on a slave $j \in S$ is $\Sigma_i F(i, j, k)$. However, on a master

(master)	a	b	c	d	e	f	g	h	i	T(L,x)
A	5	4			1				6	16
B	3		7	6						16
C	5	5	3		3					16
D					4	1		2	9	16
E				7			8			15
F				3		7	5	1		16
G		7				4	1	4		16
H			5				2	8		15
	13	16	15	16	8	12	16	15	15	T(L,x)

(slave)

(x : master or slave)

Figure 35.2   Load matrix L and total load $T(L, x)$.

bridge $x \in M_b$, it is $\Sigma_i F(i, x, k) + \Sigma_j F(x, j, k)$. Schedule F is *feasible* iff scheduled load $S(x, k)$ is at most one for all nodes $x \in M \cup S$ and all slots $k \in [0 \dots 2^n - 1]$.

Now we define the *perfect assignment scheduling problem* for scatternets as follows.

Perfect Assignment Scheduling Problem for Scatternets
Input: A feasible load matrix L.
Output: A feasible schedule F assigning load L
      perfectly, i.e. $\Sigma_k S(x, k) = T(L, x)$,
      $\forall x \in M \cup S$.

35.3 PERFECT ASSIGNMENT SCHEDULING ALGORITHM FOR BIPARTITE SCATTERNETS

A bipartite scatternet has no master bridge, so the total load on each node is computed by summing the corresponding row or column, depending on whether it is a master or a slave, respectively. The scheduling algorithm for bipartite scatternets is presented in this section. It adopts the methodology of divide and conquer. Given the initial load matrix L satisfying the constraint $T(L, x) \leq 2^n$, $\forall x$, the algorithm generates two load matrices L_1 and L_2 satisfying $T(L_i, x) \leq 2^{n-1}$, $i = 1$ or 2. In general, given a load matrix L satsfying $T(L, x) \leq 2^k$ at level k such that $n \geq k \geq 1$, the algorithm partitions it into two load matrices L_1 and L_2, each satisfying the constraint $T(L_i, x) \leq 2^{k-1}$, where $i = 1$ or 2.

In other words, this process of dividing the load matrix evenly is repeated recursively until the upper bound reaches 2^0, where total load on each node is at most one, implying that no contention exists. Thus, L at the last recursion is always a feasible assignment in itself. By assigning L into $F(*, *, l)$ for all time slices l, $0 \leq l \leq 2^n - 1$, a feasible schedule F is generated that satisfies perfect condition $\Sigma_k S(x, k) = T(L, x)$, $\forall x \in M \cup S$, since no parts of the initial load matrix entries are allowed to be dropped in the algorithm.

The proposed scheduling algorithm *Bluetooth Scheduling* implements the above process by calling procedure *Divide_Load* that recursively calls itself until the set of feasible slot assignments $F(*, *, l)$ are produced. The actual load division is done by another procedure, *Load_Partition*.

Consider a particular case that Divide_Load(L, k, l) calls Load_Partition(L, L_1, L_2). An even entry in L is divided by two and each half is set to the same entries of L_1 and L_2. Division of the odd entry in L is more complex. First, the odd entry is decremented by one and then it is divided by two. The computation result is set at the same entries of L_1 and L_2, as an intermediate value. Now, the residual value 1 can be allotted either to L_1 or L_2. All the residual values to be assigned further are represented in the 0/1 matrix A. For example, Figure 35.3 depicts A derived from load matrix L in Figure 35.2.

For a fair division of residual load, the nonzero entries at each row of A are grouped into pairs with at most one possible unpaired entry. This is repeated for

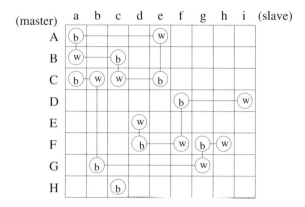

Figure 35.3   0/1 matrix A and graph G.

each column in A. Let the resulting graph be G. Later, we prove that G is always a bipartite graph for any given bipartite scatternet and load matrix. Figure 35.3 shows G computed from L in Figure 35.2, in which there is one even cycle, two linear sequences, and one isolated entry. Then, each nonzero entry of A (i.e., the vertices of G) is colored either with black (b) or white (w) so that no two directly linked entries have the same color; this rule is the key to the even partitioning of A into L_1 and L_2, that is, $T(L_1, x) \le 2^{k-1}$ and $T(L_2, x) \le 2^{k-1}$ for a given load L satisfying $T(L, x) \le 2^k$. Finally, the black or white entry in A is allotted to L_1 or L_2, respectively. For the load matrix L in Figure 35.2 and the entries in A colored like Figure 35.3, the output load matrices L_1 and L_2 are computed by Load_Partition(L, L_1, L_2), as shown in Figure 35.4 and Figure 35.5.

(master)	a	b	c	d	e	f	g	h	i	(slave)
A	3	2			0				3	8
B	1		4	3						8
C	3	2	1		2					8
D					2	1		1	4	8
E				3		4				7
F				2		3	3	0		8
G		4				2	0	2		8
H			3				1	4		8
	7	8	8	8	4	6	8	7	7	$T(L,x)$

(x : master or slave)

Figure 35.4   Load matrix L_1.

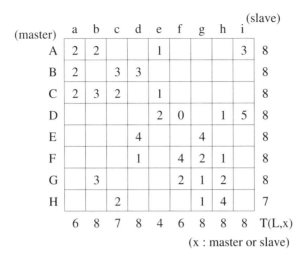

	a	b	c	d	e	f	g	h	i	T(L,x)
A	2	2			1				3	8
B	2		3	3						8
C	2	3	2		1					8
D					2	0		1	5	8
E				4			4			8
F				1		4	2	1		8
G		3				2	1	2		8
H			2				1	4		7
	6	8	7	8	4	6	8	8	8	

(master) / (slave)

(x : master or slave)

Figure 35.5   Load matrix L_2.

Algorithm Bluetooth Scheduling
Input: load matrix L
Output: a feasible schedule F
Statements:
  call *Divide_Load*$(L, n, 0)$

Procedure Divide_Load(L, k, l)
  if $k = 0$ **then**
    $F(i, j, l) := L(i, j)$ $\forall i, j$
  else
    call *Load_Partition*(L, L_1, L_2)
    call Divide_Load$(L_1, k - 1, 2l)$
    call Divide_Load$(L_2, k - 1, 2l + 1)$

Procedure Load_Partition(L, L_1, L_2)
Input: load matrix L
Output: load matrices L_1 and L_2 such that $|L_1(i, j) - L_2(i, j)| \le 1$ and $|T(L_1, x) - T(L_2, x)| \le 1$ for all links (i, j) and all nodes x.

1. For each entry $L(i, j)$, $i \in M, j \in S$, let
$$L_1(i, j) := L_2(i, j) := \lfloor L(i, j)/2 \rfloor$$
$$A(i, j) := L(i, j) \bmod 2.$$
   A is an 0/1 matrix.
2. For each row in A, group the nonzero entries into pairs with at most one possible unpaired entry; do the same for each column in A. Let the resulting graph be G. (We will show that G is a bipartite graph.)

3. Color the nonzero entries of A (i.e., the vertices of G) with black or white so that no two directly linked entries have the same color.
4. For each nonzero entry $A(i, j)$, if it is black, increment $L_1(i, j)$ by 1, else increment $L_2(i, j)$ by 1.

The following lemmas and theorem show some graphical and scheduling properties of bipartite scatternets and the algorithm Bluetooth Scheduling, and prove that the proposed algorithm solves the perfect scheduling problem for bipartite scatternets.

Lemma 1   If the scatternet is bipartite, then it has no cycle of odd length.

Proof   Proof by contradiction. Suppose that there is an odd cycle in a bipartite scatternet. A bipartite scatternet has no master bridge. Thus, there are only master–slave or slave–master links in bipartite scatternets and, thus, the sequence of nodes in the odd cycle can be enumerated alternatively as master followed by slave, followed by master, followed by slave, and so on. However, if the first node in the cycle is master (slave), then the last node in the sequence must be master (slave) because of the odd length of the cycle. Since the last and first nodes are also connected by a link, there exists a master–master (slave–slave) link contrary to the previous fact.   Q.E.D.

Lemma 2   Graph G, that is produced by step 2 of Procedure Load_Partition, is a bipartite graph.

Proof   Notice that each nonzero entry $A(i, j)$ has at most two links incident on itself, one horizontal and the other vertical. There are three possible types of isolated graph components consisting of such entries: isolated node, linear sequence, and simple cycle. Furthermore, the cycle always has an even number of vertices, since the odd cycle implies that some vertex must have two identical type of links, for example, two horizontal (vertical) links, that do not exist in G. It is easy to observe that all the above types of graphs can be arranged as bipartite graphs.   Q.E.D.

Lemma 3   If the given scatternet is bipartite and the input matrix L to procedure Load_Partition satisfies $T(L, x) \leq 2^k$, then the output matrices, L_1 and L_2, satisfy $T(L_i, x) \leq 2^{k-1}$, $i = 1$ or 2.

Proof   Suppose that input matrix L has the property $T(L, x) \leq 2^k$. If the output matrices L_1 and L_2 satisfy the relation $|T(L_1, x) - T(L_2, x)| \leq 1$, then it is evident that $T(L_i, x) \leq 2^{k-1}$, $i = 1$ or 2. Thus, it is enough to prove that procedure Load_Partition generates two load matrices L_1 and L_2 satisfying $|T(L_1, x) - T(L_2, x)| \leq 1$. Notice that $T(L, x)$ is either $L(x, *)$ or $L(*, x)$ for a master or slave x, respectively. Consider only the case of master x. Similar reasoning can be applied for the proof of the other case and we skip it here. Remember that $L(x, *)$ is $\Sigma_j L(x, j)$. In the procedure, each entry $L(x, j)$ is evenly divided into $L_1(x, j)$ and $L_2(x, j)$, except the indivisible value 1 in each odd entry of $L(x, *)$. Such entries are denoted as 1 at the same location in the 0/1 matrix A. Then, nonzero entires of A are paired and connected by horizontal links. According to Lemma 2, G is a bipartite graph in which it is always possible to color the vertices of G with black or white so that no two directly linked entries have the same color (Step 3). Since black and white vertices increment $L_1(x, *)$ and $L_2(x, *)$, respectively, by 1, and there is at most one entry remaining without pairing in the row, it is true that $|L_1(x, *) - L_2(x, *)| = |T(L_1, x) - T(L_2, x)| \leq 1$.   Q.E.D.

Theorem 1   For bipartite scatternets, a load matrix L is feasible iff $T(L, x) \leq 2^n$ for every node x. If L is feasible, then algorithm Bluetooth_Scheduling will produce a perfect, feasible schedule.

Proof   Suppose L is feasible or $T(L, x) \leq 2^n$ for every node x. We consider the case in which x is master. The other case is similar to the following proof and will be omitted here. According to algorithm Bluetooth Scheduling and Lemma 3, load matrix L' at level k, having the property $T(L', x) \leq 2^k$, is evenly partitioned into two matrices L_1' and L_2', having the properties $T(L_i', x) \leq 2^{k-1}$, $i = 1$ or 2. By induction, load matrix L'' at last level $k = 0$ has the property $L''(x, j) \leq 1, j \in S$. Remember that $F(x, j, l) = L''(x, j), \forall x, j, l$. Since $S(x, l) = \Sigma_j F(x, j, l) = \Sigma_j L(x, j) \leq 1$ and initial load is preserved in all levels of load matrices, that is, $\Sigma_k S(x, k) = T(L, x), \forall x \in M \cup S$, the schedule produced by algorithm Bluetooth Scheduling is feasible and perfect.   Q.E.D.

Notice that the algorithm distributes the original link loads evenly over the time period of 2^n slots so that the generated schedule has a regular distribution, yielding tight bounds of the delay and jitter in addition to perfect allocation of the required bandwidth. Thus, the proposed algorithm realizes QoS-aware scatternet scheduling. In a later section, QoS analysis will be presented to figure out the delay and jitter quantitatively.

35.4 DISTRIBUTED, LOCAL, AND INCREMENTAL SCHEDULING ALGORITHMS

The scheduling algorithm proposed in Section 35.3 is perfect in the sense that it yields a feasible schedule for any feasible load matrix. However, since it is a centralized algorithm, it has performance problems like low reliability, network bottleneck, and higher computation time. Hence, a distributed scheduling algorithm is introduced in this section. The proposed algorithm is local in the sense that each master schedules its own piconet links after gathering the information exclusively about the neighboring nodes within a two-hop distance. Furthermore, it can be used incrementally such that, as a new request of link bandwidth occurs dynamically, the master executes the algorithm locally to determine the schedule for the new link request without any change to the remaining link schedules.

Although the algorithm has several nice properties, it is not perfect in general. However, if the network topology is tree-shaped, as formed by many Bluetooth scatternet formation algorithms [12], then there exists a scheme that makes the proposed algorithm perfect. We will describe that scheme later in this section.

The proposed algorithm *Local_Bluetooth_Scheduling* is actually based on the local protocol proposed by Johansson et al. [6] to exchange the information necessary for scheduling. In the algorithm, each master is responsible for the scheduling of its own piconet links. To inhibit simultaneous scheduling about two links incident on a slave, the slave sends a token to one of its masters waiting for the scheduling with highest ID. A master starts the scheduling if and only if it holds the corresponding tokens from all neighboring slaves. Thus, there exists no other master simultaneously executing the algorithm within the 2-neighboring local network domain. After the scheduling, the master announces the local schedule by passing a token to the neighboring slaves. The protocol is deadlock-free and finished within a finite time. For the details of the protocol, please refer to [6].

From now on, we will concentrate on the scheduling algorithm itself executed within a master. Suppose node i is the master ready to execute the scheduling algorithm. Let $I_s(i)$ be the set of all slaves of i, and let $I_m(i)$ be the set of all masters to which i is a slave. Also, let $I(i) = I_s(i) \cup I_m(i)$, the set of all i's neighbors. Given a set of local link requests $L(i, j), j \in I_s(i)$, the local algorithm derives a feasible schedule for all links $(i, j), j \in I_s$, that is, all links in the piconet of i.

Algorithm Local_Bluetooth_Scheduling below adopts the same divide-and-conquer approach as presented in Section 35.3.

Algorithm Local_Bluetooth_Scheduling
Input: local load matrix $L(i)$
Output: a feasible local schedule $F(i, *, *)$
Statements:
  call *Local_Divide_Load*$(L(i), n, 0)$

Procedure Local_Divide_Load$(L(i), k, l)$
  if $k = 0$ **then**
    adjust L such that, if $T(0, x) = 2$, decrements
      one from $L(x, *)$ or $L(*, x)$ in a fair way
    $F(i, j, l) := L(i, j), \forall i, j$
  else
    call *Local_Load_Partition*$(L(i), L_1(i), L_2(i))$
    call Local_Divide_Load$(L_1(i), -k\,1, 2l)$
    call Local_Divide_Load$(L_2(i), -k\,1, 2l + 1)$

As in the centralized algorithm of Section 35.3, the local algorithm recursively calls procedure Local_Load_Partition to generate two evenly partitioned local loads, $L_1(i)$ and $L_2(i)$ from load $L(i)$ so as to decrement level k from n down to 1. As master i becomes ready to run the algorithm, some of the neighboring masters may already have finished their schedules. The schedule at i should be developed in the context of these established schedules to make the schedule more balanced. Before we describe procedure Local_Load_Partition, some notations imparting such scheduling information to the neighbors are defined as follows. From now on, all notations are implicitly defined on the level k and time slice l, unless explicitly mentioned.

Suppose link (i, j) is already scheduled by master $j \in I_m(i)$ such that $L_1'(j, i)$ and $L_2'(j, i)$ are generated from load $L'(j, i)$ at level k and time slice l by master j. Then, $G(i, j)$ denotes $sign(L_1'(j, i) - L_2'(j, i))$. In other words, if $L_1'(j, i)$ is greater, equal to, or less than $L_2'(j, i)$; $G(i, j)$ is equal to 1, 0, or -1, respectively. Neighboring master bridge j of i can also exist in the form of slave to i, that is, $j \in I_s(i) \cap M_b$. Since j is the slave of i on link (i, j), (i, j) is not yet scheduled. Similarly, $G(j)$ is defined to hold either 1, 0, or -1 depending on whether $\Sigma_m L_1'(j, m)$ is greater than, equal to, or less than $\Sigma_m L_2'(j, m)$, respectively. Thus, $G(j) = sign(\Sigma_m L_1'(j, m) - \Sigma_m L_2'(j, m))$.

In procedure *Local_Load_Partition,* to compensate for the load imbalance between $L_1'(j)$ and $L_2'(j)$ at master $j \in I_s(i)$, $L_1(i, j)$ and $L_2(i, j)$ are partitioned so that $L_1(i, j) = L_2(i, j) - G(j)$, if $L(i, j)$ is odd; otherwise, $L_1(i, j) = L_2(i, j) = L(i, j)/2$. Then, the loads at the remaining links with pure slaves $j \in I_s(i)$ are partitioned so as to maximize the local level of load division balance at i, or to minimize $|R|$, where R is the measure of instant local imbalance level at the scheduling time of i, $R = \Sigma_{j \in I_s(i)} C(j) + \Sigma_{j \in I_m(i)} G(i, j)$, where $C(j)$ is the balancing factor that is assigned a value in $\{1, 0, -1\}$. Notice that $C(j)$ for master bridge j is determined to enhance the load balance level at j, and $C(j)$ for pure slaves is used to balance load division at i.

Procedure Local_Load_Partition at level k and time slice l is presented as follows. Notice that the procedure cannot partition the given load matrix into two perfectly balanced loads, that is, the final value of $|R|$ after the whole scheduling process may be greater than 1.

Procedure Local_Load_Partition $(L(i), L_1(i), L_2(i))$
Input: local load matrix $L(i)$
Output: local load matrices $L_1(i, *)$ and $L_2(i, *)$ such that
$|L_1(i, j) - L_2(i, j)| \leq 1, \forall j \in I_s(i)$

1. For each $j \in I_s(i)$, let

$$C(j) := \begin{cases} 0 & \text{if } L(i, j) \text{ is even} \\ -G(j) & \text{if } L(i, j) \text{ is odd and } j \text{ has scheduled} \\ \pm 1 & \text{otherwise} \end{cases}$$

In the "otherwise" case, $+1$ or -1 is chosen so that $|R|$, the absolute value of R is, minimum, where

$$R = \sum_{j \in I_s(i)} C(j) + \sum_{j \in I_m(i)} G(i, j)$$

2. For all j in $I_s(i)$, let

$$L_1(i, j) = \lfloor (L(i, j) + C(j))/2 \rfloor$$
$$L_2(i, j) = L(i, j) - L_1(i, j)$$

Many proposed Bluetooth formation algorithms generate scatternets with tree network topology. During the tree formation stage or later, it is easy for the parent to assign a unique ID to a new node. A particular ID assignment scheme in the tree formation process, the *Hierarchic ID Assignment Scheme,* is the scheme in which a node is bestowed with an ID smaller than its parent ID.

The following theorem proves that algorithm Local_Bluetooth_Scheduling becomes perfect if all IDs in the tree scatternet are assigned according to the Hierarchic ID Assignment Scheme.

Theorem 2   If, in a tree scatternet, the ID of each node is assigned by the Hierarchic ID Assignment Scheme, then Local_Bluetooth_Scheduling is perfect.

Proof   There is no cycle in the tree network. Suppose that node i is ready to schedule its piconet link. Since node IDs are formed in the decreasing order from root to leaves by the Hierarchic ID Assignment Scheme, the parent of node i is the only possible one among the neighbors of i that may have already been scheduled. Thus, according to the rules in the procedure, the predicate $|R| \leq 1$ or $|T(L_1, i) - T(L_2, i)| \leq 1$ is preserved at this moment of scheduling of i. Later on, some child master(s) of i will do scheduling of their own. Even at such a scheduling by children of i, balancing measure R at i is always preserved such that $|R| \leq 1$. Therefore, predicate $|T(L_1, i) - T(L_2, i)| \leq 1$ is an invariant. It is easy to deduce the perfection of the algorithm using this invariant and the logic used in Theorem 1.   Q.E.D.

The proposed local algorithm can be easily modified to an incremental version in which the master schedules the dynamic bandwidth request incrementally. When a link load is canceled, the corresponding amount of assigned slots are canceled, making them free. When a new load for link (i, j) arrives, the local algorithm is applied, except that $C(j)$ is the only parameter to be determined at step 1 of Local_Load_Partition. However, the incremental version of the algorithm is not perfect even if the scatternet is a tree, since the invariant proved in the proof of Theorem 2, $|T(L_1, i) - T(L_2, i)| \leq 1$, is no longer preserved in the incremental scheduling sequence.

35.5   PERFORMANCE AND QoS ANALYSIS

In this section, we simulate the central and distributed scheduling algorithm to figure out the assignment ratio of the actually assigned slots over the initially requested slots. In a bipartite scatternet, the assignment ratio of the centralized algorithm is perfect, that is, 1.0. However, there is some chance that the distributed one will not be successfully assigned. We will show the simulation result. Then, the scheduling algorithm will be executed over an example general scatternet so as to show the effect of the odd cycle inside the general graph. Finally, QoS analysis will be done to derive the relation between delay, jitter, and the assigned load.

35.5.1 Slot Assignment Algorithm Efficiency

First, we investigate the slot assignment efficiency of the distributed scheduling algorithm introduced in the previous section. The bipartite graph configuration depicted in Figure 35.1 is selected as the simulation target. The total number of the simulation is 2,000, such that the requested load matrix is generated randomly and adjusted to satisfy the physical constraint that maximum load at a node is no greater than node bandwidth. In the simulation, the number of slots per assignment frame is fixed at 1024. Figure 35.6 shows the simulation result. Since the number of master nodes is eight, the maximum possible load request is no greater than 8192. Thus, the horizontal axis is normalized by 8192. Note that the central algorithm is perfectly assigning over all regions of request loads. On the other hand, the assignment ratio of the distributed algorithm becomes less than 100% when the load request increases over 50%. However, the unsuccessful percentage of the requested load is quite small even with an almost full request. Therefore, the distributed algorithm is a proper candidate as a scheduling algorithm for scatternets.

The maximum possible number of assigned slots is strongly dependent on the scatternet graph configuration. For example, let us examine another bipartite graph

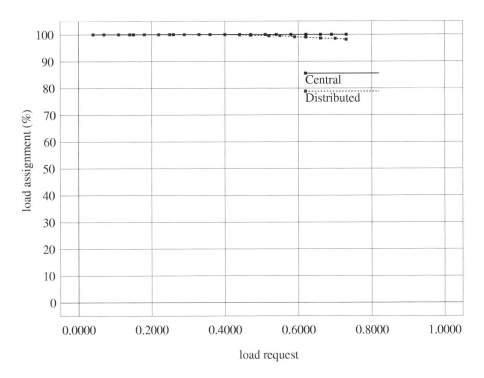

Figure 35.6 Actual slot assignment versus normalized slot request simulated on the bipartite graph of Figure 35.1.

depicted in Figure 35.7. There are four masters. Thus, if all masters would be assigned fully over all slots of one frame, say 1024, then the maximum assigned slots would be 4096. However, such assignment is impossible, no matter how a clever algorithm is employed. There are three sets of edges incident on slaves a, b, and c, that is, $\{aA, aC\}$, $\{bA, bB, bC, bD\}$, and $\{cB, cD\}$, respectively. Since any two edges in the same set share a common slave, they cannot be assigned to the same slot. Thus, at most three edges each from the sets can be assigned to one slot. Therefore, 3072 slots are the maximum possible assigned slots for Figure 35.7. Now, consider a small variation of the graph configuration such that slave b is duplicated to b_1 and b_2 and the corresponding incident edge sets are $\{b_1A, b_1B\}$ and $\{b_2C, b_2D\}$. Then, the maximum possible assigned slots increases to 4096.

Figure 35.8 shows the simulation result based on the node configuration of Figure 35.7. The horizontal axis is normalized by 4096. Thus, maximum possible load request becomes 75% or 0.75. The assignment curve is very similar to that for the previous bipartite graph except that the former has no data for the load request larger than 0.75.

All the above results are simulated on the bipartite graphs. Now, let us examine the effect of a generalized graph. In other words, some pair of master nodes have a master–slave relation such that one master becomes the slave of the other. For example, masters B and C become slaves of masters A and D, respectively, as shown in Figure 35.9.

When the centralized algorithm proposed in Section 35.3 is employed on the general graph configuration, the algorithm becomes imperfect, since the labeling cannot partition the load evenly. For example, look at the edge cycle $AB - Bb - bA$ in the figure. Suppose that each link is loaded with one slot over the time interval [0, 1]. Since the load incident on each node is two and the interval is also two, the physical constraint is cleared. However, the best partitioning of this load configuration is one (two) and two (one) into intervals [0, 0] and [1, 1]. Since one interval is loaded with two and the interval size is one, one slot request must be dropped and,

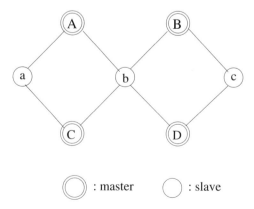

Figure 35.7 A bipartite graph with four masters and three slaves

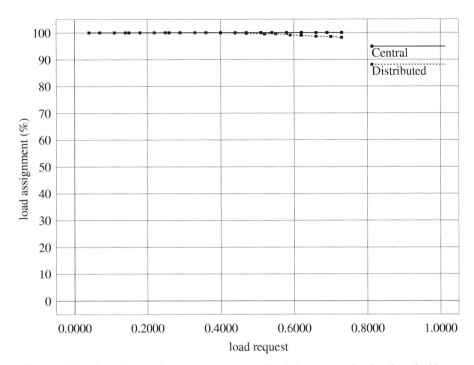

Figure 35.8   Actual slot assignment versus normalized slot request simulated on the bipartite graph in Figure 35.7.

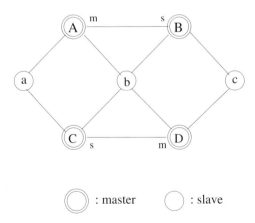

Figure 35.9   A general graph with four masters and three slaves.

thus, the centralized algorithm is not perfect with the general graph. Figure 35.10 shows the simulation result of the centralized and distributed algorithms against the general graph of Figure 35.9. As we expect, the assignment result of the centralized algorithm becomes imperfect and the distributed one shows worse performance than that of the centralized one. Also, compared to the bipartite case, the distributed algorithm has lower assignment efficiency.

35.5.2 Bandwidth

One of the most essential performance measures for QoS is bandwidth, the amount of information transferred per unit time. Since the scheduling algorithms proposed in this chapter are all reservation based, they are suitable for multimedia and real-time traffic to obtain the guaranteed bandwidths along the corresponding communication routes. Once the algorithm generates a feasible schedule from the set of link load requests, the assigned bandwidths are exclusively used for the requesting applications. In case of a bipartite scatternet (i.e., having no master bridge) or tree scatternet, the centralized and the local algorithms yield a perfect, feasible schedule.

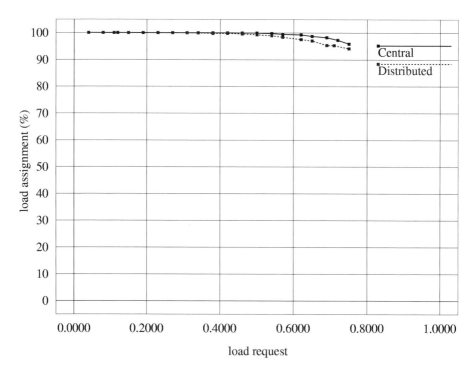

Figure 35.10 Actual slot assignment versus normalized slot request simulated on the general graph in Figure 35.9.

In summary, the feasible schedule always guarantees the allotted amount of bandwidth, which is equal to or probably less than the requested bandwidth with the perfect or local algorithm, respectively. The requesting application may accept it or not.

35.5.3 Delay and Jitter

Another two fundamental QoS measures are delay (D) and jitter (J). Multimedia and real-time data are time-critical and, hence, they should be delivered within a bounded time (delay) and distributed within a range of arrival time (jitter). Notice that in the algorithms, link load is evenly partitioned into two at each recursion until the schedule is produced. Thus, the delay and jitter are expected to be tightly bounded.

There are three kinds of delay: minimum (D_{min}), average (D_{avg}), and maximum (D_{max}) delays. Among them, average delay is the most important. The lower and upper jitters, J_l and J_u, denote the lower and the upper deviation ranges of delay from the average, that is, $J_l = D_{avg} - D_{min}$ and $J_u = D_{max} - D_{avg}$. Since J_u is much more critical to the application than J_l, J_u is used to represent the jitter.

Let t_s denote one physical slot time in Bluetooth, that is 1.25 msec. On the other hand, each logical slot used in the algorithm consists of a constant number of consecutive physical slots, v, to reduce the bandwidth loss due to phase difference. Then, the logical slot time, t_v, is $v \cdot t_s$. Remember that $L(i, j)$ is the initial link load on edge (i, j) that will be scheduled into 2^n consecutive slots. For example, if some multimedia application needs 128 kbps of bandwidth, 128 kbps/1 Mbps = ⅛ of total bandwidth, i.e. 2^{n-3} slots out of 2^n, should be scheduled for it.

We analyze a simple case in which the initial load $L(i, j)$ on link (i, j) is 2^m, $0 \le m \le n$. The general case can be analyzed in a similar fashion and will be skipped for brevity. Since the algorithm partitions the load evenly into two subloads in the lower level, from level n down to $(n - m)$, each slot span of size 2^{n-m}, called the *basic span* of $L(i, j)$ loaded with 2^m, at level $(n - m)$ contains exactly one request for link (i, j). $S(m)$ denotes this span size, 2^{n-m}. Then, $S(m) \cdot t_v$ equals the physical time of a basic span.

In scatternet analysis, it is desirable to derive the global performance measures over a route. Let $D(h)$ and $J(h)$ be the total delay and jitter along the route of h hops. First, we consider the special case of $h = 1$. The general case will be covered later. For simplicity, assume that the scheduled slot is distributed with uniform probability along the basic span. Then, $D_{min}(1) = t^v$, $D_{avg}(1) = 0.5 \cdot S(m) \cdot t_v$, and $D_{max}(1) = S(m) \cdot t_v$. According to the definition of jitter, $J_l(1) = (0.5 \cdot S(m) - 1) \cdot t_v$ and $J_u(1) = 0.5 \cdot S(m) \cdot t_v$.

Now, we consider the general case of $h > 1$. There are two different message management schemes adoptable in the intermediate nodes. In the pipelining scheme, a message arriving from an uplink node waits until the next basic span starts, even though a slot is available later in the current span. Thus, a message always advances one hop per basic span. The delay and jitter under the pipelining scheme are identified with superscript, p: $D^p_{min}(h) = [(h - 1) \cdot S(m) + 1] \cdot t^v$, $D^p_{avg}(h) = (h - 0.5) \cdot S(m) \cdot t_v$, and $D^p_{max}(h) = h \cdot S(m) \cdot t_v$. Also, according to the definion of jitter, $J_l^p(h) = [0.5 \cdot S(m) - 1] \cdot t_v$ and $J_u^p(h) = 0.5 \cdot S(m) \cdot t_v$. Notice that in the pipelining scheme, the jitter is independent of the number of hops h.

The second message management scheme is the pass-through scheme, in which a message can pass through any number of hops during one basic span if there is no other message in the buffer waiting for the available slot. Otherwise, the new message yields the slot access to the old message in the buffer. Suppose that there is no buffered message along the route to simplify the analysis. Notice that this assumption is optimistic and that the real performance measures exist somewhere between the result derived under the pass-through scheme and that under pipelining.

The location variable, x_k, $1 \leq k \leq h$, denotes the allocated slot location at the kth hop in a basic span. Let the basic span be normalized between 0.0 and 1.0 and assume that it contains many slots, that is $2^{n-m} \gg 1$ such that x_k is supposed to be uniformly and continuously distributed with uniform probability in the range [0.0, 1.0]. Then, the case that a message at the source advances k hops during one basic span occurs when the following relation is true: $x_1 < x_2 < \cdots < x_k \geq x_{k+1}$. The instant probability of such a case is represented as $(1 - x_1)(1 - x_2) \cdots (1 - x_{k-1})x_k$, for which $(1 - x_p)$ denotes the probability that x_{p+1} is greater than x_p, and x_{k+1} the probability that x_{k+1} is no greater than x_k. The average probability of a k hops advance per basic span, P_k, is

$$P_k = \int_0^1 \int_{x_1}^1 \cdots \int_{x_{k-1}}^1 (1 - x_1)(1 - x_2) \cdots (1 - x_{k-1})x_k \cdot dx_k dx_{k-1} \cdots dx_1$$

In the above, P_k is decomposed into two terms, $P_k = P_k^1 + P_k^2$, defined as follows:

$$P_k^1 = \int_0^1 \int_{x_1}^1 \cdots \int_{x_{k-1}}^1 (1 - x_1)(1 - x_2) \cdots (1 - x_{k-1})(1 - x_k) \cdot dx_k dx_{k-1} \cdots dx_1 = \frac{1}{2^k \cdot k!}$$

$$P_k^2 = \int_0^1 \int_{x_1}^1 \cdots \int_{x_{k-1}}^1 (1 - x_1)(1 - x_2) \cdots (1 - x_{k-1})1 \cdot dx_k dx_{k-1} \cdots dx_1 = \frac{2^k \cdot k!}{(2k)!}$$

L_k denotes the average location of x_k multiplied by P_k, in which k hops of advance occurs:

$$L_k = \int_0^1 \int_{x_1}^1 \cdots \int_{x_{k-1}}^1 (1 - x_1)(1 - x_2) \cdots (1 - x_{k-1})(x_k)^2 \cdot dx_k dx_{k-1} \cdots dx_1$$

L_k can be represented by P_k^1 and P_k^2 :

$$L_k = P_{k+1}^2 + P_k^2 - 2 \cdot P_k^1$$

H_{avg}, the average number of hops for a message to advance, is shown within four digits precision:

$$H_{avg} = \sum_{k=1}^{\infty} k \cdot P_k \approx 1.0868$$

L_{avg}, the average stop location of a message in a basic span, is shown within four digits precision:

$$L_{avg} = \sum_{k=1}^{\infty} L_k \approx 0.5239$$

Using H_{avg} and L_{avg}, we denote the delay and the jitter for pass-through scheme with superscript t, as follows:

$$D_{min}^t(h) = h \cdot t^v$$

$$D_{avg}^t(h) \approx \left(\frac{h}{H_{avg}} - 1 + L_{avg} \right) \cdot S(m) \cdot t_v$$

$$\approx (0.9201 \cdot h - 0.4761) \cdot S(m) \cdot t_v$$

$$D_{max}^t(h) = h \cdot S(m) \cdot t_v$$

$$J_l^t(h) \approx [(0.9201 \cdot h - 0.4761) \cdot S(m) - h] \cdot t_v$$

$$J_u^t(h) \approx (0.0799 \cdot h + 0.4761) \cdot S(m) \cdot t_v.$$

With a route of five hops, $D_{avg}^t(5)$ is reduced 8.3% in comparison with $D_{avg}^p(5)$. On the contrary, $J_u^t(5)$ increases 75% compared to $J_u^p(5)$. Notice that there is a trade-off on delay and jitter between the two schemes.

On the other hand, regardless of the message scheme applied, both the delay and the jitter are proportionally dependent on logical slot time t_v, basic span $S(m)$, and the number of hops h. As logical slot time is also proportional to the number of physical slots v, if v decreases, then the delay and jitter become shorter and smaller, yielding better performance. However, the link bandwidth utility shrinks. Remember that basic time span $S(m)$ is 2^{n-m}. Since the requested link bandwidth $L(i, j)$ is $1/S(m)$, m is dependent on the bandwidth request. Therefore, the bigger the bandwidth request, the smaller the basic time span, and better the QoS performance.

We examine the results further using some numerical examples. Suppose $L(i, j)$ is 128 Kbps. It is one-eighth of the total bandwidth, 1 Mbps. Because of phase difference, the practical minimum value of v is 2, and one-quarter of total slots, or $m = n - 2$, should be assigned to that request, 50% of which is lost due to asynchronism between two piconets. Moreover, $S(m) = 4$ and $t_v = 2.5$ msec. Thus, the delay and jitter for the requested bandwidth $2 \cdot 64$ Kbps = 128 Kbps and $v = 2$ are $D_{avg}^p(h) = 10(h - 0.5)$ msec and $J_u^p(h) = 5$ msec. If pass-through scheme is used, these measures are $D_{avg}^t(h) = 10(0.9201 h + 0.4761)$ msec and $J_u^t(h) = 10(0.0799 h + 0.4761)$ msec. If we use larger value for v, say 8, the bandwidth loss is reduced from 50% to 12.5%. However, the QoS performance becomes worse: $D_{avg}^p(h) = 80(h - 0.5)$ msec, $J_u^p(h) = 40$ msec, $D_{avg}^t(h) = 80(0.9201 h + 0.4761)$ msec, and $J_u^t(h) = 80(0.0799 h + 0.4761)$ msec.

Although the assigned link load of 2's exponential value, that is $2^k, 0 \leq k \leq n$, is evenly distributed throughout the whole time slot interval, the general link load is somewhat irregularly assigned in the frame interval. Figure 35.11 depicts the simulation result of jittering executed on the scatternet graph in Figure 35.1. The numerical data are derived from the load assignment simulation runs of 20,000. Note that the normalized jitter about the exponential link loads is within the interval [0.0, 2.0]. In the ideal case of uniform slot assignment, all the jitter values are concentrated at location 1.0. Since the 2's exponential link load has only 11 cases, the probability density curve seems to be fluctuating.

On the other hand, the probability density of the general link loads is distributed within the wider range [0.0, 3.8] that is approximately twice of that for the exponential case, although the jitter probability of link load greater than 2.0 is just 1.7%. Thus, the QoS for the general link load is almost identical to that for 2's exponential load.

35.6 CONCLUSION

In this chapter, we present two versions of QoS-aware scheduling algorithms. First of all, in a bipartite scatternet, a perfect QoS-aware scheduling algorithm is pro-

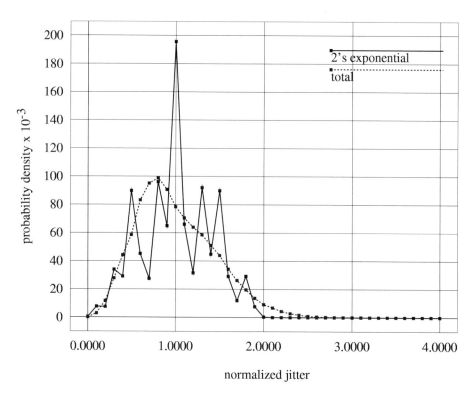

Figure 35.11   Probability density versus normalized jitter simulated on the bipartite graph in Figure 35.1

posed. In a PAN-like Bluetooth scatternet, a reliable algorithm operating over node and network failures is highly desirable, so we present a distributed, local version of the former scheduling algorithm. The algorithm can also be used incrementally when link bandwidth requests change dynamically. Both algorithms are shown to be perfect over tree scatternets.

Next, the proposed algorithms are evaluated as to slot assignment efficiency and analyzed to get their QoS behavior. It is shown that the delay and the jitter are tightly bounded.

There are several topics to be studied further. Although the bipartite scatternet has a perfect algorithm, the general scatternet with master bridge is known not to have one. Thus, it is necessary to design a heuristic QoS-aware algorithm with good schedulability.

REFERENCES

1. C. Bisdikian, An Overview of the Bluetooth Wireless Technology, *IEEE Communications Magazine,* pp. 86–94, Dec. 2001.

2. R. Kapoor et al., Multimedia Support over Bluetooth Piconets, in *ACM Workshop on Wireless Mobile Internet,* pp. 50–55, July 2001.

3. R. Nelson and L. Kleinrock, Spatial TDMA:A Collision-free Multihop Channel Access Protocol, *IEEE Transactions on Communications,* pp. 934–944, Sept. 1985.

4. I. Chlamtac and S. Pinter, Distributed Nodes Organization Algorithm for Channel Access in a Multihop Dynamic Radio Network, *IEEE Transactions on Computers,* pp. 728–737, June 1987.

5. J. Grönkvist, Traffic Controlled Spatial Reuse TDMA in Multi-hop Radio Networks, in *Conference on Personal Indoor and Mobile Radio Communications,* pp. 1203–1207, 1998.

6. N. Johansson, U. Körner and L. Tassiulas, A Distributed Scheduling Algorithm for a Bluetooth Scatternet, in *International Teletraffic Congress,* pp. 61–72, Sept. 2001.

7. N. Johansson et al., Performance Evaluation of Scheduling Algorithms for Bluetooth, *Broadband Communications: Convergence of Network Technologies,* pp. 139–150, June, 2000.

8. M. L. Garey and D. S. Johnson, *Computers and Intractability: A Guide to the Theory of NP-Completeness,* W. H. Freeman, 1979.

9. N. Golmie et al., Interference Aware Bluetooth Packet Scheduling, in *Proceedings of IEEE GLOBECOM,* pp. 2857–2863, Nov. 2001.

10. A. Rácz, et al., A Pseudo Random Coordinated Scheduling Algorithm for Bluetooth Scatternets, in *Proceedings of MobiHOC'01,* pp. 193–203, 2001.

11. N. Johansson et al., JUMP Mode—A Dynamic Window-based Scheduling Framework for Bluetooth Scatternets, in *Proceedings of MobiHOC'01,* pp. 204–211, 2001.

12. M. Sun et al., A Self-Routing Topology for Bluetooth Scatternets, to appear in *Proccedings of I-SPAN,* May, 2002.

13. Young M. Kim, Ten H. Lai, and A. Arora, A QoS-Aware Scheduling Algorithm for Bluetooth Scatternets, The Ohio State University, Technical Report, OSU-CISRC-7/03-TR41, July 2003.

## CHAPTER 36

A Workload Partitioner for Heterogeneous Grids

DANIEL J. HARVEY, SAJAL K. DAS, and RUPAK BISWAS

36.1 INTRODUCTION

Computational grids hold great promise in utilizing geographically separated resources to solve large-scale complex scientific problems. The development of such grid systems has, therefore, been actively pursued in recent years [1, 4, 7, 9, 10, 13]. The Globus project [9], in particular, has been remarkably successful in the development of grid middleware consisting of a general purpose, portable, and modular toolkit of utilities. A comprehensive survey of several grid systems is provided in [8].

Examples of applications that could potentially benefit from computational grids are abundant in several fields including aeronautics, astrophysics, molecular dynamics, genetics, and information systems. It is anticipated that grid solutions for many of these applications will become viable with the advancement of interconnect technology in wide area networks. However, applications that require solutions to adaptive problems need dynamic load balancing during the course of their execution. Load balancing is typically accomplished through the use of a partitioning technique to which a graph is supplied as input. This graph models the processing and communication costs of the application. Many excellent partitioners have been developed over the years; refer to [2] for a survey. However, the most popular state-of-the-art partitioners are multilevel in nature [11, 12, 19]; they contract the supplied graph by collapsing edges, partition the coarsened graph, and then refine the coarse graph back to its original size.

Although some research has been conducted to analyze the performance of irregular adaptive applications in distributed-memory, shared-memory, and cluster multiprocessor configurations [15, 16, 17], little attention has been focused on heterogeneous grid configurations. The design of our partitioner (called MinEX because it attempts to minimize application run time), applies specifically to applications running in grid environments and operates by mapping a partition graph (that models the application) onto a configuration graph (that models the grid), while considering the anticipated level of latency tolerance that can be achieved by the application.

The major contributions of this chapter include: (i) presenting the design of a novel latency-tolerant partitioner, MinEX; (ii) demonstrating the practical use of MinEX with an N-body application solver; (iii) presenting details of MinEX interaction with the N-body application to achieve improved performance in a high-latency, low-bandwidth grid environment; and (iv) directly comparing the performance of MinEX with METIS, a state-of-the-art partitioner, and establishing its effectiveness.

METIS [12] is perhaps the most popular of all multilevel partitioning schemes. However, when applied to a grid environment, METIS has some serious deficiencies. We enumerate below these METIS drawbacks and indicate how they are addressed by MinEX:

- METIS optimizes graph metrics like edge cut or volume of data movement and, therefore, operates in two distinct phases: partitioning and remapping. This approach is usually very inefficient in a distributed environment. MinEX, on the other hand, creates partitions that take data remapping into consideration and strives to overlap application processing and communication to minimize the total runtime of the application.

- Since the processing and communication costs are nonuniform in heterogeneous grids, the assumption of uniform weights for the underlying system (as METIS does) is insufficient. Instead, MinEX utilizes a configuration graph to model grid parameters such as the number of processors, the number of distributed clusters, and the various processing and communication speeds. The partition graph is mapped onto this configuration graph to accommodate a heterogeneous environment.

- Traditional partitioners like METIS do not consider any latency tolerance techniques that could be employed by an application to hide the detrimental effects of low bandwidth in grid environments. However, MinEX has the proper interface to invoke a user-supplied, problem-specific function that models the latency tolerance characteristics of the application.

To evaluate MinEX and compare its effectiveness to METIS for heterogeneous grids, we implemented a solver based on the Barnes and Hut algorithm [3] for the classical N-body problem. Test cases of 16 K, 64 K, and 256 K bodies are solved. We simulate different grid environments that model 8 to 1024 processors configured in 4 or 8 clusters, having interconnect slowdown factors of 10 or 100 and possessing various degrees of heterogeneity. Results show that in heterogeneous configurations MinEX reduces the run-time requirements to solve the N-body application by up to a factor of 6 compared to those obtained when using METIS. Results also show that MinEX is competitive with METIS in terms of partitioning speed.

The chapter is organized as follows. Section 36.2 presents basic concepts of partitioners and defines the performance metrics used. The MinEX partitioner is presented in Section 36.3, while Section 36.4 outlines the N-body problem and our solution procedure. Section 36.5 describes the experimental methodology, analyzes the results, and draws comparisons with METIS. Finally, Section 36.6 concludes the Chapter.

36.2 PRELIMINARIES

This section outlines some basic concepts involved in our partitioning scheme and defines the metrics used for analyzing its performance.

36.2.1 Partition Graph

Applications supply graph representations as input to the partitioners. Such graphs model the characteristics of an application so that the vertices can be assigned among the processors of a multicomputer (or a grid) in a load-balanced fashion. Each vertex v of this partition graph has two weights, $PWgt_v$ and $RWgt_v$, whereas each defined edge (v, w) between vertices v and w has one weight, $CWgt_{(v,w)}$. These weights refer respectively to the computational, data remapping, and communication costs associated with processing a graph vertex. Details of how the weights are computed for our N-body application are given in Section 36.4.2.

36.2.2 Configuration Graph

MinEX utilizes a configuration graph in order to be able to predict its performance on a variety of distributed architectures. This graph defines the heterogeneous characteristics of the grid environment and enables appropriate partitioning decisions to be made. Each cluster c is represented by a vertex, where a cluster consists of one or more tightly coupled processors; whereas an edge (c, d) in the graph corresponds to the communication link between the processors in clusters c and d. A self-loop (c, c) indicates communication among the processors within a single cluster, c. We assume that all processors within a cluster are fully connected and homogeneous, and that there is a constant bandwidth for intracluster communication.

The vertices of the configuration graph have a single weight, $Proc_c \geq 1$, that represents the computation slowdown for the processors in cluster c, relative to the fastest processor in the entire grid (normalized to unity). Likewise, edges have a weight $Connect_{(c,d)} \geq 1$ to model the interconnect slowdown when processors of cluster c communicate with those of cluster d. If $Connect_{(c,d)} = 1$, there is no slowdown, implying that it is the most efficient connection in the network. If $c = d$, $Connect_{(c,c)}$ is the intraconnect slowdown when processors of c communicate internally with one another. In addition to the configuration graph, a processor-to-cluster mapping, $CMap_p$, determines which cluster is associated with each processor p in the grid.

36.2.3 Partitioning Graph Metrics

The MinEX partitioner is unique in that its main objective is to minimize the application run time. To accomplish this goal, user programs provide partition graphs that model computation, communication, and data remapping costs. The partitioner projects expected run times by mapping these metrics onto a grid configuration graph as it executes. The following metrics are used for this purpose:

- **Processing cost** is the computational cost to process vertex v assigned to processor p in cluster c. It is given by $\mathtt{Wgt}_p^v = \mathtt{PWgt}_v \times \mathtt{Proc}_c$.
- **Communication cost** is the cost to interact with all vertices adjacent to v but whose datasets are not local to p (assuming that v is assigned to p). If vertex w is adjacent to v, while c and d are the clusters associated with the processors assigned to v and w, this metric is given by $\mathtt{Comm}_p^v = \Sigma_{w \notin p} \mathtt{CWgt}_{(v,w)} \times \mathtt{Connect}_{(c,d)}$. If the datasets of all the vertices adjacent to v are also assigned to p, then $\mathtt{Comm}_p^v = 0$.
- **Redistribution cost** is the transmission overhead associated with copying the dataset of v from a processor p to another processor q. This cost is 0 if $p = q$; otherwise it is given by $\mathtt{Remap}_p^v = \mathtt{RWgt}_v \times \mathtt{Connect}_{(c,d)}$. Here, we assume that p is in cluster c while q is in cluster d.

36.2.4 System Load Metrics

The following six metrics define values that determine whether the overall system load is balanced:

- **Processor workload** ($\mathtt{QWgt}_p$) is the total cost to process all the vertices assigned to processor p. It is given by $\mathtt{QWgt}_p = \Sigma_{v \in p} (\mathtt{Wgt}_p^v + \mathtt{Comm}_p^v + \mathtt{Remap}_p^v)$.
- **Queue length** ($\mathtt{QLen}_p$) is the total number of vertices assigned to p.
- **Total system load** ($\mathtt{QWgtTOT}$) is the sum of $\mathtt{QWgt}_p$, over all P processors.
- **Average load** ($\mathtt{WSysLL}$) is $\mathtt{QWgtTOT}/P$.
- **Heaviest processor load** ($\mathtt{MaxQWgt}$) is the maximum value of $\mathtt{QWgt}_p$ over all processors, indicating the total time required to process the application.
- **Load imbalance factor** ($\mathtt{LoadImb}$) is the ratio $\mathtt{MaxQWgt}/\mathtt{WSysLL}$ and represents the quality of partitioning.

36.2.5 Partitioning Metrics

These metrics are used by MinEX for the purpose of making partitioning decisions:

- $\mathtt{Gain}$ represents the change in $\mathtt{QWgtTOT}$ that would result from a proposed vertex reassignment. A negative value of $\mathtt{Gain}$ indicates that less processing is required after such a reassignment. The partitioning algorithm favors vertex migrations with negative or small `Gain` values that reduce/minimize the overall system load.

- `Var` is computed using the workload ($QWgt_p$) for each processor p and the average system load (`WSysLL`) in accordance with the formula $Var = \Sigma_p$ $(QWgt_p - WSysLL)^2$. Basically, it is the variance in processor workloads. The objective is to initiate vertex moves that lower this value. Since individual terms of this formula with large values correspond to processors that are most out of balance, minimizing `Var` will tend to bring the system into better load balance. ΔVar is the change in `Var` after moving a vertex from one processor to another; a negative value of ΔVar indicates a reduction in variance.

36.3   THE MinEX PARTITIONER

The main objective of the proposed MinEX partitioner is to minimize run time, as opposed to balancing processor workloads among processors. It accomplishes this by optimizing the computational, communication, and data remapping costs of the applications. The MinEX partitioner is described in detail in the following discussion.

MinEX can execute either in a diffusive manner [6], in which an existing partition is used as a starting point, or it can create partitions from scratch [15]. Similar to other multilevel partitioners, the MinEX partitioning process takes place in three steps: contraction, partitioning, and refinement. During the contraction step, MinEX shrinks the original graph by collapsing edges (v, w), removing vertices v and w, and adding metavertices, m. The partition step is then efficient because of the greatly reduced graph size. During the refinement step, MinEX expands the contracted graph to its original size by restoring the collapsed edges and replacing the metavertices by those vertices removed during contraction.

MinEX is different from most partitioners in that it redefines the partitioning goal to minimize `MaxQWgt` rather than balance the partition workloads and reduce the total edge cut. In addition, MinEX allows applications to provide a function to achieve latency tolerance, if applicable. This user-defined function is described in Section 3.3.6.

36.3.1   MinEX Data Structures

This subsection briefly describes the major data structures used for implementing the multilevel MinEX partitioner.

Graph: {|V|, |E|, *vTot*, *VMap*, *VList*, *EList*} represents the graph to be partitioned, where |V| is the number of graph vertices, |E| is the number of graph edges, *vTot* is the total vertex count (includes original and metavertices), *VMap* lists the vertex numbers that have not been merged, *VList* is a pointer to the complete list of vertices (includes original and metavertices), and *EList* is a pointer to the complete list of edges (includes collapsed and uncollapsed edges).

VMap: The list of active vertices (those that have not been compressed during multilevel partitioning).

VList: Represents the complete list of vertices, where each vertex v contains the following terms:

Pwgt$_v$ is the computational cost (refer to Section 36.2.3).

Rwgt$_v$ is the redistribution cost (refer to Section 36.2.3).

$|e|$ and *$*e$ are, respectively, the number of edges incident on v and a pointer to the first incident edge (subsequent edges are stored contiguously).

merge and *lookup* facilitate graph contraction. *merge* is the metavertex that replaces v after a pair of edges collapse. *lookup* is the unmerged metavertex that contains v in the current graph. Both *merge* and *lookup* are set to -1 if v is still part of the current graph.

$*vmap$ is a pointer to the position of v in the *VMap* table.

$*Heap$ is a pointer to v's min-heap entry. The heap orders potential vertex reassignments.

assign$_v$ and *own* are, respectively, the processor to which vertex v is assigned and the processor where the data for vertex v resides.

EList: The edges in the partitioning graph. Each vertex v in *VList* points to its first edge in *EList* using the pointer *$*e$. Each edge record is defined as $\{w, CWgt_{(v,w)}, CWgt_{(w,v)}\}$, where (v, w) is an edge in the partitioning graph. $CWgt_{(v,w)}$ is the outgoing communication weight and $CWgt_{(w,v)}$ is the incoming communication weight associated with this edge. These weights are not equal for directed graphs.

Heap: The min-heap of potential vertex reassignments. Each heap record is defined as $\{Gain, v, p\}$, which specifies the *Gain* that would result from reassigning vertex v to processor p. The min-heap key is *Gain* so the most promising reassignments can execute first.

Stack: A stack that records edges, (v, w), collapsed during graph contraction. Graph refinement restores edges in an order that is reversed from the one in which they were collapsed. The next section describes graph contraction in more detail.

36.3.2 Contraction

The first step in MinEX is to collapse the graph. This is done in multiple passes; each pass merges half of the vertices in the graph. The contraction process continues until the graph is sufficiently contracted.

Each pass of the contraction starts by executing a bucket sort algorithm to order the vertices by processor and by the number of edges each vertex contains. The sort requires accessing each vertex three times so it completes with $O(V)$ complexity. Presorting the vertices allows MinEX to quickly choose edges to collapse without employing random selection techniques.

To collapse an edge (v, w), a merged vertex M is generated. The edges incident on M are created by utilizing the edge lists of vertices v and w. *VMap* is adjusted to contain M and to remove v and w, $|V|$ is decremented and $vTot$ is incremented, $|E|$ is increased by the number of edges created for M, and the pair (v, w) is pushed onto *Stack*.

The contraction procedure uses a set Union/Find algorithm [5] so that the edges of unmerged vertices remain unchanged. For example, when an unmerged vertex that is adjacent to w accesses its *EList*, it will check whether w has been merged. If it has, *lookup* quickly locates the appropriate unmerged vertex. If *lookup* is not current (i.e., *lookup* > *vTot*), the Union/Find algorithm searches the chain of vertices beginning with *merge* in order to update *lookup*, so that subsequent queries can be performed efficiently. The pseudocode describing the Union/Find procedure is given in Figure 36.1.

MinEX favors collapsing pairs of adjacent vertices that have the least number of total edges. However, we do not claim that this choice is optimal. For example, we have experimented with the choice of adjacent vertex pairs (v, w) having the largest value of $CWgt_{(v,w)}/(Rwgt_v + Rwgt_w)$ in an attempt to minimize edge cut and data distribution cost. We also experimented with collapsing heavy edges first. However, for this application, choosing vertex pairs with the least number of total edges produces the best partitions.

Each pass of the contraction algorithm has a complexity of $O(|V|)$ and completes with a single loop through the sorted list of vertices. MinEX finds the first vertex v that is still in the graph. If the adjacent vertex w with the least number of total edges also remains in the graph, the edge (v, w) is collapsed. If not, MinEX finds and chooses the next unmerged vertex x in the sorted list. Vertices v and x are then merged to form the metavertex M.

36.3.3 Partitioning

The partitioning step follows graph contraction and reassigns metavertices among the processors. The partitioning step is efficient because the number of remaining metavertices is small. The partitioning algorithm considers every vertex of the coarse graph to find possible reassignments that are desirable. The *basic partitioning criterion* reassigns vertices from overloaded processors (where $QWgt_p > WSysLL$) to underloaded processors (where $QWgt_p < WSysLL$) whenever the projected ΔVar is negative. All possible vertex reassignments are added to the min-heap (*Heap*) with pointers from vertices in order to rapidly find the best migration and directly remove

```
Find (v)
   procedure Find (v)
   If (merge = –1) Return (v)
   If ((lookup ≠ –1) And (lookup ≤ vTot))
      Then Return (lookup =)
      Else Return (lookup = Find (merge))
```

Figure 36.1 Pseudocode for the Union/Find algorithm.

entries without searching. The min-heap is keyed by *Gain* so the reassignments that reflect the greatest reduction in QWgtTot are processed first. After each reassignment, adjacent vertices are rechecked for additional migrations and the heap is adjusted accordingly. The partitioning process ends when the heap becomes empty.

To facilitate reassignment decisions, MinEX maintains a list of processors sorted by $QWgt_p$ values that is updated after each vertex reassignment. Because only a small subset of processors change positions in this list after a vertex reassignment (3 or 4 of 32 processors in our experiments), the overhead associated with maintaining this list is acceptable.

36.3.4 Reassignment Filter

The most computationally expensive part of MinEX is the requirement that each adjacent edge must be considered to determine the impact of potential reassignments. To minimize this overhead, we have added a filter function to heuristically estimate the effect of a vertex reassignment. Reassignments that pass through the filter are then further considered in accordance with the *basic partitioning criteria* described above. The filter utilizes edge outgoing and incoming communication totals ($edgeWgt_v$) that are maintained with each vertex to estimate QWgt values for the source and destination processors ($newQWgt_{from}$ and $newQWgt_{to}$, respectively). Using these values, the pseudocode shown in Figure 36.2 is executed to decide whether to accept a possible vertex reassignment.

The reassignment filter rejects reassignments that project increases in run time. It also rejects reassignments that project a positive ΔVar value. The ThroTTle parameter controls increases in projected Gain by acting as a gate that prevent reassignments causing excessive increases in Gain. The Gain metric is squared because Var is also computed using a second-degree calculation. A low ThroTTle could prevent MinEX from finding a balanced partitioning allocation, whereas a high value might converge to a point where run time is unacceptable.

ReassignmentFilter(v)
  If $newQWgt_{from} > QWgt_{from}$ **Reject Assignment**
  If $newQWgt_{to} < QWgt_{to}$ **Reject Assignment**
  ΔVar $= (newQWgt_{from} - WSysLL)^2 + (newQWgt_{to} - WSysLL)^2$
    $- (QWgt_{from} - WSysLL)^2 - (QWgt_{to} - WSysLL)^2$
  If ΔVar ≥ 0 **Reject Assignment**
  newGain $= newQWgt_{from} + newQWgt_{to} - QWgt_{from} - QWgt_{to}$
  If newGain > 0 **And** $newGain^2 / -\Delta$Var $>$ ThroTTle **Reject Assignment**
  If *fabs*($newQWgt_{from} - newQWgt_{to}$) $>$ *fabs*($QWgt_{from} - QWgt_{to}$)
    If $newQWgt_{from} < QWgt_{to}$ **Reject Assignment**
    If $newQWgt_{to} > QWgt_{from}$ **Reject Assignment**
  Assignment Passes Filter

Figure 36.2   Pseudocode for the reassignment filter algorithm.

Table 36.1 demonstrates the effectiveness of the reassignment filter for 8, 128, and 1024 processors. We enumerate the total number of vertex assignments considered (`Total`), the number of assignments that passed through the filter (`Accepted`), and the number of potential reassignments that subsequently failed the *basic partitioning criteria* described in Section 36.3.3 (`Failed`). The partition graph represents N-body problems consisting of 16 K, 64 K, and 256 K bodies. The results clearly demonstrate that the reassignment filter eliminates almost all of the edge processing overhead associated with reassignments that are rejected. For example, for 128 processors and 256 K bodies, a total of 4608 of 51,876 potential vertex reassignments passed through the filter. Only one of these potential reassignments were subsequently rejected.

36.3.5 Refinement

The last step in partitioning is to expand the graph back to its original form through a refinement algorithm. MinEX maintains pairs of merged vertices in the *Stack* data structure so refinement of vertices proceeds in reverse order from how they were merged. Therefore, the graph is restored sequentially one graph at a time instead of in halves as is common with other multilevel partitioners. The advantage of this approach is that a decision can be made each time a vertex is refined as to whether it should be assigned to another processor, making the algorithm more flexible. If $|V|$ is the total number of vertices in the graph, the refinement requires $O(|V|)$ steps, which is asymptotically equal to the complexity of refining it sequentially in halves.

As pairs of vertices (v, w) are refined, merged edges and vertices are deallocated. The *merge* and *lookup* values are also adjusted in *VList*. The list *VMap* of active vertices is updated to delete the merged vertex M, and to restore v and w; $|V|$ is incremented and *vTot* is decremented; and $|E|$ is decreased by the number of edges created for M.

After each refinement, additional improvements to the partition are possible by reassigning either v or w. These reassignments are based on the same *basic partitioning criteria* described in the partitioning step. Each metavertex reassignment essentially migrates all of the vertices that the metavertex represents. After a reassignment, MinEX considers adjacent vertices for reassignment to determine if partition quality improvements are possible.

Table 36.1 Filter effectiveness for 16 K, 64 K, and 256 K bodies processed by 8, 128, and 1024 processors

P	16 K N-bodies			64 K N-bodies			256 K N-bodies		
	Total	Accepted	Failed	Total	Accepted	Failed	Total	Accepted	Failed
8	6011	110	0	14,991	212	0	25,183	222	0
128	19,192	2562	0	49,082	5240	4	51,876	4608	1
1024	18,555	2790	7	23,986	6569	4	35,605	12,639	2

36.3.6   Latency Tolerance

MinEX interacts with a user-defined function (called MinEX_LatTol), if one is supplied, to account for possible latency tolerance that can be achieved by the application. This is a novel approach to partitioning that is not employed by existing partitioners, including METIS. The calling signature of this function is as follows:

```
double MinEX_LatTol (User *user, Ipg *ipg, QTot *tot)
user       = user-supplied options passed to MinEX_PartGraph,
ipg        = grid configuration passed to MinEX_PartGraph, and
tot        = projected totals computed by MinEX that contains:
```
   (a) p, the processor to which the call applies,
   (b) $\mathtt{Pproc}_p = \Sigma_{v \in p} \, \mathtt{Wgt}_p^v$, the total processing weight,
   (c) $\mathtt{Crcv}_p = \Sigma_{v \in p} \, \mathtt{Comm}_p^v$, the data communication cost,
   (d) $\mathtt{Rrcv}_p = \Sigma_{v \in p} \, \mathtt{Remap}_p^v$, the data relocation cost, and
   (e) $\mathtt{QLen}_p$, the number of vertices assigned to p.

The function utilizes these quantities to compute the projected value of $\mathtt{QWgt}_p$ that is returned to the partitioner. The projected value differs from the $\mathtt{QWgt}_p$ definition given in Section 36.2.4 because some of the processing is overlapped with communication.

36.4   N-BODY APPLICATION

The N-body application is the classical problem of simulating the movement of a set of bodies based upon gravitational or electrostatic forces. Many applications in the fields of astrophysics, molecular dynamics, computer graphics, and fluid dynamics can utilize N-body solvers. The basic solution involves calculating the velocity and position of N bodies at discrete time steps, given their initial positions and velocities. At each step, there are N^2 pairwise interactions of forces between bodies.

Of the many N-body solution techniques that have been proposed, the Barnes and Hut algorithm [3] is perhaps the most popular. The approach is to approximate the force exerted on a body by a cell of bodies that is sufficiently distant using the center of mass and the total mass in the remote cell. In this way, the number of force calculations can be significantly reduced. The first step is to recursively build a tree of cells in which the bodies are grouped by their physical positions. A cell v is considered close to another cell w if the ratio of the distance between the two furthest bodies in v to the distance between the centers of mass of v and w is less than a specified parameter, say δ. In this case, all the bodies in cell v must perform pairwise force calculations with each body in cell w. However, if w is far from v, cell w is treated as a single body using its total mass and center of mass for force interaction calculations with the bodies of v. An example of a parallel Barnes and Hut implementation using message passing is described in [20]; this was later refined in

[14]. In this chapter, we modify the basic Barnes and Hut approach to construct a novel graph-based model of the N-body problem to integrate the application with MinEX and METIS partitioners. We then run the N-body solver to directly compare the run-time effects of both partitioning schemes in a distributed heterogeneous grid environment.

36.4.1 Tree Creation

The first step in solving the N-body problem is to recursively build an oct-tree of cells. The process begins by inserting bodies into an initial cell until it contains `CellMax` number of bodies. `CellMax` is set to a value that minimizes the total number of calculations required by the solver to compute the body forces. Before the next body can be inserted, this cell is split into eight octants. Each of these eight smaller cells contains the previously inserted bodies based on their centers of mass. Insertion of bodies into this tree continues until one of the cells has more than `CellMax` bodies. This cell is then further subdivided into eight octants, and the process continues. Naturally, all the bodies reside in the leaves of the oct-tree. Figure 36.3 illustrates this concept: both the spatial and tree representations are shown. The cell's center of mass is used for subsequent searches of the tree. Traversal direction is determined by the octant in which a body resides relative to this center of mass.

36.4.2 Partition Graph Construction

When the tree creation phase of the Barnes and Hut algorithm is finished, a graph G is constructed. This graph is presented to the MinEX and METIS partitioners to balance the load among the available processors. However, for METIS to execute successfully, G must be somewhat modified to another graph G_M, as described in Section 36.4.3. For direct comparisons between the two partitioners, experiments are conducted with the modified graph G_M.

Each vertex v of G corresponds to a leaf cell C_v (of $|C_v|$ bodies) in the N-body oct-tree and has two weights, `PWgt`$_v$ and `RWgt`$_v$. Each defined edge (v, w) has one

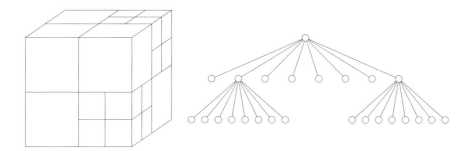

Figure 36.3 A three-level oct-tree and the corresponding spatial representation.

weight, $\text{CWgt}_{(v,w)}$. These weights (see Section 36.2.1) model the processing, data remapping, and communication costs incurred when the solver processes C_v. The total time required to process the vertices assigned to a processor p must take into account all three metrics. Their values are set as follows:

- $\text{PWgt}_v = |C_v| \times (|C_v| - 1 + \text{Close}_v + \text{Far}_v + 2)$ is the number of computations that are executed by the solver to calculate new positions of the bodies residing in C_v. Here, Close_v is the number of bodies in cells close to C_v and Far_v is the number of cells that are far from C_v. The additive factor of 2 in the equation represents the double integration of acceleration that is performed to arrive at body positions at the next time step once the effect of gravitational forces are determined.

- RWgt_v defines the cost of relocating cell C_v from one processor to another. Thus, $\text{RWgt}_v = |C_v|$, since each of the bodies in C_v must be migrated.

- $\text{CWgt}_{(v,w)}$ represents the communication cost when cell C_v is close to another cell C_w. In this case, the mass and position of each body in C_w must be transmitted to the processor to which C_v is assigned. Thus, $\text{CWgt}_{(v,w)} = |C_w|$ if C_w is close to C_v; otherwise, it is 0.

Note that the edge (v, w) is in G only if either C_v is close to C_w or vice versa. Also, G is a directed graph because $\text{CWgt}_{(v,w)} \neq \text{CWgt}_{(w,v)}$ if $|C_v| \neq |C_w|$, or whenever C_w is close to C_v but C_v is far from C_w. We do not model the cost to communicate the C_w center of mass when C_w is far from C_v because each processor contains the tree of internal nodes making these communications unnecessary.

36.4.3   Graph Modifications for METIS

The METIS partitioner has two limitations that must be addressed before its performance can be directly compared with that of MinEX. First, METIS does not allow zero edge weights; second, it is unable to process directed graphs. Both of these occur in the N-body partition graphs.

To accommodate these two limitations in METIS, a modified graph G_M is generated that is usable by both partitioning schemes. G_M differs from G in its edge weights: $\text{CWgt}_{(v,w)} = \max(|C_v|, |C_w|)$ for all edges (v, w). This guarantees that the edges in G_M have positive weights, and that the graph is undirected with $\text{CWgt}_{(v,w)} = \text{CWgt}_{(w,v)}$.

36.5   EXPERIMENTAL STUDY

In our experiments, we simulate a grid environment on a uniprocessor in which the N-body solver is executed. Our simulator models a grid using message passing primitives similar to MPI. The grid environment is modeled using discrete time simulation and uses the grid configuration graph (defined in Section 36.2.2) to account for latency and bandwidth. Experimental test cases with 16 K, 64 K, and 256 K bodies are considered that model two neighboring Plummer galaxies that are about to merge [18]. The partition graphs for these test cases respectively contain 4563, 8091, and 14,148 vertices, and 99,802, 159,496, and 236,338 edges.

Graphs labeled G in the following tables refer to the directed graph defined in Section 36.4.2 and are used only by MinEX. Graphs labeled G_M are undirected as described in Section 36.4.3 to accommodate the requirements of METIS. Both MinEX and METIS are run on G_M to obtain direct comparisons between the two partitioning schemes. Our experiments use the METIS partitioner that computes a k-way partition while minimizing edge cuts.

The grid configuration graph is varied to evaluate performance over a wide spectrum of heterogeneous grid environments, as discussed below. The total number of processors (P) varies between 8 to 1024 depending on the experiment. The number of clusters (C) are either 4 or 8, while interconnect slowdowns (I) are 10 or 100. Note that we always assume that communication overhead within clusters is constant, as is typically true for real geographically distributed grids.

Three configuration types (HO, UP, and DN) are used in our experiments. The HO configurations assume that all processors are homogeneous and grouped evenly among the clusters with intraconnect and processing slowdown factors of unity. The configurations labeled UP assume that processors in cluster i have intraconnect and processing slowdown factors of $2i - 1$. Therefore, processors in clusters with higher ids incur greater communication and processing overhead than those with lower ids. Finally, the configurations labeled DN assume that the processors in cluster i have intraconnect slowdown factors of $2C - 1 - 2i$ and processing slowdown factors of $2i - 1$. These configurations assume that clusters with higher ids incur greater communication overhead but lesser processing overhead than clusters with lower ids. The spectrum of three configuration types allows us to consider a variety of heterogeneous grid characteristics. The results of our experiments are presented in the following subsections.

36.5.1 Multiple Time Step Test

This set of experiments determines whether running multiple time steps are likely to significantly impact the overall performance. Table 36.2 presents average runtimes per step (in thousands of units) and LoadImb factors when executing 1 and

Table 36.2 Performance for 1 and 50 time steps

Type	1 time step		50 time steps	
	Run time	Load Imb	Runtime	Load Imb
MinEX—G	398	1.03	388	1.01
MinEX—G_M	413	1.05	398	1.02
METIS—G_M	1630	2.16	1534	2.03

50 time steps. MinEX is run with both the G and G_M graphs, whereas METIS is run only with the G_M graph. Both partitioners are invoked before the solver executes each time step. The partition graph represents 16 K bodies and the configuration type is UP, whereas interconnect slowdowns, number of processors, and number of clusters are respectively set as $I = 10$, $P = 64$, and $C = 8$. Results show that running multiple time steps has only little impact. Our subsequent experiments, therefore, executed only a single time step.

36.5.2 Scalability Test

The purpose of this test is to determine how the application scales with the number of processors. We process graphs representing 16 K, 64 K, and 256 K bodies using the UP configuration containing between 8 and 512 processors that are distributed among 8 clusters with an interconnect slowdown of 10. Table 36.3 reports run times (in thousands of units) and shows that the application scales well for up to 128 processors. Based on these results, our subsequent load balance comparison tests are conducted only for $P = 32$, $P = 64$, or $P = 128$.

36.5.3 Partitioner Speed Comparisons

In this section, we compare MinEX partitioning speed to that of METIS. For these experiments, P is varied between 8 and 1024 with partition graphs representing 16 K, 64 K, and 256 K bodies. The UP configuration is used with $C = 8$ and $I = 10$. Results in Table 36.4 show that MinEX executes faster than METIS in the majority of cases. For example, if $P = 128$, MinEX outperforms METIS on all graph sizes. However, METIS has a clear advantage when processing 256 K bodies with $P = 512$ or $P = 1024$ processors. In general, though, we can conclude that MinEX is at least competitive with METIS in execution speed.

Table 36.3 Run time (in thousands of units) comparisons for varying numbers of processors

Bodies	Graph type	Number of processors P						
		8	16	32	64	128	256	512
16 K	MinEX—G	2792	1445	760	398	213	124	94
	MinEX—G_M	2867	1466	780	413	206	124	94
	METIS—G_M	10384	5330	2919	1630	1619	1395	847
64 K	MinEX—G	12035	6172	3184	1625	822	716	355
	MinEX—G_M	12085	6233	3217	1656	837	716	355
	METIS—G_M	43785	23235	11738	6150	3110	3113	3735
256 K	MinEX—G	78297	39335	20038	10187	5113	2917	1756
	MinEX—G_M	78396	39448	20193	10183	5174	2927	1767
	METIS—G_M	301573	151983	76017	38379	19734	9901	5071

Table 36.4   MinEX and METIS partitioning speed (in seconds)

Bodies	Graph type	Number of processors P							
		8	16	32	64	128	256	512	1024
16 K	MinEX—G	0.17	0.20	0.23	0.33	0.53	1.09	1.58	2.36
	MinEX—G_M	0.18	0.20	0.23	0.32	0.53	1.13	1.51	2.39
	METIS—G_M	0.16	0.23	0.35	1.02	1.05	1.46	1.81	2.88
64 K	MinEX—G	0.31	0.33	0.40	0.59	1.00	1.93	3.09	4.93
	MinEX—G_M	0.35	0.37	0.39	0.58	1.05	1.99	3.09	4.73
	METIS—G_M	0.21	0.22	0.45	0.60	1.55	1.82	2.32	3.42
256 K	MinEX—G	0.48	0.53	0.57	0.71	1.08	2.27	5.37	9.08
	MinEX—G_M	0.50	0.55	0.55	0.69	1.08	2.30	5.88	9.17
	METIS—G_M	0.43	0.49	0.59	0.76	1.20	2.57	3.18	4.18

36.5.4   Partitioner Quality Comparisons

We present three tables to extensively compare the quality of partitions generated by MinEX and METIS. Tables 36.5, 36.6, and 36.7 show N-body application run times and LoadImb results for graphs representing 16 K, 64 K, and 256 K bodies. Each table contains results of runs using the UP, HO, and DN configuration types for grids. The number of processors is varied between 32 and 128, the number of clusters are 4 or 8, and the interconnect slowdowns are set to 10 or 100.

36.5.4.1   *16 K Bodies*   Table 36.5 presents results of experiments using partition graphs representing 16 K bodies. These results show that MinEX has a significant advantage over METIS in the heterogeneous UP and DN configuration types. For example, if $P = 64$, $C = 8$, and $I = 10$, MinEX shows an improvement in runtime by a factor of 4. If $P = 128$, the advantage increases to a factor of 6. In both cases, the improvement in load balance is also very significant. Results for the homogeneous configuration HO are less conclusive. Here, METIS is competitive with MinEX; however, in several cases, MinEX still has a significant advantage (e.g., $P = 64$, $C = 8$, $I = 100$). The fact that METIS is competitive is not surprising given that its strategy to minimize the edge cut should be effective in homogeneous configurations. Note that the performance of MinEX running with the graph G is in general superior to that of MinEX running with the graph G_M. This result is somewhat expected because G models the actual solver more closely than G_M does. However, MinEX using G_M still has similar advantages over METIS. One final observation is that MinEX has a significant but smaller advantage over METIS for configurations in which the interconnect slowdown is greater ($I = 100$). This is because as interconnect slowdowns increase, the communication overhead begins to dominate the application. The differences in intraconnect communication and processing speeds, therefore, become less significant and, in effect, the network becomes more homogeneous. Perhaps if MinEX is refined to put a greater focus on achieving a minimum edge cut, it could retain more of its advantage over METIS in these cases.

Table 36.5   Run time (in thousands of units) comparisons for 16 K bodies

P	C	I	Type	UP		HO		DN	
				Run time	Load Imb	Run time	Load Imb	Run time	Load Imb
32	4	10	MinEX—G	459	1.00	197	1.02	461	1.01
			MinEX—G_M	479	1.04	206	1.06	480	1.05
			METIS—G_M	1362	1.88	196	1.07	1362	1.88
32	4	100	MinEX—G	1023	1.07	921	1.02	1046	1.07
			MinEX—G_M	1157	1.22	1167	1.25	1196	1.21
			METIS—G_M	1363	1.74	1167	2.49	1363	1.73
32	8	10	MinEX—G	760	1.01	197	1.02	763	1.01
			MinEX—G_M	780	1.04	211	1.09	792	1.04
			METIS—G_M	2919	2.01	196	1.07	2919	2.01
32	8	100	MinEX—G	1347	1.03	1198	1.02	1371	1.03
			MinEX—G_M	1562	1.17	1417	1.24	1574	1.17
			METIS—G_M	2920	1.91	1182	1.67	2920	1.90
64	4	10	MinEX—G	234	1.01	106	1.08	235	1.04
			MinEX—G_M	245	1.05	109	1.11	245	1.04
			METIS—G_M	761	2.01	108	1.16	761	2.01
64	4	100	MinEX—G	620	1.10	450	1.20	634	1.11
			MinEX—G_M	737	1.28	612	1.45	746	1.27
			METIS—G_M	763	1.72	621	2.12	763	1.73
64	8	10	MinEX—G	398	1.03	109	1.11	372	1.01
			MinEX—G_M	413	1.05	115	1.15	421	1.06
			METIS—G_M	1630	2.16	108	1.16	1630	2.16
64	8	100	MinEX—G	794	1.05	549	1.03	798	1.04
			MinEX—G_M	936	1.22	685	1.39	946	1.20
			METIS—G_M	1632	2.01	841	2.01	1632	2.00
128	4	10	MinEX—G	121	1.03	94	1.80	194	1.16
			MinEX—G_M	122	1.03	94	1.44	194	1.15
			METIS—G_M	755	3.98	131	2.73	917	4.60
128	4	100	MinEX—G	353	1.32	426	1.29	493	1.22
			MinEX—G_M	425	1.40	408	1.40	482	1.20
			METIS—G_M	756	3.42	425	3.19	917	3.76
128	8	10	MinEX—G	213	1.11	94	1.80	196	1.08
			MinEX—G_M	206	1.05	94	1.55	217	1.05
			METIS—G_M	1619	4.27	131	2.73	1619	4.25
128	8	100	MinEX—G	465	1.17	428	1.23	476	1.18
			MinEX—G_M	519	1.23	633	1.82	678	1.65
			METIS—G_M	1619	3.99	604	3.19	1619	3.97

Table 36.6   Run time (in thousands of units) comparisons for 64 K bodies

P	C	I	Type	UP Run time	UP Load Imb	HO Run time	HO Load Imb	DN Run time	DN Load Imb
32	4	10	MinEX—G	1930	1.01	831	1.03	1933	1.01
			MinEX—G_M	1965	1.02	848	1.05	1974	1.03
			METIS—G_M	5574	1.82	802	1.05	5574	1.82
32	4	100	MinEX—G	3377	1.05	1529	1.06	3436	1.09
			MinEX—G_M	3812	1.18	1484	1.32	3843	1.18
			METIS—G_M	5575	1.80	1799	1.80	5575	1.80
32	8	10	MinEX—G	3184	1.00	828	1.02	3189	1.01
			MinEX—G_M	3217	1.02	851	1.05	3234	1.02
			METIS—G_M	11738	1.91	802	1.05	11738	1.71
32	8	100	MinEX—G	4882	1.08	1655	1.05	4916	1.05
			MinEX—G_M	5312	1.12	1634	1.03	5333	1.12
			METIS—G_M	11738	1.91	2079	1.68	11738	1.90
64	4	10	MinEX—G	979	1.00	417	1.02	981	1.01
			MinEX—G_M	1005	1.03	432	1.06	1004	1.03
			METIS—G_M	2878	1.85	425	1.09	2878	1.85
64	4	100	MinEX—G	1869	1.10	1042	1.03	1919	1.10
			MinEX—G_M	2297	1.28	1140	1.35	2299	1.27
			METIS—G_M	2879	1.81	1245	2.18	2879	1.81
64	8	10	MinEX—G	1625	1.01	419	1.02	1634	1.01
			MinEX—G_M	1656	1.03	432	1.06	1658	1.03
			METIS—G_M	6150	1.98	425	1.09	6150	1.98
64	8	100	MinEX—G	2705	1.07	1194	1.03	2716	1.06
			MinEX—G_M	3102	1.17	1308	1.29	3140	1.17
			METIS—G_M	6150	1.96	1434	1.47	6150	1.96
128	4	10	MinEX—G	498	1.02	265	1.24	854	1.07
			MinEX—G_M	520	1.06	265	1.24	848	1.07
			METIS—G_M	1478	1.86	276	1.38	1784	1.97
128	4	100	MinEX—G	998	1.14	854	1.38	1489	1.16
			MinEX—G_M	1177	1.31	983	1.24	1554	1.14
			METIS—G_M	1479	1.80	993	1.38	1784	1.86
128	8	10	MinEX—G	822	1.01	265	1.24	838	1.03
			MinEX—G_M	837	1.03	265	1.24	842	1.03
			METIS—G_M	3110	1.96	276	1.55	3110	1.96
128	8	100	MinEX—G	1438	1.11	1080	1.05	1436	1.10
			MinEX—G_M	1761	1.26	1330	1.34	1764	1.25
			METIS—G_M	3110	1.93	1068	1.55	3110	1.92

36.5.4.2 64 K Bodies   The experiments shown in Table 36.6 are the same as those above but with a larger partition graph representing 64 K bodies. The results are very similar to those shown in Table 36.5 but with a few surprising differences. For example, some of the MinEX results with the DN configuration are worse than the corresponding results with the UP configuration type. For example, when $P = 128$, $C = 4$, and $I = 100$ MinEX—G exhibits a run time of 998 with UP but 1489 with DN. Note that the MinEX partitioner estimated a run time of 975 and a load balance of 1.0001 in the DN case. The discrepancy is explained in that processors incur excessive idle time when processing the application with the DN configuration so that the partitioner estimates are not realized. This illustrates a potential problem for partitioners for solving grid-based applications. Even if communication costs can be exactly predicted, the dynamics of the application can still result in unexpected idle time. To further investigate this problem, we modified our simulator to accommodate multiple I/O channels at each processor (the original version assumed that each process has only one I/O channel). With two channels per processor, the solver executed the application with a runtime of 975; exactly as MinEX estimated. With four input channels per processor, the runtime was 973. These multiple channel improvements were not obtained when using METIS.

36.5.4.3 256 K Bodies   The results shown in Table 36.7 are from comparison experiments on partition graphs representing 256 K bodies. Performance with the UP and DN configuration graphs are consistent with those presented in the previous two subsections. However, the HO experiments produced additional surprises. Here, METIS has a clear advantage when $P = 32$ or $P = 64$, and $I = 100$. When investigating these cases, we discovered that MinEX converges very closely to a estimated partition (LoadImb of 1.0001) but converges at too high a value. Evidently, the partitioning criteria for vertex reassignments needs to be refined to prevent this situation. This is an open research problem that needs to be addressed before MinEX (or any grid-based partitioner) can be successfully utilized as a general-purpose tool.

36.6 CONCLUSIONS

In this article, we have proposed a novel latency-tolerant partitioner, called MinEX, designed specifically for heterogeneous distributed computing environments such as the NASA Information Power Grid (IPG). MinEX has significant advantages over other traditional partitioners. For example, its partitioning goal to minimize application run times, its ability to map applications onto heterogeneous grid configurations, and its interface to application latency tolerance information make it well suited for grid environments. In addition, MinEX is also capable of partitioning directed graphs with zero edge weights (which occur in graphs modeling N-body applications); a distinct advantage over popular state-of-the-art partitioners such as METIS.

Table 36.7 Run time (in thousands of units) comparisons for 256 K bodies

P	C	I	Type	UP Run time	UP Load Imb	HO Run time	HO Load Imb	DN Run time	DN Load Imb
32	4	10	MinEX—G	12114	1.00	5137	1.01	12122	1.00
			MinEX—G_M	12186	1.01	5178	1.02	12223	1.01
			METIS—G_M	35474	1.79	5122	1.04	35474	1.79
32	4	100	MinEX—G	12344	1.04	7239	1.19	12355	1.04
			MinEX—G_M	14089	1.09	6929	1.17	14628	1.10
			METIS—G_M	35475	1.79	5132	1.04	37475	1.79
32	8	10	MinEX—G	20038	1.00	5177	1.02	20095	1.00
			MinEX—G_M	20193	1.01	5188	1.02	20220	1.01
			METIS—G_M	76017	1.92	5122	1.04	76017	1.92
32	8	100	MinEX—G	21173	1.06	7399	1.19	21634	1.05
			MinEX—G_M	23471	1.06	7541	1.23	24136	1.06
			METIS—G_M	76018	1.93	5199	1.05	76018	1.92
64	4	10	MinEX—G	6109	1.00	2590	1.01	6124	1.00
			MinEX—G_M	6158	1.01	2625	1.03	6172	1.01
			METIS—G_M	18102	1.82	2650	1.07	18102	1.82
64	4	100	MinEX—G	6627	1.09	4231	1.22	6616	1.07
			MinEX—G_M	8237	1.11	4131	1.28	8276	1.11
			METIS—G_M	18102	1.82	3334	1.33	18102	1.82
64	8	10	MinEX—G	10187	1.01	2590	1.02	10160	1.00
			MinEX—G_M	10183	1.01	2625	1.03	10222	1.01
			METIS—G_M	38379	1.95	2656	1.07	38379	1.95
64	8	100	MinEX—G	11459	1.08	4241	1.27	11982	1.06
			MinEX—G_M	13400	1.08	4894	1.20	13797	1.08
			METIS—G_M	38791	1.95	3842	1.51	38791	1.95
128	4	10	MinEX—G	3094	1.01	1384	1.07	4362	1.07
			MinEX—G_M	3119	1.02	1384	1.07	4357	1.08
			METIS—G_M	9209	1.83	1443	1.15	10105	1.94
128	4	10	MinEX—G	3654	1.15	2324	1.24	6545	1.33
			MinEX—G_M	4284	1.09	2464	1.42	5896	1.12
			METIS—G_M	9210	1.83	2337	1.79	10185	1.91
128	4	100	MinEX—G	5113	1.01	1353	1.07	5174	1.02
			MinEX—G_M	5174	1.02	1372	1.07	5174	1.02
			METIS—G_M	19734	1.96	1443	1.15	19374	1.96
128	8	100	MinEX—G	6160	1.07	2111	1.11	6620	1.09
			MinEX—G_M	7109	1.07	2326	1.22	7421	1.12
			METIS—G_M	19735	1.96	2337	1.74	19735	1.96

Using a solver that we developed for the classical N-body problem, we evaluated and compared the performance of MinEX to METIS to determine how each partitioning scheme performs in a heterogeneous grid environment. Extensive simulation experimental results demonstrate that whereas MinEX produces partitions of comparable quality to METIS on homogeneous grids, it improves application run times by a factor of 6 on several heterogeneous configurations. The experiments demonstrate the feasibility and benefits of our approach to map application partition graphs onto grid environments, and to incorporate latency tolerance techniques directly into the partitioning process. The experiments also reveal issues that need to be addressed if a general grid-based partitioning tool is to be realized. For example, the number of I/O channels per processor affects the actual run time and load balance that is achieved by the application because the resulting idle time is directly affected. Furthermore, additional schemes for reassigning vertices in a grid environment need to be explored so that consistent results can be achieved in all grid configurations.

ACKNOWLEDGMENTS

This work was partially supported by NASA Ames Research Center under Cooperative Agreement NCC 2-5395.

REFERENCES

1. D. Abramson, R. Sosic, J. Giddy, and B. Hall, Nimrod: A tool for performing parametised simulations using distributed workstations, in *4th IEEE Symposium on High Performance Distributed Computing,* pp. 112–121, 1995.

2. C. J. Alpert and A. B. Kahng, Recent directions in netlist partitioning: A survey *Integration, the VLSI Journal, 19,* 1–81, 1995.

3. J. Barnes and P. Hut, A hierarchical $O(N \log N)$ force calculation algorithm, *Nature, 324,* 446–449, 1986.

4. H. Casanova and J. Dongarra, NetSolve: A network-enabled server for solving computational science problems, *International Journal of Supercomputer Applications, 11,* 212–223, 1987.

5. T. Cormen, C. Lieserson, and R. Rivest, *Introduction to Algorithms,* McGraw Hill, 1990.

6. G. Cybenko, Dynamic load balancing for distributed-memory multiprocessors, *Journal of Parallel and Distributed Computing, 7,* 279–301, 1989.

7. J. Czyzyk, M. P. Mesnier, and J. J. Moré, The network-enabled optimization system (NEOS) server, Preprint MCS-P615-1096, Argonne National Laboratory, 1997.

8. I. Foster and C. Kesselman, *The Grid: Blueprint for a New Computing Infrastructure,* Morgan Kaufmann, 1999.

9. Globus Project, see URL http://www.globus.org.

10. A. S. Grimshaw and W. A. Wulf, The Legion vision of a worldwide computer, *Communications of the ACM, 40,* 39–45, 1997.

11. B. Hendrickson and R. Leland, A multilevel algorithm for partitioning graphs, Technical Report SAND93-1301, Sandia National Laboratories, 1993.

12. G. Karypis and V. Kumar, Parallel multilevel k-way partitioning scheme for irregular graphs, Technical Report 96-036, University of Minnesota, 1996.

13. J. Leigh, A. E. Johnson, and T. A. DeFanti, CAVERN: A distributed architecture for supporting scalable persistence and interoperability in collaborative virtual environments, *Virtual Reality Research, Development and Applications, 2,* 217–237, 1997.

14. P. Liu and S. Bhatt, Experiences with parallel N-body simulations, in *6th ACM Symposium on Parallel Algorithms and Architectures* pp. 122–131, 1988.

15. L. Oliker and R. Biswas, Parallelization of a dynamic unstructured algorithm using three leading programming paradigms, *IEEE Transactions on Parallel and Distributed Systems, 11,* 931–940, 2002.

16. H. Shan, J. P. Singh, L. Oliker, and R. Biswas, A comparison of three programming models for adaptive applications on the Origin2000, *Journal of Parallel and Distributed Computing, 62,* 241–266, 2002.

17. H. Shan, J. P. Singh, L. Oliker, and R. Biswas, Message passing and shared address space parallelism on an SMP cluster, *Parallel Computing, 29,* 167–186, 2003.

18. J. P. Singh, C. Holt, T. Totsuka, A. Gupta, and J. Hennessy, Load balancing and data locality in adaptive hierarchical N-body methods: Barnes-Hut, fast multipole, and radiosity, *Journal of Parallel and Distributed Computing, 27,* 118–141, 1995.

19. C. Walshaw, M. Cross, and M. Everett, Parallel dynamic graph partitioning for adaptive unstructured meshes, *Journal of Parallel and Distributed Computing, 47,* 102–108, 1997.

20. M. S. Warren and J. K. Salmon, A parallel hashed oct-tree N-body algorithm, in *Supercomputing '93,* pp. 12–21, 1993.

## CHAPTER 37

Building a User-Level Grid for Bag-of-Tasks Applications

WALFREDO CIRNE, FRANCISCO BRASILEIRO, DANIEL PARANHOS,
LAURO COSTA, ELIZEU SANTOS-NETO, and CARLA OSTHOFF

37.1 INTRODUCTION

Bag-of-Tasks (BoT) applications are parallel applications whose tasks are independent of each other. Despite their simplicity, BoT applications are used in a variety
of scenarios, including data mining, massive searches (such as key breaking), parameter sweeps [1], simulations, fractal calculations, computational biology [17], and
computer imaging [15]. Moreover, due to the independence of their tasks, BoT applications can be successfully executed over widely distributed computational
grids, as has been demonstrated by SETI@home [2]. In fact, one can argue that
BoT applications are the applications most suited for computational grids, in which
communication can easily become a bottleneck for tightly coupled parallel applications.

However, few users of BoT applications are currently using computational grids,
despite the potential dramatic increase in resources grids can bring to bear for problem resolution. We believe that this state of affairs is due to (i) the complexity involved in using grid technology, and (ii) the slow deployment of existing grid infrastructure. Today, one must commit considerable effort to make an application run
efficiently on a grid. The user, who is ultimately interested in getting the application's results, seldom has the training or the inclination to deal with the level of detail needed to use current grid infrastructure. Furthermore, the existing grid infrastructure is not ubiquitously installed yet. Users often have access to resources that
are not grid-ready.

In this chapter we present MyGrid, a system designed to change this state of affairs. MyGrid aims to easily enable the execution of BoT application on whatever
resources the user has available. MyGrid chooses a different trade-off compared to
existing grid infrastructure. It forfeits supporting arbitrary applications in favor of
supporting only BoT applications (which are relevant and amenable to execution on
grids). By focusing on BoT applications, MyGrid can be kept simple to use, simple

High-Performance Computing: Paradigm and Infrastructure. Edited by L. T. Yang and M. Guo   **705**
Copyright © 2006 John Wiley & Sons, Inc.

enough to be a solution for real users who want to run their applications today and do not really care what underlying grid support they might use.

This is not to say, however, that MyGrid is a replacement for existing grid infrastructure. MyGrid uses grid infrastructure whenever available. It simply does not depend on it. MyGrid can be seen more as a representative of the user in the grid. It provides simple abstractions through which the user can easily deal with the grid, abstracting away the nonessential details (as we shall see in Section 37.4). It schedules the application over whatever resources the user has access to, whether this access is through some grid infrastructure (such as Globus [11]) or via simple remote login (such as *ssh*). MyGrid's scheduling solution is a particularly interesting contribution because it uses task replication to achieve good performance, relying on no information about the grid or the application (as we will see on Section 37.5). Note that not needing information for scheduling simplifies MyGrid usage. MyGrid is open-source software, available at http://www.our-grid.org/mygrid.

This chapter is structured as follows. Section 37.2 presents the goals that drove MyGrid's design. Section 37.3 describes the architecture created to achieve such goals. Sections 37.4 and 37.5 describe the major contributions of MyGrid to grid computing state of the art. Section 37.4 describes MyGrid's working environment, which hides details of individual machines from the user. Section 37.5 presents MyGrid's scheduling strategy, which attains good performance without relying on information about the grid or the application. Section 37.6 describes MyGrid's implementation, whereas Section 37.7 presents some experiments that evaluate its performance in practice. Finally, Section 37.8 closes the chapter with final remarks and delineation of future work.

37.2   DESIGN GOALS

We intend MyGrid to be a production-quality solution for users who want to execute BoT applications on computational grids today. Note that "today" implies that we cannot assume that some new software will be widely deployed. Our design goals were thus established with this vision in mind. We want MyGrid to be simple, complete, and encompassing.

By simple, we imply that MyGrid should be as close as possible to an out-of-the-box solution. The user wants to run her application. The least she gets involved with grid details, the better. Toward this goal, we worked on minimizing the installation effort. This is important because if the user had to manually install MyGrid on many machines, the simplicity of the solution would suffer.

Complete means that MyGrid must cover the whole production cycle, from development to execution, passing through deployment and manipulation of input and output. This goal is key for MyGrid to be useful in practice. In order to support all activities within the production cycle of a BoT application, MyGrid provides the notion of working environment, which consists of a small set of abstractions that enables the user to manipulate her files on the Grid.

Due to their loosely coupled nature, BoT applications can potentially use a very large number of processors. Therefore, we do not want MyGrid to preclude the user from using a given processor. We want MyGrid to be encompassing, in the sense that all machines the user has access to can be utilized to run her BoT applications. An important consequence of this goal is that MyGrid must be a user-centric solution, that is, MyGrid cannot assume that some given software is installed in a machine for it to be employed in the computation. Therefore, we cannot assume that a particular grid infrastructure (e.g., Globus [11]) is ubiquitously installed on all machines a user has access to. Note also that simplified installation also helps here. It does not suffice that the user potentially can employ all machines she has access to. It has to be simple to do so.

37.3   ARCHITECTURE

We assume the user has a machine that coordinates the execution of BoT applications through MyGrid. This machine is called the home machine. The user submits the tasks that compose the application to the home machine, which is responsible for farming out the tasks in the user's grid. We assume that the user has good access to her home machine, having set up a comfortable working environment on it. Moreover, the user has no problems installing software on the home machine. We envision that the home machine will oftentimes be the user's desktop.

The home machine schedules tasks to run on grid machines (see Section 37.5 for a discussion of scheduling in MyGrid). In contrast to the home machine, we assume that grid machines have not been wholly customized by the user to create a familiar working environment. Moreover, grid machines do not necessarily share file systems with the home machine, nor do they have the same software installed on them (even the operating system can differ). Ideally, the user does not want to treat grid machines individually. For example, the user should not have to install MyGrid software on them. The idea is that grid machines are dealt with through MyGrid abstractions (see Section 37.4).

Note that the differentiation between home and grid machines makes our design goals (see Section 37.2) more concrete. For example, easy installation applies solely to grid machines. On the home machine, MyGrid is software as any other and must be installed and configured. Likewise, simplicity implies that grid machines are dealt with through abstractions that hide their heterogeneity in hardware, software, and configuration.

However, enabling the user to benefit from "whatever resources she has access to" is essentially impossible in the sense that we do have to assume something about a grid machine in order to be able to use it. Therefore, our design tries to get as close as possible to this goal. This is done by defining the Grid Machine Interface as the minimal set of services that must be available in a machine for it to be used as a grid machine. These services are listed in Table 37.1.

As illustrated by Figure 37.1, there can be many ways to implement the Grid Machine Interface. Actually, the Grid Machine Interface is a virtualization [12] of

Table 37.1 Grid Machine Interface services

Task start-up on a grid machine (remote execution)
Cancellation of a running task
File transfer from the grid machine to the home machine
File transfer from the home machine to the grid machine

the access services to a grid machine. One way to implement the Grid Machine Interface lets the user furnish MyGrid with scripts that implement the four services
listed in Table 37.1. In this case, MyGrid uses the Grid Script module to access the
machine. Note that Grid Script enables the user to inform MyGrid on how to access
a given machine in a very flexible way. As long as the user is able to translate "having access to a given machine" into "providing scripts that encapsulate such access," MyGrid will be able to use the machine.

Other ways to implement the Grid Machine Interface rely on access methods that
are known to MyGrid. For example, we implemented MyGrid's Globus Proxy. The
idea is that if a grid machine can be accessed through Globus' GSI, GRAM, and
GridFTP [11], then the user does not need to supply scripts, but simply indicate that
the access is to be done via MyGrid's Globus Proxy. MyGrid also provides its own
access mechanism, called User Agent. The User Agent is useful when no service
that implements the operations described by the Grid Machine Interface (see Table
37.1) is available.

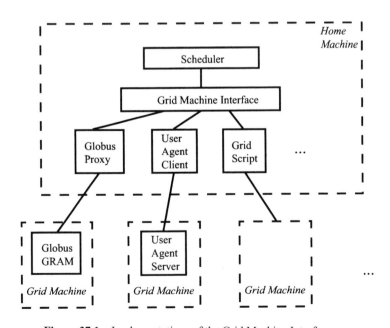

Figure 37.1 Implementations of the Grid Machine Interface.

In addition to hiding the grid machine access mechanism from the scheduler, the Grid Machine Interface provides a clean and elegant way (i) to deal with communication restrictions, and (ii) to support space-shared machines (i.e., parallel supercomputers).

Communication restrictions are a fact in today's Internet [16], where firewalls and private IP addresses are commonplace. Communication restrictions have great practical impact on MyGrid because sometimes the home machine cannot freely communicate (i.e., open a TCP socket) with a grid machine. We deal with this problem by using the Grid Machine Gateway. The Grid Machine Gateway is an application-level relay. It runs on a machine accessible to both home and grid machines (e.g., in a NAT converter) and forwards Grid Machine Interface services requests (see Table 37.1).

Space-shared machines (such as parallel supercomputers) are powerful resources the user might have access to. Using a space-shared computer, however, is different from using a time-shared workstation. In order to run a job in a space-shared computer, the user typically must submit a job request specifying how many processors are needed and the time they are to be available for the job. When no resources are currently available to fulfill the request, it sits in a wait queue until it can run.

Having to deal with two kinds of resources would complicate scheduling. In particular, directly submitting requests to a space-shared machine would imply crafting good requests (number of processors and execution time), a nontrivial task [7]. We introduced the Space-Shared Gateway to address this issue. Whenever MyGrid needs space-shared processors, the Space-Shared Gateway submits the largest request that can be fulfilled immediately, a technique introduced in [15]. Instead of submitting application's tasks, however, the Space-Shared Gateway submits instances of the User Agent, much like Condor-G's GlideIn [10]. The scheduler then farms out tasks on the space-shared processors via the User Agent. In short, the Space-Shared Gateway transforms space-shared resources in timed-shared resources that appear and leave the system, simplifying the overall system design. We should also mention that the Space-Shared Gateway is often used in conjunction with the Grid Machine Gateway. This happens because the processors of a space-shared machine typically cannot directly communicate with the outside world.

Figure 37.2 exemplifies a small but somewhat complex grid. The grid in question is composed of 18 machines, nine of which are directly accessed by the home machine. The other nine machines cannot be directly accessed. Communication to those machines is achieved with the help of the Grid Machine Gateway. Of the nine directly accessed grid machines, four employ the User Agent to implement the Grid Machine Interface, three use Globus Proxy, and two use Grid Script. Eight of the machines accessed via Grid Machine Gateway utilize User Agent. The other machine uses Grid Script. Note also that five machines accessed via Grid Machine Gateway are part of a space-shared machine and thus have their User Agents started by the Space-Shared Gateway.

One salient feature of the architecture presented here is that the home machine is a centralized component of the system. Therefore, concerns about the scalability of

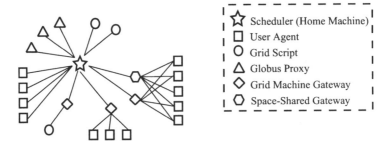

Figure 37.2   Example of a MyGrid.

our design arise naturally. Our hope is that, despite the cenralization of the home machine, MyGrid is going to be able to efficiently support most BoT applications. Such a hope is based (i) on experiments we performed (see Section 37.6), and (ii) on the fact that Condor, a successfully and mature system for the execution of BoT applications, also uses centralized job control [13]. But, of course, we intend to eventually remove such an architectural restriction from our design. The Grid Machine Gateway would be a natural place for leveraging toward a more scalable design. The challenge is to do so while keeping simple the view the user has of the system.

37.4   WORKING ENVIRONMENT

The user needs a grid-wide working environment, a set of abstractions that enable her to conveniently use her grid in the same way that files and processes make it convenient to use a single computer. MyGrid's working environment provides a common denominator that users can rely on when programming for grids, despite differences in the configuration of the multiple resources that comprise the grid. Moreover, a working environment is crucial in providing a complete solution, one that eases managing input and output files, distributing application code, and otherwise carrying on daily computational activities, now based on a computational grid.

A MyGrid task is formed by initial, grid, and final subtasks, which are executed sequentially in this order. Subtasks are external commands invoked by MyGrid. Consequently, any program, written in any language, can be a subtask. The initial and final subtasks are executed on the home machine. The initial subtask is meant to set up the task's environment by, for instance, transferring the input data to the grid machine. The final subtask is typically used to collect the task's results and send them back to the home machine. The grid subtask runs on a remote grid machine and performs the computation per se. Besides its subtasks, a task definition also includes the playpen size and the grid machine requirements, as we shall shortly see.

MyGrid abstractions allow for writing the subtasks without knowing details about the grid machine used (such as file systems organization). The abstractions provided to do that are mirror, playpen, and file transfer. Mirroring enables replication of home machine files on grid machines. Mirrored files are put in the directory indicated by the $MIRROR$ environment variable, which is defined by MyGrid by taking into account the local file system organization. Therefore, a grid subtask refers to mirrored file F through $MIRROR/F$, without having to know details about the grid machine file system. Mirroring is useful for distributing files that are going to be used more than once, such as program binaries. In fact, to ease mirroring binaries, $MIRROR$ is automatically included in the PATH by MyGrid. Mirroring is implemented efficiently by using the modification date and a hash of mirrored files, avoiding unnecessary file transfers.

Playpens provide temporary disk space independently of the local file system arrangements of a given grid machine. Playpens are directories created automatically to serve as the working directory of the grid subtask. Besides the initial working directory, a grid subtask can also refer to its playpen via the $PLAYPEN$ environment variable. MyGrid creates the playpen in a file system that can hold the amount of data specified by the user as the task's playpen size. (If there is no such file system in a given grid machine, the task cannot be scheduled to this machine.) Unlike mirroring, playpens are meant to store temporary files as well as input and output data.

Note that the name playpen makes greater sense from the grid machine viewpoint. We envision that the playpen implementer may want to protect the grid machine from a malicious task. This could be done by isolating the files that can be accessed, perfectly matching the playpen abstraction.

File transfer allows for sending files between the home machine and grid machines. They are typically used for the initial subtask to send input data to the playpen, and for the final subtask to collect output data from the playpen. In order to ease writing the initial and final subtasks, MyGrid automatically defines the environment variables $PROC$, $PLAYPEN$, and $TASK$. They respectively denote the grid machine chosen to run the task, the directory created as the playpen, and the unique task number.

For example, suppose we want to run the binary task, which has the file *INPUT* as input and the file *OUTPUT* as output. The initial subtask would then be:

```
mg-services mirror $PROC task
mg-services put $PROC INPUT $PLAYPEN
```

The grid subtask would be simply:

```
task < INPUT > OUTPUT
```

And the final subtask would collect OUTPUT to the results directory, renaming the file by appending the unique task number to its name:

```
mg-services get $PROC $PLAYPEN/OUTPUT results/OUTPUT-$TASK
```

Appending the task number to a file is useful for the quite common case in which the tasks that compose the application produce output with the same name. Appending the task number ensures the uniqueness of each output.

The final component of a task is its grid machine requirements. In MyGrid, grid machines are labeled by attributes. Attributes are user-defined strings that express the characteristics of a grid machine. For example, the user can assign the attributes "linux and lsd" to a machine named gandalf.dsc.ufcg.edu.br to denote that such a machine runs Linux and is located at LSD (Laboratório de Sistemas Distribúdos). A task's grid machine requirement consists of a Boolean expression involving the grid machine's attributes. For example, linux&&!lsd denotes machines that have been labeled with the attribute linux but not with the attribute lsd (gandalf.dsc.ufcg. edu.br would not qualify).

Any subtask can also determine the attributes of a grid machine. This makes it possible for the subtasks to adapt to different kinds of grid machines. Refining the above example, suppose that task has binaries for Linux and Solaris, placed respectively at Linux and Solaris directories. Assuming that the user has labeled each grid machine with its operating system, the initial subtask could then use attributes to mirror the right binary:

```
if mg-services attrib $PROC linux; then
        mg-services mirror $PROC linux/task
else
        mg-services mirror $PROC solaris/task
endif
mg-services put $PROC INPUT $PLAYPEN
```

37.5 SCHEDULING

Another key component of MyGrid is the Scheduler. The Scheduler receives from the user the description of the tasks that compose the application, chooses which machine runs each task, submits the tasks for execution, and monitors their progress. However, scheduling BoT applications on grids is not as easy as it might look at first. Good scheduling requires good information about the tasks that compose the application and the capabilities of grid resources. Requiring information about tasks (such as expected execution time) would make MyGrid harder to use. Information about grid resources (such as speed and load) is often difficult to obtain due to the grid's distributed and multiinstitutional nature. Moreover, we would need a richer definition of the Grid Machine Interface (see Table 37.1) in order to obtain information about grid resources. A richer definition of the Grid Machine Interface would, of course, be harder to implement, negatively affecting our goal of using whatever resources the user has access to.

An alternative is to use a scheduler that does not rely on information about tasks or resources, such as Workqueue. Workqueue only uses information absolutely necessary to schedule the application, namely, the tasks to run and the processors available to execute the tasks. In Workqueue, yet-to-be-executed tasks are chosen in an arbitrary order and sent to the processors, as soon as they become available. After the completion of a task, the processor sends back the results and the scheduler assigns a new task to the processor. That is, the scheduler starts by sending a task to every available host. Once a host finishes its task, the scheduler assigns another task to the host, as long as there are still tasks to be executed. Unfortunately, knowledge-free schedulers (such as Workqueue) do not attain performance comparable to schedulers based on full knowledge about the environment (provided that these schedulers are fed with good information) [14].

We developed the Workqueue with Replication (WQR) algorithm to deal with this problem. WQR delivers good performance without using any kind of information about the resources or tasks. Initially, WQR behaves as the conventional Workqueue. The difference appears when there are no more tasks to execute. At this time, a machine that finishes its tasks would become idle during the rest of the application execution in Workqueue. Using replication, such a machine is assigned to execute a replica of an unfinished task. Tasks are replicated until a predefined maximum number of replicas is achieved. When a task is replicated, the first replica that finishes is considered as the valid execution of the task and the other replicas are cancelled. Of course, WQR assumes that tasks are idempotent, that is, they can be reexecuted with no side effects. Since MyGrid's abstractions encourage the use of file transfer to deal with input and output, this assumption seems appropriate.

WQR minimizes the effects of the dynamic machine load, machine heterogeneity, and task heterogeneity, and does so without relying on information on machines or tasks. It improves performance in situations where tasks are delaying the application execution because they were assigned to slow hosts. When a task is replicated, there is a greater chance that some replica is assigned to a faster host. A way to think about WQR is that it trades off additional CPU cycles for the need of information about the grid and the application. Moreover, BoT applications often use cycles that would otherwise go idle [13]. Thus, trading CPU cycles for the need of information can be advantageous in practice.

We investigated the performance of WQR under a variety of scenarios in which we varied the granularity of the application, the heterogeneity of the application, and the heterogeneity of the grid [14]. Table 37.2 summarizes the results of 7885

Table 37.2   WQR simulation results

	Execution time (sec)		Wasted CPU (%)	
	Mean	Std. Dev.	Mean	Std. Dev.
Sufferage	13530.26	9556.55	N/A	N/A
Dynamic FPLTF	12901.78	9714.08	N/A	N/A
Workqueue	23066.99	32655.85	N/A	N/A
WQR 2x	12835.70	10739.50	23.55	22.29
WQR 3x	12123.66	9434.70	36.32	34.79
WQR 4x	11652.80	8603.06	48.87	48.94

simulations. Sufferage and Dynamic FPLTF (Fastest Processor to Largest Task First) are known scheduling algorithms that were fed with perfect knowledge in the simulations. The qualifier to WQR (i.e., 2x, 3x, 4x) denotes the maximum replication allowed. For example, WQR 2x allows only two replicas of each task (or the original and the replica, if you will).

Overall, the performance of WQR appeared to be equivalent to solutions that have perfect knowledge about the environment (which it is not feasible to obtain in practice), even when we were limited to two replicas of each task. On average, the wasted CPU varied from 23.5% (when using only two replicas) to 48.9% (when using four replicas, the maximum we tried).

Note also that the high values of the standard deviation suggest a great deal of variability in the results. In fact, we found that application granularity has a strong impact on the results. In our experiments, both the application size and the grid power were constant; thus, application granularity is given by the relation of machines to tasks. As can be seen in Figure 37.3(A), WQR attains better performance than the other heuristics, except for applications with very large granularity (where there are more machines than tasks). The difficulty faced by WQR when there are more machines than tasks is that the application execution takes only one "round" of tasks to processors assignments. Therefore, assigning a large task to a slow machine has a great impact on the application execution time. Algorithms based on knowledge about the application and the grid (Sufferage and Dynamic FPLTF) can avoid such bad assignments. Replication helps (as can be seen comparing WQR toWorkqueue) but not enough to overcome the problem totally. Not surprisingly, many more cycles are wasted when only a single round of tasks are assigned to processors, as shown by Figure 37.3(B). Consequently, when there are more machines than tasks, one might want to limit cycles waste by limiting replication to 2 (i.e. by using WQR 2x). Performance is still reasonable (although not as good as that achieved by scheduling algorithms with perfect knowledge of the application and the grid). Application and grid heterogeneity also influence WQR performance, but to a smaller degree. We refer the reader to [14] for a complete performance analysis of WQR.

37.6 IMPLEMENTATION

MyGrid implementation consists of two major components: the Scheduler (which runs on the home machine) and the User Agent (one of the implementations of the Grid Machine Interface). There is not much to say about the implementation of the Scheduler. The only important point that comes to mind is that we found it very hard to write automated tests for the Scheduler. This is because the Scheduler is multithreaded and its actions must be carried out in a distributed system, thereby introducing nondeterminism in the Scheduler execution and making automated testing much harder.

The implementation of the User Agent provided a much richer experience. In short, we found out that it is nowadays very difficult to develop global distributed applications. Major problems are heterogeneity (which makes installation and

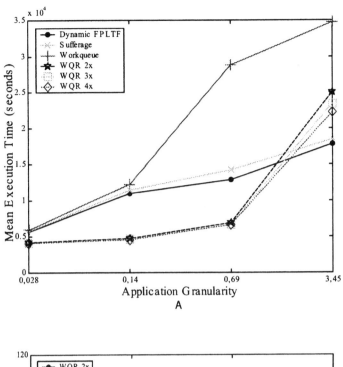

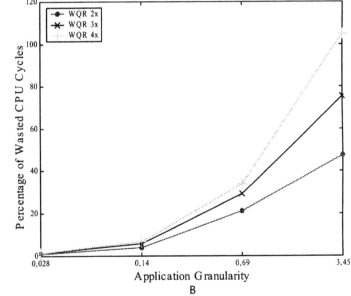

Figure 37.3   (A) Execution time versus application granularity. (B) Wasted cycles versus application granularity.

portability very tough) and lack of point-to-point connectivity (due to widespread firewalls and private IP addresses).

The User Agent is implemented in Java, which certainly helps to make it portable. However, being written in Java makes the User Agent dependent on the Java Virtual Machine (JVM). This is an annoyance because we find machines with no JVM installed, JVM not present on the *PATH*, and obsolete JVMs. We are now working on adding JVM detection (and eventual installation) as part of the User Agent's self-installation process.

The Scheduler and the User Agent communicate via Remote Method Invocation (RMI), which caused two problems. First, we needed away to authenticate the invoker of remote methods, otherwise anyone could invoke the services defined in the Grid Machine Interface, performing remote execution and file transfers as a My-Grid user. We closed this security breach by using Java's own public key authentication within RMI's socket factory. Second, we avoided using rmiregistry in order to make it easier to configure firewalls to let MyGrid traffic pass. To access an RMI service, one needs to contact two TCP ports: the well-known rmiregistry port, which informs the service port, and then the service port itself. But we found firewall managers somehow more reluctant to open two ports than one. (Maybe that is because most services only need a single port and, hence, asking to free traffic for two ports sounds suspicious.) We addressed this by writing our own implementation of UnicastRemoteObject, which can be contacted directly by providing only machine IP and port number. (Many say, "Computer Science is the science that solves problems by adding indirection levels." This is the first time we have seen something solved in computer science by removing an indirection level.)

It is also worth mentioning that we found Grid Scripts to be a source of headaches. The problem is related to the lack of strongly typed interfaces in human-oriented commands. The interfaces of commands like *ssh* are designed for software–human interaction, not for software–software interaction. It is common to find different versions of the same command with subtle variations. A human would have no problem in understanding these differences (for instance, a –*t* option becoming –*T*), but this is enough to break our scripts.

Without standard strongly typed, software-oriented interfaces, this problem is a difficult one to completely solve. We tried to minimize it by using self-installation. (Actually, this very problem was a major motivation for self-installation.) Self-installation consists of using Grid Scripts solely to install the User Agent (i.e., to transfer the software to the grid machine and start it remotely). This is not always possible (e.g., there might be a firewall that blocks User Agent traffic), but when it is, it reduces the problems caused by Grid Script, because it is much less used (only to bring the User Agent up).

37.7   PERFORMANCE EVALUATION

We ran three experiments to evaluate MyGrid's performance in practice. The first two experiments are proof of concept demonstrations. They consist of using

MyGrid to run two real applications on real grids and show that MyGrid can be useful in practice. The first experiment ran a series of simulations designed to investigate how to leverage the fact that most supercomputer jobs are moldable to improve their performance [7]. The second experiment uses MyGrid to run multiple instances of THOR, a dynamic molecular application, and investigates the impact of AIDS drugs on regional mutants of the HIV-1 [18] virus. The third experiment is different in nature in the sense that it does not execute a real application. Instead, it runs a benchmark application designed to investigate the performance bottleneck due to MyGrid's architecture, which is centralized around the home machine.

37.7.1 Simulation of Supercomputer Jobs

In 2000, we ran a large-scale experiment using Open Grid [6], a MyGrid predecessor that used traditionalWorkqueue (instead ofWQR)for scheduling and had only Grid Script to access grid machines. We conducted around 600,000 simulations to study scheduling of moldable supercomputer jobs [7] using 178 processors located in six different administrative domains (four at University of California San Diego, one at San Diego Supercomputer Center, and one at Northwestern University). The processors were in normal production (i.e., they were not dedicated to us at any point in time). The processors were either Intel machines running Linux or Sparc machines running Solaris.

The 600,000 simulations took 16.7 days, distributed over a 40 day period (the extra 23.3 days were used to analyze the latest results and plan the next simulations). In contrast, our desktop machine (an UltraSparc running at 200 MHz) would have taken about 5.3 years to complete the 600,000 simulations (had it been dedicated only to that task). Nevertheless, even more important than the achieved speed-up is the fact that we were able to use everyday machines located in different administrative domains as the platform for our application. In fact, we were required to run at lower priority in four of the administrative domains.

It is also important to stress that the machines we used shared no common software except ubiquitous Unix utilities such as *emacs*, *ssh*, and *gcc*. In particular, grid computing software (more precisely, Globus [11]) was only installed in a single administrative domain. Moreover, access mechanisms varied from one administrative domain to another. For example, one of the domains had machines with private IP (we accessed these machines via Grid Script using double *ssh*, i.e., *ssh < gateway > ssh < grid − machine >< command >*).

37.7.2 Fighting AIDS

MyGrid is being currently used by Pedro Pascutti's group [18] at IBCCF/UFRJ to support AIDS research. A single mutant protease inhibitor interaction is performed using THOR, a package for modeling molecular dynamics developed at UFRJ. Since many interactions must be tried whenever the biologist wants to examine a conjecture, the problem is amenable to be run on MyGrid.

Depending on the research analysis, a total task computing time can take from a few minutes up to many weeks. As an example, we present a typical execution that involves around 50 10 minute tasks, where each task demands the transfer of around 4 MB. For a simple test, we have submitted 60 tasks to MyGrid. Each task reads a 3.3 MB input file and writes a 200 KB output file. The grid consisted of 58 processors, distributed throughout seven independent computing sites.

There were no dedicated processors on the grid. Moreover, each task was submitted using *nice* (i.e., with low priority). Each task executed in from 4 minutes on the fastest machine in the grid to 33 minutes on the slowest machine in the grid. We performed a total of 20 executions. The total average execution time on the grid was 43 minutes.

37.7.3 Gauging the Home Machine Bottleneck

MyGrid architecture, although simple and effective, raises concerns about its scalability. Since the home machine is a centralized component, it will become a performance bottleneck sooner or latter. We here describe an experiment we devised to determine whether such a bottleneck would appear in the execution of a typical CPU-bound BoT application composed of 100 tasks.

Our experiment used three administrative domains: LSD (at UFCG, with eight machines), APE Lab (at UCSD, with 23 machines), and Grid Lab (at UCSD, with 12 machines). The home machine was at LSD. The home machine was dedicated to the experiment, but all grid machines were dealing with their normal loads. Three kinds of tasks were used: small, medium, and large. Each task was a dummy loop, which received an input determining how long the loop would run. We set up the input such that the fastest machine in our grid (AMD Athlon XP 1800) would finish tasks in 10, 100, and 1000 CPU seconds, thus creating small, medium and large tasks. Note that tasks were essentially CPU-bound. File transfer was done only for the task code, whose size was of 4 KB.

Besides task size, we had three choices for the location of the grid machines, namely at LSD (i.e., in the same LAN as the home machine), at APE Lab, and at Grid Lab. The purpose of location variation was to understand MyGrid behavior in presence of different network connectivity and machine speeds (the different domains have machines of different ages and architectures, and thus different speeds).

Combining grid machine location and task size, nine different scenarios were investigated. For each scenario, we ran a 100 tasks application 10 times. It is important to point out that the applications ran back to back in an attempt to give similar grid conditions to the different scenarios. That is, we would run an application for scenario 1, then scenario 2, up to scenario 9 before repeating the executions 10 times.

In order to determine MyGrid performance in these scenarios, we defined a task's efficiency and overhead. Let it, g_t, and f_t be the initial, grid, and final execution times of a task, respectively. Consequently, the task total execution time t_t is given by $t_t = i_t + g_t + f_t$. Efficiency e denotes the fraction of the total execution that was effectively spent on the grid subtask, $e = g_t/t_t$. Overhead o is the time spent in the initial and final subtasks, that is, $o = i_t + f_t$.

Figure 37.4 shows efficiency as a function of task size. As one would expect, due to the local connection between home and grid machines, efficiency at LSD was excellent. Also, very good efficiencies at Grid Lab and APE Lab display an interesting effect. APE Lab and Grid Lab have basically the same connectivity to LSD (where the home machine is located). However, Grid Lab machines are faster than APE Lab machines (as can be seen in Figure 37.5). Consequently, tasks finish quicker when using Grid Lab resources, thus generating greater demand on the home machine and, therefore, reducing task efficiency.

Figure 37.5 shows the overhead results. For Grid Lab, overhead decreases somewhat as task size grows. For LSD and APE Lab, overhead appears to be very stable. These results indicate that MyGrid has not reached the home machine bottleneck threshold for the scenarios here explored. It is worthy to say that efficiency was high in all scenarios.

However, an analysis of home machine's CPU usage during the experiment showed that CPU consumption peaked at 87.1% for small tasks when using LSD grid machines, indicating the bottleneck is close (at least for this scenario). A closer analysis of the CPU usage logs revealed that most of the CPU was spent starting new processes (especially the JVM). We then realized that our design decision of implementing the initial and final subtasks as invocations of external processes, while very flexible, has serious performance consequences. Since the initial and final subtasks run at the home machine, they not only have to be forked, but also need

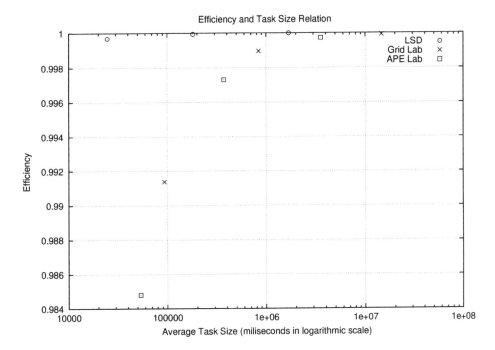

Figure 37.4   Efficiency versus task size.

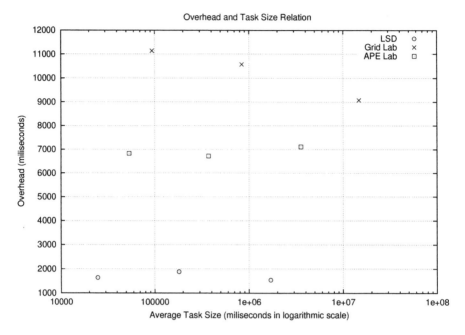

Figure 37.5   Overhead versus task size.

to fork a JVM every time they use a MyGrid service. For example, in the little initial subtask presented at the end of Section 37.4, there are 3 invocations of a JVM (not exactly a lightweight operation).

Due to this problem, we are currently working on providing an alternative to running initial and final subtasks as external processes. The idea is to embed in My-Grid a very simple script language to enable simple file transfer based on the processor's attributes, a functionality that should be enough for most applications.

After this modification, we are going to reassess when the centralization of the home machine functionality becomes a bottleneck. We hope that this point will not be reached by most applications. Nevertheless, some applications will be affected by the centralized home machine. To address this issue, we intend to investigate how to distribute the home machine functions to Grid Machine Gateways. The challenge is to do so without affecting the view the user has from the system.

37.8   CONCLUSIONS AND FUTURE WORK

MyGrid is a complete solution for running Bag-of-Tasks (BoT) applications on all resources one has available. MyGrid represents a different trade-off in designing grid infrastructure. Traditional grid infrastructure, such as Globus [11], aims to support arbitrary applications. Arbitrary applications may, of course, have complex requirements. In order to be flexible enough to deal with such potential complexity, traditional grid infrastructure leaves decisions and tasks up to the user, making it hard to use the grid. That is, the grid infrastructure typically solves only part of the problem, leaving the user to complement the solution by writing, for example, the application scheduler [3, 8]. MyGrid, on the other hand, is specific (provides support solely for BoT applications) but complete (the user does not have to add anything but the application itself). We hope that a complete solution will help to make grid technology more useful in practice, to real users. MyGrid is open-source and can be downloaded from http://www.ourgrid.org/mygrid.

From the grid research viewpoint, MyGrid's main contributions are two-fold. First, we introduce a scheduling heuristic (denominated Work Queue with Replication) that achieves good performance without relying on information about the grid state or the task execution times. Having a scheduler algorithm that works well without information about the grid or the tasks is important because such information is hard to obtain in practice. Moreover, it keeps the system easy to use (by not requiring the user to provide task execution time estimates). Second, MyGrid hides the configuration heterogeneity of the machines that compose the grid by providing working environment abstractions that are easy to use and efficiently implemented on grids.

MyGrid has currently a dozen of real users and we learned a couple of lessons from working with our users. One lesson is that today's Internet connectivity is very complex and must be taken into account when designing any widely distributed system such as grid infrastructure. The nice end-to-end connectivity implied by socket abstraction no longer works in today's Internet [16]. Firewalls, gateways, and private IPs are commonplace. This complexity has worked against our goal of creating a user-level grid infrastructure. We did our best to supply work-around solutions such as tunneling support and application gateways, but there are still situations where the user needs to involve the system administrator to make MyGrid work.

Another lesson was that, if we do not hear the user, we might create solutions for problems that do not present themselves in practice. For example, we have implemented the proportional-share ticket-based scheduler introduced in [5]. Such a scheduler is technically very interesting. It allows the user who runs more than one application simultaneously to define what fraction of her grid's resources should be allocated to each application. A bit to our dismay, however, so far none of our users found this capability useful.

As far as future work, we plan to pursue three lines of research and development. The first line is more developmental but very important for the practical success of MyGrid. Since we experienced problems with Grid Script (another generic mechanism for accessing a grid machine), we intend to extend MyGrid to directly support other kinds of resources. OGSA [12] and vCluster [9] resources are our next targets. Condor would also be a natural choice to be directly supported.

Second, we would like to have more efficient support for BoT applications that process large amounts of data. Of course, MyGrid currently runs data-intensive BoT applications, but it does not attempt to reduce the impact large data transfers have on the execution time of these applications. For example, MyGrid at this time does not exploit grid topology as in [4]. One challenge here is how to have better support for data-intensive BoT applications without making the system harder to use and/or install (by making it dependent on information about grid state, for example).

Our third future effort comes as an answer to our user community. People are not satisfied just with good grid infrastructure. They actually want the resources on which to use the infrastructure, that is, they want a grid. Therefore, we intend to create OurGrid, a peer-to-peer resource-sharing system targeted to BoT applications. OurGrid is thought of as a favor-based community, where each peer offers access to its idle resources. In return, when there is work that exceeds local capacity, a peer expects to gain access to other people's resources. The challenge is doing so in a decentralized manner. A decentralized solution is key to keep OurGrid simple, not dependent on centralized services that might be hard to deploy, scale, and trust.

ACKNOWLEDGMENTS

We would like to thank Hewlett Packard and CNPq/Brazil for the financial support. We would also like to thank Márcio Vasel, Nigini Abílio, and Nazareno Andrade for their great work on different parts of MyGrid. Thanks to Allan Snavely for the insightful discussion that gave rise to the MyGrid name.

REFERENCES

1. D. Abramson, J. Giddy, and L. Kotler, High Performance Parametric Modeling with Nimrod/G: Killer Application for the Global Grid?, in *Proceedings of the 14th International Parallel & Distributed Processing Symposium (IPDPS'00)*, pp. 520–528, Cancun Mexico, IEEE Computer Science Press, 2000. http://ipdps.eece.unm.edu/2000/papers/Abramson.pdf.

2. D. Anderson, J. Cobb, and E. Korpela, SETI@home: An Experiment in Public-Resource Computing, *Communication of the ACM, 45,* 11, 56–61, November 2002.

3. F. Berman, R. Wolski, S. Figueira et al., Application-Level Scheduling on Distributed Heterogeneous Networks, in *Proceedings of Supercomputing'96,* Pittsburgh, 1996, http://www-cse.ucsd.edu/groups/hpcl/apples/hetpubs.html.

4. H. Casanova, A. Legrand, D. Zagorodnov et al, Heuristics for Scheduling Parameter Sweep Applications in Grid Environments, in *Proceedings of the 9th Heterogeneous Computing Workshop,* pp. 349–363, 2000. http://apples.ucsd.edu/hetpubs.html.

5. W. Cirne and K. Marzullo, The Computational Co-op: Gathering Clusters into a Metacomputer, in *Proceedings 13th International Parallel Processing Symposium and 10th Symposium on Parallel and Distributed Processing (IPPS/SPDP 1999),* pp. 160–166, IEEE Computer Society Press, 1999, http://walfredo.dsc.ufcg.edu.br/resume.html#publications.

6. W. Cirne and K. Marzullo, Open Grid: A User-Centric Approach for Grid Computing, in *Proceedings of the 13th Symposium on Computer Architecture and High Performance Computing,* September 2001, http://walfredo.dsc.ufcg.edu.br/resume.html#publications.

7. W. Cirne and F. Berman, Using Moldability to Improve the Performance of Supercomputer Jobs, *Journal of Parallel and Distributed Computing, 62,* 10, 1571–1601, October 2002, http://walfredo.dsc.ufcg.edu.br/resume.html#publications.

8. K. Czajkowski, I. Foster, N. Karonis et al., A Resource Management Architecture for Metacomputing Systems, in *Proceedings of 13th International Parallel Processing Symposium and 10th Symposium on Parallel and Distributed Processing (IPPS/SPDP 1998) Workshop on Job Scheduling Strategies for Parallel Processing,* pp. 62–82, 1998, http://www.globus.org/research/papers.html.

9. C. De Rose, F. Blanco, N. Maillard et al., The Virtual Cluster: a Dynamic Environment for Exploitation of Idle Network Resourses, in *Proceedings of 14th Symposium on Computer Architecture and High Performance Computing (SBAC-PAD'2002),* p. 141. Vitória, Espírito Santo, Brazil, 2002.

10. J. Frey, T. Tannenbaum, I. Foster et al., Condor-G: A Computation Management Agent for Multi-Institutional Grids, in *Proceedings of the 10th IEEE Symposium on High Performance Distributed Computing (HPDC'10),* p. 55, San Francisco, California, August 7–9, 2001, http://www.cs.wisc.edu/condor/publications.html.

11. I. Foster, and C. Kesselman, The Globus Project: A Status Report, in *Proceedings of the 13th International Parallel Processing Symposium and 10th Symposium on Parallel and Distributed Processing (IPPS/SPDP 1998) Heterogeneous Computing Workshop,* pp. 4–18, 1998, http://www.globus.org/research/papers.html.

12. I. Foster, C. Kesselman, J. Nick et al., The Physiology of the Grid: An Open Grid Services Architecture for Distributed Systems Integration, June 22, 2002, http://www.globus.org/research/papers.html.

13. M. Litzkow, M. Livny, and M. Mutka, Condor: A Hunter of Idle Workstations, in *Proceedings of the 8th International Conference of Distributed Computing Systems,* pp. 104–111, June 1988.

14. D. Paranhos, W. Cirne, and F. Brasileiro, Trading Cycles for Information: Using Replication to Schedule Bag-of-Tasks Applications on Computational Grids, in *Proceedings of the Euro-Par 2003: International Conference on Parallel and Distributed Computing,* pp. 169–80, Klagenfurt, Austria, August, 2003, http://walfredo.dsc.ufcg.edu.br/resume.html#publications.

15. S. Smallen, W. Cirne, J. Frey et al., Combining Workstations and Supercomputers to Support Grid Applications: The Parallel Tomography Experience, in *Proceedings of the HCW'2000 - Heterogeneous Computing Workshop,* p. 241, 2000, http://walfredo.dsc.ufcg.edu.br/resume.html#publications.

16. S. Son, and M. Livny, Recovering Internet Symmetry in Distributed Computing, in *Proceedings of GAN'03Workshop on Grids and Advanced Networks,* p. 542, Tokyo, Japan, May 12–15, 2003, http://www.cs.wisc.edu/~sschang/shortGAN03.pdf.

17. J. R. Stiles, T. M. Bartol, E. E. Salpeter et al., Monte Carlo Simulation of Neuromuscular Transmitter Release Using MCell, a General Simulator of Cellular Physiological Processes, *Computational Neuroscience,* pp. 279–284, 1998.

18. C. Veronez, A. Silva, C. Osthoff, P. M. de Barros, P. Pascutti and W. Cirne, Study of HIV-1 Protease Mutants Using Molecular Dynamics in a Grid Based Computational Plataform, in *Proceedings of The First International Conference on Bioinformatics and Computational Biology—ICoBiCoBi,* Ribeirão Preto, São Paulo, 2003.

## CHAPTER 38

An Efficient Parallel Method for Calculating the Smarandache Function

SABIN TABIRCA, TATIANA TABIRCA, KIERAN REYNOLDS, and LAURENCE T. YANG

38.1 INTRODUCTION

The Smarandache function [7] is a relatively new function in number theory and yet there are already a number of algorithms for its computation. It is the intention of this article to develop an efficient algorithm to compute in parallel all the values $\{S(i), i = 1, 2, \ldots, n\}$. This is an important problem often occurring in real computation, for example, in checking conjectures on S.

To begin, the Smarandache function [7] $S : N^* \to N$ is defined as

$$S(n) = \min\{k \in N \mid n|k!\} \tag{38.1}$$

An important property of this function is given by the following:

$$(\forall a, b \in N^*)(a, b) = 1 \Rightarrow S(a \cdot b) = \max\{S(a), S(b)\} \tag{38.2}$$

Expanding on this, it is clear that

$$S(p_1^{k_1} \cdot \ldots \cdot p_j^{k_j}) = \max\{S(p_1^{k_1}), \ldots, S(p_j^{k_j})\} \tag{38.3}$$

Therefore, when trying to evaluate the value of the function at n it is possible to use the prime decomposition of n to reduce the computation. Equation (38.4) gives a simple formula for $S(p^k)$:

$$k = \sum_{i=1}^{l} d_i \cdot \frac{p^i - 1}{p - 1} \Rightarrow S(p^k) = \sum_{i=1}^{l} d_i \cdot p^i \tag{38.4}$$

High-Performance Computing: Paradigm and Infrastructure. Edited by L. T. Yang and M. Guo **725**
Copyright © 2006 John Wiley & Sons, Inc.

There have been several studies to show the connection between the function S and prime numbers. It has been proven by Ford [2] that the values of S are almost always prime, satisfying

$$\lim_{n} \frac{|\{i \leq n : S(i)\,prime\}|}{n} = 0 \qquad (38.5)$$

Several sequential methods to compute the Smarandache function have emerged since its initial definition in 1980. Ibstedt [3, 4] developed an algorithm based on Equations (38.3) and (38.4) without any study of the complexity of this algorithm. Later, Power et al. [6] analyzed this algorithm and found that the complexity is $O(n/\log n)$. The U Basic implementation that was used by Ibstedt has proved to be efficient and useful especially for large values of n. Subsequently, Tabirca [9] studied a simple algorithm based on Equation 1.1 by considering the sequence $x_k = k! \bmod n$. This proves to be a rather inefficient computation that is impractical for large values of n. It was shown that the computation has a complexity of $O[S(n)]$. However, studies [10], [11], and [5] find that the average complexity of this algorithm is $O(n/\log n)$.

38.1.1 An Efficient Sequential Algorithm

Performing the computation of the Smarandache function can be done sequentially by developing an algorithm based on Equations (38.3) and (38.4). Clearly, if an efficient method to calculate the function on a prime power exists, it is then easy to extend this to the remaining integers. It was this that prompted Ibstedt to develop an

```
static long Value (long p, long k) {
        long l, j, value=0;
        long d1 [] = new long [1000];
        long d2 [] = new long [1000];
        d1 [0]=1; d2 [0]=p;
        for (int l=0; d1 [l]<=k; l++) {
                d1 [l+1]=1+p*d1 [l];
                d2 [l+1]=p*d2 [l];
        }
        for (l--, j=l; j>=0; j--) {
                d=p/d1 [j];
                p=p%d1 [j];
                value+=d*d2 [j];
        }
        return value;
}
```

Figure 38.1 The procedure for $S(p^k)$.

algorithm for the computation of the Smarandache function. This algorithm will be briefly examined in this section.

In Equation (38.4) $(d_l, d_{l-1}, \ldots, d_1)$ is the representation of k in the generalized base 1, $(p^2 - 1)/(p - 1), \cdots, (p^l - 1)/(p - 1)$ so that $(d_l, d_{l-1}, \ldots, d_1)$ is the representation of $S(p^k)$ in the generalized base $p, p^2, \ldots, p^l$. This gives a relationship between p^k and $S(p^k)$. With this, it is possible to write a method to calculate the Smarandache function on a prime power. Once this is in place, it is then possible to calculate the function on any integer.

Note that a prime decomposition algorithm is needed for the computation of the Smarandache function, which, for these purposes, can be a simple trial division algorithm. Once a prime decomposition of $n = p_1^{a_1} \cdot \ldots \cdot p_j^{a_j}$ is available, Equation (38.3) gives $S(n) = \max\{S(p_1^{k_1}), \ldots, S(p_j^{k_j})\}$. This is described in Figure 38.2.

38.2 COMPUTING IN PARALLEL

While performing the calculation of $S(n)$ in parallel is possible (see Power et al. [6]), that is not the purpose of this chapter. Instead, it is desired that the computation of $\{S(i), i = 1, 2, \ldots, n\}$ be performed in parallel. Let us suppose that this is done by the doall loop

```
do par i = 1,n
   calculate S(i)
end do
```

```
public staticlong S (finallong n) {
       long d, valueMax=0,s=-1;
       if (n==1) return0;
       long p[] = new long [1000];
       long k[] = new long [1000];
       long value[]= new long [1000];
       for (d=2;d<n;d++)
         if (n % d == 0){
            s++;p[s]=d;
            for (k[s]=0;n%d==0;k[s]++,n/=d);
            value[s]=Value(p[s],k[s]);
         }
       for (j=0;j<=s;j++)
            if (valueMax<value[j])
               valueMax=value[j];
       return valueMax;
}
```

Figure 38.2   The procedure for $S(p^k)$.

which is computed on a parallel machine with p processors $P_1, P_2, \ldots, P_p$. The value $S(i)$ is found sequentially by calling up the function S from Figure 38.2 and this is done with a workload of $w_i = i/\log i, i = 2, 3, \ldots, n$. An important requirement of this computation is to have consecutive iterations computed by the same processor. This often occurs when it is needed to check conjectures involving consecutive terms of S.

Computing the above doall loop is a classical scheduling problem in parallel computation. Scheduling methods find a mapping of the iterations onto the processors. This means that the set of indices $\{1, 2, \ldots, n\}$ is partitioned into p sets $\{S_j, j = 1, 2, \ldots, p\}$. Scheduling methods are classified into two main categories depending on when the partition is found. Static scheduling methods generate the partition during compile time while dynamic scheduling methods find it during run time. The main advantage of the latter is that they can detect when a processor becomes idle and assign iterations to it. Studies have shown that dynamic scheduling methods achieve a good load balance of the workloads. However, they produce small scheduling overheads.

On the other hand, static scheduling methods do not give any scheduling overheads but they usually give a poor balance of the workloads. The simplest way to schedule the iterations statically is to assign n/p consecutive iterations to each processor. In this case, processor j receives the iterations $[(j-1) \cdot n/p] + 1, [(j-1) \cdot n/p] + 2, \ldots, (j \times n)/p$. This method, which is called uniform block scheduling, gives good load balance when the workloads $\{w_1, w_2, \ldots, w_n\}$ are similar. When the workloads increase or decrease, the method is clearly inefficient because there is one processor that gets all the biggest n/p workloads. Cyclic scheduling corrects this inconvenience by distributing the iterations in a cyclic fashion so that two consecutive big workloads are not assigned to the same processor. The method allocates to processor j the iterations $\{j, j + p, j + 2 \cdot p, \ldots, j + (n - j/p) \cdot p\}$. Certainly, cyclic scheduling offers an efficient load balancing when the workloads decrease or increase.

Tabirca [13] proposed a recent static scheduling method named balanced workload block scheduling (BWBS 1). This is block scheduling in which processor j receives the consecutive iterations $\{l_j, l_j + 1, \ldots, h_j\}$ so that its workload is balanced. Hence, the scheduling is defined by the lower and upper bounds $\{(l_j, h_j), j - 1, 2, \ldots, p\}$ so that

$$l_1 = 1, h_p = n, l_j = h_{j-1} + 1, j = 2, \ldots, p$$

Suppose that there is an estimation or a formula for the workloads $\{w_1, w_2, \ldots, w_n\}$. Therefore, the workload for the entire loop is given by $w = \Sigma_{i=0}^n w_i$ and the average workload per processor is given by

$$\overline{W} = \frac{1}{p} \cdot \sum_{i=0}^{n} w_i$$

Clearly, good scheduling should give bounds (l_j, h_j) for processor j such that

$$\sum_{i=l_j}^{h_j} w_i \simeq \frac{1}{p} \cdot \sum_{i=1}^{n} w_i := \overline{W}, \ \forall j = 1, 2, \ldots, p$$

To evaluate bounds for the computation, two functions are needed. First, by extending the inferior part function, define

$$f_{\square}(x) = k \Leftrightarrow f(k) \le x < f(k+1) \tag{38.6}$$

Tabirca et al. [13], show that if both $f_{\square}$ and the function $f(h) = \Sigma_{k=1}^{h} w_k$ exist or can be calculated, then the upper bounds are given by

$$h_j = f_{\square}(\overline{W} + f(h_{j-1})), j = 1, 2, \ldots, p \tag{38.7}$$

However, the method can still be applied when there are no formulas for these two functions. In this case a preprocessing step is required to calculate the average workload $\overline{W}$ and the upper bounds $\{h_j, j = 1, 2, \ldots, j\}$ using

$$h_j = h \Leftrightarrow \sum_{i=l_j}^{h} w_i \le \overline{W} < \sum_{i=l_j}^{h+1} w_i \tag{38.8}$$

The preprocessing step however gives a scheduling overhead of $O(n/p)$.

Tabirca [12] proposed an improvement on this method considering the partial sum that is closest to $j \cdot \overline{W}$:

$$h_j = h \Leftrightarrow \sum_{i=1}^{h} w_i \le j \cdot \overline{W} < \sum_{i=1}^{h+1} w_i \tag{38.9}$$

In this case, the upper bounds are given by

$$h_j = f_{\square}(j \cdot \overline{W}), j = 1, 2, \ldots, p \tag{38.10}$$

This balanced workload block scheduling (BWBS 2) method has been proven to be marginally better than the initial one.

For the loop, we study the workloads $w_1 = 0$, $w_i = i/\log i$, $i = 2, 3, \ldots, n$ increase so that the unifrom scheduling does not give an efficient solution. Certainly, the dynamic scheduling or cyclic methods can be applied to obtain a better load balance. Unfortunately, they are not suitable because the processors do not get consecutive iterations. Therefore, the balanced workload block scheduling methods remain to give an efficient solution for our problem. Since the $\Sigma_{i=0}^{n} (i/\log i)$ does not have a formula or a simple approximation, the preprocessing step must be applied to achieve the scheduling bounds.

38.3 EXPERIMENTAL RESULT

In this section, some experimental results are outlined to show how the problem is solved in parallel. The computation has been performed on a 100 node Beowulf cluster. The machine consists of 50 Dell Poweredge 1655MC servers, each of them with a dual Pentium III processor (1.26 GHz, 512 K cache, 1 GB of RAM).

The uniform and balanced workload block scheduling methods are considered to schedule the loop iterations. To test these approaches, we generate $S(i) \forall i \leq$ 100,000,000 and check whether the equation $S(i) = S(i + 1)$ has solutions. This is an old standing conjecture that has been checked by Ibstedt [3] for all the numbers $i \leq$ 1,000,000. It has been conjectured that the equation has no solutions.

The first test presents the workload distribution on processors. For that the loop is scheduled on four processors and the computation time on each processor is measured. This gives an estimation of the workload balance of each method. Table 38.1 and Figure 38.3 show the variation of these execution times. It can be seen that the uniform scheduling method generate a huge imbalance where processor four is more than six times loaded than processor one. On the other hand, the BWBS methods give an efficient load balance with a marginal advantage for the second one. The desired effect of BWBS balancing, which is to get times on each processor as "nearly" equal as possible, is clearly visible from the Figure 38.3.

The second test investigates the variation of the overall execution times when the number of processors vary. The above loop has been run using $p = 1, 2, 4, 8$, and 16 processors. The variation of the execution times is presented in Table 38.2. Examining Figure 38.4 shows, unsurprisingly, that the BWBS bounds offer not only the best balance but also the quickest computation.

38.4 CONCLUSION

This chapter has shown how the values of the Smarandache function can be found in parallel. It has been required that consecutive values have to be calculated by the same processor. This has restricted the scheduling methods that could have been used for the computation. A variation of balanced workload block scheduling has been used to achieve efficient computation. That has been possible only because the number of operations to compute $S(i)$ is known.

Based on this method, several conjectures from Smarandache's Open Problem list [8] have been verified for all values up to 1,000,000,000 using the BWBS scheduling. Unfortunately, no counterexample has been found to disprove any of them so that we can say that they are true at least for all the values under one billion. This type of computation can also be used to generate in parallel the values of some other number theory functions, for example, Erdos' or Euler's.

Table 38.1 Execution times on processors

	P_1	P_2	P_3	P_4
Uniform	225.25	611.45	971.45	1318.54
BWBS 1	787.81	780.78	777.61	785.18
BWBS 2	782.65	781.52	782.05	782.34

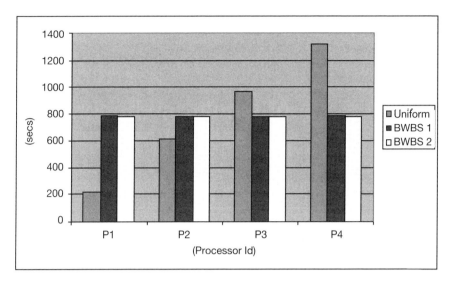

Figure 38.3   Execution times on processors.

Table 38.2   Variation of execution times

	$p = 1$	$p = 2$	$p = 4$	$p = 8$	$p = 16$	$p = 32$
Uniform	2925.62	2088.53	1215.34	718.54	434.92	271.82
BWBS 1	2925.72	1543.87	787.81	412.18	237.61	148.50
BWBS 2	2925.68	1524.25	782.65	397.34	210.53	131.58

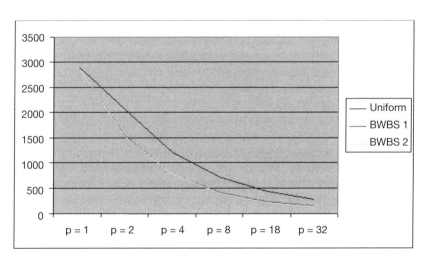

Figure 38.4   Variation of execution times.

REFERENCES

1. E. Bach and J. Shallit, *Algorithmic Number Theory,* MIT Press, Cambridge, MA, 1996.
2. G. Ford, An Asymptotic Evaluation of the Smarandache Function, *Smarandache Notion Journal, 11,* 1–2–3, 45–61, 2000.
3. H. Ibstedt, *Surfing on the Ocean of Numbers—A few Smarandache Notions and Similar Topics,* Erhus University Press, New Mexico, USA, 1997.
4. H. Ibstedt, *Computational Aspects of Number Sequences,* American Research Press, Lupton, USA, 1999.
5. F. Luca, The Average Smarandache Function, *Smarandache Notion Journal, 12,* 1–2, 134–142, 2001.
6. D. Power, S. Tabirca, and T. Tabirca, Java Concurent Program for the Smarandache Function, *Smarandache Notion Journal, 12,* 1–2, 121–132, 2001.
7. F. Smarandache, A Function in Number Theory, *Analele Univ. Timisoara,* XVIII, 142–156, 1980.
8. F. Smarandache, *Only Problems . . . Not Solutions,* Xiquan Publishing House, Phoenix/Chicago, 1993.
9. S. Tabirca and T. Tabirca, Some Computational Remarks on the Smarandache Function, in *Proceedings of the First International Conference on the Smarandache Type Notions,* Craiova, Romania, 1997.
10. S. Tabirca and T. Tabirca, Some Upper Bounds for Smarandache's Function, *Smarandache Notions Journal, 8,* 205–211, 1997.
11. S. Tabirca and T. Tabirca, Two New Functions in Number Theory and Some Upper Bounds for Smarandache's Function, *Smarandache Notions Journal, 9,* 1–2, 82–91, 1998.
12. T. Tabirca and S. Tabirca, A New Equation for the Balanced Loop Scheduling Based on the Smarandache Inferior Part Function to Loop Scheduling, in *Proceedings of the 2nd International Conference on Smarandache Type Notions,* 2001, Romania.
13. T. Tabirca, L. Freeman, S. Tabirca, and L. T. Yang, A Static Workload Balance Scheduling Algorithm, in *Proceedings of the 2nd Workshop on Parallel and Distributed Scientific and Engineering Computing with Applications (PDSECA 2001),* San Francisco, April 2001.

## CHAPTER 39

Design, Implementation and Deployment of a Commodity Cluster for Periodic Comparisons of Gene Sequences

ANITA M. ORENDT, BRIAN HAYMORE, DAVID RICHARDSON,
SOFIA ROBB, ALEJANDRO SANCHEZ ALVARADO,
and JULIO C. FACELLI

39.1 INTRODUCTION

In 1982, the number of sequences deposited in GenBank was 606, comprised of only 680,338 base pairs. By 1996, the number of sequences reached a little over one million with a total of nearly 652 million base pairs. Today, GenBank is made up of over 22 million sequences representing almost 29 billion base pairs (http://www. ncbi.nlm.nih.gov/Genbank/genbankstats.html). Behind the precipitous rise of sequencing data during the past four years has been the equally rapid improvement of DNA sequencing methodologies. Such improvements made possible what in the mid-1990s was thought to be nearly impossible: to completely sequence the genomes of multicellular organisms, including *Homo sapiens* [1]. In fact, in the next two years alone genome sequences for the chimpanzee, rhesus macaque, mouse, dog, cow, pig, chicken, zebrafish, the frog *Xenopus tropicalis,* sea urchin, honeybee, and the planarian *Schmidtea mediterranea* will be obtained and deposited in GenBank (http://www.genome.gov/page.cfm?pageID=10002154). The combined sequence data from these animals is expected to total 27 billion nucleotides, or roughly the same amount of sequence information available in GenBank today. It is clear, therefore, that the exponential growth of GenBank is unlikely to abate any time soon.

Because genetic sequences do not provide any direct biological information, researchers have to conduct elaborate experiments to determine the relationships between a genetic sequence and its biological function. This process can be significantly accelerated if one takes into account that there are important similarities between genetic sequences associated with similar biological functionality across different species. Therefore, when determining the biological functionality of a new sequence it is of great value to find homologous sequences from other organisms in which their functionality is better understood.

The tools used to find sequence similarities between a researcher's protein or DNA sequence and the entries in GenBank are the suite of BLAST (Basic Local Alignment Search Tool) programs (*blastx, blastn, blastp, tblastx*) [2] available from the National Center for Biotechnology Information (NCBI) of the National Library of Medicine of the National Institutes of Health. These programs are described in detail on the NCBI's main BLAST Web site (http://www.ncbi.nlm.nih. gov/BLAST). The NCBI also maintains a number of databases available for download that are derived from the sequences deposited in GenBank. The NCBI site offers several search methods (webblast, networkblast, and blast URL API) that are sufficient for the needs of many laboratories working on a relatively small number of genes. NCBI also offers the tools necessary for individuals and institutions to maintain their own Web site with local copies of the various NCBI databases; this can be used in order to relieve part of the high demand on the NCBI-maintained Web site. The Center for High Performance Computing (CHPC) has done this at the University of Utah. However, for laboratories in need of analyzing thousands of individual sequences on a regular basis, these tools are not sufficient. For these cases, the NCBI offers also the standalone BLAST executables necessary for any individual to establish an in-house system as described in this chapter.

Our lab has been engaged in the identification of genes that are active during a variety of biological processes such as tissue regeneration and stem cell biology in the freshwater planarian *Schmidtea mediterranea* [3]. A total over of 6500 unique cDNA sequences of expressed genes, also known as expressed sequence tags (ESTs), have been accumulated. ESTs are key reagents for printing DNA microarrays, carrying out large-scale spatial expression pattern studies, and the functional characterization of proteins. The utility of an EST collection depends in great part on determining if the obtained sequence has been identified in other organisms, as these types of comparisons allow for the refinement of functional characterization and experimental design. However, comparing over 6500 ESTs to the NCBI databases on an individual basis would take hours if not days of supervised activity, not only during the performance of the BLAST searches themselves, but also in the archiving of the results of the searches into a laboratory database known as the *Schmidtea mediterranea* Database (SmedDb) [3].

In order to overcome the difficulties described above, the SmedDb used for the storage and organization of our sequences and their BLAST results has been integrated with a low-cost, commodity-based cluster computer system that can semiautomatically process thousands of BLAST searches when the NCBI databases change. The end result for the investigator is a dynamic database that is regularly and automatically updated to obtain the most up-to-date sequence comparisons available.

Cluster computing [4] has always provided an attractive approach to provide computer resources to scientific problems. In recent years, the advent of commodity clusters using the LINUX operating system has provided special impetus to the use of cluster architectures in technical and scientific environments, including grid computing [5]. Most reports in the literature address the design and implementation of these types of architectures as general-purpose systems with an intended workload encompassing many scientific applications. Nonetheless, the ample configuration space available when designing a system using commodity hardware allows for specialization when desired. This chapter describes the design, implementation, and deployment of a computer cluster dedicated to perform periodic BLAST searches and the manner in which the output of these searches is integrated into a laboratory database, SmedDb.

39.2 SYSTEM REQUIREMENTS AND DESIGN

The design of the system proceeded using the following guiding principles derived from the scientific considerations described above, along with the financial and operational constraints:

1. All the components of the cluster should be off the shelf to keep costs within the budget typically available at most biomedical labs.
2. The initial computing capacity of the search engine for the cluster should allow processing in parallel of most of the updates to SmedDb in less than 48 hours.
3. The cluster should be scalable, so the computing capacity can be increased as the size of the SmedDb and NCBI databases increase.
4. Considering that CHPC is a central university facility, the scalability of the cluster should allow the addition of computing capacity to support other users with similar requirements.
5. The download and processing of updated NCBI databases should proceed without interfering with ongoing searches. This is important because, when performing searches lasting more than 24 hours, there is a considerable probability that updates may be occurring during the processing time.
6. Database updates, process scheduling, submission of searches and retrieval of the results should be as automatic as possible to allow for high throughput without human intervention. But the system should allow for intervention when necessary to make judicious evaluations of the results.
7. Although in this implementation the parallel cluster search system has been integrated to the SmedDb, the design should be flexible enough to permit its integration to diverse laboratory-specific data management systems.

At the very beginning of the design process, it became apparent that the fundamental constraint in the design was the data management scheme needed to update and distribute the database files containing the approximately 15 Gbytes of data deposited in the major NCBI databases. The key issue was how to move this relatively large amount of data across the system in a manner that does not create bottle-necks that may affect the scalability or run-time goals of the project. Although it was obvious that the performance targets were achievable using more expensive proprietary solutions, their use would conflict with the desire to use commodity hardware to keep the cost of the system down.

In the design of the system, there were two choices for the location of the databases: (1) to have a global repository for the data files or (2) to replicate the files locally on each compute node of the system. There are obvious disadvantages to both of these options; the first may produce an IO bottleneck when several processors try to access the same files, whereas the second may require significant time for the data migration of the files to all the nodes on the cluster and significantly increase the total amount of disk space required to implement the system. To better understand the requirements, extensive tests of the IO behavior of BLAST searches in a cluster environment were performed. The results showed that neither of the models was totally satisfactory and that the results were highly dependent on the nature of the scheduled search. We decided to implement a hybrid model in which two generations of the formatted NCBI data files are kept in globally accessible space. Searches have the option of using these copies of the databases or replicating the necessary database files on a disk local to the compute nodes at run time. If the submitted job will be running over the entire course of the nightly database update, a process that takes about three hours, the user must make a local copy; however short runs do not have to waste the computer time that making a copy takes. The use of a copy of the database on local disk also permits a user to run multiple searches on different nodes using different versions of the databases. The current implementation uses remote copy to transfer the files from the global space to the individual nodes assigned to a given search, requiring multiple reads of the globally stored files. Although this has not been a bottleneck in our relative small system, in the near future we will change this implementation by using GridFTP (http://www.globus.org/research/papers.html#Data%20Grid%20Components) for replicating the files, hopefully decreasing the load on the file server and, consequently, increasing the scalability as we increase the number of search nodes to meet the needs of additional researchers.

The next area of concern was the downloading of the daily updates of the NCBI database files without degrading the performance of the rest of the system that was running searches. To solve this problem we decided to use a separate node to process the download of the datasets. Taking advantage of the low cost of commodity disks, it was possible to acquire the large disk space that allows keeping multiple copies of the databases while using a clever update scheme that precludes interference between the updates and the searches. This scheme is explained in detail below.

The computational capacity of the cluster can be easily scaled to meet the time requirements by adding processors to the system. Note that by decomposing the input search streams as described below, it is possible to obtain almost perfect linear parallel performance improvement of the searches. This scheme makes the searches embarrassingly parallel, isolating scalability issues to the data management and IO schemes discussed above.

39.2.1 Hardware Configuration

The final hardware configuration for the cluster (see Figure 39.1) consists of eight dual-processor AMD Athlon MP 2000+ search nodes, each with 2 GB of RAM and a moderate (60 GB) amount of local disk provided for the option of using local space for storage of the database files. The core file server, used to provide the global disk space, is also a dual AMD Athlon MP 2000+ with 1 GB of RAM and 240 GB of usable space in a RAID array configuration, optimized for NFS read performance. This node is also used to provide cluster services like scheduling and accounting. A specialized node was added for processing the daily updates of the database files. The performance of this node is not relevant, as most of the delays in the downloading of the databases are introduced by the network and source host constraints. The local space in this node is used to hold the newly downloaded NCBI database files and to provide space to *untar* the files before migrating them to the global file server. The intent of this design is to keep the nightly database updates from impacting the load on the global file server as much as possible. Finally, an interactive node was added to allow users to gain a login shell access to interact with the queuing system as needed. All of the nodes in the cluster are internally connected via a GigE network using a Foundry Big Iron 15000 switch supporting jumbo frames. The internal connection of the nodes via a private vLAN makes them inaccessible from outside the cluster. The interactive node (sequence) and the node

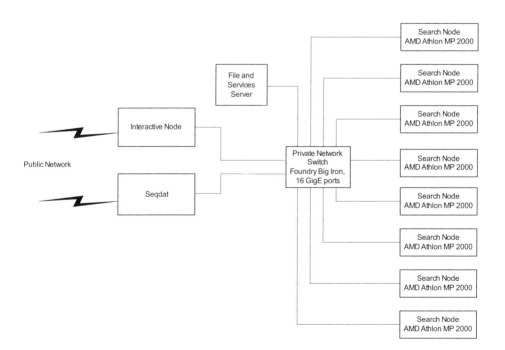

Figure 39.1 Architecture of the cluster for BLAST searches.

for database updates (seqdat) are multiported, connected to both to the campus-wide area network and to the private network with the rest of the nodes. This scheme provides a higher degree of security by concentrating the access points in two nodes and eliminating the possibility of external threats on the rest of the nodes of the cluster.

39.2.2 Software Configuration

All the nodes of the cluster are running LINUX Redhat 8.0 as the operating system. OpenPBS 2.3.16 (http://www.openpbs.org) is used for resource management, Maui 3.2.6 (http://www.supercluster.org) for scheduling the jobs, and QBank 2.10 (http://www.emsl.pnl.gov/docs/mscf) for the accounting. In its current implementation, with the system being used only by one research group, it would be possible to manage the job of scheduling manually or by some easy-to-implement *cron* job. However, OpenPBS and Maui were still implemented as feature-rich queue systems (6), allowing for a scalable software infrastructure that can be used to manage the workflow of numerous research groups when needed.

All nodes are able to run the full BLAST suite of programs that were downloaded from the NCBI site and made available via NFS. After receiving notice from the NCBI mailing list on software updates, the programs are updated manually. After installation and testing of the newest code, the *std* link is changed from the old to the new version. Using this update mechanism, there is no need to make any changes in the scripts, which use the *std* link nomenclature, preventing interference with already running jobs and providing the flexibility to run searches using previous versions of the software.

39.2.3 Database Files Refreshing Scheme

As discussed above, the task of maintenance of the database files is delegated to a dedicated node of the cluster, seqdat. The procedure to update the local databases from the NCBI ftp site is performed on a nightly basis as a *cron* job. The large database files are present on this ftp site as preformatted files in FASTA format. On seqdat, three database directories are available: ~/db, ~/db_backup, and ~/db_source. The ~/db_source directory, located on a disk local to seqdat as it is only needed for the download process, contains the compressed *tar* files as received from the NCBI ftp site. The major advantage of having this directory on a local disk versus being on a disk that is NFS-mounted across the entire cluster is that the file transfer process is extremely slow when there is a search in progress on the rest of the cluster due to the contention between reads from searches and writes from downloads to the same file system. Our tests show that moving this directory to a local disk increased the overall transfer rate by an order of magnitude, from approximately 100 to 1000 kbytes/sec. The remaining two directories, ~/db_backup, and and ~/db, are available to seqdat via a NFS mount from the file server. The directory ~/db contains the current files that are being used in the searches and are maintained in the NFS-mounted space accessible to all nodes of the cluster. The directory ~/db_backup, also on the core file server, contains the version of the databases from the previous day.

A virtual *std* link pointing to the ~/db directory with the latest NCBI database files indicates the source of the ~/db files to use in any searches. The first task of the *cron* job is to make a copy of this directory, to ~/db_backup, and transfer the *std* link to this copy. Therefore any searches running from this copy that are in progress or that may start during the nightly update will continue accessing the last static copy of the database. After making this copy, the ftp transfer is done using *ncftpget* (http://www.ncftp.com), which compares the existing compressed tar files in ~/db_source with those available for download, proceeding to download a file when they are different. Once all of the updated database files available are downloaded, the remaining task is to unpack the compressed *tar* files into the ~/db directory and move the link back to the newly created database directory. When a user starts a search that may run through a database update, the first step of the job is to make a copy, either on global or local scratch, of the databases that the user will then own. This copy takes just over three hours if the user needs all of the maintained databases for the search. The user's search is then completed on this copy of the database. This allows a user to have a static database for a search that takes multiple days in the event of an update of the NCBI databases during the duration of the run.

39.2.4 Job Parsing, Scheduling and Processing

The search sequences provided by the user are given as a set of input files. Every input files contains a number of individual nucleotide sequences, in FASTA format, each of which need to be compared to the sequences in the databases. The input files are named according to the search to be done, according to the following format: ###X12, where ### is the file index currently ranging from 1 to 164 and X = n, x, t signifies a *blastn, blastx,* or *tblastx* search, respectively. *blastn* is the standard BLAST search in which a nucleotide sequence is compared to sequences in a nucleotide database, *blastx* searches protein databases to find proteins similar to a translated form of the nucleotide query sequence and, finally, *tblastx* compares the translated nucleotide query to translated nucleotide database entries. The *blastx* searches use the nonredundant peptide sequence database, whereas the *blastn* searches against the non-redundant nucleotide, est, sts, gss, and htgs databases as provided by the NCBI. The initial search only uses *blastn* and *blastx,* and is designated as the stage-one search. Currently, this search is done on an approximately weekly basis. For sequences that do not have any hits found during the first stage of similarity searching, a second search needs to be completed. Currently, this is the case for approximately 1800 of the 6500 sequences being analyzed for similarities. This second search is the *tblastx* matching using the nonredundant nucleotide, est, sts, gss, and htgs databases, and is designated as the stage-two search. This search, due to the translation of both the query sequence and the database entries takes a significantly longer time and it is performed only on a monthly basis. For the current input files, the stage-one search takes approximately 30 total node hours, whereas the second-stage search on the 1800 "No hits found" sequences takes over 620 total node hours.

Before starting a new search, a decision has to be made as to whether or not there has been a database update since the last search, so as to not repeat an identical search. As stated above, checks are made for updates to the database available at the NCBI ftp site on a nightly basis; however, updates are not always available. If there are difficulties present at the NCBI FTP site, several days or even longer can pass between updates becoming available. In addition, a decision on the number of nodes that are available for the search needs to be made. A *perl* script was developed to create the necessary PBS script files that distribute the searches among the available nodes in the cluster. This script is based on a file structure in which there is a directory $HOME/search which contains the input files. The $HOME/search directory also contains one additional file, searchlist.in, which is a list of the filenames, one per line, of the files containing sequences on which the stage-one search must be completed. Each of these input files must exist in the $HOME/search directory. The researchers may add new search sequences by either adding them to an existing input file or creating a new input file. In the later case, the filename, which must match the existing convention and have an n or x in the name, must be added to the searchlist.in file.

The output of each of the searches is stored in a new directory inside of $HOME/search. The name of the directory of a given search is based on the date on which the search was started and is of the form yyyy-mm-dd. In each output directory the results of the search are stored, in this case as html files. There is one output file for each input file that is searched. If only stage one is being done in the search, these output files are the entire contents of the output directory. If a stage-two search is also being completed, the input files generated for this search are also stored in the $HOME/search/yyyy-mm-dd directory, along with a directory TBLASTX, which will contain the output of the second stage.

The execution of the *perl* script first checks the date of the current databases, the one to which the *std* link points. This is accomplished by running the *fastacmd-I* on the nonredundant peptide sequence database. This command returns the date of the database, *date_db*. This date is compared to the date of the databases used in the last search, *date_last*. This date is obtained by taking the last of the date directories (comparing the directory names as numbers and looking for the largest), and looking at the date posted in the output of this last search on the 1X12 input file. If *date_db* is not greater than the *date_last,* the user is told that there has been no database update since last search and that they should try again not earlier than the next day as database updates are checked on a nightly basis. The script is then exited. If *date_db* is greater than *date_last,* then the script proceeds. The user is then prompted as to whether he wishes to perform a first-stage search only or a first- and second-stage search. This is the last input required from the user. At this point, the directories under $HOME/search where the output will be stored are created—$HOME/search/yyyy-mm-dd and, if necessary, $HOME/search/yyyy-mm-dd/TBLASTX.

The remainder of the script writes all the necessary PBS script files and submits them for processing. First, the number of nodes available for the search must be determined. This is done by issuing a *showq* command and using *grep* and *cut* to pull out the number of free compute nodes, allowing for the job to be completed with as many nodes as are available in order to minimize the wall time it takes for the search to be completed. This number, #nodes, can range from zero to eight on our current cluster. If zero, the search will default to run on one node. This simplistic mechanism for choosing how many nodes to use will need to be rewritten in the advent of multiple groups using the system. In this case, there will need to be a maximum number of nodes made available to any given job, allowing for the sharing of the resources.

The *perl* script then generates the #nodes scripts, named SCRIPT-1 through SCRIPT-#nodes. The necessary PBS headers are written to each of these script files, along with the necessary environmental variables and links. In addition, the first portion of each of these scripts involves cleaning up the local scratch space from previous searches followed by installing the necessary databases for the current search onto the local scratch system of each node. This is followed by a round-robin process dividing up the searches among the #node script files, with the first input file name in searchlist.in going to SCRIPT-1, the second to SCRIPT-2, and so on, until the last PBS script file is reached, then returning to SCRIPT-1 and repeating the cycle until the end of searchlist.in is reached. Once the PBS script files are generated, they are submitted by the *perl* script. In principle, this method of dividing the workload can lead to significant unbalanced loads on the nodes, but because most of the searches being performed take the same amount of time, this static job distribution introduces only minor load imbalance. Future implementations will use a client–server model in which nodes will be able to request new files for processing from a server node when they finish their scheduled tasks. The server node will then need to maintain an updated database categorizing the individual searches processed, being processed, and waiting to be processed.

In each of these PBS scripts, the stage-one search is processed for a given input file followed by, when requested by the user, creation of the second-stage input files by parsing of the stage-one output to extract the input sequences for which the "No hits found" message is received, and then starting the second-stage search. These input sequences produced in the parsing step are collected in a new second-stage input file with the same naming scheme, but with the x replaced with a t, and the second-stage search, using *tblastx,* is then started. After all requested searches are complete on a given input file, the PBS job continues with the next input file. At any time, the user can monitor the output as well as the status of the batch queues on the system in order to track the progress of the search.

39.2.5 Integration with SmedDb

In order to become useful, the searches produced have to be uploaded and integrated to the SmedDb system. Although the implementation of the search system described above is quite general and can be integrated into any laboratory system, the integration of the search output with the SmedDb database is quite specific, tailored to the needs of the research group. Therefore, this integration is presented as an example that can be used when integrating the search system to other laboratories. SmedDb is a Web-accessible database that contains *S. mediterranea* sequences, BLAST results, reading-frame diagrams, and in situ hybridization images in one output report. Any homologous sequences are displayed with links to NCBI's Entrez and Pubmed.

The architecture of SmedDb as it relates to our cluster search system is given in Figure 39.2. The FASTA files generated from SmedDb containing the sequences (ESTs) that need to be compared with the most recently updated version of NCBI databases are uploaded manually to the cluster search system using secure copy (*scp*). Using the script described above, the required BLAST searches are executed and the output files are downloaded to the SmedDb system also using *scp*. These search results are stored with the corresponding EST as well as being parsed by a *Bioperl* [3] script. The *Bioperl* script is used to pull out the highest-scoring (lowest expectation value) match for each of the searches along with its associated description. This information is then used to update the status of the sequences in SmedDb (having a significant match, no significant match, or no match at all). If a given input sequence has a significant match in the current

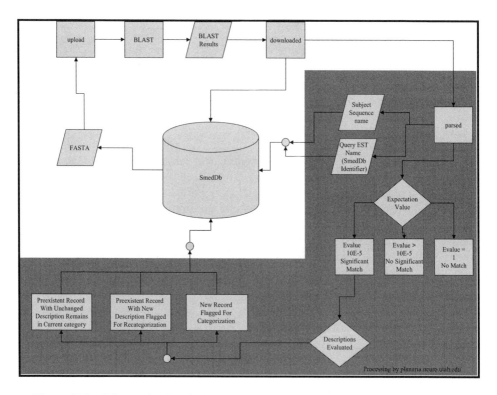

Figure 39.2   Schema showing the integration of the cluster-based BLAST search engine with the laboratory information system SmedDb.

search, further processing needs to be completed. If previous searches have not found a significant match, the search output is marked for review and possible classification by the researcher. If previous searches have already resulted in finding a significant match, the current result is compared to the old result. If the old and new descriptions are the same, no change is made in the SmedDb for the given sequence entry. If the description is different, this SmedDb record is flagged and a message is posted requesting manual intervention of the researcher to decide on its reclassification.

39.3   PERFORMANCE

The system described above is fully functional and is operating in a production environment. The system as it exists meets the design principles and requirements established in the planning stage. The total cost of the system has been estimated at $26,000, with all of the components being commodity parts.

The nightly database download process takes just over three hours for databases totaling about 15 GBytes. The copy of the necessary database files to local scratch for the project being described is approximately an hour for ~/db needed totaling about 12.5 GBytes. The database updates are performed so as not to interfere with any searches that may be in progress.

As described above, the current search is performed on over 6500 input sequences. Of these, currently about 1800 are candidates for the second-stage search. The time required for a first-stage search only is approximately 30 node hours, whereas a complete first- and second-stage search takes about 620 node hours, or slightly over 3 days if all eight nodes are used. This time is slightly longer than the criteria of most searches being done in 48 hours; however, the majority of searches are stage-one only.

39.4   CONCLUSIONS

This chapter reports a case study on the development of a dedicated commodity-based cluster for the periodic update of gene sequence comparisons. The project has been able to meet the turnaround time goals and eliminate a great deal of human labor in the periodic update of the SmedDb system. Our experience shows that it is possible to use commodity components to design and deploy a cluster with a configuration optimized for a particular task. The judicious use of low-cost hardware combined with a clever update of the databases permits the continuous operation of the system, avoiding interference among the updates and long-running searches. The cluster described here presents a low-cost model for biomedical labs requiring substantially more BLAST searches than can be reasonably performed using the existing NCBI services. As the system is highly scalable, it is possible to use this architecture to deploy systems serving from individual labs to departmental and even institutional BLAST search engines.

ACKNOWLEDGMENTS

This work was partially funded by the National Institutes of Health, National Institute of General Medical Sciences RO-1 GM57260 to ASA, and National Center for Research Resources 1 S10 RR17214-01 to JCF.

REFERENCES

1. R. Sachidanandam, D. Weissman, S. C. Schmidt, J. M. Kakol, L. D. Stein, G. Marth, S. Sherry, J. C. Mullikin, B. J. Mortimore, D. L. Willey, S. E. Hunt, C. G. Cole, P. C. Coggill, C. M. Rice, Z. Ning, J. Rogers, D. R. Bentley, P. Y. Kwok, E. R. Mardis, R. T. Yeh, B. Schultz, L. Cook, R. Davenport, M. Dante, L. Fulton, L. Hillier, R. H. Waterston, J. D. McPherson, B. Gilman, S. Schaffner, W. J. Van Etten, D. Reich, J. Higgins, M. J. Daly, B. Blumenstiel, J. Baldwin, N. Stange-Thomann, M. C. Zody, L. Linton, E. S. Lander, and D. Altshuler, A map of human genome sequence variation containing 1.42 million single nucleotide polymorphisms, *Nature, 409,* 928–933, 2001.
2. S. F. Altschul, T. L. Madden, A. A. Schaffer, J. Zhang, Z. Zhang, W. Miller, and D. J. Lipman, Gapped BLAST and PSI-BLAST: A new generation of protein database search programs, *Nucleic Acids Research, 25,* 3389–402, 1997.
3. A. Sánchez Alvarado, P. A. Newmark, S. M. Robb, and R. Juste, The *Schmidtea mediterranea* database as a molecular resource for studying platyhelminthes, stem cells and regeneration, *Development, 129,* 5659–5665, 2002.
4. G. F. Pfister, *In Search of Clusters,* Prentice-Hall PTR, Upper Saddle River, NJ, 1998.
5. F. Berman, G. Fox, and T. Hey, *Grid Computing: Making The Global Infrastructure a Reality,* Wiley, 2003.
6. D. B. Jackson, B. Haymore, J. C. Facelli, and Q. O. Snell, Improving Cluster Utilization Through Set Based Allocation Policies, presented at Proceedings of the International Conference on Parallel Computing, Valencia, Spain, 2001.

## CHAPTER 40

A Hierarchical Distributed Shared-Memory Parallel Branch and Bound Application with PVM and OpenMP for Multiprocessor Clusters

ROCCO AVERSA, BENIAMINO DI MARTINO, NICOLA MAZZOCCA, and SALVATORE VENTICINQUE

40.1 INTRODUCTION

Branch and Bound (B&B) is a technique widely used to solve combinatorial optimization problems in physics and engineering science. At the same time, B&B applications represent a typical example of irregularly structured problems whose parallelization using hierarchical computational architectures (e.g., clusters of SMPs) involves several issues, such as the sharing of global computation state and dynamic workload balancing among nodes. In this chapter we show how the combined use of PVM and OpenMP libraries can be a promising approach to exploit the intrinsic parallel nature of this class of applications and to obtain efficient code for hybrid computational architectures. Our strategy to yield an effective distributed version of a given B&B application for a distributed multiprocessor architecture was driven by the following rules: no significant variations in the original algorithm structure, reusing a large part of the available code, and exploiting the hybrid computational characteristics of the target system. With reference to this last crucial point, we needed to combine in our parallel version a coarse-grain parallelization technique, using a PVM solution of the B&B application [9] based on the coordinator/workers paradigm, together with a finer-grain parallelization approach that, using OpenMP primitives, introduces an additional dynamic and efficient workload distribution among the shared-memory nodes of the system.

The remainder of the chapter proceeds as follows. A conceptual description of the B&B technique, together with advantages and problems arising within a parallel framework, are presented in Section 40.2. Sections 40.3 describes a shared-memory extension of the sequential version and its integration into the original parallel implementation. In Section 40.4 we discuss results of tests on a local area network (LAN) of workstations. Finally, we provide some concluding remarks.

40.2 THE B&B PARALLEL APPLICATION

A discrete optimization problem consists in searching the optimal value (maximum or minimum) of a function $f : \vec{x} \in Z^n \rightarrow \mathcal{R}$, and the solution $\vec{x} = \{x_1, \ldots, x_n\}$ in which the function's value is optimal. $f(\vec{x})$ is a cost function, and its domain is generally defined by means of a set of m constraints on the points of the definition space. Constraints are generally expressed by a set of inequalities:

$$\sum_{i=1}^{n} a_{i,j} x_i \le b_j \qquad \forall j \in \{1, \ldots, m\} \tag{40.1}$$

and they define the set of feasible values for the x_i variables (the solutions space of the problem).

B&B is a class of methods solving such problems according to a divide-and-conquer strategy. The initial solution space is recursively divided into subspaces until attaining the individual solutions. Such a recursive division can be represented by a (abstract) tree: the nodes of this tree represent the solution subspaces obtained by dividing the parent subspace and the leaf nodes represent the solutions of the problem, and the tree traversal represents the recursive operation of dividing and conquering the problem.

The method is enumerative but it aims at a nonexhaustive scanning of the solutions space. This goal is achieved by estimating the best feasible solution for each subproblem, without expanding the tree node or trying to prove that there are no feasible solutions for a subproblem whose value is better than the current best value. (It is assumed that a best feasible solution estimation function has been devised, to be computed for each subproblem.) This latter situation corresponds to the so-called pruning of a search subtree.

B&B algorithms can be parallelized at a fine- or coarse-grain level. The fine-grain parallelization involves computations related to each subproblem, such as the computation of the estimation function or the verification of constraints defining feasible solutions. The coarse-grain parallelization involves the overall tree traversal: there are several computation processes concurrently traversing a different branch of the search tree. In this case, the effects of the parallelism are not limited to a speedup of the algorithmic steps. Indeed, the search tree explored is generally different from the one traversed by the sequential algorithm. As a result, the resolution time can be lower, even though the number of explored nodes can be greater than in the sequential case. As has been demonstrated in [5], this approach exhibits anomalies, so that the parallelization does not guarantee an improvement in the performance. For most practical problems, however, the bigger the problem size, the larger are the benefits of the parallel traversal of the search tree.

Parallel B&B algorithms can be categorized on the basis of four features [4]:

1. How information on the global state of the computation is shared among processors (we refer to such information as the knowledge generated by the algorithm)
2. How the knowledge is utilized by each process
3. How the workload is divided among the processes
4. How the processes communicate and synchronize among themselves

The knowledge is global if there is a single common repository for the state of the computation at any moment, accessed by all processes, otherwise it is local. In this latter case, processes have their own knowledge bases, which must be kept consistent to a certain degree to speed up the tree traversal and to balance the workload.

With respect to the knowledge use, the algorithms are characterized by:

1. The reaction strategy of processes to the knowledge update (it can range from an instantaneous reaction to ignoring it until the next decision is to be taken)
2. The dominance rule among nodes (a node dominates another if its solutions best value is better than the lower bound on the solutions of the other). It can be partial or global, if a node can be eliminated only by a dominant node belonging to the same subtree traversed by a process, or by any other dominant node
3. The search strategy, which can be breadth-, depth-, or best-first

With regard to the workload division, if all generated subproblems are stored in a common knowledge base, to each process that becomes idle the most promising subproblem is assigned (on the basis of an heuristic evaluation). If the state of the computation is distributed among processes (local knowledge), then a workload balancing strategy has to be established, consisting of a relocation of subproblems not yet traversed.

The parallel algorithm we present solves the $(0 - 1)$ knapsack problem, which can be stated as follows [6]:

$$\text{maximize} \quad \sum_{i=1}^{n} c_i x_i \tag{40.2}$$

$$\text{with} \quad x_i \in \{0, 1\} \ \forall i \in \{1, \dots, n\}$$

$$\text{subject to} \quad \sum_{i=1}^{n} a_{i,j} x_i \leq b_j \ \forall j \in \{1, \dots, m\} \tag{40.3}$$

where $a_{i,j}$ and b_j are positive integers. They have been designed for distributed memory parallel architectures, such as a network of workstations. The implementation of both algorithms has been carried out in the PVM parallel programming system [7]. In particular, the algorithms exploit the PVM primitives for interrupting sends and multicast communication.

The characteristics of the algorithm, with respect to the categorization of the B&B algorithms presented above, are the following:

1. Each processor has its own knowledge base (local knowledge);
2. Processes react instantaneously to knowledge updates (the signal primitives of the PVM environment are used for this purpose);
3. A global dominance rule is adopted since the current optimal value is broadcast to all processes as soon as it is updated;
4. The search strategy is depth-first, as it is more suited to the case of local knowledge;
5. With respect to workload sharing between processes, load balancing is provided, activated in presence of an idle process, since there is a local knowledge sharing;
6. With regard to synchronization, the algorithms are asynchronous, since there is no synchronous exchange of information and workload between executors, but this exchange is performed on the basis of executor's local events, and so asynchronously with respect to the other executors.

In the coordinator/workers concurrent programming model, a coordinator process spawns a set of worker processes, which perform the actual computation; the coordinator also manages the sharing of the global knowledge among the workers. The structure of the application is depicted in Figure 40.1.

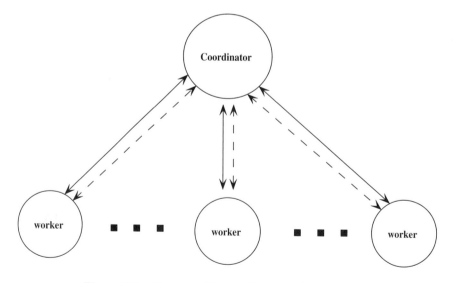

Figure 40.1   Structure of the coordinator/worker algorithm.

The algorithm consists of the following phases:

- A coordinator process produces P instances of a worker process, decomposes the assigned problem in P disjoint subproblems, and assigns them to the workers.
- Each worker explores its own subtree with a depth-first strategy and updates its local current best value, sending it to the coordinator, when it generates a feasible solution.
- When the coordinator receives a local current best value, it compares it with the global current best value and eventually updates and broadcasts it to the workers.

The load balancing among the workers is accomplished with the following strategy:

- When a worker completes the exploration of its subtree, it sends a message to the coordinator and waits for a new load share from it.
- The coordinator manages a list of idle workers. When it is not empty, it polls active workers for a share of the load until it receives a positive answer, then it assigns the share to the first idle process in the list.

Thus, the coordinator is in charge of managing the updates and the broadcast of the current best value, and of balancing the load among workers. The presence of a coordinator also allows the detection of the termination condition. This is verified when all workers are idle at the same time and there are no messages carrying work units, which have been sent but not received yet. Since the coordinator holds the global state of the computation (lists of idle workers and of workload messages), it is able to detect this situation.

40.3 THE OpenMP EXTENSION

The hybrid version of this algorithm allows many threads to solve in parallel the problem assigned to a pvm process, applying recursively the divide-and-conquer strategy (Figure 40.2). Each thread begins the traversal of the subtree assigned to the pvm process from a different node at a deeper level. The solution space is an array of Boolean values specified by an early index lsc; a feasible solution is the same array specified by the full dimension N. The solution space is divided by incrementing the index lsc and obtaining two new arrays with the value of index $lsc - 1$ equal to 1 and 0.

Similar to the actions of a group of workers, the threads divide their subspaces assigned to them and put new subproblems in the same shared bag. Every time the solution space is divided into two new problems, the thread pushes the first into the common bag and continues to explore the second one. When a branch of the tree

```
main () {
 #pragma parallel omp shared(opt,bag)
 {
while (!bagEmpty)
    {
       x = select_next_node(N);
       verify_feasibility(x);
       if "x isfeasible solution"
       #pragma omp critical(opt)
         {
           update_supposed_best
           send(new_supposed_best,coor);
         }
       else branch
     if (!branch)
       #pragmaomp critical(push)
     {
         fill_the_bag      //divide: search new feasible solutions
     }
     else
      #pragma omp critical   (pop)
      {
       if "other nodes to explore"//conquere feasible solutions
          take_from_the_bag
      }
    }//end while
}// end omp parallel

I AM IDLE !!!!
 }
```

Figure 40.2 The OpenMP implementation of the parallel algorithm with a shared bag of tasks.

occurs, a new task is taken from the common bag. When a new optimum is found, the global optimum is updated. The global optimum is shared among the threads in order to optimize the tree branching. As the bag is shared among all the workers, we do not need an inner workload balancing strategy. When the bag is empty, all the threads becomes idle and a new problem is assigned by the master thread to the PVM coordinator process. The computation of the feasible solution is performed in an OpenMP parallel section where the constraints and the function loads are shared, whereas the computations are executed on private data. The different threads concur to write the same shared data when:

- A new local optimum is found and the global one needs to be updated
- A new subproblem is pushed into the bag
- A new subproblem is taken from the bag.

In these three situations, we need to define OpenMP critical sections in order to make each of these actions atomic. In order to explain how the OpenMP support is exploited, we describe here how the sequential version has been extended. As is shown Figure 40.3, this kind of parallelization is straightforward and very simple to implement. However, in this case we have three pure parallel computations (without any concurrency on shared values):

```
main() {
 #pragma parallel omp shared(opt,bag[])
 {
while(!bagEmpty)
     {
        x = select_next_node(N);
        verify_feasibility(x);
        if "x isfeasiblesolution"
        #pragma omp critical
          {
            update_supposed_best
            send(new_supposed_best,coor);
          }
        else branch
     if (!branch){
         fill_the_bag[myid]    //divide:search new feasible solution

     else
       if "other nodes to explore"//conquere feasible solutions
       {
           omp_unset_lock(locks[myid]);
           take_from_the_bag[myid]
           omp_unset_lock(locks[myid])
       }
       else
       {
           otherid=(myd+1)%n_threads
           while((otherid!=myd)|(got_new_problem))
            {
              omp_set_lock(locks[otherid]);
              take_from_the_bag[otherid]
              omp_unset_lock(locks[otherid]);
              otherid=(otherid+1)\%n_threads
            }
         }

     }//end while
}// end omp parallel

I AM IDLE !!!!
 }
```

Figure 40.3   The optimized implementation of OpenMP-based algorithm.

1. The computation of the new optimum
2. The verification of the feasibilities
3. The branching of the tree

We have three critical sections that introduce a loss of performance when the different threads are executing the same part of the code:

1. The updating of the global optimum
2. The pushing of a new task into the shared bag
3. The extraction of a task from the shared bag

The critical sections deal with three different domains. In fact, the bag of tasks is a buffer accessed according to a first-in-first-out strategy. This means that two threads could concur to write the same data just when they are executing in the section identified by the same label `opt`, `push`, or `pop`.

First of all, we should consider that for each iteration we must enter at least one critical section. In fact, when a new optimum is found in the space of solutions two critical sections are crossed:

- We enter the first critical section in order to update the new optimum.
- We divide the problem and fill the bag in order to identify the final solution or a better value.

Instead, when the new solution is not feasible or it is worse than the current optimum, only one critical section is executed in order to take a new problem from the bag.

With regard to the scalability of the problem, when the problem size increases we see above all an exponential growth of the solution space, whose main effect is a bigger number of iterations. It means that the execution time of the critical section increases too much. Finally it easy to foresee that the degree of concurrence increases with the number of threads.

In order to overcome this kind of troubles, we tried to optimize the implementation of the algorithm described above. It is possible to reduce the concurrence among the threads by defining a shared but distributed bag. If each thread is the owner of a private repository of tasks, we have at least no executions of critical code and no more than one. We mean that the critical code is executed only when a better optimum and a feasible solution are found. The update of the global value is needfed in order to perform a more consistent pruning of the tree. When the problem size or the number of threads increase, the number of updates does not change in the same way. The number of executions of the critical code depends on just the input data and the way according to which the solution space is divided among the threads.

The pseudocode, shown in Figure 40.3, describes the implementation of the optimized approach. As we can see, we implemented the distributed bag as an array of pockets. Each thread works with its own pocket. The index of each pocket is associated with the identifier of the owner OpenMP thread. In order to perform a load balancing among the threads, when the owned pocket is empty, the worker tries to take a problem from the other pockets. The concurrent access to the same pocket takes place very seldom. Anyway, we must assure that the access to the same pocket, in order to get a new problem, is exclusive among the threads. The collision due to access to a particular pocket is prevented by an array of locks. A thread reserves and releases the lock *i* every time it needs to take a task from the pocket *i*. If the bag is empty, the thread becomes idle and waits for the others workers at the end of the parallel section.

40.4 EXPERIMENTAL RESULTS

The system used as testbed for our experimental executions is the Cygnus cluster of the Parsec Laboratory at the Second University of Naples. This is a Linux cluster with four SMP nodes equipped with two Pentium Xeon 1 Ghz, 512 MB RAM and a 40 GB HD, and a dual-Pentium Xeon 3.2 GHz front end. The nodes are interconnected by a 100 Mbit Ethernet switch. For the experiments we report in this Section, we have installed on our system the ROCKS LINUX distribution supported by NPACI, the Intel C++ Compiler version 8.0, and the PVM environment version 3.4.4. We executed first the sequential version of our application and the different parallel implementations. The results are shown in Figure 40.4 and reported in Table 40.1.

In the first two columns of Table 40.1, we have the pure OpenMP implementation using a common bag and the pure OpenMP implementation using the distributed bag, both executed on a single node. In the last columns we have the pure PVM and hybrid implementations executing on four nodes. According to the irregular behavior of the application, which is related to the kind of input data, we get very different results, even if the dimension of the original problem is always equal to $N = 40$. unknowns. The collected results rely on three different input datasets. On the first line, for each input dataset, is shown the application time required by the execution for the different implementations. On the second line, we report the total

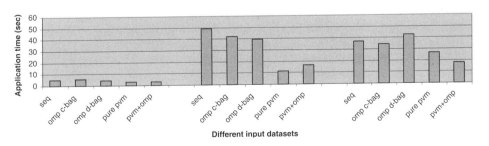

Figure 40.4   The execution time for different sets of input data.

Table 40.1 Performance results for different implementations

	seq	omp_lp	omp	pure pvm	pvm + omp
Input data 1	4779	5681	4403	3315	3363
	1,853,657	2,930,622	2,812,890	4,831,090	7,422,951
Input data 2	49,427	42,833	39,226	11,719	16,323
	19,041,082	21,515,089	25,490,114	17,169,639	38,584,062
Input data 3	36,887	34,204	42,661	26,816	17,492
	14,656,792	18,239,698	28,736,101	40,089,176	43,818,122

number of subproblems that were explored. It is reasonable that the execution time is strictly related to the number of problems that are effectively solved. The fastest execution, with the first data set, is due to the effect of a relevant branch of the tree. When a relevant pruning does not occur in the first phase of the computation, the number of solutions explored can increase a lot, as happens for the second and the third datasets.

Regarding the improvement or the loss in performance seen when a grater number of processes are involved, they depend on how the solution space is divided among the processes.

As the classical speedup measure is not meaningful because the different executions solve a different number of problems, we will provide a normalized measure of the speedup in order to remove the influence on the measures due to the irregularity of the problem.

In Figure 40.5, we compare the speedup of the pure OpenMP version executed on a single node. The optimized implementation always performs better with two threads.

In Figure 40.6 it is showed the normalized speedups for the execution of the pure PVM implementation and the hybrid one. They scales always well.

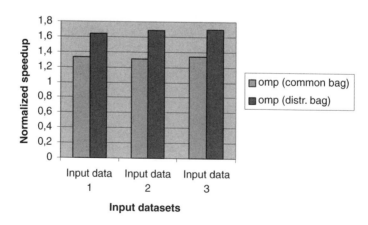

Figure 40.5 Normalized speedup for the common bag and distributed bag.

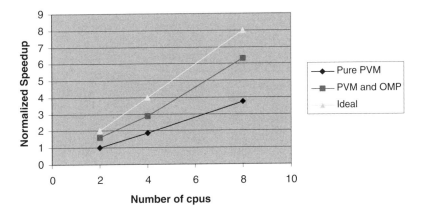

Figure 40.6   Normalized speedup for the pure PVM and hybrid parallel implementations.

40.5   CONCLUSIONS

We have presented a strategy for the parallelization of B&B algorithms for distributed-memory of SMP architectures. It is based on a coordinator/worker paradigm at a distributed level supported with a dynamic workload balancing facility. At a the shared-memory level, according a similar approach, we recursively defined a distributed bag of tasks in order to exploit the SMP architecture of the computation nodes. We described a PVM–OpenMP implementation and presented some experimental results in order to discuss the irregular behavior of the B&B application. Future work should investigate the benefit that pruning could bring to these kinds of problems by the utilization of a wider number of nodes, also geographically distributed on a grid platform. We were already able to evaluate the overhead introduced when the application is launched by the Globus v. 2.0 gatekeeper. We estimated that growth of user time is about 0.2 sec.

REFERENCES

1. J. N. Magee and S. C. Cheung, Parallel Algorithm Design for Workstation clusters, *Software—Practice and Experience, 21*(3), 235–250, Mar. 1991.

2. A. H. Karp, Programming for Parallelism, *IEEE Computer, 20,* 43–57, May 1987.

3. A. Mazzeo, N. Mazzocca, A. Sforza, and S. Russo, Algoritmi Branch&Bound paralleli per sistemi multicomputer, *Ricerca Operativa, 24,* 71, 1994.

4. H. W. J. Trienekens, *Parallel Branch&Bound Algorithms,* Ph.D. Thesis, Erasmus UniversiteitRotterdam, Nov. 1990.

5. H. T. Lai and S. Sahni, Anomalies in Parallel Branch&Bound Algorithms, *Communications of the ACM, 27,* 6, 594–602, June 1984.

6. C. Ribeiro, Parallel Computer Models and Combinatorial Algorithms, *Annals of Discrete Mathematics, 31,* 325–364, 1987.

7. A. Geist and V. S. Sunderam, Network-Based Concurrent Computing on the PVM System, *Concurrency: Practice and Experience, 4,* 4, 293–311, June 1992.

8. M. T. Heath and J. A. Etheridge, ParaGraph: A Tool for Visualizing Performance of Parallel Programs, Tech. Rep., Oak Ridge National Laboratory, Oak Ridge, TN, March 1994.

9. B. Di Martino, N. Mazzocca, and S. Russo, Paradigms for the Parallelization of Branch&Bound Algorithms, in *Applied Parallel Computing,* Springer-Verlag, Lecture Notes in Computer Science, *1061,* 161–150, 1996.

## CHAPTER 41

IP-Based Telecommunication Services

ANNA BONIFACIO and G. SPINILLO

This chapter describes an advanced telecommunication service, based on a convergent architecture between TDM networks and IP networks. The service makes use of advanced protocols and layered architecture for the fast delivery of new features and the best leveraging of existing legacy solutions. This chapter gives a short overview of advanced telephony architectures and protocols, then focuses on describing the implemented solution.

41.1 INTRODUCTION

The great spread of Internet-based services and the new features provided by IP telephony have created the best conditions for designing and deploying new convergent services. There are two different concepts that are converging and merging in new telephony services:

- Merging between different type of media (voice over TDM, voice over IP, voice and video convergence)
- Integration between phones and computers

The scope and aim of the next-generation services is to provide access to the variety of media resources available to end users, and, at the same time, also make it possible for users to more effectively manage their personal communications. Today's busy consumers need an easy-to-use method of communication that helps them interact between each other in more efficient ways and with greater impact.

Traditional legacy and monolithic networks deployed in the major network operators fields are not suitable for easily defining new services, adding new features, and reacting rapidly to new requests for new features.

True interoperability is based on the definition of and integration between different network types and protocols. In order to successfully achieve this, the use of standard protocols and third-generation APIs is required. In this chapter, we will describe a next-generation IP Centrex service based on an advanced architecture that provides end users with VOIP access and advanced call management functionality.

In the rest of the chapter, we provide an overview of:

- The target network architecture
- The advanced protocols used
- A list of features provided by the service
- Benefits for the end user
- Benefits for the service provider

41.1.1   Network Architecture

The capability of separating media from control has been notably enhanced by the introduction of the softswitch concept, which was defined around 1998.

The International Softswitch Consortium (ISC) is a nonprofit organization dedicated to promoting a worldwide, distributed architecture enabling networks to support voice, data, and multimedia communications from customer premises to the core. The original name of the consortium (ISC) has been recently changed to International Packet Communications Consortium (IPCC), whose scope is "to develop the market for all products, services, applications and solutions that utilize packet-based voice, data and video communications technologies, regardless of transport medium—wireless, copper, broadband, fiber optics, or other." [2]

The basic network architecture of Softswitch separates media from signalling and application level from call control layer. In an architecture based on the softswitch concept, softswitches handle the interworking between different types of media and different types of networks (TDM, IP), presenting to the application call control API that are media and network independent.

The application(s), mostly running on several different general-purpose computers, can handle business logic functionality and provide integration of the pure telephony network with more Internet-oriented functionality.

This type of network architecture is the voice equivalent of Web servers and it is based on:

- The use of standard hardware and software
- The use of standard transport protocols (TCP-IP/UDP)
- The possibility of leveraging Internet application development tools for telephony-based applications

Although Softswitch is strictly tied to the telephony world, the application server is a general-purpose computer, providing protocols for enabling telephony applications development and leveraging Internet application development tools.

The service selection function in Softswitch decides which application server(s) are to be involved for each specific call, based on an analysis of the caller and the called party identifier (Figure 41.1). This type of approach allows to isolate core

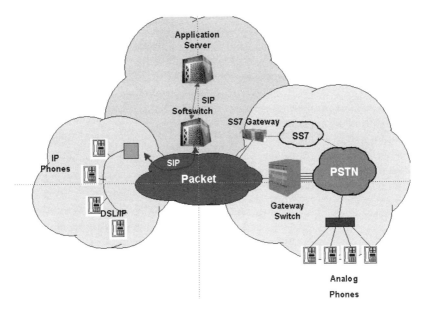

Figure 41.1

Softswitch functions and performance from demands for new services, which can be accomplished via the use of standard protocols between Softswitch and application servers. In the case of our application, the protocol used is SIP.

41.1.1.1 SIP Protocol Overview   In the past few years, SIP has became the de facto standard for voice over IP applications. The SIP stack is currently being installed on a variety of different devices and is becoming part of most diffused operating systems [1]. SIP (Session Initiation Protocol) is an RFC standard (RFC 3261) of the Internet Engineering Task Force (IETF).

SIP is an easy to use stateless protocol, extensible and available for different transport types. Moreover, SIP is continuosly evolving and being extended as technology matures and SIP products are being more used in the marketplace. SIP is a protocol for establishing communications between network endpoints. SIP can be used to create almost any kind of communication between network peers; it is not limited to establishing voice calls. It can be used also in order to establish video calls, the only difference between normal calls and video calls being just the media type used.

41.1.1.1.1 SIP Basic Call   A voice over IP call using the SIP protocol is depicted in Figure 41.2 and is basically composed of the following steps:

- User 1 picks up the phone and originates a call to User 2, whose identity according to the SIP protocol is User2@companyB.com. This results in an INVITE message being sent to the proxy authority for company A.

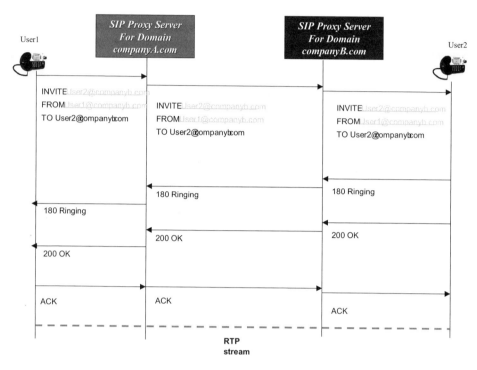

Figure 41.2

- The proxy discovers that the called user is managed by a different proxy, so it just relays the SIP message to the second proxy. Using DNS lookups, Proxy "A" determines that proxy "B" is the authority for the SIP URI being called (User2@companyB.com), and forwards the INVITE to it.
- Proxy "B" receives the INVITE, checks to see if phone "User 2" is currently registered, and, if so, passes the INVITE to phone "User 2."
- Phone "User 2" accepts the INVITE and returns a "180 RINGING" message back to proxy "B."
- Proxy "B" forwards the "180 RINGING" message back to proxy "A."
- Proxy "A" forwards the "180 RINGING" to Phone "A".
- The user finally picks up phone "B," so phone "B" accepts the call and re-turns a "200 OK" to proxy "B." The "200 OK" message includes SDP infor-mation specifying the media parameters this node supports/desires, including codecs, ports, and the IP address for the streams.
- Proxy "B" forwards the "200 OK" message back to Proxy "A".
- Proxy "A" forwards the "200 OK" message back to phone "User 1."
- Phone "User 1" returns an ACK to proxy "A." The ACK message may in-clude media information.

- Proxy "A" forwards the ACK to Proxy "B."
- Proxy "B" forwards the ACK to phone "User 2."
- The two phones are now directly communicating directly with each other. The SIP proxies are no longer involved.

The proxies are needed just in the first part of call setup until call establishment. After these steps, the two phones can communicate without involving the proxies.

The call flow described above depicts just a basic call scenario and the prerequisite is that User 1 and User 2 should be registered to their respective proxies before being able to place calls. The registration is the operation that allows the association of an abstract identity (SIP URI) with the physical IP address of the actual user, allowing user mobility and connection of users via also dialup connections.

What are the pros and cons of using the SIP protocol in order to generate calls? First of all, services may be located everywhere in the network:

- In the service provider network
- Outside of the network, controlled by third-party application developers
- At the user premises, controlled by the end user, through features available at a terminal level

Moreover, the SIP protocol is widely supported by vendors and well known in the developers community, so developing and deploying an SIP-based application is faster and cheaper with respect to proprietary protocols.

41.1.2 Service Features

The example above underlines the signaling protocol needed in order to put in place a call between two endpoints, in terms of signaling exchange and messaging between the endpoints. Besides the easy usage of the protocol and the possibility of distributing the intelligence of the network between terminals, service provider proxies, and third party application servers, we want to briefly highlight the new characteristics and new features that can provided by the services developed on top of them.

Besides the convergence between different type of telephony access, there is the need faced by enterprises to unify the different communications systems present in an enterprise, in order to decrease the costs needed to manage, maintain, and upgrade different systems (pabx, computers, telephones, etc.). There is the need to unify communication media and devices, increase manageability, and improve worker productivity. As an example, think about a user's phonebook and the different systems on which phone numbers may be stored and accessed:

- Personal user agenda (on PDA)
- Personal user agenda (on mobile phone, private numbers)
- Personal user agenda on the enterprise system
- Personal user agenda on the Web

The need for the user to learn and manage the different interfaces with different systems and for the enterprise to support different heterogeneous systems is a cost in terms of productivity for the end user and in terms of costs for both the end user and the enterprise. The final goal is to provide a unified GUI toward a host of network elements, allowing interaction between previously stand-alone systems (Class 5, Internet, wireless, PDA, e-mail, voice mail).

In this chapter, we describe such a type of application, an IpCentrex appplication, based on an advanced network architecture and aimed at providing full convergence and integration of telephony services and pure desktop applications. The phone and PC functionally are integrated and merged.

41.1.2.1   Definition and Features of a Generic IPCentrex Service   IP-Centrex is an IP based service that provided centralized call control and service logic facility to endpoints (both PSTN and IP phones). Basically, the service offers the functionality of an old legacy PBX, without the need to have hardware user equipment inside the end user premises. There is no need to buy additional pieces of hardware and configure and provide mantenance for them, since the same functionality is provided by the service on which it is centralized.

The basic functions of a typical IPCentrex service are [3]:

- Interconnect customer premises to the service provider VOIP core infrastructure

- Provide a seamless migration path from regular PBX, locally deployed in customer premises, to centrally managed advanced systems

- Define a heterogeneous group of users merging IP phones users, with traditional PSTN ones and PC phones. IP Centrex will allow the definition of a group of users belonging to branch offices and telecommuters, regardless of the specific geographical location. This will allow easier and cheaper communication.

- Define personal number-like features such as follow me diversion, alternate destination on busy, alternate destination on no answer, missed call log, and call return. Allow the user to define a treatment of the call based on time of day or day of week and customize the treatment via Web access to the user's data.

- Provide integration between end user's phone and desktop applications, in order to increase end user's productivity.

- Provide business-oriented feature such as call pickup, call park, operator features, and call transfer between different phones of the same group. These features are very useful in a business environment such as a help desk environment or a banking environment.

Besides providing the same functionality of a legacy PBX element, the service will allow final user to store in a single information system all of the settings related to his/her account. All subscriber data will be available in a centralized application server, available to be retrieved from potentially everywhere and in the same way, giving the end user the same interaction he is accustomed to via the Web paradigm [3]. Telephony features and call options can be invoked with a simple mouse click. The service merges users' telephones with their computers, resulting in synergistic new communications options [4]:

- Click to dial
- Click to add
- Click to transfer
- Call logging
- Instant messaging
- Phone presence
- Calendar
- Personal address book
- Address book synchronization
- Find me/follow me Web-based control of Centrex features
- Progressive conferencing
- Speed dial
- Secure enterprise data option
- High availability
- Integration with desktop applications (e-mail, calendar, etc.)

41.1.3 Market Targets

41.1.3.1 Telecom Service Provider Benefits   In addition to enabling carriers to add advanced features besides pure voice functionality, the bigger benefits for the carriers will be:

Additional revenue generation. As shown by past experience, customers are willing to pay additional fees in order to receive services that provide convenience.

Cost reduction. Services are centralized on the application servers, so this approach reduces the need to introduce additional hardware and local knowledge of the platform.

Market targets. It addresses market needs of both single office, multiple office entreprises and big corporations markets needs.

Customer loyalty. As providers begin to offer services that add control and choice in addition to baseline connectivity, customers may become more invested in their communications provider and less likely to switch based on factors like cost or connection speed.

41.1.3.2   End User Benefits

- Calls and call features are invoked through the friendly graphical user interface inreal time.
- Logs of unsuccessful calls, voice mail, corporate directories, and personal directories are viewable from anywhere.
- Allows better retention of phone history by logging incoming, outgoing, missed, and voice mail calls in a format that allows workers to record notes of calls (including conference calls) in the call log.
- Simplify the logistics of organizing meetings of coworkers.
- Control voice communication system with a user-friendly, browser-style interface instead of using hard-to-remember "star code" key sequences.
- Reduce or eliminate the costs related to maintaining legacy PBX.

REFERENCES

1. IETF, *Session Initiation Protocol (SIP)*, RFC 3621
2. IPCentrex Organization, *What is IP Centrex*, www.ip-centrex.org.
3. IPCC, *IPCC Scope and Network Architecture*, www.packetcomm.org.
4. A. Johnston and S. Donovan, *Session Initiation Protocol Service Examples*, 06-MAR-03, draft-ietf-sipping-service-examples-04.txt.

INDEX

Address resizing, 250
Affine functions, 139–140, 143–144, 148–149
Affinity relation, 139
Alchemi, .NET-based framework:
  application models, 409–411
  applications, 419–421
  design, 416–419
  desktop grid framework, 408–415428–429
  desktop grid middleware, 405–406
  development of, 404–405
  distributed components, 411–413
  features of, 404
  performance evaluation, 421–425
Alignment:
  axis, 145–146, 171
  data, 171, 173
  data realignment, 145
  implications of, 136–137, 139
AMD Athlon, 737
ANDF, 245
Andrew File System (AFS), 481
ANSI C, 120, 232
APIs:
  shared-memory, 32–34
  standard high-level for HPC, 34–35
Application I/O:
  characteristics of, 496–497
  interface for databases, 498
  parallel system software, 497–498
  standard UNIX and parallel I/O, 498–507
Architecture, *see specific computer programs*
ARF, 136, 154, 160, 172
ARF/PARTI, 152–153
Artificial neural networks:
  ART (adaptive resonance theory), 387
  ART–2A, 387
  characteristics of, 388
ASIC (application-specific integrated circuits),
  defined, 277
AS Model, 581
Asynchronous PRAM, 73
Atomic computation constraint, 148–149, 172

Autonomic group protocol (AGP), P2P
  computing systems:
  evaluation of, 622–625
  global protocol instance, 618–620
  local protocol instance, 617–618
  protocol profiles, 617–618
AVIDD, 511–512, 517, 521
AVTree, 567–568
Axis alignment, 139, 145–146, 171

Balanced workload block scheduling (BWBS),
  728, 730
Benchmark:
  BBMA, 317, 319–320, 327–329
  Linux cluster, 511
  NAS, 316
  nBBMA, 317, 320–321, 328–329
  Splash–2, 316
  STREAM, 317
Beowulf, 279, 284, 729–730
Binding of LPs to graph nodes, VisualGOP, 8–9
Bipartite scatternets:
  perfect scheduling algorithm for, 665–669
  perfect scheduling problem for, 663–665
Bitstream, 286
BLAS:
  ATLAS, 514
  high-performance, 514–515
  LINPACK performance and, 519
BLAST (Basic Local Alignment Search Tool):
  defined, 734
  IO behavior of, 736
  searches, 742
Blind flooding, unstructured P2P computing
  systems, 575, 577, 579, 583
Block(s):
  defined, 57
  distribution, 27, 29, 39
BlueGene (IBM), 24
Bluetooth:
  defined, 661
  scatternets, QoS-aware scheduling algorithm: